About the Author

Gordon Stein is an assistant professor and health sciences bibliographer at the University of Rhode Island. He is a graduate of the University of Rochester, received his masters of library science from the University of California at Los Angeles, and received his Ph.D. in physiology from Ohio State University.

He is the author or editor of seven previously published books, including *An Anthology of Atheism and Rationalism, Encyclopedia of Unbelief, Freethought in the United Kingdom and the Commonwealth, Freethought in the United States, Robert G. Ingersoll,* and *A Second Anthology of Atheism and Rationalism.*

ENCYCLOPEDIA OF HOAXES

ENCYCLOPEDIA  OF HOAXES

GORDON STEIN

Foreword by Martin Gardner

 **Gale Research Inc.**   **Detroit • Washington D.C. • London**

Encyclopedia of Hoaxes

Gale Research Inc. Staff:

Lawrence W. Baker, *Senior Developmental Editor*
Peg Bessette, *Developmental Editor*
Jane Louise Hoehner, *Associate Developmental Editor*

Mary Beth Trimper, *Production Director*
Evi Seoud, *Assistant Production Manager*
Mary Kelley, *Production Assistant*

Cynthia Baldwin, *Art Director*
Barbara J. Yarrow, *Graphic Services Supervisor*
Tracey Rowens, *Cover Designer*
Nicholas Jakubiak, *Desktop Publisher*

Benita L. Spight, *Data Entry Supervisor*
Gwendolyn S. Tucker, *Data Entry Group Leader*
Tara Y. McKissack, *Data Entry Associate*
Nancy K. Sheridan, *Data Entry Associate*

ISBN 0-8103-8414-0

Printed in the United States of America by Gale Research Inc.
Published simultaneously in the United Kingdom
by Gale Research International Limited
(An affiliated company of Gale Research Inc.)

The trademark **ITP** is used under license.

For Susan—my anchor in reality

Populus vult decipi, ergo decipiatur.

Contents

Foreword

About forty years ago, after my *Fads and Fallacies in the Name of Science* was published, I proposed a book on hoaxes to a major publisher. The editor was about to give me a contract when he discovered that Curtis MacDougall's *Hoaxes* had recently been published, and he didn't think the market was ready for a similar book. Although I continued to collect materials on hoaxes and practical jokes, I never considered the project again. I am glad now that I didn't. My files are sparse compared to Dr. Gordon Stein's, and I never could have treated the topic so thoroughly, or organized it as well as he has done.

It is high time that a scholar with a broad range of interests and knowledge assemble a massive collection of hoaxes, describing them in a carefully referenced and eminently readable volume. No one could be better qualified for such a monumental task than Gordon Stein.

After obtaining his Ph.D. in physiology at Ohio State University, he wrote seven books about the history of ideas, most of them covering the development of religious skepticism. Among his books is the two-volume *Encyclopedia of Unbelief* (Prometheus, 1985), which has become one of the most useful of recent philosophical and theological references. For two decades he has been collecting material on hoaxes of all varieties, from early times until the present, and from all parts of the world.

A hoax can be funny, like H.L. Mencken's famous bathtub hoax, or the reported discovery that T.S. Eliot wrote unpublished poems about quantum mechanics. It can be criminal, like the spurious biography of Howard Hughes. It can be socially devastating, like the phony *Protocols of the Elders of Zion*. Dr. Stein has covered them all. The *Encyclopedia of Hoaxes* is not only a splendid resource for historians of bizarre and, at times, abnormal and reprehensible human behavior, it is also a work that anyone can open at random and read with great pleasure, surprise and amusement.

Books about hoaxes have been written before—the most recent a coffee table book that consists largely of splashy color pictures with a modicum of text—but all these earlier studies combined cover only a small fraction of a much more vast field. Dr. Stein's net is incredibly wide. And, unlike his previous encyclopedia, on which numerous experts collaborated, almost all of the entries in *this* encyclopedia are by Dr. Stein himself.

I must confess that I once perpetrated a wild hoax of my own. In an April Fools' Day column in *Scientific American*, I reported on non-existent scientific discoveries. Although most readers were amused, it brought down on my head considerable wrath. One mathematician who took my column seriously wrote to the Mathematical Association of America, urging them to expel me.

This reminded me of Ogden Nash's poem ''What's the Matter, Haven't You Got Any Sense of Humor?'' It tells of a prankster who had himself lowered from the roof of a hotel so that he could see into the bridal suite. His plan was to clash a pair of cymbals at the proper moment.

And he weighed two hundred and eighty pounds, and the rope broke.
And that to my mind is the perfect practical joke.

Not until now has the curious topic of hoaxes been treated so comprehensively. No library can afford not to own this volume. It will be *the* classic reference on the subject for many decades to come.

Martin Gardner

Introduction

Hoaxes hold a certain fascination for people. This may be because they involve the successful fooling of at least some people for some time, and we all like to fool people. It is a test of how gullible people are and, in a sense, is a way of testing or comparing one's gullibility (and, therefore, intelligence) with theirs. To successfully fool someone implies (but of course does not prove) that the fooler is somehow smarter than the foolee.

Hoax—The Art of Deception

What exactly is a hoax? *Webster's Unabridged Dictionary* (2nd ed.) defines it as "a deception for mockery or mischief; a deceptive trick or story; a practical joke." This, although technically correct, does not give hoaxes their proper flavor. *The Random House Dictionary of the English Language* (2nd ed.) does even worse. It says a hoax is "something intended to deceive or defraud. Synonym: deception, fraud, fake, imposture, humbug." Each of the aforementioned definitions fails to distinguish a hoax from a swindle. *Random House 2*, in fact, defines swindle as "a fraudulent transaction or scheme. Anything deceptive; a fraud." Thus, it makes swindle and hoax synonyms, which they are not (as will be seen). *Webster's Unabridged* simply defines swindle as "a defrauding; a cheat."

In the *Encyclopedia of Hoaxes*, hoaxes are distinguished from swindles (which are *not* included here) by the element of money. A swindle is *a deception done exclusively or primarily to make money*. A hoax, on the other hand, *may* involve money as an element, but has an enduring quality that involves more than just money. Sometimes this is a fine distinction, while at other times, the distinction is clear and obvious. An example or two will help. Someone who tries to sell the Brooklyn Bridge (in the guise of its owner) is perpetrating a *swindle*. Yes, if you buy it, you will have been both swindled and momentarily hoaxed. Still, there would have been little or no point in the swindler claiming ownership of the Brooklyn Bridge unless he or she were trying to sell it for money. After the "sale," you will not own anything, nor will the Brooklyn Bridge continue to be anything that it wasn't before.

In contrast, a hoax would be done *regardless* of the financial return, and its deception would continue until exposed.

For example, a forger of a Rembrandt painting probably wants to achieve fame for having artistic ability equal to Rembrandt's, even if it is only obtained anonymously. Yes, there is money to be made by selling the painting, but that is probably not the major motive for the forgery. Besides, once the painting is hanging in a museum or on a private collector's wall, the hoax *continues*, without financial motivation, while a swindle ends.

The hoax only ends when it is definitively exposed to the public as a hoax. Often, this never occurs. Even though a few experts may be aware of the hoax, if the public is not, it will continue to be deceived.

In the case of art, the ground rules and definitions break down. In a way, all (or at least *most*) art is a sort of conscious deception when compared to the reality it depicts. In that sense, the terms hoax and fraud do not really apply to art. Even if an artist intentionally copies the style of Monet, for example, unless he or she signs Monet's name to a work that he or she has painted, even the copying of the style (but not the exact subject) of Monet does not constitute a fraud. The work is merely a stylistic imitation, but still an original work of art. It is only when a forgery of the artist's name or of the exact content of an artist's given work *and* style is done, that a fraud has actually been committed by the standards applied to art in this book.

With some movements in art (for example, surrealism), the artist may intentionally want to deceive us about what he or she is showing. The point the artist may be making has to do with the fickleness of perception. Clearly art and photography are special cases, and those chapters present their own special criteria for hoaxes.

Believability and Discovery

A major element needed to have a successful hoax is believability. The subject of the hoax must be something that the listener can accept as being both possible and even likely. Playing to the preconceived notions of the listener is a good way to insure believability. If he or she thinks that all rich people are greedy, then a hoax story about greed motivating a rich person will be easier to believe.

Does a hoaxer want his or her hoax to be discovered? Sometimes yes and sometimes no. It depends largely upon what the original motivations of the hoaxer were. Often there is a desire on the part of the hoaxer to make the "victim" appear stupid, either in public in private. In that case, this goal will only be achieved if the victim and/or the public discovers the hoax. The simplest example is one of the many April Fools' Day hoaxes, such as giving someone the phone number of a zoo (without telling that it *is* the zoo, of course), and having the caller ask for Mr. Fox. Many zoos get hundreds of such April Fools' calls. Clearly, the point of this hoax requires that the victim find out that he or she has been hoaxed into calling the zoo to make a fool of him or herself.

At other times, publicity would completely destroy the point of having done the hoax. In cases such as these, the motivation of the hoaxer is different. It may involve power, fame, sex, fortune, or something similar. An example of such a hoax would be the Donation of Constantine. In this hoax, a forged document, purportedly signed by the Emperor Constantine, gave the Catholic Church ownership of a large part of

Italy, later known as the Papal States. Obviously, for this hoax to succeed, its fraudulent nature had to be kept secret, as it was for hundreds of years.

Fraud vs. Hoax

What is the difference between a fraud and a hoax? This distinction is not as clear cut as the distinction between a swindle and a hoax. All hoaxes are frauds, but not all frauds are hoaxes. A fraud is basically a legal concept, defined by *Black's Law Dictionary* (6th ed.) as "an intentional perversion of truth for the purpose of inducing another in reliance of it to part with some valuable thing belonging to him or to surrender a legal right. A false representation of a matter of fact, whether by words or by conduct, by false and misleading allegations, or by concealment of that which should have been disclosed, which deceives and is intended to deceive another so that he shall act upon it to his legal injury. Anything calculated to deceive, whether by a single act or combination, or by suppression of truth, or suggestion of what is false, whether it be by direct falsehood or innuendo, by speech or silence, word of mouth, or look or gesture."

From this we can see that the elements of intention and of deception must be present in a fraud (and also in a hoax). Yet, there are many frauds that would not be called hoaxes. An example would be when an item of men's clothing is advertised for sale at a very reasonable price by mail order. You order several and instead receive several child-size shirts in the mail. It is not a mistake, but an intentional deception. This is a fraud (and perhaps a swindle), but not a hoax.

Often, in order to know whether a hoax was really intended, we must explore the motivation of the purported hoaxer. For example, did Immanuel Velikovsky *purposely intend* to deceive people when he wrote his books or developed his ideas of the origins of the solar system? Perhaps he was merely a deluded crank? Perhaps he was merely mistaken?

Certainly many "discoveries" in science turn out to be errors and are discarded. Does that mean that they were hoaxes? Much of the time it is impossible to know the true motivation of a person or persons who may have perpetrated a hoax. In cases like this, where there is a *distinct possibility* that a hoax has occurred, I have chosen to examine the evidence on both sides without making a definitive judgment.

Cranks, Myths, and Legends

Three other terms should be distinguished from a hoax. The first is a crank—an odd or eccentric person, or one who has odd or eccentric ideas. The element of sincerity distinguishes a hoaxer from a crank. A crank believes what he or she is saying is true. There is no conscious intention to deceive, no matter how outlandish the crank's ideas may be. In contrast, hoaxers consciously intend to deceive their victims. The work of true cranks is excluded from this book, except when subsequent generations have made their work into hoaxes by consciously deceiving.

The second and third terms to be distinguished from hoaxes are myths and legends. A myth is a story of unknown origin that ostensibly relates historical events or is a veiled explanation of a truth. A legend is a story handed down from early times and popularly regarded as historical, although not entirely verifiable. In addition, when a person is referred to as "legendary," he or she could have existed, whereas a person referred to as "mythical" had no real historical existence.

As I see it, here is the connection between a myth or legend and a hoax. When a hoax perpetuates for years and is not discovered to be a hoax, it can turn into a myth or a legend. This is especially true when we can no longer identify the hoaxer or the exact facts, but we know that the incident could not logically be true. In these cases, an old hoax may have turned into a myth or legend. A good example is Atlantis, which was turned into a hoax by early misinterpretation of Plato, and then embellished by subsequent writers. The antiquity of the story and a clear lack of its origins have turned it into a legend. Yet, a hoax element is present as well, especially in some of the nineteenth-century elaborations of the Atlantis story. Therefore, some myths and legends that appear to include hoax elements are also included in this book.

In the past, the literature on hoaxes has not been united in any one place. Rather, it has been scattered, often appearing only in newspaper articles. In recent years, some well-known hoaxes, such as the Clifford Irving/Howard Hughes biography and the Hitler Diaries, have been well documented in entire books. These, however, are exceptions. The major goal of the *Encyclopedia of Hoaxes* is to bring together in one place many of history's most interesting deceptions. Some of these hoaxes are extremely clever, funny, or outrageous. Others have changed the course of world history. Others started out as mere pranks, but

got out of hand. Still others seem to have no discernable motivation.

Often the base motives that govern many human activities—greed, lust, power, etc.—were the primary motivations for a hoax. At other times honor, loyalty, pride, and reverence were the "noble" motivations. In each of the hoaxes presented here, I will try to delineate not only the course of events, but also the motivation of the perpetrators. And while, in some cases, the motivations may not be discernable, we can still enjoy these hoaxes for their cleverness or humor.

Hoaxes have been perpetrated in almost every field. In the *Encyclopedia*, you will find instances of hoaxes in politics, medicine, law, athletics, entertainment, history, science, literature, religion, journalism, business, and more. Few areas are immune from hoaxes, and the more sensitive the area, the more likely that the hoax will be memorable.

Features

Organization and coverage: The book is organized by 27 subject chapters. Most chapters begin with a brief introduction which covers the history or highlights of hoaxes within that subject area. This is followed by descriptions of nearly 150 well-known, or major, hoaxes. These entries include pertinent background information, how the hoax was played out, how it was discovered (*if* it was discovered), and any after effects. One chapter, **The Sociology and Psychology of Hoaxes**, helps explain why hoaxers do what they do. Following the major hoaxes, over 100 smaller, lesser known hoaxes are briefly covered.

Sources: Sources used to compile major hoax sections and the collections of minor hoaxes are included.

Cross references: Within entries, cross references to other chapters are indicated.

Bibliography: A general bibliography, arranged by subject, consisting of all sources used in compiling this book is included.

Illustrations: About 80 photographs and line drawings augment the text.

Index: An index provides quick access to names, subjects, individual hoaxes, and more. In addition, the highlighted terms refer to pages where you'll find entire entries on that subject.

Inclusion Criteria

There may well be some disagreement over whether every entry *should* have been included in a book on hoaxes. While there is no universal agreement about exactly what should be called a hoax, even by those who adhere to the definition explained earlier, I have tried to justify each hoax by strictly and thoughtfully applying the criteria I have indicated. Occasionally, a hoax was not actually perpetrated by the originator of the idea. For example, Nostradamus' predictions were made by him originally to cover local events in the immediate future. After his death, new "translations" of his writings were made in which the prophecies were expanded from local to worldwide events and the time extended far into the future. Thus, the hoax element did not occur until after Nostradamus was dead.

Additional subjects that some would call hoaxes are not included in the *Encyclopedia* due to their controversial nature or because of a lack of a substantial body of evidence that the incident was grounded in a hoax. Among them are 1) the existences of witches, 2) various parapsychological or occult phenomena, 3) the founding events of a number of religions, and 4) the basic assumptions of a number of political and social movements.

Although I have tried to cover all the important hoaxes, some may have escaped me. I'd be glad to learn about any that I have missed. I can be reached at P.O. Box 20446, Cranston, RI 02920 USA.

We should never lose sight of the fact that reading about hoaxes is supposed to be *fun*. There are some very clever, humorous, and rather wicked hoaxes in this book. I do hope that they are as much fun to read as they were to write about.

Gordon Stein, Ph.D.

Acknowledgments

In a project as large as this one, many people helped out. I will try to thank as many as I can remember, but I extend my thanks to all who helped, even if I have inadvertently forgotten to mention them.

Parts of several of my entries appeared previously in the form of magazine articles. I would like to thank *The American Rationalist* for permission to reprint (in modified form) the article on Noah's Ark. I would like to thank the editor of *Fate* for permission to reprint the article on fire immunity and a small part of the articles on the Amazing Medium Mirabelli and human monsters. I would like to thank the editor of *The Skeptical Inquirer* for permission to reprint (in modified form) the article "The Lore of Levitation."

I would like to thank the following individuals for their kind assistance: Martin Gardner, Marcello Truzzi, James Randi, Jerry Clark, Joe Nickell, C. J. Scheiner, Robert Gutchen, Robert Weisbord, David Salamie, Larry Baker, Chris Nasso, Peg Bessette, Judy Haughton, Vicki Burnett, Marie Rudd, Martha Ott, Ken Morse, Geoffrey Gibbs, Klaus Baernthaler, Charles Daniel, the late D. Scott Rogo, Jan Harold Brunvand, Silvia Berti, Richard H. Popkin, Richard J. Wolfe, Mark Oliver, and Judith A. Sundell.

A scholar would be at a complete loss without the help of many libraries. I would especially like to thank Brown University Library, Countway Library of Medicine, Los Angeles County Medical Association Library, New York Public Library, British Library, Bibliothèque Nationale, Library of Congress, American Antiquarian Society Library, University of California at Los Angeles Library, Harvard University Library, Boston Public Library, Cambridge University Library, Harry Price Collection at the University of London, the library of the International Instituut voor Sociale Geschiedenis, and the University of Rhode Island Library.

Contributors

Jerome Clark—Author of the *UFO Encyclopedia* and Gale's *Encyclopedia of Strange and Unexplained Physical Phenomena*, Clark is an internationally recognized authority on UFOs. He is also the editor of the *International UFO Reporter*. *Contributions:* "UFO Hoaxes" and "Hollow-Earth Hoaxes."

Denis Dutton—Author of *The Forger's Art* and an expert on the philosophy of art forgery, Dutton is a member of the faculty of fine arts of the University of Canterbury in New Zealand. *Contributions:* "Art Hoaxes" and "Han van Meegeren."

Martin Gardner—Author of *Fads and Fallacies in the Name of Science* and many other books on the rational examination of science and the paranormal, Gardner has long been interested in hoaxes. *Contribution:* Foreword.

Arnold Bruce Levy—A collector of books on literary hoaxes and an editor and bookseller, Levy has studied literary hoaxes for over twenty-five years. *Contribution:* "Other Literary Hoaxes."

Joe Nickell—A former private investigator and professional magician, Nickell is now an instructor at the University of Kentucky, where he investigates literary forgery and solves historical mysteries such as the Shroud of Turin. *Contributions:* "The Shroud of Turin," "Outlaw Impostors," "Disappearance Hoaxes," "The Beale Treasure," "The Bermuda Triangle," and "Poltergeist Hoaxes."

Marcello Truzzi—A professor of sociology at Eastern Michigan University, Truzzi is the coauthor of *The Blue Sense* and editor of *The Zetetic Scholar*. His interest in hoaxes extends back many years. *Contribution:* "The Sociology and Psychology of Hoaxes."

Photo Credits

Photographs appearing in the *Encyclopedia of Hoaxes* were received from the following sources:

Author's Collection 4, 16, 19, 28, 29, 47, 57, 79, 106, 107, 114, 116, 140, 143, 149, 151, 153, 172, 175, 184, 187, 223, 225, 240, 241, 265, 289

Barnum Museum 285

British Library 81, 145, 249

Brown University Library 142

Jerome Clark 267, 268

S. Peter Dance 259, 260, 261, 262

Fortean Times 256

Free Library of Philadelphia 254

Paul Higdon/*New York Times* 186

Kansas Historical Society 165

Library of Congress 34, 40, 52, 54, 82, 89, 113, 115, 124, 145, 146, 167, 173, 199, 221, 222, 225, 263, 299

Madison *Capital-Times* 187

Metropolitan Museum of Art 22

Minnesota Historical Society 56

New York Public Library 62, 214, 257

Smithsonian Institution 11, 12, 72, 123

Spencer Productions 209, 210

University of Leeds Library 182

Anthropology Hoaxes

Carlos Castaneda and Don Juan

The don Juan story formulates the best-selling series of books in the history of anthropology. It probably established the validity of ethnomethodology (a research technique used to study and explore a group's culture) and it certainly made a lot of money for its author, Carlos Castaneda, as well as earning him his doctorate from the University of California at Los Angeles (UCLA). Unfortunately for all, it appears that don Juan Matus, the Yaqui sorcerer, never existed and that the whole series of adventures that occurred with don Juan was a hoax.

It should be made clear from the beginning that Castaneda has many supporters, including professional anthropologists. They, and others, have pointed out that it doesn't really matter to them whether Castaneda's writings are fact or fiction, because they contain important truths. Whether Castaneda's books are fact or fiction doesn't necessarily alter their importance. It does, however, explain whether the work is written by a great field anthropologist or a science fiction writer.

Richard de Mille, editor of *The Don Juan Papers*, has been Castaneda's harshest critic. He insists on knowing whether Castaneda is writing fact or fiction. In his intensive investigations of Castaneda, he has found only one obvious mistake in his writings, but quite a few lies in Castaneda's description of his own life. The only factual contradiction de Mille could find in any of the four Castaneda books is this: in October 1968, Castaneda and don Juan drove into Mexico to visit don Juan's friend and fellow sorcerer, don Genero. They left their car and walked two days further to reach don Genero's shack. After staying with don Genero for a few days, they decided to visit don Genero's two apprentices, Nestor and Pablito. Castaneda wrote, "Both of them got into my car." However, the car was left a two-day walk away. It is a minor point, but internal contradictions may be a way to test the truth or falsity of the don Juan books.

The contradictions in Castaneda's biography, as told by Castaneda himself, are important mainly in what they disclose about his truthfulness. According to Castaneda, he was born in Sao Paulo, Brazil in 1935. His father was only seventeen when he was born, his mother fifteen. His mother died six years later, and his father became a professor of literature. The biography says Carlos was raised by his grandparents on their chicken farm in the Brazilian countryside. There he learned Italian and Portuguese. He was later sent to school in Buenos Aires, where he learned Spanish. At the age of 15, he was sent to the United States to live with a foster family in Los Angeles. He attended Hollywood High School, from which he graduated in two years. He then went to Milan, Italy, where he studied sculpture at the Academy of Fine Arts. At some point, he returned to the United States, and served in the U.S. Army, stationed in Spain. Eventually, he enrolled at UCLA, where he obtained his doctorate in anthropology.

Except for his UCLA schooling, *all* of this autobiography is demonstrably false. As an investigation by *Time* magazine in South America revealed Carlos Arana Castaneda was born in Cajamarca, Peru, in 1925. His father was a goldsmith and watchmaker named Cesar Arana Burungaray, and his mother was named Susana Castaneda Novoa. He went to high school in his hometown, although he moved with the family to Lima in 1948. He graduated from the Colegio Nacional de Nuestra Senora de Guadalupe, and then attended the National Fine Arts School of Peru. A fellow student there remembered him as a resourceful blade who lived mainly off horses, dice, and cards. He was described as "witty, imaginative, cheerful—a big liar and a real friend."

After his mother died in 1949, Castaneda announced he was going to leave home. He arrived in San Francisco in 1951 and was enrolled at Los Angeles City College between 1955 and 1959 (the four previous years are still a mystery). In 1960, he married Margaret Runyon, a distant cousin of Damon Runyon. He divorced her in 1973. There is no evidence that he was in the military service at all, or that he knew Italian or Portuguese.

Castaneda entered UCLA as an undergraduate in 1959, received a B.A. in anthropology in 1962 and a doctorate in anthropology in 1973. He published no scholarly papers other than his dissertation. The "structural analysis" section, found at the end of the first don Juan book, *The Teachings of Don Juan: A Yaqui Way of Knowledge,* may have served as the equivalent of his master's thesis, although that degree was never formally awarded. The text of his third book, *Journey to Ixtlan,* appears to be his Ph.D. dissertation republished in popular form.

Castaneda explains the contradictions in his biography as an attempt to minimize his factual role in this world, stressing his role as a sorcerer in a different reality.

Richard de Mille listed the problems with treating the four Castaneda books as non-fiction in his own book, *Castaneda's Journey.* The major problem was that the third book, *Journey to Ixtlan,* contradicts the time flow of the other three books. In other words, in order for all the books to be true, Castaneda would have to be two different individuals, who existed simultaneously in two different places, doing two different things. De Mille thinks that Castaneda got himself into this bind by trying to assign exact dates to the events in the first two books (to make them appear to have been transcribed from field notes), thereby not allowing any time period for the events in the third book, which was supposed to have occurred during the same period as the first two books. Castaneda avoided this problem in his fourth book, *Tales of Power,* by not dating *anything* in the book.

There are many other problems in the books, including language. don Juan never speaks in Yaqui, nor does he show any indication that he is familiar with his own native language. Castaneda does not use don Juan's Spanish for any peculiar words for which it might be useful to know his actual words. In cases where words and phrases such as "ally," "stop the world," and "not-doing" are used, it is common for scholars to indicate what the original word was in instances in case another translation may make more sense. In fact, de Mille makes a strong case that *none* of the material in the book was ever said in Spanish; in other words, don Juan always spoke in English, and

suddenly seemed to switch to a slang-filled English in the fourth volume. This would mean, most likely, that a person named don Juan Matus (a pseudonym) never existed, since his native language was not English, and he did not speak English well, according to Castaneda.

On the other hand, when R. Gordon Wasson, the pioneer investigator of hallucinogenic mushrooms (and a sort of hero to Castaneda), wrote to him to ask for the Spanish notes for a particular section, Castaneda sent him photocopies of a neatly written set of pages in Spanish. These were likely not his original field notes, but rather some recopied or just-written version. It does show that *perhaps* a part (or all) of *that* book was originally written in Spanish.

Wasson, too, disputed the truthfulness of the books at first because of the fact that Castaneda had been instructed by don Juan to cut magic mushrooms into slivers that would pass through the neck of a gourd vessel. They were to be left there for a year, until they were reduced to powder. Wasson had never heard of such mushrooms. His own hallucinogenic mushrooms were still intact after drying for ten years. Later, Wasson met with Castaneda and became convinced of his truthfulness, although his reasons are not clear.

How Castaneda managed to get his work approved by a committee of scholars, and receive his Ph.D. for it, is a complex problem, which de Mille addresses at length. His explanation is feasible though no one from the dissertation committee will talk about it publicly. De Mille thinks the committee was pressured by Castaneda and one professor who was trying to teach traditional anthropologists a lesson. Once they were cornered, the safest way for the committee to free itself was to approve the dissertation.

As an aside on the "scholarly value" of Castaneda's work, de Mille points out that his "structural analysis" section at the end of the first book may have been an attempt to seem scholarly, but it really serves as a sort of satirical comment upon scholarship, contradicting the whole theme of the rest of the book.

Another fact that points to the suspect nature of the four books, as the product of field research in Mexico is that no names of plants or animals are provided other than the Jimson weed, mescal, and the mushrooms which are not clearly identified. Surely a Yaqui Indian would have a local name for each plant, either in Yaqui or Spanish. Yet none of these names were given. Also, the foremost authority on the Yaquis at the time, Edward Spicer, says that he never heard of the Yaquis using *Datura* (Jimson weed) ointment to achieve the feeling of flying, yet Castaneda treats this as common practice.

Suspicion surrounds the entire apprenticeship of Castaneda to don Juan. Most Mexican Indians would be hesitant to reveal that they were practitioners of sorcery, but not don Juan. In addition, don Juan decides to reveal his secrets to someone who is 1) not an Indian, 2) not a neighbor, 3) not a relative, and 4) not someone whom he knew well or long. All of this is highly suspect behavior for a Yaqui or *any* Mexican Indian.

Castaneda never presented his field notes to his dissertation committee at UCLA, or let anyone see them. (He did send supposed copies of a few pages to the aforementioned mushroom expert, R. Gordon Wasson). As part of his field experience, Castaneda claims to have hiked for days with don Juan across the Sonoran desert in June, July, August, and September. Experienced desert scouts, such as desert expert Hans Sebald, say this is virtually impossible. Even the most experienced desert people avoid hiking in the Sonora during the summer, for one can die in a few hours from the heat.

Castaneda's depiction of plants and animals in the desert is one of the strongest reasons for concluding that he was never there for any length of time. As Sebald points out in *The Don Juan Papers*, pumas are quite scarce there, and will not come near a human, yet Castaneda says he was attacked by one and climbed a tree. Most trees in the Sonora are unclimbable, although Castaneda climbs them with ease. He notes a "chubby squirrel-like rodent" that is unknown there. At the same time, he *fails* to encounter some of the most common creatures of the desert, namely scorpions. He also never encounters the saguaro fruit fly, which swarms throughout the desert in May, repeatedly getting into human eyes, ears, and nostrils.

Castaneda grabs a male rabbit with his bare hands, a virtual impossibility. Although he worries unnecessarily about pumas, he does not mention the wild pig, javelina, which *is* quite dangerous. Castaneda also seems to forget about king snakes, gila monsters, centipedes, and tarantulas, all of which are quite common.

Castaneda's books may contain *valid* information, that is, information that is factually correct. However, this information may have been "lifted" from other published sources, and not authentic—the result of his field research. Although something cannot be valid without authentic reporting by someone, a report can be valid and still be unauthentic if the reporter did not obtain the information from the sources *claimed*.

So where does that leave the claim that Castaneda made up the persona of don Juan and used him to convey anthropological "truths" from Castaneda's mind and from his wide reading? Perhaps the best answer is that there is significant circumstantial evidence that the

don Juan books are hoaxes, but no "smoking gun" that proves the hoax hypothesis. Castaneda's dissertation committee at UCLA has—to this day—refused to admit that it erred or awarded a doctorate for a fraudulent piece of research. Perhaps the committee knows more than it is willing to reveal.

Sources:

Castaneda, Carlos. *Journey to Ixtlan: The Lessons of Don Juan.* New York: Simon & Schuster, 1972.

———. *A Separate Reality: Further Conversations with don Juan.* New York: Simon & Schuster, 1971.

———. *The Teachings of Don Juan: A Yaqui Way of Knowledge.* Berkeley, CA: University of California Press, 1968.

de Mille, Richard. *Castaneda's Journey: The Power and the Allegory.* Santa Barbara, CA: Capra Press, 1976.

———, ed. *The Don Juan Papers: Further Castaneda Controversies.* Santa Barbara, CA: Ross-Erikson Publishers, 1980.

Drury, Nevill. *Don Juan, Mescalito and Modern Magic.* London: Routledge & Kegan Paul, 1978.

Noel, Daniel. *Seeing Castaneda: Reactions to the "Don Juan" Writings of Carlos Castaneda.* New York: Capricorn/G.P. Putnam's Sons, 1976.

The Native of Formosa

Cases of imposture rarely make much of a lasting impact upon history. The case of George Psalmanazar, as he called himself, was a rare exception to that rule. He had Europe puzzled, and singlehandedly set the world of anthropology and geography back a number of years. Later he felt remorse for having fooled people for so long, and wrote what he thought was a full confession of his deceit. Even with this more than 300-page-long published confession, almost nothing is known about the real George Psalmanazar. He admits that was not his original name. His real name, birth place, and ancestry are all unknown. According to information from Psalmanazar's own memoirs, he was born somewhere in the south of France in 1679. The town of Sluis, in Holland, where he first became known as Psalmanazar, was destroyed, including its archives, in World War II, and along with it any evidence of Psalmanazar's existence.

The story began in April 1704, in London, when Psalmanazar published his book, *An Historical and Geographical Description of Formosa*. The book was well-written, and soon became a best seller. The book was a travel account of the then little known island of Formosa (today Taiwan), purportedly written by Psalmanazar, a

George Psalmanazar, "The Native of Formosa."

former native of the island. The book was actually promoted by an "author tour," involving personal appearances and lectures by Psalmanazar in Oxford and London. The author's fame as a source of information about this mysterious country continued for years.

Psalmanazar was able to successfully write about and act as a native of Formosa, because so little was known about the land in 1704. The only people who had visited Formosa were a few Jesuit priests. One of them, Father Jean de Fontaney, was living in London when the book was published. His confrontation of Psalmanazar is addressed later in this section.

Psalmanazar's confession piece, *Memoirs of ****,* reveals that he studied under Franciscans in France as a child, learning Latin quite well. When he was 16, his mother sent him on foot—a 500 mile distance—to find his father in Germany, hoping his father could support him. When Psalmanazar reached Germany, he found that his father was just as poor as his mother. He supported himself by begging from priests whom he addressed in Latin. At his father's suggestion, Psalmanazar travelled to Holland. On the way, he decided to pretend to be oriental. Accordingly, he invented a language, a calendar, and a new religion as he walked to Holland. He was to be a Japanese converted to Christianity by missionaries. This was the beginning of the Formosan hoax. By the time he reached Holland,

Psalmanazar was posing as a pagan of good morals, who worshiped the sun and the moon. At Sluis, the governor, George Lauder, the chaplain of the Scots regiment, Alexander Innes, and a local Huguenot pastor Isaac D'Amalvi, all became associated with Psalmanazar, and tried to convert him to Christianity. At first these attempts were rejected with gusto, as Psalmanazar said that Christianity appeared even more unreasonable than his paganism. Finally, he did convert to Anglicanism, although why is not clear. His conversion prompted a call to visit from the Bishop of London, who would later become one of his sponsors. Before he went to London, however, Reverend Innes had him translate a passage of Cicero from Latin to "Formosan." Psalmanazar readily did so. Almost immediately after that, Innes asked him to do so again. Psalmanazar could not reproduce the first translation, and as a result, the second translation of the same passage differed by more than fifty percent from the first. After looking over both translations, Reverend Innes, rather than unmask Psalmanazar as an impostor, merely suggested that he take better care with his translations in the future. The Bishop of London still wanted to see the Formosan, and Psalmanazar left for England to visit him.

A number of things that Psalmanazar said in his book contradicted what was known about Formosa. For example, he said that Formosa was a dependency of Japan. Those who had been there said it belonged to China. Psalmanazar's skin was white, whereas visitors to Formosa said the natives had dark skin. On the other hand, Psalmanazar *did* speak, read, and write a language incomprehensible to anyone else. He also ate raw meat, convincing people that he couldn't be European! Among other odd things that Psalmanazar said occurred on Formosa was that a convicted murderer was hung upside down by the feet for a period of time and then shot full of arrows. Further, there was a yearly sacrifice of 18,000 young boys to appease one of the gods. Polygamy was allowed, as long as the man could support all of his wives.

Although much of the "information" in the book was not especially remarkable, it was often translated from English. There were illustrations of the typical clothing worn by Formosans, of their houses, boats, temples, and alphabet.

When Psalmanazar arrived to see the Bishop of London, those who saw him seemed skeptical. People found his consumption of raw meat and herbs convincing, and eventually persuaded that charges made against him were not true. (Some pointed out that he was a drunkard and knew the languages of Europe too well.) People concluded that he must really be from Formosa. When absurdities such as the annual sacrifice of the 18,000 male children described in his book were questioned, Psalmanazar refused to retract what he had said or written.

The Bishop of London had set Psalmanazar up at the University of Oxford, where he was to translate religious literature into "Formosan," and lecture on the Formosan language. It seems, however, that he wound up doing mostly, or entirely, private study, as he did not actually instruct anyone in the Formosan language. He left Oxford after six months.

The Jesuits were quick to respond to the rather negative things that Psalmanazar said about them in his book and lectures. The Jesuits published a refutation of much of what Psalmanazar said, written by the Jesuit Father Fontaney, who had recently returned from Formosa. When Father Fontaney and Psalmanazar faced each other publicly at the Royal Society, "the Formosan" triumphed each time, at least according to him. People supposedly believed the impostor and rejected the knowledge of the man who had actually been to Formosa. Although no independent verification of this exists, it *is* possible that the public believed Psalmanazar.

However, the Royal Society itself later published a one sentence statement in which it decided that the account of Formosa given to them by a Mr. Griffith, who lived there for some time, ". . . does in these letters [Mr. Griffith's] contradict the account later given of it by Mr. George Psalmaanasaar [sic]."

What eventually caused Psalmanazar to recant was, according to him, a reading of Law's *Serious Call to a Devout Life.* He devoted the next sixty years of his life to frantic editing and writing "hack" work. Much of it was noted for its lack of influence or real content. One of the works to which he contributed was called *Geography of the World.* Psalmanazar contributed, among other things, the section on Formosa, only this time he researched and correctly described what was known of the island.

While working closely on his writing and editing, Psalmanazar managed to devote a little time to writing his autobiography. This work, which he wished to be published after his death, is called *Memoirs of ****, Commonly Known by the Name of George Psalmanazar.* It is a sincere attempt at a confession, written as the author himself put it " . . . to undeceive the world, by unravelling that whole mystery of iniquity in a posthumous work, which would be less liable to suspicion, as the author would be far out of the influence of any sinister motives that might induce him to deviate from the truth."

Sources:

Foley, Frederic J. *The Great Formosan Impostor.* St. Louis, MO: Jesuit Historical Institute, 1968.

"George Psalmanazar." *Temple Bar* (July 1865): 385–395.

Maycock, A.L. "The Amazing Story of George Psalmanazar." *Blackwood's Magazine* 235 (1934): 797–808.

Psalmanazar, George. *An Historical and Geographical Description of Formosa. . . .* 1704. Reprint. Edited by Norman M. Penzer. London: Robert Holden & Co., 1926.

———. *Memoirs of ****. Commonly Known by the Name of George Psalmanazar.* London: Printed for R. Davis, 1765.

T. Lobsang Rampa

T(uesday) Lobsang Rampa (1911?–1981) was the author of such best-selling books as *The Third Eye* (1956) and *The Rampa Story* (1967). His more than thirteen books are all purported to be autobiographical, and tell of his mastery of Tibetan Buddhism after long years of study and apprenticeship. Rampa claimed to be the son of a wealthy Tibetan family, and to have studied in Lhasa to become a lama (Buddhist monk). Part of his preparation included an operation to open up his "third eye" in the middle of his forehead to give him psychic powers.

Although his British publisher claims to have made an attempt to authenticate the manuscript, he did not come to a definitive conclusion. Most experts on Tibet Buddhism said the book was a hoax, but Rampa steadfastly maintained that his book was true. A group of suspicious Tibetan scholars in Britain hired a detective named Clifford Burgess to try to determine if Rampa was authentic. Burgess discovered that Rampa's real name was Cyril Henry Hoskins, and that he was the son of a plumber named Joseph Henry Hoskins.

Cyril was born in Devon, England. During the period he was supposed to be apprenticing in a Tibetan monastery, he was actually working at his father's plumbing store in Plympton, England. It seemed that Hoskins had neither been to Tibet nor had an operation on his forehead. He later worked for a surgical instrument company, studying the occult in his spare time. Eventually, he grew a beard, shaved his head, and started calling himself "Dr. Kuan-suo." He later moved to Ireland, where Detective Burgess eventually found him.

When the detective confronted "Rampa" with the information about his family background, Hoskins' reply was that his body had been taken over by Rampa's spirit. Rampa proceeded to write more than twelve additional books, still maintaining that he was Rampa and that his books were true. Although the later books did not sell as well as *The Third Eye*, they collectively sold millions of copies.

When Tibetan scholars examined *The Third Eye*, they spotted a number of obvious errors. For example, the Tibetan highlands are not at 24,000 feet altitude, but rather at 14,000 feet. Also the eye operation described by Rampa never would have been done, as the "third eye" is a *psychical* center, to be "opened" only by meditation, and never by surgery. The concept Rampa employs, of a "silver cord" joining the real body with the astral body, although found in western occult literature, is completely alien to Buddhist thought. Also his statement that apprentices must memorize every page of the *Kan-gyur* (or *Bkah Hygur*) to pass a test is false. Not only is this book of Buddhist Sutras *not* memorized, it is not even read by apprentices. Only a few advanced lamas read it, and then only for reference. Prof. Chen Chi Chang, an expert on Tibet and Buddhism, points out a number of other serious errors in his 1958 article.

Hoskins and his wife moved to Canada in the early 1970s, becoming Canadian citizens in 1973. He died in 1981, still proclaiming his books and identity as Rampa authentic. It is now well established by many experts in this field that all of his books are hoaxes. The books should not be relied upon for authentic statements about the Tibetan lama experience.

Sources:

Chang, Chen Chi. "Tibetan Phantasies." *Tomorrow* 6 (1958): 13–16.

McIlroy, William. "Jottings." *The Freethinker* (March 1981): 39.

Rampa, T. Lobsang [Cyril Henry Hoskins]. *The Rampa Story*. London: Souvenir Press, 1960.

——. *The Third Eye*. Garden City, NY: Doubleday, 1956.

"The Tibetan Lama Hoax." *Tomorrow* 6 (1958): 9–13.

The Tasaday

The discovery of a whole tribe of people who had never had contact with the outside world before would be an anthropologist's dream. This would provide a chance to see a group uncontaminated by modern civilization. Therefore, when such a tribe in the Philippines was announced to the press in the spring of 1972, the anthropological world and the general public were keenly interested. The tribe was called the Tasaday, and they reportedly lived in the remote rain forest of Mindanao, the southernmost island in the Philippines.

Immediately reporters, journalists, and even school children were taken to see the Tasaday people. Eventually, a helicopter pad was built in the jungle to enable visiting dignitaries to be brought in. The Tasaday numbered twenty-six individuals living in caves. They had been discovered by Manuel Elizalde, Jr., a Philippine Cultural Minister in charge of minorities, who announced that he had found them with the help of a hunter named Dafal in 1971. The Tasaday supposedly lived by eating tubers dug from the forest floor, berries, frogs, crabs, bananas, and grubs. They neither farmed nor hunted. They had no method for calculating time, no woven cloth, no metal, no art, no weapons, no pottery, no domesticated animals, and no knowledge of the sea. Their language contained no words for war. Their clothes were made of orchid leaves. The Marcos government, in an attempt to protect the tribe from logging interests, established a tribal preserve of 46,300 acres in 1973. When martial law was proclaimed in the Philippines in 1974, media attention to the tribe ended.

A Swiss journalist, Oswald Iten, went into the jungle to see the Tasaday only one month after Ferdinand Marcos was overthrown. What Iten found stunned him. The same people who were wearing loincloths of orchid leaves, were now wearing colored T-shirts, sleeping in log houses on wooden beds, and using metal knives. The caves were deserted. He pronounced the whole thing a hoax, devised by Elizalde and Marcos to make them look like protectors of the minorities, while scheming to get control of the valuable mahogany and gold in the land preserves. The "former" Tasaday told Iten that Elizalde told them to remove their clothes, put on leaves, and sit in the caves. If they did so, he would give them money and guns. They complained that they never got either, although Elizalde was able to honor his word that he would always give them advance warning when visitors were about to come. This was easy as Elizalde controlled the helicopter that was the only way in.

A few weeks after Iten's visit, a team of German reporters for the magazine *Der Stern* were accompanied by Dafal into the jungle. They found the Tasaday in their caves and loincloths, as if nothing had happened. Underneath their leaves, however, the Germans noted the men wore colored underwear, and the women wore brassieres. Their number had swelled to forty-one, even though there seemed to be no place for the men to meet potential wives. The Germans were later captured and held for ransom—probably by Philippine government agents—when it became clear they questioned the authenticity of the tribe. Yet the Tasaday have had their defenders among anthropologists. Before 1974, a number of anthropologists and linguists spent from a few days to two weeks with the tribe. Several of them said that the linguistic evidence in Tasaday speech supported the idea that they had been isolated from their neighbors for at least several hundred years. Other anthropologists said their language marked them as fakes. For example, there were words for house roof, and for agricultural terms that had no place in a cave-dwelling, non-planting tribe that had been isolated from its neighbors. Their language was largely similar to the South Cotabato Manobo language of the neighboring region, with only a few different words.

Several heated sessions at meetings of the American Anthropological Association have dealt with the Tasaday issue. There is strong disagreement among some anthropologists about the authenticity of the Tasaday. The following points support the hoax theory: 1) a number of the alleged Tasaday individuals (e.g., Lobo, Gintui, Adug) admitted *on camera* to a crew from the television show "20/20" that they were hoaxers, 2) no refuse heaps or garbage dumps exist in or near the caves that the Tasaday claim to have occupied for centuries, 3) the amount of food available in the area for non-hunters and non-farmers appears to be insufficient to sustain the tribe, 4) the "tools" the Tasaday claim they made were inadequate for use and cannot be found, 5) the number of tribesman is too small to be self-sustaining, but the other tribes that the Tasaday claim they used as "kin" groups and sources for mating cannot be located, and the Tasaday claim to have never been in contact with another group that had food and is only a three-hour walk away. These are powerful objections. Until they can all be answered, it seems that the best conclusion is that the Tasaday are a hoax.

Sources:

ABC News. "The Tribe That Never Was." Transcript of "20/20" television program for August 14, 1986.

MacLeish, Kenneth. "The Tasadays: Stone Age Cavemen of Mindanao." *National Geographic* 142 (August 1972): 219–49.

Marshall, Eliot. "Anthropologists Debate Tasaday Hoax Evidence." *Science* 1 (December 1989): 1113–14.

Molony, Carol. "The Truth About the Tasaday." *Sciences* 28 (September/October 1988): 12–20; Letters in response, 29 (March/April 1989): 8, 10.

Nance, John. *The Gentle Tasaday.* New York: Harcourt Brace Jovanovich, 1975.

Other Anthropology Hoaxes

Margaret Mead and the Samoans. Margaret Mead (1901–1978) was long considered one of America's outstand-

ing anthropologists. To criticize her work was unpopular, yet in 1989, Derek Freeman published an article in *American Anthropologist* that raised some discrepancies in Mead's work. He went back to Mead's original informants for *Coming of Age in Samoa* (based on Mead's dissertation research) and found that the information saying that teenaged Samoan girls were sexually promiscuous prior to marriage was based on a "joke" played upon Mead by a number of Samoan teenagers. In Samoa, it is considered rude and improper to question teenagers about their sexual activities. Virginity prior to marriage is highly valued. It is also considered good fun to tease a foreigner by telling them playful lies. This practice is called *ta fa'ase 'e* or *tau fa'alili.*

When Mead arrived in American Samoa in 1926, as a student of Franz Boas, one of the Samoans who acted as an informant was Fa'apua'a Fa'amu. In 1987, Freeman found her, at age 86. She readily admitted to him that she had lied to Mead, and was in fact sorry. Because of that lie, misinformation about the promiscuity of Samoan teenagers was widely believed. This led to the myth of free pre-marital sexuality in Samoa, which was virtually the opposite of the truth. Margaret Mead had been hoaxed by several conspiring Samoan teenagers, and that delusion has come to be accepted as anthropological "truth."

Old Age Attained by Ecuadorian Villagers. The Ecuadorian village of Vilacabamba was thought for a number of years to have a disproportionately large population of people more than 100 years old. A 1971 census showed nine of 819 residents of the village to be over 100. As anthropologists came to the village to study why so many lived so long there, it became apparent that many of these elders had been lying about their age. A careful examination of the baptismal certificates of the people who claimed great age showed that no one in the village was more than 96 years old. It is suspected that a scrutiny of the demographic documentation for Armenians in other Ecuadorian villages who also claim great age would result in similar findings. The anthropologists who examined the documentation in Ecuador say that the motive for the hoax was to attract tourists to the area.

Grimm's Fairy Tales. The Grimm's Fairy Tales are regarded both as delightful children's stories *and* as tales based on the folklore of Germany and Europe. The Grimms claimed to have based their stories upon traditional German folktales, which they supposedly collected from all over Germany through field work. However, author John M. Ellis in his book *One Fairy Story Too Many: The Brothers Grimm and their Tales,* raised serious questions about whether the Grimms ever did any field collection, or whether they simply fabricated their stories.

The first German edition of their *Kinder- Und Hausmachen (KHM)* (Child and Household Tales) was published in 1812. The Grimms destroyed all of the manuscripts they used to prepare the first edition of *KHM*. This seems suspect, unless they were trying to hide something. The sources of the stories cannot be documented anywhere in their records.

Early copies of some of their tales were sent to Clemens Brentano, who was preparing a collection of fairy tales. Brentano saved the Grimm papers. A comparison of the material the Grimms sent to Brentano to the published version of the same tale by the Grimms showed vast differences. It appeared that the Grimms completely rewrote the stories between the time they sent the manuscript to Brentano and the time the first edition of *KHM* was published. This is especially peculiar *if* the tales are in fact a written rendering of oral folktales, wherein fidelity to the original story is critical. This supports the notion that the Grimms may have written the stories themselves, and therefore felt no compunction about revising them. Although the mate-

rial to compare the two texts has been publicly available since 1924, no one brought attention to the differences until Ellis did in 1983.

Examination of the Grimm brothers' own copy of the *KHM*, with marginal notes indicating which brother had written which story (made available for scrutiny in 1899), should have settled the matter back then. No one was willing to make the serious accusation that the Grimms were not the folklore collectors they claimed to be, but rather were literary hoaxers.

Sources:

Ellis, John M. *One Fairy Story Too Many: The Brothers Grimm and Their Tales.* Chicago: University of Chicago Press, 1983.

Freeman, Derek. "Fa'apua'a Fa'amu and Margaret Mead." *American Anthropologist* 91 (1989): 1017–22.

"High Hoax: Those Not-So-Old Ecuadorians." *Time* (March 27, 1978): 87–88.

April Fool's Day Hoaxes

Richard Dimbleby is one of the British Broadcasting Corporation's (BBC) most distinguished television broadcasters. In 1957, he was responsible for a classic April Fool's hoax. He told the evening news viewers about the bumper spaghetti harvest in southern Switzerland, and was shown walking among trees that were growing spaghetti. Workers were gathering the pasta into baskets. Many viewers called the BBC's to ask how they could grow spaghetti plants. The BBC answer was to "place a sprig of spaghetti in a tin of tomato sauce and hope for the best." Eventually, Dimbleby admitted his prank.

Esther Rantzen's "That's Life" program featured an English sheepdog who could drive a car. The dog was shown driving in a sports car. This was accomplished by filming a woman wearing a dog costume, mixing the shots in with film of a real sheepdog. The result was convincing enough that the station's switchboard was flooded with calls from people saying that dogs should not be allowed to drive on public roads.

Another British hoax was executed by the *Daily Mail* newspaper in 1982. The article claimed that widespread television interference had been caused by a brassiere manufacturer who made 10,000 brassieres using a special treated copper wire as the support. This wire was originally designed to be used in fire alarms. When body heat and the nylon surrounding the wire came together, static electricity was produced. Collectively, all of these bras were causing massive television interference. The article was so convincing that the chief engineer of British Telecom ordered that all female laboratory employees be asked whether they were wearing bras containing the treated metal.

An Australian April Fool's incident was done by Dick Smith of Sydney in 1978. Smith allegedly had a giant iceberg towed into Sydney. The radio reported that Smith intended to moor the iceberg near the Opera House. There it would be cut up into ice cubes, and these sold for ten cents each. This never happened, as the iceberg was really a barge covered with white plastic sheets and foam used to fight fires. The incident cost Smith $1,450 to stage.

The British Broadcasting Corporation (BBC) was involved in another April Fool's Day hoax in 1980, when they announced that Big Ben, the clock, was going digital. They offered to give the clock's hands away.

An April Fool's Day prank went awry for Linas Gylys of Chicago. When he noticed that a bank computer error gave his checking account a balance of $4,757,000, instead of the sixty-seven cents the account actually held, he went to the bank to get a personal check for $4.5 million certified. The check was made out by John H. Perkins, the president of the Continental Illinois National Bank. Gylys had checked with the state attorney's office first to make certain that he would not be breaking the law.

When he presented the check to the teller to be certified, she checked his balance and went to get a couple of bank officials. One of these, claiming to be his "personal account officer," actually was the bank's fraud investigator. Gylys was taken into an office and grilled for an hour. The fraud officer wanted to know if Mr. Perkins was associated with Mr. Gylys. Gylys wouldn't talk. As a result, he was presented with a certified check for sixty-seven cents, and told that his account was closed. When Gylys introduced the man with him as a newspaper reporter, things improved considerably. He was told that his account was reopened, and that he could keep the $4.5 million check as a souvenir.

Sources:

Calonius, L. Erik. "Stiff Upper Lips Get a Bit More Relaxed on the First of April." *Wall Street Journal* (March 30, 1984): 1, 17.

Cohen, Hennig and Tristam Potter Coffin, eds. *The Folklore of American Holidays.* Detroit: Gale Research Inc., 1987: 147–49.

Hatch, Jane M. *The American Book of Days.* New York: H.W. Wilson Co., 1978, 3rd ed.: 314–16.

Phillips, Richard. "April Fool's Prank Catches Bank Off Balance." *Chicago Tribune* (April 3, 1977): I3.

Archaeology Hoaxes

Ancient Astronauts and Erich von Däniken

At first glance, the great architectural feats of the past, such as the pyramids, Stonehenge, and the Easter Island statues, appear as though they could not have been built without modern technology. Nevertheless, those structures exist. One explanation of their existence is that visitors from outer space ("ancient astronauts") were responsible. The attraction of this idea stems from the thought that "higher intelligences" not from earth are interested in human beings, and also from the idea that today's society dismisses "primitive" people as being incapable of building such magnificent structures.

The foremost proponent of the ancient astronaut idea is Swiss hotelman Erich von Däniken. His books have sold more than 40 million copies worldwide since 1970. They have been translated into a score of languages and remain in print after many years. Those books are marked by a peculiar and scientifically disconcerting style. Questions are asked but never answered. For example, "The pyramids could not have been made by earthlings, could they?" The implied answer—no—may lead a person to accept the necessity for ancient astronauts, but the evidence required to prove this assumption is never offered. If it *had*, then the obvious answer to the pyramid question would be "yes," since "earthlings" *could* easily have made the artifacts. In addition, most archaeologists simply do not think it worthwhile to respond to von Däniken, even though the public was deceived by the misinformation he supplied.

There are so many different examples of structures and carvings that could not have been made by earthlings, according to von Däniken, that the only way to show how mistaken he is may be to go over a number of his examples and show how each explanation he gives is flawed.

King Pacal's futuristic coffin lid.

The first demonstrable case is the lid of the funeral chamber of the Mayan King Pacal. This tomb is in the Yucatan, in what once was the ancient city of Palenque. Von Däniken says that the stone carving on this lid represents an ancient astronaut operating his spacecraft. According to von Däniken, the carving shows a man with his hands manipulating controls. With his heel, he is operating a pedal of some sort. He has something resembling an oxygen mask on his nose. Outside the "frame" of the vehicle is a small flame-like exhaust.

Careful examination of the carving actually reveals something different to those familiar with the Mayan culture. The king is clad only in what appears to be shorts. The "mask" is a piece of the ornament around the king, and does not actually touch his nose. The ornamental enclosure itself represents corn leaves. The "controls" are representations of the Mayan Sun God in the background. The "pedal" is a sea shell (the Mayan symbol for death). The flame is the roots of the

Erich von Däniken.

corn plant. In short, this is a religious motif, illustrating the life-giving properties of the corn plant, and has nothing to do with a space ship. Yet von Däniken's "explanation" is just plausible enough to fool the naive reader who is not archaeologically sophisticated and may believe what he says is true.

Another alleged example of feats earthlings are not capable of are the so-called Nazca Lines. These are long lines scraped in the desert of Peru, which von Däniken says are the markings or landing strips for a spaceport designed for alien visitors. The inaccuracy of this conclusion is evident when one considers that spacecraft are vertical takeoff and landing devices. Unlike airplanes they do not require a landing strip. Furthermore, the lines scratched in the desert are far too long, to be airplane landing strips, the soil is much too sandy and soft to be used by airplanes. The lines were much more likely to be processional pathways for religious marches.

The Nazca Lines also include spirals and animal figures. How they were created is not as much of a puzzle as von Däniken would have people believe. Author Joe Nickell showed in his 1983 article how they can be created *on the ground* with the use of a few stakes and pieces of rope. In addition, it is quite possible that the Incas had crude hot air balloons, since they had mastered the art of weaving and basketry, both of

which are needed to make a serviceable balloon. Regardless, ascending in a hot air balloon is not necessary to the production of the figures, as Nickell illustrated.

Related to the Nazca Lines is the so-called Trident of Pisco Bay. This is a pitchfork-shaped hillside carving more than 490 feet high. Von Däniken makes three claims about the trident: 1) it cannot be seen from the nearby sea, but only from the air, 2) it is carved into solid rock, and 3) it points directly towards the Nazca "spaceport." He is wrong on all three counts. It *is* clearly visible from the sea, for up to twenty miles. It does not point to the Nazca area, but is off by several degrees. It is scratched into the salt that lies beneath the surface soil, not into rock. The trident actually represents the tree of life and death that is common to many religions. It signifies that the area is a burial ground. In fact, it marks the site of two of the largest ancient burial grounds in Peru.

Perhaps the most outrageous claim made by von Däniken is that he personally visited the "Caves of Gold" under Ecuador, where the gold treasure of the Incas is hidden. These caves are mythical according to most archaeologists. In fact, the man who von Däniken says led him through the caves, Juan Moricz, denies that he ever took von Däniken there. Although Moricz claims to have discovered the caves, he was unable to lead an expedition there in 1969, perhaps because he had never discovered them. The "gold" objects that von Däniken claims to have photographed in the caves were actually brass and imitation objects from the collection of an eccentric priest, Father Carlo Crespi. They are actually located behind his church in Cuenca, Ecuador.

The Piri Re'is map, dated 1513, indicates the map's cartographer—according to von Däniken—had a vantage point in outer space to accurately reproduce the map of the world, given what was known at the time. He claims that Antarctica is shown minus its ice cap, and that the outline of the rest of the continents is almost perfect. What he does not tell is the map shows that Antarctica is located 4,000 miles from where it really is, the Amazon River appears twice, the Drake Passage between Cape Horn and the Antarctic is missing, 900 miles of South American coast is missing, and the Mediterranean Sea is also missing. It's not accurate, but it is what would be expected from sixteenth-century cartography.

The large statues on Easter Island are widely known. It may seem beyond the abilities of the early inhabitants of the island to quarry the stone, haul it several miles and erect the completed statues. However, there is an explanation. Several descendants of the early natives are still alive, and they have demonstrated exactly how the statues were quarried, moved and erected. The process is slow, but does not require many people.

Thor Heyerdahl's book, *Aku-Aku*, details the results of his investigation of the method by which the statues were made. He found that seven men could build a rough version of a statue in three days with the old stone tools. It was estimated that it took two teams of six men each about a year to complete a statue.

Von Däniken claims that the stone tools found around the quarry were not used. Rather, he suggests, ancient astronauts carved the statues, then discarded their work. The natives used stone tools to try to finish the statues not completed. They found this impossible, and abandoned the job and their tools. Thus, he uses the evidence of the stone tools to try to prove the exact opposite of what the evidence would seem to indicate.

To move a statue over the sand, about 180 natives were required; about half that number could move it over harder ground. The job was far from impossible. It is estimated that at least twenty times this many people were available.

To erect a statue, only twelve men were required. It would take them eighteen days. They must have used log levers to raise the top of the statue, at first lying on the ground, a few inches. Then a rock would be inserted under the raised part. Gradually, a pile of rocks was made that raised the statue to a near-vertical position.

Von Däniken attested that the Egyptian pyramids could not possibly have been built by the ancient Egyptians. He makes the statement that ancient Egypt appears a ready-made civilization, without a pre-history. This cannot be true. Pyramids, for example, evolved from burial mounds and tombs. Mud-covered structures followed these simple mounds and tombs, then brick, and finally stone blocks. The first pyramids were the step pyramids. It was only later that the steps were filled in to produce the classic pyramid shape. In this explanation, von Däniken brings in Charles Piazzi Smyth's about the use of mathematical constants in the construction (*See* King Tut's Tomb Curse, p. 15).

There are fairly sound theories explaining how even the biggest pyramids were constructed. It was not by ancient astronauts, but by ancient Egyptians. Huge rollers were made from logs imported from Lebanon and elsewhere. They were used to move the large blocks of relatively soft limestone that had been quarried with hard stone tools and water application. Also, there is a long sloping causeway leading from the banks of the Nile to the base of the Great Pyramid. The large blocks of stone took this path up the Nile on rafts. Sledges of wood were constructed to carry the stone blocks over land, and ramps of earth were constructed to ease the blocks up to their position in the pyramid. It took the Egyptians a long time, but did not require any astronauts. In fact, the first pyramid, known as the ruined Pyramid of Meidum, almost collapsed during construction. As these examples illustrate, von Däniken's books are basically untrustworthy and indicate that he is worthy of being included among the hoaxers.

Sources:

Bainbridge, William Sims. "Chariots of the Gullible." *The Skeptical Inquirer* 3, no. 2 (Winter 1978): 33–48.

Nickell, Joe. "The Nazca Drawings Revisited: Creation of a Full- Sized Duplicate." *The Skeptical Inquirer* 8 (Spring 1983): 36–47.

Story, Ronald. *Guardians of the Universe?* New York: St. Martin's Press, 1980.

———. *The Space Gods Revealed: A Close Look at the Theories of Erich von Däniken*. New York: Harper & Row, 1976.

Wilson, Clifford. *Crash Go the Chariots: An Alternative to Chariots of the Gods*. New York: Lancer Books, 1972.

The Cardiff Giant

The Cardiff Giant is perhaps the best-known American hoax. Many people know of this large stone figure of a human that was unearthed and supposed to be a fossilized man. Although partly true, this is far from what really happened. The story is rather complicated.

George Hull, a cigar maker from Binghamton, in upstate New York, had a brother-in-law named William C. Newell. Newell had a farm at Cardiff, New York, twelve miles south of Syracuse. In October of 1869, Hall asked Newell to dig a well on his property, precisely twenty feet behind his barn. Although this was a rather odd spot for a well, Newell agreed, and hired two local men, and on October 16 they began to dig. At three feet down, they struck stone that was shaped like a large human foot. Soon the body of a ten-foot-long naked and anguished-looking stone giant was uncovered.

Public exhibition of the giant began almost at once. Newell bought a large tent and charged fifty cents per person to view the giant, hear a fifteen-minute talk, and have questions answered. Although the Newell farm was not easy to reach, people took the train from all over the northeast to Syracuse, and then rode by wagon to the farm. Stagecoaches soon ran from Syracuse to Cardiff every day. The Cardiff Giant was first exhibited while still in its pit. Noting that the average number of visitors was 300 to 500 per day (2,600 on one

Sunday), Hull and Newell decided to move the Cardiff Giant to a more accessible place, even though the two men had already made $12,000 from the giant. A 3/4 interest in the giant was sold to some area businessmen for $30,000, and Syracuse was chosen as the new place of exhibition. The giant was moved on November 5. Attendance increased, and the New York Central Railroad even arranged a special ten-minute stop so that passengers could go across the street and view the giant.

Business boomed, both for the giant exhibition and for local shopkeepers. Several experts on fossils and ancient man came to see the giant. One of the first was Dr. John F. Boynton. He pointed out that there was no precedent for the transformation of human or animal flesh into stone. He concluded the giant must be a statue carved by early Jesuit missionaries to impress the Indians. Prof. James Hall, the New York State Geologist, agreed that the giant was a statue. The local newspapers carried arguments from both sides, with those opposed to the statue idea pointing out that there was no pedestal. It was also noted that it would be odd to sculpt a naked man writhing in agony, as the giant was. Those on the other side pointed to the natural striations indicating that the giant had been carved from a single block of stone.

Esteemed Yale paleontologist Othniel C. Marsh finally looked at the giant. After one look at it, he said in his report "It is of very recent origin and a most decided humbug . . . I am surprised that any scientific observers should not have at once detected the unmistakable evidence against its antiquity." He pointed out the fresh tool marks and the presence of smooth, polished surfaces, which would have been roughened by any lengthy burial. Dr. Boynton took another look and agreed.

The evidence that finally discredited the giant's authenticity was the story from the Onandaga County Bank that Newell had withdrawn a sizable sum from his account and paid it to Hull. People then began to remember that a very large wooden box was hauled over backroads south of Cardiff by wagon the previous year. Some quarrymen in Iowa recalled selling a large block of Iowa gypsum to George Hull about two years earlier. Finally, two men in Chicago were identified who claimed to have carved the giant.

About this time, the New York *Herald* ran a story claiming that the statue had been carved previously by a Canadian sculptor who thought he was as good as Michaelangelo. This story was supposedly based on the sculptor's deathbed confession; it, too, was a hoax.

The hoax was actually conceived by George Hull after he had an argument with a clergyman over the

phrase in Genesis "there were giants in the earth in those days." Hull decided to find amusement and fortune by creating and burying a "giant" in the earth. He bought the stone block in Iowa, secretly shipped it to Chicago, where it was carved—also in secret—and then shipped by train to a depot near Binghamton, New York. The crate made its way by backroads to Newell's farm in Cardiff, where it was buried a year before it was unearthed. Hull took care to ensure that no hair was carved on the giant, because he had read that hair did not "petrify." He also "aged" the giant with acid, and put "pores" in the skin by hammering the giant with a mallet studded with darning needles. The giant's burial site was a lucky choice because there were a number of caves, abundant with fossils, in the area. Furthermore, a pattern of finding unusual buried things (Joseph Smith and the Golden Plates) and religious oddities (e.g., the Millerites and the Fox sisters) existed.

Rather than ignoring the giant as just another hoax after its exposure, the public remained fascinated. The giant was moved to New York City, where attendance soared at the Apollo Hall at Broadway and 28th streets. P.T. Barnum (*See* P. T. Barnum's Hoaxes, p. 284) made an offer of $60,000 to lease the giant, but was refused. He had his own copy carved and put on exhibit in New York. Barnum's giant was on display only two blocks from the original. The imitation fake drew more people than the "real fake," undoubtedly due to Barnum's promotional skills.

In February of 1870, the giant was moved to Boston, where it again drew many visitors. A less successful tour of New England and Pennsylvania followed. The giant ended up in a barn in Fitchburg, Massachusetts in about 1880. It stayed there for more than thirty years, with one viewing at the Pan-American Exposition in Buffalo, New York, in 1901. Hull himself tried "finding" another giant (this one made of clay) in Colorado, but that hoax was exposed quickly by the same Professor Marsh, and the public lost interest. The giant was bought in 1913 for $10,000 by a carnival owner. He showed it at small carnivals and state fairs around the country until the 1930s, when he went bankrupt. The giant was then bought by publisher Gardner Cowles, who kept it in his home in Des Moines, Iowa. The New York State Historical Association tried for four years to get Mr. Cowles to sell it to them. He finally agreed in 1948. The giant was transferred to the Farmer's Museum in Cooperstown, New York, where it remains on display.

Sources:

Dunn, James Taylor. "The Cardiff Giant Hoax." *New York History* 29, no. 3 (1948): 367–77.

Franco, Barbara. "The Cardiff Giant: A Hundred Year Old Hoax." *New York History* 50, no. 4 (1969): 421–40.

Sears, Stephen W. "The Giant in the Earth." *American Heritage* 26, no. 5 (August 1975): 94–99.

King Tutankhamen's Curse and the Pyramids

Legend had it that anyone who entered the tomb of King Tutankhamen, commonly called "King Tut," was soon dead from an ancient curse that was inscribed as a warning at the entrance to the tomb. The whereabouts of this inscription today, is uncertain and was perhaps never known. Also, some of the people who first entered the tomb, for example Howard Carter, the first one in, lived many years after their entrance.

The story began with the death of Lord Carnavon's pet canary. The Lord, sponsor of an expedition to the tomb, died shortly thereafter. At this point, a French Egyptologist and occultist, J. S. Mardus, stated in a Paris news conference that the tomb contained " . . . all the things which the priests and masters of the funeral ceremony were able to place in the way of protection against profaners." He suggested that other curses had protected other tombs in the past. Mardus cited a number of other deaths at other tombs reinforcing the validity of the curse concept. Although a number of people reportedly involved with the tomb *did* die within a few years of its opening, many who were involved did *not* die shortly thereafter. Further, many who were mentioned as having died were *not* involved in the tomb's opening.

Herbert E. Winlock, director of the Metropolitan Museum of Art tallied the number of people, present at the 1922 opening of the tomb, who died by 1934. There were twenty-two people present at the opening, and by 1934, six had died. Of the separate group of twenty-two present when the King's sarcophagus was opened in 1924, two died during the next decade. Of the ten present when the mummy was unwrapped in 1925, all were still alive in 1934. The deaths of those present at the various openings were from natural causes. Few were victims of Egyptian diseases, which is logical because they were foreigners unused to Egyptian conditions.

Reports that a curse was inscribed on the entrance of the tomb, or somewhere inside, were completely false. Although the text of the curse was *somehow* provided by journalists, a carved or written curse was not found on or in the tomb.

Another aspect of ancient Egyptian life that has taken on the elements of a hoax is the legendary power of pyramids. The original idea was that the dimensions of the Great Pyramid (the Pyramid of Cheops) mirrored great mathematical relationships (Pi, or a significant relationship with the size of the earth). From this came the idea of the structure itself forming some sort of cryptogram about the earth's future. Some journalists reported that this was all possible because the Great Pyramid was actually constructed by ancient astronauts (*See* Ancient Astronauts and Erich von Däniken, p. 11).

The foremost proponent of the idea of mathematical truths embodied in the construction of the Great Pyramid was Charles Piazzi Smith, who wrote *Our Inheritance in the Great Pyramid* in 1864. He came up with a unit of measurement he called "the pyramid inch," which corresponded to 1.001 English inches. Author Robert Menzies later added the idea of "immortal truth," that prophecies and biblical history were recorded on the pyramid through the use of the pyramid inch. One pyramid inch represented one year, and the length and size of the pyramid's internal passages represented the scale of time.

Immediately, two schools of thought developed. One claimed that time measurement should start with the birth of Jesus, projecting the Second Coming in 1911. The other school said that the chronology should start with the Resurrection, which would make the Second Coming a 1936 event. Obviously, both were wrong; in fact, there is no evidence to support the idea that the constructors of the Great Pyramid intended to prophesize through it.

Modern pyramid studies assert that placing a sharp object under a pyramid will preserve its sharpness, despite repeated use. Also, if placed under a pyramid perishables such as fruit will not rot. Another assertion is that sleeping under a pyramid shape is somehow beneficial to one's health. These ideas have been promoted in recent years without any solid verification. Most writers who assert these as truths are reporting on flawed experiments. Presently, no reliable evidence exists to support the assertion that pyramid shapes have any protective effect.

Sources:

Brackman, Arnold C. *The Search for the Gold of Tutankamen.* New York: Mason/Charter, 1976.

Carter, Howard. *The Tomb of Tut-ankh-Amen.* 3 vols. New York: Cooper Square Publishers, 1963.

Hoving, Thomas. *Tutankhamun: The Untold Story.* New York: Simon & Schuster, 1979.

Vandenberg, Philipp. *The Curse of the Pharaohs.* Philadelphia: J.B. Lippincott Co., 1975.

West, J. A. "Pyramidology." In *Man, Myth & Magic* 17 (1970): 2313–14.

The Lying Stones of Dr. Beringer

Occasionally, prominent scientists have been the *victims* of complex hoaxes; this is one of those cases. The victim was Dr. Johann Bartholomew Adam Beringer (1667–1740). Beringer was well-versed in all areas of science. In addition to being a respected physician, Beringer was an amateur geologist and archeologist. His title at the time of this hoax (1725–1726) was Dean of the Faculty of Medicine at the University of Würzburg in Germany. Junior faculty at Beringer's university at the time, the perpetrators were J. Ignatz Roderick, professor of geography, algebra, and analysis and Georg von Eckhart, university librarian.

Beringer hired three local youths, Christian Zenger (who was seventeen), and Niklaus and Valentin Hehn (brothers, ages eighteen and fourteen), to dig on a nearby mountain and bring him any objects of geologic or archeological interest. Zenger was also employed by the professors to either plant items on the mountain, or to bring them directly to Beringer. The objects (carved stones) were made by Roderick and polished by Zenger. The small stones bore images of insects, lizards, crabs, frogs, flowers, birds, fish, and even Hebrew letters.

When Roderick and Eckhart's hoax got uncontainable, having learned that Beringer was about to publish a book on his findings, they grew alarmed. They spread rumors that the stones were fakes, even showing Beringer how they "could have been" made, but Beringer would not listen. Beringer knew that others had accepted similar stones as genuine. Supposedly the hoaxers then made a stone that bore Beringer's own name, but this cannot be documented. It is known that judicial proceedings started on April 13, 1726, at Beringer's request. His book was published earlier that same year, and Beringer frantically tried to buy up all of the copies once he realized that he had been hoaxed. The original edition of that book, *Lithographiae Wirceburgensis*, is quite rare today, but has been reprinted—most recently in an English translation in 1963. This work brings all the essential items on this hoax together in one place.

In the book, Beringer discussed the pros and cons of the stones' authenticity. He questioned why they often appeared to show the flesh of the creatures and not just the bones. Further, Beringer was actually present at the alleged unearthing of several stones, convincing him of their authenticity. Again, he did not seem to consider that this was a plot to deceive him. The fact that other scientists found stones on the same mountain that also had images on them was enough to convince Beringer of their genuineness. As revealed at the legal

Dr. Beringer's lying stones.

hearing, the boys hired by Beringer had given one or two stones to two other scientists. Only Christian Zenger admitted that he knew the stones were hoaxes.

Although Beringer's reputation was temporarily ruined by this hoax, he soon recovered. He lived for fourteen years after the hoax, and wrote two additional books, both of which were received as valid scholarly works. Today, however, he is remembered largely for his role as the victim of this hoax.

Sources:

Beringer, Johann B.A. *The Lying Stones of Dr. Johann Bartolomew Adam Beringer Being His Lithographiae Wirceburgensis.* Translated and annotated by Melvin E. Jahn & Daniel J. Woolf. Berkeley, CA: University of California Press, 1963.

The Piltdown Man

The hoax of the Piltdown Man is one of the best known of all hoaxes, and certainly has been the subject of many books and articles. During 1911–15, Piltdown, England was the site of the discovery of jawbone and skull segments originally claimed to originate from a human-like ancestor of man. However, although it is recognized as a hoax, the identity of the perpetrators has remained a subject of much speculation. To this day, although fairly convincing cases have named instigators, no one suspect has emerged as unchallenged.

Among the suspects are Charles Dawson, the solicitor and amateur paleontologist who found the first specimen fossils; Sir Arthur Keith, a famous anatomist; Pierre Teilhard de Chardin, Jesuit priest and paleontologist; Lewis Abbott, fossil collector; Martin Hinton, zoologist; Arthur Smith Woodward, anatomist; Sir Arthur Conan Doyle, a doctor and creator of the Sherlock Holmes character; Grafton Elliot Smith, anatomist; Frank Barlow, museum technician; and William Johnson Sollas, geologist.

The motivations and rivalries among these men were complex, and any one or a combination of them could have perpetrated the hoax for reasons varying from jealousy to desire for fame and acceptance. There is a large amount of literature on the subject of the hoax, beginning in 1953 after anthropologist Joseph Weiner first publicly disproved the find. The Piltdown Man's remains were actually a part of an orangutan jawbone and a fairly recent human skull.

Almost all involved in the investigation agreed that Charles Dawson was the principal conspirator. He obtained the fossils by trading with other collectors or buying them. He and Abbott experimented with chemically aged bone specimens. Abbott was involved to give Dawson someone to accuse of fraud if the hoax were discovered prematurely. Dawson, had taken considerable pains to insure that his hoax would not be readily discovered. He evidently stole a medieval orangutan jawbone from a collection. He then broke off the condyle (where the jaw joins the skull), which is distinctive in an ape jawbone, filed the teeth so that they appeared worn as human teeth do, not ape teeth (wear is different due to different diets). He then stained the bone with potassium dichromate to "age" it. The human skull was an unusually thick one, possibly from an Australian aborigine. It, too, was aged with chemicals. All that remained was to plant the bones in a barren gravel pit near Piltdown that would be checked for fossils if Dawson suggested that it might contain them.

Dawson told a number of his collector friends that workmen digging for gravel in the pit found an object "something like a coconut." They probably wondered if it was a fossil skull. Dawson acquired a human skull in 1906 and showed pieces of a human skull (probably the Piltdown skull) to others in the period between 1908 and 1911. Around 1910, he asked the chemist Samuel Woodhead how to treat a bone to make it appear older. It is known that Abbott soaked some of Dawson's skull pieces in potassium dichromate "to harden them." Finally, the fact that the "Heidelberg Jaw" and other remains of man's early ancestors had been found throughout Europe, but not in Great Britain, meant the mood was ripe for a British humanoid find. All of this set the stage for Dawson's 1912 "find." He later brought Teilhard to the pit where Dawson found another skull fragment and Teilhard a part of an elephant molar.

In May 1913, the first doubt on the genuineness of the find was cast by two amateur archaeologists, Guy St. Barbe and Reginald Marriot. They observed Dawson experimenting with pieces of bone soaked in chemical solutions. They kept their doubts private but they were discovered when Weiner investigated in 1953. William King Gregory, anatomist at the American Museum of Natural History, also expressed doubts about the find in late 1913. However, he finally endorsed the find as genuine. Gregory later changed his mind several times about the fossils.

The discovery of the Peking Man's remains, as well as several other fossil finds, showed that the primitive jaw of the Piltdown Man was odd when placed beside the rather modern skull. It was not until the thorough reinvestigation of the fossils in 1953, by Weiner and anthropologist Kenneth Oakley, that the hoax was uncovered. Oakley's chemical analysis of the bones showed staining by potassium dichromate. The tooth discovered later at the site was not an elephant tooth but came from a modern ape and was painted with brown artist's pigment. A "fossil" elephant femur that was later found in the pit by workers had been cut with a steel knife. The alleged elephant molar came from a site in Tunisia.

Dawson's motive is far from clear. He apparently wanted to be respected as a legitimate scientist, and accepted as a member of the Royal Society. Perhaps the others became involved because the find suited their own needs and ambitions.

The exact roles of people other than Dawson in the hoax may never be clearly known. A case can be made that Dawson involved Teilhard, at first innocently. After Teilhard realized that he was trapped as a coconspirator, he played along passively. Dawson's fellow scientist and acquaintance Martin Hinton may have detected the hoax early and, in an attempt to show Dawson that he knew what was going on, planted the elephant femur and tooth, more or less as obvious hoaxes. When they, too, were taken as serious finds, he did not know what to do. Dawson diverted suspicion by discovering additional fossils in another location nearby. Dawson died suddenly in 1916. Hinton still kept silent. The hoax remained concealed until the 1953 reexamination. The Piltdown Man remains the longest held and most deceptive hoax in paleontology.

Sources:

Blinderman, Charles. *The Piltdown Quest*. Buffalo, NY: Prometheus Books, 1986.

Booher, Harold R. "Science Fraud at Piltdown: The Amateur and the Priest." *The Antioch Review* 44 (Fall 1986): 389–407.

Costello, Peter. "The Piltdown Hoax Reconsidered." *Antiquity* 59 (1985): 167–73. See also letters in response to this article in vol. 60 (1986), p.59–60, and Costello's response, p. 145–47.

Grigson, Caroline. "Missing Links in the Piltdown Fraud." *New Scientist* (January 13, 1990): 55–58.

Matthews, L. Harrison. "Piltdown Man: The Missing Links" (multiple-part article). *New Scientist* (April 30, 1981): 280–82; May 7, 1981, p. 376; May 14, 1981, p. 430; May 21, 1981, pp. 515–16; May 28, 1981, pp. 578–79; June 4, 1981, pp. 647–48; June 11, 1981, pp. 710–11; June 18, 1981, p. 785; June 25, 1981, pp. 861–62; July 2, 1981, pp. 26–28.

Oakley, Kenneth P. "The Piltdown Problem Reconsidered." *Antiquity* 50 (1976): 9–13.

Shipman, Pat. "On the Trail of the Piltdown Fraudsters." *New Scientist* (October 6, 1990): 52–54. Also letters in response on October 20, 1990, p. 59.

Spencer, Frank. *Piltdown: A Scientific Forgery*. London: Oxford University Press, 1990. See also the companion volume of documentation, *The Piltdown Papers*.

Thomson, Keith Stewart. "Piltdown Man: The Great English Mystery Story." *American Scientist* 79 (May/June 1991): 194–201.

Weiner, J[oseph] S. *The Piltdown Forgery*. Oxford: Oxford University Press, 1955.

Other Archaeology Hoaxes

The Kinderhook Plates. In April 1843, a set of six brass plates was discovered buried in an Indian mound near Kinderhook, Illinois. The plates were unearthed by Robert Wiley, a local merchant and amateur archaeologist. Each plate was shaped like a flat bell, with narrow top and wide bottom, and each had a small hole bored at the top. Through this hole ran an iron ring, which bound all of the plates together. The plates, when cleaned with diluted sulfuric acid, revealed "hieroglyphics."

Although the plates excited much controversy when they were first made public, an 1855 letter written by W.P. Harris, who was present at the discovery of the plates), contained details of how the plates were made by Robert Wiley, blacksmith Bridge Whitton, and conspirator Wilbur Fugate. Whitton cut the plates out of a copper sheet. Wiley and Fugate made the hieroglyphics on a sheet of wax, and then put it against the plate, filling the cut out letters with acid to etch the plates. They were then covered with dirt, aged with acid and buried.

From 1844 to 1920, the location of the plates was unknown. In 1920, one of the plates was given to the Chicago Historical Society. Its origin was traced back to the original set.

In 1980, definitive tests at Northwestern University showed that the markings were etched with nitric acid and made from brass with few impurities, unlike ancient brass. Rumors that Joseph Smith, the founder of Mormonism, proclaimed the plates authentic and "translated" them, were also negated. Although the plates *were* shown to Smith in 1843, he never did any follow-up on them, and he was killed the following year. Whether the intention of the hoaxers was to trick and embarrass Joseph Smith or to seek fame and fortune for the discovery, is not known.

The Calaveras Skull A human skull was found inside a mine in Calevaras County, California, in February of 1866. At first, the skull was said to be from the Pliocene Age, which would make it more than two million years old—the oldest human remain ever found. Part of the reason for the claim of such great age was that the skull was found beneath some lava 130 feet below the surface. The skull was eventually sent to J.D. Whitney, the California State Geologist, who found that the skull had fossilized. At a meeting of the California Academy of Science, the find was announced and denounced by opposing groups.

The skull appeared to be from an American Indian. Several people said that it had been planted in the mine, as a hoax, but others defended the skull's authenticity. Finally, archeologist W.H. Holmes, after extensive study, declared that nothing about the skull prevented it from being of recent origin. In 1901, he eventually determined that it definitely was *not* of great age.

The whole issue was complicated further by the fact that two skulls were being identified as the one found in the mine. One skull was described as having been covered with black earth when it was found. The other was white and covered with "a limey encrustation." There is fairly reliable evidence that the skull examined by Whitney was *not* the skull found in the mine. In any case, both skulls were fairly contemporary, and were different hoaxes involving the same supposed ancient skull.

The Himalayan Fossils Hoax. Professor Viswa Jit Gupta of Panjab University in India has been accused of falsifying more than 450 research papers over a period of more than twenty-five years. Many of the reports involved the "finding" of fossil remains in the Himalayan regions, where those particular specimens were never found before. The fossils, it is claimed, really came from other places, and were planted at the Himalayan sites. After an investigation by the Indian National Academy of Science, Professor Gupta was suspended from his position at the university.

The Glozel Inscriptions. Glozel is near Vichy, France. In 1924, a farmer found two bricks with an incised design on them while he was plowing. He returned later and started digging, finding a layer of the same bricks about three feet below the surface, and another brick with strange markings on it. Although this was the remains of a glass kiln, it was not interpreted as such at first. The farmer, Emile Fradin, produced additional tools, and pebble artifacts inscribed with letters or symbols. A visitor to Fradin's stable discovered pebbles with steel files and drills next to them. Yet, this was not enough to cast suspicion on Fradin at the time. The incomprehensibility of the inscriptions, however, should have done that. Fradin's collection consisted of more than 2,000 pebbles—some with cuneiform (late Phoenician) hieroglyphics, others with meaningless symbols and ''squiggles.''

A commission arrived in Glozel to investigate. They decided that ''everything we were able to study in Glozel was of no very great age.'' The technical director of the Museum of National Antiquities in France declared that Fradin's discovery of so-called stone tools had been altered by steel files. The engravings were done with steel needles, and the holes in the pendants had been made with steel drills. More items, fired in a kiln, were discovered in 1928.

In France, on February 25, 1928, the Prehistoric Society started court proceedings against an ''unknown person'' for fraud. Fradin's house was searched, and ''artifacts'' in various stages of production were found. Among the elements that comprised the artifacts (which should not have been present if the items were of great age) were chlorophyll, grass, moss, and cotton threads. Although no one was caught in the act of forgery, suspicion rested heavily upon Fradin. Some ''experts'' continued to defend the authenticity of the finds, but most declared that they were hoaxes.

Translations of some of the ''Phoenician'' inscriptions were issued when a clay box with inscriptions similar to those of the Glozel items was unearthed at Bautzen, Germany, in November of 1927. Dr. Morlet, one of the strongest defenders of the authenticity of the Glozel items published an article advocating the authenticity of the box. Shortly after, a Dresden schoolmaster came forward with proof and admitted that *he* made the box years earlier, decorating it with ancient letters he was shown while in school.

The Redman's Pictographs. Peculiar to this hoax is its pricy execution, which leads to questions about the motivation of the perpetrator, supposedly a priest. The Abbe Emmanuel Domenech (1825–1905) was a priest

Supposed Indian Pictographs.

who spent a considerable amount of time in the first half of the nineteenth century exploring the American Southwest and Mexico. He wrote several books about his explorations. Hence, when he published his *Manuscrit Pictographique Americain* in 1860, heavily illustrated with ''pictographs'' supposedly found on rocks and walls in America, the response was favorable. Domenech had apparently managed to have the illustrations, and possibly the entire book, published at French government expense by the Ministry of State. Again, this may be a part of the hoax, or may explain how the great expense of the printing was covered.

The illustrations found in his book appear simplistic—almost ''stick figure,'' and not look anything like what is genuinely attributed to American Indians. Many of the pictographs have a distinctly sexual, often sadomasochistic flavor, including whipping, urinating, and the figures with large genitals. The text makes it fairly clear to the person familiar with ancient cultures in North America, that the author is uninformed.

There are references in Domenech's book to Juan de Torquemada (1540?–1617?), a Franciscan missionary in Mexico, who published a three-volume work on the Indians in 1615. He supposedly discovered the pictographs, though they appear to be of much later generation, perhaps late eighteenth or early nineteen century. Who actually fabricated them is not known, nor is the exact motive or involvement of the Abbe Domenech. It is also conceivable that he was not the author, but that the book's attribution to him was simply part of the hoax.

The Taughannock Giant. Shortly after the Cardiff Giant (*See* Cardiff Giant, p. 13) was "discovered" in 1869, another giant was also discovered in upstate New York in Ithaca. The discovery of the Taughannock Giant came in 1879. On the morning of July 4th, a stone giant weighing about 800 pounds and measuring nearly seven feet tall, was unearthed on the shores of Lake Cayuga in Ithaca. The discovery was described as "a human figure lying on its back, arms nearly straight and the legs crossed at the ankle . . . well proportioned with the exception of the feet, which appear more like those of an ape." Scientists and physicians examined the giant, pronouncing it an authentic fossilized man. The presence of an easily identifiable local mineral rock incorporated in the crotch region of the stone man, helped geologists pronounce the figure authentic.

The giant was actually the work of Ira Dean, who spent months carving the giant in the basement of his home. His motivation merely was the desire to fool someone. Although this particular hoax was much less publicized and of shorter duration than the Cardiff Giant hoax, it remains another example of a fake, stone, giant "fossilized man."

The Wooly Mammoth Hoax. In 1864, Edward Lartet discovered a picture of a wooly mammoth scratched upon a mammoth tusk in a cave at La Madeleine, France. In 1889, another mammoth picture (called "the Holly Oak Pendant") scratched on a shell was produced. The claim was that the pendent was originally found in 1864, in Delaware. The importance of these two finds was that they would associate the existence of early man with the existence of the now-extinct mammoth. Mammoths supposedly became extinct in North America about 2,000 B.C. In 1986, a radiocarbon analysis of a small piece of the Holly Oak Pendant was made, showing an age of about 885 A.D. for the shell of the pendant. Although the shell came from an archeological site, it was estimated that the carving was made in approximately 1880 by Hilborne T. Cresson, using the La Madeleine tusk art as a model. Cresson was a field assistant at the Peabody Museum of Harvard University, and was fired from his position in 1891 for stealing artifacts. He killed himself in 1894. The mammoth in North America must have become extinct long before 885 A.D.; thus the Holly Oak Pendant is a hoax.

Sources:

Anderson, Ian. "Himalayan Scandal Rocks Indian Science." *New Scientist* (February 9, 1991): 17.

———. "Researcher Faces Charges Over Himalayan Fossils Scandal." *New Scientist* (February 23, 1991): 17.

Cazeau, Charles J., and Stuart D. Scott, Jr. *Exploring the Unknown: Great Mysteries Reexamined.* New York: Plenum Press, 1979.

Dexter, Ralph W. "Historical Aspects of the Calaveras Skull Controversy." *American Antiquity* 51, no. 2 (1986): 365–69.

Domenech, Em[manuel]. *Manuscrit Pictographique Americain.* Paris: Gide Librare-Editeur, 1860.

Feder, Kenneth L. *Frauds, Myths, and Mysteries: Science and Pseudoscience in Archeology.* Mountain View, CA: Mayfield Publishing Co., 1990.

Griffin, James B., and others "A Mammoth Fraud in Science." *American Antiquity* 53, no. 3 (July 1988): 578–82. "Himalayan Hoax." *Nature* (April 20, 1989): 604.

Kimball, Stanley B. "Kinderhook Plates Brought to Joseph Smith Appear to be a Nineteenth-Century Hoax." *The Ensign* (Salt Lake City) (August 1981): 66–74.

Meissner, J.P. *Erklärung des "Buches der Wilden."* Leipzig: Friedrich Ludwig Herbig, 1862.

Munro, Robert. *Archeology and False Antiquities.* London: Methuen & Co., 1905.

Petzholdt, J. *"Das Buch der Wilden" im Lichte Französischer Civilization.* Dresden [Germany]: G. Schönfeld's Buchhandlung, 1861.

Rieth, Adolf. *Archeological Fakes.* New York: Praeger Publishers, 1970.

Talent, John. "The Case of the Peripatetic Fossils." *Nature* (April 20, 1989): 613–15.

Vayson de Pradenne, Andre. *Les Fraudes en Archeologie Prehistorique, avec quelques examples de comparison en archeologie genereale et sciences naturelles.* Paris: E. Nourry, 1932.

Williams, Stephen. *Fantastic Archeology: The Wild Side of North American Prehistory.* Philadelphia: University of Pennsylvania Press, 1991.

Art Hoaxes

Artists and art dealers often hope for recognition and wealth, while art collectors are likely to acquire works more for their intrinsic aesthetic merit than for their investment potential. In such a climate of values and desires, poseurs and frauds flourish. The monetary value of painting and sculpture is often derived from two factors: 1) aesthetic quality and 2) who made them when. It is the second of these two factors that comes into play in most art hoaxes, which are cases of forgery.

I

A forgery is normally defined as a work of art presented to a buyer or audience with the intention to deceive. Fraudulent intention is necessary for a work to be a forgery, which distinguishes forgeries from honest copies and mistaken attributions. Usually a forger paints a work in the style of a famous artist and tries to sell it, often in conjunction with an unscrupulous dealer, claiming it is from the hand of a famous artist. Forgers seldom try to execute exact copies of existing authentic paintings; such works are practically impossible to sell to informed buyers.

Because of the cautious expertise of dealers and curators, the creation of plausible forgeries is a demanding process. If a forger wishes, for example, to fake an important seventeenth-century painting, he must begin with a seventeenth- century canvas, as the production of an old-looking canvas from modern materials is virtually impossible. He will have to find an unimportant, but sufficiently old, painting and either paint over it or dissolve and scrape away the old painting. If he paints over it, he faces the possibility that an X-ray will reveal the underpainting. Trying to remove the old paint from the canvas may be nearly impossible, as chemicals might fuse with the fibrous material. Sometimes forgers leave parts of the underpainting that cannot be removed and try to incorporate them into the design of the new forgery.

In selecting paints and brushes, the forger of a seventeenth-century painting must know the history of pigment formulae and carefully avoid paints invented later that would reveal his fraud. For example, the color ultramarine did not come into general use until 1838, and Prussian blue does not predate 1800. Other colors in use today are clearly from the late nineteenth and twentieth centuries. The notorious Dutch forger of Vermeers, Han van Meegeren (*See* Han van Meegeren, p. 26), in addition to using only badger hair brushes lest a single modern bristle be found embedded in the paint, also studied old pigment formulae, grinding his own lapis lazuli, for instance, to produce blue.

Style is of great importance; a forger must study the brush techniques, typical subject matter, and stylistic qualities of the artist to be forged. Many forgeries are pastiche works—paintings that draw together miscellaneous elements from a number of authentic paintings in a way that fits perfectly into the established style of the older artist. Style, however, is where even the most technically accomplished forgers usually fail. It is almost impossible for a modern painter, no matter how conscientious the attempt, to fully back into the representational conventions of a previous century. Thus, even so cautious a forger as van Meegeren produced, from the beginning of his forgery career, paintings that—though they were supposed to be by seventeenth-century hands—displayed elements of twentieth-century style. For example, the faces in his 1937 Vermeer forgery, *Christ and the Disciples at Emmaeus*, are strongly influenced by photography. One of the faces even resembles that of Greta Garbo. These stylistic features were much less apparent to the trained eye of the 1930s, precisely because they seemed so "normal." In retrospect, they are quite obvious.

The pigment of old paintings, acquired through time, has two characteristics: it becomes quite hard and shrinks slightly, causing a network of fine cracks called

A forged El Greco.

craquelure. Depending on how thick the pigment is, it may take ten years or more for a forgery in oils to dry to the hardness of an old work. Forgers, impatient to cash in on their work, will add solvents to their paints to increase the drying speed. Craquelure presents a more serious problem, as the cracks on old paintings blacken with dust and dirt. Craquelure can be mimicked by painting fine, black cracks over the surface. This technique will not, however, get past the experienced eye of a dealer or curator. The forger may try to induce cracking in the paint surface by slow baking. But even if the baked-and-cooled painting is rolled on a tube, the cracks will tend to line up in one direction, rather than extend randomly in all directions. Rolls at right and diagonal angles must be attempted, however, the first rolling will tend to make more cracks than subsequent rolls, making a completely random pattern nearly impossible to produce. The forger may attempt to achieve the effect of a cracked surface by scratching into the pigment with a needle. When the resulting surface is wiped with black ink, the result can look excellent, but the "cracks" will not extend all the way into the canvas, which may reveal the fraud. It is possible to achieve a more natural cracking by mixing egg white with pigment; this is difficult, however, because it dries faster and requires the forger to work quickly.

Once a satisfactory appearance of craquelure has been produced by one or more of these techniques, a final varnishing is required. Many collectors of old art consider it a mark of authenticity when a painting is obscured by a cloudy, dark varnish, which the forger applies with coats of a brownish substance. Finally, a bit of attic dust is convincing.

Although many old paintings of little value have been "recycled" by forgers, occasional mistakes are made. One story involved a dealer who tried to sell an "eighteenth-century French" painting to the wealthy industrialist Alfred I. duPont in 1931, claiming it was a portrait of one of duPont's ancestors. The asking price was $25,000, a large sum at the time. When duPont grew suspicious the painting dropped to $10,000, and eventually to a mere $1000. DuPont considered the frame alone to be worth $400, so he bought the portrait and showed it to a curator who determined that the work had been altered by overpainting. The curator suggested the overpainting be removed, which was easily done, revealing beneath a magnificent Madonna and Child by the seventeenth-century Spanish painter Murillo, valued at $150,000. The forger had cheated himself.

II

When a painting is finished, the forger faces what may be his most difficult task—creating a story that explains where the painting came from and why it remained undiscovered. The forger needs a plausible story about the painting's whereabouts for the last few centuries. In this respect, the forgery of works of art resembles hoaxes in other fields; the faker needs to invent an origin for the object. This may involve forging one or two official museum certificates with old wax seals to be affixed to the back of the canvas. For a serious forger, skilled enough to fake a seventeenth-century painting, old certificates of authenticity pose little difficulty. If the forgery is of a twentieth-century work, perhaps the artist's relatives can be tricked, via flattery or money, into signing a letter of authenticity. The forger—or his dealer/partner—now needs a story of how it came into his hands. This has resulted in variations of the following theme: "An old Italian family, which owned this masterpiece for generations, has fallen on hard times and must sell it. They insist on utmost discretion; they do not want to be named."

Perhaps one of the most clever and audacious origin-establishing routines was that used in the 1960s by two confederates of the modern Hungarian forger, Elmyr de Hory. They searched secondhand bookshops in France for out-of-print art books of the 1920s and 1930s. They looked for books on modern art of the time that were illustrated with color plates that had been glued onto the text paper of the books (a common procedure for art books of the time). For example, they might find a book with a plate that was described in the text or caption, "Raoul Dufy, *The Reception at Elysee Palace*, 1928 oil on canvas, 87 X 133 mm, signed in lower left corner." They would then telephone de Hory and ask him to produce a forgery that exactly matched the description of the plate. After de Hory delivered his painting, his partners would have it photographed and printed on a paper stock that closely matched the other plates in the book. They would remove the original plate, replace it with their color reproduction of the forgery, creating an old art book containing the very painting they were selling! As another copy of the book would be next-to-impossible to locate in Texas, South Africa, or wherever the painting was bound to be sold, there was little chance of being found out. They would even give the doctored art book to the buyer of the forgery to proudly place on his coffee table.

The price at which a forgery is offered to potential buyers is often an indication of its true status. Authentic masterpieces are always expensive—honest copies are cheap. Forgeries offered by fraudulent dealers tend to be priced far too high for copies, but considerably under the market for authentic work. Along with the phony origin, the dealer might explain that the owner has large debts and needs immediate payment, and at this special bargain price, the painting must be bought immediately. Paintings, and other collectibles prone to fakery with prices too good to be true are probably fakes.

III

Described above was a clear case of intentional deception where a forger produces a pastiche work and tries to establish it as the creation of another artist. But many cases that might be treated as forgery are not so clear cut. For example suppose a nobleman of the Italian Renaissance might admire a painting owned by a neighboring duke. He accordingly instructs his personal court painter to produce a copy of the painting for himself. It may be that neither the original nor the copy is signed and, as both works are Italian Renaissance paintings, later scientific tests will be no help in distinguishing them. If the original is signed, a later owner of the copy may surreptitiously sign it with the original artist's signature. Thus, over the years, what started off as an innocent copy is turned into a forgery by a later owner. To further confuse matters, a later owner of the original may, if it was originally unsigned, forge on it the signature of the original artist in order to protect the reputation and value of his painting. In such a misty and confused historical context, it may be impossible to determine which is the original and which the copy.

Historically, many paintings, such as those of the Flemish artist Peter Paul Rubens (1577–1640), were produced in workshops. In such circumstances the credited artists paint only the most important parts of the work, leaving minor portions to his assistant. The artist may even provide no more than a sketch or outline that is completed by an assistant. This compromises exclusive creative responsibility for a work of art. Also, it is possible that workshop assistants falsely signed their own private output with the names of their more famous employers in order to increase the price of their paintings. To add to the ambiguities, Rubens himself often employed assistant artists of the calibre of Van Dyck, Teniers, and Jan Breughel.

In the past art training relied much more on copying than it does today. Although in European museums one still occasionally sees art students with easels set before Old Master paintings executing exact copies; such sights were more common in the nineteenth and early twentieth centuries. This indicates two considerations important in the history of forgery. First, there were several well-executed copies made of old paintings both famous and obscure. Some of these training copies have been passed off as authentic, if their canvas and materials resemble the original. Second, the general prevalence of copies is a reminder that many artists' training centered on perfecting the ability to copy or mimic another artist's style. Many of these artists would have been perfectly able to forge, given sufficient motivation. One of the most copied paintings of history was Leonardo's *Mona Lisa*. Hundreds of copies of this work of art are known to exist. Some of these are nearly as old as the original and a few are thought by their owners to be the original *Mona Lisa*. They believe the one in the Louvre to be a copy.

Perhaps the most forged painter in history was the French landscape artist, Jean-Baptiste-Camille Corot (1796–1875). It has been jestingly said that of the 3,000 or so paintings he produced in his career, about 10,000 are now in the United States alone. Actually, the number of Corot fakes has been estimated at more than 100,000. Besides being an extremely popular and prolific artist of his time, Corot was generous to the point of occasionally signing his own signature to his student's paintings. Many of his paintings feature a loose, sketchy, spontaneous style which lends itself to casual forgery. The body of work claimed for Corot is now so clogged with fakes, some obvious, but others quite subtle and apparently respectable, that it might never be possible to precisely sort out the authentic from the forged paintings.

IV

Forgers, in general, produce their fakes for money. Although, especially in the twentieth century, they have also tried to find moral justification for their activities. Van Meegeren, for example, claimed that he originally intended with his first great Vermeer forgery, *Christ and the Disciples*, to take revenge on the critics who humiliated him. He planned to wait until the painting was lauded by critics and historians, and then reveal to the world his scam. He made so much money on the painting, however, that he kept his cover and painted more forgeries. Similar claims have been made by other forgers, including more recently the British forger Eric Hebborn. He expressed a desire for revenge against the British class establishment and art dealers as a prime motive for a thirty-year string of forgeries which began in the 1950s. In taking such a stand, forgers are often cheered on by a public eager for the embarrassment of the rich elite of the art world. During his trial in 1949, van Meegeren became a folk hero, not only for having humiliated art snobs, but for having scammed the Nazi leader Hermann Göring, who paid a high price for one of van Meegeren's phony Vermeers. Even van Meegeren's forgeries began to sell for substantial amounts, though nothing near the prices of Vermeers'.

In fact, a vague pattern can be detected by studying the more noted forgers of the last century. They tend to be artists whose careers have foundered after a promising start. Most are men, though some women also forge, such as Madame Claude Latour, convicted by a French court in 1947. Some of her Utrillo forgeries were said to be so accurate that even Utrillo himself could not be sure he hadn't painted them. Successful forgers often exhibit impressive technical skill, yet as artists seem to have no original ideas. They use talent to imitate another's style, and though the outcome will have a superficial resemblance to their target artist, the overall work will seem to lack the inner passion and vision that makes great art so perpetually fascinating. The imitative ability of the forger succeeds best where a single fake is seen in isolation. A whole gallery or portfolio of forgeries, on the other hand, will begin to betray itself more clearly as fraudulent. Where an original artist may attack a canvas with uninhibited enthusiasm, the forger tends toward deliberation and care. Picasso could, with one bold gesture, create a powerful line. The forger may painstakingly try to achieve the same, with a resulting sense of constriction and lack of freedom. This is one of the reasons why many forgers attempt to fake sketches and "early works" of an artist—if the work does not look quite right, it is explained that it was done before the artist established his mature, more confident style.

Observing the monetary excesses of the art market and the occasional foolishness of art historians and critics, the so-called educated eye of the connoisseur is not to be completely disregarded. Though *Christ and the Disciples at Emmaus* received high praise when it was unveiled in 1937, it was also seen by the Paris representative of the New York dealers, Duveen Brothers. He wired to his bosses the following cable: "Seen today at Bank large Vermeer . . . Christ's Supper at Emmaus supposed belong private family certified by Bredius who writing article . . . stop price pounds ninety thousand stop picture rotten fake."

V

The same features that may immediately mark a forgery to the educated eye may be the same ones that make a forgery appealing to a particular time or age. Such indications as physical posture or the style of an eyebrow may make a fake Botticelli or Picasso slightly more palatable to the contemporary eye. These features may seem almost imperceptible but, once fashion changes, they become immediately apparent. As mentioned, shades of Garbo are present in van Meegeren's Vermeers, but their most apparent stylistic quality is the way in which they resemble the German Expressionist style of their time. Faces in the van Meegeren forgeries evoke the work of the German Expressionist artist Emil Nolde.

Another result of van Meegeren's forgery is the eventual acceptance of his style as that belonging to Vemeer. The first of van Meegeren's widely known Vermeers, *Christ at Emmaeus*, was close enough to Vermeer to fool some experts, but it also had unmistakable aspects of van Meegeren's own style. Nevertheless, since the painting was praised as a fine Vermeer, the van Meegeren aspects of it were henceforward accepted as Vermeer's stylistic features. In his next Vermeer forgery, van Meegeren included more of himself and less of Vermeer, gaining more acceptance each time that his own style was actually Vermeer's. His last forgeries were hardly anything like authentic Vermeers, but because curators and buyers had their understanding of the Vermeer style warped by earlier forgeries, van Meegeren was undetected. In the unlikely event that his forgeries had remained undiscovered, today's view of Vermeer's art would be wildly distorted.

The great age of forgeries was the nineteenth century. Through this era, interest in classical antiquities and the Middle Ages increased. The market for Old Masters paintings flourished, while imperial expansion meant a new fascination for art and craft objects from cultures beyond the accepted edge of civilization. Wealthy art collectors, not always expert in spotting fakes, combined with hungry dealers and highly skilled craftsmen caused forgery to prosper as never before. Objects purporting to be from ancient Egypt, India, and the Far East were especially popular, as well as works from medieval Europe. The diverse range of art interests inspired forgers to create new genres. For example, ivory was coming into Europe in considerable quantities. This influx, combined with the popularity of medieval carving, resulted in vast outputs of religious carvings in ivory purporting to be from the Middle

Ages. Medieval ivories eventually lost much of their popularity among collectors because of the confusion.

With the rise of modern art in the twentieth century and the subsequent decline of painting technique, craftsmanship, and historical copying as a teaching method, the era of forgery of old works of art is probably past. The forgery of contemporary works will continue, and it is expected that forgers will try to go into fields that are as lucrative, but less labor intensive than forgery of old European art. One area where forgeries are currently surfacing in large numbers is African art. Workshops within Africa are producing forgeries of nineteenth-century masks, ancestral figures, and artifacts capable of fooling even the most knowledgeable experts. Since the styles of African art are various, artificial aging techniques straightforward, and prices high, the current market supports a number of "old" African pieces of dubious authenticity.

VI

Different opinions exist in the area of art as to whether it matters or not that a forgery is a forgery. One strand of thought holds that a work's status as a forgery makes no difference to its aesthetic value. If one cannot see a difference in a copy, or if a work of art is pleasing, it is aesthetically irrelevant who created it or when. If experts and the public at large both enjoy a van Meegeren as much as a Vermeer, then the paintings are of equal value. According to this view, to affirm the value of a work of art and later deny its value once it is known to be a forgery amounts to hypocrisy and snobbery. If one can't see a difference between two objects no aesthetic difference exists between them.

While the aesthetic-value school of thought enjoys wide popular acceptance, it is disputed by a number of philosophers. Author Nelson Goodman argues that if he is presented with an original and a copy are indistinguishable, the fact that he knows one is a copy should still make an aesthetic difference to him. Though he cannot at present see a difference, no matter how hard he looks now he cannot rule out the possibility that sometime in the future he might be able to see a difference. Differences between the two works that elude him now may at a later time, and with greater sophistication and eye training, seem obvious. This is a lesson of the van Meegeren episode; at first his fakes fooled experts, but later even novices could pick out the characteristics that distinguished van Meegerens from authentic Vermeers. Moreover, looking for the difference has the benefit of training the eye.

The other line of argument holds that admiration for a work of art includes more than what simply meets the eye. If people listen to a recording of a pianist who amazes them with her virtuosity and later discover that the speed and accuracy of her runs were electronically faked, they are justifiably disappointed. This shows that attitude toward a work of art is in part determined by what is known about the circumstances under which it was produced. The Victorian painter J. M. W. Turner, for instance, is often praised for being ahead of his time in adumbrating, the loose-brush technique and hazy character of later Impressionism. But no twentieth-century Turner forgery—however appealing to the eye—could be praised as "ahead of its time." Part of what individuals admire and enjoy in art is innovation and originality; forgery by its nature is derivative and unoriginal. Historically speaking the artist is an imaginative and revolutionary creator; the forger is always a parasite.

Finally, a major objection to forgery is the way it distorts the understanding of an original artist or a historical time. As the forger's aim is to sell to his own contemporaries, he only wishes to mimic the appearance of his model artist. Once a forgery is accepted as genuine, it will inevitably affect the historical understanding of art from that time. Nevertheless, it is fair to ask if a perfect, undetectable forgery is possible. The answer is, curiously, that one can never be sure. The truly successful forgeries, if they exist, hang to this day on the walls of museums.

Denis Dutton

Sources:

Arnau, Frank [H. Schmitt]. *The Art of the Faker*. Boston: Little Brown, 1961.

Bredius, Abraham. "A New Vermeer." *Burlington Magazine* 71 (November 1937): 210–11.

———. "An Unpublished Vermeer." *Burlington Magazine* 61 (October 1932): 145.

Bulley, M. H. *Art and Counterfeit*. London: Methuen, 1925.

Coremans, P. B. *Van Meegeren's Faked Vermeers and de Hooghs*. Translated by A. Hardy and C. Hutt. London: Cassel, 1949.

Drachsler, Leo M., ed. *Forgery in Art and the Law: A Symposium*. New York: Federal Legal Publishers, 1956.

Dutton, Denis, ed. *The Forger's Art: Forgery and the Philosophy of Art*. Berkeley, CA: University of California Press, 1983.

Friedlander, Max J. *Genuine and Counterfeit*. New York: A. & C. Bonni, 1930.

Gerald, W. R. *The Eye of the Beholder: Fakes, Replicas, and Alterations in American Art.* New Haven, CT: Yale University Press, 1977.

Godley, John. *Van Meegeren, Master Forger.* New York: Charles Scribner's Sons, 1967.

Goodman, Nelson. *Languages of Art.* Indianapolis: Hackett, 1976.

Goodrich, David L. *Art Fakes in America.* New York: Viking Press, 1973.

Goodrich, Lloyd. *The Problem of Authenticity in American Art.* New York: Whitney Museum, 1942.

Hollander, Barnett. *The International Law of Art.* London: Bowes and Bowes, 1959.

Irving, Clifford. *Fake! The Story of Elmyr de Hory, the Greatest Art Forger of Our Time.* New York: McGraw-Hill, 1969.

Jones, Mark, ed. *Fake? The Art of Detection.* Berkeley, CA: University of California Press, 1990.

Koestler, Arthur. *The Act of Creation.* New York: Macmillan, 1964.

Koobatian, James, ed. *Faking It: An International Bibliography of Art and Literary Forgeries, 1949–1986.* Washington, DC: Special Libraries Association, 1987.

Kurz, Otto. *Fakes: A Handbook for Collectors and Students.* New York: Dover, 1967.

Reisener, Robert George, ed. *Fakes and Forgeries in the Fine Arts [1848–1948]: A Bibliography.* New York: Special Libraries Association, 1950.

Sachs, Samuel. *Fakes and Forgeries.* Minneapolis: Minneapolis Institute of Arts, 1973.

Savage, George. *Forgeries, Fakes, and Reproductions.* London: Barrie and Rockliff, 1963.

Tietze, Hans. *Genuine and False.* London: Max Parrish & Co., 1948.

Van Bemmelen, J. M., and others, eds. *Aspects of Art Forgery.* The Hague: Martinus Nijhoff, 1962.

Biographical Memoirs of Extraordinary Painters

What began as a joke, became a hoax that still amuses and confuses people. William Beckford (1760–1844), a British writer best known for his novel, *Vathek*, was also an art collector. Visitors to his large house admired his art collection, which his housekeeper was often asked to show. One day she approached Beckford, wanting to learn about the artists and paintings in the collection so she could more competently show it. Beckford composed his *Biographical Memoirs of Extraordinary Painters,* in manuscript, to guide his keeper. At least that is the story Beckford told; it is most likely untrue.

Rather, according to Robert J. Gemmett's introduction to the reprint of Beckford's *Biographical Memoirs,* they are an "ingenious burlesque of artistic excesses propagated by various schools of painting, most notably the Dutch and Flemish, and a masterful parody of certain biographies dedicated to capsulizing the life and work of individual artists."

In fact, the book was probably composed between 1777 and 1780, when it first appeared in print. The work itself is entirely a product of the author's imagination, although it purports to contain genuine biographical sketches of little-known, but important, artists. Beckford wrote about the lives of six artists—all imaginary—Watersouchy, Aldrovandus Magnus, Andrew Guelph, Og of Basar, Blunderbusiana, and Sucrewasser. The mere names of the artists ought to reveal that the work was a satire.

Each section of the book contains additional names that smack of satire: "Insignificanti," "Zigzaggi," and "Boccadolce." The only reason that the work was taken seriously was because many of the incidents and titles of pictures were closely modelled after real ones. Beckford's reputation as an art connoisseur also lent the book authenticity. These ingredients helped to produce Beckford's satire.

Sources:

Beckford, William. *Biographical Memoirs of Extraordinary Painters.* Rutherford, NJ: Fairleigh Dickinson University Press, 1969 (reprint).

Chapman, Guy. *Beckford.* London: Rupert Hart-Davis, 1952.

Gemmett, Robert J. "Introduction" to Beckford's *Biographical Memoirs.* Rutherford, NJ: Fairleigh Dickinson University Press, 1969, 11–31.

Redding, Cyrus. *Memoirs of William Beckford of Fonthill: Author of Vathek.* 2 vols. London: Charles Skeet, 1859.

"William Beckford, Esq., of Fonthill." *European Magazine & London Review* (September 1797): 147–150.

Han van Meegeren

The most notorious and celebrated forger of the twentieth century, Han van Meegeren (1889–1947), was born in the Dutch town of Deventer. He was fascinated by drawing as a child, pursuing it despite his father's disapproval and sometimes spending all his pocket money on art supplies. In high school he was finally able to receive professional instruction and went on to study architecture, according to his father's wishes. In 1911, he married Anna de Voogt. Soon after, his artistic talents were recognized when he won first prize and a gold medal from the General Sciences Section of the Delft Institute of Technology for a drawing of a church interior. He agreed to sell this drawing, but his wife discovered him making a copy of it to sell as the original. She dissuaded him from carrying out this small swindle, but the incident was the first evidence of his interest in forgery, even if he was forging his own work.

The Van Meegerens moved to The Hague where he received his degree in art in 1914. For the next ten years he sold his own work and supported himself by giving drawing lessons. He held fairly well-received exhibitions in 1916 and 1922. In 1923, he divorced Anna and became involved with Johanna Oerlemans, the estranged wife of art critic Karl de Boer. They were married in 1929.

Van Meegeren's artistic style was essentially conservative: misty interiors of old churches, Dutch scenes, religious paintings, sentimental portraits, and paintings in the mystical symbolism genre. One animal drawing, *Queen Juliana's Deer*, enjoyed great popularity on calendars and postcards. His political outlook was Catholic, anti-Semitic, and extremely conservative. He was opposed to all modernist tendencies in art. Though van Meegeren was successful as an artist, critics in the 1920s were increasingly negative and condescending about his work. He became bitter toward critics and promoters of modern art, whom he called a "slimy little group of woman-haters and negro-lovers."

By 1923, van Meegeren produced his first forgery, a *Laughing Cavalier*, presented as the work of Frans Hals. This was authenticated by an expert and fetched a good price at auction, but was detected as a forgery some months later. Van Meegeren's involvement went undiscovered. From this episode, van Meegeren learned lessons that helped him succeed in his first Vermeer forgery, *Lady and Gentleman at the Spinet*, which was produced in 1932 and praised by the eminent art historian Prof. Abraham Bredius as a fine Vermeer. The same year he left Holland and moved with wife Johanna to southern France.

For the next four years, he supported himself by painting portraits. During this time he studied formulae for seventeenth-century paints and experimented with ways to produce a pigment surface that had the hardness of old paint and displayed "craquelure," the system of cracking normally found on the surface of old paintings. Using volatile flower oils, he managed to perfect the technique he employed in his greatest Vermeer forgery, *Christ and the Disciples at Emmaeus*, which he painted from 1936 to 1937.

The 1932 Vermeer forgery was pastiche of elements from known authentic works, but van Meegeren's strategy for the second forgery was much more subtle. Though most extant Vermeers were small paintings of interior domestic scenes, Vermeer had earlier produced large religious paintings. Professor Bredius had theorized that other large, early Vermeers of religious themes might yet turn up. Accordingly, van Meegeren painted a work that exactly fulfilled Bredius' scholarly hypothesis. Other art historians also suggested that Vermeer traveled through Italy early in his life. The *Emmaeus* canvas, which showed possible influence of Carravagio, was designed to confirm an academic conjecture.

Van Meegeren invented a story about a destitute Italian family that owned the painting for generations and did not want the family name revealed. He then set out to sell it through Dutch dealer G. A. Boon. When the painting was presented to Bredius for authentication, he beamed, publishing news of this "wonderful moment in the life of an art lover" in 1937 in the *Burlington Magazine*. He wrote,

> we have here a—I am inclined to say—the masterpiece of Johannes Vermeer of Delft . . . quite different from his other paintings and yet every inch a Vermeer. . . . In no other picture by the great Master of Delft do we find such sentiment, such a profound understanding of the Bible story—a sentiment so nobly human, expressed through the medium of the highest art.

Though doubts about the painting persisted in some quarters (the agent of the New York dealer Duveen Bros. called it a "rotten fake"), with Bredius' authentication the painting was sold by Boon to the Boymans Museum in Rotterdam for a sum equivalent to approximately two million U.S. dollars (1992 value). Van Meegeren received about two-thirds of this amount. From this point Van Meegeren, who now had more money than ever before, began to abuse alcohol and drugs, becoming a morphine addict. Though he originally planned to confess his forgery to humiliate the critics who had lauded it, he instead forged two more Vermeer paintings.

Van Meegeren was arrested only days after the end of World War II on the serious criminal charge of having sold a Dutch National Treasure to the enemy. One of his fake Vermeers, *The Adulteress*, had ended up in the personal art collection of the Nazi Reichsmarshall Hermann Göring. In order to save himself from serving a long sentence for collaboration with the Nazis, he pleaded guilty to the lesser crime of forgery. At first his claim to have forged not only *Emmaeus* and *The Adulteress*, but also four other "authentic" Vermeers, was met with disbelief. A scientific commission was set up and

Han van Meegeren and one of his forged paintings.

van Meegeren himself proposed that he paint a new Vermeer while in jail awaiting trial. The resulting painting, *The Young Christ Teaching in the Temple,* was clearly by the same hand as all the other fakes.

His trial received international coverage. Van Meegeren portrayed himself as a man who merely loved to paint and whose career had been ruined by malicious critics. Having embarrassed eminent scholars and curators with his forgeries, he became a folk hero. The court treated him leniently, sentencing him to the minimum one year in prison on November 12, 1947. But van Meegeren's debauched life, coupled with a heart condition, led to a fatal cardiac arrest on December 29.

Today it seems almost impossible that the van Meegeren forgeries were mistaken for Vermeers. The faces seem influenced by photography. The sentimental eyes and awkward anatomy are more reminiscent of German expressionist works of the 1920s and 1930s than they are of the works of Vermeer. One of the faces in the *Emmaeus* painting resembles Greta Garbo. Yet the very characteristics that identify the paintings as works of their time, rather than Vermeer's, also made them immediately appealing to their 1930s audience.

The first major forgery, *Emmaeus,* was closer to a Vermeer than any of the others. Once it was firmly accepted as an authentic Vermeer, the next forgery could afford less Vermeer and more van Meegeren. The last of the fakes, *The Adulteress,* is far from Vermeer, but once scholarship incrementally accepted its predecessors, it was a small step to validate it.

The van Meegeren case, with its elements of vanity, gullibility, artistic skill, perfectly captured problems that haunt the art world to this day. Han van Meegeren may not have been a great artist, but he made

Han van Meegeren's self-portrait.

people think much harder about what they value in art and why. (*See* Art Hoaxes, p. 21).

Denis Dutton

Sources:

Bredius, Abraham. "A New Vermeer." *Burlington Magazine* 71 (November 1937): 210–211.

———. "An Unpublished Vermeer." *Burlington Magazine* 61 (October 1932): 145.

Coremans, P. B. *Van Meegeren's Faked Vermeers and de Hooghs.* London: Cassel, 1949.

Godley, John [John Raymond Godley Kilbracken]. *Van Meegeren, Master Forger.* New York: Charles Scribner's Sons, 1967.

Jones, Mark, ed. *Fake? The Art of Detection.* Berkeley, CA: University of California Press, 1990.

Tietze, Hans. *Genuine and False.* London: Max Parrish & Co., 1948.

Werness, Hope B. "Han van Meegeren Fecit." In *The Forger's Art: Forgery and the Philosophy of Art.* Edited by Denis Dutton. Berkeley, CA: University of California Press, 1983.

Two Hoaxers: Smith and de Hory

Paul Jordan Smith (1885–?) was the author of a number of books of fiction. He disliked Picasso and other artistic innovators and tried to found a new school of art, the "Disumbrationist School," in 1924. Masquerading as a Russian named Pavel Jerdanovitch, he entered a painting of his, done in the "Disumbrationist School," into a French exhibition in the spring of 1925. The painting was called "Exaltation." A French art journal wrote and asked for photographs of his other work. Smith replied that he was too poor to afford the photographs, but did submit a fanciful biographical sketch.

Several French art journals gave his now four paintings favorable mention. The art looked like "Gauguin, pop art, and Negro minstrelsy" combined, according to one art critic. After three years, Smith tired of his double life and confessed to a feature writer for the *Los Angeles Times*. The paper printed an exposé on August 14, 1927.

Elmyr de Hory (b. 1906), was born in Hungary. His early life is a mystery, complicated by his many pseudonyms, including Von Houry, Louis Cassou, L.E. Raynal, Hoffman, Herzog, and Dory-Bouton. He probably inherited some significant amount of money because no one ever saw him work at anything but art.

In 1946, he sold one of his paintings to a woman who thought it was a Picasso. She subsequently sold it to a dealer *as* a Picasso, which gave de Hory the idea to forge the works of other artists. He moved to the United States, where he used direct mail to sell forged Degas, Modigliani, Matisse, Renoir, and Braque paintings. In 1968, one of his customers noticed that some of the paint was still wet on one of the paintings, and the forgeries were exposed.

De Hory later moved to the Mediterranean island of Ibiza in the Balearics. It was here that Clifford Irving

One of Paul Jordan Smith's Disumbrationist paintings.

(*See* Howard Hughes' Autobiography, p. 72), also a resident there, met him and decided to write a book about him. Whether de Hory supplied the information, or the information came from elsewhere, Irving's book is not entirely reliable. It does tell of the intricate network of art dealers and middlemen who later sold de Hory's forgeries to trusting art lovers. According to Irving, someone made a lot of money from de Hory's forgeries, though probably not de Hory.

Sources:

Checkland, Sarah Jane. "Works of a Great Faker Come to Auction." *London Times* (March 30, 1990): 4.

Irving, Clifford. *Fake! The Story of Elmyr de Hory, The Greatest Art Forger of Our Time.* New York; McGraw-Hill, 1969.

MacDougall, Curtis D. *Hoaxes.* New York: Macmillan, 1940.

Business Hoaxes

The Bank of Portugal

Artur Virgilio Alves Reis (1896–1955) had the Bank of Portugal's currency printer produce genuine Portuguese 500 escudo notes for him in one of the most ingenious financial hoaxes of all time. This was *not* counterfeiting, as the notes were both genuine and authorized, but rather deception by semi-official permission, with a little larceny involved.

Born in Portugal, Reis was married there, and after buying a phony engineering diploma, left for the Portuguese colony of Angola in 1916. He must have had innate engineering skill, because he quickly became known as "the man who made the trains run." Reis had an uncanny knack for figuring out how to solve various locomotive operation problems. He rose to become Inspector of Public Works and Acting Chief Engineer of the Angola Railways.

In 1919, he resigned from his position and sought his fortune by buying and selling crops. Prosperity resulted. In late 1919 Reis went to Europe intending to capitalize on the war surplus business. A deal involving non-functioning German tractors, which he repaired, made him a wealthy man. Returning to Lisbon, he became an international trader, but legal prohibition of currency transfers between Portugal and Angola in 1923 ruined him.

He discovered how to "float" checks on a New York bank for up to twenty-four days before he had to cover them. By doing so, he was able to buy control of his company, tapping into the $100,000 the Portuguese government had given the company to pay off bonds. With that money, he covered his checks. Reis was later arrested and held in jail, pending trial, for a board of directors' complaint that he embezzled the $100,000. In jail he thought up the scheme that would make him a wealthy man and hoax the Portuguese government out

of millions of dollars. At his trial, Reis was acquitted of embezzlement, convicted of one count of fraud, and released on bail.

Reis discovered that the Bank of Portugal had the exclusive right to issue banknotes in Portugal. After 1891, the Portuguese government did not need to cover its banknotes with gold or silver. It often issued notes for which it had no backing. In short, millions of escudo notes were technically worthless, their value dependent on the implied good faith of the government. Reis also discovered that no department of the bank or government checked to verify that currency serial numbers were not duplicated.

Reis' initial plan was to draw up a contract by which an international group of financiers would lend Angola one million pounds sterling (then about $5 million). In return, the financiers would obtain the right to issue banknotes for Angola in that amount. Reis realized that any document written upon official government stationery would likely have authority, even if unauthorized. He obtained the stationery, drew up the contract, and had it notarized by a compliant notary. He then went to the British, French, and German consulates and had them place their seals on the document, indicating that they recognized the notary's seal and signature as authentic. A forged signature of the High Commissioner of Angola, and the Minister of Finance were added to the document. As a final touch, he attached two new Portuguese banknotes, one for 1,000 escudos, the other for 500 escudos. These were the notes to be duplicated.

Reis then met with Karel Marang, a minor diplomat who was to finance the deal. He also brought in Adolf Gustav Hennies, a German with ties to the banking world. They agreed that a Dutch firm of banknote printers, Enschede, would be approached to do the job. The Dutch firm would only agree to be the intermediaries with the British firm of Waterlow & Sons, the company that actually printed Portugal's regular currency.

Marang visited Waterlow & Sons. When Sir William Waterlow was shown the contract, letters, and the two attached Portuguese banknotes, he immediately recognized that those particular notes had been printed by his arch rival in the banknote business, Bradbury Wilkinson. The business was declined unless one of the notes Waterlow printed, a 500 escudo note, was used. In any case, new authorization from the Bank of Portugal would have to be obtained.

New forged contracts were written by Reis, along with a forged letter of authorization from the governor of the Bank of Portugal to use their printing plates. Now the plan could proceed.

A number of problems, such as the number and order of bank directors' signatures to appear on the printed banknotes, had to be worked out. Reis improvised from available information, and made some lucky guesses. In February, 1925, the first 20,000 banknotes were printed and hand-delivered by Marang to Holland. A contract was drawn up among the four principals, dividing the profits up at twenty-five percent each, after expenses were reimbursed.

Much of the money was "laundered" through the foreign exchange marts in the Portuguese city of Oporto. The escudos were converted to pounds of sterling and deposited in a special account. A second batch of 30,000 notes was delivered, then one of 40,000 notes. By the time all of the ordered notes were obtained, $5 million of escudos were in circulation. Although rumors sprung up that counterfeit 500 escudo notes were in circulation, every time the Bank of Portugal had its experts examine batches of new 500 escudo notes, they were pronounced genuine.

The plot began to unravel when Sir William Waterlow noticed a discrepancy in a new order for banknotes, and wrote to the governor of the Bank of Portugal. Naturally, the governor knew nothing about any such order for banknotes since his signature was forged on the order by Reis. Luckily, it was Marang's official duty, so the letter was forwarded to Marang for delivery to the governor. Reis replied without the governor seeing the letter. However, it was soon noticed that the new order for banknotes contained notes with the same serial numbers as those previously printed. The London printer wondered how this could be. The printer also noticed that the name of one of the bank directors who signed the notes was incorrect.

Reis decided to use some of his funds to buy up shares of stock in the Bank of Portugal, hoping to eventually be part of the bank's board of directors. This was a difficult feat, as shares of stock in the bank rarely came on the market.

Reis went to Angola and started buying up land and properties there. He noticed for the first time that he was under surveillance, but reasoned that it was probably people with financial interests in Angola that were having him observed. Reis began financing the construction of a new railroad in Angola, thus returning to his roots.

Diario de Noticias, the leading daily newspaper in Lisbon began running stories about all the new capital flooding into Angola. Reis' bank—Oporto Commercial Bank—was under suspicion. The newspaper also revealed that this bank was buying shares in the Bank of Portugal, even though they were not a lucrative investment. Suspicions were aroused that the source of the bank's wealth was counterfeit 500 escudo notes. Rumors mushroomed, and experts from the Bank of Portugal were sent to Reis' bank to investigate. The experts pronounced all the 500 escudo notes genuine, amidst much consternation. The experts finally noticed that the new notes were still wrapped in a band that had been applied at the mint, yet the notes were *not* in consecutive serial number order, as they should have been if coming untouched from the printer. The notes were sent back to the Bank of Portugal for further examination.

On December 6, 1925, Alves Reis was arrested. The directors of the Bank of Portugal withdrew all 500 escudo notes from circulation, as there was no way of telling the genuine notes from the "fakes." The bank promised to exchange these notes for notes of other denominations. The governor and vice governor of the Bank of Portugal were arrested as accomplices, since it was not understood how the scheme succeeded without their help.

Reis was held incommunicado in jail for 106 days. During that time, he manufactured a number of forged documents that would implicate other innocent high officials. One of Reis' victim was the Attorney General of Portugal, the very man heading the investigation against Reis. Reis was able to forge, and smuggle out of jail, a receipt for a $25,000 gift to the Attorney General from Reis. The Attorney General was removed from the investigation. The two governors of the Bank of Portugal were exonerated.

The investigation and trial of Reis and the others lasted several years. In 1930, Reis finally confessed all, even framing the attorney general. Marang was tried in Holland and sentenced to eleven months in jail for receiving stolen property. Sir William Waterlow was dismissed as director of the banknote printing firm. A few years later, he served as Lord Mayor of London. All the while, Reis remained in jail, which was rather comfortable for him. He had money and could afford to have his food sent in. He had a crack team of lawyers, and spent his time implicating others, denying his guilt (until 1930), and writing a book.

In May 1928, Reis was transferred to a harsher prison. He attempted suicide by drinking a poison, after leaving a note of confession. Reis survived, however, and the prison doctors were convinced he was diseased. Reis managed to destroy the confession before it was found.

In May 1930, a special court heard the case of Alves Reis and some of his conspirators. The twelve charges against Reis included conspiracy, forgery, bribery, and fraud. Mrs. Reis was charged for receipt of stolen property. Reis testified that he was solely responsible for the plot, having only received minor assistance from two of the other defendants. Some defendants were found guilty, and Reis received an eight-year sentence, followed by twelve years of exile. An alternative was twenty-five years in exile, to be spent in Angola. However, rather than go back to Angola in shame, Reis chose to spend his time in a Portuguese prison. This was just as well, as the governor of Angola protested to Portugal that he did not want Reis to come there.

Waterlow & Sons was fined a substantial sum and had to pay the costs of the investigation and prosecution. On appeal, the fine was reduced to only the cost of replacing the "fake" banknotes—some 9,000 pounds sterling. Sir William Waterlow died shortly after this appeal verdict. Reis remained in jail until May of 1945. He became a lay preacher for evangelical Protestantism. He died of a heart attack in July, 1955. Reis had served twenty years in jail, but had pulled off the most complex and successful banking hoax of all time. Safeguards have now been installed by Portugal and Britain to guard against this happening again.

Sources:

"Admits $5,000,000 Fraud." *New York Times* section 2 (May 25, 1930): 1. See also other reports of the case in the *New York Times*, as follows: December 11, 1930: 12; December 12, 1930: 18; December 24, 1930: 13; and March 27, 1931: 11.

Bloom, Murray Teigh. *The Man Who Stole Portugal.* New York: Charles Scribner's Sons, 1966. [This book is virtually the only extended treatment of the case. The rest of the documentation consists of legal documents and news accounts.]

Cassie Chadwick

Rich people are often targets of hoaxers. The extremely rich are often special targets. Andrew Carnegie (1835–1919) was a prime target, and although he did not suffer in any measurable way from Cassie Chadwick's actions, others were injured more seriously. The definitive biography of Carnegie to date, by Joseph Frazier Wall, does not mention Chadwick. In fact, Chadwick gets little coverage in the literature, yet she was an audacious impostor and hoaxer.

Chadwick (1857–1907) was born Elizabeth Bigley, near London, Ontario in Canada. Eventually, she present herself as the illegitimate daughter of Andrew Carnegie. By telling people that she was paid well by Carnegie to cover his youthful indiscretion, Chadwick managed to relieve banks, investors, and individuals of about $2 million.

From a poor family, fifteen-year-old Chadwick managed to get a local farmer to mortgage his land to buy her a diamond in return for spending a night with him. When he then proposed marriage, she declined, telling him that was not part of the deal. At eighteen, Chadwick went to nearby London and bought clothes beyond her means. When asked for identification, she produced a business card that simply said "Miss Bigley. Heiress to $15,000." The store owners accepted her credit. When the banks notified them that she held no account, the police were summoned, but charges were dropped and she was allowed to keep the clothes.

Chadwick tried the same scam in Toronto four years later. The judge was sympathetic and found her not guilty by reason of insanity. He later pronounced her sane, telling her to go home. Her parents were not so forgiving, and sent her to live in Cleveland with her sister. Chadwick married a physician named Springsteen, but soon divorced. She then moved to Toledo, where she started a business as a fortune teller named Lydia Devere. There she ran afoul of the law and was sent to jail for nine and one-half years for forgery. She was released early from prison having written moving letters to the parole board. Chadwick moved back to Cleveland, adopting the identity of Cassie L. Hoover, a widow.

Three years later (1896), she met and married surgeon Leroy Chadwick. A period of hostessing lavish parties followed, but Chadwick began to grow bored with this life; she longed to pull a grand imposture.

In 1901, Chadwick became friendly with the pastor of a local Baptist church, Rev. Charles Eaton. She then hired a gossipy lawyer from Cleveland to accompany her to New York City. They rode in a coach up Fifth Avenue, stopping at Andrew Carnegie's man-

Andrew Carnegie.

sion. She stepped out of the carriage, telling the lawyer that she would only be a few minutes. Chadwick knocked at Carnegie's door and was admitted. She pretended that she wanted to check the reference of a maid who claimed to have worked for Carnegie. When she was told that no one of that name had worked there, she left, taking a paper-wrapped package out of her large purse as she left the house. The lawyer asked what was in the parcel. Chadwick swore him to secrecy, certain he would talk freely later.

Andrew Carnegie was her father, she said. This surprised the lawyer since Carnegie had never married. Chadwick showed him two notes, apparently signed by Carnegie, stating that he promised to pay her $25,000 in one note and $500,000 in the other. She told him the parcel contained $5 million in negotiable securities.

As she predicted, this news, including Carnegie's role, was widespread through Cleveland by the next day. A few days later, Chadwick called on the treasurer of one of Cleveland's most respected banks. He had heard the story, as she expected. She gave him the parcel in return for a receipt stating "I hereby certify that I have in my possession $5,000,000 in securities belonging to Mrs. Cassie L. Chadwick, and that neither myself nor the Wade Park Bank nor any other person has any claim upon the same. Iri Reynolds." Mr. Rey-

nolds never opened the package. Cassie then went to Reverend Eaton and "confessed" to being Carnegie's illegitimate daughter. Eaton, glad she trusted him, decided to help her raise some immediate cash. Reverend Eaton contacted his brother, who was a Boston lawyer.

Chadwick soon received a note from a Boston investment banker who offered to lend her money. Chadwick went to Boston and left with a check for $79,000 and a note for an additional $50,000. To get this $129,000, Chadwick signed a promissory note for $190,000, due in one year. This was fifty percent interest, but legal then.

The parties at the Chadwick house became more and more lavish. The increased spending required more cash. She approached a bank in Oberlin, Ohio. Soon she was regularly borrowing from the officer's personal funds at a high rate of interest, and then from the bank itself. She used the Carnegie note for $500,000 as collateral, borrowing $900,000 by the time she was through. She bought lavish gifts for her friends, including twenty-seven pianos, and toured Europe.

When the loans came due, she paid only the interest, extending the terms of the loans. Cassie borrowed more from banks and wealthy individuals, all on the strength of her Carnegie notes. By the end of 1903, she had borrowed $2 million. By this time, only her husband and Andrew Carnegie himself had not heard of her source of wealth.

By Spring of 1904, her borrowing schemes began to collapse. A $61,000 interest payment came due on her original $129,000 loan in Boston. She couldn't pay, and the banker worried about her stalling. He asked Iri Reynolds' bank in Cleveland to open the package containing the $5 million in securities. The bank refused and when word leaked out, a run on the Cleveland and Oberlin banks began. The Oberlin bank failed, having loaned Chadwick more than forty times the maximum amount allowed by law.

Andrew Carnegie finally heard about Chadwick. His only comment was "I have never heard of Mrs. Chadwick!" A judge ordered Reynolds to bring Chadwick's package to court. It contained nothing but worthless paper. Reynolds cried openly in court. Chadwick was arrested at a hotel in New York City. Her return to Cleveland was marked by 10,000 angry citizens, demanding their money back.

Carnegie publicly announced that he had not fathered any children, and Chadwick was tried and found guilty. She was sentenced to ten years in jail. Dr. Chadwick had his marriage annulled and moved to

Florida. After two and one-half years in jail, Chadwick died in the prison hospital at age fifty. Although parallels with the case of Madame Humbert (*See* Thérèse Humbert, this page) are striking, Chadwick actually began her scheme six months before Madame Humbert's frauds were revealed, so Chadwick did *not* copy from Madame Humbert, nor she from Chadwick. They were independent hoaxers.

Sources:

Mehling, Harold. *The Scandalous Scamps.* New York: Henry Holt, 1959: 69–86.

Various articles in the *New York Times* about Cassie Chadwick, as follows: December 9, 1904: 1; December 10, 1904: 1; December 12, 1904: 1; December 23, 1904: 1; February 22, 1905: 2; March 12, 1905: 1; March 28, 1905: 1.

Wall, Joseph Frazier. *Andrew Carnegie.* New York: Oxford University Press, 1970.

Thérèse Humbert

A shrewd understanding of the psychology of greed enabled a humble washerwoman, Thérèse d'Aurignac Humbert, to borrow millions of dollars from leading bankers in France with no visible collateral. This ruse went undetected for more than twenty years.

On the surface, the story of the hoax is simple. Humbert was the nurse to a man named Henry Robert Crawford. After he died at Nice in 1877, he left her a fortune in his will. Just before she was to collect the money from his estate, a second will was found, dated the same as the first. The second will left most of Crawford's estate to his two nephews, plus a large annuity to Humbert's younger sister, Marie. However, in order for Humbert to acquire anything, her then thirteen-year-old sister, allegedly had to marry one of the nephews. Until then, Humbert was to procure $100,000 per year and maintain physical custody of the $20 million in bonds and securities that made up the estate.

The nephews waged a legal battle to have the first will declared void and only the second one probated. Both nephews and Crawford were Americans, so they had American attorneys representing their interests. The probate was scheduled in New York City. No sooner had the legal battle become public than Frederic Humbert, son of a former justice minister of France, married Thérèse. Perhaps the only attraction to the peasant washerwoman was her newfound wealth. Nevertheless, the marriage brought her instant status. What

happened next was the beginning of a tangled web from which it would take Humbert over twenty years to extricate herself.

Humbert originally met Robert Henry Crawford, who was a Chicago millionaire, on a train in France. They had been sharing a compartment when Crawford became deathly ill from food poisoning. Humbert had nursed him back to health, both on the train and for several days afterward; rumors surfaced that they had been lovers, but that is unclear.

Although the first notification that she was a beneficiary of Crawford's estate had been accompanied by a signed and witnessed copy of Crawford's will, there was little Humbert could show to document her impending wealth. When the second will was discovered, entitlement became more questionable. Humbert had a copy of Crawford's death certificate and letters from the American attorneys.

Frederic Humbert had money of his own that they used to buy a luxurious mansion on the Avenue de la Grande Armée in Paris. French bankers saw an opportunity to make money by offering to lend Madame Humbert money at high rates of interest until her fortune materialized. When the bonds, constituting Crawford's $20 million fortune were received by Humbert for safekeeping, she made an event of depositing the heavily sealed packages into a large safe built into the wall of her bedroom. Before witnesses, one of the sealed parcels was opened by an official notary. The parcel had its contents (bonds) confirmed in writing, and a certificate was prepared stating that nothing in the packet of bonds had been removed. The parcels were sealed in the safe with the understanding that Humbert would forfeit all claim to the estate if she tampered with the safe.

Over the years, as the settlement of the Crawford estate dragged on, Humbert was able to borrow more and more money from banks and institutions on the strength of the sealed papers. Eventually, she borrowed more than $12 million, often paying substantial interest.

Between 1882 and 1902, Humbert continued to invent new reasons why the Crawford will could not be settled. Eventually, when it began to look as though she did not want it to be settled, suspicions were aroused. It was the bankruptcy of a number of merchants, putting some of the same bankers who had loaned Humbert money into near financial collapse, that brought an end to the hoax. Humbert was forced to agree to open the safe in front of legal authorities, a move that would *not* forfeit the estate. She had a fire in her house, which did not damage the safe, but gave Humbert an excuse to flee. She, her husband, and her two brothers fled the country. When the safe was opened, it contained 5,000 francs in genuine securities (worth about $1,000), several worthless deeds, and many packages of old newspaper.

The fugitives were soon caught in Spain. The Crawford nephews were searched for in New York but were nowhere to be found. In fact, they did not exist. Agents in the United States had handled the "nephews'" correspondence, using Crawford legal letterhead.

The trial was a sensation in most newspapers around the world. They were all found guilty, and the Humberts each were sentenced to five years in jail. The brothers received three-year terms. Upon her release from jail, Humbert insisted that the Crawfords come forward for her to receive her inheritance. Both the press and the public had long since lost interest in her case. She had executed one of the longest-lasting and most financially rewarding hoaxes in history, and refused to reveal many details of how it was done.

Sources:

Klein, Alexander. *Grand Deception.* Philadelphia: J. B. Lippincott, 1955: 370–80.

Phillips, Perrott, ed. "Crooked Washerwoman Cleaned Up a Fortune." In *Out of This World: The Illustrated Library of the Bizarre and Extraordinary.* New York: Columbia House, 1978, vol. 5: 75–78.

Various newspaper articles on the case. *Times* (London), May 8, 10, 1902; August 8, 10, 11, 12, 13, 14, 15, 18, 19, 20, 21, 22, 24, 1903; November 18, 1903.

Other Business Hoaxes

Subliminal Advertising. Research done in the late 1950s showed that flashing rapid ("subliminal") messages reading "Eat Popcorn" or "Drink Coke" on the screen of a movie theater while patrons watched the movie, resulted in a large increase in popcorn and Coke sales. Although James Vicary claimed to have conducted this research, and announced its results to the popular media, his data never appeared in any scholarly journal. When asked to repeat his experiment in a theater setting, the equipment either malfunctioned, or the results came out negative. Vicary never researched what he claimed. It is now known that when this research *is* done, no subliminal effects are obtained. In short, both Vicary's research *and* subliminal advertising are hoaxes.

The Federal Communications Commission witnessed several demonstrations of Vicary's equipment

in response to public outcry against the perceived immorality of using subliminal advertising. A Federal Communications commissioner concluded "I refuse to get excited about it—I don't think it works." Independent investigators tried to replicate Vicary's work with no success. For example the Canadian Broadcasting Corporation flashed "Phone Now" on the screen 352 times during a popular Sunday-night television show. Nobody called the station and telephone usage did not increase among viewers. When the audience was told of the experiment and asked to guess the message, more than 500 viewers wrote to the station. Not one correctly identified the message. In 1962, Vicary finally admitted publicly that he had not done the research he had claimed.

Interestingly, many of the "subliminal learning" tapes marketed today cite the non-existent Vicary study. *No* scientific data exists that shows a person can increase concentration, improve memory, learn, stop smoking, or do anything better as a result of listening to subliminal messages. Although subliminal *perception* may occur, subliminal *persuasion* or *influence* apparently does not.

The Field of Diamonds. In 1871, Mr. Arnold and Mr. Slack, prospectors in California, told a small group of investors that they had stumbled upon a field strewn with diamonds, somewhere in California or Nevada. They offered to take investors there, and produced diamonds they claimed were from the field. These diamonds were appraised at $125,000.

The prospectors were first contacted by William C. Ralston, a California banker, after they had deposited the stones in a safe deposit box in his bank. George D. Roberts, who was in mining, also contacted them. A number of investors were eventually taken to the field, blindfolded until they arrived at the site. Many diamonds *were* lying on the field, waiting to be picked up. The prospectors brought back an entire sack of stones, which were appraised as genuine by Charles Tiffany of New York. When investor Asbury Harpending, who later wrote about the hoax, went with some additional investors to the field, they found diamonds, rubies, emeralds and sapphires.

The "San Francisco and New York Mining and Commercial Company" was incorporated and issued 100,000 shares of stock at $40 each. Business was steady until in 1872, the president of the company, Clarence King, stated that the diamond fields were fraudulent, and had been "salted" (placed with the intent to deceive). King concluded this after he picked up a diamond in the field that was partially "cut" by a diamond cutter. Another party went to the field and, now looking for evidence of fraud, found plenty of it. Holes existed where gems had evidently been pushed in with a stick. Some stones were not even buried. Evidence of salting was plentiful. Many of the previously found stones turned out to be of low quality.

The premise that diamonds, rubies, emeralds, and sapphires were found together in the field should have made investors suspicious. The geological conditions needed to produce each of these gems vary greatly. Tiffany had appraised rough stones, *not* his expertise. Arnold and Slack, good prospectors, had made $50,000 selling several mines. They used this money to buy rough diamonds with which to salt the field. For their $35,000 investment, the two received more than $660,000 in cash from wealthy would-be partners.

Arnold was tracked to Kentucky, where he was sued for the profits he had made. A deal was arranged in which Arnold turned over $150,000 in return for immunity from further prosecution. Slack disappeared and was never located again. The diamond field was only a clever hoax.

The Paper Empire Hoax. Keith Gormezano claimed to be the chief executive officer of a publishing company named Le Beacon Presse, which did $666 million in business in 1986. The company published *Who's Who*-type directories for regions all over the world. To back up this statement was the company's listing in Dun & Bradstreet's *Million Dollar Directory*. Many of the company's alleged books were listed in *Books In Print*, complete with Library of Congress numbers. A listing of its subsidiary, Gormezano Reference Publications, in Standard & Poor's 1986 directory of businesses also proved Le Beacon's fruitful existence. Dun & Bradstreet listings require a credit rating, which in this case was done by Arthur Anderson & Co.

However, when *Forbes* writer Carol Monkman checked bookstores to find copies of the company's publications, she was unable to do so. A phone call to the company in Seattle produced a recording saying "leave a message and we will call you back." When she was called back by the company's president, Keith Gormezano, he explained that he had 398 employees, 150 of them in Seattle. The company was forty-nine percent employee-owned. He received so many calls asking about employment that the real business phone number was unlisted. He refused to divulge it to Monkman, who found that the company was listed as a sole proprietorship in the state of Washington.

The Library of Congress, responding to an initial inquiry, said that the issuance of Library of Congress numbers meant that the books were published. In *this* case, however, the numbers were requested but never used for actual books. Arthur Anderson denied it certified the credit rating for a company named Le Beacon

Presse. Marquis *Who's Who*, which *would* be Le Beacon Presse's main competitor, never heard of Gormezano's company. Finally, Gormezano complained to Monkman that Arthur Anderson called him to complain about the misuse of their company name. Gormezano admitted that their name was on his credit ratings "by mistake."

Under Monkman's inquiries, he finally admitted that the company was non-existent, the product of a hoax that became unmanageable. He had made a bet with someone five years previously that he could get himself listed in a *Who's Who* directory. It was now an obsession with him to see in how many reference works he could get his "company" listed. Actually, he was a second-year law student and part-time apartment building manager. The "company headquarters" were in the apartment building. When it was pointed out that Gormezano had himself illegally listed as an attorney in the 1985 *Legal Directory of Washington State*, he left law school without finishing. The paper empire of Keith Gormezano had been a hoax.

The Tropical Fantasy Hoax. A hoax was employed to drive the manufacturers of Tropical Fantasy, a new soft drink product, out of business. In September 1990, the Brooklyn Bottling Company produced a new soft drink called Tropical Fantasy. They tried to carve out a piece of the market by offering a twenty-ounce bottle for forty-nine cents. This bargain price soon led the soda to become the number one selling soda in "mom and pop" stores, especially in low-income areas of New York City. Soon, however, leaflets began appearing in neighborhoods throughout the Northeast. The leaflets claimed that the soft drink was manufactured by the Ku Klux Klan and "contained" stimulants to sterilize the black man." Although the Klan denied any connection, people in the neighborhoods took the leaflets seriously. Angry customers threatened distributors, and sales plummeted. A seventy percent decline was noted, and some stores refused to stock the drink. Although the FDA did an analysis of the drink and found nothing improper, little could be done to repair the damage of the flyers. Another drink, Top Pop, also reasonably priced, faced similar accusations in flyers. The main beneficiary of a decline in the sales of the two sodas would be another bottling company, but there is no proof that another company was responsible for the flyers.

The Proctor & Gamble Logo. Between 1980 and 1984, the Proctor & Gamble Company (P&G) received literally *millions* of letters about its "Man in the Moon" corporate logo. Word was spread that the logo was a satanic symbol (*See* Satanism Hoaxes, p. 237). The rumor gained momentum with the report that the president or chairman of P&G had appeared on television saying that he was a satanist and that ten percent of the company profits were going to the Church of Satan.

The shows he *reportedly* appeared on denied that any such appearance was made by anyone from P&G. Nevertheless, these rumors were spread by word of mouth and through church newsletters, especially Fundamentalist church newsletters.

Proctor and Gamble hired a staff to answer the mail and field the phone calls about this issue. Although the P&G logo was designed in the last century, and represents nothing more than a stylized man in the moon, the rumors continued to grow. Finally, P&G filed lawsuits against people it caught spreading the rumor about the logo. The firm had hired investigators to track down active rumor mongers. Those caught were Fundamentalists. Letters written by Jerry Falwell and Billy Graham, denying the P&G rumor, were published in a number of religious magazines and newsletters. Eventually, the rumors stopped, but it took considerable years and expense.

Sawing Off Manhattan. "Lozier" was a retired contractor in New York City. In 1824, he reported to friends that he had just been summoned to city hall to consult with his friend, Mayor Stephen Allen. The mayor was worried because Manhattan Island had apparently become much too heavy on the south (Battery) end due to all of its large buildings. The island had already begun to sag and the mayor was concerned that part might break off and sink.

The solution they came up with was to saw off the island, tow it out past Governor's Island, turn it around, and replace it on its moorings, therefore redistributing its weight. Because of his reputation for seriousness, and his experience as a contractor, Lozier's friends believed him. There was much talk about the scheme among New Yorkers.

A few days later, Lozier appeared with a large ledger at the Centre Market. He recruited 300 volunteers to work on the project. Lozier began to make arrangements to feed his work crew, and number of people were hired to build barracks for them. Others were signed up to build the iron "sweeps," designed to help turn the sawed-off island around. All along, Lozier refused to set an exact date at which work would begin, but was finally forced to do so.

He split his "crew," directing half of them to come to the corner of Bowery and Broadway, while the other half were directed to assemble at Bowery and Spring Streets. Hogs to be used for food, wagons to transport them and other supplies, and the workers arrived at the given spots, but Lozier did not. He hid out for several weeks, until their anger subsided.

The Neiman Marcus Cookie Recipe. A 1992 article in the *Christian Science Monitor,* reported the rumor that Neiman Marcus made fabulous cookies. When asked for the recipe, employees replied that they would sell it, but not give it away free. The price: $250. This is the story as reported. The facts, as journalist Daniel Puzo discovered, are as follows: Neiman Marcus does not sell or serve cookies in any of its restaurants. Any recipes for food served in its restaurants are given away free to anyone who asks. There is no such thing as a "Neiman Marcus cookie." The hoax in circulation for a number of years, was apparently spread via electronic bulletin boards and word of mouth.

Sources:

DeVoe, Thomas F. *The Market Book, Containing a Historical Account of the Public Markets. . . .* 1862. Reprint. New York: Augustus M. Kelley, 1970: 462–64 on "Sawing Off Manhattan" hoax.

Harpending, Asbury. *The Great Diamond Hoax and Other Stirring Incidents in the Life of Asbury Harpending.* Norman, OK: University of Oklahoma Press, 1958.

Madigan, Charles. "A Story of Satan that is Rated P&G." *Chicago Tribune* (July 18, 1982): 1, 12.

Monkman, Carol Smith. "The Case of the Paper Empire." *Forbes* 138 (October 27, 1986): 354–55.

Moore, Timothy E. "Subliminal Perception: Facts and Fallacies." *Skeptical Inquirer* 16, no. 3 (Spring 1992): 273–81.

"P&G Rumor Blitz Looks Like a Bomb." *Advertising Age* (August 9, 1982): 1, 68–69.

Pratkanis, Anthony R. "The Cargo-Cult Science of Subliminal Persuasion." *Skeptical Inquirer* 16, no. 3 (Spring 1992): 260–72.

Puzo, Daniel P. "The Great Neiman Marcus Cookie Recipe Hoax." *Providence Journal* (February 12, 1992): F7. From the *Los Angeles Times.*

"A Storm Over Tropical Fantasy." *Newsweek* (April 22, 1991): 34.

Disappearance Hoaxes

Ambrose Bierce and Derivative Disappearance Tales

The strange case of Mr. James Phillimore, "who, stepping back into his own house to get his umbrella, was never more seen in this world," is briefly mentioned in the Sherlock Holmes story "The Problem of Thor Bridge." That fictional case recalls the reportedly real-life cases of David Lang and young Oliver Larch (sometimes called Lerch), each of whom, quite literally, stepped off the face of the earth.

The disappearance of 11-year-old Oliver Larch occurred in the late evening of Christmas Eve, 1889. While snow fell outside, the Larch family and some friends gathered around the parlor organ singing Christmas songs. Just before eleven o'clock, Oliver's father sent his son to the well for some water. Almost immediately the adults heard the boy's frantic cries for help.

Grabbing a kerosene lamp, they rushed outside. The boy's cries, which seemed to come from the darkness overhead, began to grow faint. Lamplight revealed that his tracks went only halfway to the well, where they ended abruptly. According to writer Frank Edwards, "There were no other marks of any kind in the soft snow. Just Oliver's footprints . . . and the bucket . . . and silence." Edwards claimed that subsequent investigation confirmed the witnesses' testimonies. He ruled out certain explanations of Oliver's disappearance, such as a balloon or eagles "because they defied logical explanation." "The disappearance of this boy was quietly filed away and forgotten."

A markedly different version of the story places the events a year later, giving Oliver's last name as Lerch and his age as twenty. It reports that his tracks ended 225 feet from the well. The author of this version, reported by Joseph Rosenberger, alleged: "The facts in this case are clearly written down for everyone to see in the police records of South Bend, Indiana, and have been attested by levelheaded persons. . . . These witnesses include lawyers, Rev. Samuel Mallelieu, the local Methodist minister, and responsible citizens who actually witnessed the weird disappearance."

Neither version is true. A thorough search of police files and other area records revealed that no such incident was ever reported and that no Larch or Lerch family ever lived in the South Bend area during the late nineteenth century.

Another version of a remarkable disappearance, attributed to Oliver Thomas, and set in Rhayader, Wales, in 1909, was similarly debunked. The mayor of Rhayader, Eddie Collard, thoroughly investigated the story, as related in Brad Steiger's *Strangers from the Sky*, and found "no evidence" to substantiate the alleged facts. He concluded the tale was simply a hoax.

Actually, these and other versions of the tale are derived from a short story by American writer Ambrose Bierce. Titled "Charles Ashmore's Trail," it is one of a trilogy of stories headed "Mysterious Disappearances" and published in Bierce's collection of horror and mystery tales, *Can Such Things Be?* In fact, one version of the hoax tale transforms Bierce's "Charles Ashmore" into "Charlotte Ashton" and places the alleged vanishing in London in 1876. All of the versions are linked by similar details, notably the abruptly-ending tracks.

While the tale is obviously fiction, David Lang's story is quite different. Lang was a Tennessee farmer who walked into his pasture on September 23, 1880, and, in full view of his wife, children, and a family friend, vanished. Although the shocked onlookers immediately ran to the spot where he was last seen, no trace of him was found. There was no hole or any other clue as to what caused his disappearance. As time passed, a circle of stunted grass came to mark the spot of Lang's last appearance, and sometimes from within the circle family members heard his voice faintly calling for help.

Once again, however, historical research fails to substantiate the alleged facts in the story, including the existence of farmer Lang. There is, however, a first-person account by Sarah Emma Lang, who claimed to be David Lang's daughter. Her account, "How Lost Was My Father?," appeared in the July, 1953 issue of *Fate* magazine, carrying the byline of Stuart Palmer. Unfortunately, Sarah Lang's story turned out to be fictitious also, even though she claimed to communicate with her father through "automatic writing" (a form of mediumship in which one enters a disassociated state of consciousness, allowing the hand to write without conscious action).

As with the stories of Oliver Larch and the others, the Lang tale derives from Ambrose Bierce's trilogy—in this case from the story entitled "The Difficulty of Crossing a Field," which describes the witnessed vanishing of an Alabama planter named Williamson. Jay Robert Nash, in his book *Among the Missing*, maintains that the Williamson narrative is true. He claims that it was fictionalized in 1889 by a traveling salesman who, having nothing better to do during a snowstorm, penned it between drinks in a hotel bar. The salesman changed the man's name to David Lang, and the locale to Tennessee. Although it is not mentioned in Bierce's story, Nash uses Williamson's first name, asserting: "Orion Williamson was no figment of the imagination but a real, live resident of Selma, Alabama—until, of course, he slipped into eternal mystery."

Investigation shows that Bierce's tale has no basis either. In a postscript, "Science to the Front," Bierce relates the crackpot theories of a "Dr. Hern of Leipsic." Hern, a product of Bierce's imagination, theorized that "in the visible world there are void places," rather like "cells in Swiss cheese," that are somehow responsible for "mysterious disappearances."

In a sidelight to Bierce's fictional trilogy, another mysterious disappearance was added to the collection of tales. It too was a hoax. But this time the protagonist was not fictitious; it was Ambrose Bierce. Bierce (1842–1913) was known in literary circles as a journalist, wit, cynic, and writer of sardonic tales of death and horror. He is more popularly known for having vanished in 1913. Rarely recognized is Bierce's identity as an inveterate hoaxer—a fact that would have profound implications for his mysterious disappearance.

In *Can Such Things Be?* Bierce convinced many that his tales were authentic accounts, or at least *based* on true events. Research indicates otherwise. As Bierce himself wrote about some of his fiction: "With a hardy

Ambrose Bierce.

mendacity that I now blush to remember I gave names, dates and places with a minute particularity which seemed to authenticate the narratives that I came near to a belief in some of them myself." In another example of Bierce's proclivity for hoaxing, Bierce coauthored a book, *The Dance of Death*, in which he pretended to condemn the waltz as "shameless." Then, under a pseudonym, he wrote a column angrily rebutting, and panning the book.

Considerable evidence suggests that "the Old Trickster," as he was called by Paul Fatout, planned his own disappearance. Once having written an essay advocating suicide as a means of avoiding the debilities of old age, Bierce told his publisher that he possessed a German revolver for the purpose. He had selected a location in the Colorado River gorge where his corpse would be protected from vultures. He wrote farewell letters to friends, making such statements as "This is to say good-by at the end of a pleasant correspondence" and "My work is finished, and so am I." To his daughter he wrote, in giving up his cemetery plot, that he did "not wish to lie there. That matter is all arranged and you will not be bothered about the mortal part of [signed] Your Daddy."

Bierce created the illusion that he was traveling to Mexico, possibly to serve with Pancho Villa. Privately he confessed, "You need not believe *all* that these newspapers say of me and my purposes. I had to tell them *something*." After Bierce disappeared, supposedly after leaving Chihuahua, Mexico, the American consul investigated and was unable to find any evidence that Bierce had been there. Bierce earnestly promised in a letter, "And nobody will find my bones." Certainly, no one ever has.

Joe Nickell

Sources:

Bierce, Ambrose. "Mysterious Disappearances" In *Can Such Things Be?* New York: Albert & Charles Boni, 1924.

Edwards, Frank. *Strangest of All.* New York: Signet Books, 1962: 102–03.

Nash, Jay Robert. *Among the Missing.* New York: Simon and Schuster, 1978: 327–30.

Neale, Walter. *Life of Ambrose Bierce.* New York: AMS Press, 1969.

Nickell, Joe. *Ambrose Bierce Is Missing and Other Historical Mysteries.* Lexington, KY: University Press of Kentucky, 1991.

———. "The Oliver Lerch Disappearance: A Postmortem." *Fate* (March 1980): 61–65.

Rosenberger, Joseph. "What Happened to Oliver Lerch?" *Fate* (September 1950): 28–31.

Schadewald, Robert. "David Lang Vanishes . . . Forever." *Fate* (December 1977): 54–60.

The Bermuda Triangle

The "mystery" of the Bermuda (or Devil's) triangle—an alleged area of the Atlantic Ocean where ships and planes supposedly vanish without a trace—is a mixture of hype and hoax.

The term "Bermuda Triangle" was coined in 1964 by the late Vincent Gaddis to describe an area roughly bound by Puerto Rico, the Bahamas, and the tip of Florida. Gaddis, a self-styled "researcher" who promoted such alleged mysteries as "spontaneous human combustion," later regretted using the term "since a triangle implies boundaries that contain the phenomena." Indeed, others have called it an oval or even a trapezium (a figure with four unequal sides). Author Richard Winer prefers the latter term, emphasizing that "the first four letters of the word *trapezium* more than adequately describe it." Winer, Gaddis, and other popular writers have suggested that, whatever term is used to describe it, the Bermuda Triangle means doom for

those who venture into its domain. As a result of several dozen ships and planes vanishing in the region, Gaddis and others have speculated about "time warps," UFO kidnappings, and other bizarre "theories."

For example, they cite Flight 19, a group of Avenger torpedo bombers, that vanished on the "clear and sunny" afternoon of December 5, 1945. The five bombers left Fort Lauderdale Naval Air Station for a routine two-hour patrol. Instead, following brief radio exchange with other planes and ground receivers, all five planes disappeared. Headed for the last estimated position of Flight 19, a giant Martin Mariner plane with a crew of thirteen also vanished. No trace of any of the six planes was ever found and their collective vanishing represents one of the Bermuda Triangle's greatest mysteries.

However, in his book *The Bermuda Triangle Mystery—Solved*, research librarian Lawrence David Kusche concluded that the so-called Triangle represented "a manufactured mystery." For instance, citing a Navy investigation's report on the fate of Flight 19, Kusche showed that the patrol comprised rookies and a leader who became disoriented and changed direction a number of times during the more than four hours the squadron was lost. The approach of bad weather, poor radio reception, a failed teletype, the military rule that kept the planes together, and other factors contributed to the squadron's desperate situation. Kusche argues that the planes ran out of gas and were forced to ditch at sea during a stormy night. He says, "Had any one of these factors not prevailed, the flight might have ended differently. One or more of the planes might have made it back, and the event would have been forgotten, rather than becoming known as the strangest flight in the history of aviation."

As to the disappearance of the Martin Mariner, such planes were dubbed "flying gas tanks" because of dangerous fumes often present in the fuselage. The fumes were subject to ignition by a mere spark or a crew member smoking a cigarette. In fact, after twenty-three minutes of flight, the airplane was actually seen to explode! Contrary to the impression given by some Triangle researchers, the Mariner was not the only plane that searched for the lost patrol. Other planes left both before and after it, escaping the Triangle unharmed.

Another case cited by Triangle researchers was the *S.S. Marine Sulphur Queen*, a tanker that supposedly vanished in the Triangle in early February, 1963. En route from Beaumont, Texas, it was last heard from at 1:25 A.M. on February 4, nearing the Straits of Florida. The tanker became the focus of an air and sea search on February 9, one day overdue at Norfolk, Virginia. The search was widened over the following days, but no corpses, lifeboats, or oil slicks were discovered to provide a clue to the tanker's fate.

In fact, a piece of an oar and other debris from the tanker was found, including a name board bearing the letters "ARINE SULPH" between its shattered ends. The wreckage proved the vessel did not vanish, as some articles and books imply. Moreover, the lack of any distress message from the tanker indicates that whatever happened to it occurred suddenly. The vessel was structurally weak, plagued by fires, and was believed to have encountered rough weather. Perhaps, with a cargo of 15,260 tons of molten sulphur, the ship exploded, as did a similar vessel carrying liquid benzene in 1972, or it could have sank in deep water.

Still another touted Triangle mystery occurred in December of 1967, when a twenty-three-foot cabin cruiser named *Witchcraft* disappeared with its two-man crew just off Miami Beach. The men reported a damaged propeller to the Coast Guard and asked to be towed back to port. The men reported that the boat's hull was intact and in any case, built-in floatation chambers rendered the craft virtually unsinkable. Yet, when the Coast Guard reached the location, after only nineteen minutes, there was no trace of the boat, men, or life preservers. It seemed the Triangle claimed two more victims.

Actually, contrary to the way the incident is usually portrayed, the craft was disabled in rough weather amid waves that were as high as six feet. Without use of its engine propeller to maintain proper heading into the waves, the boat could have been swamped. Also, the craft's exact position was actually unknown and the Coast Guard conducted a nighttime search over what Kusche observes was "an enormous area." When such particulars are factored into the case, the specter of the Triangle is again deflated.

Other cases have similarly suffered from Kusche's penetrating investigation. For example, the 1944 mystery surrounding an abandoned ship found drifting off the Florida coast evaporated when a hurricane—which was omitted from most writers' accounts—was restored to the scenario. A plane that allegedly vanished in the Triangle in 1950 actually exploded in 1951, some 600 miles west of Ireland. Another plane, a British troop transport that disappeared in 1953 "north of the Bermuda Triangle" probably crashed in icy wind and torrential rain some *900 miles north* of the Triangle! According to the U.S. Coast Guard, even when the vanishings actually occur within the Triangle, "there is nothing mysterious about disappearances in this particular section of the ocean. Weather conditions, equipment failure, and human error, not something from the supernatural, are what have caused these tragedies."

Concluded Kusche, "Previous writers, either on purpose or because they were gullible, created the mystery. I found that many things writers call mysterious really aren't if you take the trouble to dig for some information. Previous writers on this topic had to be either very poor researchers with little curiosity, very gullible, or outright sensationalists. They've been passing off their own lack of information as mysteries."

Joe Nickell

Sources:

Berlitz, Charles. *The Bermuda Triangle*. New York: Doubleday, 1974.

Gaddis, Vincent. *Invisible Horizons: True Mysteries of the Sea*. Philadelphia: Chilton, 1965.

Kusche, Lawrence David. *The Bermuda Triangle Mystery—Solved*. New York: Harper & Row, 1975.

Parrott, Wanda Sue. "Public Mystery Number One—Or Just a Hoax? An Interview With Lawrence David Kusche." In *The Riddle of the Bermuda Triangle*. Edited by Martin Ebon. New York: Signet Books, 1975: 39–50.

Winer, Richard. *The Devil's Triangle*. New York: Bantam Books, 1974.

Education Hoaxes

Fake Students. Perhaps the first reported fictitious student was "George P. Burdell," created at Georgia Technological University in about 1927 by Ed Smith. Smith derived the name from his cat "Burdell," and George P. Butler, his prep school principal. Burdell hoaxes became a tradition at Georgia Tech. Burdell continued to "attend" Georgia Tech for the next forty years! In 1969, at Spring registration, Burdell signed up for 3,000 hours of class. Students subscribed to magazines in Burdell's name. He gave glittering parties that were reported in the society pages of Atlanta newspapers, and he became engaged to a socially prominent woman astronomer. Burdell finally "graduated" from Georgia Tech, with the administration's knowledge and agreement. Now graduated, he is occasionally listed as an alumnus of the Class of 1930 or 1970. Georgia Tech has received requests for Burdell's transcripts from potential employers.

Cal Tech University Hoaxes. A hoax was perpetrated against an unpopular university administrator by three faculty members at California Technological University (Cal Tech) in 1970. They obliterated the administrator's named parking space by repainting all of the parking space lines. Each space was made a little wider, with the administrator's space completely eliminated. The other name plates were placed before the wider spaces, except his. There is no record of the administrator's reaction when he arrived at work the next morning.

In a separate Cal Tech hoax in 1972, Cal Tech freshman Chuck Conner took a week off from school to visit a girlfriend. While he was gone, his dormmates removed all physical traces of his existence at the school. They plastered over the door to his room, even moving a lighting fixture to the new wall. None of his dormmates claimed to remember his name or face when he returned.

Benefactor Hoax. Not only students, but rich benefactors have been "created" at colleges. At Dartmouth, a fictitious millionaire named "Nelson Billings" was created. As Billings was planning a large bequest to the college, Dartmouth organized a reception, complete with a band and a police escort for the actor hired by the students to impersonate Billings. The actor addressed the reception, telling them how his son had planned to go to Dartmouth, but had died before he could attend. Billings presented to the college "the 1934 football team." Onto the stage came five unemployed farmers and three students dressed as bums in tattered old football uniforms. The administration, realizing it had been hoaxed, was redfaced.

MIT Hoaxes. The Massachusetts Institute of Technology (MIT) has a long tradition of hoaxes and pranks. Putting animals or other hard to move objects into places difficult to remove them from, is particularly popular at MIT. Perhaps the two most famous such stunts were the 1928 placement of a cow named "Maisie" onto the roof of a dormitory and that of a working telephone booth onto the Great Dome in 1972. Contrary to popular opinion, a *live* cow was never placed onto the Great Dome at MIT, but a full-sized *plastic* cow was in 1979.

Death of the Dean. One of the most difficult obituary pages to fool is that of the *New York Times*. The obituaries staff thoroughly checks facts. On January 2, 1980, Alan Abel (*See* Alan Abel's Hoaxes, p. 209) was one of the few to successfully have his own obituary published in the *Times* while still alive. Another false obituary appeared in the *Times*, this one involuntary. On May 9, 1942, the *New York Times* published the obituary of 37-year old Dr. William Baer, dean of the College of Arts and Science at New York University (NYU). Fortunately for the dean, he was still very much alive. Some NYU students submitted the obituary as a hoax. A retraction was published the next day.

Sources:

Bear, John. *How to Get the Degree You Want.* Berkeley, CA: Ten Speed Press, 1982. See pages 199–232 for diploma mills, degree mills, etc.

Leibowitz, Brian M. *The Journal of the Institute for Hacks,*

Tomfoolery & Pranks at M.I.T. Cambridge, MA: M.I.T. Museum, 1990.

Poundstone, William. *The Ultimate.* New York: Doubleday, 1990: "Judging How Easy," 91–104.

"A Question of Degree." *Time* (February 5, 1979): 125.

Exploration and Travel Hoaxes

Christopher Columbus Hoaxes

Christopher Columbus (1451–1506) did not personally perpetrate any hoaxes that have been recorded. Rather, some hoaxes were committed in his name by others long after he was dead. They are gathered here, although no known connection exists between them.

One hoax involves the final resting place of Columbus' body. Tradition has it that he was buried in the Cathedral of Santo Domingo, Dominican Republic. His remains were brought from Seville, Spain, in the 1540s, along with those of his son, Diego Columbus, at the request of Diego's widow, who then lived in Santo Domingo. In 1655, the British attacked Santo Domingo, and the remains in the Cathedral were concealed and then forgotten. Some remains (but whose was not definitely known, although "tradition" made them Christopher Columbus') were exhumed and taken to Havana, where Columbus was to be memorialized, in 1795.

The facts appear to be (as stated by author Walter M. St. Elmo) that from the 1540s until 1795, there were *two* Columbus family vaults in the Cathedral at Santo Domingo. One housed the body of Christopher Columbus, and the other, his son Diego. It appears that Diego's remains, which had been buried on the other side of the church's presbytery, were exhumed and taken to Havana. In 1899, the remains at Havana were returned to Seville, since Cuba had just been given to the United States as a result of Spain's loss in the Spanish-American War, and Spain wanted Columbus' remains to stay in Spanish territory.

The hoax appears to have originated due to the inability of the Archbishop of Santo Domingo to find the actual coffin of Christopher Columbus in 1795. All that could be found was Diego's coffin, which lacked a nameplate. This coffin was therefore (intentionally or

unintentionally) said to be Christopher's. In 1917, the two vaults were destroyed during remodeling of the cathedral. Of course, one of these vaults (the only one known about at the time, and in reality formerly Diego's) was thought to be empty. The other, whose location was forgotten, still contained the real remains of Christopher Columbus. So, although Diego Columbus' remains were returned to the cathedral in Santo Domingo before going to Seville, the remains of Christopher Columbus have been lost. The claim of the cathedral to have those bones is a hoax.

A more complex hoax involving Columbus has to do with the letter he supposedly wrote to his friend Luis de Sant Angel in 1493, describing his first voyage to the New World. The letter was purportedly several pages long, and told of the native peoples Columbus encountered. A printed version of this letter was supposedly published in 1493 and resides in the archives of Simancas, Spain. There is another letter, written by Columbus to his friend Gabriel Sanchez at the same time, the authenticity of which is not in question. These letters would represent the only writings of Columbus. The text was first mentioned in nineteenth century Spanish travel writer Navarrete's *Colleccion de Viages*, published in Madrid in 1825. The printed text was known only from a copy found at the Ambrosian Library in Milan, to which it had been bequeathed in 1852 by Baron Pietro Custodi. At first, this text was thought to be the same as the Sanchez letter. Several editions of the Sanchez letter, translated into Latin, were published, some as early as 1493. Neither printed Spanish text lists a publisher, place of printing, or a date of printing. Although the contents of the two letters are similar, they were supposedly addressed to different people and written separately. Evidently, Sant Angel had the text of his handwritten letter from Columbus printed in an effort to have its contents disseminated. This is the opinion of Julia Rae, who edited an English and Spanish edition of the letter in 1889. She published a facsimile of the original printing (claimed to have been about 1493), an exact type version, a modern Spanish version, and an English translation of the modern Spanish version.

Author Henry Harrisse examined the Sant Angel letter carefully, and concluded that it was a hoax. It was, he claimed, produced in the nineteenth century, probably using the text of the Sanchez letter as a basis. It takes a great deal of knowledge of fifteenth century Spanish typography to produce the original version, claiming a 1493 imprint date, and the forger made some mistakes. His job was made much easier, however, by the publication of a facsimile of the Sanchez letter, issued in 1866 in Milan. That facsimile was produced by lithography. Perhaps the forged version was also so produced, although this cannot be determined without looking at the original.

The copy used to produce the facsimile in the London edition of 1889 was sold to an American for a large sum in 1891 (900 pounds sterling, or about $5,000). A lawsuit was eventually brought by the American in a New York court on the grounds that he was sold a forgery. A number of bibliographers were brought in to testify. Few of these had any real expertise in fifteenth century Spanish printing, however. It was pointed out that the spacing between the lines in the printed letter was irregular. How this could occur in set type was argued, although it really cannot occur intentionally. Various typographical anomalies were also pointed out, especially the presence of letters and letterforms that were not used in the 1490s. More damning still was the same problem that Mark Hofmann's forgery of *The Oath of a Freeman* (See Mark Hofmann and the Mormon Forgeries, p. 81) had, namely descending letters (''g,'' ''p,'' ''j,'' and ''y'') whose descenders fell into the space occupied by preceding letters. Since each letter is set on a block of lead, it is not possible for *set type* to have descenders from one letter in a previous letter's space. The fact that some letters did have this is an indication that some photographic process or artistic process was used, rather than typesetting. Of course, no such process was available in the 1490s, so anything printed that was produced by a non-typesetting method *must* be a fake.

In fact, there are now known to be at least three different versions of the fake letter from Columbus to Sant Angel. These can be distinguished by different errors made on the part of various forgers. One corrected the errors of another, but then introduced new errors. It is thought by Harrisse that the original forger was Enrico Giordani of Milan.

Sources:

Harrisse, Henry. *Apocrypha Americana: Examen Critique de Deux Decisions de Tribunaux Americains en Favor d'une Falsification Enhontée de la Lettre Imprimée de Christophe Columb en Espagnol Annonçant la Decouverte de Nouveau Monde, et Vendue Comme Authentique un Prix Enorme.* Leipzig [Germany]: Otto Harrassowitz, 1902.

''Ives v. Ellis.'' 370 *New York State Reports & Session Laws 399*, (April Term, 1900).

Rae, Julia E. S., ed. *The Letter in Spanish of Christopher Columbus, Written on His Return from His First Voyage, and Addressed to Luis de Sant Angel, 15 Feb.–14 March, 1493. Announcing the Discovery of the New World.* London: Ellis & Elvey, 1889.

St. Elmo, Walter M. *The Alleged Remains of Christopher Columbus in Santo Domingo. Removing the Mask from this Most Amazing Hoax.* San Juan, Puerto Rico: Author, 1929.

The Cruise of the *Kawa*

The *Kawa* was an alleged ship captained by Walter E. Traprock. ''Traprock'' was the pseudonym of George Shepard Chappell, of *Vanity Fair* magazine. In fact, Traprock's book about his adventures aboard the *Kawa*, *The Cruise of the Kawa*, is a hoax. Two of the book plates show impossible things. The plate of ''Captain Ezra Triplett'' shows him holding a flintlock pistol carved out of wood. Why someone in the twentieth century would use a flintlock is not clear, especially an obviously fake wooden one. The other plate was of the alleged nest of the Fatu-Liva bird, found on the island of ''Filbert,'' supposedly discovered by the crew of the *Kawa*. This bird lays dice-like eggs, including the spots. Page 147 has an ad listing eight other books supposedly written by Traprock, including *Through Borneo on a Bicycle* and *Around Russia on Roller Skates*. All except *Curry-Dishes for Moderate Incomes* are out-of-print, says the ad. The curry book is available for $200. None of the books are real. A notice to sign up with Traprock for a new cruise to the South Seas to ''see the cute cannibals'' also appears at the end of the book.

The author's purpose seems to have been to mock glamorized, exotic travel books. Some book reviewers recognized that the book was a ''burlesque,'' as one called it. Others liked the writing, but apparently showed no recognition that the book was a hoax. Worst of all, Traprock did two other hoax travel books during the next two years. Apparently his first hoax was not enough to stop the American people's fascination with overdone, exotic travel books. After the three books by ''Traprock,'' the genre declined.

Nest, with the Fatu-Liva bird's supposed eggs.

Sources:

"Chappell, George Shepard (Walter E. Traprock)." *Book Review Digest* (1921): 79.

Traprock, Walter E. [pseud.]. *The Cruise of the Kawa.* New York: G.P. Putnam's Sons, 1921.

Edgar Allan Poe's Balloon Hoax

The April 13, 1844 issue of the *New York Sun*, reported that a balloon had crossed the Atlantic Ocean in three days. The balloon, named *Victoria*, had taken off from England on a trip to Paris. Well known balloonist Monck Mason was the pilot and eight others were aboard. The bag of the balloon was made of silk coated with rubber. Coal gas was used to fill the balloon. There was a propeller, activated by a "clockwork mechanism," along with one rudder for steering.

According to the *Sun*, shortly after takeoff, a high wind came up. The propeller shaft slipped out of place, disabling the propeller. As it was out of reach, no one could repair it. Prevailing winds carried the balloon across the Atlantic in seventy-five hours. It landed on Sullivan's Island, near Charleston, South Carolina. The *Sun* article contained extracts from the log of the *Victoria*, including details of the icing that occurred in mid-trip.

In 1836, Mason and a man named Charles Green ballooned from London to Weilburg, Germany. Mason published an account of this voyage in London in 1836, and in New York in 1837 in a book entitled *Account of the Late Aeronautical Expedition from London to Weilburg*. The details and names of passengers in Monck's book are the same as those in the *Sun* story. The *Sun* account turned out to be an imaginary voyage. No actual attempt at crossing the Atlantic by balloon took place until 1873, and it ended in failure. There has never been to date a successful balloon crossing of the Atlantic from Europe to America. The first successful powered airship crossing of the Atlantic occurred in 1919 from England.

Another publication existed, an anonymous pamphlet (probably by Monck), entitled *Remarks on the Ellipsoidal Balloon, Propelled by the Archimedean Screw, Described as the New Aerial Machine* (London, 1843). The two Monck publications, taken together, form about twenty-five percent of the balloon hoax article in the *Sun* in paraphrased form. The illustration of the *Victoria* accompanying the *Sun* article appears to be a redrawn version of the frontispiece engraving of the *Remarks* pamphlet.

The author of the *Sun* story is now known to be Edgar Allan Poe (*See* Edgar Allan Poe's Hoaxes, p. 141). Poe was an inveterate hoaxer, and also a borrower of others' material. At the same time, he was keenly interested in science. Poe followed the latest developments in astronomy and aeronautics closely. The Great Moon Hoax (*See* Great Moon Hoax, p. 252) severed Poe's own projected hoax before he was able to follow through on it. Perhaps the balloon hoax was Poe's attempt to make amends for being "scooped" by Richard Adams Locke on the Great Moon Hoax. On the other hand, perhaps it was the $50 Poe received for the article that motivated him. It is also difficult to explain why Poe stood on the steps of the *Sun* building on the day the story was published, telling crowds that his own story was a hoax. Poe was a strange and complex man, often given to self-destructive behavior.

Sources:

Falk, Doris V. "Thomas Low Nichols, Poe, and the 'Balloon Hoax'." *Poe Newsletter* 5 (1972): 48–49.

Norris, Walter B. "Poe's Balloon Hoax." *The Nation* (Oct 27, 1910): 389–90.

[Poe, Edgar Allan]. "The Atlantic Crossed in Three Days!" *New York Extra Sun* (April 13, 1844): 1.

Scudder, Harold H. "Poe's Balloon Hoax." *American Literature* 21 (May 1949): 179–90.

Wilkinson, Ronald Sterne. "'Poe's Balloon-Hoax' Once More." *American Literature*, 32 (November 1960): 313–17.

Hollow-Earth Hoaxes

In 1692, the great English astronomer Edmond Halley, best known for predicting "his" comet, theorized that the earth was a hollow shell within which three smaller concentric spheres, each separated by 500 miles of atmosphere, float. Halley's revisionist geology failed to persuade his colleagues, but it bears the distinction of being the first "scientific" attempt to prove the hollowness of the earth—a notion that until then was confined to religious belief (in the theory that hell existed inside the hollow earth, for example) and folklore (which held that fairies and other supernatural entities dwelled underground).

When the hollow-earth theory was revived in the 1820s, Halley's model was modified to incorporate a 4,000-mile hole at each pole. The hollow-earth's new champion was American retired soldier and eccentric John Cleves Symmes, who maintained, to the amusement of many of his countrymen, that the earth's interior is the abode of an advanced civilization. Until his death in 1829, Symmes lobbied vigorously for official and private-funding for an inner-earth expedition intended to open up "new sources of trade and commerce" with the subterraneans. Symmes was immortalized in Edgar Allan Poe's proto-science-fiction novella, *The Narrative of Arthur Gordon Pym* (1838), but is otherwise forgotten—except by a small band of hollow-earth advocates whose enthusiasm remains undiminished to this day. Classic works in this genre of esoteric literature include Frederick Culmer's *The Inner World* (1886), William Reed's *The Phantom of the Poles* (1906), and Marshall B. Gardner's *A Journey to the Earth's Interior* (1913).

The Word from the Spirit World

The Hollow Globe, an important early hollow-earth book, was published in 1871, and purported to be a communication from the spirit world as dictated to medium M. L. Sherman. Sherman was one of the legion of mediums who appeared in the late 1840s following the celebrated "spirit rappings" of the Fox sisters of Hydesville, New York. Eventually he told his publisher and collaborator "Professor" William F. Lyon that his public powers failed him, and he retreated into years of private communion with discarnates. In 1868, he had called on Lyon, a stranger to him at that time, at the latter's Sacramento office and told him, "You are the man that I have been looking for . . . and we have a large amount of business to transact."

The result was *The Hollow Globe*, a treatise on spiritual cosmology. After detailing at great length the supernatural underpinnings of the physical universe, the book says that the restlessness and curiosity most characteristic of the "American or Anglo-Saxon race" will eventually lead explorers through the "warm Oceanic current through Bering's Straits" into the "beautiful" interior world whose inhabitants live "in a more highly developed condition" than their counterparts on the surface.

Another hollow-earth visionary, physician Cyrus Teed, related that while meditating one night in October of 1869, he saw the "Mother of the Universe" emerge from a "sphere of purple and golden light." In the ensuing conversation Teed learned that the earth contains the entire universe within its interior, which has a diameter of 8,000 miles; in other words, the universe is inside out, and human beings live on the inside of the outer shell. Armed with these and other revelations (including the news that he was Christ in his Second Coming), Teed rechristened himself Koresh (the Hebrew name for Cyrus) and established his own religion, Koreshanity.

Koreshanity got off to a slow start, first in Moravia, New York, then in Syracuse, with a tiny band of believers. After Teed delivered a powerful lecture to the Chicago convention of the National Association of Mental Science in September of 1886, all that changed and Koreshanity units sprouted up across the country. Teed envisioned a world under his control, following socialist economics and political arrangements. He preached celibacy but apparently did not practice it, as he lived with a woman for more than fifteen years, and was reportedly sexually active with some of his followers. Soon a utopian community was set up in south Florida. A huge sign declaring "We live on the inside" was put up by the entrance. In 1898, Teed and his chief follower, Ulysses Grant Morrow, wrote *The Cellular Cosmogony, or the Earth a Concave Sphere*. Teed died ten years later, but a diminishing group of Koreshans kept the faith alive until the 1970s.

Far more successful and influential than Koreshanity, Theosophy was the creation of medium Helena Petrovna Blavatsky, cofounder of The Theosophical Society, who "precipitated" (produced out of thin air) letters from "Tibetan Masters." (*See* The Mahatma Hoax, p. 223) The two prominent masters, Koot Hoomi and Morya, purported to reside in a hidden Himalayan valley, under which, in tunnels, chambers, and a vast library, all human knowledge was stored. Under the Gobi Desert and beneath the mountains of Peru and Bolivia lay the remains of mighty civilizations, guarded by the Masters who hid them from the prying eyes of the spiritually unqualified. Among these lost civilizations was Lemuria, the Pacific Ocean's version of Atlantis.

After Blavatsky, Lemurians and Tibetan Masters figured prominently in the stories of those who said they had had personal contact with the inner-earthers. A widely read 1934 book, *Unveiled Mysteries*, recounted author Guy Warren Ballard's adventures and out of body experiences, with Tibetan Masters, Lemurians, and even Venusians under the earth. Ballard (writing as Godfre Ray King) penned another book, *The Magic Presence* (1935), full of even more implausible tales, such as that in which the Tibetan Master St. Germain drew a cloak of invisibility around a car he was riding in. Ballard toured America with his wife Edna and son Donald promoting their occult group, The "I Am" Religious Activity. Though Ballard died in 1939, his claims would serve as the model for flying-saucer contactees such as George Adamski, whose Venusians were clearly patterned after Ballard's.

Though usually depicted as advanced and benevolent by other hollow earthers, the demonic creatures whom Richard Sharpe Shaver claimed the misfortune of having met were out of a pre-Symmes vision of the inner earth. Shaver may have lived and died in obscurity if Ray Palmer, the Chicago-based editor of *Amazing Stories, Fantastic Adventures,* and other Ziff-Davis publications, had not taken an interest in a letter to him from Shaver, that included an ancient alphabet from Lemuria. The alphabet was published in the January 1944 issue of *Amazing Stories,* by which time Palmer had met with Shaver and his wife, Dorothy at their Pennsylvania farmhouse. There, Palmer would insist until his death in 1977 that he heard voices. They were discussing their favorite subject, torture which Palmer inferred they were actually practicing on a young woman.

As Shaver told it, sometime in the 1930s—although there are different versions of the story—he heard voices and experienced visions that led him to believe that under the terrestrial surface, in huge caves, lived the survivors of a race of giants who once occupied the exterior. Solar radiation forced most of the giants, called Titans or Atlans, to escape the earth in spaceships 12,000 years earlier. Some stayed, adapted, and became the ancestors of the present human race. Others went underground, taking the machines and other sophisticated Titan technology with them. Most of these degenerated into sadists who used the machines to cause havoc on the surface, to enhance sexual pleasure during orgies, and to torture humans. In time, their wretched habits caused them to become hideously deformed. These creatures were called deros, short for detrimental robots, though they were not robots in the literal sense. A small, embattled minority of underground dwellers, the teros (so-called integrative robots, who were not robots either), were fighting valiantly but losing the war with the deros.

The "Shaver mystery" was introduced to the world in a 30,000-word novella, "I Remember Lemuria!", in the March 1945 issue of *Amazing Stories.* The story had Shaver's byline, but was written as science fiction by Palmer. All of this was based on Shaver's memories of life as "Mutan Mion, who lived many thousands of years ago in Sub Atlan, one of the great cities of ancient Lemuria!" Palmer claimed that this and other subsequent Shaver mystery stories brought 50,000 new readers to the magazine over the next three years. Another Ziff-Davis editor, Curtis Fuller, who saw the circulation figures, says readership rose only slightly.

The Shaver material, however, indisputably received attention and revived interest in the hollow earth and other esoteric claims. Some readers claimed to have been inside the caves and seen the deros, and one reader, Fred L. Crisman, recounted an incident in which he shot his way out of a dero cave in Borneo with a machine gun. In 1947, Crisman would be the instigator of the first major hoax of the UFO era, when he and an associate, Harold Dahl, reported seeing a flying saucer dump materials into Puget Sound. Crisman subsequently peddled the stories to Palmer. Science-fiction fans were outraged by Shaver's stories. They were afraid they would portray science-fiction enthusiasts as unable to tell the difference between fantasy and reality. They embarked on a letter-writing campaign to get the series stopped and Palmer fired. In 1948, publisher William B. Ziff ordered Palmer to publish no new Shaver material.

Undaunted, Palmer moved to rural Wisconsin to join the Shavers, who were already established there because a tero colony lived nearby. By then Palmer had co-founded *Fate* magazine with Curtis Fuller, but the latter's lack of enthusiasm for the Shaver mystery ensured that *Fate*'s focus would be on "true mysteries." Notwithstanding, the deros were scarcely mentioned. Palmer sold his share of the magazine to Fuller, then started his own magazine, *Mystic* (later called *Search*) and *Flying Saucers. Flying Saucers* featured Shaverian claims and other hollow-earth notions, including the story that in 1947 Adm. Richard E. Byrd and his expedition to the North Pole entered the interior realm and met its inhabitants (in fact, that year Byrd visited the South Pole). Between 1961 and 1964, Palmer published a quarterly magazine in trade-paperback format, *The Hidden World,* which brought together old and new writings by or about Shaver.

To those who knew him, even those who questioned the Shaver mystery, Shaver was a pleasant, manifestly sincere individual, a man who apparently could not tell the difference between fantasy and reality. Critics almost always put the blame on Palmer, a chronic promoter, who they were certain was exploiting Shaver for financial gain. Palmer made no secret of his interest in using Shaver to stir controversy and increase sales of his magazines, but he also insisted that his endorsement of the "mystery" was sincere—and it may well have been. Palmer generously supported the Shavers and remained close to Byrd long after Shaver's name could be used to sell anything.

Still, if the Shaver mystery was not itself a hoax in the strict sense, it inspired plenty of hoaxers, including the science-fiction fans who delighted in writing Palmer to tell of their inner-earth encounters and, upon the publishing of their letters, announced that they had lied. A hoaxer with another sort of motive was Claude Doggins, who used the pseudonym Maurice Doreal. Doreal headed the Brotherhood of the White Temple, a religious sect. In this capacity he had frequent dealings with the Tibetan Masters who lived under Mount Shasta in northern California. He also had occasion to observe the operations of the deros who, he said, were evil Lemurians. Doreal had his own complex science-fiction cosmology, in which inner-earthers and extraterrestrials interacted and engaged in conflict over thousands of years.

There was also W. C. Hefferlin, who informed *Amazing Stories'* readers of the abandoned Martian colony, Rainbow City, under the Antarctic ice. Hefferlin learned of it after meeting an agent of the Tibetan Masters, and in turn he met three Masters personally. Hefferlin dropped out of sight in the late 1940s, but in 1951 the Rainbow City story was revived in *Agharta: The Subterranean World*, a self-published book by Robert Ernst Dickhoff. In 1960, Michael X. Barton, in *Rainbow City and the Inner Earth People*, reported that Venusians and Tibetan Masters had formed an alliance to defeat the deros. Iowa evangelist Theodore Fitch, author of *Our Paradise Inside the Earth* (1960), told of the "little brown men" who piloted flying saucers from bases under the surface. The Garden of Eden was inside the earth, according to Fitch.

The Siegmeister Saga

Of all modern hollow-earth writers none has had the impact of "Raymond Bernard," the pseudonym of Walter Siegmeister. Born in New York City in 1901, Siegmeister developed unusual interests. Fascinated, yet repelled by human sexuality, he believed that women needed to be free of menstruation. He also held that men were a threat to the survival of the race since, through degrading women, they would eventually cause the human race to degenerate. These were themes with which he would be obsessed all his life. He wrote forty volumes on "biosophy" wherein he addressed such issues as diet (advocating not only vegetarianism but abstinence from all cooked food), occultism, and humanity's fall from its lofty past in Atlantis and Lemuria.

After attaining a Ph.D. in education from New York University, he drifted to Florida, established a small utopian colony, and published a health-food newsletter. In the 1940s Siegmeister got into trouble with the U.S. Postal Service for promoting, with unacceptable hyperbole, a "super-race" outpost in Ecuador. He moved to California, then to Hawaii, Guatemala, and Puerto Rico before settling permanently in 1955 off the coast of southern Brazil on Sao Francisco do Sul Island. He occupied his time with a fruitless quest for secret entrances to the interior world. When he was not looking for Atlanteans, he wrote about flying saucers, imminent nuclear war, the super race, the supernatural—and the hollow earth.

The most widely read of all books on the subject, *The Hollow Earth* (1964) is also among the least original. It is a synthesis of previous writings on the subject, including whole blocks of prose from nineteenth-century works. Writing as Raymond Bernard, Siegmeister (a reader of *Amazing Stories* during the Shaver years) revived the nearly forgotten Shaver mystery, rehashed Palmer's ruminations on the pole holes, and exposed the "conspiracy" (some earthlings don't want to know the "truth") to keep the truth from surface earthlings. The publisher vigorously promoted the book in the United States and elsewhere, and it went through numerous printings.

For most readers it was an introduction to a concept of which they had never heard before, and it led to something of a hollow-earth revival. Siegmeister was not around to enjoy it, however. He died in September of 1965.

In the 1970s the hollow earth became a theme in neo-Nazi literature. In *UFOs—Nazi Secret Weapon?* (1976) and *Secret Nazi Polar Expeditions* (1978), a Canadian writer, Christof Friedrich (the pseudonym of Ernst Zundel), asserted that Hitler and a corps of elite troops had escaped after World War II to Argentina. From there they made their way to the South Pole, entered the earth through the hole, and established a base. From this location they flew the saucers they developed during the war. World governments knew of the base, but helpless to do anything about it, conspired to keep its existence a secret. Friedrich contended that the Nazis owed their racial superiority to their genetic ties to the advanced people of the inner earth. Zundel and his associates solicited funds for their own through-the-pole-hole expedition, to be accomplished in a chartered airliner with a large swastika on its fuselage (presumably to assure the inner-earthers of the visitors' amiable intentions), but the effort got nowhere.

Jerome Clark

Sources:

Bernard, Raymond [Walter Siegmeister]. *The Hollow Earth: The Greatest Geographical Discovery in History.* New York: Fieldcrest Publishing, 1964.

Kafton-Minkel, Walter. *Subterranean Worlds: 100,000 Years of Dragons, Dwarfs, the Dead, Lost Races and UFOs from Inside the Earth.* Port Townsend, WA: Loompanics Unlimited, 1989.

Ley, Willy. "For Your Information: The Hollow Earth." *Galaxy Science Fiction* 2, no. 5 (March 1956):71–81.

Mamak, Zbigniew. "Is the Earth Hollow?" *Fate.* Part I, 33, no. 7 (July 1980): 47–52; Part II, 33, no. 8 (August 1980):80–86.

Michell, John. *Eccentric Lives and Peculiar Notions.* San Diego, CA: Harcourt Brace Jovanovich, 1984.

Shaver, Richard S. "I Remember Lemuria!" *Amazing Stories* 19, no. 1 (March 1945):12–70.

Walton, Bruce A. *A Guide to the Inner Earth.* Jane Lew, WV: New Age Books, 1983.

Lost Continent Hoaxes

Both the Atlantis and the Lemuria, or Mu, stories were fiction based upon possible truth. That truth was probably the volcanic explosion on the island of Thera. The island of Thera (or Thira) is located 100 kilometers (60 miles) north of Crete in the Mediterranean Sea. On the island was a volcano called Santorin (or Santorini). Today, Thera is shaped like a horseshoe. The center is ocean. The proper geologic term for this structure is a volcanic caldera—the remains of a volcanic cone that exploded. The explosion may have been due to accumulated gases and lava that filled a cavern under the center of the island.

It is estimated that the explosion of the volcano on Thera occurred about 1400 B.C. The rim of the caldera is about ten kilometers (six miles) in diameter, indicating that much land was destroyed and replaced by ocean as a result of the explosion. There as an extensive city on the island. Archaeologists have worked for some time uncovering the city. It seems to have been a fairly modern city for the time, with running water, sewers and a thriving economy. Pellegrino has presented some of the most recent archeological findings in his book.

Perhaps the most famous "lost continent" is Atlantis. Another is its Pacific Ocean counterpart, Lemuria (or MU). The literature on Atlantis alone is enormous, while other works often combine both Continents. The first mention of Atlantis was in two of Plato's dialogues, *Kritias* (or *Critias*) and *Timaios* (or *Timaeus*).

These were written in about 355 B.C., and refer to events occurring about 9,000 years earlier when Atlantis was supposedly destroyed. Plato's description of Atlantis has served as the blueprint for almost all subsequent speculation about Atlantis.

The Lost Continent of Atlantis

Atlantis, as described by Plato, was a large island as big as Spain or France, located in the Atlantic Ocean just outside the Straits of Gibraltar. It was ruled by kings, with the king of the largest city as the leader. The supposed source of Plato's information was the Greek statesman Solon, although this seems unlikely since Plato didn't have known contact with Solon.

The destruction of Atlantis occurred after it lost a war with Athens 9,000 years earlier. Prior to the war, Atlantis extended her power from Egypt to central Italy. Both Athens and Atlantis were destroyed by earthquakes and floods, disappearing within 24 hours. The area of the Atlantic Ocean where Atlantis was located is now unnavigable because of shallow water and mud. Athens was rebuilt; Atlantis never was.

The problem with Plato's account is that virtually *every* statement in it is either demonstrably false or highly unlikely. For example, 9,000 years previously, Athens existed not as a city, but as caves and rock shelters housing early man. Also, according to oceanographers, no large, shallow, unnavigable area of the Atlantic Ocean near Gibraltar exists. Plato, in reality, may have used the fictional government of Atlantis to represent his ideal form of government.

When Heinrich Schliemann, the discoverer of ancient Troy died, he left a sealed envelope relating to Atlantis with the proviso that anyone in the family who opened the envelope must first pledge to devote his or her life to resolving the Atlantis mystery. Schliemann's grandson, Paul, took the pledge and opened the envelope. Inside was a small sealed vase, with instructions to break it open. The vase contained several square coins made of a platinum/aluminum alloy, inscribed in Phoenician "Issued in the Temple of the Transparent Walls." Young Schliemann published the results of his long "research" on Atlantis, which turned out to have been copied from many other writers on the subject (without acknowledgment). Paul claimed to have read the ancient Mayan *codex* (a manuscript book, usually of Scripture, or ancient annals), the *Troano Codex*, at the British Museum. this would have been doubly difficult, as that codex is at the National Museum in Madrid, and also because at that time no one knew how to read Mayan hieroglyphics. What he says it contained appears to have been plagiarized from the writings of Augustus Le Plongeon, who claimed to be able to read Mayan.

It was later revealed by author L. Sprague de Camp, among others, that Le Plongeon could not read Mayan. Although Paul Schliemann promised to write a definitive proof of his ideas about Atlantis, the book never appeared. No one saw the claimed vase or the platinum coins, and according to de Camp and others, it now appears that they were hoaxes. The entire story of Heinrich Schliemann's sealed envelope rested entirely upon the writings of grandson Paul, who did not tell the truth.

Ignatius Donnelly (1831–1901) was a journalist who turned to politics in his native Minnesota. As a U.S. congressman, Donnelly spent his spare time at the Library of Congress doing research on Atlantis. After his defeat for a third term in 1870, Donnelly returned to Minnesota where he spent the next twelve years working on his book about Atlantis. The book, *Atlantis: The Antediluvian World*, was published in 1882. It was the most popular book on Atlantis, and is still in print.

Donnelly's ideas about Atlantis can be summed up as follows: 1) Plato's information was basically correct, 2) Atlantis was the site of the Garden of Eden and was where mankind first emerged from barbarism to civilization, 3) Atlantis became a mighty nation, 4) the gods and goddesses of ancient Greece and Rome, as well as of the Hindus and others, were really the actual rulers of Atlantis, 5) the original religion of Atlantis was sun worship, 6) the alphabet was invented on Atlantis, and 7) a few people escaped the destruction of Atlantis in ships and rafts to tell the story.

Donnelly's sweeping linkage of many areas of mythology, history, and religion verified Plato's story of Atlantis. Therefore, it was highly appealing to many people, in spite of the fact that most of what Donnelly said was highly questionable or downright wrong. Author L. Sprague de Camp noted may of these errors in his 1970 book, *Lost Continents*.

The next great popularizer of Atlantis was Lewis Spence, a Scottish mythologist and occultist. Spence wrote five books on Atlantis, the most important of which was *The Problem of Atlantis* (1924). Spence tried to prove the following: 1) There was a great continent in the north Atlantic (Atlantis) that underwent frequent submergences over time, 2) in ancient times, a section of that continent emerged near the entrance to the Mediterranean Sea, and 3) the final disaster overtook Atlantis in about 10,000 B.C., when it was totally destroyed.

The Lost Continent of Mu

The second great lost continent is that of Mu or Lemuria. Stories of Mu and its people became known only in the nineteenth century. They started when

Ignatius Donnelly.

Bishop Diego de Landa of Yucatan published an alphabet that could be used to translate Mayan hieroglyphics into English. The alphabet was discovered by Abbé Charles-Etienne Brasseur in 1864. Brasseur used the alphabet to translate the three surviving Mayan codices. He claimed they told of a volcanic destruction of a land called Mu. Brasseur thought this land was identical to Atlantis.

Augustus Le Plongeon also used de Landa's alphabet to translate his own version of the codices. He provided much more detail on Mu, which he also thought was identical to Atlantis. He placed the continent to the east of Central America. Experts now agree that de Landa's Mayan alphabet was wrong, and that therefore both Le Plongeon and Brasseur were wrong in their "translations." It turns out that the *Troano Codex* is really a book about astrology.

Author James Churchward was the man who really moved Mu to the Pacific. He published a number of books, beginning with *The Lost Continent of Mu* in 1926. His information supposedly came from ancient tablets found in a Tibetan temple. Churchward called them the "Naacal Tablets," and said that after he befriended the priest at the temple, the priest taught him how to read the tablets, and showed him where additional tablets were stored. Judging solely from his writings, it is difficult to assess whether Churchward really believed what he said about Mu, or whether he was knowingly writing fiction. Regardless, insight can be gained from the fact that Churchward felt he could understand the meaning of a page of symbols by merely staring at it.

John Newbrough, in his book *Oahspe*, told about a lost continent called Pan. It was located between Alaska, Japan and Australia, and was of enormous size. Newbrough's book was dictated by him through "automatic writing" (a form of mediumship in which one enters a disassociated state of consciousness and allows the hand to write without conscious action) in 1882. It contained so many factual errors and unfulfilled prophecies that it is no longer taken seriously.

The name Lemuria was first suggested as a possible place (a Pacific continent) through which lemur monkeys may have travelled to get from Asia to Madagascar, near Africa. The suggestion was supported by German naturalist Ernst Haeckel. It was not purported to have human civilization until Madame Helena Petrovna Blavatsky of the Mahatma Letters (*See* Mahatma Hoax, p. 223) exposed it as such. In Blavatsky's book *The Secret Doctrine*, she mentions both Atlantis and Lemuria as the original home of the Mahatmas (Hindu saints, also called "Ascended Masters"). A follower of Blavatsky, W. Scott-Elliot, fleshed out her Lemuria in his 1896 book, *The Story of Atlantis and the Lost Lemuria*. These Lemurians were twelve to fifteen feet tall, had a third eye in the back of their heads, and had no foreheads. In short, they were barely human, and actually were egg-laying hermaphrodites (having both male and female reproductive organs). Although the Lemurians eventually "learned" about sex, they chose to mate with the great apes, eventually producing humans, but also incurring the wrath of the Lhas, who were supernatural beings hoping to incarnate themselves in human bodies. Other writers, such as Annie Besant, Rudolf Steiner, and Edgar Cayce contributed to the further elaboration of these stories.

Sources:

Babcock, William H. *Legendary Islands of the Atlantic.* New York: American Geographic Society, 1922.

de Camp, L. Sprague. *Lost Continents: The Atlantis Theme in History, Science and Literature.* New York: Dover Publications, 1970.

Donnelly, Ignatius. *Atlantis: The Antediluvian World.* New York: Harper Brothers, 1882.

Mavor, James W. *Voyage to Atlantis.* New York: G.P. Putnam's Sons, 1969.

Pellegrino, Charles. *Uncovering Atlantis.* New York: Random House, 1990.

Ramage, Edwin, S., ed. *Atlantis: Fact or Fiction?* Bloomington, IN: Indiana University Press, 1978.

Spence, Lewis. *The Problem of Atlantis.* London: H. Rider & Son, 1924.

Robert Peary and the North Pole

On April 6, 1909, Admiral Robert E. Peary (1856–1920) claimed he was the first person to reach the geographic North Pole. His claim was accepted, despite some questionable documentation, and he was hailed as a hero. Another who claimed to have really been the first to reach the pole was Frederick A. Cook (1865–1940). His claim was made on April 21, 1908, nearly a year *before* Peary. The matter is in such dispute because of questionable documentation and a fierce rivalry between the two men. This rivalry led Peary to try both fraud and character assassination in an attempt to hoax his way into the record books as the first man to reach the Pole.

Peary led several previous expeditions that tried to reach the North Pole. The first of these was in 1891, then in 1892–93, when he tried an overland route through northern Greenland that failed. He tried again in 1893–95, and by ship in 1905–06. During that last voyage, he came within 174 miles of the Pole. After his try in 1908–09, for which he claimed success, he learned that five days before his announcement of reaching the pole Frederick Cook, a surgeon on Peary's 1891 expedition, had announced that he (Cook) had reached the Pole in 1908.

Of course, there was mass confusion. Two believable explorers were undercutting each other's claims to have been first. Peary's supporters undertook a massive campaign to discredit Cook's claim. The National Geographic Society was the strongest supporter of Peary, and continued to defend him until 1988. At that point, the evidence no longer substantiated Peary. In the meantime, Cook's life was intentionally ruined by Peary and his agents. He was jailed for financial fraud and discredited. The man commissioned by the National Geographic Society to investigate (and buttress) Peary's claim, Wally Herbert, was so shocked when he examined the poorly documented records, that he wrote a book that conceded that Peary did not reach the Pole. Herbert still attributed this failure to document as incompetence, not malice. Author Dennis Rawlins then claimed to have found the records made by Peary on the day Peary said he reached the Pole. These were records that Peary claimed had never existed. Rawlins showed that Peary's own calculations on that day had him 121 statute miles (or 105 nautical miles) short of the Pole on April 6, and that was the most northerly point he ever reached.

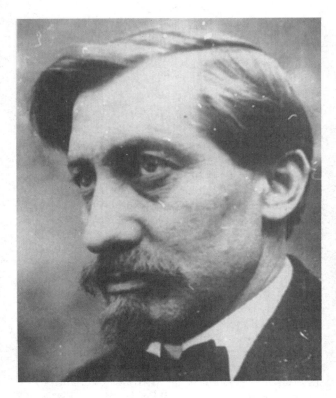

Frederick Cook.

William Peary.

Once this new material was discovered by Rawlins, Peary's subsequent behavior began to make sense. Peary apparently *knew* that he had not reached the Pole. He gave a document to his wife, who was unable to understand it. She put it in a bank safe deposit box. Peary had told her the document was important and would destroy Cook's claims. In 1935, fifteen years after Peary's death, his daughter sent a copy of the paper to Melville Grosvenor, director of the American Geographical Society. Both Peary's daughter and his widow thought that the document supported Peary's claim. The document was finally deciphered by Harry Raymond, an astronomer. It consisted of sextant readings showing that Peary was about 200 nautical miles from the North Pole. Although it had been deciphered, the contents of the document was sealed and not revealed at that time. Rawlins finally found the document again in 1973 and released the information.

The Peary family then opened the archives to the public in 1984. Rawlins showed that Peary was, by his own calculations, never actually closer than 121 statute miles from the Pole. Because Peary was apparently so inept at using his instruments, he never knew exactly where he was, although he clearly knew he had not reached the Pole. This was obvious since the sun was still rising and falling in the sky, something that would not happen right at the Pole. Interestingly, Rawlins also believes that Cook did not make it to the Pole. A number of other Arctic experts accept Cook's claim, based upon his accurate description of the area around the Pole.

Sources:

Abramson, Howard S. *Hero in Disgrace: The Life of Arctic Explorer Frederick A. Cook.* New York: Paragon House, 1991.

Eames, Hugh. *Winner Lose All: Dr. Cook and the Theft of the North Pole.* Boston: Little Brown, 1973.

Freeman, Andrew A. *The Case for Doctor Cook.* New York: Coward-McCann, 1961.

Herbert, Wally. *The Noose of Laurels: Robert E. Peary and the Race to the North Pole.* New York: Atheneum, 1989.

Rawlins, Dennis. *Peary at the North Pole: Fact or Fiction?* Washington DC: Robert B. Luce, 1973.

Weems, John Edward. *Peary: The Explorer and the Man.* Boston: Houghton Mifflin, 1967.

Viking Hoaxes

Many assert that the Vikings or others came to North America before Christopher Columbus, but evidence of a pre-Columbus "discovery" is hard to find. In search of such evidence, some, like Barry Fell, Harvard marine biologist and amateur archeologist, have mistaken natural markings for inscriptions in stone. As Fell is not generally held in high regard by archaeologists, the vast bulk of them reject his "evidence" as poor. Yet, there are some pieces of evidence that cannot be so easily dismissed. The Kensington Runestone, clearly inscribed, is obviously a stone object carved by man. The only question is how old is it? The Vinland Map is also a man-made item; again how old is it? Another possible Viking structure is the Round Tower at Newport, Rhode Island.

In 1948 and 1949, the entire area around the tower, which is of haphazard fieldstone masonry, was excavated by William S. Godfrey, Jr., an amateur archaeologist. He discovered colonial artifacts (such as clay pipes, glass fragments, ceramic shards, and a gun flint) *under* the stone foundations that support the tower. Gun flints date *after* the Viking era, yet they were found *beneath* the supposed Viking construction. This proves that it was built during the American colonial period, probably in the 1650s. It certainly rules out a pre-Columbian construction date.

The Vinland Map

The Vinland Map, named after a territory in the New World, was found bound into a volume with two manuscripts, one dating from the fifteenth century, the other from the thirteenth century. It was clear that the map had been in the bound volume for some time since worm holes through the manuscript pages were contiguous with those in the map. The map is drawn on a single piece of vellum measuring about eleven by sixteen inches, folded down the center. The map itself is drawn in ink depicting the three known parts of the medieval world—Europe, Asia and Africa. From its style, it appears to date from about 1440. The striking thing about the map is that in the upper left corner there are two large islands indicated. One is clearly Greenland (called Gronelada). The other, further west, is labeled "Vinlanda Insula." This representation of land west of Greenland in the period before Columbus lent credence to the theory that the Vikings (or others) travelled to the New World before Columbus. It should be noted that the names on the map are in Latin and that the map was based on the kind of circular or oval prototype that was popular until the second half of the fifteenth century. Although a number of map experts have argued that the nomenclature, wormholes, and style of the map argue strongly in favor of its authenticity, Yale University, which acquired the map in 1957, decided to have a microscopical and chemical investigation of the map carried out in 1972 by McCrone Associates of Chicago. This firm specializes in scientific testing of suspected art and other forgeries.

A microscopical examination of the map indicated that the ink line that formed the outline of the countries was bordered along its length by a yellowish discoloration. At first this was attributed to the tendency for old ink to become discolored along its edges because parts of it have migrated into the fibers of the paper. After additional observation, it was noted that the discoloration was not that, but rather had a "body" of its own. In fact, pieces of the "yellow" could be flecked from the line with a fine needle. A careful examination showed that the black ink line had been drawn over a slightly wider yellow line that had been laid down first. In fact, in one spot the black line had been carelessly drawn out of register with the yellow line. Higher magnification and the use of polarized light showed particles of what turned out to be anatase in the yellow "ink." Anatase is a mineral, but the small regular size of the anatase particles showed that these were from a precipated (man-made) variety. Anatase is a "titanium white" pigment that has been only available since 1917. The levels of titanium (of a natural sort) that were found in the inks of the two manuscripts with which the Vinland Map was bound were several orders of magnitude lower. These match the levels found in real aged iron gallate inks used at the time of supposed composition. In other words, the two manuscripts are genuinely old, but the Vinland Map could not have been drawn any earlier than 1917. McCrone Associates also noted that the coastline of Greenland was accurately drawn and was shown as an island—both facts were likely unknown in the fifteenth century. The forger's only serious mistake was using a yellow ink too modern for the 1400s!

The Kensington Runestone

The Kensington Runestone was a piece of flat sandstone about six inches thick and thirty inches by fifteen inches in dimension. It was found in 1898, entangled in the roots of a tree no more than thirty years old. The farmer who found it, Olof Ohman, had bought his farm in Kensington, Minnesota in about 1889. The stone was covered on one side with what appeared to be sharply cut runes, the writing of the ancient Scandanavians. The writing has been translated by several Norwegian experts, including Erik Wahlgren, as follows:

> 8 Goths and 22 Norwegians on an exploration journey from Vinland to the west. We had camp by 2 skerries one day's journey north from this stone. We were to fish one day after we came home found 10 men red of blood and dead AVM [Ave Maria]. We have 10 men by the sea to look after our ships 14 days' travel from this island Year 1362

The stone was brought to Prof. G.O. Curme, an expert in Germanic languages at Northwestern University. He examined it and remarked that it was odd that

Kensington Runestone.

the stone dated itself to 1362, yet was written in modern Swedish with recent runes. He also noted that the cuts that formed the runes did not look old. The stone was returned to Ohman.

Nine years later, a book salesman named Hjalmar Holand rediscovered the stone and spent the rest of his life proclaiming its authenticity. He used sources that really did not support his thesis defending the stone's authenticity, but the sources were misquoted and not readily available to those who listened to Holand's defense of the stone. Yet, for all his efforts, Holand did not impress the experts. After all, according to Wahlgren, the type of Swedish on the stone was a version of that language that had never been spoken anywhere outside the American Midwest!

It now looks as though Ohman, a self-educated man, carved the stone himself. It even appears that his own speech peculiarities, reflected in his Halsingland dialect, were also present on the Runestone. Ohman finally did admit that he knew how to read and write modern runes, and that he was trained originally as a stone mason. He also possessed several books that illustrated runes. Perhaps the hoaxer in this case can be identified. It looked as though he may have been helped by Sven Fogelblad, a former minister in Sweden, turned teacher, who knew runes well. He died before the stone was found (and perhaps before it was

carved), but could have drawn the pictures of the runes to be carved by others.

Sources indicate that a fair number of local Minnesota residents knew how to read runes. Soon after the stone was found, several locals made fair translations of the runes. Another school of thought says that *because* the runes are so carelessly done, they must represent a real fourteenth century Swede of limited education. No knowledgeable hoaxer would make such an obviously wrong inscription.

There are a great many more supposed Viking artifacts from North America. Among these are spears, axes, and swords. The axes are almost all of a variety that are called socket paring axes, a form of lumbering tool that have extra weight added to the butt for balance. This is strictly an American innovation, therefore ruling out a Viking origin. The small halberds (nineteenth-century tobacco-cutting swords) discovered in many places are not Scandinavian at all. Such halberds were not in use in Scandinavia until after 1500. Rather, they are plug tobacco cutters, made in the nineteenth century in Ohio. Several genuine Norse weapons of great antiquity, found in Canada, were later shown to have been brought there from Norway in the early twentieth century.

Lest the idea forms that *no* Viking or Scandanavian settlement occurred in North America before Columbus, it should be noted that at L'Anse au Meadow in Newfoundland the apparent remains of the only genuine Viking settlement in North America have been found. Further exploration is being done in the area.

Sources:

Blegen, Theodore C. *The Kensington Rune Stone: New Light on an Old Riddle.* St. Paul, MN: Minnesota Historical Society, 1968.

McCrone, Walter. "The Vinland Map." *Analytical Chemistry* 60 (1988):1009–18.

Skelton, R. A., T. E. Marston, and G. D. Painter. *The Vinland Map and the Tarter Relation.* New Haven, CT: Yale University Press, 1965.

Wahlgren, Erik. "The Case of the Kensington Rune Stone." *American Heritage.* 10, no. 3 (April 1959):34–35, 101–05.

Wallace, Birgitta. "Viking Hoaxes." *Vikings in the West.* Edited by Eleanor Guralnick. New York: Archeological Institute of America, 1982.

"Wrong Way" Corrigan

In July of 1938, Douglas (born Clyde) Corrigan thrilled Americans by landing in Ireland after flying solo across the Atlantic on the mistaken assumption that he was heading for California from Long Island, New York. Corrigan said it was all due to his broken compass. His backup compass was also malfunctioning. Interestingly enough, Corrigan was refused permission by the Federal Aviation Administration (FAA) at Long Island to fly the Atlantic because of the condition of his poorly constructed plane.

Corrigan would not have made it to Ireland had he not been an extremely resourceful and determined pilot. After ten hours of flight (out of twenty-eight hours total time to cross to Ireland), he noticed that his feet were getting quite cold. He looked down and saw that his feet were sitting in an inch deep pool of gasoline. The leak pooled right over the exhaust pipe. Corrigan cleverly punctured a small hole in the floor of the plane with a screwdriver to allow the gasoline to drain out at a point that was away from the hot exhaust pipe.

When Corrigan came out of the clouds, he noticed several small fishing boats on the water. He was surprised to find himself over water, but followed the coastline to what appeared to be a city and then to an area marked "Baldonnel" in the grass. He recognized this as the name of the Dublin airport and landed. When he landed, he was met by a man who asked him his name. "Corrigan" he answered. "Oh, just another Irishman coming home," the man replied.

Corrigan was warmly received by people in Dublin. As he had no passport, and had entered the country illegally, he could have been in trouble. His plane was confiscated, and Corrigan was turned over to the American ambassador. The ambassador questioned Corrigan, but he stuck to his story that his compass had malfunctioned. Corrigan was taken to see Prime Minister Eamon De Valera. De Valera decided that since Corrigan had come into Ireland without any papers, he should be allowed to leave without any papers. De Valera appreciated the publicity that Corrigan's flight had generated for Ireland.

Corrigan was immediately deluged with offers for personal appearances in the United States. His airplane was dismantled and loaded on a boat. After a short visit to London as a guest of U.S. Ambassador Joseph Kennedy, Corrigan sailed back to the United States on the steamer *Manhattan*. While on board, he was informed that, due to his illegal flight, the U.S. government had suspended his pilot's license until his arrival in New York!

Corrigan was treated as a hero upon his arrival in New York. He was given a ticker tape parade that was said to be bigger than the one given Charles Lindbergh

Douglas "Wrong Way" Corrigan.

after his solo flight across the Atlantic. Corrigan received many gifts of airplane compasses. He claimed in his book, *That's My Story*, (1938), that it was not his compass that was faulty, but his *reading* of his compass. This was impossible to believe from an experienced pilot.

With analysis over whether Corrigan's story was a hoax come incongruities. The first was the changed story about the compass. The second was the fact that Corrigan accepted a job as a test pilot with Douglas Aircraft after his return, not the kind of job offered to someone who couldn't read a compass.

After World War II, Corrigan bought an orange grove in Southern California and dropped from sight until 1988, on the fiftieth anniversary of his famous flight, when the 81-year-old Corrigan came out of seclusion and told the *Los Angeles Times*, that his "mistake" was intentional. "Wrong Way" Corrigan was never really in doubt about which way he was headed.

Sources:

Corrigan, Douglas. *That's My Story*. New York: E. P. Dutton, 1938.

Dean, Paul. "Return of 'Wrong Way,'" *Los Angeles Times* Sect. V (August 16, 1988): 1, 3.

Other Exploration and Travel Hoaxes

Prester John and John Mandeville. The works of both Prester John and John Mandeville were two of the earliest and most influential travel books. Actually, Prester John did not write anything himself, and probably never existed at all. He seems to be a conglomeration that built upon the appearance in Rome, in 1122 of an Oriental clergyman called "John, the patriarch of the Indians." This man told many tales of life in India. About twenty-five years later, Prester John appeared in the character of a Christian who combined the roles of priest and king. He was first mentioned in the chronicle of Otto, Bishop of Freisengen, in which John tells "tall tales" about his kingdoms far away. A number of people have been suggested as the model for Prester John, but, in any case, his stories are almost entirely fictional.

John Mandeville (Jehan de Mandeville) had a book of travels, written in French, issued in manuscript copies between 1357 and 1371. The author claimed to be a British knight, who travelled throughout much of Asia and the Middle East. Stories of his adventures are similar to Prester John's in that they involve fabulous beasts, monsters, locations, and events that likely never existed. On his deathbed in 1372, French physician, Jean de Bourgogne, confessed that he wrote the Mandeville book.

The Travels of Sebastian Cabot. One of the first exploration hoaxes that can be examined is the 1508 voyage of Sebastian Cabot (1476?–1557) from Bristol, England to Northern Canada. Cabot, the son of famous explorer John Cabot, claimed to have visited Hudson Bay in Northern Canada and Newfoundland. He then sailed along the east coast of North America as far south as Florida. Of course, these places did not have those names at that time. Cabot then returned to England. There is reason to believe that Cabot did not make as extensive a trip to North America as he claimed, and that he may not have voyaged to North American waters at all.

Sebastian Cabot claimed that he travelled with his father as a young man. This is unlikely, as Sebastian was prone to bragging and exaggeration. Unfortunately, the British did not make careful records of their explorers' trips, as did the Spanish, Portuguese and Italians. It was not until the 1540s that the British started compiling exploration records, mostly from people's memories. Because of the unreliability of human memory, these reports are questionable. Author Henry Harrisse argued strongly against Cabot's claims in his 1896 book.

Louis Hennepin's Travels. Father Louis Hennepin (1640–1701?) is known as an explorer of the American Mid-

west. He started as a member of French explorer Renè La Salle's expedition, but left the expedition before it descended down the Mississippi River to its mouth—thereby establishing the vast Louisiana claim for France. In 1697, Hennepin published a book in which he claimed that he and two comrades (not La Salle) canoed all the way down the Mississippi and back in 1680. This would have been two years *before* La Salle.

Hennepin was a member of the Recollet order, arch-rivals of the Jesuits, the latter of whom did much of the exploration in North America. He often minimized or falsified the accomplishments of the Jesuit explorers. He also lied in his own writings, making it difficult to know what to believe. Hennepin claimed that he and his two companions disobeyed La Salle's orders to travel down the Illinois river to the Mississippi and then go north up the Mississippi to the Wisconsin River. Although Hennepin followed the route La Salle asked, Hennepin claimed that before this, he and his companions went south on the Mississippi as far as its mouth. However, that would mean they paddled 3,000 miles, much of it upstream against a flooding Mississippi, in less than 43 days—paddling 70 miles a day downstream (possible) and 190 miles a day upstream (not possible). In his writings Hennepin complains that his canoes could barely make 30 miles a day upstream. In those days, the full length of the Mississippi was not known or appreciated. With today's knowledge, it is clear that his claimed feat was impossible. In 1941, writer Jean Delanglez revealed through careful analysis of claims of Hennepin that the father was a hoaxer.

Travels of Jonathan Carver. The Travels of Jonathan Carver (1732–1780) was one of the most widely reprinted travel books in pre-1800 America. Unfortunately, Carver appears to have put it together from plagiarisms of earlier travel books. Among his favorite sources are Charlevoix's *Journal of a Voyage to North-America*, and La Hontan's *New Voyages to North-America*.

Writer Edward Bourne has shown that Carver did not have the background to write the book, and that he simply lifted whole passages from both of the mentioned books, sometimes changing a few words.

The Vizetelly Hoax. In January of 1849, British publisher David Bogue released *Four Months Among the Goldfinders in Alta California . . .* , by "J. Tyrwitt Brooks, M. D." The author's real name was Henry Vizetelly and his book helped start the gold rush in California. The author, however, had never been to North America, much less California. The book was quickly translated into German, French, Spanish and several other languages, and has been an historical source for more than a century. It is largely based upon a few works, such as John

Fremont's *Report*, glorified by liberal use of the author's imagination.

Vizetelly admitted the hoax in his 1893 autobiography, *Glances Back Through Seventy Years*. Actually, the hoax had been exposed by Friedrich Gerstaecker in 1853, but almost nobody discovered the work in which he exposed it, namely *Narrative of a Journey Around the World*. Gerstaecker had translated Vizetelly's work into German shortly after it was first published. He also *really* visited the goldfields. Gerstaecker showed a copy of Vizetelly's book to Captain Sutter, on whose property gold was first discovered. Vizetelly mentioned in the book that John Augustus Sutter was an acquaintance of his. Sutter denied knowing Vizetelly, and told Gerstaecker that what was said about Sutter's family in the book was totally false. Gerstaecker soon discovered many other falsehoods. Unfortunately, Hubert Bancroft, in his great history of California, unfamiliar with Gerstaecker's autobiography, treats the Vizetelly book as genuine.

Imaginary Voyages After Defoe. After novelist Daniel Defoe wrote about Robinson Crusoe (*See* Hoaxes that Were Not Hoaxes, p. 95), many books were printed based upon other travelers' accounts. The books were about places the purported author had never visited, despite his or her insistence at having done so. Among the books in this category were Thomas Aubury's *Travels Through North America* (1789), Johann Bueschel's *Neue Reisen . . . in England* (1784), and P.N. Chantreau's *Voyage Philosophique, Politique, et Litteraire fait en Russie . . .* (1794).

The case of St. Jean de Crevecoeur and his *Le Voyage dans la Haute Pennsylvanie et dans l'état de New York* is complex because the author does not claim to have visited the places he describes. Rather, he claims to have found the anonymously authored manuscript in a shipwreck. Actually, Crevecoeur plagiarized everything from earlier travel books, without giving credit.

Crevecoeur was also purportedly responsible for creating a speech made by Benjamin Franklin (*See* Benjamin Franklin's Hoaxes, p. 139) at the dedication of Franklin College in Lancaster, Pennsylvania on June 5, 1787. Neither Franklin nor Crevecoeur was present. This is a case where a master hoaxer (Franklin) was himself the subject of a hoax.

The Mystery of the Mary Celeste. In 1872, the ship *Mary Celeste* was found abandoned on the high seas with all of its cargo intact, no damage to the ship itself, no crew, and no indication of what became of them. The ship was spotted moving erratically in the mid-Atlantic by another ship, the *Dei Gratia*, captained by David Read Moorhouse. He sent out a boarding party, which found the ship deserted. Captain Moorhouse ordered several

members of his crew to sail the abandoned ship into Gibralter, and claim it as a derelict. They turned the ship over to British authorities in Gibralter and layed claim to the value of the ship and its cargo. A lengthy hearing followed. Eventually, Moorhouse was awarded the salvage value of the ship.

Author Laurence J. Keating claims this was a hoax concocted to defraud the insurance companies of a large sum of money. Both ships were docked near each other when they were in New York a few days earlier, and Keating suggests the plot was hatched at this time. The *Dei Gratia* simply followed the *Mary Celeste* out to sea and in mid-Atlantic transferred its crew to the *Dei Gratia*. The crew of *Mary Celeste* was dropped off in another port, prior to arriving in Gibralter. While this "explanation" is both simple and logical, it is not accepted by everyone. After all, none of the crew of the *Mary Celeste* was ever seen again. Perhaps they used the money from the salvage to settle on land.

Frederick Cook and Mount McKinley. In 1906, Frederick Cook (1865–1940), who later claimed to have reached the North Pole (*See* Robert Peary and the North Pole, p. 53), maintained that he scaled Mount McKinley, the highest mountain in North America. Although Cook never confessed to lying about scaling Mount McKinley, later explorers located the real sites from which his photographs, supposedly shot from the summit, were taken.

Cook first tried to climb Mount McKinley in 1903. He attempted it from the north, where he ran up against the Wickersham Wall, the largest precipice in North America. The expedition failed. He tried again, he claimed, in September of 1906, in the company of Montana blacksmith Edward Barrill, and reached the summit. This would have been the first successful scaling of the mountain. He brought back a photo taken at the summit. In 1910, Belmore Browne and Herschel Parker tried climbing the mountain. Although unsuccessful, they were able to conclusively show with their own photographs that Cook's photo had been taken at a lower point on the mountain. Cook claimed to have been the first to reach what has been called the Great Gorge, located fifteen miles south of the summit. From there, it is almost impossible to get to the summit without using alpine rockclimbing gear, which Cook did not have with him. (No one, in fact, scaled Mount McKinley from this direction until 1954.)

Cook described his ascent in his book *To the Top of the Continent*. His book has been analyzed by subsequent climbers, and some claim they can pick out the exact sentence where the book departs from the truth. On October 15, 1906, it was revealed that Barrill signed a sworn statement that he and Cook were never near the summit of McKinley. Barrill claimed that he maintained a daily diary, with the entries dictated by Cook on the expedition. Four days before Cook claimed they reached the summit, Cook ordered Barrill to stop making entries in the diary, and to leave some pages blank. On September 16, Cook asked for the diary, and added to the blank pages fabrications about reaching the summit. Cook claimed later that he never knew Barrill kept a diary. Cook refused to defend his case in front of the Explorer's Club. When Cook's photos were taken on the 1910 expedition and compared with the actual terrain, it was soon discovered that the "summit" photo had been taken on what is called "Fake Peak," a 6,000-foot-tall projection from the glacier at the base of Mount McKinley. Cook had never been closer to the summit on this trip than the 6,000- foot level. McKinley is more than 20,000 feet high.

Donald Crowhurst and the Atlantic. Donald Crowhurst (1932–1969) was a champion sailboat pilot. On October 31, 1968, he set sail from England on a round-the-world solo sailing attempt. He kept logs and tape recordings of his progress. Occasionally, he had radio contact with ships, although his radio only worked intermittently. On November 15, he claimed that he covered 243 miles in a single day, which would have been a new world record for a small sailboat. This was later proven to be a hoax. On December 12, Crowhurst stopped writing in his official logbook, and started writing in a blue examination booklet, commonly used in college examinations. This seems to have marked the start of his greater hoax, namely his claim to the fastest solo trip around the world in a sailboat. On December 17, he sent a radio message, falsely claiming he was over the Equator. He was soon claiming to be off Brazil—a full 550 miles ahead of where he really was. He then made an aimless series of zig-zags off the coast of Brazil. On January 19, 1969, he radioed a position 4,000 miles ahead of his actual position. He then went into radio silence for months.

On June 22, he indicated he was in the mid-Atlantic, on the way back to England. On July 10, his boat was found 1,800 miles from England, without him on board. The logbooks on the boat showed that he would have beaten the old record for an around-the-world sailboat trip, but the last few pages of the log also contained a confession that his entries were a hoax. Whether Crowhurst jumped overboard intentionally, or was accidently swept overboard may never be known. Why he carried out his hoax and then confessed all before his presumed death, is also unknown. Nicholas Tomalin and Ron Hall, in their definitive work about Crowhurst, feel that he started his trip around the world honestly, but faced financial ruin due to the fame, endorsements, and future sponsors he would never realize if he did not complete the course successfully. That may have driven him to undertake the hoax.

Sources:

Adams, Perry G. *Travelers and Travel Liars, 1660–1800*. New York: Dover Publications, 1980. Originally published by the University of California Press in 1962.

Bourne, Edward Gaylord. "The Travels of Jonathan Carver." *American Historical Review*, 11 (1906):287–302.

Delanglez, Jean. "Hennepin's *Description of Louisiana*: A Critical Essay." *Mid-America* 23, no. 1 (1941):3–44; 23, no. 2 (1941):99–137.

Gudde, Erwin G. "The Vizetelly Hoax." *Pacific Historical Review*, 28, no. 3 (1959):233–36.

Harrisse, Henry. *John Cabot the Discoverer of North America and Sebastian Cabot His Son*. London: B. F. Stephens, 1896.

Keating, Laurence J. *The Great* Mary Celeste *Hoax: A Famous Sea Mystery Exposed*. London: Heath Cranton, 1929.

Roberts, David. *Great Exploration Hoaxes*. San Francisco: Sierra Club Books, 1982.

Tomalin, Nicholas, and Ron Hall. *The Strange Last Voyage of Donald Crowhurst*. New York: Stein & Day, 1970.

Watson, Douglas. "Spurious Californiana." *California Historical Society Quarterly* 11 (1932):65–68.

Historical Hoaxes

Aimée Semple McPherson's Kidnapping

In the 1920s and 1930s Aimée Semple McPherson (1890–1944) was America's best-known woman evangelist. In 1926, at the peak of her fame, she suddenly disappeared. According to newspaper reports she had been swimming in the Pacific Ocean off Los Angeles when she vanished. Five weeks later, she suddenly reappeared in the desert of Mexico. For many weeks, both before and after her return, the newspapers gave the event extensive coverage. Yet the entire disappearance was a hoax.

On May 18, 1926, McPherson invited her mother, Minnie Kennedy, to accompany her to the beach. Her mother declined. McPherson went with her secretary, Emma Schaffer. Schaffer saw McPherson far out in the water, but then she lost track of her. As McPherson did not come back on shore Schaffer spread the word that McPherson had drowned. An extensive search turned up no body. Newspapers raised questions and reported sightings of her in small California towns. Although several demands for ransom were received, the police felt these too, were hoaxes. Kennedy offered a $25,000 reward for the return of her daughter alive.

Five weeks after the disappearance, the Los Angeles police received a call that McPherson had surfaced in Douglas, Arizona. McPherson called her mother shortly thereafter to confirm this. Although Kennedy told her daughter on the phone not to talk to anyone about the events, by the time Kennedy reached Arizona, McPherson had talked to the media quite a bit. She claimed she was abducted and tortured, but had finally escaped. She said she was lured to a car parked by the beach when someone told her the story of a dying infant. Once inside the car, she was overcome by chloroform. She awakened bound to a cot somewhere in northern Mexico.

McPherson claimed that two men and one woman had been involved in the kidnapping. She had escaped by rolling off the cot, cutting her bonds with a discarded tin can, and climbing out a window. She walked through miles of desert to the Mexican border town of Agua Prieta, just across from Douglas, where she collapsed.

Immediately, the press questioned her story. McPherson was not sunburned, injured, or even thirsty when she was found. Her clothing was not torn, and there were grass stains on her shoes. Word spread that Kenneth Ormiston, McPherson's radio station engineer, had been seen with her at a seaside resort during the time she was missing. Ormiston and McPherson had been linked romantically before, and his wife had threatened to name McPherson as the reason she was seeking a divorce from her husband. Kennedy stopped this scandal by forcing Ormiston out of his job and then, after he had left the area, paying him to come back to Los Angeles during a time when it was rumored he was traveling in Europe with McPherson.

McPherson claimed that her kidnappers had cut off some of her hair to send to her mother, along with a demand for a $500,000 ransom. An envelope containing a lock of hair, purported to be McPherson's *was* received by Kennedy, along with a demand for that amount of money. If the ransom was not paid, the note said, McPherson would be sold into white slavery in Mexico. The police questioned the note's authenticity.

Both Kennedy and McPherson were called before a Los Angeles grand jury formed to investigate the incident. The grand jury found enough evidence to try them for "conspiracy to perpetuate a hoax" although it was more likely obstruction of justice. Kennedy was, in fact, arrested on obstruction of justice. The judge, Carlos Hardy, accepted a check for $2,500 from the Angelus

Aimée Semple McPherson.

Temple, McPherson's church organization, although this was not revealed until much later.

Other exchanges of money for influence were transpiring. The district attorney, on the last day possible to make his decision, finally decided that no one would be well-served by a trial. He dropped all charges. The public, however, did not forget and reporters kept asking about the contents of a "little blue trunk." The trunk contained fancy undergarments and was found at the site of the seaside cabin occupied by McPherson and Ormiston. Several years later, Hardy was tried at an impeachment hearing for having accepted the check and for other unprofessional conduct. At that hearing, the memory of many of the witnesses from the kidnapping case several years earlier, seemed to improve. They could now clearly identify the woman with Ormiston at the seaside cottage as McPherson. Previously, Hardy had instructed some of the witnesses to be certain of their identification. The judge was impeached and summoned to trial. He was tried and acquitted by a close margin. However, California had recently gone to a system of electing judges, and Hardy was defeated at his first attempt at re-election.

Sources:

Bahr, Robert. *Least of All the Saints: The Story of Aimée Semple McPherson.* Englewood Cliffs, NJ: Prentice-Hall, 1979.

Thomas, Lately. *Storming Heaven: The Lives and Turmoils of Minnie Kennedy and Aimée Semple McPherson.* New York: William Morrow & Co., 1970.

———. *The Vanishing Evangelist: The Aimée Semple McPherson Kidnaping Affair.* New York: Viking Press, 1959.

The Amityville Horror

The facts are far from clear about most of the things that purportedly happened at the Dutch colonial house on Ocean Avenue in Amityville, New York in 1975 and 1976. Despite a best-selling, supposedly non-fiction book and a popular movie on the matter, it appears that little of what was *supposed* to have happened really did. Few facts are agreed upon. Ronald DeFeo *did* kill six members of his family in the house on November 13, 1974. He *was* tried, convicted, and sentenced to six consecutive life terms, despite his insanity plea in which he claimed voices in the house told him what to do.

In November of 1975, George and Kathy Lutz were shown the house by a realtor and told that murders had taken place there. They decided to purchase it anyway, especially since the price was reasonable. The Lutzes moved in with their three children on December 18. Reportedly they had the house blessed by a priest that day. During his blessing, the priest supposedly heard a loud voice say "Get out!" The Lutzes moved out 28 days later, temporarily leaving their possessions. They later claimed that they were tormented during their brief stay by a wide variety of supernatural events. Among their complaints were an infestation by hundreds of flies in the middle of winter, a malfunctioning telephone, moving statues, windows and doors opening and breaking, green slime oozing from the ceiling, a constant chill, apparitions, and mysterious music. Pecorara, the priest who blessed the house (called Father "Mancuso" in the book and film) also experienced strange phenomena at the house during this time.

Prior to buying the house, the Lutzes lived in Deer Park. They financed the $80,000 home in spite of the fact that George Lutz' business was not doing well. In over his head with the unsound purchase, he soon realized he could not keep up the payments. The Lutzes needed a way to get out of their financial crisis, and since They didn't even have decent furniture for their new home, it was easy to abandon. Later, they came back to hold a garage sale, where most of the items were passed over due to their poor quality. Meanwhile, William Weber, the lawyer for murderer Ronald DeFeo, was trying to acquit DeFeo on the murder charges by reason of insanity. When that didn't work, he planned an appeal based on the "devil made me do it" defense.

Although it is unclear who came up with the idea of a haunting first, it seems to have gradually evolved among the Lutzes, Weber, and Paul Hoffman, the first writer to publish anything about the mysterious happenings in the house. As skeptic Frank Zindler notes in his article, there is a transcript of the Lutz vs. Hoffman, trial held in September of 1979, in which the Lutzes admitted that almost everything in the book by Jay Anson was fiction.

Anson, a writer who had worked on the screenplay of *The Exorcist*, was brought in to tell the Amityville story. He was not allowed to enter the house. He never even interviewed the Lutzes, but was given a series of tapes made by them in which they gave the outline of their story. Anson, apparently borrowing heavily from *The Exorcist*, literally let his imagination run rampant. He did not do a careful job, however. In his rush to complete the book, he allowed all sorts of contradictions to remain. The floor plan of the house, for example, changes several times in subsequent printings of the book, specifically the paperback's floor plan and that in the hardbound version.

Many outright falsehoods are stated in Anson's book. For instance, the face of a pig was never really seen, Lutz admits. There was no band marching through the house, and the carpet and furniture were not moved to accommodate it. No heavy door was torn off its hinges. No levitation occurred while Lutz was awake, although Lutz says he might have dreamed it. No priest was called in to bless the house the day they moved in. No windstorm or heavy snow storm occurred on the nights that the book says they did. The house is not built upon a graveyard of the Shinnecock Indians. No policeman was ever called to witness the cloven-foot tracks in the snow (in fact, there was no snow, and therefore no tracks). No phenomenon of any sort occurred to the next family, the Cromartys, who moved into the house. In fact, the Cromartys sued the Lutzes over the problem they had with sightseers stopping to see the famous house. The Lutzes settled out of court for an undisclosed amount.

In effect, whenever the Lutzes, Anson, Weber had to swear under oath about the so-called facts in the Anson book, none of the phenomena described could be confirmed as stated. The plot was designed to extract money from a credulous public.

The campaign to sell this hoax to the public was masterfully handled. To this day, few people know that the whole episode was a hoax, yet a number of exposures of the hoax are offered. The exposures did not realize the broad publicity that the book or movie did.

Sources:

Anson, Jay. *The Amityville Horror: A True Story.* Englewood Cliffs, NJ: Prentice Hall, 1977.

Harris, Melvin. *Sorry—You've Been Duped.* London: Weidenfeld and Nicholson, 1986: 1–9.

Lowe, Ed. "The Relentless Horror of the Amityville Tourists." *Chicago Tribune Magazine* (May 2, 1980): 13, 42–43, 47.

Morris, Robert L. "The Amityville Horror." *The Skeptical Inquirer* (Spring/Summer 1978): 95–102.

Zindler, Frank. "The Amityville Humbug." *American Atheist* (January 1986) 28: Part I: 20–24; Part II (February 1986): 23–26; Part III (March 1986): 29–33.

Appleton's Cyclopedia of American Biography

When a major new reference book appears, most people do not realize the vast amount of planning that went into the successful completion of the project. Sometimes, there is a flaw in the planning. In the case of the important American biographical set, *Appleton's Cyclopedia of American Biography*, a major planning flaw allowed the perpetration of an extremely devious hoax.

The *Appleton's Cyclopedia* is a six-volume set that was the first major American biographical dictionary, published from 1887 to 1889. It is still somewhat useful because it covers in detail a number of obscure individuals not profiled elsewhere. It also covers non-Americans who worked, mostly in botany, in South and Central America and are not mentioned in other, earlier sources. Unfortunately, some of these individuals *are* mentioned in later reference books. Their coverage in other biographical works is unfortunate largely because more than 100 of these entries are for nonexistent people.

The situation developed from the errant way in which entries were selected. Ideally, an editor or editorial board decides who or what will be included in an encyclopedia or biographical dictionary. The specific pieces from the list of final topics can then be assigned to a staff or to freelance writers.

In the case of *Appleton's Cyclopedia*, this procedure was not followed; instead, an elementary error was made. A team of writers, many with subject-area expertise, was assembled. They were then told to select the subjects for their biographical sketches and to submit those completed sketches. Contributors were then told that they would be paid a stipend for each sketch submitted. At that point, one or more quickly realized that the more sketches were submitted, the more they would be paid. False entries were passed off and printed as fact. Because reference source authors often borrow from previous reference sources, there was a considerable risk that the entire information "stream" would have become polluted, had the hoax had not been detected in about 1919. Even so, one still has to use *Appleton's Cyclopedia*, with extreme caution, although the fake biographies are almost all of biologists.

Although a long list of contributors is given in each volume, the contributor or contributors who fabricated the entries remain unknown, since the individual entries were unsigned. A few of the contributors' sketches are listed after their names, but the hoaxer was careful not to falsify any of the more prominent entries. In fact, it would have been easiest to manufacture a biography completely from scratch for the "unknowns." In the process, the hoaxing compiler invented a number of individuals who never existed.

The author or author of these faux biographies must have studied the *real* botanists and other scientists who did their work in Latin America, because among the concocted details were titles of publications that sounded authentic, perhaps even to a scientific historian. For example, Charles Henry Huon de Penanster is identified as an entomologist who smuggled specimens of the cochineal insect and the plant upon which it feeds (nopal plant) from Mexico in 1755. He was then supposed to have introduced them into Santo Domingo, thereby breaking the Spanish monopoly on the cochineal dye industry. This was actually done by Nicolas Joseph Thiery de Menonville in 1777. In fact, the hoaxer has split up the lengthy title of a book by Thiery to give Huon de Penanster credit for *three* books based upon this one title.

Botanist John Hendley Barnhart discovered the botanist hoaxes when he was unable to locate even a single copy of many of the books attributed to the biographies. Eventually he realized that neither the books nor the persons existed.

Barnhart discovered fourteen fake biographical entries, but historian Margaret Castle Schindler then examined all of the entries under the letter "H" in detail to determine the extent of the fakery. She took all articles under "H" about people who were born from 1800 to 1850, and examined them carefully. Only sources available in New York City were checked since the work had been compiled in the New York City area, and on a fairly tight schedule in the 1880s. That made it unlikely for material available elsewhere to be used. Only sources published before 1886 were checked, to eliminate the possibility that later sources may have relied on *Appleton's* for their information. In that subsection of "H" alone, fifteen false entries were identi-

fied. Other editors, working on Sabin's *Dictionary of Books Relating to America*, examined the letter "V" in *Appleton's*, after noting some otherwise unknown book titles listed among the biographical entries. Those editors were able to identify seventeen more false articles. The number of false entries, even in these small samples, is probably larger since no one person could necessarily spot all of these "additions" to real life. Although an accurate estimate of the total number of fake biographical entries in the set is unknown, if the rate is uniform throughout all the letters of the alphabet, there are several hundred false entries.

Appleton's also carries at least one grossly errant article about a *real* person. An example is the article about Huet de Navarre, an early French governor in the West Indies. No one has identified a pervasive pattern of this type of fraud in *Appleton's*, but the lack of cautious planning from the onset has forever ruined the utility of the work.

Sources:

Barnhart, John Hendley. "Some Fictitious Botanists." *Journal of the New York Botanical Garden* 20 (September 1919): 171–81.

Schindler, Margaret Castle. "Fictitious Biography." *American Historical Review* 42 (1937): 680–90.

The Beale Treasure

An area in Virginia's Blue Ridge Mountains continues to lure treasure hunters in one of the costliest quests for hidden wealth in American history. Enlisting such devices as dowsing pendulums, metal detectors, computers, and backhoes, treasure seekers have sought the bonanza described in documents known as the Beale Papers.

The papers tell a fanciful tale about a Virginia adventurer named Thomas Jefferson Beale who, with a company of thirty comrades, went west to hunt buffalo and grizzly bears in 1817. The following year, some 300 miles north of Santa Fe, New Mexico, the men accidently discovered a fabulous lode of gold and silver, worth an estimated $20 million in today's market. They transported it by wagon to a secret location in Bedford County, Virginia, where they hid it in a subterranean, rock-lined vault.

As a contingency plan, should some misfortune befall the men, Robert Morriss of Lynchburg, Virginia, was to transfer the treasure to their families. Morriss was given a strongbox, and instructed not to open it for ten years, yet, inexplicably, he waited twenty-three years before unlocking the box and discovering its contents—the Beale Papers. The papers consisted of a letter accompanying three documents in cipher (a method of transforming text to conceal its meaning). Morriss never received the promised key to the cipher and was unable to solve it himself, but sometime before his death in 1863 he allegedly passed the papers on to James B. Ward.

Ward claimed to have solved the cipher of the document which described the vault's contents, and he published the results in a pamphlet in 1885. However, a fire at the printing plant destroyed most of the copies of the pamphlet, along with, supposedly, the "original" Beale papers.

The tale is almost certainly a hoax. Not only is it implausible at face value—burying the treasure and creating a cipher seem unnecessary to say the least— but more serious problems are present in the Beale Papers. There is no proof that their alleged author ever existed and the papers (now available in pamphlet form only) contain textual anachronisms: certain words in the documents, such as stampeding, postdated the 1820 date of the documents. Furthermore, no proof exists to verify that Thomas Jefferson Beale actually lived.

Suspicion that James Ward perpetrated the hoax begins with his having supposedly solved one of the ciphers. The noted cryptanalyst George Fabyan as mentioned in *Gold in the Blue Ridge*, found it highly improbable that such a complex cryptogram "could be deciphered by a novice without the key, regardless of whether he put 20 years or 40 years into it." Ward claimed to have solved the second of the three cryptograms by using the text of the Declaration of Independence as the key.

Linguistic analysis was revealing. Linguistic detective, Jean Pival (Nickell, 1982) noted that "Although two writers might share one idiosyncratic characteristic, the sharing of several extraordinary features constitutes, I think, conclusive evidence that the same hand wrote both documents." She concluded that the same person wrote both the Beale Papers and the Ward pamphlet.

The exact motive for the hoax is unclear, but a clue may come from the fact that the papers contain clever allusions to the secret fraternal society, Freemasonry. Beale's hidden "vault" equates with Masonry's allegorical "secret vault," a subterranean depository of certain great secrets. Beale supposedly found the treasure in "a cleft of the rocks," a Masonic term. And Ward's statement that he was publishing the ciphers "with the hope that all that is dark in them may receive light" recalls the Masonic concept of "light out of darkness." James Ward was, in fact, a Freemason. The pamphlet's representation of Masonic values—including the contrast between the futile search for gold and more spiritual concerns—suggests that the hoax may

have been a pious one. No one appears to have solved the other two ciphers correctly (or to have found the treasure), despite occasional claims by amateur cryptographers to have solved them.

Joe Nickell

Sources:

Daniloff, Ruth. "A Cipher's the Key to the Treasure in Them Thar Hills." *Smithsonian Magazine* (April 1981): 126–128, 130, 132, 134, 136, 138, 140, 142, 144.

Hammer, Carl. "Signature Simulation and Certain Cryptographic Codes." *Communications of the ACM* 14 no. 1 (January 1971): 3–14.

Innis, Pauline B. and Walter Deane Innis. *Gold in the Blue Ridge: The True Story of the Beale Treasure.* Washington, DC: Robert B. Luce, 1973. Contains a complete reprint of James Ward's *The Beale Papers* pamphlet.

Nickell, Joe. "Discovered: The Secret of Beale's Treasure." *The Virginia Magazine of History and Biography* 90 no. 3 (July 1982): 310–324 .

The Blue Laws of Connecticut

A man kissing his wife on Sunday in Connecticut is supposedly prohibited by a "Blue Law" that regulated morality dating back to the 1600s. There were a few morality laws like that, but most were hoaxes promulgated by Rev. Samuel Peters (1735-1826) in his book *General History of Connecticut* (1782).

The name "Blue Laws" was attached to the laws of New Haven in about 1762, in an anonymous pamphlet (probably written by Rev. Noah Wells of Stamford, CT) called *The Real Advantages Which Ministers and People May Enjoy, Especially in the Colonies, by Conforming to the Church of England.* However, actual examples of these laws were never published before 1782, when Samuel Peters' book was published in London. Since Peters' book is the only source for the text of these laws, their very existence is suspect.

An acquaintance of Peters called him factually unreliable, especially with regard to storytelling (Trumbull). In fact, even Peters' L. L. D. and D. D. degrees are inauthentic. He falsified his family history as well, claiming that he had a brother, early Connecticut settler Hugh Peters.

Peters was also accused of having "punished" the state of Connecticut by writing its history. The work was really intended for a British audience, but they received it quite cooly, recognizing its lack of credibility. A critique of Peter's book in the *Monthly Review,* stated "we do not hesitate to pronounce it altogether unworthy of the public attention."

Of the New Haven colony laws, Peters says "They consist of a vast multitude and were properly termed *Blue Laws,* i.e., *bloody laws;* for they were all sanctified with excommunication, confiscation, fines, banishment, whippings, cutting off of the ears, burning the tongue, and death. . . And did not *similar laws still* [i.e., in 1782] *prevail over New England as the common law of the country,* I would have left them in silence." In fact, such laws did not exist in 1782, and the term "Blue Laws" was not derived from "bloody laws."

Here are some of Peters' Blue Laws: "no one shall run on the Sabbath-day, walk in his garden or elsewhere, except to and from meeting [i.e., church]. No one should travel, cook victuals, make beds, sweep house, cut hair or shave on the Sabbath-day. That no woman should kiss her child on the Sabbath or Fasting-day. That no one should keep Christmas or Saint days; and that every male should have his hair cut round, according to a cap. Married persons must live together, or be imprisoned."

Peters' Blue Laws have been reprinted a number of times. Although the genuine *Connecticut Code of 1650,* is often cited as the source of Peters' Blue Laws, this is not so as Peters' laws no do not cite any source. Peters called his Blue Laws the code of the New Haven colony. There actually *was* a code of New Haven laws from 1655, but it did not contain any of the Blue Laws. The true source of these laws seems to have been Peters' imagination. His motivation remains obscure, but to this day few people know that the Blue Laws of Connecticut are an elaborate hoax.

Sources:

Kingsley, William L. "The Blue Laws." *The New Englander and Yale Review* (April 1871): 243–304.

Peters, Samuel. *General History of Connecticut. . . .* Freeport, NY: Books For Libraries Press, 1969.

Trumbull, J. Hammond. *The True Blue Laws of Connecticut and New Haven and the False Blue Laws Invented by the Rev. Samuel Peters to Which are Added Specimens of the Laws and Judicial Proceedings of Other Colonies and Some Blue-Laws of England in the Reign of James I.* Hartford, CT: American Publishing Co., 1876.

The Donation of Constantine and the False Decretals

The hoax that has most affected world history has been the *Donation of Constantine.* Due to this forgery, a good part of Italy was ruled by the Vatican for nearly 1,200 years. It was only in 1929, under pressure from Mussolini, that the Vatican ceded the so-called Papal States back to Italy. This action was in return for a promise by Mussolini to allow the Catholic Church to exist undisturbed in fascist Italy and to have sovereignty over Vatican City.

The genesis of the *Donation of Constantine* is not completely clear, but it appears to have been written circa 750 A.D. Since Constantine I died in 337 A.D., he apparently had nothing to do with the *Donation* that bears his name. The document grants Pope Sylvester I (Pope from 315–335 A.D.) and his successors all palaces in Rome and its provinces and districts, and the regions to the west of Italy. In effect, this gave the Pope dominion over a large part of Central Italy around Rome, the Papal States, an enlarged area of the older "Patrimony of Peter."

The Papal States were officially constituted and recognized in 756 A.D., just about the same time as the forging of the *Donation.* Constantine supposedly granted the Pope these lands in gratitude for the Pope baptizing him into Christianity and curing Constantine of leprosy. These actions were attested to in a fifth century document (of dubious authenticity) called *Legenda S. Silvestri.* The text of the *Donation* exists in several different versions. It was first published as a part of the *Pseudo-Isidorean Decretals* in the mid-ninth century. The full text is about ten pages long, written in Latin.

The first monarch to reject the *Donation* was Emperor Otto III, who reigned from 983–1002 A.D. Critical examination of the document did not occur until 1440, when Lorenzo Valla published his *Declamitio de falso credita et ementia donatione Constantini (Discourse on the Forgery of the Alleged Donation of Constantine).* As Valla noted one indication that the *Donation* was a fraud was the total absence of any recorded acceptance by Sylvester of the document. Neither the biography of Sylvester, nor any extant document, mentioned any response to the *Donation.* Valla also pointed out a number of historical anachronisms in the *Donation,* including reference to Byzantia as a province instead of Byzantium as a city as it then was. Other mistakes asserted that temples were present in Rome dedicated to Peter and Paul when they were not, and that "Judea" existed; it didn't then. The phrasing of the document is also not in keeping with a member of the ruling class, such as an Emperor.

Some have suggested that the *Donation* first saw publication as one of the *Pseudo-Isidorean Decretals,* otherwise known as the *False Decretals of Isidore.* These were a mass of documents (perhaps more than eighty items), probably compiled between 847 and 853 A.D. and written at Mainz and Reims. The compiler calls himself "Isidorus Pecator" or "Mercatus," but these are almost certainly pseudonyms according to author Schafer Williams. Many of the documents are genuine items of the 840 A.D. period, made to appear to be from 340 A.D. Much of the text has to do with canon law. These *False Decretals* colored, and confused the canon law of the period by making it appear that the justifications of many actions were quite ancient, irrefutable tenets when they were not. It is not known who forged the *False Decretals*, but they are historically related to the *Donation* only in their false publishing history as ancient Catholic forgeries.

Sources:

Brooke, Christopher. *Medieval Church and Society: Collected Essays.* London: Sidgwick & Jackson, 1971.

Coleman, Christopher B., ed. *The Treatise of Lorenzo Valla on the Donation of Constantine. Text and Translation into English.* New Haven, CT: Yale University Press, 1922.

Davenport, E.H. *The False Decretals.* Oxford, UK: B. H. Blackwell, 1916.

Goffert, Walter. *The Le Mans Forgeries.* Cambridge, MA: Harvard University Press, 1966: 66–69.

Huyghebaert, Nicolas. "La Donation de Constantine ramenée a ses veritables dimensions." *Revue d'Histoire Ecclesiastique.* 71 (1971): 45–69.

Tout, T. F. "Medieval Forgers and Forgeries." *Bulletin of the John Rylands Library* 5 (1919): 208–34.

Williams, Schafer. "The Oldest Text of the 'Constitutum Constantini'. "*Traditio* 20 (1964): 448–61.

———. "The Pseudo-Isidorian Problem Today." *Speculum* 29 (1954): 702–7.

The Eikon Basilike

The *Eikon Basilike* (*The King's Image*) was a book attributed to King Charles the First of England (1600–1649). One group of historians claims, however, that he may not have written the book. Authorship is most often attributed to Bp. John Gauden (1605–1662), who claimed that he wrote the book in an attempt to inspire sympathy for Charles I by revealing his pious and forgiving disposition, thus arousing public sentiment against the king's execution. Charles had made a deal with the Scot's army that parliament did not agree to, and he refused to agree with parliament. If this was truly the intent it failed, as Charles I was executed in 1649. Further, according to writer Almack, the first edition of the book was published just a few hours *after* Charles I was executed in 1649, lending no credence to Gauden's claim.

Another possibilty is that Gauden copied the manuscript of *Eikon Basilike* longhand. Reportedly, a copy in his handwriting did exist. Yet the printer of the book, Richard Royston, said that the manuscript he worked from was in the handwriting of Nicholas Oudart, secretary to Sir Edward Nicholas, who was Charles I's Secretary of State. Both the printer and Mrs. Gauden agree that the manuscript was sent via Edward Symmons, rector of Raine, a town in England. There is testimony, according to writer Wordsworth, that Gauden copied the manuscript while it was briefly on loan to him from Symmons.

Still another possibility is that Gauden, working from drafts by Charles I, incorporated parts of Charles' work into a final version of his own, making them joint authors. This theory would account for the testimony of a number of witnesses who claimed to have seen Charles working on the manuscript at various times and places, including prison.

The case for Gauden's authorship, as stated by author C.E. Doble, seems strong. The points advanced in Gauden's favor are: 1) the *Eikon* is full of alliteration, as was Gauden's known writing, whereas King Charles I was not known to have used it; 2) there are many puns in the *Eikon*, as in Gauden's known writing, while the king's writing was not noted for this; 3) popular Scottish words often used by Gauden are found in the *Eikon*, but were not in Charles' writings; 4) Bible quotations used in the *Eikon* were among John Gauden's favorites, as seen in his other writings; 5) the *Eikon* and John Gauden's known works frequently quoted Virgil; 6) both bodies of work include nautical and medical metaphors; 7) the contents of the *Eikon* and a work called *A True Parallel Betwixt the Sufferings of Our Savior and Our Sovereign, In Divers Particulars . . .* are similar. The latter work, *Sufferings*, is sometimes attributed to Edward Symmons, who took the *Eikon* manuscript to the printer. This supports Gauden's authorship since the *Sufferings* volume is often attached as a supplement to another work known as *A Vindication of King Charles. . . . Vindication* is about the forgery of a document in the King's name. Gauden is thought to have had a role in writing *Vindication*, which was published in 1648. Perhaps it and *Sufferings* provided the plot and part of the text for the whole *Eikon Basilike*.

Although much has been written on this controversy, the true author of the *Eikon* it is still unknown. If Gauden did write it or co-write it, the hoax lies in Charles' claim as author. If Charles I *did* write the book, then Gauden's claims to authorship are a hoax.

Sources:

Almack, Edward. *Bibliography of the King's Book or Eikon Basilike.* London: Blades, East & Blades, 1896.

Almack, Edward., ed. *Eikon Basilike, Or The King's Book.* London: Alexander Moring, 1904. See especially the preface (ix–xxiii) and appendices I–IV (286–99).

Doble, C.E. "Notes and Queries on the 'Eikon Basilike'." *The Academy* (May 12, 1883): 330–332; May 26, 1883: 367–368; June 9, 1883: 402–3; June 30, 1883: 457–59.

Goodwin, Gordon. "John Gauden." *Dictionary of National Biography.* Oxford: Oxford University Press, 1922.

Wordsworth, Christopher. *King Charles the First. Author of Icon Basilike.* London: John Murray, 1828.

———. *Who Wrote Eikon Basilike? Two Letters to the Archbishop of Canterbury.* London: J. Murray, 1824.

The Hitler Diaries

In April of 1983, the world was stunned by a massive publicity campaign announcing the discovery and immediate publication of a series of diaries supposedly kept by Adolph Hitler throughout his years in power. The world was promised new information that would require rewriting the history of that period. The editor of *Der Stern*, a popular West German magazine, claimed he had discovered the diaries and would publish their content. *The Times* of London, and a number of other publications, struck deals for rights to the publication of parts of the diaries. Although *Der Stern* claimed to have a number of expert testimonies attesting to the authenticity of the diaries, the entire scheme began to unravel as additional experts called the diaries a fraud and existing experts changed their minds about the authenticity of the diaries.

Gerd Heidemann was a top reporter for *Der Stern*, where he did many investigative reportings on historical subjects. He grew interested in the search for Nazis who had escaped after World War II, and actively collected materials on Nazism. He even bought Nazi Hermann Göring's old yacht and planned to fix it up and sell it for profit. When the cost of repairs turned out to be far more than he could afford on a reporter's salary, he suddenly needed to raise money; this set the stage for what was to follow.

Konrad Kujau was a petty forger and antique dealer, who dealt in Nazi military memorabilia as well. Much of what he sold was fake or forged, often a rather ordinary item bearing a forged note from German Nazi leader Martin Bormann, or someone similar, verifying that the item belonged to Hitler, Himmler, or Göering. In 1978 he forged a single diary volume, which he claimed was by Hitler, for Fritz Stiefel, a wealthy manufacturer who collected Nazi memorabilia.

When Heidemann saw Stiefel's collection, he wanted to know if other volumes of Hitler's diary existed. He sensed a good story, but at first Stiefel would not reveal where he acquired the volume. Heidemann finally tracked down the diary's source as a "Fischer,"—actually Konrad Kujau.

Heidemann was able to establish that Hitler had become quite upset when told in late April of 1945–just days before his death—that one of the planes filled with materials from his Berlin bunker had crashed. As it turned out, this plane was said to carry his personal archives. Although the plane had burned upon crashing in Bavaria, Heidemann located the crash site, found the graves of the crew, and located one person who survived the crash. He also found a window from the plane. Fischer told Heidemann that locals at the crash site salvaged some of the materials on board.

After Heidemann located Kujau, whom he knew as Fischer, he pestered him for additional Hitler materials until Kujau finally agreed to supply them to him at a high price. Kujau claimed that his brother, a general in East Germany, could smuggle out the diaries a few at a time. Heidemann photographed the graves at the crash site, and located a statement by Hitler's personal pilot about Hitler's reaction to news of the crash. Using all of this information, Heidemann persuaded top management at *Der Stern* to finance the delivery of the Hitler diaries. The price started out at about two million marks, but rose considerably as more and more volumes of the diaries were later "discovered."

Meanwhile, Kujau practiced Hitler's handwriting until he had mastered it. He eventually became so skilled he could write using it, as fast as he could his own. He then bought some old notebooks and proceeded to turn volume after volume of Hitler's purported diaries. The contents of the diaries came entirely from information gleaned from published sources. The number of words in each diary was fewer than 5,000, with only a short paragraph for most entries. Ironically, this helped "authenticate" the diaries, as Hitler was notoriously adverse to writing by hand. The handwriting was in old German script, no longer taught, which was quite difficult for most modern Germans to read. This also prevented the fraud from being immediately discovered.

As Heidemann received the money for each diary, he skimmed off a good percentage for himself, giving Kujau about half of what he received from the magazine. It was Heidemann's sudden wealth that eventually made the publishers of *Der Stern* suspicious.

The management at *Stern's* parent company, Gruner & Jahr, were anxious to recapture the money spent for the diaries once they had almost all of them in hand. They decided to cut deals with several international publishing houses for partial rights. Rupert Murdoch's conglomerate and *Newsweek* both entertained the deal, then backed out.

Authentication had been done by Hugh Trevor Roper (for the handwriting and general contents—his German was not that good), before Murdoch and *Newsweek* backed out, although he never carefully read the text. Photocopies of certain parts of the diaries had been the only things supplied at first, so no lab tests on the notebooks themselves were possible. When the final syndication deals were in progress, actual notebooks were finally turned over for examination, but it took some time to get the results back.

Meanwhile, Eberhard Jaeckel, a history professor at the University of Stuttgart, voiced his suspicions on the basis of his examination of photocopies; Kenneth Rendell, an autograph dealer concurred. Rendell had done what no one else had thought of doing. He cut out various capital letters from the photocopy of the manuscript and pasted them next to the same letters on the page for comparison. Rendell, having had a look at the original volumes, thought they looked suspicious (cheap paper, modern ink, unblotted writing, etc.)—not as though they were Hitler's. When Rendell attained photocopies of twenty-two pages of the 1932 diary, he conducted his capital letter comparison. The results were conclusive to him; the diaries were a rather clumsy forgery.

When the results of the tests on the notebooks came in, the overwhelming verdict was forgery. The paper contained whitener not used until 1955. The binding of the notebooks also contained whitener. The seals were fastened with thread containing synthetic fibers not marketed until after World War II. The paper labels for all volumes were typed on the same typewriter, even though the volumes were supposedly written over a period of more than twelve years.

The deal with Murdock and *Newsweek* had foundered on the question of the price. *Der Stern's* management kept raising the price until both parties backed out. When the remaining deals were totaled, *Stern* was going to take a significant loss. It would be worse if the diaries were proven to be forged, as there was an authenticity clause in the contracts granting money back if the diaries were not authentic.

In the midst of growing doubt about the diaries' authenticity (early in that process), Hugh Trevor Roper, who had come out early in favor of authenticity, started wavering and finally came out *against* authenticity. His original opinion was one of the prime reasons why the production and sale of the diaries went so far and his switch of opinion came too late to stop *Der Stern's* large capital losses.

The final indignity—was that the diaries proved to be dull. There were almost no personal comments by Hitler. Almost all of the "facts" seemed to have come from Max Domarus' two-volume edition of *Hitler's Speeches and Proclamations.*

Heidemann was fired, later arrested, and the Hitler memorabilia he had collected was confiscated. He was accused of having stolen at least 1.7 million marks (and possibly as much as 4.6 million) of the 9.9 million marks that *Der Stern* had paid for the diaries. Konrad Kujau was charged with fraudulently receiving 1.5 million marks. Both men were convicted. Heidemann was sentenced to four years and eight months in prison, Kujau four years and six months. More than five million marks of *Der Stern's* money remains unaccounted for.

The circulation of *Der Stern* dropped from a peak of 2.1 million copies per week to fewer than 1.5 million. Their total losses from all sources in this matter were estimated at 19 million marks, or more than 46 million dollars. Hugh Trevor Roper's post-trial was a collection of his essays, entitled *Renaissance Essays.* The Hitler diaries were not mentioned.

Sources:

Binyon, Michael. "Hitler's Secret Diaries: Germans Greet Find With Great Skepticism." *Times* London (April 25, 1983): 1–2.

Hamblin, Dora Jane. "Anyone for Fake 'Duce' Diaries?" *Life* (May 3, 1968) 73–74, 77–78.

Hamilton, Charles. *The Hitler Diaries: Fakes that Fooled the World.* Lexington, KY: University Press of Kentucky, 1991.

Harris, Robert. *Selling Hitler.* New York: Pantheon Books, 1986.

Hitler Survived World War II

Powerful people often inspire rumors concerning their lives and deaths. Few people were present at the end of Adolph Hitler's life, and they were all loyal Nazis, so their stories are open to suspicion. It was Russians who took Berlin and entered the bunker in which Hitler was last seen, and perhaps they had ulterior motives for proclaiming Hitler dead.

Certain facts are established about the events of April 30, 1945. Hitler was in his bunker under the Reichs Chancellery in Berlin, along with his mistress Eva Braun; Nazis Joseph Goebbels and Martin Bormann; two Hitler secretaries; Hitler's chauffeur Erich Kampka;

Heinz Linge, Hitler's servant; and several guards. The Russians were advancing within Berlin, and were close to the Chancellery. Hitler was in poor health; his hands trembled severely, possibly because of Parkinson's disease, or possibly because of his chronic abuse of amphetamines.

The Russians overran the rest of Berlin that day. The first announcement of Hitler's death from the Kremlin was made on May 2. In this announcement, Tass, a Russian News Service, stated that the Germans reported that Hitler died at noon the previous day, and that he named Admiral Doenitz his successor as chancellor. The Tass statement added that "By spreading the news of Hitler's death, the German Fascists apparently wish to give Hitler the means of leaving the stage and going 'underground'."

Stories were widespread that Hitler and Bormann had escaped from Germany and went by submarine to South America. Hitler was also, according to some accounts, in Antarctica. The Russians delaying the release of the autopsy report on Hitler's body until 1968, didn't help squelch the rumors. The report was buried in a Russian book by a former Soviet intelligence officer named Lev Bezymensky.

The book gave details that Russian Counter-Intelligence (SMERSH) captured the guard who witnessed the bodies of Hitler and Eva Braun being taken from the bunker to the garden and burned. SMERSH discovered the bodies of Goebbels and his wife. On May 4, 1945, SMERSH dug up the bodies of a male and female that had been buried in the garden outside the bunker. At first these weren't thought to be the bodies of Hitler and Eva Braun, but their bodies were not found within the bunker after a careful search. When the guard who witnessed the burning later added that he saw the burnt bodies placed in a bomb crater and covered with dirt, SMERSH carefully examined the exhumed bodies. The autopsy report said that both died by biting into a poison capsule (cyanide), as glass fragments were found in the mouths of the two corpses. The male body had also been shot in the head, although undoubtedly *after* taking the poison. The male—like Hitler—had only one testicle. Using the remains of Hitler's extensive dental work, the Soviets matched Hitler's teeth with records from his dentist's office. The dentist's assistant was able to make a solid match. Eva Braun's body was also identified from her dental work. After the autopsy, the book reports that the bodies were cremated and the ashes scattered.

Although there was hope that Bezymensky would appear in front of reporters to defend his book and answer questions, the Soviets allowed no such appearance. Hitler's former servant, Heinz Linge, whom the Soviets had said was the one who shot Hitler at his instruction after he took the poison, was found alive. He denied having shot Hitler. Both Linge and another present at the time said Hitler had not taken poison, but had shot himself. The issue was perceived by some as one of bravery or cowardice. To shoot oneself was brave; to take poison was cowardly. Regardless, Hitler's death *did* occur.

Some of Hitler's deputies did escape, such as Mengele and Eichmann. Martin Bormann escaped, but was evidently captured and killed shortly thereafter. His skull was identified in 1972. Hitler did not escape.

Yet the myth of Hitler's survival was well established. He was "sighted" in nearly every country of the world (except Russia) at some point after World War II. Scenarios of his escape were constructed. A fanciful movie of *The Boys From Brazil* was made, with the premise that Mengele took cells from the live Hitler and used them to clone replicas. All this aside, whether or not Hitler died in his bunker, he would now be more than 100 years old if he were still alive.

Sources:

Ainszstein, Reuben. "How Hitler Died: The Soviet Version." *International Affairs* 43 (April 1967): 307–18.

Bezymensky, Lev. *The Death of Adolf Hitler: Unknown Documents From Soviet Archives*. New York: Harcourt, Brace & World, 1968.

McKale, Donald M. *Hitler: The Survival Myth*. New York: Stein and Day, 1981.

Trevor-Roper, H. R. *The Last Days of Hitler*, 3rd ed. New York: Macmillan Co., 1965.

H. L. Mencken's Bathtub Hoax

Henry Louis Mencken (1880–1956) was a social critic without peer. His iconoclastic writings held America's attention especially in the 1920s and 1930s. One of the most famous of Mencken's witty ideas was his bathtub hoax. It began as a Mencken article in the New York *Evening Mail* of December 28, 1917, with the title "A Neglected Anniversary." The article purported to tell the history of the bathtub in America.

According to Mencken, 1917 was the seventy-fifth anniversary of the bathtub's introduction into the United States, but almost no one had noticed. The first bathtub in the United States was installed by Adam Thompson in his home in Cincinnati in December of 1842. He was a wealthy merchant; his tub was built of mahogany, lined with sheet lead. It was big enough to hold the entire body of a large adult male. It was filled with water piped in from a large tank in the attic. After using it twice, Thompson then invited a group of men to dinner, showing them the tub. Four of them then took baths. The local newspapers reported it and received letters from readers, detailing the effect of baths upon the health. There was much opposition from physicians and from those who opposed the bathtub as an "obnoxious toy from England, designed to corrupt the democratic simplicity."

Mencken reported that in 1843 controversy had spread to Baltimore, where an ordinance prohibiting bathing was barely defeated. In Virginia, there was a tax of $30 per year attached to tubs installed in the state. High water rates were imposed upon tub owners in Hartford, Connecticut, Charleston, South Carolina, Wilmington, Delaware, and Providence, Rhode Island. Boston made bathtub use illegal from 1845 to 1862, when the law—which was never enforced—was repealed.

The price of a tub was $500 in 1845, but the invention of an all-zinc tub in 1848 was responsible for greatly reducing the price. In 1859, at the American Medical Association annual meeting, fifty-five percent of the physicians attending said they regarded bathing in a tub as harmless, while an additional twenty percent said it might even be beneficial. President Millard Filmore, gave the bathtub its final push towards respectability when he installed a tub in the White House in 1851. By 1860, newspaper ads showed that nearly every hotel in New York City had a bathtub, and some had several of them.

Mencken's entire account is false. He *thought* his history was so obviously false that no one would take it seriously. Unfortunately, people believed it. The "facts" in the hoax were soon reprinted in other newspapers, magazines, books, and eventually even in reference books. In May of 1926, Mencken wrote an article confessing that the original bathtub article had been a hoax. This confession was printed in his syndicated column that reached an audience of millions.

He admitted that he was reluctant to tell the truth because so many people, especially in Cincinnati, were bragging about their role in the introduction of the bathtub. He thought that physicians would also be angry with their obstructionist portrayal. Mencken realized, however, that he had to say something even though the truth might be unsettling.

Despite the confession, other continued to cite the dubious information in Mencken's original article. In July of 1926, he tried again to rectify that situation in an essay called "Hymn to the Truth." Thirty major newspapers, including the Boston *Herald*, ran this article. Yet, just three weeks later the *Herald* reprinted Mencken's original hoax article as if it were true.

In 1927, a rewritten version of the confession appeared in the sixth book of Mencken's *Prejudices* series. Again, its appearance had little effect in curbing the erroneous citing. In August 1935, the *New York Times* continued to be fooled, citing many of Mencken's "facts." The CBS Evening News presented the "facts" again in 1976. ABC and NBC also repeated the idea that Filmore had introduced the bathtub into the White House. It was actually Andrew Jackson in about 1829. Prior to that, the presidents used personal portable tubs. Even in the 1980s Mencken's history continues to be cited. He truly created a classic hoax that would not die.

Sources:

Fedler, Fred. *Media Hoaxes*. Ames, IA: Iowa State University Press, 1989: 118–28.

Mencken, H. L. *The Bathtub Hoax and Other Blasts and Bravos*. New York: Alfred A. Knopf, 1958: 4–10.

————. "A Neglected Anniversary." New York *Evening Mail* (December 28, 1917): 9.

Smith, Beverly. "The Curious Case of the President's Bathtub." *Saturday Evening Post* (August 23, 1952): 25, 91–94.

Stefansson, Vilhjalmur. *Adventures in Error*. New York: Robert McBride & Co., 1936: 279–99.

The Hope Diamond Curse

The Hope Diamond was originally a 112.5 carat blue diamond. It was brought from India to France by John Baptiste Tavernier in the sixteenth century. Tavernier would not reveal where he found the diamond, but it was rumored to have been stolen from an idol's eye in a temple in Mandalay, Burma. It was eventually taken to the Smithsonian Institute in Washington, D.C., where it remains today, although in its changes of ownership its size has been cut to 44.5 carats. Along the way, it was reputed to have a curse that brought an early death to anyone who owned it.

When Tavernier first brought the stone to France, it was purchased by the only man in France who could afford it, King Louis XIV. Tavernier had a business failure and died in Russia. Louis lived on into old age and passed the stone on to his descendants. When Louis XVI inherited the diamond, he presented it to his wife Marie Antoinette. Both of them died in the French Reign of Terror.

The diamond disappeared; it was probably stolen during the French Revolution. It surfaced in London, reduced to 44.5 carats in size. What happened to the remainder of the stone is unknown, but it could have been cut into some fairly small fragments. Banker Henry Hope bought the diamond, which bears his name, and lived without any noticable ill effects from its "curse." After his death, the diamond was passed on to members of his family without incident. Only May Yohe, wife of Lord Francis Hope, complained of the diamond bringing her bad luck. The Hope family had sold the jewel in 1901, and Yohe died in poverty due to bad investments in 1938. Of the next two owners, both jewelers, one went bankrupt and the other killed himself. The Russian nobleman who owned it next was stabbed to death by Russian revolutionaries. A Greek jeweler who owned it fell off of a cliff. A Turkish sultan who owned it was removed from his throne.

The jewel was finally sold by Cartier's to Edward B. McLean, an American newspaper heir. McLean's only son was struck and killed by a car. Further, McLean's wife divorced him and he was committed to a mental hospital where he died. Mrs. McLean, however, still wore the diamond though her daughter committed suicide, and Mrs. McLean died the following year, 1947, at an advanced age.

New York jeweler Harry Winston bought the diamond and displayed it for several years before donating it to the Smithsonian Institute in 1958. Winston sent the diamond from New York to Washington via ordinary U.S. mail, although he registered and insured it for $1 million. The stone arrived safely.

Many who owned the diamond—Louis XIV, Evelyn McLean, Henry Hope, and Harry Winston—did not die young. Others who briefly owned the diamond were also unscathed by the experience. Others appear to have suffered adversity, but often after they no longer owned the stone. There does not seem to be a concrete connection between ownership of the Hope Diamond and early death, debunking the idea that the Hope Diamond has a "curse" on it.

Sources:

Bracker, Milton. "The Hope Diamond is Off in the Mail." *New York Times* (Nov 9, 1958): 56.

———. "Winston Gives Hope Diamond to Smithsonian for Gem Hall." *New York Times* (Nov 8, 1958): 1, 28.

Cohen, Daniel. *Encyclopedia of the Strange.* New York: Dodd, Mead & Co., 1985: 254–58.

Howard Hughes' Autobiography

The elusive billionaire Howard Hughes (1905–1976) has long fascinated people. When he became a recluse during the last twenty years of his life, it only

The 44.5 carat Hope diamond.

piqued the public interest. So when publisher McGraw-Hill announced on December 7, 1971 that it would publish Howard Hughes' autobiography, public curiosity soared. The press release from McGraw-Hill explained that Hughes spent most of 1970 working on his memoirs, with the help of Clifford Irving, an American writer. The two men reportedly had 100 work sessions together, often in parked cars. Irving taped all of these sessions. The memoir, which was 230,000 words long, would be published on March 27, 1972. *Life* magazine would publish three 10,000-word installments from the book, plus a separate article by Irving on the interviews.

Howard Hughes' supposed reasons for breaking his long silence to write his autobiography were also laid out in the press release. As reprinted in Fay's co-authored book, they are:

I believe that more lies have been printed and told about me than about any living man—therefore it was my purpose to write a book which would set the record straight and restore the balance . . . .

Biographies about me have been published before—all of them misleading and childish. I am certain that in the future more lies and rubbish will appear. The words in this book—other than some of the questions which provoked them—are my own spoken words. The thoughts, opinions and recollections, the descriptions of events and personalities, are my own. I have not permitted them to be emasculated or polished, because I realized, after many interviews had been completed and transcribed, that this was as close as I could get to the elusive, often painful truth.

I have lived a full life and, perhaps, what may seem a strange life—even to myself. I refuse to apologize, although I am willing now to explain as best I can. Call this an autobiography. Call it my memoirs. Call it what you please. It is the story of my life in my own words.

Irving was identified in the press release as the author of several books, including *The Losers* and *The Thirty-eighth Floor*. His latest book, *Fake!*, a study of the art forger Elmyr de Hory (*See* Two Hoaxers: Smith and de Hory, p. 29), was *not* mentioned. It was later claimed that *Fake!* was the book that convinced Howard Hughes to choose Irving as his collaborator.

Since Howard Hughes had not been photographed or interviewed since 1958, it was virtually impossible for any reporter to confirm the press release contents with him. At that time Hughes was living on a sealed floor of the Britannia Beach Hotel in Nassau, Bahamas, but calls to his hotel were not put through. Callers were told "We don't have a Mr. Hughes registered here."

Those reporters who called Hughes' public relations firm reached jammed switchboards and confused personnel. The firm had no information, although the *idea* of a Howard Hughes autobiography reportedly seemed absurd to them. Yet, they could not deny the story without checking. Shortly thereafter word was released that the Hughes Tool Company denied that Howard Hughes was writing an autobiography. The reason why the information was released from the tool company was that Hughes' application for a gaming license in Nevada was under consideration. Normally, an applicant *must* put in a personal appearance before the Nevada Gaming Commission. Hughes was released from the obligation on the grounds that he had not appeared in public for years, and doing so would impose great hardship. Yet, according to the press release, he was meeting all over the country with Clifford Irving. The Nevada Gaming Commission did not look kindly on this contradiction, and was in the process of requiring Hughes appearance, when the denial from Hughes Tool Company was made public.

Meanwhile, Ralph Graves, the managing editor of *Life* magazine, was holding a meeting with his editorial board. They wanted to know why *Life* was publishing excerpts from the book if it wasn't by Hughes. Graves told the board of a letter he had from Hughes, although it was actually from Hughes to McGraw-Hill. In the letter, Hughes agreed to publication of his autobiography. The letter was handwritten, had been authenticated by handwriting experts, he said.

The vice president for public relations at McGraw-Hill, Ted Weber, received messages from wire services and networks, asking about the Hughes Tool Company denial. He referred questions to Albert Leventhal, general books vice president at McGraw-Hill. Leventhal assured the press that they had " . . . gone to considerable efforts to ascertain that this is indeed the Hughes autobiography." One weekend, the press' attempts to contact Clifford Irving were rebuffed by McGraw-Hill. Apparently Irving told McGraw-Hill that on that particular weekend he must not be disturbed. He was to be in Florida seeing Hughes, giving him a $350,000 check from McGraw-Hill, and getting his signature on the preface. Irving later reported that his mission was successful.

It is at this point that the two major sources of information about the Howard Hughes autobiography, namely Clifford Irving's book *What Really Happened*, and Fay et al's *Hoax* begin to differ. Irving says that he reports the truth, while Fay implies that Irving is a con man. As other sources are less credible, they cannot point to where the whole truth lies.

According to Irving, the plot was hatched on the island of Ibiza, in the Balearic Islands off Spain, where Irving was then living. He and his "researcher," Richard Suskind, were discussing ways a publisher might be fooled by an author. Irving surmised that if the subject of a biography were afraid to go public, a book might be written about him without his knowledge or approval. Suskind was reading a *Newsweek* article about the secretive Howard Hughes, when it occurred to Irving that Hughes would be the perfect subject for an "unauthorized autobiography," since he would never come forward in public to deny his authorship.

As the plan evolved, it was decided that Irving would propose the idea of an authorized biography of Howard Hughes to McGraw-Hill, his regular publisher. Irving would mention that he was in contact with Hughes. Then Irving would forge a letter from Hughes, open a bank account in Switzerland in Hughes' name, and deposit any advance money paid to Hughes. Other advance money would also be made payable to Irving as the co-author.

Irving mentioned the idea to one of his contacts at McGraw-Hill, who was interested. He then forged some letters from Hughes to himself, using a bit of a real Hughes letter that had appeared in *Newsweek* as a model. When he was in New York shortly thereafter to attend his mother's funeral, he stopped at McGraw-Hill and showed them the phony material. The publisher was impressed. Later, Irving found a photograph of a longer letter from Hughes in an issue of *Life* magazine, and realized how bad his forgery really was. Fortunately McGraw-Hill had nothing to compare Irving's forgery to, so thought it genuine.

Irving told them he was meeting Hughes that weekend. When he came back from what was really a weekend with his mistress, Nina van Pallandt, he had modified copies of the contract, adding alleged annotations from Hughes. In another meeting with McGraw-Hill's management, the publisher insisted that Hughes' signature be notarized. Irving flew back to Ibiza thinking the scam was over. Subsequently, McGraw-Hill changed its mind and said that Irving merely had to witness Hughes' signature and sign a statement saying that he had done so. The scam was back on.

Irving then "met" with Hughes in Puerto Rico then obtained the agreement with *Life* magazine, through managing editor Ralph Graves, to do a secret excerpt from the book in the magazine. *Life* would also make its files on Hughes available to Irving. There would be a $500,000 advance from McGraw-Hill, with Hughes getting $400,000, Irving $100,000, and all royalties going to Irving. Irving's willingness to take only a small part of the royalties helped convince the publisher that the contract was legitimate, and that Irving would work hard to craft a successful book.

McGraw-Hill gave Irving a check—made out to Irving—for $97,500 as he already had a small advance on his advance and he took the check to the issuing bank in New York and, after some argument, had the check broken into two cashier's checks, one for $50,000, payable to "H. R. Hughes," the other, for the balance payable to himself.

Irving researched Hughes at the New York Public Library, then went to Washington, where he uncovered a useful file on the Hughes Aircraft Company at the Pentagon. At the Library of Congress, he found congressional testimony by Hughes, and a thesis that discussed the role of Trans World Airlines (TWA)—then a Hughes' company) in the development of Ethiopian Airways. Suskind and Irving examined newspaper files in Houston and Las Vegas for any items on Hughes or his family.

Edith Irving, Clifford's wife, was Swiss. Clifford altered an old passport of hers, changing the name to "Helga R. Hughes." Edith then took the $50,000 check made out to "H. R. Hughes" and opened an account in a Zurich bank, using the altered passport as identification. Although she was nervous, everything went well. They had now established a conduit to convert any money paid to Howard Hughes by McGraw-Hill or *Life* into their own account.

On a trip to Los Angeles to obtain information about Hughes' Hollywood years, Suskind and Irving had a breakthrough. They were offered a look at the manuscript of the unpublished biography of Howard Hughes by Noah Dietrich, his long-time financial chief. The information they gleaned from this unauthorized look greatly helped their own work, as did a look at the *Time/Life* files on Hughes, and the *Los Angeles Times'* files.

With this and other material, Suskind and Irving were able to produce a book-length manuscript biogra-

phy of Hughes. Since their work was supposed to be from the tapes dictated by Howard Hughes, Suskind and Irving took turns dictating what they had learned into a tape recorder. Although it wasn't Hughes speaking, it did help to produce the flavor of a dictated book. It also allowed them to produce the transcripts used to prove to McGraw-Hill that the conversations had taken place. Many of the incidents described in the book were fabricated, but many others came from their research and had never been made public before.

In the course of their writing, they learned that Howard Hughes had signed a contract with Robert Eaton to do his autobiography. The book was well underway, according to a contact at McGraw-Hill. Irving, stumped for a while about what to do, finally decided that he would "ask Hughes," and report back to McGraw-Hill that Hughes denied Eaton's claim. Irving told McGraw-Hill that the publisher of Eaton's "biography" was being hoaxed. He also pointed out that Hughes was incensed because he had heard that first serial rights to the book had been sold to *Life* magazine. Hughes had a professional quarrel with *Life's* owner, Henry Luce, because of what Hughes considered a "hatchet job" that Luce had done on Hughes years earlier. Irving told McGraw-Hill that Hughes was angry when he found out about the deal for the publication of excerpts from the book in *Life*, especially since he was neither told about them, nor offered any money for them. Irving said that Hughes wanted *all* subsidiary income or his share of the advance money for the book to be raised to one million dollars.

Although Irving was really bluffing on all of these things, after much argument and consultation, McGraw-Hill offered Hughes $750,000 as an advance (if the transcripts were satisfactory) instead of the original $400,000. Irving, of course, reported that "Hughes" agreed, and insisted that the check be made out to "H. R. Hughes." Another deposit was made by Mrs. Irving to the Swiss bank account. Throughout this time, the deal could have collapsed and Irving would have had to return the money. Contingency plans on returning the money to the right accounts, so the money could be paid back to McGraw-Hill if necessary, were constructed.

Finally, the transcript of all the interviews was completed. It came to 950 typed pages. Copies were made, and McGraw-Hill and *Life* brass gathered to read them. The original tapes were destroyed, so there was no evidence that Hughes did not dictate the material in the transcripts. The McGraw-Hill and *Life* people who read the transcripts thought they were terrific, and decided to keep the book in its "interview" format. In fact, it was the quality of the transcripts that persuaded McGraw-Hill to raise the advance to $750,000.

Then came devastating news; *Ladies Home Journal* announced that it would be publishing excerpts from the rival Eaton Hughes biography. Panic set in at McGraw-Hill and *Life*. They decided to move publication of Irving's work up. Irving commissioned an artist friend to do some paintings of Hughes, basically from his imagination, but conforming to general speculation about Hughes' appearance. A handwriting expert employed by McGraw-Hill authenticated the last few alleged letters from Hughes regarding the publication date and the increase in advance. The press release explaining the accelerated schedule was issued; at that point the hoax began to unravel.

The Hughes Tool Company denied the authenticity of the book. However, Noah Dietrich, for reasons unknown, said that he knew, on good authority, that Hughes *had* met with Irving at least once. Irving and Suskind had finished the manuscript by now. At a publishing party, it was announced that the Book-of-the-Month Club had agreed to feature the Irving book, and to pay a $350,000 advance for the right to do so. Dell bought the paperback rights for $400,000.

At this point the first surprise from the *real* Howard Hughes occurred. A spokesman for Hughes told Frank McCulloch New York bureau chief of *Time* magazine, and the last journalist to actually interview Howard Hughes (in the late 1950s), that Hughes wanted to talk to him on the phone, in part about the biography. Irving and Suskind were invited in, but did not stay to hear the call. They were informed later that McCulloch was convinced that he *was* speaking to Howard Hughes, and that he asked two trick questions, (which Hughes answered correctly), to make certain. Hughes said that he never met or heard of Clifford Irving, and that he certainly was not working with him on his autobiography.

The next day Irving was summoned to a meeting with McGraw- Hill and *Life* executives. McCulloch said that although the facts in the Irving biography checked out, anyone might have been able to dig them up. However, the one thing Irving couldn't duplicate was Howard Hughes' style of speaking and, in McCulloch's opinion, that style was reflected in the interview transcripts. McCulloch said he thought that Irving's biography was authentic in spite of what Howard Hughes said. What most convinced him was Irving's ability to quote what Hughes had said to McCulloch on the phone during their last conversation in the late 1950s. McCulloch thought no one but he and Hughes could have known that, but he had evidently forgotten that a transcript of the conversation was made for the president of *Time/Life*. It made its way to Noah Dietrich somehow, and had been in the Dietrich manuscript, where Irving had come across it. McGraw-Hill and *Life*

decided to stand by the authenticity of the Irving manuscript.

Irving then had a private meeting with Frank McCulloch, leaving McCulloch further convinced that Irving had met with Hughes. All of the written material alleged to be by Hughes was resubmitted for examination by a firm purported to be the finest handwriting experts in the United States. They compared the Mc-Graw-Hill samples with material written by Hughes while in Las Vegas. They too confirmed that Hughes had written all of the McGraw-Hill material. Irving was given a rushed lie detector test, with inconclusive results, as Irving was so nervous during *all* the questions that no usable results were obtained. The test was not repeated.

The only piece of the manuscript left to write was the introduction. The first *Life* article was to be excerpted from this account of Irving's meetings with Howard Hughes. He finished it, only to be told that the real Howard Hughes would hold a telephone news conference with seven journalists from Los Angeles. During the conference the voice purporting to be Howard Hughes told the journalists and the television audience that he did not know Irving and had never worked with him on a book. Clifford Irving's response was to say that the voice was *not* Hughes', but only a fair imitation of how Hughes sounded a few years ago.

Evidence began to work against Irving. Mike Wallace was scheduled to interview Irving for "Sixty Minutes." Word was in from Zurich, Switzerland that the "H. R. Hughes" who opened the bank accounts and deposited the checks for Howard Hughes was not Howard Hughes. The Swiss police issued a warrant for the arrest of Edith Irving, having identified her as the "Helga R. Hughes" who had opened the Zurich bank account.

Irving's plan readily collapsed. He was referred to two lawyers by a friend when it was rumored that the New York District Attorney and possibly the United States Attorney for New York, were about to arrest Irving for fraud. Although he continued to deny his guilt, Irving finally confessed to his longtime friend and attorney Philip Lorber. He admitted it was a hoax. This took the pressure off Irving, but put it on his attorneys who spent many hours getting his confession transcribed. Irving's mistress, Nina van Pallandt, was located and interrogated. She lied at first, but then admitted that she had known—almost from the beginning—that Irving's book was a hoax.

The prosecution offered a deal if Clifford Irving would plead guilty: no prosecution for wife Edith, who was merely a courier, and a minimal sentence for Dick Suskind. The Swiss authorities at first refused to drop charges against Edith, then agreed, but finally decided to charge her. McGraw-Hill finally admitted it was hoaxed, and returned the money it received from *Life* for the serial rights.

On March 9, 1972, the day originally projected for the publication of the McGraw-Hill/ Hughes biography, Clifford Irving was indicted on federal conspiracy to defraud, forgery, the use of forged instruments, using the mails to defraud, and perjury charges. Dick Suskind was only indicted as a co-conspirator on the federal charges. In New York State court, charges of grand larceny, conspiracy and a few minor charges were placed against Irving, his wife and Dick Suskind. They pleaded guilty to all charges. Clifford Irving was sentenced to two-and-a-half years in jail. Edith Irving was sentenced to two years, with all but two months suspended. Richard Suskind was sentenced to six months in prison.

Edith Irving served her two months, then Clifford Irving began his sentence at the Allenwood Federal Prison in Pennsylvania. He actually served about seven months before he was released on parole. Edith Irving then went voluntarily to Zurich, where she was tried for forgery, embezzlement, and theft. She was convicted and sentenced to two years in jail, which she served. Some of the money, $650,000 of it, was returned to McGraw- Hill. The publisher had won a judgement against Clifford Irving in court for the $776,000 paid. Later Irving repaid McGraw-Hill $130,000 for expenses paid for his travel.

Clifford Irving's hoax biography of Howard Hughes has never been published. He *did* write a history of his involvement with the biography. Of course, McGraw-Hill would not publish it. Nina van Pallandt, as a result of all the publicity, had a short singing career. After that, she faded from public attention.

Sources:

Clarity, James F. "Swiss Give Edith Irving 2 Years." *New York Times* (March 6, 1973): 47.

Corry, John and Richard Eder. "Irving: Gulling Experts for Fun and Fame." *New York Times* (March 12, 1972): 68.

Fay, Stephen, Lewis Chester, and Magnus Linklater. *Hoax: the Inside Story of the Howard Hughes-Clifford Irving Affair.* New York: Viking Press, 1972.

Irving, Clifford. *What Really Happened: His Untold Story of the Hughes Affair.* New York: Grove Press, 1972.

[Morrow, Lance and Frank McCulloch]. "The Fabulous Hoax of Clifford Irving." *Time* (February 21, 1972) 12–18, 21.

Jack the Ripper Hoaxes

Although the murders of at least five women in London in 1888 were not hoaxes, the killer (who *may* have called himself "Jack the Ripper," although the name itself may be a hoax), was never publicly identified, and perhaps never caught. Over the years, a number of books and articles have been written purporting to solve the killings and identify the Ripper. Some of these "solutions" have been deliberate hoaxes. The hoax does not surround the Jack the Ripper killings, but has to do with the solution to the crimes.

The generally accepted outline of what happened and to whom follows. Although some attribute as many as eighteen murders to the Ripper, only the five listed can definitely be attributed to the same killer.

The first killing was that of 43-year-old Mary Ann(e) Nichols, on August 31, 1888. The body was found in Buck's Row (now Durward Street) in the East End of London. This Whitechapel area was the scene of all of the killings then a dangerous slum. Nichols, a prostitute, was killed by having her throat cut, as did all the victims. In addition, there were several deep slashes in the abdomen, but no organs were removed.

The second killing was that of prostitute Annie Chapman, age 47, found murdered on September 8, on Hanbury Street. Her body had been terribly mutilated, the intestines strewn about and the uterus removed. The third victim was Elizabeth Stride ("Long Liz") on September 30. She had also been a prostitute, and was found with her throat cut, but her body was otherwise unmutilated. It was believed that her killer had been interrupted before he could mutilate her. Prostitute Catherine Eddowes ("Kitty Kelly"), age 46, was also killed that night in Mitre Square. She was severely mutilated and cut about the face, with her uterus and one kidney removed.

After these four killings, the news agencies and police received several infamous letters signed "Jack the Ripper." The letters boasted that he would not be caught and said that he was going to cut off the ears of one of his victims and send them to the police. A following letter enclosed a piece of a human kidney, although whether it was the one removed from Catherine Eddowes can not be determined.

The final, and the most horrific murder, occurred inside the room where prostitute Mary Jane Kelly, about 25, lived. On November 9, her body was found in her bed, terribly mutilated. The public was outraged, but this was the last killing. Explanations range from the sudden death of the killer, to his secret capture and commitment to an insane asylum, to the possibility that all his targeted victims were now dead.

The list of suspects is long. Suspects appearing on more than one list include a mentally-ill barrister (Druitt), a royal physician (Gull), a butcher ("Leather Apron," possibly John Pizer), a mad poet (Stephenson), the father of a man who caught syphilis from a prostitute (Stanley), a Russian physician (Pedachenko or Ostrog), a royal grandson (Eddy, the Duke of Clarence), a mentally ill surgeon (Cream), and a Pole (Kosminski). There is evidence in favor of each, and against each. This has not stopped people from distorting or fabricating cases against each.

The first such hoax has the best explanation of the clues, tying together facts for which there had previously been no explanation. The trouble with this "solution," posed by Stephen Knight, is that there aren't any facts to sustain it. The main witness admitted that he made up this story. Knight's idea was that all five of the victims knew each other and were specific targets of the killer, who was trying to dispose of witnesses who were trying to blackmail the queen.

The story held that Queen Victoria's grandson, Prince Edward Albert, second in line for the throne, secretly married a Catholic girl and had a baby girl with her. This child, third in line for the throne, was a Catholic (by birth) and would have destroyed the entire Anglican basis of the monarchy had she ever become queen. The order, therefore, was issued by the Home Secretary to kidnap the woman and kill the child. The five women murdered by the Ripper were eyewitnesses to the kidnapping and were trying to blackmail the queen to keep silent. This story proposes that three men acted as the murderers. They included Sir William Gull, the Queen's physician and a Freemason, John Nettey, the Queen's coachman, and Robert Anderson, an Assistant Commissioner of the Metropolitan Police. The murders were committed inside of a royal coach, hence the fact that no one witnessed them. The bodies were then dumped in an alley. It was easy to lure a prostitute into a royal coach by rolling down a window and extending a hand with a gold coin in it. The murder was committed by Dr. Gull in order to make it seem the work of a madman and show his own secret revenge for a personal betrayal. This ties in the chalk inscription found on a wall near one of the killings which mentioned "the Juwes." It read, "The Juwes are the men that will not be blamed for nothing." Prior to author Stephen Knight's insight, writers have thought that this was an illiterate attempt to spell "Jews," but Knight shows that "the Juwes" was a masonic term meaning a high Masonic official, known to those in the upper ranks of Freemasonry. Mary Jane Kelly's killing occurred indoors, according to this scenario, because she had been mistaken for another Mary Kelly (also known as Katie Kelly) who was accidentally killed. When the mistake was noted, Mary Jane Kelly was tracked down at home and killed. With her death, all the blackmailers were dead. Distraught, Prince Eddy's wife was confined to a mental asylum, where she died. The exact fate of the child is unknown.

Although this story, supposedly told to its author by the son of artist Walter Sickert, had a lot going for it, it unravels upon close investigation. The strongest evidence against the story is that two laws existed that prevented any possibility of the throne of England ever being occupied by a Catholic. With the existence of those two laws (the Royal Marriages Act, which allowed any secret marriage of the Royal family to be set aside as invalid if the Royal was under age twenty-five, or had married without the Queen's consent—both of which were the case; and the Act of Settlement of 1700, which expressly excludes any person who married a Roman Catholic from inheriting the crown), motivation for the entire murder plot crumbles.

In addition, Walter Sickert's son Joseph admitted that the whole story was a fraud. Further, an intensive search produced no record of a marriage of Prince Eddy or of the birth of a child to the woman whom he supposedly married. The woman, named Ann Elizabeth Crook, was real, but any marriage between her and Prince Eddy was imaginary. Eddy was bisexual, possibly exclusively a homosexual, and died quite young from what was probably influenza, but may have been paresis, or syphilis of the brain.

Another hoax explanation of the Ripper killings was that given by Robert J. Lees, a medium (1849–1931). A story appeared in the *Chicago Sunday Times & Herald* of April 28, 1895, that Lees had a vision of one of the killings before it occurred. He went to the police, but they readily dismissed him. The following night, a murder occurred in the precise place and time and in the manner he had foreseen. The next time he went to the police with another vision, he told them that the killer would cut off the ears of his victim. The police listened more attentively this time because they had just received the letter signed "Jack the Ripper" in which he threatened to cut off the ears of his next victim and send them to the police. Lees supposedly accompanied the police to the scene of the next Ripper killing and received a strong enough impression of the killer to enable him to trace the killer back to his house. This turned out to be the home of a prominent physician, who is not named, but is *suspected* to be William Gull. After much cajoling, the police interviewed the physician's wife and were told that her husband had a strange character defect that caused him to go into rages and behave in a sadistic manner at times. The physician was taken before a panel of physicians, judged insane, and committed to an asylum, where he soon died.

There are several problems with the story. First, the police, backed by their files, deny any of this happened. The files have no record of an R. J. Lees and no one connected with the case ever mentioned him at the time of the murders. Secondly, William Gull was never judged insane, nor committed. Intensive search failed to find any such records for any London physician. A British journalist, Edwin T. Woodhall, took the original 1895 Chicago newspaper article and reworked it in the 1930s. It was accepted to be true and was reprinted in many books and magazines. There seems to be no truth to the story, however. Many other suspects have been postulated as Jack the Ripper. The cases for those suspects are flawed but not because of a deliberate intention to deceive. Rather, inconvenient evidence is downplayed and weak evidence is built up to strengthen it. It is unlikely that the Jack the Ripper killings will ever be solved. London files that were unsealed after 100 years did not even produce the solution many thought they contained. Rather, several of the usual suspects were listed as possibilities, with none a good fit.

Sources:

Begg, Paul. *Jack the Ripper: The Uncensored Facts.* New York: Robson/Parkwest Publications, 1989.

Harris, Melvin. *Jack the Ripper: The Bloody Truth.* London: Columbus Books, 1987.

Kelly, Alexander. *Jack the Ripper: A Bibliography and Review of the Literature.* London: Association of Assistant Librarians, 1973.

Knight, Stephen. *Jack the Ripper: The Final Solution.* New York: David McKay Co., 1976.

Rumbelow, Donald. *The Complete Jack the Ripper.* Boston: New York Graphic Society, 1975.

West, D. J. "The Identity of Jack the Ripper." *Journal of the Society for Psychical Research* 35 (1949): 76–80.

The Life of Charles Bradlaugh, M. P.

Among British and American radicals of the nineteenth century, there were two schools of thought about birth control. One school was represented by Charles Bradlaugh, Member of Parliament and a well-known atheist. He and Annie Besant, a leader of the Theosophical Society, favored birth control, even to the extent of fighting a court battle over their publication of *The Fruits of Philosophy*, by Charles Knowlton, an early birth control book. On the other side was editor William Stewart Ross, known as "Saladin," who was strongly against birth control on the grounds that it was likely to stimulate sexual promiscuity. Both men were leaders in the freethought movement, a form of eighteenth-century Deism.

Ross decided that Bradlaugh's power and influence (then much greater than his own) would be neutralized by a book in which the true moral consequences of following those who favored birth control could be seen. Since Bradlaugh sought a life that was blamelessly moral (except for his atheism) a few "liberties" would have to be taken with the facts. To protect against the inevitable libel suit from the litigious Bradlaugh, a pseudonym would have to be attached to the book, as well as a phony publisher's imprint. Charles Mackay, a local man otherwise barely known, was listed as author. The name "D. J. Gunn & Co." was chosen as the imaginary publisher. With that in place, the book was written, printed in Scotland, and issued as *The Life of Charles Bradlaugh, M. P.* in 1888.

Bradlaugh was outraged. He was especially upset about the intentional disregard for the truth evident on every page of the book. He immediately filed a libel suit, but did not know against whom the suit would be charged. No one could find Charles Mackay or D. J. Gunn and Company.

Although there is considerable confusion about exactly who was responsible for what in the production of the title, one can sort out a few things. In sworn depositions, the four main candidates accused one another. Each was quick to swear, under penalty of perjury, that the other was responsible. The four suspects were William Stewart Ross, also known as "Saladin," Charles R. Mackay, G. C. Griffith-Jones, also known as "Lara," and—peripherally—William Harral Johnson, also known as "Anthony Collins."

Ross swore that he was not involved and that all of his past animosities with Bradlaugh were long over. Bradlaugh, however, did not feel that way; Ross was sued for libel. Ross insisted that the book was written by Johnson, at Mackay's urging, and that Mackay made all the publishing arrangements. Ross admitted that he introduced Mackay to James Coulston, the Edinburgh printer who printed the book. Ross also testified that he was present when Mackay first met Johnson and when Johnson was approached to write the book for fifty pounds. Ross also helped Mackay get an office on Fleet Street, but Mackay defaulted on the rent.

Johnson admits that he wrote *most* of the book but insists, as does his daughter who acted as his secretary, that Mackay added a number of libelous passages to the book. Some were removed when both Johnsons protested, but others remained, having been added after the Johnsons read and approved the proofs. Lara claimed no involvement, but he was the one who boasted that the purpose of the book was to stop

Charles Bradlaugh.

Bradlaugh before he used his freethought connections to climb to higher political power and the one who wrote two pamphlets—*Monkanna Unveiled* and *Balak Secundus*, (which lists C. R. Mackay as author). Both pamphlets indicate a deep knowledge of classified aspects of the case and show hostility for Bradlaugh. It is difficult, therefore, to believe that Lara played no role in the case.

Ross was apparently shown some of the book's galleys, and made some corrections or comments on them. This bit of Ross's handwriting was later used by Mackay to implicate Ross. Ross later sued Mackay for "conspiracy," but that was not the appropriate charge and the case was dismissed. As a result, Mackay sued Ross for malicious prosecution. Eventually, the whole mess was sorted out. All of the charges against Mackay were dismissed, which greatly angered Ross. Ross held that Mackay had been the instigator of the book scam. In fact, Ross argued, this biography was only the first of several scandalous biographies planned by Mackay. The next two, never published, were of Edward Albert, the Prince of Wales, and of Jehovah. Eventually, Bradlaugh stopped pursuing Mackay as Mackay had declared bankruptcy.

Mackay's version of the story is that Ross approached him, saying that Johnson agreed to write the biography for fifty pounds. Mackay denied having threatened to give Bradlaugh's solicitors a manuscript in Ross's handwriting. Mackay sued Ross for 570 pounds for publishing expenses, which he claimed Ross was supposed to pay. Mackay also said that Ross assured the printer that there was nothing libelous in the book. Johnson asserted that he wrote the book, except for a few passages inserted by Mackay without his knowledge, and that Ross was not involved.

Bradlaugh's friend John Lees discovered who had printed the book in Edinburgh and began legal action against the printer. Bradlaugh obtained an injunction against the sale of the book and had a libel writ issued against Charles Mackay, W. S. Ross, and "D. J. Gunn," assuming the latter to be a real person. "Gunn" was eventually dropped from the writ. The conspirators began to quarrel. Johnson, a trained solicitor who had never practiced, wanted to handle the legal defense. Ross denied all involvement, and said his magazine would not review the book. He did, however, reprint comments and reviews made elsewhere. This bit of hypocrisy overwhelmed Lara, who sued Ross for the return of various manuscripts. Mackay sued Ross for the 570 pounds of publishing expenses, thereby apparently implicating Ross in the book's production. Ross settled with Mackay out of court for 225 pounds for the return of what Ross viewed as incriminating manuscripts. Ross then sued Mackay for the return of the money, claiming that not all the manuscripts were returned as agreed. The dismissal of this case led all the other defendants to sue Ross for malicious prosecution. One of Ross' solicitors sued him for his legal fees. Bradlaugh sued the *Dumfries Standard* and the *Warrington Observer* newspapers for reprinting excerpts from the book.

In the final resolution before hearing officer Master Butler, Ross agreed to destroy all copies of *The Life of Charles Bradlaugh* that he had or found, donate fifty pounds to Bradlaugh's favorite charity (the Masonic Boys' School), and pay Bradlaugh's legal costs of 190 pounds. The Edinburgh printer was ordered to pay twenty-five pounds to the Boys' School, issue an apology, and pay legal costs. Copies of the book were destroyed, although about twenty copies escaped destruction. Bradlaugh continued to serve in Parliament until his death in 1891. Just before his death, all traces of the five years of struggle it took him to be sworn in as a legitimate member of Parliament after his election were expunged from the official record. The effort to destroy Bradlaugh through this libelous biography failed. Bradlaugh is still remembered as Britain's greatest atheist spokesman.

Sources:

Griffith-Jones, G. C. *Monkanna Unveiled: An Essay on Charles R. Mackay's "Life of Charles Bradlaugh, M. P."*

with an Addendum on Secularism and Politics. London: D. J. Gunn [false imprint c. 1889].

Mackay, Charles R. *Balak Secundus: Being a Preliminary Exposure of William Stewart Ross, Trading as W. Stewart & Co. . . .* London: D. J. Gunn [false imprint c. 1889].

———. *Life of Charles Bradlaugh, M. P..* London: D. J. Gunn [false imprint], 1888.

Ross, William S. *Bradlaugh Papers,* Item 1631, Bishopsgate Institute, London, or microfilm of same.

Tribe, David. President Charles Bradlaugh, M. P. London: Elek Books, 1971: 264–69.

The Map of Roman Britain

Once incorrect information has been "authenticated" by an eminent authority, it is difficult to get it removed from source books, even after the information has been shown to be spurious. The hoax about the location of Roman sites in Great Britain perpetrated by Charles Bertram in the mid-1750s, still results in erroneous information in current textbooks.

Bertram (1723–1765), who was also known as Charles Julius Bertram, was an English teacher at a Danish school for naval cadets in Copenhagen. Although British by birth, Bertram was raised in Copenhagen. He wrote to Dr. William Stukeley, a celebrated local British historian, who was thrilled to hear that Bertram had a friend who possessed an old manuscript describing Roman antiquities in Britain. Stukeley urged Bertram to send him the manuscript. Bertram copied sections of the manuscript and sent them to Stukeley, who had a short facsimile verified as being "over 400 years old."

Bertram claimed that the Latin manuscript was written by "Richard of Westminster." Stukeley identified this man as "Richard of Cirencester," who, at the time of the supposed composition, was a monk at Westminster. Richard of Cirencester never wrote the manuscript in question. He did, however, write historical works in Latin. Judged by today's standards, the Latin manuscript is about what a high school Latin student would write if trying to convert a text in English, medieval style, into Latin. At the time (c. 1750), studies of comparative linguistics were in their infancy, and the Latin "passed."

There are many quotations in this work taken from Tacitus, Julius Caesar, and other ancient historians. As author Woodward points out, these quotations come from rather inaccurate seventeenth and eighteenth century editions of Tacitus and other ancient writers. All of the "modern" errors are retained, which is suspect if Richard of Cirencester, writing in the fourteenth century, was the author.

Woodward further establishes the contents of the work are erroneous. It is purportedly a description of Roman settlements, roads, construction, and remains in Britain. It is almost impossible that this information could have been passed down through the centuries; Richard must have borrowed from ancient historians. Further, the work encompasses folk traditions and ideas from nearly every part of Britain. It is highly unlikely that a fourteenth century monk could have done this.

The manuscript refers to six Roman provinces in Britain, while there were five. The borders of two of these were known in the 1700s, but the other three were of unknown size. Much of the conjecture and many of the ideas in the manuscript seem to have come from William Camden's *Britannia.*

The roads that appear in *De Situ Britaniae,* as Richard's manuscript is entitled, must come from the author's imagination. A map is included in the copy of the manuscript sent by Bertram to Stukeley. However, when Stukeley printed the edition of the work in 1759, he included a map that is quite different from that in Bertram's manuscript.

The reasons for rejecting the authenticity of the supposed work of Richard of Cirencester on Roman Britain are:

1) No original copy of the manuscript has ever been found, despite an intensive search in Copenhagen and elsewhere after Bertram's death. Only Bertram's supposed transcriptions of the work are known.

2) The facsimile of the map sent by Bertram is based upon sixteenth or seventeenth century knowledge of the topography of Britain and full of inconsistencies.

3) The manuscript's Latin reads like bad medieval English translated into bad Latin.

4) The way in which Richard of Cirencester describes himself in works known to be by him and in *this* work differ. Bertram calls him "Ricardus Corinensis" whereas Richard called himself "Ricardi de Cirencestria."

5) The feelings the author expresses in the work are not characteristic of a fourteenth century man, but of a much later period, such as the seventeenth century.

zine & Historical Review. 1 (1866): 301–8, 617–24; 2: 458–66; 4 (1867): 443–51.

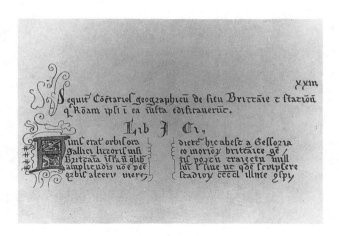

A page supposedly from *De Situ Britaniae.*

This is particularly true of the self-descriptive passages.

6) The sources taken from ancient writers were taken from editions of those writers printed between 100 and 300 years after Richard of Cirencester, who supposedly quoted them, lived.

7) The map and descriptions of Roman roads appear to be borrowed largely from the work of William Camden.

8) Much of the acceptance of the work appears to be based upon the authority of William Stukeley, who must have been thoroughly hoaxed by Charles Bertram.

As recently as 1872, the work was translated to English, and published in the "Bohn's Antiquarian Library" series, as one of the *Six English Chronicles.*

Sources:

Bradley, Henry. "Charles Bertram." *Dictionary of National Biography.* London: Oxford University Press, 1922.

Mayor, J. E. B., ed. *Ricardi de Cirencestri Speculum Historiale, Vol. 2.* London: Longmans Green, 1869: xvii–clxiv.

Randall, H. J. "Splendide Mendax." *Antiquity* 7 (1933): 49–60.

Stukeley, William. *An Account of Richard of Cirencester . . . With His Ancient Map of Roman Brittain . . . The Itinerary Thereof, . . .* London: Richard Hett, 1757.

Woodward, B. B. "A Literary Forgery: Richard of Cirencester's Tractate on Britain." *Gentleman's Maga-*

Mark Hofmann and the Mormon Forgeries

Often, when an organized religion has a lengthy history and a considerable amount of money, they seek out important historical documents of their origin. The Mormon Church has done just this. Because the Mormons then lock up the documents they find, especially the critical ones and let but a few trusted officials and historians see them, some question their motives. This very practice allowed the career of Mark Hofmann, perhaps the greatest American forger and hoaxer of historical documents, to flourish.

Mark Hofmann was born in 1954 in Utah. He was raised as a Mormon and remained outwardly devout until young adulthood, completing his missionary service. Evidence of his first doubts about his beliefs seem to have also surfaced while he was fulfilling his missionary service. While in high school, he became interested in Mormon history, and avidly sought out and read books critical of Mormonism.

After dabbling in a few occupations after high school, Hofmann decided to buy and sell Mormon historical books, documents, and currency. His first great find was the sheet of paper upon which the founder of Mormonism, Joseph Smith had copied some of the hieroglyphic characters he transcribed from the Golden Plates of the Book of Mormon. This transcript was then taken by early Mormon disciple Martin Harris to Prof. Charles Anthon at Columbia University in New York City. Harris said he was assured by Professor Anthon that Joseph Smith's translation was correct. On the basis of this, Harris mortgaged his farm to pay for the printing of the Book of Mormon. Professor Anthon later denied that he had authenticated the translation. This, of course, throws Smith's "translation" of the Book of Mormon into doubt. The Mormon church bought the Anthon transcript that stated he had *not* authenticated the translation, from Hofmann.

Hofmann's success was followed up in 1983 by his discovery of what has been called the "White Salamander Letter." This was a letter written by Martin Harris to W. W. Phelps in 1830. In it, Harris tells of Smith's discovery of the Golden Plates. He says that in the hole dug to find the plates, there appeared a white salamander, which transformed itself into a spirit and struck Smith three times. Again, this letter reflects unfavorably upon Smith because he appears to be involved in magic and fortune hunting by use of crystals. While a few people, such as skeptical author Tanner thought the salamander letter was not authentic, the Mormon church's own experts pronounced it authentic and the Church immediately bought it from Steven Christensen, the man to whom Hofmann sold it.

This was only the beginning of a steady stream of documents discovered by Mark Hofmann. He was soon selling a number of documents to the Mormon church, most of them casting an unfavorable light upon Mormonism.

One significant recurring feature in Hofmann's discoveries was that, often, one discovery could be used to "authenticate" later discoveries. For example, Martin Harris' handwriting was unknown until Hofmann first "discovered" a bible with Harris' signature in it. Later he found the Salamander letter in Harris' handwriting. Each authenticated the other, and both set the stage for the alleged discovery of the missing first draft of the Book of Lehi (part of the Book of Mormon) in Harris' handwriting. This was dictated by Joseph Smith to Harris, and subsequently lost by Harris in 1829. It remains lost, although Hofmann claimed as early as 1982 that he had spent thousands of dollars looking for the lost manuscript pages.

The first recorded piece of printed material in the United States, was a single sheet, or "broadside," on which *The Oath of a Freeman* was printed by Stephen Daye at Cambridge, Massachusetts in 1638–39. There were no first-run copies of the *Oath* known, despite intensive searches. However the text of the *Oath* was known since it had been reprinted later. The *Oath* was something that every freeman in Massachusetts had to swear to attain full citizenship. Since the oath could only be sworn in person before an official, the printed oath was probably used by local officials to read to the petitioner.

In March of 1985, Mark Hofmann contacted Justin Schiller, a New York City dealer in rare children's books, from whom Hofmann had bought items before. Hofmann called Schiller from Utah after having picked up an auction catalog at Schiller's store. The catalog listed for sale a copy of *New Englands Jonas,* the 1647 British book that first reprinted the *Oath.* Hofmann told Schiller that he had found a copy of a small broadside mounted on cardboard in one of the bins at the Argosy Bookstore in New York a few days before. It had been titled "Oath of a Freeman," but he pretended it was not anything special. He had paid $25 for the item, and had a handwritten receipt. When he saw the description of the *Oath* in the auction catalog, he realized that he might have something valuable. Hofmann brought his copy of the broadside to New York to show Schiller. The broadside had been removed from the cardboard backing by Hofmann, who had soaked it in water to do this. On the back of the broadside was some handwriting. A number of experts were shown the document. No one could find anything wrong with the broadside,

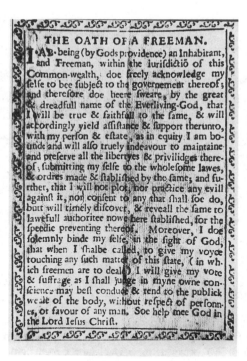

"The Oath of a Freeman."

but since no known copy of the *Oath* was available for comparison, most examinations were made comparing it with a copy of *The Bay Psalm Book,* printed by Stephen Daye two years later than the supposed broadside publication date. Comparisons of the paper, type, ink, and the writing on the back were done.

Eventually, the Library of Congress was offered the *Oath* by Hofmann, Schiller and Schiller's partner. The idea was to let the Library of Congress test the *Oath* for a month, and then decide whether they wanted to purchase it. The partners agreed to a $1,500,000 price. The Library of Congress could not find anything wrong with the broadside, but still thought the price too high. The partners then offered it to the American Antiquarian Society (AAS). While they were examining it, the bombs made by Hoffman went off in Utah. These bombs killed Hofmann's business partner Steven Christensen and Kathy Sheets, the wife of another partner Gary Sheets, for whom the second bomb was intended. A third bomb exploded Mark Hofmann's car, seriously injuring him. Hofmann immediately became a bombing suspect as the bomb seemed to have "accidentally" gone off in his car. The AAS offered $250,000 for the *Oath,* but was turned down, and the bombings put off all further negotiations.

Once suspicion was cast upon Hofmann, and while his house had been searched, a photographic negative of what appeared to be the *Oath of a Freeman* was found.

As evidence of Hofmann's involvement in a large-scale document-forgery scheme grew, the motivation for the bombings began to surface. Hofmann had been advanced $185,000 to buy the "McLellin Collection" of Mormon documents. This collection, which Hofmann claimed to have located, did not exist. Apparently, Hofmann had also been advanced several hundred thousand additional dollars from other sources. These advances were partly secured by the *Oath* manuscript, with its pending purchase by the Library of Congress. When that purchase fell through, Hofmann was in a financial bind. He had spent lavishly when he first got the money, buying, among other things, an expensive house. He could not pay back his loans, and probably would not be able to in the near future. In addition, suspicions about some of the documents he *had* sold were emerging. He needed to buy time and divert suspicion from himself, hence the bombings. Steven Christensen was the original purchaser of the Salamander Letter, and Gary Sheets was involved in financing other purchases, so these were logical Hofmann targets. But when the bomb exploded in Hofmann's own car, either accidently (en route to another destination) or intentionally, the incident was perhaps his worst miscalculation. He pled guilty to two counts of murder without standing trial and was sentenced to life in prison where he still resides.

Nonetheless, the way in which the *Oath of a Freeman* was forged was ingenious. Each letter of the words needed to form the text of the *Oath* was cut from a facsimile edition of the *Bay Psalm Book*. The words were enclosed in a border also cut from the *Bay Psalm Book*. A photograph was taken of the assembled mocked-up version, and a metal etching was made of that. The type images on the plate were then carefully filed or sanded to resemble uneven inking. This was necessary to duplicate Stephen Daye's usually poor inking. In addition, the ink was made from carbon black, obtained by burning paper from the 1600s, in case carbon dating would be done. Hofmann used ink that he made from a 1600s recipe. It was a simple ink, and Hofmann was careful not to use tap water in its formula. He also made certain that there was type "bite" (an impression made by the type on the paper) showing through the back of the paper, although how this was accomplished is not clear. This "bite" made it appear that the document had been printed by letterpress and not by offset printing. The paper used was cut from books of the 1620–40 period found at the University of Utah or Brigham Young University libraries. He looked for quite a while before he found paper with chain lines similar, but not identical, to those in the *Bay Psalm Book*. He was also careful not to use watermarked paper, as

that could be traced to papermakers that Stephen Daye could not have used. The only major error that Hofmann made in his *Oath* forgery, which was not noticed until it was too late, was he contracted the word "established" to "stablished," something that Stephen Daye never did.

Sources:

Gilreath, James. *The Judgment of Experts: Essays and Documents About the Investigation of the Forging of the Oath of a Freeman.* Worcester, MA: American Antiquarian Society, 1991.

Hewett, David. "Is the White Salamander Letter a Fake? Many Don't Think So." *Maine Antiques Digest* (April 1986): 10–13.

Lindsay, Robert. *A Gathering of Saints: A True Story of Money, Murder and Deceit.* New York: Simon & Schuster, 1988.

Naifeh, Steven. *The Mormon Murders: A True Story of Greed, Forgery, Deceit and Death.* New York: Weidenfeld & Nicholson, 1988.

Sillitoe, Linda and Allen Roberts. *Salamander: The Story of the Mormon Forgery Murders.* Salt Lake City: Signature Books, 1988.

Tanner, Jerald. "LDS Documents & Murder." *Salt Lake City Messenger* no. 59 (January 1986): 1–25.

The Mecklenburg Declaration

It is widely held the Declaration of Independence, proclaimed on July 4, 1776, was the first attempt to declare America free of European colonial powers. The Mecklenburg Declaration, it is claimed, was announced on May 20, 1775, in Mecklenburg County, North Carolina, predating the Declaration of Independence by more than a year. The Mecklenburg Declaration was supposedly published in an issue of the *Cape Fear Mercury*, a newspaper of the area, in an issue that has not survived.

In 1800 notes were made from memory by John McKnitt Alexander, one of the participants in the meetings that led to the "resolves" produced at Mecklenburg. These notes placed the date of the declaration as May 20, 1775, although the series of resolves were adopted in Mecklenburg County on May 31, 1775.

During the winter of 1818–19, there was much discussion in Congress about an assertion that the people of Mecklenburg, North Carolina had declared themselves free of England before July 4, 1776. The text of the Mecklenburg Declaration was eventually produced for inspection. It follows, in its entirety, except for the list of signers and a description of the circumstances:

1. *Resolved,* That whoever directly or indirectly abetted or in any way, form or manner, countenanced the unchartered and dangerous invasion of our rights, as claimed by Great Britain, is an enemy to this country—to America—and to the inherent and inalienable rights of man.

2. *Resolved,* That we the citizens of Mecklenburg County, do hereby dissolve the political bands which have connected us to the Mother Country, and hereby absolve ourselves from all allegiance to the British Crown, and abjure all political connection, contract, or association, with that nation, who have wantonly trampled on our rights and liberties—and inhumanly shed the innocent blood of American patriots at Lexington.

3. *Resolved,* That we do hereby declare ourselves a free and independent people, are, and of right ought to be, a sovereign and self-governing Association, under the control of no power other than that of our God and the General Government of the Congress; to the maintenance of which independence, we solemnly pledge to each other, our mutual co-operation, our lives, our fortunes, and our most sacred honor.

4. *Resolved* That as we now acknowledge the existence and control of no law or legal officer, civil or military, within this county, we do hereby ordain and adopt, as a rule of life, all, each and every of our former laws, wherein, nevertheless, the Crown of Great Britain can never be considered as holding rights, privileges, immunities, or authority therein.

5. *Resolved* That is is also further decreed, that all, each and every military officer in this country, is hereby reinstated to his former command and authority, he acting comformably to these regulations. And that every member present of this delegation shall henceforth be a civil officer, viz, a Justice of the Peace, in the character of a *"Committeeman,"* to issue process, hear and determine all matters of controversy, according to said adopted laws, and to preserve peace, and union, and harmony, in said county, and to use every exertion to spread the love of country and fire of freedom throughout America, until a more general and organized govenment be established in this province.

The declaration was carried to the Philadelphia Congress, with a letter addressed to the three North Carolina representatives. The individual members of Congress agreed with the sentiments of the declaration, although it was decided that it was premature to lay the entire document before the House. The three North Carolina delegates recommended perseverence.

All of this information was made public in 1819, and was extensively circulated in the newspapers around the country. John Adams noticed an article about the declaration in his local Massachussets newspaper. Ad-

ams wrote to Thomas Jefferson and exclaimed that it was a mystery to him. Jefferson said that he thought the document was spurious, basing his opinion on the complete lack of evidence he found from the 1775 period, coupled with no mention of the document in the eighteenth century. Adams was convinced by Jefferson's reply, even though he initially leaned towards accepting the declaration as genuine.

North Carolinians accepted the document, and were upset when Jefferson's opinion on the matter became widely known through the 1829 publication of the first edition of his *Works of Thomas Jefferson.* To attempt to meet Jefferson's demand for additional proof, the North Carolina legislature in 1830–31 appointed a committee to "examine, collate and arrange" all obtainable evidence about the declaration. This committee reported in 1831 that the declaration was genuine. Shortly after this report appeared, Peter Force, working on his book *American Archives,* discovered a proclamation issued by the royal governor of North Carolina, Josiah Martin, on August 8, 1775, stating that he had "seen a most infamous publication in the *Cape Fear Mercury* importing to be resolves of a set of people styling themselves a committee for the county of Mecklenburg, most traitorously declaring the entire dissolution of the laws, government, and constitution of this country, and setting up a system of rule and regulation repugnant to the laws and subversive of his majesty's government. . . ." The original proclamation book of Governors Tryon and Martin was found. Then Peter Force found the text of the preamble and the first four resolutions in the *Massachusetts Spy or American Oracle of Liberty* of July 12, 1775. Other supporting articles were found during the next few years. However, the text of the resolutions was different from the version reconstructed from memory; it was broader, applying to all the colonies. Others disagreed with Force on the scope of the resolutions. Today, advocates of the authenticity of the Mecklenburg declarations say that the May 31 Resolves were never adopted in that form, but were amended on May 20 into a declaration of independence.

This version of the Resolves of May 31, 1775 took the following form:

WHEREAS by an Address presented to his Majesty by both Houses of Parliament, in February last, the American colonies are declared to be in a state of actual rebellion, we conceive, that all laws and commissions confirmed by, or derived from the authority of the King or Parliament, are annulled and vacated, and the former civil constitution of these colonies, for the present, wholly suspended. To provide, in some degree, for the exigencies of this county, in the present alarming period, we deem it proper and necessary to pass the following Resolves, viz:

I. That all commissions, civil and military, heretofore granted by the Crown, to be exercised in these colonies, are null and void, and the constitution of each particular colony wholly suspended.

II. That the Provincial Congress of each province, under the direction of the great Continental Congress, is invested with all legislative and executive powers within their respective provinces; and that no other legislative or executive power does, or can exist, at this time in any of these colonies.

III. As all former laws are now suspended in this province, and the Congress have not provided others, we judge it to be necessary, for better preservation of good order, to form certain rules and regulations for the internal government of this county, until laws shall be provided for us by the Congress.

IV. That the inhabitants of this county do meet on a certain day appointed by this Committee, and having formed themselves into nine companies (*to wit*) eight in the county, and one in the town of Charlotte, do chuse [sic] a Colonel and other military officers, who shall hold and exercise their several powers by virtue of this choice, and independent of the Crown of Great-Britain, and former constitution of this province.

V. That for the better preservation of the peace and administration of justice, each of those companies do chuse [sic] from their own body, two discreet freeholders, who shall be empowered, each by himself and singly, to decide and determine all matters of controversy, arising within said company, under the sum of twenty shillings; and jointly and together, all controversies under the sum of forty shillings; yet so as that their decisions may admit of appeal to the Convention of the Select-Men of the county; and also that any one of these men, shall have power to examine and commit to confinement persons accused of petit larceny.

VI. That those two Select-Men, thus chosen, do jointly and together chuse[sic] from the body of their particular company, two persons properly qualified to act as Constables, who may assist them in the execution of their office.

VII. That upon the complaint of any persons to either of these Select-Men, he do issue his warrant, directed to the Constable, commanding him to bring the aggressor before him or them, to answer said complaint.

VIII. That these eighteen Select-Men, thus appointed, do meet every third Thursday in January, April, July, and October, at the Court-House, in Charlotte, to hear and determine all matters of controversy, for sums exceeding forty shillings, also appeals; and in cases of felony, to commit the person or persons convicted thereof to close confinement, until the Provincial Congress shall provide and establish laws and modes of proceeding in all such cases.

Articles IX through XVI, deal with trials, debtors, taxes, and a militia. The concluding articles follow:

XVII. That any person refusing to yield obedience to the above Resolves, shall be considered equally criminal, and liable to the same punishment, as the offenders above last mentioned [held to be delt with 'as prudence may direct.'].

XVIII. That these Resolves be in full force and virtue, until instructions from the Provincial Congress, regulating the jurisprudence of the province, shall provide otherwise, or the legislative body of Great-Britain, resign its unjust and arbitrary pretentions with respect to America.

XIX. That the eight militia companies in the county, provide themselves with proper arms and accoutrements, and hold themselves in readiness to execute the commands and directions of the General Congress of this province and this Committee.

XX. That the Committee appoint Colonel Thomas Polk, and Doctor Joseph Kennedy, to purchase 300 lb. of powder, 600 lb. of lead, 1000 flints, for use of the militia of this county, and deposit the same in such place as the Committee may hereafter direct.

Signed by order of the Committee

This set of "resolves" is quite different from the other. In fact, this set seems to deal largely with the local administration of law and order, giving some support to dissatisfaction with British administration of the colony. It does not, however, call for independence from Great Britain. The first declaration was much stronger in this respect, actually calling for a dissolution of the political "bands" connecting Great Britain and North Carolina.

These are the established facts surrounding the Mecklenburg Declaration. The signature or issue of a declaration that proclaimed independence of Great Britain rests on the memory of a number of people who claim to "remember" the declaration many years previously. The original documents were supposedly destroyed in a fire in 1800. A fire *did* occur, but no one knows what was destroyed. There is no contemporary record of the declarations, as the *Cape Fear Mercury* "article" was a fake. Thomas Jefferson denounced the declaration as spurious. The first actual document of the period that mentions the declaration is a Charleston newspaper (*The South-Carolina Gazette and Country Journal*) of June 16, 1775, giving full text of the Mecklenburg Resolves adopted on May 31, 1775. These do not declare independence of Great Britain, (see the second set of text given above).

With regard to the first set of text above, which is more a declaration of independence from Great Britain, the papers of then-Governor Martin of North Carolina show that more than a month after this declaration was supposedly issued and published in the *Cape Fear Mercury*, Governor Martin was apparently unaware of their existence in a proclamation he issued at Fort Johnston. James Iredell of North Carolina, an associate justice of the U.S. Supreme Court, and eyewitness to North Carolina events in 1775, said in 1776 that "we [North Carolina] have never taken any one step which really indicated such a view [independence]."

The copy of the declaration made from memory by John McKnitt Alexander in 1800, after his house burned down, is the first version quoted above. This is the only source of the first version, and is quite different from the second. It is likely that his memory failed him when he tried to reconstruct the document. He probably had a vague memory of the *second* document, and created the first from it. The real May 31 "Resolves" were loosely called a "declaration of independence" as people forgot their exact thrust. This is probably the source of the idea that there had been a Mecklenburg Declaration of Independence before the Congressional Declaration of Independence. Evidence does not illustrate that the Mecklenburg version was the first declaration of independence.

Sources:

Ford, Worthington Chauncey. "Dr. S. Millington Miller and the Mecklenburg Declaration." *American Historical Review* 11 (April 1906):548–58.

Graham, George W. *The Mecklenburg Declaration of Independence. May 20, 1775 and Lives of Its Signers.* New York: Neale Publishing Co., 1905.

Graham, William A. *The Address of Hon. Wm. A. Graham on the Mecklenburg Declaration of Independence of the 20th of May 1775.* New York: E. J. Hale & Son, 1875.

Hoyt, William Henry. *The Mecklenburg Declaration of Independence.* New York: DaCapo Press, 1972. Reprint.

Nostradamus's Predictions

In this case, the hoax was not the work of the person it is named after. Rather, it was the work of people who followed Nostradamus and tried to take advantage of his reputation. Michael Nostradamus (Michel de Notredame), 1503–1566, was a French physician of probable Jewish ancestry. His prophetic work was called *The Centuries,* and was probably first published in 1555. Today no known copies of this edition exist. The work consisted of quatrains, or four-line verses, each of two rhymed couplets, and was written in a form of Medieval French that was antiquated even when Nostradamus wrote it. The text was ambiguous, and easily translated in different ways.

Further, not all verses present in modern editions of Nostradamus go back to Nostradamus's time. In fact, there are 942 quatrains, or nine groups of 100 each, and one of 42. The 42-verse piece, or Century number VII, has been expanded upon in some editions—adding 58 spurious quatrains, and bringing the total up to 100.

Perhaps the best-known quatrain, interpreted as predicting, in detail, the death of King Henry II of France, is as follows in the original:

Le lyon jeune le vieux surmontera.
En champ bellique par singulier duelle.
Dans caige d'or les yeux luy creuera:
Deux classes une, puis mourir, mort cruelle.

This has been translated as follows:

The young lion shall overcome the old
On the field of battle in single combat;
In a cage of gold he shall burst his eyes–
Two fleets one, then to die, a cruel death.

Supposedly, Henry II was killed by being pierced through the eye by a lance when jousting, his head encased in a gold helmet. Henry *was* killed while jousting with a captain of his guard who was only a few years younger than Henry. The lion was not the emblem of either. Henry died when a splinter from the captain's lance penetrated his brain (other sources say his throat), but not his eye. Henry's helmet was not gold. The word "fleets" was subsequently changed to "wounds," but there was only one wound. In short, the verses were not prophetic. In addition, another quatrain predicted great things for Henry II (see VI:70). It states that he will be "chief of the world" and have the title of "Victor." These predictions were made in 1558, and Henry died as described in 1559.

This brings up the issue of the time frame of Nostradamus' predictions. As author James Randi has convincingly argued, Nostradamus was only interested in predicting things that would happen in his local area in the next few years. Indeed, most of the references in the *Centuries* refer to events and places in France in the sixteenth century. Randi backs up his litany of incorrect predictions made by Nostradamus with an example found in a manuscript source dating directly to Nostradamus' lifetime. This document is from Catherine, mother to King Charles IX and Francis II, and was written in 1564 to Conetable, Catherine's godfather. In the document she says that Nostradamus has just personally predicted to her that Conetable would live to be ninety (he died at the age of seventy-seven) and that her son Charles would also live to be that old (he died at the age of twenty-four in 1574).

Another famous quatrain is IX:20, usually translated as a prediction of the escape of Louis XVI and

Marie Antoinette from Paris. If that was intended then the prediction was wrong on almost every count. Contrary to information in the verse, the queen was dressed in gray, not white. They did not take a detour, and although there is a reference to the the town of Varennes, there are more than twenty towns of that name in France.

Another example of how the quatrains have multiple interpretations has to do with VIII:1. Some have taken "PAV, NAY, LORON" at the beginning of the quatrain to be an anagram for "Napoleon," when they actually are the names of three neighboring towns (Pau, Nay and Oloron) in southwestern France.

Karl Ernest Krafft, an astrologer to the Nazi party, wrote a small book called *Nostradamus prophezeit den Kriegsverlauf (Nostradamus Predicts the Course of the War)* in 1943. The book contains a great many "improvements" of Nostradamus' verses, and illustrates that they can be translated to predict any number of things— even that Germany would win World War II. Among the verses that supposedly predict Hitler's involvement, and this is not due entirely to Krafft's improvements, is II:24, which reads as follows:

Bestes farouches de faim fluues tranner,
Plus part du camp encontre Hister sera.
En caige de fer le grand fera treisner,
Quand rien enfant de Germain obseruera.

Despite those who argue that "Hister" is "Hitler," it is actually an old name for a portion of the Danube River. Further, "Germain" does not mean "Germany," but "brother" in Medieval French. The corrrect translation of this quatrain is as follows:

Beasts mad with hunger will swim across rivers,
Most of the army will be against the Lower Danube.
The great one will be dragged in an iron cage
When the child brother will observe nothing.

While it is difficult to know what all of this means, educated guesses say that it refers to the Turkish advances in Hungary that occurred during the mid-sixteenth century. The other so-called "Hitler" quatrain is IV:68, which also refers to the Lower Danube. Further examination of other quatrains have revealed no clear set of predictions shown to apply to anything past the mid-sixteenth century. Even in most of *those* predictions, Nostradamus was wrong. Many generations of forgers and hoaxers are responsible for the idea that Nostradamus was a prophet.

Sources:

Cazeau, Charles J. "Prophecy: The Search for Certainty." *Skeptical Inquironer* 7 no. 1 (Fall 1982): 20–29 .

Leoni, Edgar. *Nostradamus and his Prophecies.* New York: Exposition Press, 1961.

LeVert, Liberte [Everett Bleiler]. *The Prophecies and Enigmas of Nostradamus.* Glen Rock, NJ: Firebell Books, 1979.

Randi, James. *The Mask of Nostradamus.* New York: Charles Scribner's Sons, 1990.

The Protocols of the Elders of Zion

Some hoaxes are harmless and can be considered for their humor alone. The *Protocols of the Elders of Zion* hoax (hereafter called the *Protocols*) is another matter altogether. This hoax had serious, even deadly consequences. Lives were lost as a result because of this hoax, although it is impossible to estimate how many.

The *Protocols* have a tangled and mysterious history. Many scholars have worked to untangle this history, but the greatest credit goes to Norman Cohn, author of *Warrant for Genocide.* Other major contributions were made by Herman Bernstein and Philip Graves, each of whom identified one of the two novels that were major sources for the *Protocols.*

While not all the steps by which the *Protocols* arrived in final form are known, it appears that production started in Russia in about 1895. However, The true origin of the *Protocols,* lies in Paris, 1864. In that year, a political satirist named Maurice Joly published his book. Although the book was actually published in Brussels, its title page said it was published in Geneva. Joly's book, *Dialogue aux Enfer entre Montesquieu et Machiavel (A Dialog in Hell Between Montesquieu and Machiavelli),* openly criticized Emperor Napoleon III— which, at the time, was criminal. The author put the emperor's words into the mouth of political philosophers Machiavelli and Montesquieu, using the latter to present the case for liberalism. The book was smuggled into France, but was seized at the border. Joly was arrested and tried. On April 25, 1865, he was sentenced to fifteen months imprisonment. The book was banned and copies confiscated, making it a rare work. This rarity has helped hide the fact that large sections of the imagined dialog have been lifted and grafted on to the work that became the *Protocols.*

In Berlin, during 1868, Hermann Goedsche, a minor official in the German Postal Service, who wrote under the pseudonym of Sir John Retcliffe, published a novel called *Biarritz.* The novel contained a chapter called "In the Jewish Cemetery in Prague." In this chapter, he tells of a secret nocturnal meeting held in the cemetery during the Feast of Tabernacles. There the heads of the twelve tribes of Israel gather to meet with the Devil. The leaders report on their activities during the century that has elapsed since their last meeting. The reports assert that the Jews are making great progress towards taking over the world, since they have accomplished such things as putting all the princes and governments of Europe into their debt by means of the stock exchange. They discuss a scheme for getting all land in the hands of Jews, and outline plans to undermine the Christian Church. A plea to gain control of the press is presented, as well as schemes to obtain high governmental positions. They renew their oath and agree to meet again in 100 years. Although *Biarritz* is fiction, this chapter summarizes many of the fears that anti-semites have exhibited for hundreds of years.

Another *Protocols* conspirator, Pyotr Rachkovsky, was the head of the foreign branch of the Russian secret police from 1884 to 1902. The Okhrana (secret police) had its overseas headquarters in Paris. Rachkovsky organized the overseas operations in Paris, Switzerland, London, and Berlin. He also spearheaded the transformation of the two fictional works by Joly and Goedsche into the *Protocols*. In 1887, he planted a forged letter in the French press, claiming that the majority of the terrorists then active in France were Jews. In 1892, Rachkovsky published a book in Paris entitled *Anarchie et Nihilisme*, telling how the French Revolution made the Jew "the absolute master of the situation in Europe . . . governing by discreet means both monarchies and republics." The one remaining goal of the Jews was domination of Russia, the book claimed, and this was being planned. The book urged the creation of a Franco-Russian league to combat the power of the Jews. In 1902, Rachkovsky tried to create such a league, but failed. In 1905, he created the Union of the Russian People, that would later help circulate the *Protocols* and conduct other anti-Jewish activities.

In 1902, Rachkovsky was involved in a court intrigue in St. Petersburg with Sergey Nilus. Nilus was a former landowner, who had lost his entire fortune while living in France. He wandered in Russia from monastery to monastery. In 1900, Nilus published a book explaining how he had been converted from an atheist to an Orthodox Christian. The book was called *The Great in the Small.*

At this point, it is speculated that Rachkovsky sent Nilus a manuscript version of the *Protocols*. They may have planned to use it in a continuation of their St. Petersburg court intrigue. In 1905 Nilus published a second edition of *The Great in the Small*, containing an addendum of the *Protocols*. Nilus apparently believed a worldwide Jewish conspiracy was taking place, but the materials comprising the "documentation" of that conspiracy, namely the manuscript of the *Protocols*, was evidently supplied to him by Rachkovsky. Evidence also suggests that copies of the *Protocols* in manuscript or in mimeograph were circulating in Russia in the late

1890s, although no copies seem to have survived. Whether Rachkovsky was also the source of these copies is unknown.

Author Norman Cohn feels "practically certain" that the *Protocols* were fabricated sometime between 1894 and 1899 in Paris. That would correspond with the time of the Dreyfus Affair, when a Jewish army captain was accused of treason in an anti-semitic incident. The copy of Joly's book in the Bibliotheque Nationale bears markings that indicate that it was the copy used to lend information to the *Protocols*. The fabrication was undoubtedly done by a Russian.

Once Nilus' version of the *Protocols* was published in 1905, the work took on a life of its own. The *Protocols* were widely circulated in right-wing circles in Russia. Tsar Nicholas II read and accepted the *Protocols* as genuine. An investigation later showed that the work was fraudulent, however, and Nicholas ordered that they no longer be used for anti-Semitic propaganda. When the Tsar was overthrown in the Russian Revolution, the situation changed, and the *Protocols* were widely read by the "White" army that lost to the "Red" army during the revolution. The losers blamed the revolution on the Jews and used the *Protocols* as the document explaining their motivation. Thus was started the myth of the Jewish-Communist conspiracy that helped fuel the German campaign of anti-Semitism.

Translations of the *Protocols* began to circulate in Europe around 1919. Publication in Germany began in 1920, although the earliest title page is dated 1919. The first edition was called *Die Geheimnisse der Weisen von Zion* (*The Mystery of the Sages of Zion*). Sales quickly reached 120,000 copies. The assassination of German Foreign Minister Walther Rathenau in 1922, was motivated by the idea that Rathenau, a Jew, was one of the "Elders of Zion."

An English translation, entitled *The Jewish Peril*, was published in 1920 by Eyre & Spottiswoode, publishers of the Authorised Version of the Bible and Anglican Prayer Book. Most reviewers accepted the work as authentic, although the newspapers published letters from readers to the contrary . In America, the work was also published in 1920. Henry Ford's newspaper, *The Dearborn Independent*, published a long series of articles in 1920, justifying the authenticity of the *Protocols*. These were republished as a book, *The International Jew*. Hitler later had copies of this book translated and circulated throughout Germany.

Back in Germany, the German National People's Party (DNVP) used racist propaganda—including the *Protocols*—in its election campaigns beginning in 1920. The "Jewish World Conspiracy" was allegedly due to an inborn destructiveness in all Jews, who were con-

Henry Ford.

spiring to destroy the "Aryan," or Germanic race. A combination of the "volkisch-racist" (nationalist) tradition in Germany and the *Protocols* produced an inflammatory combination that reinforced the kind of attitudes that led to the Holocaust. Alfred Rosenberg, propagandist of Nazi anti-Semitism, was apparently influenced by the *Protocols* when writing his *Myth of the Twentieth Century,* which became known as the source-book of Nazism. Hitler's explanation of the great economic inflation of 1923 was that "According to the *Protocols of Zion* the peoples are to be reduced to submission by hunger. The second revolution under the Star of David is the aim of the Jews in our time."

Therefore, what started out as a hoax, probably for Russian political reasons, became perhaps a key piece in the genocide of the Jews. The *Protocols* are still in print, and still being issued as genuine documents in some places. This was certainly the most deadly hoax ever conceived.

Sources:

Bernstein, Herman. *The Truth About "The Protocols of Zion; A Complete Exposure.* New York: Ktav Publishing House, 1971.

Cohn, Norman R. C. *Warrant for Genocide: The Myth of the Jewish World Conspiracy and the Protocols of the Elders of Zion.* New York: Harper & Row, 1967.

Graves, Philip. *The Truth About "The Protocols": A Literary Forgery.* London: Times Publishing Co., 1921.

Gwyer, John. *Portraits of Mean Men: A Short History of the Protocols of the Elders of Zion.* London: Cobden-Sanderson, 1938.

[Nilus, Sergey, ed.] *The Protocols and World Revolution, Including a Translation and Analysis of the "Protocols of the Meetings of the Zionist Men of Wisdom".* Boston: Small, Maynard & Co, 1920.

Wolf, Lucien. *The Myth of the Jewish Menace in World Affairs, or The Truth About the Forged Protocols of the Elders of Zion.* New York: Macmillan, 1921.

The Three Impostors

The existence of the blasphemous book, *The Three Impostors* (*Les Trois Imposteurs* in French, and *De Tribus Impostoribus* in Latin) has been debated in Medieval and Renaissance studies. The issue is resolved to have been one of the most enduring and complex hoaxes ever devised.

In 1229, Pope Gregory IX excommunicated his opponent, Emperor Frederick II, only to have Frederick win a victory over the Turks and recover the Holy Lands. In another attempt to discredit Frederick, the pope issued an encyclical accusing the emperor of blasphemy. The pope said that Frederick described the world as deceived by three "worthless fellows," namely Jesus, Moses, and Mohammed. Frederick denied the charge, but it stuck, even though there was no evidence that he wrote anything of the sort. Nevertheless, he became the first candidate for the authorship of the book *De Tribus Impostoribus* (*The Three Impostors*). Others who would later be accused of writing it included Italian philosophers Vanini, Giordano Bruno, Machiavelli, and Campanella, Italian writer Boccaccio, Dutch humanist Erasmus, and English poet Milton. During the seventeenth century, most of the talk was not about the book itself, but about who wrote it.

There were a few who doubted the existence of the book at this early date. Among them were Dutch scholar Grotius, who argued that since no one saw the book, it did not exist. French philosopher and critic Pierre Bayle also had his doubts. After he expressed these doubts in an essay on Aretino (also known as Leonardo Bruno), Bayle received a manuscript from de La Monnoye in which all of the evidence was weighed and it was concluded that the book never existed. A *Reponse* to La Monnoye's essay was written in 1716 by a "J. L. R. L." This anonymous author said in his manuscript that he knew the book existed because he had a copy of it in his library. Although J. L. R. L. says that the work states that the original was copied from one in Emperor Frederick's library, this appears to be a weak attempt to shift authorship back to a man who had been dead for 500 years. J. L. R. L. inserts excerpts in his manuscript; especially convincing is the second part of the work entitled *La Vie et l'Espirit de Spinoza*. Author Ira Wade attributes this work (in J. L. R. L.'s alleged longer original) to Henry de Boulainvillier. Others, such as writer Margaret Jacob, disagree. Printed in 1719, the whole work is the first biography of Benedict Spinoza, but the part formed into the *La Vie et l'Espirit* is really a sloppily constructed set of supposed excerpts from Spinoza's thought. Although this work has been reprinted many times under the title *Les Trois Imposteurs*, it is not the original source for the stories about the book.

The original Latin version may have been discovered and reprinted in the mid-nineteenth century by author Gustave Brunet, among others. Allegedly, the original is dated 1598 and is a small book of forty-six pages, printed on gray paper with blunt type. Typography officionados have determined that the paper and type point to a book published east of the Rhine River in the eighteenth century. The work is composed of poor Latin, without much logic or philosophy. It is anti-religious, but resembles, as writer Allen says, the oration of an atheist speaker more than a profound analysis of the theist position.

Margaret Jacob in *The Radical Enlightenment* has come up with what appears to be a solution to at least the origin of the version of *Les Trois Imposteurs* that goes back to *La Vie et l'Esprit de Spinoza*. She says that *La Vie* was a separate manuscript from *L'Esprit*. The one called *L'Esprit* appears to have been virtually identical to *Les Trois Imposteurs*. Gaspar Fritsch, a leader of the Knights of Jubilation (an early Freemasonry group), says in correspondence quoted by Jacob, that the original of this work came from freemason Jean Rousset de Missy. Don Cameron Allen also suggests Rousset, although for different reasons. Rousset also appears to be the true author of the *Reponse*. The Knights of Jubilation may have been involved in making copies of various heretical books (including *L'Esprit*) and circulating them throughout Europe. This was a dangerous business, punishable by jail if one was merely caught in possession of a copy of such a book.

The Latin version of *De Tribus Impostoribus* may have been written by Peter Friedrich Arpe, at least according to Jacob. She does not present much of a case for his authorship, except that the Royal Library in The Hague possesses a copy of *Les Trois Imposteurs* bound together with Arpe's essay on Vanini and a copy of the Latin *De Tribus Impostoribus*. Some disagree with Jacob, such as Silvia Berti, who feels that Jan Vroesen, a Dutchman was the actual author of *Les Trois Imposteur's* section called *L'Esprit*.

No version of the work dates back much before 1700. Before that, the book did not exist, and all its attributions before then are hoaxes. When the work was created, perhaps in response to Queen Christina's desire to comb all the existing libraries to find a copy, it was made from two different sources. Regardless, the book was not penned by any of the famous authors to whom it was attributed. The work is basically a hoax, manufactured to meet an existing reputation, and consequent demand.

Sources:

Allen, Don Cameron. *Doubt's Boundless Sea: Skepticism and Faith in the Renaissance*. Baltimore, MD: Johns Hopkins Press, 1964. 224–43.

Berti, Silvia. "The First Edition of the *Traité des Trois Imposteurs* and its Debt to Spinoza's *Ethics*" in Michael Hunter and David Wootton, eds. *Atheism from the Reformation to the Enlightenment*. Oxford, UK: Clavender Press, 1992: 182–220.

———. "Jan Vroesen, Autore del 'Traité des Trois Imposteurs' *Rivista Storica Italiana* 8 no. 2 (1991): 528–43.

Jacob, Margaret C. *The Radical Enlightenment: Pantheists, Freemasons and Republicans*. London: George Allen & Unwin, 1981.

Nasier, Alcofribas [pseud.], ed. *De Tribus Impostoribus, A. D. 1230. The Three Impostors translated (with notes and comments) from a French manuscript of the work written in the year 1716, with a dissertation on the origin of the treatise and a bibliography of the various editions* by Alcofribas Nasier, the Later. Privately printed, 1904.

Philomeste Junior [Gustave Brunet]. *Le Traite Des Trois Imposteurs (De Tribus Impostoribus, MDIIC)*. Paris: La Libraire de l'Academie des Bibliophiles, 1867.

Presser, J. *Das Buch "De Tribus Impostoribus" (Von Den Drei Betrugern)*. Amsterdam: H. J. Paris, 1926.

Vale, Gilbert, ed. *The Three Impostors. Translated (with notes and Illustrations) from the French edition of the works, published at Amsterdam, 1776*. New York: G. Vale, 1846.

Wade, Ira O. *The Clandestine Organization and Diffusion of Philosophic Ideas in France from 1700 to 1750*. Princeton, NJ: Princeton University Press, 1938. 124–40.

Wolf, A[braham], ed. *The Oldest Biography of Spinoza*. New York: The Dial Press, 1928.

Vrain Lucas' Hoaxes

The hoaxes of Denis Vrain Lucas (also Vrain-Denis Lucas or Vrain Lucas), perpetuated largely against the mathematician Michel Chasles, must rank near the most incredible. Chasles' intellect should have, but did not, protect him against the "original" autograph letters he was offered by Lucas.

In 1851, Lucas, a completely self-educated young man from Lanneray in the Loire region of France, moved to Paris. He was interested in history, but also wrote poetry. He took a job in the offices of a geneologist, researching coats of arms. Here he evidently learned something about human vanity—which he would utilize to his advantage later. His opportunity came when he met Michel Chasles, a mathematician and a trusting man. Chasles was a collector of autographs and books, which Lucas endeavored to supply to him.

Chasles later said that he thought Lucas would be incapable of deceiving him, nonetheless Lucas did. Soon he was showing Chasles letters from great men and women of the past, including Joan of Arc and Charlemagne. Lucas claimed that these letters had come from the collection of Blondeau de Charnage, whose collection was lost in a shipwreck enroute to America. In the course of a few years, Lucas sold him 27,472 letters for 150,000 francs. The letters' authors included Sappho, Virgil, Julius Caesar, St. Luke, Aristotle, Montaigne, and Rabelais. They all wrote in French and always on the same paper, watermarked with a fleur-de-lis. Each author's historical praise of France appealed to Chasles' patriotism.

Events climaxed when Chasles decided to publish some of the letters in 1867. He shared their contents with the French Academy. Surprisingly, the contents were praised by scholars and all detractors were dismissed. The situation was different in England, however. There, Sir David Brewster denounced the letters to and from Isaac Newton as forgeries. The arguments continued for two years, but the academy pronounced the letters genuine.

In 1869, an official of the French Observatory discovered the text of sixteen of the letters from Pascal and one from Galileo in a book published in 1761. Chasles claimed that the author of that book had stolen his originals without his knowledge. Lucas was always prepared, willing to produce a letter from anybody to anybody, documenting anything that needed to be documented. Chasles was not suspicious. Lucas had been turning out about eight letters a day for almost eight years.

The frenchman Le Verrier finally convinced Chasles that he had been duped. Lucas was arrested and charged with fraud. About $30,000 had been paid for the letters; this was a fortune in the 1860s. In February of 1870, Lucas was sentenced to two years in jail. When Lucas was arrested, he had already written and was preparing to convince Chasles of the authenticity of the next item he had penned. It was the original manuscript (in French, and on the same paper) of Jesus' "Sermon on the Mount," signed by Jesus.

Sources:

Girard, Georges. *Le Parfait Secretaire des Grandes Hommes, ou Lettres de Sapho, Platon, Vercingetorix, Cleopatre, Marie-Madeleine, Charlemagne, Jeanne d'Arc et Autres Personnages Illustres, Mises en Jour par Vrain-Lucas.* Paris: La Cite des Livres, 1924.

Mann, Georg. "Literary Hoaxes Live On!" *Science Digest* (August 1948): 57–61.

Whibley, Charles. "Of Literary Forgers." *Cornhill Magazine* 12 (1902): 625–36.

Other Historical Hoaxes

The Great Berner Street Hoax. In 1810, Theodore Hook made a wager with a friend that he could make sedate, out-of-the-way Berner Street the most talked about street in London. His bet was taken. Hook made all of the arrangements, and this is the sequence of events that an observer on the street, early one morning in 1810, would have seen:

A coal cart pulled up to the door of a widow named Tottingham at number 54 on the street. A dozen chimney sweeps appeared to clean the chimney. They were quickly followed by a hearse and a furniture van. Mourning coaches drew up in a line. Two physicians pulled up in separate vehicles. Then came a dentist and a man who assisted at childbirth. Next came a brewer's van, unloading beer barrels. The street was rapidly becoming clogged, but more vehicles appeared. An organ was delivered. Butlers, maids, footmen and cooks came to the door of the widow's house and tried to gain admittance. Finally, the Archbishop of Canterbury, the Lord Mayor of London, the Lord Chief Justice of England, the Duke of York, and other dignitaries arrived. All wanted to know what was really happening. They had all been summoned by notes. The dignitaries' notes stated that the inhabitant of the house, now near death, had important revelations to make. The physicians had been asked to attend a lady in her illness. The servants had been promised jobs in advertisements. It took most of the day for the police to straighten out the mess. Mr. Hook had succeeded in making Berner Street the most talked about street in London, and he watched the whole thing from an upper story window across the street from the widow's place.

The Libyan Chemical Warfare Plant Fire. On March 14, 1990, the large plant near Rabata, Libya, which was suspected by the Central Intelligence Agency (C.I.A.) and the media to be Muamar El-Khadafi's chemical warfare plant, was reported to be on fire. Libyan security officials reported that the plant burned to the ground. Since the West had sought to stop the Libyans from producing chemical weapons at the plant, sabotage, or perhaps a planned accident, was at first thought to be the cause of the blaze. Later reports said that the main building was "extensively damaged." Several nearby buildings were also damaged. Colonel Khadafi said, "If the current investigations prove that West German intelligence is involved in any act inside Libya, then Germany's economic presence in Libya will be eliminated." Germany was suspected by the C.I.A. of having helped Libya build the factory. An American official said that the "damage was very extensive. They will not be producing anything there for a very long time." By the end of March, U.S. officials were suspecting that the fire might have been a hoax by Colonel Khadafi to fool the West into thinking that the plant was destroyed or put out of production. It later turned out according to the *New York Times*, that the Libyans hauled a large number of used car tires to the plant and set them on fire to produce black smoke. The plant was not seriously damaged, but Khadafi succeeded in delaying demands for an inspection of the plant by foreign investigators.

Father Burgos and the Philippines. Father José Burgos (1837–1872) was a Jesuit priest who lived in the Philippines during the 1872 Cavite Mutiny. The mutiny was a local revolt against Spanish rule at the arsenal across the bay from Manila. The Spanish governor treated the mutiny as if it were a national revolt, and that led to the evolution of the Philippine need for independence. Father Burgos was one of the priests accused of leading the Cavite Mutiny. He was tried by court martial (along with three others), convicted and sentenced to death. The records of the court martial have never been found, but recently uncovered documents show that Burgos was really *not* involved. The writings of Father Burgos, it now turns out, are most likely spurious. Writer John Schumaker has concluded that *none* of the extant works supposedly written by Burgos were authentic. Most appear to be the work of José E. Marco, a Philippine historian. Although Marco also forged other works that were attributed to other notable Philippine writers, it is not clear what his motivation in doing this was.

The Horn Papers. The *Horn Papers* were early records of the history of the area comprising western Pennsylvania, southeastern Ohio, western Maryland and northern West Virginia, from 1765 to 1795. These papers were written or collected by Jacob Horn and transcribed and edited by his great, great, great grandson,

W. F. Horn, of Topeka, Kansas. The papers were published in several newspapers in western Pennsylvania from 1933 to 1936. W. F. Horn wrote to the editors of several papers, telling them of the great amount of historical material he had about the newspapers' local areas. The newspapers *were* interested in printing articles by Horn based on the historical papers, especially after he mentioned that he had plates and descriptions of the lost early Pennsylvania towns of Razortown and Augusta Town. No one locally knew exactly where these towns had been before their destruction, so this was welcome information.

As the *Papers* were published in newspapers, a minority of opposition began to form. So much of Horn's information contradicted what was published in Boyd Crumrine's *History of Washington County, Pennsylvania*. A number of incidents recounted in the *Horn Papers* did not look as if they could have happened, or happened as described. When additional documentation was requested, Horn replied that since the material came from his ancestors' papers, no further authentication was required.

The unearthing of several lead plates with symbols on them in 1936, at the exact site the *Horn Papers* said they would be, greatly strengthened support for the authenticity of the papers. Nobody seemed suspicious of the fact that it was Horn himself who supposedly unearthed the lead plates.

The *Horn Papers* were finally published as a book. A committee of representatives from the historical societies of Pennsylvania, Maryland, Ohio, Virginia and West Virginia was set up simultaneously to look into the authenticity of the papers. The committee's report was published in 1946, one year after the papers were published as a book. Its report (as given by history professors Middleton and Adair) faulted the *Horn Papers* on the following grounds: "1) evidences of ineptitude in copying the original manuscripts, 2) anachronisms and doubtful words and phrases, 3) biographical anomalies, 4) historically incorrect or doubtful statements, 5) internal discrepancies, and 6) internal similarities of documents purporting to be of different authorship."

As an example of "impossible" words for an eighteenth century document, the committee mentioned "hometown," "race hatred," and "frontier spirit." The committee pointed out that a diary, which Horn's records were considered to be, would have to be true throughout, although it did not have to report every event. The writer might be misinformed about something, of course, but "an authentic diary would under no circumstances record the appearance and activities . . . . of a person . . . . known to have been elsewhere or . . . . known to have died." There are many such irregularities in the *Horn Papers.* An example would be the case of Christopher Gist, who is mentioned in the *Papers* until his death in 1769. It is known, however, from unimpeachable courthouse death records that Gist died in 1759. Further, when the few papers reputed to be originals (not copies) were examined by document experts, the ink and paper were pronounced to be from the late 1800s. In other words, they were fakes.

And so, the *Horn Papers* turn out to be a hoax. Why and how anyone would devote so much time and energy to the careful production of such a large mass of fake material, is difficult to understand. W. F. Horn never told why he or his agents did the massive forgery.

Sources:

Bridgeman, William S. "Famous Hoaxes." *Munsey's Magazine* 29 (August 1903): 730–34.

Gordon, Michael R. "Plant Said to Make Poison Gas in Libya is Reported on Fire." *New York Times* (March 15, 1990): 1, no. 6; (March 16, 1990): 3; (June 19, 1990): 8.

Horn, W. F. *The Horn Papers: Early Westward Movement on the Monongahela and Upper Ohio, 1765–1795.* 3 vols. Scottsdale, PA: Published by a Committee of the Greene County Historical Society, by the Herald Press, 1945.

Middleton, Arthur Price & Douglass Adair. "The Mystery of the Horn Papers." *William & Mary Quarterly,* 4 no. 4 (1947):409–45.

Schumaker, John N. "The Authority of the Writings Attributed to Father José Burgos." *Philippine Studies* 18 no. 1 (1970): 3–51.

Hoaxes That Were Not Hoaxes

This section is reserved for perhaps the most peculiar of all hoaxes—namely events or things identified as hoaxes, or that were widely believed to have been hoaxes, but which later were proven not to be hoaxes. Among the most famous of these was the "War of the Worlds" Broadcast (See "War of the Worlds," p. 100) by Orson Welles. This was not a hoax because it was made clear at the beginning of the broadcast that the broadcast was fiction, based upon the H. G. Wells novel. It was the fact that many people tuned in after the opening announcement that led to the belief that this was a real news event and resulted in a panic.

Archeopteryx

The first fossil of what would later be called Archeopteryx (literally, "the ancient wing") was found in a Bavarian quarry in 1861. The piece of slate, when split, appeared to have the imprint of a pigeon-sized dinosaur on both sides. This dinosaur, then called a Compsognathus, showed clear marks of a long feather tail, wings, and other feather imprints.

At that time, Darwin's theory of evolution was two years old. Although the discovery of this fossil *did* strongly support the idea of evolution (clearly a transitional form between reptiles and birds), it did not especially support Darwin's version of evolution. The fossil was sold to the British Museum (Natural History) in 1862 by Karl Haeberlein, a German physician. The purchase was quite expensive, and was largely supported by the director of the museum, anatomist Richard Owen, at the time a bitter opponent of Charles Darwin.

The fossil was accepted as authentic for more than 100 years. Then, in 1985, astronomer Fred Hoyle and his co-author, Chandra Wickramasinghe, claimed in the *British Journal of Photography* that the original fossil and another example found a year after the first in the same quarry, were forgeries. It was not the fossils that were hoaxes, said Hoyle, but rather the feathers. They were added, he claimed, by grinding up the same rock, making it into a paste, then applying it to one side of the fossil imprint, and pressing feather impressions into it. The scientific community was outraged at the idea of the hoax. Hoyle could not access the original fossil to examine it carefully.

Hoyle claimed that the motivation for the hoax was to discredit Darwin and Thomas Henry Huxley in their strong support for the theory of evolution. This assumes that the instigator (who Hoyle claims was Richard Owen) was not an evolutionist, but a creationist. Owen's idea would then be for Huxley to loudly support a "new" fossil, then for Owen to reveal it as a fake, thus discrediting Huxley, and by implication, evolution.

Unfortunately, as Stephen Jay Gould has convincingly shown, Owen was *not* a creationist, but simply an evolutionist of a slightly different sort than Darwin or Huxley. In addition, the British Museum (Natural History) conducted extensive tests of the original Archeopteryx fossil. They used a scanning electron microscope and found that 1) there were exactly matched hairline cracks on the surfaces of both halves of the fossil block of stone, showing that the two surfaces were not tampered with, 2) there were no traces of any "cement" (the alleged paste made from ground rock) on either half of the stone slab, 3) the two halves of the slab fit together perfectly, showing that there was no material added to either half, 4) the three more recently discovered fossils of Archeopteryx (found in the 1950s) also showed feather impressions, although not as distinctly, and 5) the fossils showed other distinctly bird-like such as a "wishbone," a perching foot, and a retroverted pubis (tilted back pelvic bone). Thus it was not simply a "dinosaur" upon which feathers could be "grafted." The Archeopteryx fossils are genuine transitional forms, showing the characteristics of both reptile and bird.

Sources:

Charig, Alan, and others "Archeopteryx is Not a Forgery." *Science* 232 (May 2, 1988): 622–25.

Gould, Stephen Jay. "The Archeopteryx Flap." *Natural History* 95 no. 9 (September 1986): 16–25.

Hoyle, Fred and C. Wickramasinghe. *Archeopteryx, the Primordial Bird: A Case of Fossil Forgery.* Swansea, UK: C. Davies, 1986.

Wellnhofer, Peter. "Archeopteryx." *Scientific American* 262 (May 1990): 70–77.

Cannibalism

In 1979, William Arens startled the anthropological world by claiming, in his book *The Man-Eating Myth*, that human cannibalism was never a social custom of an entire tribe anywhere. Of course, individuals driven by desperate hunger or psychosis had occasionally been guilty of this practice. However, Arens claimed that cannibalism was largely a charge leveled by one tribe toward another (often when missionaries were asking), in an attempt to disgrace or discredit.

When extensive literature on the subject is reviewed, it becomes obvious that cannibalism is widespread among animal species. Printed reports from missionaries and explorers testify to the fact that certain tribes either said *they were* cannibals many years ago, *or*, more commonly that their neighboring tribes were *still* cannibals. When Arens looked at these reports he noted that they did not contain *any* eyewitness accounts of cannibalism.

One of the common misconceptions used to "prove" cannibalism as a tribal norm was described in the work of D. Carleton Gajdusek. His study, for which he won the Nobel Prize, was of the disease kuru and its transmission. This disease of the central nervous system *could* be spread by handling the infected brains of those who died of the disease. As a part of the funeral preparations for the victims, their brains *were* handled by their relatives. Whether the slow virus that causes the disease could be spread by *eating* the infected brains is not known, as it is unknown whether the virus could survive passage through the stomach acid. It was thought that ritual eating of the brains of the victims *might* be a method of transmission. Gajdusek only suggested this as a possibility. However, since this was never observed, it is unlikely that the transmission of kuru can be used to document the occurrence of cannibalism. It is much more likely that the transmission of the disease occurs when infected brain tissue is handled and contaminated fingers are rubbed on the eyes or on breaks in the skin.

The first source of cannibalism stories that came to the attention of anthropolgists was the reports of Hans Staden, an explorer who visited the South American coast in the mid-sixteenth century. A sailor on a Portuguese ship, he was shipwrecked and then captured by an Indian tribe (the Tupinambas). Staden claimed that he witnessed these Indians preparing a cannibal feast. Allegedly, Staden was to be able to immediately converse with the Indians in their native tongue, even though his native language was German. Other explorers quote Staden's words as their own in describing *their* visits to the Tupinambas. The tribe was wiped out by the end of the sixteenth century. Much of what Staden wrote is therefore unsubstantiated. Other anthropologists feel that corroborative evidence from other explorers verifies Staden's accounts of the Tupinamba's cannibalism.

Margaret Mead writes about cannibalism in New Guinea in her *Sex and Temperament in Three Primitive Societies.* However, she admits that she did not actually witness any cannibalism among the Mundugumor people, as the practice had been outlawed by the Australian authorities three years before she arrived there.

Arens' comments are carefully analyzed and shown to be mistaken by author Donald Forsyth. He indicates Staden could have understood the Tupi language from the moment he was taken captive, for he was in the jungle dealing with the indians for two years before he was captured. Tupi was then the most prevalent language in Brazil, replaced only in the nineteenth century by Portuguese. Since Staden was not an uneducated "seaman" as Arens claims, one can expect that he could read and write.

Staden's claim regarding the Tupinamba Indians were, in fact, supported by the evidence of other explorers. Others who supported his claims in the sixteenth century included Manuel da Nobrega, Jose de Anchieta, and Pero Correia. The complete citations are given by Forsyth. Evidence is strong in favor of the basic accuracy of Staden's observations.

Arens' statement that there are no other eyewitness accounts of cannibalism is also false. Especially strong is the evidence from Fiji. Marshall Sahlins, in his essay reprinted in Brown and Tuzin's book, discusses the evidence that more than 500 people were eaten during a five year period in the 1840s, as counted by John Hunt, who was in Fiji at the time. Richard Burdsall Lyth also kept a journal in which he noted each of the cannibal feasts that occurred in the 1840s. He was a physician, and recorded in detail the preparation of a body for a feast to which he was an eyewitness.

When the other eyewitness testimonies that Arens apparently missed are added in, tribal cannibalism proves to be a reality among tribes in the last century, and perhaps in the early part of this century.

Sources:

Arens, W[illiam]. *The Man-Eating Myth: Anthropology and Anthropophagy.* New York: Oxford University Press, 1979.

Brown, Paula and Donald Tuzin. *The Ethnography of Cannibalism.* Washington, DC: Society for Psychological Anthropology, 1983.

Forsyth, Donald W. "Three Cheers for Hans Staden: The Case for Brazilian Cannibalism." *Ethnohistory* 32 no. 1 (1985): 17–36.

Kolata, Gina. "Are the Horrors of Cannibalism Fact—or Fiction?" *Smithsonian* (March 1987) 17: 150–70.

Sanday, Peggy Reeves. *Divine Hunger: Cannibalism as a Cultural System,* Cambridge, UK: Cambridge University Press, 1986.

Steadman, Lyle B. and Charles F. Merbs. "Kuru and Cannibalism?" *American Anthropologist* 84 (1982): 611–27.

Cyril Burt

Sir Cyril Burt (1883–1971) was a highly regarded British psychologist. His studies of the effect of heredity on IQ, largely based on studies using twins separated at or near birth, were regarded as classics; then they began to unravel. Burt was accused of fraud and largely discredited. However, that discredit may have been unwarranted, as recent evidence suggests.

The issue of whether IQ is more dependent on heredity or environment is lively. Few definitive studies on the subject had been done until Burt's identical twin separation studies in 1966. The study demonstrated that environmental factors were not correlated with IQ. In other words, heredity was more important than environment. This position is called the "hereditarian position." The opposite viewpoint (that environment is the most important influence upon IQ) is called the "environmentalist position."

Burt has been accused of several major types of fraud. Each of these needs to be examined separately to see if it is valid. The major charges are as follows:

1) Burt invented two or more research assistants (whom he called Miss Conway and Miss Howard), who never existed. He also published papers under their names.

2) Burt's raw data does not exist. His statistics indicate this since the numerical result of his statistical analysis does not change over time, even with more data entered for analysis.

3) Burt's results were calculated backwards from the results he wanted from the data, which he then concocted.

4) These actions were deliberate, calculated fraud, as opposed to mere carelessness.

Burt's twin study was ongoing and long-term. Burt did a great deal of looking to find each of the pairs of twins and test their IQs. Because of this the study, which began with fifteen pairs of twins in 1943, was not completed until 1966, when he had located and tested 148 pairs of identical twins. Of these, fifty-three sets had been reared apart.

A few significant historical events occurred during the long period of time Burt's study spans. The most important of these was World War II since Burt was forced to move his offices several times during the war when London was under German air attack. Burt relocated to Wales. During the moves, Burt claimed that some of his data was misplaced and lost for more than ten years. Assuming this was possible (there *is* evidence that his secretary at the time was an incompetent filer), this could have affected Burt's subsequent actions. A case can be made that it did.

Much of the suspicion against Burt was solidified by Hernshaw's supposedly definitive biography of Burt, published in 1979. Hernshaw had access to Burt's diaries, which was thought to be significant, although subsequent examination of the diaries by others has shown nothing incriminating there. Nevertheless, Hernshaw said that he was convinced that Burt had fabricated his postwar data, since the original data was lost in the bombings. Because of Hernshaw's conclusion, the British Psychological Association declared that Burt was guilty of fraud.

Joynson's biography of Burt reexamined the case for fraud for the first time in 1989. In the biography, Joynson submits that Burt is innocent until proven guilty, and examines anew the evidence offered in favor of Burt's guilt. Joynson argues that if there is plausible explanation favoring Burt's innocence, it should be considered as Burt *was* an honored and towering figure in psychology.

Joynson comes up with the following set of hypotheses. The vast majority of Burt's twin studies data was collected before World War II. Miss Conway and Miss Howard were perhaps unpaid volunteers that helped with the fieldwork. When Burt's department was evacuated to Wales, he extracted some data from his files and published it later, but a good part of the data was misfiled and temporarily lost. After the war, he attempted to continue publishing his data, only to discover that much of the data was missing. When it was finally found, ten years later, Burt was so embarassed at his secretary's incompetence that he refused to publicly state that fact. Instead, he credited his prewar collaborators Conway and Howard and included the previously calculated correlation figures. He failed to indicate the sample sizes that these correlations were measuring. On Burt's death, these old data files were probably destroyed (probably by Burt's coworker Liam Hudson), so Hernshaw never saw them.

While much of this scenario is speculative, it *is* plausible. Although it shows a sloppy approach to old data, it does not involve deliberate fraud. Since Burt may be the uncredited discoverer of applying correlation coefficients as part of factor theory to psychological data (Blinkhorn) some of this sloppiness would appear unforgivable. In fact, some might throw out Burt's results on the twin studies as too subjective, poorly documented, inadequately reported, and perhaps insufficiently rigorous. Nevertheless, some of his conclusions have been supported by better-conducted studies.

It would appear that Burt *could* have been sloppy, faced with missing data, and expedient. He may not have been deliberately fraudulent, and others' accusations of his hoaxing the psychological world may themselves be fraudulent, or at least unjustified. There is no way of definitively settling this matter other than discovering the missing data, or discovering a confession from someone involved in a deception.

Sources:

Blinkhorn, Steve. "Was Burt Stitched Up?" *Nature* 340 (August 10, 1989): 439–40.

Burt, Cyril. "The Genetic Determination of Differences in Intelligence: A Study of Monozygotic Twins Reared Together and Apart." *British Journal of Psychology* 57 (1966): 137–53.

Fletcher, Ronald. *Science, Ideology & the Media: The Cyril Burt Scandal.* New Brunswick, NJ: Transaction Publishers, 1991.

Gillie, Oliver. "Burt: The Scandal and the Cover-Up" in *A Balance Sheet on Burt*, edited by H. Beloff. Supplement to: *Bulletin of the British Psychological Society*, vol. 33 (1980): 9–16.

Hearnshaw, L. S. *Cyril Burt: Psychologist.* Ithaca, NY: Cornell University Press, 1979.

Joynson, Robert B. *The Burt Affair.* London: Routledge, 1989.

Kamin, Leon J. *The Science and Politics of IQ.* New York: John Wiley, 1974.

McAskie, M. "Carelessness or Fraud in Sir Cyril Burt's Kinship Data: A Critique of Jensen's Analysis." *American Psychologist* 33 (1978): 496–98.

Firewalking

Firewalking is not a hoax, yet for hundreds of years skeptics thought that human skin was unable to withstand contact with hot coals. Firewalking exhibitions usually involved preparing a long trough, perhaps ten feet by thirty feet, by burning wood until it was reduced to glowing embers. People would then walk—barefoot—the length of the trough and emerge with no blisters or burns on their feet. Of course, occasionally a person *was* burned, which made it seem that there was trick to it.

Firewalking has been used as a religious ceremony for centuries. When people did not get burned, it was perceived as a sign that the gods were with them. In the Old Testament (Proverbs 6:28), is the question "Can one go upon hot coals, and his feet not be burned?" Isaiah (43:2) answers this by stating that since the Lord redeemed Jacob, he would be protected " . . . when thou walkest through the fire, thou shalt not be burned; neither shall the flame kindle upon thee." The relationship of this to modern firewalking is not clear, as there is no longer a tradition of firewalking in the Judeo-Christian world.

A long tradition of firewalking is known in the Eastern religions, stretching back to Hindu references from 800 B.C. These traditions have extended into the present. There are a number of published reports from this century of observed firewalks in Singapore, Fiji, Sri Lanka, and India. Many photographs and films exist of these ceremonies. It is not a question of whether people *can* walk through beds of hot coals without getting burned, but rather *how* they are able to do so. It was assumed that the feet must be prepared in some way with a chemical solution, or that the coals must be treated in some way. Both of these "explanations" turned out to be incorrect.

The explanation of firewalking is strictly a matter of physics and a bit of psychology. No physical burning occurs because the hot embers or hot rocks have a low heat capacity and poor thermal conductivity. At the same time, human feet have a fairly high heat capacity. The embers are poor retainers of heat and poor conductors of heat, while the feet are slow to heat up. During the quick contact of the feet and the coals, not enough heat is transferred to produce a burn.

An analogy might be made to a cake baking in an oven. Upon opening the oven door when the cake is almost done, one can put one's hand inside the hot oven without getting burned. Although the air in the oven is the same temperature as the cake pan, one can touch the air without getting burned. If one touches the pan, however, one will be burned. All are at the same temperature, but the metal pan has a high heat capacity and a high thermal conductivity, while the air has a low heat capacity and a low thermal conductivity.

One physical principle offered as an alternative explanation for the reason why the feet are not burned is the Leidenfrost effect. This is the "dancing" seen by drops of water upon a hot griddle or other surface. The water "balls up" and is protected from direct contact with the hot surface by a layer of water vapor. The water vapor, a gas, is a relatively poor conductor of heat. So, too, a layer of moisture upon the feet protects them from burning. While some firewalkers wet their feet before the firewalk, others dry them carefully on the theory that a hot ember is more likely to stick to a wet foot than to a dry one. If an ember sticks, it is likely to remain in contact with the foot long enough to produce a burn. It would seem from careful observation of many firewalks by authors Leikind and McCarthy that the Leidenfrost effect is not an important factor in preventing the burning of the feet. Other irrelevant factors include callouses, endorphins, hypnotism, and religious states of grace.

Although people have paid hundreds of dollars for "self-confidence" courses that conclude with a firewalk, it is possible for anyone to firewalk without getting burned—without prior courses or psychological conditioning. To firewalk, a person must keep the feet flat and walk briskly. It also helps to wipe the feet off on grass after reaching safety. Psychologically, it is a matter of self-confidence and calm. If a person self-assuredly walks across the coals without panic or hesitation, one will not get burned.

Firewalking is neither a hoax nor something that science cannot explain. It is merely an action that most people have never actually done. It appears dangerous enough for people to doubt the relatively simple explanation that physics has to offer.

Sources:

Dennett, Michael R. "Firewalking: Reality or Illusion?" *The Skeptical Inquirer* 10 no. 1 (Fall 1985): 36–40.

Leikind, Bernard J. and William J. McCarthy. "Firewalking." *Experientia* 44 (1988): 310–15.

———. "An Investigation of Firewalking." *The Skeptical Inquirer* 10 no. 1 (Fall 1985): 23–34.

Lewis, L. E. "The Fire-walking Hindus of Singapore." *National Geographic* 59 (1931): 513–22.

The Shapira Affair

This is a case in which false accusations of a hoax led to a man's suicide. The objects in the hoax were fragments from ancient scrolls, similar to the Dead Sea Scrolls.

Moses Wilhelm Shapira (1830–1884) was born in Kiev, the Ukraine. He was from a Jewish family, but converted to Christianity after he moved to Jerusalem. He married a Lutheran woman, and had two daughters. His younger daughter, using the pseudonym Myriam Harry, wrote a disguised biography of her father under the title *La Petite Fille de Jerusalem*—The only early source on Shapira. Shapira ran a shop in Jerusalem in which he sold tourist trinkets in the front and rare Judaic manuscripts and books in a back room.

In 1868 a German pastor made an expedition to the east side of the Dead Sea, where he found a black basalt steele, or carved stone, lying half buried in the sand. He dug it up. The stone measured three-and-a-half feet tall, by two feet wide, and was covered with ancient Semitic writing in rows. When translated, the text told of the revolt of King Moab against the Israelites in the ninth century B.C. Shapira heard of the discovery and hoped to make a similar discovery himself. Unfortunately, his knowledge of Semitic linguistics was not adequate. As a result, he became the unwitting accomplice of forgers.

He had already sold the German government pottery inscribed with similar characters, believing that they came from the excavations he sponsored in the area near the Dead Sea, called Dhiban. In fact, the pottery was manufactured near Jerusalem, then planted in the area where his men were excavating.

After hearing from an acquaintance that parts of an old manuscript were found not far from his excavations, he used an intermediary to purchase a number of pieces of the manuscript. It consisted of fifteen strips of parchment, mostly about three-and-a-half by seven inches in size. The parchment was dark, and the writing almost impossible to see. Shapira found that if he moistened the parchment, the writing became more visible. He translated the ancient writing up to the point at which he believed it was an early and variant text of the Old Testament book of Deuteronomy. He sent his transcription to a professor of Old Testament at the University of Halle, who wrote back that his text could not be authentic because it differed too much from the accepted text of Deuteronomy. Shapira agreed, and locked his parchments in a bank vault.

Some years later Shapira read a book on modern biblical criticism. He was astonished to learn of the idea that several different sources were used to compile the five books of Moses. Even Deuteronomy had its Javist and Priestly sources. The possibility that his manuscript of Deuteronomy might be authentic reoccurred to him. He spent hours examining and cleaning the parchment strips that comprised the manuscript.

In June 1881, Shapira departed for Europe to show his manuscript to scholars there. In Berlin, he showed a committee of experts the manuscript and in an hour-and-a-half they decided that the manuscript was "a clever and impudent forgery." They did not tell him so immediately.

Shapira went on to London, writing home that he was much encouraged by his reception. In London, Walter Besant arranged for two leading authorities to examine the parchments. One did an extensive study for the British Museum, which considered purchasing the material. An old enemy of Shapira from France made a cursory examination of a few of the fragments and pronounced them forgeries. The British expert said they must be forgeries because no parchment could survive that long in the damp Palestinian climate. He also claimed that the forger made many errors in the Hebrew, revealing that the forger was a Jew who had learned Hebrew in Northern Europe. The manuscript was pronounced a hoax.

After wandering around Europe for another nine months, trying to defend the authenticity of his manuscript, and receiving only further rebuffs, Shapira arrived at a small hotel in Rotterdam, where on March 9, 1884, he killed himself with a pistol shot to the head.

The tragedy of all of this is accentuated by the fact that Shapira's manuscript was *genuine*. The later discovery of the Dead Sea Scrolls showed that parchment or leather could survive in the environment of a cave for more than a thousand years. The Shapira manuscript was sold at auction by Sotheby on July 16, 1885. The manuscript brought ten pounds, five shillings.

After the Dead Sea scrolls were found between 1947 and 1952, the reason for the experts' confusion became clearer. The Shapira manuscript's text was not intended to be a complete version of Deuteronomy, but rather a compilation of texts from Deuteronomy and other parts of the Torah for a specific purpose.

A similar manuscript was found among the Dead Sea Scrolls. It was an attempt to bring together biblical writing on a particular issue—in the Dead Sea Scrolls' case, about debts and their legal status. With regard to the dark color of the parchment, parts of the Dead Sea

scrolls' parchment are also quite dark. Shapira died in vain; his manuscripts were not hoaxes.

Sources:

Allegro, John Marco. *The Shapira Affair*. Garden City, NY: Doubleday & Co., 1965.

Harry, Myriam [pseud]. *La Petite Fille de Jerusalem*. Paris: Librairie Artheme Fayard, 1925.

"The War of the Worlds" Broadcast

The broadcast of H. G. Wells' "The War of the Worlds" in October of 1938, caused widespread panic throughout the United States. It is considered perhaps the most famous publicly perceived hoax. Yet, this broadcast was *not* a hoax, as the term is used in this encyclopedia. There was absolutely no intention to deceive. It was made clear at the beginning of the broadcast that this was the Mercury Players' dramatization of H. G. Wells' novel. Unfortunately, many listeners missed the beginning of the broadcast. Since the format of the dramatization was that of a newscast, the listeners who missed the beginning thought they were listening to a real newscast. In addition, three announcements were made *during* the broadcast stating that it was fiction.

The high "believability quotient" stems from the fact that it was late in 1938 and radio was just coming into its own as a source for "on the spot" news. H. V. Kaltenborn and Edward R. Murrow had recently begun broadcasts from Vienna and London about Hitler's warlike intentions. The public trusted radio then in a way that neither radio nor televison today would be trusted. This fact alone explained why the most quoted response from people who were asked later *why* they panicked was "I knew it was true because I heard it on the radio newscast."

People packed up clothes, ran into the street in their nightclothes, piled furniture on top of their car, and held wet handkerchiefs over their faces for prevention from gas attacks. Switchboards were tied up, police stations crowded, and traffic snarled. Newspaper articles about the incident went on for three weeks and numbered more than 12,500. Letters to the Federal Communications Commission (FCC) were sixty percent against the broadcast and forty percent in favor. Letters to the radio station WABC, with tie-in to all the CBS network stations across the country, ran 1,086 in favor, and 684 against the show. The Mercury Theater received 1,450 letters, with ninety-one percent favorable and only nine percent opposed to the program. Authorities learned from the public's reaction how to better prepare for real emergencies in the future.

Overlooked in most of the writings about the broadcast of "The War of the Worlds" were two later incidents that happened in Santiago, Chile, when the play was broadcast there in November 1944, and in Quito, Ecuador, when the show was heard on the radio there in February of 1949. In Santiago, there were panic, injuries, and heart seizures. In Quito, the situation was far worse. After the panic, word was spread that the whole thing was a hoax. As a result, a huge angry crowd surrounded the building that housed the radio station and the newspaper, and began throwing rocks. Soon the building was set on fire and nearly destroyed. At least twenty people were killed in the fire, many by jumping from upper story windows, where the radio station was located. The response of the Ecuadorean government was to arrest the director of the newspaper and the two writers of the modified radio script on charges of inciting riot. Some of the rioters were also arrested. In the case of the South American broadcasts, not much warning (if any) that this broadcast was only fiction was announced.

Sources:

Cantril, Hadley. *The Invasion from Mars: A Study in the Psychology of Panic, With the Complete Script of the Famous Orson Welles Broadcast.* Princeton, NJ: Princeton University Press, 1949.

Koch, Howard. *The Panic Broadcast: Portrait of an Event.* Boston: Little, Brown & Co., 1970.

"'Mars Raiders' Cause Quito Panic; Mob Burns Radio Plant; Kills 15." *New York Times* (February 14, 1949): 1, 7.

"Martian Invasion Terrorizes Chile." *New York Times* (November 14, 1944): 1.

"Radio Listeners in Panic, Taking War Drama as Fact." *New York Times* (October 31, 1938): 1, 4.

Zombies

The zombies of old horror movies were cursed by voodoo practitioners, killed, then brought back from the dead to work as slaves of the living in Haiti. Zombies are a quaint piece of folklore, but undoubtedly a hoax. Many were surprised then, when Wade Davis, an ethno-botanist at Harvard, announced the results of his field work in Haiti. His book *The Serpent and the Rainbow* became a best seller and was made into a rather distorted movie. Although scientists don't rely on popular treatments of scientific research, Davis' work *does* give a real basis to the zombie phenomenon. Davis' zombie was never *really* dead, so in that way it is different from its reputation. However, the zombies he and others discovered were *declared* dead (really in a drug-induced cataleptic state), buried, and then dug up again.

According to author Diederich, the Haitian psychiatrist Lamarque Douyon reported on at least three cases of what he considers genuine zombies. These people were all "poisoned" by bocors, or witch doctors, at the request of a family member.

People are made zombies to *punish* them for something they have done or will not do. The poison is absorbed through the skin, or through a cut in the skin. It produces a slow paralysis that lowers the body's metabolic rate in such a way that the heartbeat virtually ceases, no movement is possible, the pupils of the eye are fixed and dilated, and yet the mind is still conscious. Without an electroencephalogram, the person *appears* dead.

Burial must not exceed eight hours or there is danger of suffocation. When the potential zombie is dug up, there is a ceremony wherein others beat of the earth above the casket with sticks. This is said to keep the spirit from returning to the body of the zombie, but it actually seems to calm the rather manic phase of excitement that develops in the victim as he or she comes out of the paralysis phase. The business about zombies serving as slaves is open to dispute. Some former zombies confirm this, others do not.

Interviews with former zombies have revealed that a zombie must be fed a salt-free diet in order to maintain the zombie state. The mind of a zombie is reported to function at a low level; any task seems to be impossible. Giving them salt brings them out of their state, as possibly do other drugs. Recovery of most mental functions may be possible eventually.

Wade Davis tried for quite some time to get a sample of the powder that produces the paralysis. He was defrauded by some bocors, but eventually obtained some *probably* authentic powder. Analysis showed that it contained hallucinogenic extract of a toad's skin, hallucinogenic extract of the plant Datura stramonium, and extract of puffer fish. This extract is a tetrodotoxin, similar to that found in the fugu fish. It is a powerful nerve toxin that produces a creeping paralyis, usually fatal by itself. The other ingredients in the powder serve to moderate its effects.

The idea of zombies is *not* a hoax, but a kind of folkloric explanation of a real phenomenon or condition, slightly distorted by a lack of scientific information. The ingredients in the zombie powder might have uses in modern medicine, especially in surgery. Further work is being done on these compounds with those applications in mind.

Sources:

Davis, E. Wade. "The Ethnobiology of the Haitian Zombie." *Caribbean Review* 12 no. 3 (Summer 1983): 18–21, 47.

———. *The Serpent and the Rainbow.* New York: Simon & Schuster, 1985.

Diederich, Bernard. "On the Nature of Zombie Existence." *Caribbean Review* 12 no. 3 (Summer 1983): 14–17, 43–46.

Koper, Peter. "In Search of Zombies: A Tale of Voodoo Potions and the Curse of Living Death." *Chicago Tribune* (August 21, 1983) Sect. 15: 1, 4.

Other Hoaxes That Were Not Hoaxes

Floyd Collins and the Crystal Cave. Floyd Collins was trapped in Crystal Cave in Kentucky on January 30, 1925. The attempts to rescue him received nationwide publicity. Reportedly, a large boulder was pinning Collins' foot, preventing him from being pulled out of the narrow cave passage in which he was trapped. Many attempts to move him were made in vain. Having a surgeon amputate his foot was discussed, but it was not possible. Collins' body was blocking access to the narrow passage and his foot was too far from the entrance to the cave. As the turmoil at the site continued, stories were printed that Collins' entrapment was a hoax. He was either never in the cave or was quickly rescued. The purpose of the hoax, it was reported, was to advertise cave country. Other newspapers, said that Collins was murdered in the cave. When rescuers finally reached Collins by digging a new shaft from the surface, he was dead—although it is unclear how he died. Collins had died about five days before but was not murdered. His body was left where it was trapped. There was no hoax.

The "Myth" of the Holocaust.

The Holocaust, the methodical killing of millions of Jews by the Nazis during World War II, is a true historical event. It is recent history, involved millions of people, and was heavily documented. While a few people have written that the Holocaust was an exaggeration, the fact that millions of Jews died in the concentration camps at the hands of the Nazis during World War II is supported by the following types of evidence: 1) captured Nazi documents that mention the statistics of the destruction of European Jewry (e.g., the Korherr Reports), or discuss the "final solution" to the Jewish problem, 2) the testimony of several thousand eyewitness prisoners who saw mass killing in the death chambers and the piles of bodies, 3) the testimony of former Nazis, such as Adolph Eichmann, who participated in the genocide, 4) the documents at Yad Vashem in Israel, which record the names and deaths of more than three million Jews, and 5) the photographs—and physical existence—of the death camps themselves, along with uncovered evidence of human remains. Clearly the Holocaust was not a hoax. The motivation of the historical "revisionists" who would deny the reality of the Holocaust is itself suspect.

William Lauder and Milton's Plagiarism. William Lauder who died in 1771 was a Scottish scholar of Latin who sought to prove that John Milton had plagiarized *Paradise Lost* from a variety of ancient poems. Among the techniques that Lauder used to stage his hoax was deliberate falsification of the evidence. He inserted Latin lines into manuscript versions of ancient poems, additions Lauder took from *Paradise Lost.* Lauder then claimed that Milton had taken these "additions" from the ancient poems, when the reverse was true.

John Douglas (1721–1807) exposed Lauder's false charges against Milton. Author Marcuse examined the claim that Douglas was singlehandedly responsible for Lauder's exposure and found that this was not so. Rather, Lauder confessed in a publication entitled *Letter to the Reverend Mr. Douglas Occasioned by His Vindication of Milton* (1751). In 1749, Douglas made his accusations against Lauder in an article in five parts in the *Gentlemen's Magazine.* These articles were later enlarged and published as a book called *Essay on Milton's Use and Imitation of the Moderns in His Paradise Lost* (1749).

Lauder published a list of twenty-five falsifications he had made in his plagiarism charges, appended in his *Letters.* Richard Richardson at Cambridge and John Bowle at Oxford were also responsible for exposing Lauder. John Milton, of course, was completely innocent of any plagiarism in *Paradise Lost.*

Acupuncture. Although acupuncture has been practiced in China for more than 2,500 years, when it was first examined by Western medical authorities in the nineteenth century, it was pronounced a hoax. The "experts" rejected the idea that, for example, sticking a needle into the hand could stop pain coming from a toothache. It was the use of acupuncture analgesia, allowing painless operations to be performed with no other form of anesthesia, that really caught the attention of Western medicine. Using acupuncture in surgery was actually a fairly recent development, dating from about 1960.

When China was opened up to the West after Pres. Richard Nixon's visit in 1972, the interest in acupuncture grew. At first, providers of Western medicine, observing the use in surgery, suggested that acupuncture must be similar to hypnosis. This, however, cannot be the case, as infants and animals can be successfully treated for pain by acupuncture. Acupuncturists disagree about the "points" at which needles should be inserted for pain control. Traditional Chinese acupuncturists do *not* say that the entire body can be mapped out on the human ear. That is an idea from a twentieth-century German acupuncturist. In addition, the Chinese have "streamlined" the number and location of the best "points" during the past generation.

The Chinese theory of *how* acupuncture works is not supported by Western anatomical or physiological knowledge. Identifiable nerve tracts do not run from the "points" to the area whose pain they control. That aside, acupuncture *does* work. It is *not* a hoax, although neither Chinese nor Western medical experts are able to explain *how* it works, although endorphins (natural pain blocking substances produced by the body) may play a role.

Mary Chestnut's Diary. The diary of Mary Chestnut (1823–1886), also published as *A Diary from Dixie*, has been called a hoax, purporting to be the diary of a woman from South Carolina during the Civil War. In the diary she tells of conditions in the South during the War, showing how its affects on the well-to-do and ruling class. The reason the work is neither a diary nor a hoax, lies in the peculiar way in which the finished work was composed.

During the Civil War, Chestnut had only a few minutes each day to make notes of her activities. She did not put in many details, nor any lengthy descriptions of the people she encountered. All of that was done a number of years later after 1876, when she sat down and "fleshed out" her original entries. It was the publishing history of the finished book (Chestnut died long before its publication) that caused some concern that the work was a hoax. Chestnut tried several formats for the finished work before finally deciding on the diary format. She then added to her original entries from memory. However, she found that her original entries from 1862–1863 had been destroyed. Therefore, she reconstructed those entries from memory, and called that section of her book "Memoirs." In short, the first two editions of *The Diary from Dixie* (1905 and 1949) were badly edited and organized, leading to apparent contradictions in the text, which in turn led to the idea that the book was a hoax. The 1984 edition by Woodward and Muhlenfeld amends this problem through meticulous editing. Mary Chestnut was guilty of nothing more than a rather ponderous method of constructing her final written work, but not of a hoax.

The Duckbilled Platypus. The duckbilled platypus, found only in Australia, is a real animal, but when it was first discovered in 1797, it was thought to be a hoax. Stuffed specimens reaching England were thought to be composites (*See* Plant and Animal Hoaxes, p. 259) of several different species. The problem was the combination of a ducklike beak, poison spurs found on the male's rear legs, fur, mammary glands, and a flat beaverlike tail. It was the fact the animal laid eggs (mammals do not lay eggs, with two exceptions, of which the platypus is one), that inspired the most skepticism. The platypus was first described in scientific literature by George Shaw in the *Naturalist's Miscellany*, volume X, in 1799. The first living platypus seen outside of Australia was shown at the New York Zoological Park ("The Bronx Zoo") in 1922. By then, other live specimens had been examined in Australia, so it was apparent that the platypus was *not* a hoax.

Defoe and Madagascar. One unresolved question concerns the authorship of an exploration and travel book called *Madagascar: Or, Robert Drury's Journal* (1729). This book, at first thought to be by Robert Drury, was later widely attributed *as a work of fiction* to Daniel Defoe. Due to the work of historian Arthur Secord, however, scholarly opinion is shifting toward Drury. Secord discovered, by searching public records in England, that Robert Drury *did* exist, and that many factual statements he made in the work can be independently confirmed.

If the work is indeed by Defoe, it is an extremely clever and well-done hoax. If it is by Drury, it is a peculiar book, for he claims to have spent fifteen years in Madagascar yet gets many simple facts about the country wrong. It *is* possible that Drury's information was correct, and the so-called "experts" did not know as much about the early history of Madagascar as they thought. The issue is yet to be resolved.

Sources:

Griffiths, Mervyn. *The Biology of the Monotremes.* New York: Academic Press, 1978: 1–19, 43–55, 162–81, 209–32.

Klarsfeld, Serge, ed. *The Holocaust and the Neo-Nazi Mythomania.* New York: Beatte Klarsfeld Foundation, 1978.

Lesy, Michael. "Dark Carnival: The Death and Transfiguration of Floyd Collins." *American Heritage* 27 no. 6 (October 1976): 34–45.

Lynn, Kenneth S. "The Masterpiece that Became a Hoax." *New York Times Book Review* (April 26, 1981): 9, 36.

Marcuse, Michael J. "The Scourge of Impostors, the Terror of Quacks: John Douglas and the Expose of William Lauder." *Huntington Library Quarterly* 42 no. 3 (1979): 231–61.

Pomerantz, Bruce and Gabriel Stux, eds. *Scientific Bases of Acupuncture.* Berlin and New York: Springer Verlag, 1989.

Secord, Arthur W. *Robert Drury's Journal and Other Studies.* Urbana, IL: University of Illinois Press, 1961: 1–71.

Woodward, C. Vann and Elisabeth Muhlenfeld. *The Private Mary Chestnut: The Unpublished Civil War Diaries.* New York: Oxford University Press, 1984: especially introduction, ix-xxix.

Impostors

Impostors are people who pretend to be someone they are not. Actors and actresses are impostors of a sort, but audiences are aware that they are playing a role. True impostors, as considered here, do not reveal their assumed identity. In fact, they would be annoyed to be unmasked. They do not act for entertainment, but are motivated by complex and varying situations. The actions and true identity of the better-known or more audacious impostors will be examined in this article.

Imposture has a long history. Impostors have been around at least since Old Testament days. The case of Esau and Jacob (Genesis 27:19–27), where Esau impersonates his brother Jacob to fool their father Isaac exemplifies the ancient history of imposture.

The most skillful—or perhaps lucky—impostors are never unmasked. Since all incidents of imposture are not known, it is difficult to estimate its frequency. In many cases, the unmasking took place long after the act was completed. Sometimes truth was revealed by voluntary confession. In a number of other cases, courts have ruled that a person was an impostor, but no confession was ever made. People have opted for long jail terms rather than admit that they were impostors. Their motivations can include money, power, sex, fame or ego gratification.

Psychiatrists Deutsch and Greenacre have examined the psychology of the impostor in some depth. Only the most unusual, or recent cases will be covered here.

Anastasia and Anna Anderson

Anna Anderson claimed to be Anastasia, daughter of Czar Nicholas II. The immediate Romanoff family was supposedly shot to death in the cellar of a house in Ekaterinburg in the summer of 1918. Anastasia alone may have survived, falling down at the first shots, then shielded by her sister's body.

Anna Anderson's story allegedly begins, in 1920, three years after the shooting, when a bedraggled woman was pulled by the police from a Berlin canal. She had tried to kill herself. She was taken to the hospital, with no identification papers or money. The next day, the patient was transferred to the Dalldorf Psychiatric Hospital. Three psychiatrists said she was in deep depression, probably affecting her memory. Weeks later, still in the psychiatric hospital, an inmate read an article about the Czar's murder. There was a picture of Anastasia included. The inmate noticed that the nameless patient in the next ward closely resembled Anastasia, especially given the three years difference between the time the photograph was taken and now. The hospital doctors were informed and they called one of the former Czarina's ladies-in-waiting, now living in Berlin. She came to the hospital to meet the patient. There was no doubt—the nameless patient was the Princess Anastasia.

From that point on, the story changed. Shortly afterward, Anna Anderson (as she later called herself for privacy), suddenly had her mental block lifted. She remembered falling down at the time the family was shot in the basement of the house, but then remembered nothing until awakening in a cart driven by two soldiers. The cart continued via backroads for a number of days, after which she heard mention that they had crossed the Romanian frontier. The two soldiers were brothers, Alexander and Serge Tschaikovsky. They were present at the execution and were Red Guards (anti-Czarists), but were still loyal to the Czar. When they saw that Anastasia was still alive, they wrapped her body in a blanket and put it into a cart instead of into the truck bound for the burial site.

In Romania, Alexander and Anastasia were married. That is why Anna Anderson often called herself "Mrs. Tschiakovsky." She had a child, but within a year, her husband was mysteriously shot on the street

Anastasia Romanoff (age 17).

and died. The baby was placed in an orphanage, and Anna went with her brother-in-law to Germany. She lived from the sale of jewels she had stitched inside her undergarments, but in Germany, she sold the last of these. The brother-in-law went out one day and never returned. After searching for him for many hours, she came to a bridge from which she impulsively threw herself into the canal.

For the next seven years, after her "discovery" as Anastasia, she was in and out of hospitals and nursing homes, still recovering from the after-effects of the stress she had been through. Thorough physical examination showed that Anna had the following characteristics that Anastasia also had: bunions, a small scar on the right shoulder from the removal of a mole, a scar on the left hand middle finger, and one on the forehead (both from childhood accidents). On the other hand, she could not speak a word of Russian. She claimed that the amnesia caused her to forget it, but there were unconfirmed reports that she spoke Russian in her sleep.

In 1927, a private detective claimed that Anna was really a peasant girl named Franziska Senanzkovsky. She disappeared in Berlin three days before Anna was found in the canal. Franziska's landlady was found and identified her. Anna denied the identification and left for the United States. There she stayed with her cousin,

Princess Xenia. Xenia, who had not seen Anastasia since they were small children, agreed that Anna *was* Anastasia. She remembered where and when they had played together as children.

In an attempt to collect the Czar's fortune, Anna Anderson returned to Europe and filed the first of many lawsuits. It was not until 1967 that the final verdict of the German courts was rendered; her claims were all rejected. After retiring in the Black Forest of Germany, while her claims were considered, at age sixty-seven she married an American history professor named John Manahan. She lived with him in Charlottesville, Virginia, until she died in her 80s in 1984. She insisted to the end that she was Anastasia. Also in favor of her claim was the agreement of at least a dozen Romanoff relatives, although several others, including her Swiss tutor and her godmother, rejected her claims. An ear identification test was done by Moritz Furtmayer. This "PIK" test, which he claimed was as definitive as fingerprints in identifying a person, was done in 1977. Using a good photograph of the real Anastasia's ear, a comparison was made with Anna Anderson's. The results showed that Anna Anderson was Anastasia.

The answer to the question was recently revealed. In a front page article in the *Sunday Times* of London, writers Bahn and Rayment reported that the graves of Czar Nicholas II and his family were discovered and opened in Russia. Among the skeletons found at the site was one identified as Anastasia. She had been stabbed by a bayonette.

The remains, found near the assassination site at Ekaterinburg, were those of eleven bodies, as was reported in the first investigation of the killings in 1919. The bodies identified as the two daughters, Tatiana and Anastasia, were found just outside the pit holding the other nine bodies. This was interpreted by archeologists at the scene as evidence that the daughters were still alive after the shooting, protected from the bullets by the jewelry that they had hidden in their underclothes. That was why the bodies were not thrown in the pit in the forest near their home, but stabbed with bayonettes by the side of the pit. Previous reports were correct, indicating that the bodies were stripped and burned, doused with acid, and hidden when the ground above the site was crushed by driving a heavy truck over it several times.

More detailed forensic studies have been promised, in which the DNA in hair samples from the real Anastasia will be compared to bone DNA from the skeleton that is thought to be hers. Without having these results, it still seems likely that Anna Anderson was an impostor.

Sources:

Bahn, Paul and Tim Rayment. "Remains of Tsar and Family Found in Forest Grave." *London Sunday Times* (May 10, 1992): 1, 22.

Barringer, Felicity. "The Czar? Sverdlovsk Keeps Its Secrets." *New York Times* (September 23, 1991): A-12.

Botkin, Gleb. *The Woman Who Rose Again: The Story of the Grand Duchess Anastasia.* New York: Fleming Revell, 1937.

Kurth, Peter. *Anastasia: The Riddle of Anna Anderson.* Boston: Little, Brown & Co., 1983.

Lovell, James Blair. *Anastasia: The Lost Princess.* Washington, DC: Regnery Gateway, 1991.

Nogly, Hans. *Anastasia.* London: Methuen, 1959.

Summers, Anthony and Tom Mangold. *The File on the Tsar.* New York: Harcourt Brace Jovanovich, 1978.

Wilton, Robert. *The Last Days of the Romanovs.* New York: G. Doran, 1920.

Emperor Joshua Norton.

Emperor Norton I

Joshua Abraham Norton (1818–1880), also known as Norton I, Emperor of North America and Protector of Mexico, was a colorful American character. Whether he was a hoaxer as well, is now difficult to say. He was rational, all his life, with the single exception of the legitimacy of his emperorship. Whether his refusal to discuss his emperorship rationally was a clever way to maintain his ruse or not is open to question. Most writers have said he was insane. It seems unlikely however, that an insane person would have acted as he did or been as successful in an emperor role. All that separates Norton from a hoaxer is the question of his sanity. Regardless, Norton was a sort of imposter and was therefore included here.

Norton was born in England to a Jewish family, but was taken to South Africa by his parents when he was a small child. The details of this period of his life are rather obscure, but he left the Jewish faith as he grew up. Perhaps the only important fact that has been unearthed about his South African years (he left at thirty-one), was that at this time Norton lived in Cape Town. Also living there was an elderly German named Isaac Moses, a long-retired captain who walked around town in a faded army uniform, ate at the officers' mess, and slept in the old barracks. Everyone saluted him and treated him with respect.

In 1849, Joshua Norton embarked on a ship bound for Rio de Janeiro and finally to California. He arrived there with *some* money (often stated to be $40,000) and became a partner with Peter Robertson in the firm of Joshua Norton & Company, general merchants.

Norton dabbled in real estate and in the rice market. At first he did well and in 1851, he was reportedly quite wealthy. Then he tried to corner the rice market in San Francisco. Rice was scarce because China had just banned its export due to internal famine. Norton found out that Peruvian rice was available and bought it at a good price, but still less than he could sell it for on the open market if the scarcity continued. Norton invested much of his fortune in the rice, but the bottom fell out of the market as two ships loaded with rice arrived in San Francisco. Norton was wiped out financially. He soon staged a partial comeback as a commission agent, handling other people's goods. In 1856, he filed the equivalent of a bankruptcy petition, listing $55,000 in liabilities and only $15,000 in assets. In 1857 and 1858, his finances grew worse.

In 1859, Norton left a document at the editorial offices of the San Francisco *Bulletin* newspaper, asking that it be published. It was a proclamation, as follows:

At the premptory request of a large majority of the citizens of these United States, I, Joshua Norton, formerly of Algoa Bay, Cape of Good Hope, and now for the past nine years and ten months of San Francisco, California, declare and proclaim myself Emperor of these United States, and in virtue of the authority thereby in me vested, do hereby order and direct the representatives of the different States of the Union to assemble in the Musical Hall of this city on the 1st day of February next, then and there to make such alterations in the existing laws of the Union as may ameliorate the evils under which the country is laboring, and thereby cause confidence to exist, both at home and abroad, in our stabilty and integrity. (signed) NORTON I, Emperor of the United States.

The paper printed the proclamation under the headline "Have We an Emperor Among Us?" His proclamations abolished the federal Congress, then the California Supreme Court, and finally discharged the present Governor of Kentucky and replaced him with another man. The readership of the newspaper increased because of the proclamations. Finally, Norton I, seeing that his order to disband Congress was not being obeyed, ordered the Commander-in-Chief of the army to clear the halls of Congress. Norton then dissolved the Republic of the United States, in a proclamation, and established an absolute monarchy under his direction. The only effect of these proclamations was that Norton was evicted from his boarding house and moved elsewhere.

In 1861, Norton decided to wear a uniform befitting his rank, so he assembled one. It consisted of blue pants and tunic, a sword, a tall beaver hat with feather plumes, gold epaulets and buttons, plus a fresh flower in his buttonhole.

For the next twenty years or so, Norton I was a San Francisco attraction. He walked many miles each day, often accompied for the first few years by his two dogs, Bummer and Lazarus. They were devoted to him and to each other, and would wait to share the food he got from the many restaurants that in those days offered him a free meal with a purchased drink. Although it has been reported that Norton had free food at any restaurant he wanted by a sort of silent agreement among the restauranteurs of San Francisco, this was not really the case. It is not mentioned in any contemporary source about Norton, and was only reported after his death.

Norton I arranged for a new uniform when the old one became too frayed. He also issued "bonds," usually for fifty cents face value. Interested parties promised a pay back of fifty cents in about ten years, with interest. Unfortunately, none of them were paid off, but rather replaced with new bonds when the old ones came due.

Norton lived in a simple rooming house and did not become wealthy through his activities. In fact, he barely scraped by. Yet for more than twenty years he was able to live off the largesse and goodwill of the San Francisco community. In fact, he became so popular that practical jokers forged new Norton I proclamations and had them published in the newspaper. Today, his published proclamations are easily mistaken for the fake ones. Generally, the "authentic" proclamations are much better written than the fakes.

Norton read several newspapers daily and was often a participant in public debates. He was considered well-informed about world events, and generally knowledgable. If he was insane, his intellect seems to have remained intact.

Each morning as he left his lodgings, Norton stopped to have a slightly wilted carnation pinned on his lapel by the neighborhood flower seller. This, in turn, allowed that vendor to post a sign on his flower barrow saying "By Appointment to Norton I." Many restaurants also advertised the fact that Norton I ate there. Both Mark Twain and Robert Louis Stevenson used Norton as a character in their fiction.

On January 8, 1880, Emperor Norton was walking through the rain on his way to attend a lecture at about 8 P.M., when he evidently suffered a heart attack or stroke. He collapsed on the pavement and died. When his body was taken to the morgue he had a $2.50 gold piece and about $3 in silver coins on him, as well as a number of unissued "bonds." Also present were a number of telegrams from famous people, most of them sent by other hoaxers. Among the "senders" were Czar Alexander II of Russia and the President of France.

The newspapers heavily covered Norton's death. He had become one of the city's most popular tourist attractions. More than 10,000 people attended Norton's funeral. The funeral expenses, including his burial in the Masonic Cemetery were paid for by charitable contributions. Years later, the body was moved to Woodlawn Memorial Park in Colma, when the Masonic Cemetery was demolished. His monument reads "NORTON I EMPEROR OF THE UNITED STATES AND PROTECTOR OF MEXICO—JOSHUA A. NORTON 1819–1880."

Supposedly, "Emperor Norton" brand cigars and coffee are still available in San Francisco.

Sources:

Cowan, Robert Ernest. "Norton I Emperor of the United States and Protector of Mexico." *California Historical Society Quarterly* 2 (1923): 237–245.

Dressler, Albert. *Emperor Norton.* San Francisco: Albert Dressler, 1927.

Drury, William. *Norton I: Emperor of the United States.* New York: Dodd, Mead & Co., 1986.

Lane, Allen Stanley. *Emperor Norton, the Mad Monarch of America.* Caldwell, ID: The Caxton Printers, 1939.

Ferdinand Waldo Demara

Ferdinand Waldo Demara (1922–1982) has been called "The Great Impostor." Demara had claim to this title, as he successfully impersonated many individuals including a surgeon, psychologist, college dean, professor, Trappist monk, and dentist.

Demara grew up in Lawrence, Massachusetts. He ran away from home at age sixteen to join a Trappist monastery. He stayed there for two years, finally finding the discipline too rigorous. He then enlisted in the U.S. Army. Assigned to Kessler Field in Biloxi, Mississippi, he realized almost at once that he had made a mistake. The army was coarse; soon Demara discovered that the orderlies who rounded up recruits for transfer to other units seemed to avoid the worst duties. Soon he was masquerading as an orderly, complete with fake armband, clipboard, and officious air. This marked the beginning of Demara's life of imposture.

Demara was then invited to the home of a fellow soldier, and shown the soldier's diplomas and certificates by his proud mother. This inspired Demara to adopt the soldier's identity by using the credentials he was shown—an idea he used repeatedly later in life. Demara went back to the house of the soldier and purloined enough material to create a new identity for himself as that soldier. Under the new identity he obtained admission at another monastery. His imposture went well until he was recognized by a former student at the first Trappist monastery he joined.

Demara fled after only a week. He enlisted in the U.S. Navy and was sent to Hospital School just after the bombing of Pearl Harbor. At Hospital School, he received first aid training which interested him in the medical field. When his application to receive advanced training was turned down on the grounds that he did not have enough education, he obtained the credentials of Dr. Robert Linton French, a psychologist. Using these credentials, he secured a teaching position in science at a boy's school run by a Catholic order.

Demara stayed one lesson ahead of his pupils. The abbot eventually checked his credentials and Demara was fired. He left, stealing the abbot's car. In Chicago, he started training for the priesthood, but left when it looked as if he would have to go through another rigorous training period including self-denial. Demara, using his psychology "credentials," became dean of the School of Philosophy at Gannon College in Erie, Penn-

sylvania. His grandiose schemes for improving the college (and his position there) led to his dismissal. He then travelled to an abbey in Washington, where he successfully ran a student psychological counseling center. Demara's downfall came when he was appointed deputy sheriff; a background check turned up his criminal past. Demara was arrested and led away in handcuffs—charged with deserting the navy in wartime, a capital crime. He served eighteen months in prison after conducting a memorable self-defense.

Upon being freed, he enrolled as a law student in Boston, completing his first year of law school using the credentials of a biology professor. Demara then left for Maine, where he became a biology teacher at a small college, again using the biologist's credentials. He helped turn the college into a university, but left angrily when he was informed that at the new university *he* would be only an instructor in biology. Demara managed to leave with copies of the credentials of the physician who treated some of the college's faculty. The physician's name was Joseph Cyr.

The "new" Dr. Joseph Cyr enlisted in the Royal Canadian Navy as a surgeon lieutenant. For six months he bluffed his way through diagnosis and treatment without losing a patient, and even performed a number of difficult operations successfully. When his ship was sent to Korea, he removed a bullet near one patient's heart and removed another patients lung that had been pierced by a bullet. When a story was written about his medical triumphs—despite his protests—his past caught up with him. The real Dr. Cyr read the story and knew an imposture was taking place. Demara was dismissed from the navy for entering under false pretenses. The more serious charge, practicing medicine without a license, was not raised in order to spare the navy from charges that it provided improper care.

Demara sold his story to *Life* magazine for $2,500. This turned out to be one of his worst mistakes—one that would resurface. Public knowledge of his appearance and background proved fatal to his impostures. Demara was appointed a prison officer under the name Ben W. Jones. He was soon made warden of the maximum security block at the Huntsville, Texas jail. When a prisoner saw the article in *Life*, Demara's prison career was over. He returned to Maine, where he ran a local school until he was arrested. The local townspeople rallied to his defense, saying what a good teacher he was. The charges were dismissed and Demara left town.

After Robert Crichton's book *The Great Impostor* appeared in 1959, Demara's career as an impostor suffered. After a movie was made of the book, starring Tony Curtis, it was all but impossible to continue the masquerade. Demara used only his own name from then on. He moved to California, where he worked in various youth counseling positions. He was twice charged with child molestation, but was defended successfully by attorney Melvin Belli. Demara's final position was as a visiting counselor at Good Samaritan Hospital in Anaheim, California. He worked there until illness forced him to retire. Demara died at age sixty on June 8, 1982.

Sources:

Crichton, Robert. *The Great Impostor*. New York: Random House, 1959.

"Ferdinand Waldo Demara, 60, An Impostor in Varied Fields." (obituary) *New York Times* (June 9, 1982): Section 2, 16.

Garvey, Jack. "Ferdinand Demara, Jr.: His Undoing Was Usually that He Did So Well." *American History* (October 1985): 20–21.

McCarthy, Joe. "The Master Impostor: An Incredible Tale." *Life* (January 28, 1952): 79–86, 89.

Long Lance

Among the Indian impostors in American history, we can count Grey Owl (*See* Imposters, p. 105) and Long Lance as the most prominent. In the early 1930s Chief Buffalo Child Long Lance (1890–1932) was one of the most popular and recognized American Indians in the United States. He starred in a movie, *The Silent Enemy* (1930), was a war hero, and published a best-selling autobiography in 1928 (*Long Lance*). In fact, this appears to be the only hoax autobiography written by its subject since Psalmanazar (*See* The Native of Formosa, p. 3) wrote his in the 1700s. True, there have been other hoax "autobiographies" (*See* Howard Hughes' Autobiography, p. 72), but this appears to be the only one in the past two centuries that is *completely false*. Frank Harris' (*See* Literary Hoaxes, p. 139) autobiography contained some false incidents, but the basic outline of the author's life was true.

Sylvester Clark Long was born in Winston, North Carolina on December 1, 1890. His parents owned a farm and they were white and Indian, rather than black. Sylvester's maternal great-grandfather was a white plantation owner who kept an Indian woman as a slave and concubine. With him she bore twenty children, among them Sylvester's grandmother. The grandmother, although not black, was born into slavery. The grandmother gave birth to Sylvester's mother, whose father was a neighboring white plantation owner. Sylvester Long's father was reputedly half Indian and half Caucasian, so, he was at least partly Cherokee Indian.

The Longs lived and associated with blacks in Winston, as there was no classification except "white" or "black," and they were not considered white. Sylvester attended black schools, but was unhappy being classified as black. He longed to escape from Winston. The Carlisle Indian School in Pennsylvania seemed to be the solution. He ran away with the circus, and became an adept horse rider. He also learned some Cherokee. Long applied for admission to Carlisle in 1909, reporting his age as eighteen rather than nineteen. He stated that he was of Cherokee origin on his father's side and Croatian origin on his mother's. Sylvester was admitted to the school, where he succeeded. Within a year after graduation, he was calling himself "Long Lance."

After a time at St. John's Military Academy Long Lance applied to West Point via a letter to Pres. Woodrow Wilson. He lied about his age, claiming to be twenty-one when he was actually twenty-four, and his percentage of Indian ancestry. After several genuine letters of recommendation supporting his application, Sylvester was admitted to West Point. The newspapers made much of the first American Indian—"a full-blooded Cherokee"—to attend West Point. However, Sylvester failed three of his six entrance examinations for West Point. This may have been deliberate, as he usually did well in the subjects he flunked on the exams. Perhaps the reason was that he heard that the authorities in Washington were inquiring about his background and he knew that it would not be long before they found out about his real age, which would have disqualified him for admission. His background was also being investigated.

Because of his poor exam grades, he was denied admission to West Point, and joined the Canadian army. Posted to England and then France, he fought in a number of bloody battles in France. Wounded twice, he emerged a sergeant, although newspapers in the United States reported him as a lieutenant.

After discharge in 1919, Sylvester headed for Calgary, Alberta, Canada. While there Long Lance claimed he was born in Oklahoma. After a while, he obtained a job as a reporter on a Calgary newspaper. There he invented stories, about himself and others; he was fired in March, 1922, for setting off a smoke bomb in the office of the mayor of Calgary.

Long Lance then worked for a newspaper in Vancouver, writing stories about the Indians. Finally, in Winnipeg, Long Lance began a public speaking career on behalf of Indian causes and was soon a recognized spokesman. He picked up a chiefdom and became known as "Chief Buffalo Child Long Lance." His "chiefdom" was supposedly of the Blood tribe of Alberta. Long Lance also became a sportswriter for a number of newspapers, and "resident Indian" at the

Banff resort in Alberta. In interviews, his lies ballooned. For example, he became chief of all of the Plains Indians. He was now a Blackfoot Indian, raised in the plains of Western Canada.

Long Lance wrote his "autobiography" in 1928. It was based in part on some articles he wrote for *Cosmopolitan* magazine. It was almost entirely fiction. The book sold well, was well-reviewed, and was probably believed by most. Even Donald Smith, the author of the definitive expose of Long Lance was moved by Long Lance's autobiography when he read it as a boy.

The book's success led Long Lance to his movie role in *The Silent Enemy*, filmed in Canada in 1929. The silent film received good reviews. However, the legal counsel for the film, who was concerned with protecting the studio from bad publicity and scandals, was informed by an Indian that Long Lance was a fake. Long Lance was summoned to the lawyer's office in February of 1930. Confronted with the truth of his North Carolina origins, Long Lance remained adamant in his lies. He "conceded" that he was a Blackfoot and not a Blood Indian from Alberta, but this was merely *another* lie. An on-the-spot investigation in North Carolina cleared Long Lance of the most serious charge against him in the studio's mind—that he wasn't black.

The fear of exposure was with Lance all the time now. On March 19, 1932, he shot and killed himself in Arcadia, California.

Sources:

Long Lance, Chief Buffalo Child [pseud]. *Long Lance.* New York: Cosmopolitan Book Corporation, 1928.

Smith, Donald B. *Long Lance: The True Story of an Impostor.* Toronto: Macmillan of Canada, 1982.

Martin Guerre

The case of Martin Guerre (b. 1525) is one of the most famous and complex of all recorded cases of imposture. A French movie "Le Retour de Martin Giuerre" ("The Return of Martin Guerre") was made of the case, which still continues to be of interest. Although the story told in the film is basically accurate, the facts of the case will be taken from historian Natalie Zemon Davis' book. At least one *major* point is disputed between Davis and another historian, Finlay (who may be backed up by court official Coras' original report on the case).

The basic story is simple. A woman named Bertrande de Rols Guerre was married to Martin Guerre. They lived in the village of Artigat in southern France and were married for nearly ten years. Martin Guerre

disappeared in about 1553. Four years later, a man claiming to be Martin Guerre appeared in the village. He looked something like Martin and Bertrande accepted him as her husband. This Martin knew a lot about Martin, Bertrande, and Martin's past life. If he was *not* Martin, he prepared well for his imposture. Bertrande lived with Martin for three years; they had two children. Many people accepted him as the original Martin. When they expressed doubt to Bertrande, she always reassured them that this *was* the original Martin.

Then Martin began asking Bertrande's relatives about how much property she owned and what it was worth. This aroused the suspicions of relatives who informed the authorities that something was amiss. The new Martin (whose real name was Arnaud du Tilh) was arrested and brought to trial for adultery and imposture. He was convicted and sentenced to death by hanging. During the trial, the original Martin Guerre returned to the village. He had lost a leg in battle, but was otherwise recognized and accepted by both the Guerres family—Bertrande—and the villagers. Arnaud du Tilh died insisting that he was Bertrande's legitimate husband.

Martin Guerre had lost his leg fighting for Spain, and against France. (Their home was near the French/Spanish border.) The court, although suspicious of Martin for this reason and for deserting his family long ago, decided not to prosecute him. The court also had to decide whether Bertrande was consciously aware of Arnaud's deception and whether she was a willing participant in adultery. This is the point upon which Davis and Finlay disagree. Finlay thinks Bertrande was an innocent victim, while Davis thinks Bertrande was a willing participant.

As Davis points out in her 1988 rejoinder to Finlay, the court, as reported by Coras, deliberated long and hard over the issue of whether Bertrande was an accomplice. In the end, the judges decided to accept that she had been deceived by Arnaud for more than three years. Still, the court's reasoning seemed more like a pardon than a verdict of innocence. In fact, the court ordered Bertrande to pardon her husband, and to accept reconciliation with him, as she was led too easily into fraud with Arnaud. So, although there is room for dispute, it *appears* that Bertrande may not have been entirely innocent in this matter.

Sources:

Davis, Natalie Zemon. "AHR Forum: The Return of Martin Guerre 'On The Lane.'" *American Historical Review* 93 no. 3 (1988): 572–603.

———. *The Return of Martin Guerre.* Cambridge, MA: Harvard University Press, 1983.

de Coras, Jean. *Arrest Memorable, du Parlement de Tolose* [Toulouse], *Contenant une Histoire Prodigieuse, de nostre temps.* . . . Lyon, [France]: Antoine Vincent, 1561.

Finlay, Robert. "AHR Forum: The Return of Martin Guerre—The Refashioning of Martin Guerre." *American Historical Review*, 93 no. 3 (1988): 553–71.

Outlaw Impostors

The desire to pose as someone else—which hoax authority Curtis MacDougall suggests "often seems to fill an overpowering psychological need"—leads impostors to target not only the noted but the notorious as well. Famous outlaws are especially popular subjects for such imposture.

Many people believe that one of the nation's most infamous outlaws, Pres. Abraham Lincoln's assassin was not the man shot in a Virginia barn on April 14, 1865. Over subsequent decades, some forty persons, shortly before their death, "confessed" that they were John Wilkes Booth. One even confessed posthumously. Known as David E. George, he committed suicide in 1903 at Enid, Oklahoma. Finis Bates, a shrewd lawyer from Memphis, Tennessee, obtained George's long-unclaimed, but remarkably embalmed body, identified it as John St. Helen, and claimed that—years before— St. Helen had confessed his secret identity to Bates. Bates published an account of this "true" story, *The Escape and Suicide of John Wilkes Booth,* and for many years the mummy of "Booth" was exhibited at carnival sideshows. Although it superficially resembled the actor-turned-assassin, even carrying fractures and wounds similar to Booth's, the mummy was investigated and debunked by the *Dearborn Independent* in 1910.

The death of outlaw and Missouri bank robber Jesse James was also popularly doubted, despite a positive identification by a coroner's jury. The corpse identified matched James' in several important respects, including two scars on the right side of the chest, and the missing tip of the middle finger on the left hand. Scarcely a year had passed since the reported death however, when a Missouri farmer claimed he had seen James alive. Eventually, men claiming to be James came forward. According to folklorist Richard M. Dorson, "In the tradition of the Returning Hero, who reappears after his alleged death to defend his people in time of crisis, ancient warriors have announced that Jesse James lives in their emaciated frames." Some seventeen such claimants have been counted. They were especially popular during the late 1920s and 1930s as part of travelling tent shows.

Kentucky writer Joe Creason tells how one forgetful James pretender showed up in a Kentucky town whose bank had once been robbed by the James gang. "Are you Jesse James?" the U.S. Marshall asked. When the man avowed that he was, the marshall pulled an old, yellowed document from his pocket. "In that case," he said, "I have here a warrant for your arrest, charging you with the robbery of the Bank of Columbia and the murder of the cashier." The confessed outlaw paled. "However," continued the marshall, "on the off chance that you just might not be Jesse James, I'm giving you ten minutes to get out of town." Replied the impostor, as he fled "Marshall, I can beat that time with five minutes to spare!"

The last man to claim that he was James was one J. Frank Dalton. Although his story was inconsistent and inaccurate, and his handwriting was unlike James', Dalton managed before his 1951 death in Texas, to convince many people that he was the legendary American outlaw.

Dalton's success with James was paralleled by a Texan who insisted he was Billy the Kid. The claimant—Ollie L. "Brushy Bill" Roberts, who died at Hico, Texas in 1950, only a week before his nineteenth birthday—was the best known of several claimants. Supposedly, the twenty-two-year-old Kid, whose real name was William Bonney, escaped the trap set for him by Sheriff Pat Garrett at Fort Sumner, New Mexico, and subsequently lived to a ripe age in the guise of "Brushy Bill." Skeptics pointed out that Roberts had also claimed to be Frank James. Using authenticated photographs of the Kid and "Brushy Bill" to compare twenty-five facial "landmarks," a computer photo analysis proved that the two men were clearly two different individuals. In discussing the "Brushy Bill" case—and the claim that Butch Cassidy survived his death in a shoot-out in Bolivia in 1908, dying in Seattle as a businessman in 1937—author Gregory Byrne concluded, "It seems bad guys, or at least their legends, don't want to die."

Joe Nickell

Sources:

Byrne, Gregory. "Did Billy Really Die a Kid?" *Science* 243 (February 3, 1989): 610.

"Computer Upholds Billy the Kid Legend." *Lexington Herald-Leader* (March 4, 1990).

Creason, Joe. *Joe Creason's Kentucky.* Louisville: The Courier-Journal and the Louisville Times, 1972: 230.

Dorson, Richard M. *American Folklore.* Chicago: University of Chicago Press, 1959: 243.

MacDougall, Curtis. *Hoaxes.* New York: Dover Books, 1958: 164–65.

Billy the Kid.

Settle, William A., Jr. *Jesse James Was His Name.* Lincoln, NB: University of Nebraska Press, 1977.

The Tichborne Claimant

The Tichborne Claimant case was a complex and puzzling one in the nineteenth century. In 1854, the ship *Bella* left Rio de Janeiro for Jamaica and New York. On board was Roger Charles Doughty Tichborne, who was twenty-five years old. Tichborne had gone to South America a year earlier to forget his cousin, Kate Doughty, with whom he was in love, but whose mother refused to let marry so close a relative. He was the heir to a large British fortune. The ship *Bella* sank off South America. All aboard were presumed lost.

Twelve years passed since the *Bella* sank. Roger Tichborne's mother never gave up hope that Roger might still be alive. She advertised in the newspapers in Britain and abroad for news of her son. Many sailors came to the Tichborne home with tales, usually second or third hand, that kept Mrs. Tichborne's hopes alive. She finally saw an advertisement by a missing persons firm in Australia, where several British people had disappeared. Mrs. Tichborne described her son, and the search firm came up with Thomas Castro, a butcher. He was willing to impersonate Tichborne, although he eventually became convinced that he *was* Tichborne. In Australia, Castro ran into a former Tichborne servant,

Andrew Bogle. Castro pumped Bogle for useful information—information that would prove critical to the initial success of the imposture.

Castro made many mistakes in "remembering" his past life, both before and after he went to England. His mother overlooked his errors, so joyous at the return of her son. Castro went to England with Bogle at the Tichborne's expense in 1866. By now Bogle was convinced that Castro was the missing Roger Tichborne. Although at first "Roger's" facts about his early life were confused, his mother helped him with his old diaries and letters. Soon "Roger" was more familiar with the facts of his life.

Many Tichborne relatives and friends agreed that the claimant was indeed Roger Tichborne. However, others, including his former tutor and cousin Kate, came out against him. Castro claimed that he was on one of the two lifeboats of the *Bella* that were launched. After two days, the people on his lifeboat were rescued by a British ship bound for Australia. Although there was such a British ship, no one could confirm that it had picked up any survivors of the *Bella*. Once in Australia, he adopted the name Thomas Castro because he liked it and had known a man of that name in South America.

Although Castro resembled some of the Tichbornes, he was grossly fat; Roger had been quite slim fourteen years earlier. In addition, Roger spent his earliest years in France; French was his native language. He did not learn English well until he was fifteen. Yet, the claimant knew no French. Roger had a tattoo, the claimant had the remains of what appeared to be a different tattoo.

The case went to the courts, as a posthumous son of Roger's brother who stood to inherit the Tichborne fortune if Roger were really dead. The case remained in the British legal system for the longest time of any case until then. More than 100 witnesses said Castro was Roger. It was pointed out in court that when he came to England, Castro first visited a family named Orton in Wapping. A man was found who named the claimant as his brother, Arthur Orton. Some independent evidence supported the idea that Castro's real name was Arthur Orton, and that he travelled from Britain to Chile, and finally to Australia.

After the protracted trial, Castro was found guilty of perjury and sentenced to fourteen years in jail. Many other people connected to the case also went to jail for perjury or contempt of court. After serving ten years in jail, he was released. For the next eleven years, he toured England giving talks about the terrible miscarriage of justice that had befallen him. In May of 1895, he confessed his imposture in a publication called *People*. He died in 1898. On his deathbed, Orton recanted his confession, saying he had only made it for money. He

The Tichborne claimant, otherwise known as Arthur Orton.

claimed he really was Roger Tichborne. A careful evaluation of the evidence, has confirmed that he really was Arthur Orton. Roger Tichborne evidently did die when the *Bella* sank.

Sources:

Atlay, J[ames] B. *The Tichburne Case.* London: W. Hodge, 1916.

Finger, Charles Joseph. *Romantic Rascals.* Freeport, NY: Books For Libraries, 1969: 127–56.

Maugham, Lord [F.H.]. *The Tichborne Case.* London: Hodder & Staughton, 1936.

Woodruff, Douglas. *The Tichborne Claimant.* New York: Farrar, Straus & Cudahy, 1957.

Other Impostors

Billy Tipton. Jazz musician Billy Tipton (1914–1989) was noted for his saxophone and piano playing, often with the Billy Tipton Trio. When he died on January 21, 1989, it was discovered that Billy Tipton was a woman. His three adopted sons were shocked, and Kitty Oakes—his wife from 1960 to 1979—would not talk about their life together. Tipton, ill towards the end of his life, would not go to a doctor, perhaps to guard his true sexual identity. Tipton evidently adopted the male persona because it was difficult for women to become professional jazz musicians when Tipton began in the music business.

Dr. James Barry. Dr. James Barry (1794–1865) was a British army physician who rose in the ranks to become the Inspector General of the British Army Medical Department. Barry was a legitimate physician—a graduate of Edinburgh University's medical school. Barry fought at least three duels. He had one major secret and that was discovered upon his death. Barry was a woman. Barry managed to keep the secret through fifty years of army service. She had evidently adopted a male role before admission to medical school, as women were not admitted to medical school in 1808. Nothing could be learned about Barry before medical school, despite intensive army inquiries. Barry went directly into the army after graduating from medical school. She fulfilled service in the Peninsular War and in Capetown South Africa. She had a high-pitched voice and dyed hair, but that was not that unusual. She told of her success as a ladies' man, but not many believed her.

She was largely responsible for the legislation that required druggists to be given an examination and licensed. The post-mortem examination showed that Dr. Barry had given birth to a child at least once, but no one knew when. She was buried with full military honors at Kensal Green Cemetery in London.

Deborah Sampson. Deborah Sampson (1760–1827) distinguished herself in combat during the Revolutionary War as a male soldier named Robert Shurtliff. Sampson was born in Massachusetts. Her father died when she was five, and her poor mother had to "bind her out" as a servant until she was seventeen. At that point, Deborah became a school teacher until she decided to enlist in the Continental army in 1781. She was tall and strong, with a large frame, so the masquerade was not difficult on a surface level. Sampson simply dressed in a man's suit of clothes and cut her hair, enlisting in Captain Webb's company of the Fourth Massachusetts Regiment.

Sampson served with great valor, receiving several commendations, and suffering a sword wound to the head and a bullet through the shoulder. When a bout with "brain fever" caused her hospitalization, her true sex was discovered by the army physician. After her recovery, she was sent to George Washington's headquarters in Philadelphia with a letter to him explaining the situation. Washington saw that she was honorably discharged from the army with a pension. A life pension was later given her by Congress. Sampson returned to her hometown in Massachusetts. She married Benjamin Gannett in 1784, and had three children. Deborah Sampson successfully achieved her dream of

Deborah Sampson.

serving as a soldier in battle by means of her clever imposture.

Caspar Hauser. Caspar Hauser (1812?–1833) remains a mystery. It is still unknown whether he was an impostor, the illegitimate son of royalty, or merely an abused child. Hauser wandered into Nuremberg, Germany on May 26, 1828. He could hardly speak German and was unable to read or write. Hauser was educated as a special project by Georg Friedrich Daumer, who found Hauser a bright pupil. Although Hauser was unable to shed much light on his early life (he claimed he was confined in a cell without human contact), he became almost a polite gentleman. In 1833, he was stabbed fatally in an unsolved attack in a park. The mystery of Hauser's real identity has never been resolved; it is unclear whether he was an impostor or not.

David Hampton. A young black man named David Hampton claimed several times that he was the son of actor Sidney Poitier in the 1980s. Poitier has six daughters, but no sons. Hampton also approached wealthy parents of college students, claiming he was a friend of their son or daughter from college. He was then usually invited to dinner and as an overnight guest. He also managed to "borrow" as much as $350 from his victims.

Hampton's exploits started when he obtained the address book of a Connecticut College student, and

began contacting the parents of the student's friends. Hampton was eventually arrested for attempted burglary and grand larceny. His story was made into a Broadway play, "Six Degrees of Separation." Hampton tried to extort money from the playwright, John Guare, but was unsuccessful. He later filed a civil suit to get money from the proceeds of the play, but again lost. This last suit was not settled until May of 1992, when the New York Supreme Court dismissed it.

Grey Owl. One of the many American Indian hoaxes involved Grey Owl, whose real name was Archie Belaney (1888–1938). Belaney was a strange boy. Born in Hastings, England, he was sent to live with his maiden aunts when he was four, after his parents separated. Belaney had one passion from the very beginning—the North American Indians. When he was eighteen, after a year of being forced to work at an unpleasant job in England, Belaney left for Canada to live with Indians. He was tall and thin, with long hair that he dyed black and skin that he tanned with a rinse of alum. He looked every bit the Indian, except for his gray eyes. He told of being born in Mexico, the child of a Scottish father and an Indian mother. He was soon adopted by the Ojibwe Indians, who taught him everything they knew about woodcraft, Indian lore, and trapping. After World War I, Belaney returned to Hastings under his Grey Owl identity to convalesce. He married his childhood sweetheart, undeterred by the fact that he had a common-law Indian wife and two children.

Grey Owl became an ardent defender of the forests and animals. After his return to Hastings, he wrote four bestsellers: *The Men of the Last Frontier, Pilgrims of the Wild, The Adventures of Sajo and Her Beaver People,* and *Tales of an Empty Cabin.* Strangely, one of Grey Owl's strongest defenders, the British publisher Lovat Dickson, who had written a biography of Grey Owl after Belaney's death, made the necessary investigations to reveal the imposture to the world. Perhaps it was because he had been so badly fooled.

Harry Domela. Harry Domela (1903–?) played a small role in deflating the Germans' high regard for their royal family. Fifteen-year-old Domela lost his father and older brothers in World War I. He wound up on the streets of Berlin, homeless and unemployed. Down and out, he began to call himself Baron Wolf Luederitz, and had doors open to him as soon as people heard the word "Baron." Harry's first attempt at using a title other than his own ended in disaster. He became a "count" for a while, but was discovered and sent briefly to jail.

Next, Domela became "Baron Korff." Attempting to impress people, he made a phone call to the ex-Kaiser's son, Prince Louis Ferdinand, whom he did not know. Fortunately, the prince was not home. Soon,

Harry Domela.

however, word spread that the "Baron" was really the grandson of the Kaiser, namely Prince Wilhelm.

Domela actually bore a resemblance to the prince. In addition, he had learned the appropriate manners and demeanor. Everyone in the region of Thuringia and Prussia *knew* that Harry was really Prince Wilhelm. At each town he visited, he was was called "your highness" and given free lodging and meals. Harry heard eventually that Von Berg, the chief administrator of the Royal Estates was looking for him. Harry worriedly left Weimar, in Thuringia. It was actually another man named Von Berg who was looking for him.

Domela thought that he was a wanted man and knew that any further newspaper publicity would ruin him. He therefore approached the colonel in charge of the district and asked him to keep publicity about "Prince Wilhelm's" visit to the area out of the local newspapers. His request was scrupulously obeyed, thus gaining some additional time for Harry to play the prince.

In January of 1927, the newspapers finally printed the details of his imposture. The public was both amused and ashamed. On his way to board a train after joining the French Foreign Legion, Domela was arrested by two German plainclothes detectives. During his time in prison, awaiting trial, he wrote his autobiography, which became a bestseller in Germany. At his trial,

all witnesses said that they suffered no harm, financial or otherwise, by Domela's imposture. He was sentenced to seven months already served, and released. Domela opened a movie theater in Berlin with the money from his book sales. A movie comedy called *The False Prince*, starring Harry Domela, was made and shown in the theater. Domela disappeared from recorded history in 1930 and no one knows what happened to him.

Princess Caraboo. In 1817, in the British village of Almondsbury in Gloscestershire, a strange woman appeared. She spoke no recognizable language and was dressed in a turban and Far Eastern clothing. No one could communicate with her in anything other than sign language. It was determined that she was named "Caraboo" and that she could write her language, which looked oriental, but was not Chinese or Japanese. A specimen of her writing was shown to Oxford University language professors, who were unable to identify the language. Finally, a Portuguese sailor was found who claimed that he recognized the language as Malay. He could understand some of it, having visited the region.

Princess Caraboo's father was a local king on the island of Javasu in the Malay archipeligo. The princess claimed she was kidnapped by Malay pirates and was kept prisoner on their ship until she jumped overboard into the Bristol Channel. Learned English men visited her to observe her dancing and discuss her country with her through the Portuguese sailor, who acted as interpreter.

Everything fell apart when a young journeyman looking for work came to the village. He was shown the princess, whom he quickly identified as Mary Baker of Witheridge in Devon. He had met Baker earlier while they were both "trampling the countryside." A woman who ran a lodging house also identified Caraboo as Mary Baker at almost the same time. When the lodging house owner confronted Caraboo, she at first tried to bluff, but then confessed. The sailor/interpreter, she admitted, was only another hoaxer who had agreed to cooperate with her. The spoken and written "language" she had used was nonsense she had made up (*See* Native of Formosa, p. 3 for a similar case). Mary Baker was basically a wanderer who went to Almondsbury to raise the five pounds that it would cost to buy her passage from nearby Bristol to America. Surprisingly enough, the woman with whom she had been staying in Almondsbury gave her the five pounds for her trip to America. Mary Baker was last heard from publicly as she boarded the ship "Robert and Ann" for the United States.

Buckwheat from "Our Gang". The staff of the television show "20/20" was hoaxed in 1990 by a man who claimed to have been the child star "Buckwheat" in the "Our Gang" movie comedies. Buckwheat was really played by William (Billy) Thomas, who died in 1981. On the "20/20" segment, host Hugh Downs claimed that Buckwheat was working as a grocery bagger in Tempe, Arizona. The man claiming to be Buckwheat was actually Bill English, an imposter.

Lord Gordon Gordon. The complete solution to the mystery of Lord Gordon Gordon is unresolved. No one knows his real name, when he was born, or where. It is known that he stole $125,000 worth of diamonds in Edinburgh, Scotland, where he called himself "Lord Glencairn." He appeared in Minneapolis in 1871, calling himself "Lord Gordon Gordon" and claimed he was head of the Gordon clan. He was reportedly worth millions, and intended to invest much of his money in land in Minnesota. He claimed that the people in Scotland were running out of room to farm. Lord Gordon, therefore, was in the market for large tracts of land to resettle Scotsmen on in Minnesota. To bolster his legitimacy, he deposited $40,000 in a Minneapolis bank, and presented letters of introduction, later shown to have been forged, from a number of prominent English noblemen.

Lord Gordon was accepted as a distinguished and possibly quite profitable visitor. He was treated well and his every whim was satisfied. After seeing the state thoroughly, and selecting numerous parcels of land, he announced that he would have to go to New York to get the money needed for his purchases. He left, carrying a warm letter of introduction from his hosts to Horace Greeley, editor of the New York *Tribune*.

Lord Gordon told Greeley that he was the secret owner of more than 60,000 shares of the Erie Railroad, which would qualify as a controlling share. This was good news to Greeley, who was trying to stop financier Jay Gould's growing railroad empire. Gordon offered Gould the right to approve the members of the board of directors of the Erie in return for Gordon securities and money totalling $500,000 to be held as security for the impending deal. Gould had no control over the stock and money once it was given to Lord Gordon, but had to rely on his trustworthiness.

Gordon began cashing in the stock almost immediately. When word of this reached Gould, he became suspicious. After asking Gordon for the return of the stocks and money, Gordon gave him all of it back except the part he had already sold. This amounted to about $150,000 worth. Gould had Lord Gordon Gordon arrested. One of Gould's rivals paid his bond, and Gordon was freed. At his trial, Gordon was haughty and had an explanation for everything. The judge was impressed and leaned towards finding him not guilty.

Gould cabled England to check on Gordon's references, and found out that no one knew him. When the judge heard this and learned that Gordon had fled in the middle of the trial, he declared the proceedings over. Gould issued a $25,000 reward for the return of Lord Gordon. The citizens of Minnesota, upon hearing the true status of Lord Gordon, resolved to capture him from just across the border in Manitoba, Canada. A party of prominent citizens there set out to find him. They did, and when they just made it over the U.S. border, the party from Canada freed Gordon and took the Minnesotans back to Canada in chains. The Canadians were evidently ashamed to admit that they had been hoaxed. This was a sort of cover-up. An international incident was threatened. The Canadian prime minister was called upon to resolve the issue, and he ordered everyone freed. Lord Gordon moved near Toronto where bounty hunters, seeking the $25,000 reward, tried to capture him.

Finally, an extradition warrant was obtained, and the police came to arrest Gordon. He asked for a few minutes to pack his things. As he was doing so, a shot rang out. Lord Gordon killed himself, taking his secrets with him to the grave.

Stanley Clifford Weyman. Stanley Clifford Weyman (1890–1960) was one of the most resourceful of the short-term or "event" imposters. That is, he rarely tried to impersonate anyone for more than a single day or event. Nevertheless, he was a master at it. His successes included nearly becoming a diplomatic representative from Thailand to the United States; many medical impersonations, including physician to Pola Negri, Rudolph Valentino's girlfriend at the time of his death; and holding audience with Secretary of State Charles Evans Hughes and Pres. Warren G. Harding. Weyman was also "Rumanian Consul General" in New York, a Lieutenant Commander in the United States Navy, an Undersecretary of State, and a military attache from Serbia.

His facility with languages was an advantage and he occasionally became the interpreter for a visiting celebrity as a way of doing his impostures. Weyman was born as Stephen Weinburg in Brooklyn, New York. His parents were too poor to send him through college and medical school as he wished and he spent most of his life in a series of menial jobs. His hobby was executing impostures of someone who usually took years to get where he was going.

One of Weyman's best impostures was when he befriended the Princess Fatima of Afganistan on a visit she made to the United States in 1921. The princess was ignored by the State Department, which did not consider her important. Weyman went to her hotel as a representative of the Secretary of State to apologize for not having given her a proper reception. He told the princess that he was going to take her to Washington to meet the secretary and the president. However, she would be expected to give $10,000 to purchase gifts for state department employees. Weyman used the money to hire a private railroad car to Washington and to pay for a hotel suite for the princess.

Then, clad in the uniform of a lieutenant commander in the Navy, he called upon the State Department, dropping the names of a number of influential senators who wanted the secretary to meet with the princess. When they met with Secretary Charles Evans Hughes, Weyman suggested that the princess meet President Harding; this was also arranged at short notice. When Weyman, in naval uniform, passed certain verbal pleasantries with Harding, suspicions were aroused. A true naval officer would not do this with his commander-in-chief. An investigation subsequently determined the fact that Weyman was an impostor. Weyman served a two-year jail term as a result of this incident; he had served many short ones in the past.

The longest stretch that Weyman spent in jail was six years, for being a "physician" who counselled young men on how to get a medical deferment from the draft during World War II. Yet, his finest moment was when, as Pola Negri's physician, he sheperded her to Rudolph Valentino's funeral, past the adoring crowd, even administering smelling salts to a woman who fainted in the excitement. Weyman issued press statements about Negri's condition and basked in the limelight. Strangely enough, Weyman died defending a safe from robbers at the motel where he worked. This little bit of "terminal heroism" did much to rescue the rather bad image that Weyman managed to build for himself over the years.

Medical Impostors. There have been many medical impostors (*See* Ferdinand Waldo Demara, p. 109 for example). Some used purchased credentials or, in earlier days, were simply quacks. Sometimes the difference is not clear among these types. Only a few modern medical imposters will be considered here. In each case, they were blatant repeat offenders, with no possible claim to legitimate credentials.

Harold Rain was a man from Iowa who masqueraded for a number of years under the name of a real physician, Samuel Hall, who was not aware that someone was using his name and credentials. Williams wrote an extensive article revealing the ease with which Rain was able to obtain employment as a physician. The restrictions have tightened up since the 1950s when Rain was at his prime.

Freddie Michael Brant, a convicted bank robber, was successful in posing as physician Reid L. Brown.

He was eventually caught only because both Dr. Browns tried to order pharmaceuticals from the same company. David William Baker used his real name, but never attended the medical schools or studied at the hospitals he said he had.

Perhaps the medical imposter who was most successful at being a practicing physician, until he was finally caught thirty years later, was "Dr. James H. Phillips." This was the name used by Arthur Osborne Phillips (1894-?). He served in World War I as a medical orderly. After a string of bad checks and other minor infractions, he found out that his old boss in the army, Dr. James H. Phillips, was confined to a mental institution. He called Phillips' family, and managed to steal Phillips' medical license. Using that, he obtained a copy of Phillips' diploma. This began a period of thirty years of imposture, although it was interrupted by many cases in which he had to flee or face exposure.

When he was involved in a serious automobile accident, however, he went too far. He was sued by the other party involved, and he countersued for $40,000, which included losses from his inability to practice medicine. An insurance adjuster investigated and the masquerade ended. Phillips was sentenced to three concurrent fifteen-to-twenty-year sentences in jail for perjury. All of the above medical imposters were eventually caught, tried, convicted, and jailed. Many others continue to practice.

Student Imposters. Many people have falsified their credentials in order to get into particular schools. In fact, some "students" have been made up by others and do not even exist. (*See* Education Hoaxes, p. 43). Recently, two notable cases received publicity in the United States. One was the case of "Baron Maurice Jeffrey Locke de Rothschild," who attended Duke University from 1988 to 1990. He was eventually unmasked as Mauro Cortez, Jr., a thirty-seven-year-old from El Paso, Texas, with no connection to the Rothschild family.

The other was the case of Princeton track star Alexi Indris-Santana, who was eventually revealed at a track meet by a spectator from Yale. She recognized him as James Arthur Hogue, who was expelled from her high school in California a few years previously. Hogue, who had served time in a Utah prison, was really thirty-one—not twenty-one as he claimed. He was expelled from Princeton.

Count Carlos Balmori. In 1926, Mexico City first heard about Carlos Balmori, a wealthy Spaniard who just moved to Mexico. He threw lavish parties at his large chateau. The count was known for his impulsive spending and would readily part with money. However, he usually demanded that the recipient of his charity perform some humiliating act as a condition for receiving the money. Among the humiliations, one general agreed to lead a revolution against his country, a diplomat stripped off all of his medals, and communists denounced Karl Marx. Often, after performing the humiliating act, the count's secretary would tear up the check that was just written. After that, the "count" would remove her hat, gloves, and moustache to reveal herself as Conchita Jurado, a school teacher. The checks were worthless.

The entire idea was hatched by Luis Cervantes, a local physician who saw Conchita do a male impersonation and was impressed. He plotted out the various victims and their humiliations, and rehearsed Conchita. The hoaxes continued for five years, until an enraged chief of police (a victim) staged a hoax police raid on the club where Conchita/Count Balmori was "entertaining." She was so scared by the raid that she abandoned the impersonation from then on. Conchita died only a few months later.

Louis de Rougemont. Although the story of Louis de Rougemont (real name probably Louis Grin) crosses between "Exploration and Travel Hoaxes" or in "Imposters," he has been placed here because his whole adult life seems to have been an imposture, even though the stories he told were mostly about exploration. In August 1898, *Wide World Magazine* published an article about de Rougemont's thirty years as a cannibal chief in Australia.

He and a dog were marooned on an island near New Guinea when the ship they were on disappeared in a storm. He remained on the island, using the ship's wreckage for supplies for two years. Then four "savages," Australian aborigines, were shipwrecked on the island as well. They decided to build a boat, sail to Australia, and appoint de Rougemont king of the aborigine tribe. Thus began what de Rougemont called his "Cannibal Chief" period. After arriving by boat in Australia, he married Yamba, the woman who was among the four shipwrecked companions.

He described his life as chief, including the occasional cannibal feasts on the bodies of fallen enemy warriors. One of the first suspicious signs in de Rougemont's account came with his description of the thousands of "flying wombats" he encountered. Wombats were described as small bears, although they are actually more like large woodchucks and cannot fly.

Eventually, the series of articles about de Rougemont's adventures became the object of suspicion among the reading public. A number of people challenged him to provide proof of his adventures. It was demanded that he appear in person before an audience to answer questions. He did appear, an elderly man, and gave ready replies to all questions asked. Nevertheless, several journalists were suspicious and made a thorough investigation. As author Barton relates, Louis de Rougemont turned out to be a Swiss butler, probably named Louis Grin originally, who wandered the world, including Australia, but who had never been any closer to cannibals thatn the British Museum, where he read extensively about them. He died in 1920, then claiming the name Norris Redmond. His coffin reads "Louis Redman."

Literally thousands of other imposters existed—more than could be addressed here. Although many had their stories told in articles and books, there has never yet been a thorough coverage of a majority of impostors in a single volume. There are also "fringe impostors," such as professional gate crashers who like the challenge of attending inaugural balls and other events to which they are not invited.

Sources:

"At Duke U., Bogus Baron Fit Right In." *New York Times* (February 20, 1990): A18.

Barron, James. "Princeton Man is Held as Fugitive, Unmasked and Undone." *New York Times* (February 28, 1991): B1–B2.

Barton, Margaret. *Sober Truth: A Collection of Nineteenth Century Episodes, Fantastic, Grotesque and Mysterious.* London: Duckworth, 1930.

Caraboo: A Narrative of a Singular Imposition Practiced Upon the Benevolence of a Lady Residing in the Vicinity of Bristol. Bristol [U.K.]: J.M. Gutch, 1817.

Croffut, W.A. "Lord Gordon-Gordon: A Bogus Peer and His Distinguished Dupes." *Putnam's Magazine* 7 (January 1910): 416–428.

Deutsch, Helene. "The Impostor: Contribution to Ego Psychology of a Tupe of Psychopath." *Psychoanalytic Quarterly* 24 (1955): 483–505.

Dickson, Lovat. *Wilderness Man: The Strange Story of Grey Owl.* Toronto: Macmillan of Canada, 1973.

Domela, Harry. *A Sham Prince: The Life and Adventures of Harry Domela as Written by Himself in Prison at Cologne, January to June, 1927.* London: Hutchinson, 1928.

"Dr. Reid L. Brown." *Life* (June 12, 1968): 32–32A.

Greenacre, Phyllis. "The Imposter." *Psychoanalytic Quarterly* 27 (1958): 359–82.

———. "The Relation of the Imposter to the Artist." *Psychoanalytic Study of the Child* 13 (1958): 521–40.

Hynd, Alan. "The Fabulous Fraud from Brooklyn." *True* (March 1953): 55–56, 68–71.

Larsen, Egon. *The Deceivers: Lives of Great Imposters.* New York: Roy Publishers, 1966: 58–60.

(Mann, Herman). *The Female Review: Life of Deborah Sampson, the Female Soldier in the War of the Revolution.* Boston: J.K. Wiggin and Wm. Parsons Lunt, 1866.

"Musician's Death at 74 Reveals He Was a Woman." *New York Times* (February 2, 1989): A18.

Oulahan, Richard, Jr. "Barrel of Fun for Cynics." *Life* (December 7, 1962): 25.

"'Our Gang' Imposter Dupes Staff of '20/20'." *New York Times* (October 8, 1990): A15.

Racster, Olga and Jessica Grove. *Dr. James Barry: Her Secret Story.* London: G. Howe, 1932.

Smith, Ralph Lee. "Strange Tales of Medical Impostors." *Today's Health* 46 (October 1968): 45–47, 69–70.

Wasserman, Jacob. *Caspar Hauser: The Enigma of a Century.* New York: Horace Liveright, 1928.

Williams, Greer. "The Doctor Was a Fake." *Saturday Evening Post* (November 13, 1954): 17–19, 53, 55, 57–58, 60.

Witchel, Alex. "The Life of Fakery and Delusion in John Guare's 'Six Degrees.'" *New York Times* (June 21, 1990): C17, C20.

Wyden, Peter. "Thirty Years a Fake Doctor." *Coronet* (August 1953).

"Young Man Claiming to be Son of Sidney Poitier Hits Rich New Yorkers for Loans." *Jet* 65 no. 9 (November 7, 1983): 59.

Invention Hoaxes

Inventors often get bad press. Some have been portrayed by Hollywood and the press as oddballs or crackpots, but were geniuses. For inclusion here, those whose inventions did not work, or never could work, are excluded under the "crank" rule. "Cranks" are people who believe in the idea or ideas they are promoting, and are not guilty of conscious deception; therefore they are not hoaxers. Nevertheless, some "inventions" were crafted with intent to deceive.

Perpetual Motion Machines

It is natural for humans to look for ways to profit from their efforts. People want interest on the money they deposit. They want more for what they sell than what they paid to buy it. Similarly, humans have sought a machine that will give more output than what is put into it. Perpetual motion machines are devices of this kind. Without being connected to an electrical outlet, they never stop running. They put out more energy than it takes to start them or keep them running.

The First Law, a law of thermodynamics says energy can be neither created nor destroyed, but only converted from one form to another. This is also called the Law of Conservation of Energy. There seem to be no exceptions to this law, as it describes the way matter behaves on earth. In order for perpetual motion to occur, this law would be violated. Energy would have to be created to get more out than was put in. Scientists and engineers are united in thinking that perpetual motion is impossible. The U. S. Patent Office will not even consider inventions that claim to get more energy out than is put in, unless a working model accompanies the patent application. This last requirement has greatly cut down on applications. Before 1830, the Patent Office granted about ten patents for devices that would today be called perpetual motion machines, although early records were destroyed in a fire, so the exact

number of patents granted for such devices is not known exactly. That was before the requirement for models.

The designers of perpetual motion machines have fallen into three categories as defined by author Martin Gardner: 1) the inventor, ignorant but honest, who simply doesn't know enough about physics to understand why his or her invention *can't* work; 2) the confidence man who *knows* his invention cannot and will not work, but wants investors to give money; and 3) the "pious fraud," who is sincere, but also seeks as much money or fame as he or she can.

The earliest type of perpetual motion machines were designed to move water uphill, as a kind of early pump. The design for these machines goes back to Medieval times and probably earlier. However, the first person usually credited with designing a useful perpetual motion machine was Robert Fludd (1574–1637), a British physician. Fludd's machine was a "closed cycle mill," driven by water elevated by a kind of screw. The water flowed downwards over a water wheel, driving a mill grindstone. The device, which was apparently never built, would not work theoretically because the amount of energy generated by the water would be insufficient to keep elevating enough water to turn the water wheel. Friction would overcome and the wheel would stop turning.

Connecticut machinist E. P. Willis belongs in the confidence man category. He built an elegant pair of large gear wheels. They were fitted with a system of weights and rods, and displayed in a glass case. Willis charged admission at a New Haven exhibition to see the device. The wheels turned with no apparent motivating force or energy. Later someone observed that one of the gear wheels was resting unnecessarily on a support in a corner of the glass box. Compressed air was being passed at that point into the hollow inside of one of the gear wheels. The escape of that air at another point was what kept the wheels turning.

Another famous machine was invented by John Worrell Keely, between 1875 and 1898. The machine was a complex but ran powerfully with no apparent energy source other than one gallon of ordinary tap water and thirty seconds worth of human breath that Keely supplied before each run. Keely formed the Keely Motor Company and capitalized at $1 million to perfect and produce the device. When the breath and water were supplied, Keely turned on the device and opened valves. A gauge showed a "vapor pressure" of 10,000 pounds per square inch. Keely said this was due to "the power in the water." By 1881, Keely was attributing the power to "vibratory energy." There was power, because the device could, in its later versions, fire a ball 500 feet with a respectable muzzle velocity of 500 feet per second.

Keely appeared to be an honest man who wanted to use his device to benefit mankind. After years of tinkering, the device was still not ready and many of the investors became disgusted. Clara Bloomfield-Moore, a wealthy widow, then became a donor. She advanced Keely more than $100,000 to meet "research expenses." After Keely's death in 1898, Bloomfield-Moore's son, angered at being largely disinherited, made a thorough examination of Keely's laboratory. He found a huge air tank and compressor in the basement and a system of tubes to lead the compressed air to the device. A number of the machine's supports had hollow centers used to conduct the compressed air into the device.

Lester J. Hendershot claimed to have invented a motor that ran on the earth's magnetic field. In 1928, he was endorsed by the commandant of the U. S. Army's Selfridge Field test facility for his motor. A scientist called a press conference shortly thereafter to announce that his examination revealed a battery concealed within the motor. Hendershot replied that he put it there just to steer scientists away from "the true secret." He faded from the scene shortly thereafter.

Another perpetual motion hoaxer was Charles Redheffer (or Redheifer). In Philadelphia in 1812, he revealed a machine that ran with no visible source of energy. Inventor Robert Fulton finally unmasked the fraud. He guessed that the irregular motion of the wheel disclosed the fraud. Fulton offered to demonstrate this or pay for any damage he caused trying to do so. He soon discovered catgut belt drive hidden in the framework of the device. It led into the wall and then upstairs in the house. Tracing the belt, Fulton found a room upstairs in which an elderly man sat eating bread and turning a crank that ran the catgut belt. The angry crowd below demolished the machine. Redheffer fled

for his life. In spite of the widespread record of failure, and the certainty that perpetual motion is a theoretical impossibility, the public continues to be occasionally fooled by new claims of the invention of a perpetual motion machine.

Sources:

Angrist, Stanley W. "Perpetual Motion Machines." *Scientific American* 218 (January 1968): 114–22.

Bloomfield-Moore, C. S. *Keeley and His Discoveries.* Secaucus, NJ: University Books, [1972]. Reprint.

Dircks, Henry C. E. *Perpetuum Mobile.* London: E. F. Spon, 1861 (Vol. 1), 1870 (Vol. 2).

Gardner, Martin. "Perpetual Motion: Illusion and Reality." *Foote Prints* (Exton, PA), 47 no. 2 (1984): 21–35.

Jones, David "Daedalus". "I, Fraudulous." *New Scientist* 100 (December 1983): 915–17.

Ord-Hume, Arthur W. J. G. *Perpetual Motion: The History of an Obsession.* New York: St. Martin's Press, 1977.

Other Invention Hoaxes

Flight Hoaxes. The first successful airplane flight was the Wright brothers' flight at Kitty Hawk, North Carolina, in 1903. That does not mean that all previous, unsuccessful, makers of airplanes of different designs were hoaxers. A *conscious intention to deceive* has to be present for there to have been a hoax. Yet, some attempts at flight *do* qualify as hoaxes.

Anatomists and physiologists have pointed out that the human body is too heavy to be lifted by human arm and chest muscles, no matter how large or well-designed the set of bird-like wings is when it is strapped to the arms. Flying birds have hollow bones, organs that minimize weight (air sacs instead of lungs, only one ovary, etc.), and never weigh more than thirty-five pounds (an albatross). In spite of the knowledge that man-powered flight is impossible, people continue to design and promulgate flying devices.

A man-powered aircraft with movable wings is called an "ornithopter." It should be distinguished from such feasible man- powered aircraft as the "Gossamer Condor," which is basically a bicycle-pedal-powered fixed wing aircraft. One of these crossed the English Channel.

The theme of man flying by using wings is common in mythology and other literature. In fact, all

Marriott's aerial steam carriage, an example of an early flying device.

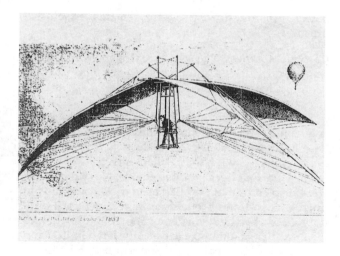

Leturr's flying machine, another example of a man-powered aircraft.

attempts to fly using movable, strapped-on wings have led to immediate—and often—fatal plunge to the ground. One of the earliest "birdmen" was Eilmer of Malmesbury, who strapped on wings circa 1010. He supposedly flew more than 607 feet or "stadium," in Roman measure, before crashing and breaking his legs. Author Lynn White states that he probably used rigid, strapped-on wings. Eilmer's feat was described by William of Malmesbury, writing in his *De Gestis regum Anglorum* in 1066. There appears to be about a forty-five-year gap between the event and the time it was first recorded. The time gap is probably responsible for the improbably large distance covered by Eilmer in his flight. Although there *may* not be any conscious deception here, it is apparent that the distance has been exaggerated in the retelling.

The other major "birdman" of the period before 1600 was Giovanni Battista Danti (c.1477–1517). Leonardo da Vinci, although he designed ornithopters, parachutes, and helicopters, apparently never used them himself. Danti, in contrast, was reported to have made several flights. His main flight was described in the book *Elogia Civicum Perusinorum* by Caesar Alesi in 1652. The flight purportedly took place in 1498 or 1499. Danti made the wings that he wore, perfecting his control over their use with flights over Lake Trasimeno. In his major flight, which occurred in Perugia, Italy, Danti flew across the public square, where a great crowd was gathered for a wedding. During the flight, one of the iron struts that controlled the left wing broke. As a result, Danti was thrown onto the roof of St. Mary's Church, injuring his leg. The total distance he covered in his flight was not stated. The written version of these "facts" did not appear until 150 years after the event. Again, it appears that some exaggeration occurred.

Anti-Gravity Devices. Although one of the fondest dreams of many inventors is to find a device which can neutralize gravity, it seems almost theoretically impossible. Gravity is by no means well-understood, but *is* not a bipolar force. In other words, while magnets have a north and south pole, with like poles repelling and opposite poles attracting, gravity is apparently a force in only one direction. It is unlikely that any anti-gravitational force can exist, except of course for something like a rocket exhaust *thrusting against* gravity. What is being sought is a *reactionless* thrust against gravity. A mere cancellation of gravity would not provide any propulsive force pushing against the earth, so a "gravity shield" would be of limited use. None of the above has stopped inventors from producing devices they claimed were anti-gravity or gravity shields.

The "Dean Drive," invented by Norman Dean of Washington, D.C., in the 1950s, is essentially an "anchorless winch." It converts rotary motion into unidirectional thrust. Dean's device was actually awarded a U.S. patent. There were a number of engineers who have looked at the tiny amount of thrust developed by the device, and have thought that it could be developed into a useful machine. Others have analyzed the force produced and said that it was present because static friction in one direction (the unidirection thrust direction) is less than in another direction. In other words, something is not being gotten for nothing, and gravity is not really being cancelled out. Others disagree, but since the early 1960s, nothing further was heard of the Dean Drive, raising suspicion that perhaps it really didn't work as advertised.

No other anti-gravity device obtained a U.S. patent, which means that no working model of the device could have been presented as required for a patent. An anti-gravity device remains an elusive dream.

Gasoline Additives. The search for inexpensive energy has extended to the automobile. Many purported inventors have claimed to have invented an automobile engine that runs on water or some sort of additive that can be mixed with gasoline to fuel an automobile engine that gets hundreds of miles per gallon. In 1917, John Andrews demonstrated to the U. S. Navy a mysterious green powder that, when mixed with water, made a fuel that ran a gasoline engine. Navy personnel were suspicious that they had been tricked and did not pursue it. Andrews brought no more inventions forth until 1935, when he again demonstrated the powder for the Bureau of Standards. He was murdered in 1937 and his powder and papers stolen from his home in Pennsylvania.

In 1973, Guido Franch of Chicago gave demonstrations of a similar powder to automobile companies and others. His terms for the invention put people off, however. He wanted $250,000 up front, with $10 million put into an escrow account that became his as soon as the secret of producing the powder was revealed. He then wanted one cent per gallon of fuel made. No one would agree and analysis of the fuel showed that it was nothing but a substance similar to lighter fluid. The powder was not available for analysis. Franch claimed he did not make the powder, but got the idea—and perhaps a supply of the powder—from a German chemist named Kraft. He knew Kraft's mistress, who had been given the powder. Franch claimed he did not know John Andrews, but thought Kraft may have also given Andrews some of the powder. When pressured, Franch claimed that the secret of the powder actually came from "the Black Eagles," a group of spacemen from the planet Neptune. It is all rather suspect of a hoax.

The Death Ray. Rumors surrounded Grindell H. Matthews, a British scientist, when, in 1924 he claimed to have invented the death ray—the ultimate battlefield weapon. The reports turned out to be false. T. F. Wall applied for a patent on a death ray in 1924, but it was not granted. Supposedly the Germans also invented such a weapon at about this time but, again, nothing further came of it. In 1924, electrical genius Nikola Tesla supposedly claimed that *he* invented a death ray capable of stopping an airplane in mid-flight. Nothing further surfaced about this until 1934, when Tesla was quoted as saying that his ray worked on an entirely new principle of physics. He claimed that his ray could destroy 10,000 planes at a distance of 250 miles. Each ray would require the construction of a $2 million plant, located at a high, strategic point. A network of twelve such plants would protect the United States from aerial invasion. Two years later, Tesla was still

Nikola Tesla, supposed death ray inventor.

talking about his ray to a now disinterested public. The military was also strangely disinterested. Tesla's invention got no further and no papers on it were found after his death in 1943. The laser, first put on the market in 1960, has been called an intellectual child of Tesla's death ray, but this seems doubtful.

Sources:

Beller, William. "Consultant's Report Overrides Dean Space Drive." *Missles and Rockets* 9 (June 12, 1961): 24–25, 42.

Gibbs-Smith, C[harles] H. *Flight Through the Ages.* New York: Thomas Y. Crowell, 1974.

Haining, Peter. *The Compleat Birdman: An Illustrated History of Man-Powered Flight.* New York: St. Martin's Press, 1977.

Hart, Clive. *The Dream of Flight: Aeronautics from Classical Times to the Renaissance.* London: Faber & Faber, 1972.

Hunt, Inez and Wanetta W. Draper. *Lightning In His Hand: The Life Story of Nikola Tesla.* Denver: Sage Books, 1964.

LaFond, Charles D. "The Controversial Dean System Space Drive." *Missles and Rockets* 8 (May 1, 1961): 24, 34, 46.

[Stewart, Oliver], Frank Howard, and Bill Gunston. *The Conquest of the Air*. New York: Random House, 1974.

Valentine, Tom. "The Man Below is Turning Tap Water Into Gasoline." *The National Exchange* 1 no. 3 (June 1977): 6–7.

White, Lynn, Jr. "Eilmer of Malmesbury, an Eleventh Century Aviator." *Technology and Culture* 2 (1961): 97–111.

Journalism Hoaxes

Journalists have an ethical code that prevents them from fabricating a story they know to be untrue (See Janet Cooke and the Pulitzer Prize, p. 130). This was not always the case. In fact, in the 1800s, when there were no wire services to supply news from around the world, it was often difficult to find much to report. As a result, journalists were tempted to invent news on a slow day. Some of the hoaxes in this section were the result of such temptations. Others were attempts at humor, while still others had more deceptive motives.

The Central Park Zoo Escape

The New York *Herald* of November 9, 1874 ran a five-column article on page one in which it reported the escape of many animals in the Central Park Zoo. The purported eyewitness account said that many people were dead, listing twenty-seven of them. It said that perhaps 200 people were injured. Headlines read "Awful Calamity" and "Terrible Scenes of Mutilation."

The anonymous article reported that at least twelve animals were still at large. Most had been captured or shot during a hunt on Broadway and Fifth Avenue, and in several churches. Participating in the "roundup" were Chester A. Arthur, Samuel J. Tilden, Governor Dix, and several other prominent people. The mayor urged citizens, except for National Guard members, to stay home for their own safety.

The reporter said that the zoo's most dangerous animals were kept in a single building. The doors to this building had been locked as usual at 5 P.M. An attendant named Chris Anderson was observed by a zoo keeper to be poking a rhinoceros named Pete with his cane. After the attendant accidently poked Pete in the eye, the enraged animal charged, smashing the front of his cage and killing Anderson. Pete then smashed open the cages of several other animals. A panther was freed; the rhinoceros killed another keeper. A freed lion crashed through a window in the building, killing several spectators. Although wounded by a bullet, the lion continued its rampage. Other animals escaped through the broken window.

The lion and a Bengal tiger ran out onto Fifth Avenue. Several other large cats killed giraffes, ostriches, and pelicans. An elephant destroyed several cages and a zebra escaped into the city streets. Someone finally lassoed the elephant by the legs, and he was tied up. The rhinoceros left Central Park, attacked other people, and finally fell into a deep sewer excavation, where it died from injuries.

The lion and tiger fought with each other. After killing eighteen people, the lion was shot by a party of hunters. After the Bengal tiger killed twenty people, it was finally shot by Gov. John A. Dix, an experienced big-game hunter. One of the tigers entered the open door of a church, causing a panic and at least one death. People started firing at the animals from their apartment windows, adding to the panic and danger. One tiger jumped aboard the 23rd Street ferry, spooking the horses from the wagons being carried by the ferry. The horses leapt overboard, pulling the wagons and their human occupants into the river with them. Other passengers were also mangled by the tiger.

The *Herald* published a list of some of the casualties. They listed at least twenty-seven people killed, eighteen injured, and fifty-nine animals killed, and suspected the total was closer to 200 injured, and many more than thirty-two killed. The wild animals still at large included a cheetah, a panther, a Cape buffalo, a puma, and a black leopard.

The last paragraph of the article gave away the fact that it was all a hoax. It was headed "The Moral of the Whole" and mentioned that the story was written to point out the deplorable condition of the zoo, with the real possibility that the animals could escape. It read:

> The entire story given above is pure fabrication. Not one word of it is true. Not a single act or incident described has taken place. It is a huge hoax, a wild romance, or whatever other epithet of utter untrustworthiness our readers may choose to apply to it. It is simply a fancy picture which crowded upon the mind of the writer a few days ago while he was gazing through the iron bars of the cages of the wild animals in the menagerie at Central Park.

The story idea was that of managing editor Thomas B. Connery. He ordered two reporters to write it, and gained the approval of the paper's owner, James Gordon Bennett, Jr., to run it. Neither thought that the effect on the public would be so profound. When Connery saw the frightened people in the streets, he stopped the presses.

The other New York newspapers criticized the *Herald* for running the hoax article. The *Herald's* circulation, however, increased. The strongest criticism came from the *New York Times*, whose editor had run outside with two pistols after reading the *Herald's* story. He made a further fool of himself by berating the police at the local station for not telling the *Times* about the incident while it was occurring.

Sources:

"Awful Calamity." New York *Herald* (November 9, 1874): 1.

Connery, Thomas B. "A Famous Newspaper Hoax." *Harper's Weekly* (June 3, 1893): 534–35.

Fedler, Fred. *Media Hoaxes.* Ames, Iowa: Iowa State University Press, 1989: 84–96.

The Federal Communications Commission Petition

One of the most widespread modern hoaxes has an origin that can be pinpointed, but the hoaxers have eluded identification. The hoax consisted of a 1974 rumor that the Federal Communications Commission (FCC) was about to cancel all religious broadcasts as a result of a petition by atheist Madalyn Murray O'Hair. The FCC, as of late 1988, received over 21 *million* letters asking that religious broadcasting *not* be cancelled.

Since 1974 the 21 million letters received by the FCC have been an enormous disposal problem. Several staff members do nothing but open these letters, put them into a pile, and have them hauled away. They were put into warehouse storage for a while, but now the letters are so numerous that they are taken away for recycling.

The hoax started with an authentic petition in 1974. It was filed by two California broadcasters, Jeremy Lansman and Lorenzo Milam, and was given the FCC number "RM-2493." The petition asked the FCC to investigate the practices of non-commercial radio and television stations, including religious broadcasters.

The wording used by Lansman and Milam was rather strong. It said that scarce FM radio and educational TV frequencies were being monopolized by religious groups "locked into a bleak, self-centered and miasmic view of man's capability for knowledge." The letter went on to say that religious broadcasters presented "one-sided, blind and stultifying" programming.

The FCC denied this petition in August of 1975. By then, they received 750,000 protest letters. After the petition was denied, someone "attached" Madalyn O'Hair's name to this petition, or at least to *some* petition that was supposedly still pending at the FCC. This was when the mail *really* increased. Mrs. O'Hair had supposedly filed 27,000 signatures on behalf of her "petition." She wanted to stop all religious broadcasting. Various Fundamentalist and other churches as well as well-meaning but misinformed clergy spread the message that action had to be taken to stop her.

Even the major newspapers were partly responsible for fueling the O'Hair rumors. Despite the fact that the *Chicago Tribune* ran an article on April 3, 1977 debunking the rumor, it then ran a December 19 column contributed by an undergraduate student at Boston College that said that Mrs. O'Hair had filed the petition. The next day a small correction was issued; the entire basis of the previous day's story was denied by the FCC. How the *Tribune* had been hoaxed was not explained.

The letters continue to stream in to the FCC, although there are sporadic decreases and increases in the volume.

Sources:

Castelli, Jim. "The Curse of the Phantom Petition." *TV Guide* (July 24, 1976): 4–6.

Dart, John. "Rumor of Atheist Radio Move Proves Persistent." *Los Angeles Times* (December 1, 1964) II: 6.

Federal Communications Commission. *Fact Sheet RM-2493.* Washington, DC: Federal Communications Commission, 1990.

Hirsley, Michael. "Rumor That Wouldn't Die." *Chicago Tribune* (December, 1988).

The Phantom Phenomenon Christiansanity Strikes Again!
   Austin, TX: American Atheist Center, [ca. 1982]: 29.

The Floating Cafe or the Sin Ship

On August 16, 1924, the *New York Herald Tribune* reported that during Prohibition there was a large ship flying a British flag, anchored outside the twelve-mile limit of New York harbor. This ship served as a speakeasy, where drinks—though expensive at one dollar each—were freely served to a wealthy clientele. People were delivered to the ship on small boats from the south shore of Long Island.

The article on the ship was entitled "New Yorkers Drink Sumptuously on 17,000-Ton Floating Cafe at Anchor 15 Miles Off Fire Island." The article contained a map showing the location of the ship and claimed "unemployed chorus girls" were aboard. Many small boats loaded with eager New Yorkers set out to find the "sin ship." They searched in vain.

The story was invented by reporter Sanford Jarrell, who was subsequently fired by the *Tribune* after his hoax became unmanageable. However, other New York newspapers picked up the story, as did the Customs Service and the Coast Guard. They all searched for the ship, thought at first to have been the former German liner *Friedrich de Grosse*. It wasn't the German liner— identified as having sunk off California—or any other. Jarrell's second article had the Coast Guard cutter *Seneca* trying to track down the ship. A third article said that the Coast Guard had been unable to find the ship.

At first, the *Tribune* editors defended the authenticity of their reporter's story. They even ran an editorial praising the reporter. When finally confronted by his editors, Jarrell admitted that he had "embellished" the truth, although he insisted his fundamental "facts" were true. After reflection, he sent in a written confession, admitting he fabricated the story. He was subsequently fired. The other newspapers that ran the story were surprisingly gracious at the news of the hoax. Several apologized for misleading their readers.

Sources:

"Coast Guard Acts to Close Cabaret 15 Miles Out at Sea." *New York Times* (August 17, 1924): 1.

Jarrell, Sanford. "New Yorkers Drink Sumptuously on 17,000-Ton Floating Cafe at Anchor 15 Miles Off Long Island." *New York Herald Tribune* (August 16, 1924): 1.

Smith, Jack. "The Great Gambling Ship Hoax and How it Was Blown Out of the Water." *Los Angeles Times* (July 11, 1984): Section 5: 1.

The Georgia Train Duels

Many of the more "civilized" people of Europe, especially in England, harbored the thought that parts of the United States in the 1850s were uncivilized or inhabited by little more than savages. Therefore, they readily accepted a story that appeared in the London *Times* of October 15, 1856.

The story was submitted by "an English gentleman" who appeared trustworthy and went as follows. A writer left Macon, Georgia on a train for Augusta on August 1, 1856. There were only two cars on the train, a passenger car and a mail/luggage car, with room for a few passengers who smoked. Soon after departure, a man argued with two other men over two women seated next to them. This led to a challenge for a duel with pistols. It was suggested that the conductor be asked to stop the train and let the two men off to have their duel. Neither man would agree to this. Two *other* men, arguing over the merits of dueling itself, challenged each other to a duel. The train was stopped, both men got off, and the train left them behind. A telegraph report later said one man killed the other in the duel. Meanwhile, the original two antagonists got off the train to have their duel. The train continued on. That left only one of the original antagonists, who managed to challenge *another* passenger to a duel. The train stopped; they duelled. The original antagonist won, and got back on the train uninjured. The body of the other man was left behind.

The most recent loser's father began to insult one of the women who had been the subject of the original disagreement. She found someone to defend her honor in a duel, but the conductor refused to stop the train again, as they were already late. Instead, the two duelers went into the luggage car. They duelled there and the younger man she enlisted to defend her was killed. Finally, the young child of one of the men killed was told to avenge his father's death. He evidently made a remark to the man who killed his father. As a result, that man killed the child and threw his body from the train.

The correspondent reported says that he read nothing about any of this in the Georgia newspapers and was even told that duels like this were fairly common events on trains in Georgia—scarcely a week passed without a death on the train.

The *Times* thought that these killings reflected badly upon the United States. No one was caught, tried or convicted. The events had occurred at the beginning of August and the *Times* article was published in mid-October. The *Times* sarcastically said that if this continued, the railroad should provide pistol stands and surgeons at each stop. They might even provide certain cars marked as shooting cars, with appropriate facilities.

Americans living in Europe were angry. One person from the South, who knew the trains in Georgia, wrote that the story was "a miserable hoax." He questioned many of the details and noted that all the events could never have happened. The conductor would have ejected the unruly passengers long before they started dueling. The lack of specific details, including names, spoke against the truth of the story. The Southerner thought that the story might be a fabrication of a Northerner trying to influence the upcoming presidential elections. A man from New England also wrote to say that the incidents could not have happened as described. He pointed out that there was no five P.M. train listed in the timetables as leaving Macon. There were several other errors in the correspondent's description of the route.

The correspondent who had written the original story finally identified himself as John Arrowsmith of Liverpool, England, restating in a letter that his narrative was truthful. The *New York Times* reprinted the original Arrowsmith story, commenting that it was obviously was a hoax. The president of the Georgia railroad called Arrowsmith's story an insulting fabrication. He insisted that the laws against dueling in Georgia were so strict that no duels had been fought for twenty years. No passenger had *ever* been killed while riding a train in Georgia, by duel or otherwise.

The London *Times* said that it found Arrowsmith's letter and story more believable than the Georgia railroad president's. The president of the Central Railroad of Georgia denied there was any truth in it. The letter from *this* gentleman was transmitted to London by the British consul in Georgia, who swore that he had known the Central Railroad president for more than thirty years and that he was of fine character.

This, and much criticism from American newspapers, at last convinced the London *Times* that it had been the victim of a hoax. Finally, the Central Railroad president obtained depositions from seven people who had been aboard the train. All seven denied that any of the events mentioned had happened. These people included the firemen, the engineers, the conductor, and the mail clerk. The story *was* a hoax.

Sources:

Arrowsmith, John. "Railways and Revolvers in Georgia." London *Times* (October 24, 1856): 7.

[Arrowsmith, John]. "Railways and Revolvers in Georgia." London *Times* (October 15, 1856): 6.

Fedler, Fred. *Media Hoaxes*. Ames, Iowa: Iowa State University Press, 1989: 69–83.

[H. C. W.]. "Railways and Revolvers in Georgia." London *Times* (October 18, 1856): 8.

"A Prodigious Hoax." *New York Times* (November 1, 1856): 4.

[Untitled letter]. London *Times* (October 18, 1856): 8.

Janet Cooke and the Pulitzer Prize

The Pulitzer Prize is among the most prestigious prizes a journalist can win. In April of 1981, *Washington Post* reporter Janet Cooke won a Pulitzer Prize for her story about Jimmy, an eight-year-old heroin addict. A few days after the announcement, the *Post* discovered that Jimmy was imaginary and that the entire story was a hoax. True to its reputation as a great newspaper, the *Post* launched an intensive investigation of how the hoax story made it to print. Their own articles on the results of this investigation are masterpieces.

This was the first time in the sixty-four-year history of the Pulitzer Prize that a prize was declined because the story was shown to be false. The *Post* declined the award and insisted it be returned after their own investigation.

The hoax was quickly exposed because reports of the award contained background information about reporter Janet Cooke. She falsified her résumé, and told the Pulitzer Committee that she graduated from Vassar College magna cum laude in 1976 and received a master's degree in journalism from the University of Toledo in 1977. Spokesmen for the two schools said that Miss Cooke had only attended Vassar her freshman year. She received a B.A. degree in 1976 from the University of Toledo.

When doubts about the story were raised the previous year, Miss Cooke was asked to take another reporter to the apartment where Jimmy lived. She was unable to find the building, but the accompanying reporter attributed this to a confusing neighborhood to which she had only been once before. When Miss Cooke was asked—before the story was published—to identify her sources and Jimmy, she said that she promised them anonymity and her life was threatened by the drug pushers involved. The *Washington Post* did not insist that she reveal their identity.

Janet Cooke's story, "Jimmy's World," was originally published in the *Post* on September 28, 1980. It told of the life and views of "Jimmy," identified as an eight-year-old heroin addict. He allegedly became an addict at the age of five, when his mother's live-in boyfriend—a heroin dealer—let him sniff some heroin. Cooke's story added that both Jimmy's mother and grandmother were heroin addicts. Jimmy was quoted as saying that the only reason he went to school was to learn math, which would help him in his future as a heroin dealer. Cooke told her editors that the mother's boyfriend threatened her life if she revealed Jimmy's whereabouts.

The published story hit a nerve; there was clamor to find Jimmy and save him from his environment. Mayor Marion Barry of Washington, and the police chief, launched an intensive search for Jimmy. Both Barry and a drug-addiction expert at Howard University claimed they knew who "Jimmy" was. They later denied their claims. Ben Bradlee, the executive editor at the *Washington Post*, stated *after* the scandal broke, that he was still convinced that there was such a boy in the Washington area. Some have since claimed that "Jimmy" was a composite of several people.

Post editors claimed afterward that suspicions were always present about the truth of the Jimmy story. When the reporter who accompanied Cooke on her search for Jimmy's residence was later asked by their editor to find Jimmy, Cooke claimed that she recently checked the residence and found it vacant. She learned that the family moved to Baltimore.

When Janet Cooke was confronted by Ben Bradlee about her false credentials from Vassar she denied everything, then finally admitted she went to Vassar for only a year. She was less forthright about the Jimmy story, however. She stuck to the story's authenticity for many hours. Eventually, it was made clear to her that the only thing that held the story together was her support from the *Post*. Now that *that* was in doubt the Jimmy story was collapsing.

Bradlee gave Cooke twenty-four hours to prove the Jimmy story true. Bob Woodward, *Post* Metro section editor, requested Cooke's notes, which were stored at a law firm after the Jimmy story was published. He and others went through the 145 pages of notes and the tape recorded interviews. Although Woodward said he found "echoes" of the Jimmy story all through the notes, there was no indication that she actually interviewed a heroin-addicted child.

Although Cooke stuck to her story for a while longer, the evidence against her was getting stronger. She finally confessed to David Maraniss, the Maryland state editor, that Jimmy was a fabrication and a composite. Cooke resigned from the *Post* as requested. The Pulitzer was returned. The *Post* conducted extensive meetings and postmortem examinations of what had gone wrong, and emerged with their reputation intact.

Sources:

"The Confession." *Washington Post* (April 19, 1981): A12–A15.

"The Conclusions." *Washington Post* (April 19, 1981): A12–A15.

"The Doubts." *Washington Post* (April 19, 1981): A12–A15.

Griffith, Thomas. "The Pulitzer Hoax—Who Can Be Believed?" *Time* 117 (May 4, 1981): 50–51.

Munson, Naomi. "The Case of Janet Cooke." *Commentary* 72 no. 2 (August 1981): 46–50.

Noah, Timothy. "Jimmy's Big Brothers." *New Republic* 184 (May 16, 1981): 14–16.

"The Ombudsman." *Washington Post* (April 19, 1981): A12–A15.

"The Players." *Washington Post* (April 19, 1981): A12–A15.

"The Pressures." *Washington Post* (April 19, 1981): A12–A15.

"The Prize." *Washington Post* (April 19, 1981): A12–A15.

"The Publication." *Washington Post* (April 19, 1981): A12–A15. "Pulitzer Board Withdraws Post Reporter's Prize." *Washington Post* (April 16, 1981): A25.

"The Reporter." *Washington Post* (April 19, 1981): A12–A15.

"The Story." *Washington Post* (April 19, 1981): A12–A15.

Other Journalism Hoaxes

The Great Wall of China Hoax. In 1899, four reporters, one from each of Denver's four newspapers, were having drinks together. They agreed to concoct a story that would impress people, yet be hard to verify. The basic story would be that China had decided to demolish the Great Wall and recruited a group of American engineers to plan the job. These engineers were in Denver enroute to China. The Chinese would demolish the Wall as a gesture of international good will—to show that they now welcomed foreign trade.

After working out the details, the reporters went to the best hotel in Denver and, with the cooperation of the desk clerk, signed the four fictitious engineers' names in the hotel register. The clerk agreed to tell questioners that the engineers were interviewed by the reporters, but had left for California on their way to China. The story ran in the Denver papers under various headlines, one of which was "Great Chinese Wall Doomed! Peking Seeks World Trade!"

Although Denver soon forgot about the story, the rest of the world didn't. Two weeks later, a large east coast newspaper carried the story. Worse yet, the story reached China. The Chinese government knew *they* had not contracted to have the Great Wall taken down. Therefore, it must have been the idea of the Americans. The Chinese were furious at this intrusion into their sovereignty.

Although China had been sensitized to this by the previous intrusion of the Russians and British, this American "intrusion" was not—as has been claimed—the final straw that helped start the Boxer Rebellion. The Boxers, a secret Chinese society opposed to foreign intrusion into China, caused people to riot. Foreign embassies were put under siege. Hundreds of missionaries were killed. French, British, American, Russian, and Japanese troops rushed in. The Emperor's palace was looted. Finally, the Chinese were subdued. They had to pay $320 million in "fines" and grant further economic concessions.

Although several sources, including writer Mark Muldavin, claim that hoax triggered the Boxer Rebellion, there is no proof of this. No evidence indicates that the average Boxer knew anything about the American's "plan" to demolish the wall. The story that the Boxer Rebellion resulted from the hoax may have come from Henry White Warren, an American missionary in China, who was perhaps trying to minimize the role of the missionaries in causing the ill will that provoked the rebellion. He may have been the source of the widely quoted Harry Lee Wilber article in *The North American Review* in 1939. The article claims that the hoax started the rebellion.

The Chicago Theater Fire. The nineteenth-century Chicago press was especially notorious for the liberty they took with the facts of a story in order to sell newspapers. Some of this was due to the fierce competition among the many Chicago newspapers of the time. Wilbur Storey (1820–1884) became publisher of the *Chicago Times* in 1861. On February 13, 1875, Storey wrote a page-one article about a theater fire. There were eleven levels of headlines above the story, commonly used for emphasis in those days. The eleventh said "Description of a Suppositious Holocaust Likely to Occur Any Night." The hoax was announced right in the story, if anyone had bothered to read the last headline. The theater was never identified by name, but that didn't seem to bother the readers.

The article stated that the theater was almost full. At about 10:30 P.M., a fire broke out on the stage just before the curtain was going to rise. The flames and smoke spread quickly, the audience panicked, and many lives were lost. More than 200 people died. The *Times* published the names of 108 victims, but many of the names were incomplete, obviously misspelled, or quite common.

After giving all the details, the paper reported that its story was untrue. It urged the people of Chicago to work for safer theaters. The newspaper's architect inspected every theater in Chicago and found that *none* was safe. Problems included narrow exit stairs, doors that opened inwards, and lack of ample exits.

The rival *Chicago Tribune* called the *Times'* story "worse than murder." It told of a woman who collapsed and became insane after reading her husband's name among the list of fire victims. Further her mother collapsed and *died* when she saw the name. The *Tribune* admitted in the last paragraph of the story that *its* report was also a hoax.

In December of 1903, there was a *real* fire, much like the one in the hoax story, in Chicago's Iroquois Theater. The report stated that 571 people died and another 350 were injured. Many of the conditions mentioned as unsafe in the 1875 story contributed to the high death toll. All of Chicago's theaters were closed after the Iroquois fire, and the safety changes that had been recommended in 1875 were made.

The Nineteenth Century News. Before 1900, newspaper reporting was a much more different business. Facts could not be easily checked by telephone. Even though most newspapers had telephones, most of the people to whom reporters had to speak *did not*. Automobiles were not prevalent yet, so to get one name correct could involve hours riding on streetcars. In addition, reporters were not particularly respected; when interviewed, people often refused to answer questions. Journalists were simply not respected, as the job required no degree. As a result, many reporters were tempted to manufacture the "facts" of a story and sometimes fabricate the whole story.

An additional complication, was that many reporters were "stringers." Stringers were paid an amount of money for the length of stories. The length was measured with a piece of string. The more "facts" a story had, the higher the amount paid. Reporters from several different papers in the same city would often get together over drinks to "fill out" an insignificant story into a front-page article. As a result, many of the stories in nineteenth-century newspapers were hoaxes.

Lou Stone's Hoaxes. Lou Stone was a reporter for the Winsted, Connecticut *Evening Citizen*. He was responsible for hundreds of stories about the animal life around Winsted, almost all hoaxes. One of his most famous hoaxes was the 1895 story of the Winsted Wild Man—a naked, hairy man who jumped out and screamed at people. The alleged Wild Man was soon spotted by many other people in the area. Other newspapers also carried the story of the hundreds of people who sought the Wild Man, and often spotted him. The story finally ended when it was reported that a jackass belonging to a local man named Mr. Danehy was shot. It was apparently responsible for most of the "sightings."

Other Lou Stone stories included the river that ran uphill, the dog that talked, a tree that grew baked apples, a man who caught a fish with his red nose as "bait," and several stories about chickens with unusual eggs and cows that gave butter instead of milk.

T. Walter Williams's Hoaxes. Williams was a *New York Times* reporter for many years. At a loss for fascinating people to write about, he began to invent them. Author Fred Fedler states Williams' stories are the only instances where the *Times* knowingly published fiction in its news columns. Williams specialized in marine and maritime stories. One of his best involved a sixty-five-foot sea serpent supposedly spotted in the Caribbean. He also had stories about a monkey in the zoo who learned to play the ukelele, and an imaginary Marmaduke M. Mizzle, a caraway seed merchant, who traveled the globe.

The Recruiting Proclamation. On May 18, 1864, a proclamation by President Lincoln, calling for 4,000 new recruits between the ages of eighteen and forty-five for the Union Army reached newspaper offices. The proclamations were written on regulation manifold paper, customarily used for Associated Press dispatches. The New York *World* and the *Journal of Commerce* printed the proclamations as authentic, as did the New Orleans *Picayune*. The proclamation, which also called for a day of fasting and prayer, was the work of Joseph Howard of the Brooklyn *Eagle*; he was arrested and imprisoned. Both northern newspapers printed an immediate retraction, but were each closed down by the government for four days. The New Orleans paper was closed for two weeks by General Banks.

Sources:

Bird, S. Elizabeth. *For Enquiring Minds: A Cultural Study of Supermarket Tabloids.* Knoxville, TN: University of Tennessee Press, 1992.

"Burned Alive!" *Chicago Times* (February 13, 1875): 1.

Felder, Fred. *Media Hoaxes* Ames, IA: Iowa State University Press, 1989: 97–109, 110–17.

Lancaster, Paul. "Faking It." *American Heritage* 33 no. 6 (October/November 1982): 50–57.

Muldavin, Mark. "The Fake that Made Violent History." *The Double Dealers*, Alexander Klein, ed. Philadelphia: J. B. Lippincott, 1958: 301–4.

"'The Winsted Liar.' A News-Fictionist Whose Fame Is In Whoppers." *Literary Digest* (September 11, 1920): 62.

Language Hoaxes

Although language is involved to some extent in almost every hoax, this section focuses on those in which language itself is the key element. For other hoaxes involving language as a significant but not exclusive part of the hoax, see The Native of Formosa, p. 3, and Viking Hoaxes, p. 54.

The Eskimo Words for Snow

It is widely believed that the Eskimo culture looks at the world differently than others. For example, it is said that the Eskimo language has anywhere from 23 to 200 words for different kinds of snow. They perceive differences where most do not. Actually, this whole idea is a hoax. It developed gradually, and perhaps unintentionally, but now is imbedded in the popular mind.

Anthropologist Laura Martin traced the misunderstanding back to a statement made by the famous anthropologist Franz Boas in the introduction he wrote to the *Handbook of North American Indians* in 1911. He claimed there were four etymologically unrelated words for snow in the Eskimo language, namely "aput," meaning snow on the ground; "qana," meaning falling snow; "piqsirpoq," meaning drifting snow; and "qimusqsuq," meaning a snow drift. His apparent point was that language structures were not comparable. In that he was incorrect, at least in the example cited. English does the same thing with *water*, although not with snow (e.g., river, stream, rain, flood, lake, ocean). English uses an unrelated different word for each form of water. For snow, English attaches a modifying noun to the word "snow" (snowdrift, snowbank, snowfall).

The next step in the creation of the hoax was the work of Benjamin Lee Worf, an amateur language theorist, and author of the widely quoted article "Science and Linguistics." Worf's article cites as many as seven different words for snow in Eskimo, although he doesn't say what they are. He merely implies that they mean things like "slushy snow," "wind-driven flying snow," and "snow packed hard like ice." Various other popular language books picked up the idea from Worf, although the number of words for snow in Eskimo varied considerably. The highest number cited was 200 in a Cleveland TV weather forecast in 1984, followed by an editorial in the *New York Times* of February 9, 1984, stating it was 100. The *Times* quickly had second thoughts, as the number dropped to forty-eight in a February 9, 1988 Jane Brody article.

Eskimos are commonly expected to be interested in snow, but there is no reason why they should have more words for it than any other language group has that experiences snow. Since a root word can have any number of endings expressing variations of that concept, there is no limit to the number of words based on one root that a language *could* have. The Eskimo languages, such as West Greenlandic, have only two roots referring to snow. These are "qanik," which means snow in the air and "aput," which means snow on the ground. All other "snow words" are formed by adding to these, as in English.

Sources:

Adler, Jerry and Niko Price. "The Melting of a Mighty Myth. Guess What: Eskimos Don't Have 23 Words for Snow." *Newsweek* (July 22, 1991): 23.

Martin, Laura. "Eskimo Words for Snow: A Case Study in the Genesis and Decay of an Anthropological Example." *American Anthropologist* 88 (1986): 418–23.

Pullum, Geoffrey K. "The Great Eskimo Vocabulary Hoax." *Natural Language and Linguistic Theory* 7 (1989): 275–81.

Worf, Benjamin Lee. "Science and Linguistics." *Technology Review (MIT)* 42 (1940): 229–31, 247–48. Reprinted in S. I. Hayakawa's *Language in Action*.

Other Language Hoaxes

Lake Webster. Allegedly, there is a lake in Massachusetts commonly called "Lake Webster" with the real name "Chargoggaggoggmanchaugagoggchaubunagungamaug"—an American Indian word of record length. This supposedly means "You fish on your side, I'll fish on my side, nobody fish in the middle." The whole story is a twentieth-century hoax.

Earliest records call the lake Chabungungamaug Pond. An 1881 work on Indian place names in New England translates this as "boundary fishing place." Larry Daly, former editor of the Massachusetts' *Webster Times*, apparently began the hoax around 1921. Although the pond's name is from the extinct Nipmuck language, it is now translated as "a lake divided by islands." The long version of the name was coined by Daly as a joke, but people took it seriously.

Channeling. Channeling—a process in which information is accessed and expressed by someone who is convinced the source is not their ordinary consciousness—is an historical descendant of the seances of spiritualist mediums (*See* Spiritualistic Hoaxes, p. 204). The question here is whether the language used by the channeler—reproducing the speech of the entity—makes any sense linguistically. As reported by author Roberts, tapes of the entities' speech and accents were studied. They all cast doubt on the validity of the entity's speech patterns.

The use of words that did not exist at the time the channeled entity supposedly lived is a clue that a hoax is being perpetrated. One entity named Matthew, supposedly lived in "The Firth of Forth," (a body of water) in sixteenth-century Scotland. However, he used words like "rapscallion," which did not appear in the language until 200 years later. Matthew also used a silent "gh" in such words as "neighbor" and "lighter," something no Scotsman would do, then or now.

Ramtha, perhaps the most famous of present channeled entities, is purportedly a 35,000-year-old entity from Atlantis. Other than the fact that Atlantis did not exist 35,000 years ago (*See* Lost Continent Hoaxes, p. 51), the language Ramtha uses is inappropriate. This is also the case for almost every channeled entity. That situation does not bother some believers in channeling, as they claim it should be the *content* that is important, and not the language. In most cases, the content is mainly platitudes, but perhaps that *is* what is significant.

That Thusendigste Jär. *That Thusendigste Jär* is the name of a purported Old Saxon chronicle from about the year 1000 A.D. It was published in 1957 in a Dutch and Saxon edition by Gerben Colmjon. The work, as author Shetter shows, is a hoax. It contains a number of modern Dutch words in the "Saxon" part, which did not exist in 1000 A.D. Also, the piece indicates an awareness of classical learning that did not exist then and a knowledge of world geography then impossible. It also includes predictions of the modern world that seem startlingly accurate (e.g., "a thousand years from now, people in Europe might be flying across the sky too"). The book glorifies the Saxon people, especially those living in what is now the Netherlands. The introduction to the book reveals the editor's grudge against other Dutch literary and classical scholars, and provides a probable motive for this expensively produced hoax.

Sources:

Goddard, Ives. "Time to Retire an Indian Place Name Hoax." *New York Times* (September 29, 1990): 22.

Roberts, Majory. "A Linguistic 'Nay' to Channeling." *Psychology Today* (October 1989): 64–66.

Shetter, William Z. "That Thusendigste Jär." *Language* 34 (1958): 131–34.

Legal Hoaxes

This section will not include criminal hoaxes which, if done with the exclusive or primary aim of making money, are identified as swindles, and are not included in this encyclopedia. Hoaxes included here are those relating to the law or containing a substantial legal issue around which the hoax revolves.

Howard Hughes' Will

When reclusive billionaire Howard Hughes died on April 5, 1976, an intensive search was made for his will. Hundreds of millions of dollars were at stake, and California, Nevada, or Texas stood to gain millions of dollars in inheritance taxes, depending on which was declared Hughes' legal residence. The fact that Hughes died in an airplane enroute from Mexico complicated the situation further due to the resulting jurisdictional question.

Within a month, a copy of a three-page handwritten will was found sealed inside two envelopes on a desk in Mormon headquarters in Salt Lake City, Utah. The outer envelope was addressed to Spencer Kimball, the president of the church. When Kimball's secretary opened the envelopes she found the will. Apparently, a public relations staffer discovered the envelope earlier on his desk and forwarded it to Kimball's office. How the six-year-old document, got onto the desk was not explained. The will was taken to the Clark County clerk in Las Vegas, Nevada, and filed for probate.

Although Hughes did not belong to it, the terms of the will gave the Mormon Church a one-sixteenth share of his estate. This could have amounted to more than $100 million. One-quarter of the estate was left to the Howard Hughes Medical Institute. Others sharing in the balance were Hughes' former wives, Jean Peters and Ella Rice, as well as Melvin Dummar who once found Hughes injured along a Nevada highway and gave him a lift to safety in Las Vegas.

Some details of the will raised immediate suspicions that it was not authentic. For example, it referred to Hughes' wooden airplane as "The Spruce Goose," a nickname Hughes detested. According to the 1968 document, the plane was to be donated to the city of Long Beach, California. This too was odd because in 1968 Hughes did not own the plane. The will also spelled his cousin William R. Lummis' name as "Lommis," and appointed former Hughes aide Noah Dietrich to be executor. Dietrich and Hughes had a serious falling out years before. Dummar's name was misspelled as "Dumar," and a number of other words (e.g., "revoke" as "revolk") were misspelled. Hughes was not known to be a poor speller.

However, there was evidence for the will's authenticity. The number of the postage meter used to seal the inner envelope containing the will was registered to the Desert Inn, the place where Hughes was living when the will was drawn. Handwriting experts verified that the will was in Hughes' handwriting.

Complicating the issue was the appearance of more than thirty-five *additional* wills, all of them dismissed as hoaxes. The so-called "Mormon Will" remained the only possible authentic will. Reportedly Hughes wrote another will years previously, but never signed it. Intensive searching failed to produce that will, which reportedly left everything to the Hughes Medical Institute. If that will had been found and probated, there would have been no federal estate tax, and possibly low state taxes. Instead, with the "Morman Will" there was a prolonged fight over which state was Hughes' legal residence, with Texas and California finally settling their differences in 1984 when both were awarded a portion of the money.

The value of Hughes' estate declined from an initial estimate of $1.6 *billion* to the value accepted by the IRS as $460 *million*. The decrease was due to poor management by Hughes and his staff during the last three years of his life. In any event, the estate was considered the largest in American history ever probated without a definite will.

In fact, in 1981 the probate judge in Texas ruled that no valid will was left by Howard Hughes. He rejected the "Mormon Will" as a forgery—as did a Las Vegas judge previously. The unsigned will, never produced in court, was also ruled by the judge not to exist for probate purposes.

Sources:

Rhoden, Harold. *High Stakes: The Gamble for Howard Hughes Will.* New York: Crown Publishers, 1980.

Turner, Wallace. "Ex-Aide to Hughes Is Seeking Probate of Purported Will." *New York Times* (May 1, 1976): 1, 20.

———. "Probate Judge in Texas Rules that No Will Was Left by Howard Hughes." *New York Times* (February 19, 1981): A21.

———. "Purported Will of Hughes Found at Mormon Office." *New York Times* (April 30, 1976): 1, 17.

———. "Students of Hughes's Life Doubt Will's Authenticity." *New York Times* (May 3, 1976): 1, 40.

Other Legal Hoaxes

Captain Kidd and the Astor Fortune. Frederic Law Olmsted (1822–1903) is primarily remembered as the landscape architect who designed New York City's Central Park. He was also the descendant of an old American family that owned land in Maine, including Deer Isle at the mouth of the Penobscot River. The island was given to Olmsted's ancestor in 1699 by the Indians. Later the Secretary of the Treasury in George Washington's administration affirmed the legality of the deed.

On the Deer Isle property was a small cave beside the ocean; it was here that Mr. Olmsted made a discovery. He found a mark on a rock that looked like it was created by a human. Digging beneath the mark, he found a sand-filled hole in hard clay. When the sand was removed, it revealed the perfect impression of a metal box studded with large bolt heads. The box was no longer there, but its impression remained.

Olmsted was intrigued and began a long investigation that revealed that John Jacob Astor had owned the Isle in around 1799. At that time, a man named Jacques Cartier lived in a cabin on a part of the Isle he bought from Astor. According to a receipt, Astor paid Cartier $5,000 for something in 1801—probably the iron box—and within the next year Astor's bank deposits and records from Streeter's jewelry auction house in London showed that Astor sold many gold coins and jewels there. Olmsted was able to tie this together by means of old bank records and other documents, and was even able to locate the old iron box in a metal scrap dealer's stock.

Olmsted concluded that Cartier had discovered the box, which hid a part of Captain Kidd's treasure. He was unable to open the sealed box and sold it unopened for $5,000 to Astor. When Astor had it cut open he found it contained a fortune in gold coins and jewels. The proceeds of the treasure were invested in Astor's fur business and in Manhattan real estate, thus making Astor one of the city's richest men.

Since the land where the treasure was found belonged to Olmsted's ancestors, and since Kidd hanged for piracy and left no descendants, Olmsted filed suit against Astor's heirs. Olmsted sued for $1,300,000, the value of the Kidd treasure, plus interest from the year 1801 on the sum. The case was based on the statute of limitations, the treasure trove laws, the validity of old land grants, and other legal issues.

This was the state of affairs until 1931, when an 1894 note from Olmsted revealed that the entire story was a hoax. He had included the story in a talk at a luncheon in Chicago in 1894, and it spread slowly since then. Olmsted died in 1901, but the story and the lawsuit's resolution were still alive in 1931.

Sources:

"As Barnum Said." *New Outlook* (October 29, 1924): 317–18.

Head, Franklin H. "Captain Kidd and the Astor Fortune." *The Forum* (July 1931): 56–64.

Literary Hoaxes

This section includes works of literature issued under deceptive circumstances. Authors using a pseudonym will not be included here, unless the literary work is falsely issued under the name of a well-known author. Non-fiction literary hoaxes will be found under their appropriate subjects.

The literary hoax predates the printing press. Author Farrer observed that "all this miserable history [prior to Guttenberg— where printing from mobile type manuscript forgeries occurred] was the direct product of a series of forgeries . . . [O]ne is disposed to wonder whether falsehood rather than truth has not had the more permanent effect on the destinies of mankind."

The most famous English author, William Shakespeare, has been the subject of a number of hoaxes. Perhaps the two most famous hoaxes were those of William Henry Ireland and John Payne Collier. These are covered in a separate article (See Shakespeare Hoaxes, p. 148). Others tried to capitalize on Shakespeare's reputation in a minor way. Among these was the deceitful Irish printer Jacob Tonson, who used his printing press to pass off "The Widow of Watling Street," and "The London Prodigal, A Comedy" as bona fide Shakespearean plays.

In the early 1800s, the boy poet Thomas Chatterton, afraid that his poetry would not be accepted because of his age, pretended that it was found and translated by him, but that it was written by monk William Rowley. Again, there is a separate article about him (See Thomas Chatterton's Hoaxes, p. 150).

Benjamin Franklin's Hoaxes

The same Benjamin Franklin who played such an important role as a Founding Father of the United States, also possessed a mischievous sense of humor. This led him to perpetrate a number of hoaxes, mostly literary, but nearly all with a moral lesson attached to them.

Franklin's first known hoax was a series of letters, written in 1722 when he was sixteen years old and published in the *New-England Courrant*. In these fourteen letters, Franklin posed as a cheerful but shrewd rural widow, named Silence Dogood. Silence poked fun at drunkenness, pride, and hoop petticoats. She also advocated life insurance to help support widows. Benjamin's brother James was the editor of the *Courrant*, but there is no evidence that he knew who the real author was.

In *Poor Richard's Almanac* Franklin, using the name "Poor Richard Saunders," satirized astrology by predicting that death on a specific date at a specific hour would occur to a rival almanac editor named Titan Leeds. When the announced time passed, Leeds was vigorous in denying that he was dead. Poor Richard, however, was equally adamant in insisting that he *was* dead. For eight years Saunders continued to insist that Leeds was dead. When Leeds finally *did* die, Saunders said that the friends of Titan Leeds finally decided to admit that he was dead.

In 1730, Franklin published a hoax in his own paper, the *Pennsylvania Gazette*. It was called "A Witch Trial at Mount Holly" and purported to be a news story from New Jersey. It said that about 300 people gathered at the town of Mount Holly in order to watch a test of a man and a woman accused of witchcraft. They were accused of "making their neighbors' sheep dance . . . and with causing hogs to speak and sing Psalms. . . ." The test involved placing the accused on one pan of a large balance scale, with a large Bible placed on the other pan. Supposedly, the Bible would weigh more than the person if the person were a witch. In the actual test, the witches each weighed much more than the Bible. The spectators insisted that the suspected witch-

Benjamin Franklin.

es be given the water test. The suspects were therefore thrown into a pond. Both floated. This was usually a sign of guilt, as an innocent person was supposed to sink. It was decided to test them again without their clothes on when the weather was warmer. At this point, Franklin's parody of a witchcraft trial ended.

Franklin's skills as a printer helped him succeed with another hoax that he utilized on several occasions. He wrote in the proper biblical style—and printed in the proper place in the Bible—a fifty-first Chapter to Genesis, normally not found in the Old Testament. This chapter tells the story of how Abraham offered a stranger shelter, but after the stranger told Abraham that he worshiped a different god, Abraham drove him from his house. God then appeared to Abraham and told him that he had done the wrong thing. Abraham found the man and returned him to the hospitality of his home. Although people claimed they never saw the chapter of Genesis before, they could not dispute that it sounded authentic. It *was* in Franklin's copy of the Old Testament.

Another Franklin hoax was a satirical attack on slavery, exposing to Americans its immorality. Franklin wrote to the *Federal Gazette*, which had recently published an article reporting an emotional speech by a Georgia congressman urging Congress not to interfere with the slave trade. Franklin wrote that the congress-

man's speech reminded him of a similar speech, one hundred years earlier, by Sidi Mehemet Ibrahim of Algeria. In that speech, Sidi defended the enslavement of Christians in Algeria. The letter said the Algerian's speech noted that enslaving the Christians was not bad because they were slaves in their own countries, under governing despots. Those who proposed that the Christians be set free were misguided, he said, because the Christians were too ignorant to govern themselves. If the slave Christians were freed, Sidi claimed, they would start insurrections and endanger the government. The unstated parallel with the congressman's claims was obvious, although there was never a speech by an Algerian of that name. Franklin fabricated him to make a point.

To emphasize the evil of recruiting Hessian soldiers to fight with the British against the Americans, Franklin wrote a hoax letter, purported to be from "Count Schaumbergh" (Count Schaum*burg* was actually in charge of recruiting the Hessians). "Schaumbergh" reported that he was angry because the figures stating how many Hessians were killed in battle were understated. Since he received money for each Hessian killed, he wanted the correct figures, so he wouldn't be cheated out of any money. Although the British replied that the undercount was due to a number of wounded not being counted as dead, the count insisted that since they could no longer fight, the surgeons should make no effort to save them. Thus, Franklin portrayed the count as an amoral trafficker in human flesh. This helped rally sentiment against the continued recruitment of the Hessians.

Perhaps Franklin's most influential hoax was called the Polly Baker case. Polly Baker was a woman who was convicted five times of fornication, once after each of her five children were born out of wedlock. The children were each used as indisputable evidence of their mother's misdeeds. Polly made a speech to the court after her last conviction. The speech was recounted in articles that began appearing in 1760, and were reprinted many times. That speech could serve even today as a plea for equal treatment of women before the law. She pointed out that she supported all of her children, never turned down a proposal of marriage (the one she accepted led to her first pregnancy, at which point her fiancee abandoned her), thought more people were needed in the country, and would have supported her children better had the court not fined her heavily each time. Her actions hurt no one, she insisted. No action was taken against the men in each case, who were equally responsible. In fact, the first one was now a magistrate, but he would not testify on her behalf.

Polly Baker's speech must have touched a sensitive nerve, for it was republished in newspapers and magazines all over the world for many years thereafter. Benjamin Franklin wrote the original article about Polly. He seems to have modelled her upon a real woman in Worcester, Massachusetts (Eleonor Kellog), who was convicted of fornication five times between 1733 and 1745. The speech to the court did not occur in that case, however. It was Franklin's way of commenting upon the injustice of the situation. Max Hall wrote an entire book about this case, showing the prodigious amount of research needed to untangle the facts.

Franklin also executed a few other hoaxes, including one in which he recounted what happened to all the scalps taken by the Indians in America. In the story, the scalps were sent to the British King, Queen, and members of Parliament in little assorted packets. This helped turn public opinion against the British. As with all of his hoaxes, Franklin used them to teach a point. They are perhaps, another illustration of his wisdom.

Sources:

Aldridge, Alfred Owen. "A Religious Hoax by Benjamin Franklin." *American Literature* 36 no. 2 (May 1964): 204–09.

Fedler, Fred. *Media Hoaxes.* Ames, IA: Iowa State University Press, 1989.

Hall, Max. "An Amateur Detective on the Trail of B. Franklin, Hoaxer." *Massachusetts Historical Society Proceedings* 84 (1972): 26–43.

———. *Benjamin Franklin & Polly Baker: The History of a Literary Deception.* Chapel Hill, NC: University of North Carolina Press, 1960.

Edgar Allan Poe's Hoaxes

In his short life, Edgar Allan Poe (1809–1849) left an indelible mark upon literature. He was also responsible for at least six hoaxes. In return, at least one hoax was played upon him, after his death.

A poem named "Leonainie" was repeatedly attributed to Poe, even though he had nothing to do with it. The poem was actually written by James Whitcomb Riley (1849–1916), a fair poet in his own right. Riley tried to imitate the style of Poe, but not well in this poem. In addition, Riley claimed anonymously that the poem was found written in a book that was left in a hotel room in lieu of payment for room and board. The poem, in handwriting similar to Poe's, was signed "E. A. P." The book containing the poem was real enough, but the poem—a number of Poe experts testified—was not by Poe. In spite of the fact that Riley confessed and included the poem among his own in his anthology *Armazindy*, the authorship of the poem was repeatedly attributed to Poe.

Among the reasons for this errant attribution was the stubbornness of Alfred Russel Wallace, the co-discoverer of evolution. He refused, in spite of overwhelming evidence, to admit that Poe did not write the poem. Long after the poem was correctly attributed to Riley, Wallace received a handwritten copy of the poem from his brother in California. Wallace said that his brother attributed the poem to Poe. Wallace was unaware that the correct authorship of the poem had been revealed twenty years before. As author Joel Schwartz points out, Wallace could not be moved from his position. Wallace even went so far as to say that Riley had tried to pass the poem off as his own, but it really *was* Poe's.

A similar hoax on Poe was engineered after Poe's death by Ambrose Bierce (*See* Ambrose Bierce and Derivative Disappearance Tales, p. 39). In this case Bierce conceived a plan to publish a poem called *The Sea of Serenity*—actually by Herman Schaffauer—as a poem of Poe's. The poem was written in Poe's style and appeared, with Bierce's connivance, in the *San Francisco Examiner* newspaper of March 12, 1879. Contrary to what Bierce had expected, almost no notice was taken of the poem. No one seemed to care.

Poe began a Moon Hoax, similar to Richard Adams Locke's "Great Moon Hoax" (*See* Great Moon Hoax, p. 252). However, Poe found out that Locke's hoax was being published, just when he had started his story, "The Unparalleled Adventures of One Hans Pfaall," in installments in the June, 1835 *Southern Literary Messenger*. The story is basically about a man who builds a balloon and takes off for the moon to escape his creditors. After many adventures, he arrives there and lives among its inhabitants for five years. A moon person is sent back to the earth with a message that Pfaall would like to return to the earth but would only do so if he was paid a large sum for his story and absolved of all of his past crimes, including the murders of three of his creditors. Although the earth officials are willing to do this, the moon person becomes afraid of the earth inhabitants and leaves without waiting for an answer. Although Poe was going to describe the moon and its inhabitants in detail in a later installment, the success of Locke's moon hoax at exactly that moment caused Poe to abandon his story at this point.

Poe's next hoax was the Balloon Hoax (*See* Poe's Balloon Hoax, p. 47), followed by the "discovery" of gold in California in 1849, a hoax designed to slow the rush of people to California in search of gold. The title

Edgar Allan Poe.

Sources:

Felder, Fred. *Media Hoaxes*. Ames, IA: Iowa State University Press, 1989: 17–33.

Hall, Carroll D. *Bierce and the Poe Hoax*. San Francisco: Book Club of California, 1934.

Schwartz, Joel S. "Alfred Russel Wallace and 'Leonainie': A Hoax that Would not Die." *Victorian Periodicals Review* 17 (1984): 1–2, 3–15.

Silverman, Kenneth. *Edgar A. Poe: Mournful and Never-Ending Remembrance*. New York: Harper-Collins, 1991.

Thomas, Dwight and David K. Jackson, eds. *The Poe Log: A Documentary Life of Edgar Allan Poe*. Boston: G.K. Hall, 1987.

Weissbuch, Ted N. "Edgar Allan Poe: Hoaxer in the American Tradition." *New York Historical Society Quarterly* 45 (1961): 290–309.

The Fortsas Catalog

Jean Nepomucene-Auguste Pichauld, Comte de Fortsas, was a peculiar book collector. From his home near Binche, Belgium, the Comte (1770–1839) pursued his unique hobby of collecting books of which there was only one known copy in the world. Since there were so few books such as this, the Comte's collection was small. In fact, every time he found that another copy of one of his books existed, he purged his copy of that volume from his library. The mere sight of one of "his" books mentioned in a bibliography as existing elsewhere caused him to remove his copy. In fact, when Brunet's *Nouvelles Researches* was published in 1834, he "lost" one-third of his library, since many supposedly unique items were shown by Brunet to exist in duplicate copies. This loss was disheartening to the Comte, and he ended his acquisitions at this point. At the time of his death in 1839, there were fifty-two unique items in his collection.

A year after his death, his executors put the entire collection up for auction. Bookseller Emmanuel Hoyois in the city of Mons, Belgium, was chosen to compile the catalog. He published an auction catalog entitled *Catalogue d'une tres-riche mais peu nombruse collection de livre de feu M. le Comte J-N-A de Fortsas*. The catalog stated that the auction would be held on August 10, 1840, at 11 A.M. in the offices of Maitre Mourlon, a notary public, in the town of Binche. The books would be exhibited on the afternoon preceding the sale. Those who couldn't attend the auction were told in the catalog that Mr. Hoyois would execute their bids for them.

The *Catalogue* contained complete descriptions of each volume (in French). although the authors must

of the story was "Von Kempelen and His Discovery," which appears to have been published posthumously. The idea was that Von Kempelen discovered a way to make gold in the laboratory, which alchemists had long sought. People were hesitant to migrate to California, as they feared that gold would become much less valuable as a result of Von Kempelen's discovery.

Poe's hypnotism hoax was entitled "The Facts in the Case of M. Valdemar," which appeared in the *American Review* in 1845. Here Poe claimed to have hypnotised—with his permission—a dying acquaintance. As a result Valdemar appeared dead, but could still talk. This allegedly went on for several months, with a result that Valdemar begged to either be awakened or allowed to die. When an attempt was made to awaken him, his body disintegrated as if he had been dead for some time. It was a gruesome story, but many people took it for a fact. Poe refused to comment either way, leaving the impression that it was indeed fact.

Poe's other hoaxes were the long story (almost novel-length), "The Narrative of Arthur Gordon Pym," which was presented as an authentic adventure story, and "The Journal of Julius Rodman," an unfinished "true" story of a trip across the country to California. The Rodman story was dropped while Poe was in the Rockies, when he evidently either got bored with it or became ill.

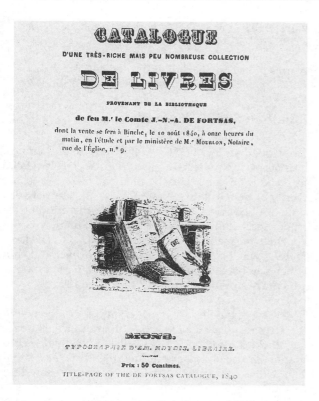

Title page from Fortsas' auction catalog.

have seemed familiar to the readers of the catalog who knew books, the titles of the works were largely unknown.

Here is a sample entry from the *Catalogue*, translated into English:

35. *Poesies de Careme [du sieur Poisson]*, a la Trappe, chez Lafriture. [Mons: Henri Bottin], 1779. (A small book of 264 pages, volume incomplete; half-binding, back and corners of blue morocco.) By Francois Auguste Poisson, called "the Poet," born at Mons in 1725, and died in the same city in 1788. The favorite genre of this Montois poet was satire and epigram, the wit of which all too frequently depended on naughtiness. Not content with having given wide dissemination to his manuscript, and with having read it everywhere, Poisson, just like anyone else, eagerly desired to see himself printed. Unfortunately for his fame, the Council got wind of this private edition and, since some of the old fogies of that respectable body had been badly treated in his rhymes, they caused the book to be seized before it saw the light. My copy, the sole to escape the flames, came from the author's heirs. Poisson was celebrated as much for his puns as for his verses; and that he might die in a manner worthy of that in which he had lived; he desired to expire with a witticism: While extreme unction was being administered to him he exclaimed "Poor Poisson, you are done, for you are being dressed with oil!"

The receipt of the *Catalogue* caused consternation and great interest throughout Europe. Many famous book collectors prepared to attend the auction, in order to complete an extensive collection on a subject or by an author. Others planned to go to buy up a particular item and destroy it to protect a family member's reputation. The keeper of the Royal Library at Brussels managed to convince the Cabinet that many of the books were so important to Belgian history that the state should appropriate them to ensure that they wouldn't leave the country. The sum of 1800 francs was earmarked for this purpose by the Cabinet. The Belgian ambassador to England was so impressed that he wanted to buy the entire collection and left instructions to this effect with Hoyois. Some of the bibliophiles and book collectors who came to Binche for the auction were Brunet, "the Bibliophile Jacob," Techener, Audemarche, and Baron de Ruffenberg. The collectors disputed whether all of the items offered were indeed unique. A number of frantic searches for second copies were undertaken among the stock of various booksellers and publishers—all to no avail.

When various attendees arrived at Binche for the auction, they gathered by the church in the central square to inquire as to the location of the "Rue de l'Eglise," where the notary's office was located. Each time someone asked a townsman for the location of the Rue de l'Eglise or of Mr. Moulon, the notary, they were politely told that there was no such street, nor any such person in Binche. When they asked for the residence of the Comte de Fortsas, the town people replied that they had not heard of him either.

A man went through the gathering crowd passing out handbills stating that the auction was cancelled. The notice actually read (in translation) as follows:

The public is informed that the choice library of the Comte de Fortsas will not be sold at auction. Amateurs doubtless will hear of this with regret. But his precious collection will not be lost to our land: it has been acquired by the town of Binche for its public library.

Several of the collectors made immediate inquiries as to the location of the Binche public library so they could actually see some of the unique items. All who inquired were told that the town of Binche did not have a public library.

At last the collectors realized they were the victims of a carefully planned and well-executed hoax. Many of the collectors returned home silently, later denying that they went to Binche for the auction.

It soon became clear that the perpetrator was Renier-Hubert-Ghislain Chalon, a retired army major, numismatist, and practical joker. He took special pleasure in vexing academic types. He evidently did a considerable amount of "homework" in preparing this hoax, including interviewing a number of prominent book collectors about their collections and interests. He was able to include seemingly-real items in the catalog, and every book in the catalog was specifically aimed at two or three collectors. Several other people, notably Henri Delmotte and Etienne Henaux, may have been accomplices as they suggested several items for the catalog.

A few people who received the catalog were not fooled by it. A number of the original recipients of the catalog also received a copy of the handbill announcing the cancellation of the auction. The handbill was mailed only a few days before the auction, reaching only those who were close enough to Binche not to require a journey of several days by coach to get there. The point of sending the "Advis" handbill before the auction was to help deflect some of the anger that would be felt by the attendees when they realized that they were hoaxed. Although it didn't work as intended, most of the victims took the hoax relatively well.

M. L. Polain saw through the hoax before the auction. He wrote an article, published in the August 10 issue of a Liege (Belgium) newspaper (the day of the auction, but obviously written *before* it was to occur), that detailed what happened during the sale of many of the books. Of course, the auction was never held, so Polain was making a small hoax about the larger hoax.

Although no collector actually lost money or was defrauded by false merchandise as a result of the Fortsas hoax, there were some unexpected side effects. Ketele a portly collector apparently lost more than fifty pounds because of the heat and effort involved in his journey to Binche. Copies of the Fortsas *Catalogue* became "hot" items for collectors. Castiaux, one of the victims of the hoax, took advantage of this fact by collecting all the copies he could find. Several years later the sale price for copies had gone so high that he made a tidy profit. The *Catalogue* has been reprinted several times since then, but original editions are highly sought. The Fortsas bibliohoax remains one of the best thought-out and effective hoaxes ever perpetuated.

Sources:

Klinefelter, Walter. *The Fortsas Bibliohoax.* New York: Press of the Wooly Whale, 1942: 72.

Lethwidge, Arnold. "The Library of M. Le Comte de Fortsas." *Literary Collector* 7 (November 1903): 6–11.

Rosenwald, Lessing J. *The Fortsas Catalogue: A Facsimilie With an Introduction by Lessing J. Rosenwald.* North Hills, PA: Bird & Bull Press, 1970.

Van Der Bellen, Liana. "The Fortsas Catalogue." *Osler Library Newsletter* no. 9 (February 1972).

Wormser, Richard. "Fabulous Fiction." *Papers of the Bibliographical Society of America.* 47 (1953): 231–47.

Jonathan Swift's Hoaxes

Jonathan Swift (1667–1745) was one of the finest satirists ever to write in English. Satire is closely related to hoaxing, except that the element of deceit is not clearly present in satire. Nevertheless, the line between satire and hoaxing is often blurred in the mind of the reader, especially when the satirical intention is unknown to the reader. A good example is Swift's *Gulliver's Travels,* which was intended as satire by Swift, but which was occasionally taken by the reader to be a true adventure story (*See* Literary Hoaxes, p. 139).

One of the literary productions of Jonathan Swift is more easily classified as a hoax than a satire. This was his "Bickerstaff Hoax." On April 1, 1708, Swift—celebrating April Fool's Day—issued the *Predictions for the Year 1709* by Isaac Bickerstaff. Swift had prepared for this hoax by writing several supplementary pieces to the *Predictions.* One of these was called *An Answer to Bickerstaff,* another the *Elegy,* and another *The Accomplishment of the First of Mr. Bickerstaff's Predictions.* Bickerstaff was purportedly an almanac writer, and the *Predictions* was an almanac. Among the events Bickerstaff (Swift) predicted for 1709 was the death of John Partridge, almanac maker, astrologer, and apparent quack. Swift did not like the man and thought that the weapon to use against him was an almanac similar to the ones Partridge made himself.

In Swift's almanac, Partridge is to die on March 29 of 1709. When the day arrived, Swift issued a previously composed verse, called the *Elegy,* which commemorated Partridge's death. This verse, which sold well in both London and Dublin even though John Partridge was alive was followed by Swift's *The Accomplishment of the First of Mr. Bickerstaff's Predictions.* The anonymous author (Swift) makes much of the fact that Bickerstaff's prediction was off by four hours.

Swift studied Partridge's own *Merlinus Liberatus* almanac for 1708 carefully before he wrote the Bickerstaff almanac. He noted that Partridge predicted an epidemic of fever to rage through London in early April. Swift therefore had Partridge die "by a raging fever." Bickerstaff made a prediction that Cardinal de Noailles, the Archbishop of Paris, would die on Easter Sunday, April 4, 1708. Since the information from Paris would take at least two weeks to reach London, the "facts" about the Cardinal would not be known until some time later due to wartime conditions. This timing was

Jonathan Swift.

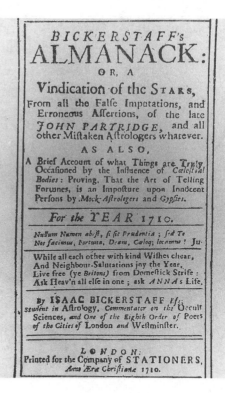

Bickerstaff's Almanac.

important because Swift wanted Partridge to wake up on April 1 and be the laughingstock of London.

Partridge, however, didn't understand he was being hoaxed. He loudly insisted that he was still alive. Others such as Richard Steele and Nicholas Rowe, *did* catch on to the prank and joined in. Reverberations from Swift's hoax extended as late as 1712, with involvement along the way from the Lord Chief Justice of England and the Grand Inquisition of Portugal. The latter put the Bickerstaff book on a list of forbidden heretical writing.

Sources:

Bickerstaff, Isaac [Jonathan Swift]. *Predictions for the Year 1708.* London: John Morphew, 1708.

Mayhew, George P. "Swift's Bickerstaff Hoax as an April Fool Joke." *Modern Philology* 61 (May 1964): 270–80.

Partridge, John. *Merlinus Liberatus for 1709.* London: John Partridge, 1709.

Mark Twain's Hoaxes

Early in his career, Samuel Langhorne Clemens (1835–1910), better known as Mark Twain, lived in

Virginia City, Nevada. He was a reporter on the *Virginia City Territorial Enterprise* during that period. Ethical standards in journalism then were different from what they are today. Many reporters saw nothing wrong with inventing the details of stories and it was often looked at as entertainment for the readers.

Twain's hoaxes consisted of untrue stories that were passed off as true. An example was "A Petrified Man," which appeared in the *Enterprise* in 1862. Twain reported that a petrified man was found south of the town Gravelly Ford. The age of the mummy was estimated at 100 years old and even the wooden left leg had turned to stone. A judge and jury went to the scene to hold an inquest. Their verdict was that the man died of exposure. The mummy was fastened to the bedrock by an encrustation of limestone. The judge refused to allow the use of explosives to free the body. There was no truth to any of this.

Another hoax by Twain took place when he was left in charge of the paper for a few days while the editor was on vacation. Twain, overwhelmed by work, urged the editor to return quickly. He sent off an issue to the vacationing editor. The issue libeled twenty prominent Nevadans on page one and questioned the morals of most of the town's women. The editor hurried back to town, only to find that Twain printed up one special copy of the paper just for the editor. The

Mark Twain.

libelous statements were not in the real issue published for distribution.

In another hoax, Twain insisted that a man who had murdered two police officers was hiding in a mine tunnel. Afraid to enter the tunnel, citizens sealed the mouth of the tunnel with rocks. The next day, a strong posse rolled away the stones and entered the tunnel. The posse found five dead Indians, including women and children, who had gone inside to sleep. None of this was true, although Twain insisted that it was.

Still another hoax was Twain's story of a man who went berserk and killed his whole family after his wealth was lost to a crooked water company in which he had invested heavily. The company had "cooked its dividends." He wanted to have the water company criticized publicly and he knew his story would be picked up by the San Francisco papers, where the water company was located. By picking the name "Philip Hopkins" for the berserk man, he also poked fun at a local tavern owner of that name, who could not have been the man involved.

Also, Twain fought a supposed duel with a Mr. Gillis, that never occurred, discounting any and all of the several accounts as hoaxes. Twain moved on from Nevada and from journalism to fiction writing, where his tendency to hoax found a later expression in his imaginative fiction and his social satire.

Dan De Quille, Mark Twain's sometime roommate and fellow reporter on the *Enterprise*, was even more adept at hoaxes than Twain. Perhaps his most famous hoax involved Mr. Jonathan Newhouse's invention of "solar armor." This was clothing to protect travellers crossing the desert. It was made out of sponge material and was soaked in water before its wearer crossed the desert. A reservoir of water suspended under the arm was squeezed to keep the suit wet. De Quille told that Newhouse wore the suit to cross Death Valley. An excited Indian reported to local residents that Newhouse was found frozen in the middle of Death Valley, his beard covered with frost. His "armor" worked too well. Other newspapers, including some abroad, picked up the story. De Quille then added an addendum that Newhouse used ether to mix with the water to get extra cooling and that the combination was responsible for the great effect.

Sources:

Fatout, Paul. *Mark Twain in Virginia City*. Bloomington, IN: Indiana University Press, 1964.

Fedler, Fred. *Media Hoaxes*. Ames, IA: Iowa State University Press, 1989: 34–50.

Ferguson, DeLancy. "Mark Twain's Comstock Duel: The Birth of a Legend." *American Literature* 14 (1942): 66–70.

Lillard, Richard G. "Dan De Quille, Comstock Reporter and Humorist." *Pacific Historical Review* 13 no. 3 (1944): 251–59.

Loomis, C. Grant. "The Tall Tales of Dan De Quille." *Western Folklore* [*California Folklore Quarterly*] 5 no. 1 (1946): 26–27.

The Old Librarian's Almanack

Around Christmas 1909, the Elm Tree Press of Woodstock, Vermont published a new thirty-two-page edition of *The Old Librarian's Almanack*, of which there were supposedly only two copies surviving from the original printing at New Haven, Connecticut in 1773. The justification in reprinting it (as the first number in a projected six-volume "Librarian's Series") was that it presented, in the style of Poor Richard's Almanac, "the opinion and counsel of the librarian and book lover of 140 years ago. It is of interest to the librarian today for its striking contrast with modern ideas of library administration."

The existence of the original was first pointed out by Edmund Lester Pearson in his column in the *Boston Evening Transcript* of July 24, 1907. In that column,

Pearson, known for his wit about librarianship, quoted from the *Almanack*. The quote was a recommendation that the library be closed for six weeks during the summer so that all books may be examined, reshelved, repaired, or replaced.

The "Old Librarian" urged his peers to

> Cast out and destroy any book which is merely frivolous, and empty of all serious meaning, for the true object of literature is to instill wisdom and to lead to habits of grave meditation, and there always are those whose vapid minds will feed, if it be allowed, on nothing but that which amuses for the moment.

Pearson later quoted from the "Old Librarian" again whenever he needed a source that defended the love of books he thought should be a characteristic of librarians, but which he felt was often no longer common among them. Pearson also used the "Old Librarian" to embody the clerical functions of librarianship that he so despised; these he made the object of gentle ridicule. One of these responses (to Thomas H. Briggs) was read by John Cotton Dana, a librarian at the Newark, New Jersey Public Library, and the proprietor of the Elm Tree Press in Woodstock, Vermont. Dana was in the process of selecting items for reprinting in a "Librarian's Series" and suggested to Pearson that *The Old Librarian's Almanack* be included. If it did not exist, he said, it ought to. Pearson was told that it would be well-printed, but that he would not profit from it. The two men then agreed that the *Old Librarian's Almanack* would be reprinted in its entirety as the first number in the Librarian's Series.

This put Pearson in a quandary because the *Almanack* did not exist. Dana finally found a suitable model for the *Almanack* at the Connecticut State Library. It was a New Haven almanac done by Joseph Perry in 1773. Dana subsequently found a copy at a Brooklyn book sale, and sent it to Pearson. Pearson lifted all the astronomical and meteorological data from the Perry almanac and substituted his own "Old Librarian's" wisdom for the rest of the text. It was difficult to fit all of his material precisely into the space available.

Dana had a friend at the American Type Founders Company design a title page into the "long S" type that was used in the eighteenth century. Pearson wrote a preface to the "reprint" in which he explained how he found the original of the almanac among the books of a deceased lawyer. Pearson created "Jared Bean," the purported real author of the original *Almanack*, under the pseudonym "Philobiblos." He fabricated a biography for him, which was included in the reprint. Throughout Pearson's preface and biographical sketch, real places are mixed with fictitious people and fictitious book titles.

As the date for the announced publication of *The Old Librarian's Almanack* approached, Dana got nervous. After all, he was a librarian perpetrating a literary hoax. He instructed his brother at the Elm Tree Press to insert a slip in each copy of the *Almanack* admitting that the work was Pearson's creation. Dana's brother disagreed and stalled. The inclusion of the slip became moot when an employee of the press sent a copy for review to the *New York Sun* without the slip. The review appeared treating the book as a reprint of a rare pamphlet. At that point, plans to include the slip were dropped. The *Sun's* review was favorable.

Pearson, ever the joker, wrote to the *Sun* to thank them for their review and to contrast their attitude with that of the local paper in Newburyport, Massachusetts. Newburyport was where he discovered the original almanack in the lawyer's library. Pearson *claimed* the newspaper was doubting the existence of the lawyer and of the Newburyport Antiquarian Society, which supposedly had possession of the original. The lawyer and the society, and the newspaper's "doubts" were fictitious. The *Sun* supported the hoax. It claimed to know Jared Bean's grandfather, Rev. Calabar Bean, who wrote *Marginalia on the Witchcraft in Salem Village and the Black Man in Connecticut, With Some remarks on the Moodus Noises*. Other Beans were noted approvingly. The *Sun* concluded by stating that another copy of the original of the *Almanack* had been found "in the library of Dr. Bowles, the well-known Springfield, Massachusetts Arctic explorer."

Other newspapers and magazines were fooled by the *Almanack*. Their reviews all treated it as authentic. Curiously, when the *Newburyport Daily News* actually reviewed the *Almanack*, it did not question the existence of the lawyer or the antiquarian society, both *supposedly* local and both fictitious. Many other reviews of the *Almanack* were published and were almost all favorable. A letter sent for publication by Pearson appeared in the *Boston Evening Transcript* which reported that the original printer of the *Almanack*, Benjamin Mecom (a real printer), had really moved back to New Haven in 1773–74, and could have printed the original pamphlet.

A former editor of *Library Journal*, Helen E. Haines, finally revealed the hoax in a letter to the editor of *The Nation*. That magazine had favorably reviewed the *Almanack*. She explained that the Newburyport Antiquarian Society and the lawyer did not exist, and she revealed several other frauds. She insisted (to further the joke) that Jared Bean had not remained a bachelor, but married late in life. His wife left him after a year, however. Pearson responded, with additional information about Bean, and the hoax went on again. Haines again reviewed the *Almanack* in *Library Journal*, where she hinted at a hoax, but perpetuated it.

The magazine *America,* in its issue of February 12, 1910, finally took a tough stance against the hoax. It stated that the motivation for the hoax could probably be found in an earlier statement of Dana's in which he took the reviewing media to task for their lack of critical reviews. Too often, he claimed, a review becomes merely a "puff" for the publication being reviewed. Although Pearson responded that the pamphlet was so transparently a fake that he was surprised it was not unmasked earlier, he did offer a money back refund.

After this point, the controversy died down. The *Almanack* was accepted finally for what it was, namely a clever hoax. The publisher G. K. Hall reprinted the *Almanack* in 1962 as a Christmas keepsake.

Sources:

Durnell, Jane B. "An Irrepressible Deceiver." *PNLA Quarterly* 36 (Fall, 1971): 17–23.

Haines, Helen E. "The Old Librarian's Almanack." *The Nation* 90 (February 24, 1910): 185.

[Pearson, Edmund Lester] "Philobiblos." *The Old Librarian's Almanack.* Woodstock, VT: Elm Tree Press, 1909.

Sullivan, Howard. "The Old Librarian and His Almanack." *Library Journal* 89 (March 15, 1964): 1188–92.

Wiegand, Wayne A. *The History of a Hoax: Edmund Lester Pearson, John Cotton Dana, and The Old Librarian's Almanack.* Pittsburgh, PA: Beta Phi Mu, 1979.

Shakespeare Hoaxes

Although William Shakespeare (1564–1616) was arguably the greatest writer in the English language, little is known about him. What *is* known does not reveal a man educated or "wise" enough to have written his brilliant plays, so many attempts have been made to "prove" that someone else wrote the plays attributed to Shakespeare. The fact that only six authentic signatures of Shakespeare are known—and little else in his handwriting—has opened the field to a large number of forgers, hoaxers, and deceivers. Some of these will be discussed here.

Samuel Ireland, a retired silk weaver, was comfortably situated. He had enough money to indulge his hobbies of rare book and curio collecting. His special interest, however, was William Shakespeare. Ireland longed for Shakespearean relics. His son, William Henry Ireland (1777–1835), was eager to help his father. Since the real Shakespearean items were not available, William Henry created them. He forged a deed with Shakespeare's name on it, a Confession of Faith by

Shakespeare, and a love letter to Anne Hathaway. Although Samuel Ireland was convinced of the authenticity of these items, they now appear clumsy forgeries, even though there are still so few samples of Shakespeare's handwriting.

William Henry Ireland's biggest hoax was the production of previously unknown Shakespearean play, *Vortigern and Rowena.* When it was "discovered," Ireland tried to get it produced on stage. He was successful in getting Richard Brinsley Sheridan to produce it, and the great Shakespearean actor John Philip Kemble to star in the play. The play was scheduled to open on April Fool's Day, 1796, but was postponed until April 2. Two days previous to this, a prominent Shakespearean scholar of the time, Edmund Malone, published a book in which he denounced *Vortigern* a forgery and a hoax. The performance was sold out. The audience thought the play was so bad that they applauded the announcement that it would not be performed again. Although a number of stories relating to the poor quality of the play were told (some of the actors' lines—especially "Oh that this solemn mockery should end."—were repeated back by the audience at the actors), this does not seem true. Nevertheless, the play was not performed again.

Ireland never sold any of his forgeries. They were produced for the benefit of his father, and perhaps for his own gratification. For this reason, no criminal proceedings were ever instituted against him. Although suspicion was raised against both William Henry and Samuel Ireland as forgers, the son admitted to the forgeries to protect his father. He wrote a short confession as a pamphlet in 1796, and a longer, book-length, confession in 1805.

The second major hoaxer of Shakespeare materials was a highly respected scholar. In fact, it has been difficult for people who investigated the case of John Payne Collier (1789–1883), to understand Collier's motives. It appears that Collier was first suspected of deception in 1852, when an annotated copy of Shakespeare's Second Folio was examined. There were supposedly thousands of corrections in the book in a hand contemporary with Shakespeare's. Collier "discovered" the book, which was known as the Perkins Folio from the ownership inscription in the book. Since the First Folio printing of Shakespeare's collected works contained so many printing errors, the presence of "corrected" text, supposedly from an authoritative hand, was quite important.

Although looking back at the Perkins Folio, it is difficult to see why it aroused so much interest in light of the anonymity of the "corrector." Collier caused much of the interest by touting his discovery and by incorporating the corrections into a new edition of

William Henry Ireland.

Shakespeare that sold well. In addition, Collier, at first, never allowed the Perkins Folio to be examined out of his sight, and eventually refused to have it examined *at all*. In 1858, Collier had to surrender and the book was finally examined by the staff at the British Museum. It was pronounced a forgery and a hoax. Collier's reputation took an immediate plunge, and his earlier work on Shakespeare was carefully reexamined. Twenty years earlier, Collier had printed some documents relating to Shakespeare that he claimed to have found in the Bridgewater Library. These were also pronounced forgeries, as were many of the manuscripts upon which Collier had based his three most famous books on Shakespeare. It was charged that Collier, who had access to all of the famous collections of Shakespeare materials, had planted forgeries among them. Collier protested his innocence, but the last thirty years of his life were spent in disgrace.

Dewey Ganzel reexamined the evidence in the Collier case, and felt that Collier was really an innocent victim. Collier's chief accuser was Clement Ingleby, a man who was involved in a conspiracy against Collier. In fact, says critic Dewey Ganzel, Ingleby knew that Collier was innocent. Ingleby was convinced that the only way the "corrections" to the Shakespeare text that the public had accepted from the Perkins Folio could be removed, was by completely discrediting Collier. Ingleby felt that the corrections were corruptions of Shake-speare. Although Ganzel makes a good case that Ingleby was dishonest, the final verdict on John Payne Collier is not in. Either Collier was a hoaxer, or Ingleby and the forger of the Shakespeare text—possibly Sir Frederic Madden—were hoaxers, or all of them were.

A final group of Shakespeare hoaxes comprises the Cunningham Papers. These were "Revels Accounts," or lists of the dates of performances of Shakespeare's plays in the years 1604–05 and 1611–12. A young man named Cunningham declared that he had found the accounts in an attic at Somerset House, the British records archive, in 1842. In 1880, a single sheet of paper was found among the Edmund Malone papers at Oxford which supported the list of plays found in the Revels Accounts. Author Tannenbaum convincingly demonstrated that not only were the Revels Accounts forgeries, but the paper supporting them from the Malone collection was also forged. Although Tannenbaum thinks that John Payne Collier was also involved with these forgeries, it may not be the case. They may have nothing to do with Collier and *still* be forgeries. Shakespeare's works remain a fertile ground for deceptions of all sorts.

Sources:

Ganzel, Dewey. *Fortune and Men's Eyes: The Career of John Payne Collier.* New York: Oxford University Press, 1982.

Grebanier, Bernard. *The Great Shakespeare Forgery.* New York: W. W. Norton & Co., 1965.

Hamilton, Charles. *In Search of Shakespeare: A Reconnaissance Into the Poet's Life and Handwriting.* San Diego: Harcourt Brace Jovanovich, 1985.

Ingleby, Clement M. *A Complete View of the Shakspere [sic] Controversy Concerning the Authenticity and Genuineness of the MS. Matter Affecting the Works and Biography of Shakspere, Published by Mr. J. Payne Collier as the Fruits of His Researches.* London: Nattali & Bond, 1861.

Ireland, William Henry. *Confessions of William Henry Ireland Containing the Particulars of His Fabrication of the Shakespeare Manuscripts; Together With Anecdotes and Opinions of Many Distinguished Persons in the Literary, Political and Theatrical World.* New York: Burt Franklin, 1969. Reprint of 1879 edition.

Malone, Edmund. *Inquiry Into the Authenticity of Certain Miscellaneous Papers.* New York: A. M. Kelley, 1970. Reprint of 1796 edition.

Tannenbaum, Samuel A. *Shakespeare Forgeries in the Revels Accounts.* Port Washington, NY: Kennikat Press, 1966. Reprint of 1928 edition.

Thomas Chatterton's Hoax

This literary hoax had fatal consequences for its author. Thomas Chatterton (1752–1770) was the child of a twenty-one-year-old mother who was six months pregnant when her husband—a schoolmaster—died. She also had a two-year-old daughter. Thomas, was loved by his mother and sister. At around age four, he became interested in reading, and soon taught himself to read from old manuscripts his father had gathered. Once he learned to read, he read voraciously, with a special interest in ancient history. At age seven, he explored the attic of his house and found bundles of old parchments that his father had brought home. His mother used them to hold patterns that she drew for the embroidery work she did to support the family. Thomas was fascinated by the writing on the old parchments. He also spent considerable time with his uncle, the sexton (janitor) of the St. Mary Redcliffe Church, where wealthy five-time mayor Mr. Caynge was buried in the churchyard.

At age eight, Chatterton was admitted to Coulston's Charity School, where he stayed for seven years. He was then apprenticed to an attorney in Bristol. At age eleven, his first poem was published in a Bristol newspaper, and at age twelve, one of Thomas' schoolmasters praised him for a supposed translation he wrote of a poem by monk Thomas Rowley. This set the stage for the triumph and tragedy that was to come and end Chatterton's life at age seventeen.

William Caynge—the wealthiest merchant during the time—was the five-time mayor of Bristol, and the man whose grave was in the churchyard. Within the church tower, was a room called the muniment room. Here old papers and records were stored, many quite old, but then considered of little value. Chatterton explored these papers, and claimed that he found among them a manuscript volume of poems by the "secular priest" Thomas Rowley. Thomas Rowley lived in Bristol about the time St. Mary Redcliffe Church was built; he was bailiff in 1466–67, and sheriff in 1475–76. Rouley died in 1478. He may have served as a *model* for Chatterton's character Thomas Rowley, who did things Thomas Rouley never did. The fifteenth century manuscript was "translated" by Chatterton. It was still, however, largely in medieval English, making it difficult to understand. Allegedly, it was Caynge who inspired Rowley to write.

Chatterton's first literary hoax was written in 1768, on the occasion of the opening of the new Bristol Bridge. To celebrate the event, Chatterton wrote a spurious history of the opening of the *first* bridge in 1248. He relied on his knowledge of those times to make it seem authentic.

George Catcott and William Barrett, older men whom Chatterton knew, were interested in local history and soon received copies of Chatterton's translations of Rowley's poems. They were impressed. Chatterton wrote to novelist and essayist Horace Walpole. Walpole indicated that he thought the poems ought to be published. Walpole sent one manuscript (not a poem) to some experts for examination who reported that it was a forgery. Thus alerted, Walpole's interest in Chatterton faded.

The first published edition of "Rowley's" poems was issued in 1777. Prior to that, individual poems were published in magazines. Chatterton adopted the "cover" of Rowley because he feared his own work would not be taken seriously because of his youth. The imposture was debated for many years. The truth was finally uncovered in the early 1800s. Chatterton wrote all of the "Rowley" poems and transcribed some of them onto old parchment. Others were merely written as "translations" by Chatterton. In fact, Chatterton often made up the "medieval" words when he didn't know the proper word for the idea he was trying to express.

Chatterton's poems fall into three major groups: the "Rowley poems," the satires, and the lesser occasional verses. Even if the Rowley poems had not survived, it is likely that Chatteron would still be remembered as an important poet for his satires. They influenced the Romantic school, including such poets as Keats, Byron, and Coleridge.

Chatterton got out of his servile law apprenticeship by making up his last will and testament, in which he sarcastically left his honor to one person, his vigor to another, and his debts to a third. His employer let him go.

Chatterton left for London in April of 1770. There, he thought he would be able to earn his living by his pen. Chatterton almost succeeded. Many of his articles and poems were published in leading Whig journals. Then the government—in the midst of political rivalry with them—arrested the editors of those journals and put the journals out of business.

Many of the journals owed Chatterton money for his work and did not pay. His finances looked grim. He became friendly with the Lord Mayor of London, William Beckford, who soon died. Alone, broke, and without much hope of a better future, Chatterton sunk into a depression. His physician friend refused to take him on as an apprentice to study medicine. Thomas moved to a garret apartment, and did not eat or sleep well. He refused help when it was offered. Finally, in August of 1770, Thomas Chatterton took arsenic that he obtained from a pharmacy, ostensibly to kill rats in his apartment. His corpse was found in his bed, amidst a litter of torn-up poems and manuscripts.

Sources:

Chatterton, Thomas. *The Complete Poetical Works of Thomas Chatterton.* 2 vols. London: George Routledge & Sons, 1906.

Haywood, Ian. *The Making of History: A Study of the Literary Forgeries of James Macpherson and Thomas Chatterton in Relation to Eighteenth-Century Ideas of History and Fiction.* Rutherford, NJ: Fairleigh Dickinson University Press, 1986.

Kaplan, Louise J. *The Family Romance of the Impostor-Poet Thomas Chatterton.* New York: Atheneum, 1988.

Meyerstein, E. H. W. *A Life of Thomas Chatterton.* New York: Russell & Russell, 1972. Reprint of 1930 edition.

Newell, John Cranstoun. *Thomas Chatterton.* Port Washington, NY: Kennikat Press, [ca. 1970]. Reprint of 1948 edition.

Russell, Charles Edward. *Thomas Chatterton: The Marvelous Boy.* New York: Moffat, Yard & Co., 1908.

Taylor, Donald S. *Thomas Chatterton's Art: Experiments in Imagined History.* Princeton, NJ: Princeton University Press, 1978.

Thomas James Wise and His Forgeries

Thomas James Wise (1859–1937) was a self-educated book collector and bibliographer who made his money in the essential oils business and spent much of that money buying rare English literature. As happens with many owners of fine collections, Wise soon learned that he knew more about this subject than anyone who has previously written about it. Wise began to write articles on the subject in an effort to make what he knew available to others.

For many years Wise did not earn enough money at his regular job to support his lavish taste in rare books. He began to make extra money by two means. First, he bought imperfect copies of rare books cheaply, and "fixed" them by inserting the missing pages from those he stole from copies of the books in the British Museum. He then sold the "fixed texts. Although he was never caught doing this during his lifetime, the case was proven from circumstantial evidence by David Foxon.

The second method Wise used to make money required many years of sharp detective work, principly by John Carter and Graham Pollard, to uncover. Wise published a number of definitive bibliographies of the

Thomas J. Wise.

works of such important British authors as Swinburne, Ruskin, Coleridge, Tennyson, Robert Browning, Wordsworth, Byron and Elizabeth Barrett Browning. In his bibliographies he included a number of rare pamphlets by these authors. The pamphlets' existence was unknown to collectors and their dates of publication predated what was known to be the first publication of the poetry contained in them. Wise then sold a few copies of these rare items to his fellow collectors, who were delighted to have such rare items, especially since Wise had pronounced the items genuine.

The production of these pamphlets served several other functions for Wise. He appeared an even better bibliographer than he was (and a better collector), since he discovered, described, and collected these rare items. The pamphlets helped authenticate his bibliographies. On the other hand, producing the items was fraught with danger. The slightest slip would have attracted publicity that would have ruined his reputation in the book world. Yet, until late in his life, when the secret was suspected, Wise managed to effectively conceal his activities.

Bookseller George D. Smith suspected something was wrong with the pamphlets, but he did not know the scope of the activity or who was involved. It took years of detective work, largely based upon the type style used in most of the pamphlets (the same typeface was used, a font called Long Primer No. 3). Carter and Pollard traced this font to Richard Clay & Sons, a printer. They used it exclusively. The pamphlets were unrecorded by anyone—including their authors—until Wise "discovered" them. Also damning was the fact that the paper used in the pamphlets contained esparto grass, which was not introduced into good paper in Britain until at least twenty years *after* the purported date at which some of the pamphlets were printed. The facts proved the pamphlets were forgeries.

The identity of the forger, however, remained only circumstantially demonstrated. Therefore, Carter and Pollard only hinted that it was Wise, fearing a libel suit. The fact that all of the pamphlets were first discovered by Wise, described by Wise, and sold originally by Wise, implicated him irrevocably in their production. The "smoking gun" was only found later by Fannie Ratchford, in the form of a letter called the Pforzheimer Document, in which Harry Buxton Foreman—another prominent book collector and bibliographer—was implicated along with Wise in the actual forgeries. Of the approximately 400 items with which Wise was associated as author, editor, reprinter, and discoverer, approximately sixty were identified (as of 1960) as almost certain Wise forgeries.

Thomas Wise was in an advantageous position when he made these forgeries. He was the only authority who could legitimize his own work. This was a tenuous situation—potentially fraught with abuses—and Wise utilized it to produce and get away with perhaps the largest and most widespread literary hoax of all time.

Sources:

Barker, Nicolas and John Collins. *A Sequel to An Enquiry Into the Nature of Certain Nineteenth Century Pamphlets by John Carter and Graham Pollard: The Forgeries of H. Buxton Forman & T. J. Wise Re-Examined.* London: Scholar Press, 1983.

Carter, John and Graham Pollard. *An Enquiry Into the Nature of Certain Nineteenth Century Pamphlets.* London: Constable & Co., 1934.

———. *The Firms of Charles Ottley, Landon & Company: A Footnote to an Enquiry.* London: Rupert Hart-Davis, 1948.

Collins, John. *The Two Forgers.* Newark, DE: Oak Knoll Publications, 1992.

Foxon, D[avid] F. "Another Skeleton in Thomas J. Wise's Cupboard." *Times Literary Supplement* (Oct 19, 1956): 624.

Partington, Wilfred. *Forging Ahead: The True Story of the Upward Progress of Thomas James Wise, Prince of Book*

Collectors, Bibliographer Extraordinary and Otherwise. New York: G. P. Putnam's Sons, 1939.

Todd, William B., ed. *Thomas J. Wise Centenary Studies.* Austin, TX: University of Texas Press, 1959.

Other Literary Hoaxes

Longfellow Hoax. Henry Wadsworth Longfellow was also a literary victim. The spurious title, *The Blank Book of a Country School Master,* along with other pseudo-Longfellows, found its way into the nation's bookshops. Among them was the handsome gift book with gold-stamped binding, *A Book of Beauty: A Souvenir.* This ornate coffee table book of its time was "Edited by Henry *Wordsworth* [sic] Longfellow."

Roth and Harris. The convicted pornographer/pirate, author/publisher Samuel Roth turned out his own writings under his real name. He also wrote—under the illustrious name of Friedrich Nietzsche—a trashy, incest-themed novel entitled *My Sister and I.* When Roth wanted to capitalize on the notorious banned erotic autobiography of the controversial Irish writer Frank Harris, he commissioned hack writer Clement Wood to turn out *The Private Life of Frank Harris* under Samuel Roth authorship. The ghostwriter was still able to get his licks in with the dedication of the book: "To Clement Wood: The only man I know who could have turned this trick . . . " Curiously, the Roth biography wasn't the only time Harris had his name and reputation tied to a literary hoax.

Harris retired to a villa on the French Riviera in the late 1920s, where he began to write *My Life and Loves,* his erotic and boastful autobiography. As fast as Harris fed it to his publishers, they issued it, one volume at a time. Regretfully, Harris died before he could finish and deliver his fifth—and last—volume. Gathering together all the scribblings, memoranda, and scraps that her late husband set aside for the volume, his widow stuffed everything in a large manila folder and left for Paris. She delivered what she had to Harris' French publisher, Jack Kahane, of the Obelisk Press. Going through the mass of Harris papers at his desk, Kahane realized that they would not make a complete volume in that form. Desperate, he commissioned Alexander Trocci, a writer of erotic fiction whom he had used before, to use whatever he could from Harris' folder to deliver a fifth volume of *My Life and Loves.* It was only many years later when Maurice Girodias, Kahane's son and heir, reprinted the fifth volume as its own entity in his Traveller's Companion series, that it was labelled correctly as *What Frank Harris Did NOT Say,* by Frank Harris and Alexander Trocci. A decade later, Grove Press printed the definitive edition of *My Life and Loves;* the Trocci additions to the Frank Harris material in volume five were edited out.

Frank Harris.

Hoax upon Ben Franklin. Benjamin Franklin was also the victim of spurious writings attributed to him. In the early 1930s, a pro-Nazi group concocted some fictitious anti-Semitic quotations and attributed them to Franklin. The Franklin Institute showed that, on the contrary, Franklin had contributed to the building fund of the Hebrew Society of Philadelphia. Franklin himself, however, was a seasoned hoaxer (*See* Benjamin Franklin's Hoaxes, p. 139).

Gentle Hoaxers. Poets Elizabeth Barrett Browning and Edward FitzGerald were both gentle literary hoaxers. Mrs. Browning's *Sonnets from the Portuguese* were mainly from her own head and heart, while so much of the "translation" of *The Rubáiyát of Omar Khayyám* was really Edward FitzGerald's writing.

Jean Shepard Radio Hoax. A radio-spawned literary hoax was *I, Libertine*, by "Frederick R. Ewing." It was the brainchild of brash, irreverent, and brilliant radio personality Jean Shepard. Musing to himself out loud, Shepard wondered what would happen if everybody in his audience would descend on their local bookshops and ask for a non-existent book. He promptly made up a title, and an author, and sent his listeners to the bookshops. The demand was huge. In fact Ballantine Books immediately commissioned Shepard and noted science fiction author Theodore Sturgeon to actually craft a paperback potboiler under that title. Because of the unprecedented demand for the softcover, Ballantine did an extraordinary thing in publishing; it released a *hardcover* edition of *I, Libertine* after the printing of the *softcover* edition. Both of them made money.

Naked Came the Stranger. Second only to the Howard Hughes hoax (*See* Howard Hughes' Autobiography, p. 72) in recent newsworthiness was the 1969 story behind the publication of *Naked Came the Stranger,* the steamy sex novel by "Penelope Ashe." It was actually thrown together by twenty-four staffers of Long Island's *Newsday* newspaper. "Penelope Ashe" was actually the sister-in-law of Mike McGrady, columnist for the newspaper and the mastermind behind the hoax. Each of the "authors" was assigned to turn out one chapter. McGrady's guidelines were that there had to be at least two kinky sex scenes in each chapter and a warning that "fine writing would be *ruthlessly* expurgated." When *Life* magazine found out about the hoax, they featured all concerned in a five-page photo story, that propelled *Naked Came the Stranger* straight onto the best-seller lists. McGrady himself relates the tale, in full hilarious detail, in his lively book about the making of the hoax, *Stranger than Naked, Or How to Write Dirty Books for Fun & Profit*. The spoof book was translated into more than a dozen languages and published on six continents.

Russian Author Hoax. Perhaps the most elaborately plotted literary hoax was concocted by the prestigious Author's Club of New York in 1917. Two of the members—annoyed by the fad of pseudo-intellectuals fawning over every obscure Russian author that surfaced—turned out an elaborate and respectful tribute to *Feodor Vladimir Larrovitch: An Appreciation of His Life and Work*. The in-depth scholarly study actually a hoax, included a manuscript page from his masterpiece *Crany Baba*, a select bibliography (in both Russian and English), and pictures of his gravesite at Yalta, Larrovitch as a young man, his parents, the room in which he died, and his embroidered shirt. The *Boston Transcript* reviewed the title, as did several New York newspapers. The club itself threw one of its biggest dinners ever on April 17, 1917, when over 300 members attended a lavish, catered affair to honor "their" Larrovitch.

The Mannix Hoaxes. Unlike the Larrovitch affair, the caper pulled by William Francis Mannix—convicted forger, check "kiter," and phony war correspondent—was of an entirely different breed. Dodging a Philadelphia newspaper, where his reckless reporting ended in a million-dollar libel suit, he fled to Hawaii, and found a job under an assumed name with the *Honolulu Advertiser*. While there he eventually forged a check, which earned him a term in the Honolulu jail. It was in jail that he wrote *Memoirs of Li-Hung Chang*, "researched" from the confines of his prison cell. At the time, Li was lionized in the Western World as both a great Chinese general and as a statesman. He was the chief negotiator, serving along with the American Secretary of State John W. Foster, at the peace talks that ended the Sino-Japanese War of 1896. Mannix fooled the Secretary of State into writing an introduction to the spurious memoirs. Recognizing a hot seller when it saw one, Houghton Mifflin published the "memoirs" in 1916. The hoax came apart when an official of the Imperial Chinese Customs Service wrote a scathing letter to the publisher, and included a list of discrepancies in the book. To the publisher's credit, they issued a new edition of the book, containing a long explanatory introduction, which told the whole story of Mannix and his literary hoax.

Third Eye Hoax. The Lobsang Rampa titles (*See* T. Lobsang Rampa, p. 5) brought forth a number of satirical treatments. For example, "Dr. Boyd Boyland & Dr. Rex Lode" (pseudonyms) turned out *The Third Eye of America*, published by Lyle Stuart. Outside of a brutally sharp satirical text on the Lobsang Rampa books themselves, the dust jacket of the book listed on its flaps almost two dozen cleverly titled—but non-existent—books on Third Eye subjects.

Compulsive Gambler Hoax. A curious "memoir," the *Compulsive Gambler*, was an anonymous confession book by "Bernie P," allegedly a reformed compulsive gambler. After a number of anachronisms, contradictions, misstatements, and lies that peppered the book were pointed out to the publisher, they withdrew the book from future publication in both the mass market paperback and foreign rights markets, and ceased the hardcover publication as well.

A Hoax of Manners. The *Diary of a Young Lady of Fashion, In the Year 1764-1765*, a charming account of eighteenth-century society and manners was written by Cleone Knox, who was privy to the royal courts of pre-French Revolutionary Europe. The excess and ceremony of royalty, reigned supreme, as recorded in the young girl's colorful diary. Only when serious questions arose concerning some of the entries and witnessed events, did the truth come to light. Magdolen King-Hall, the nineteen-year-old daughter of a British admiral, wrote it over a two-month period. All the information in the book was culled from the books and magazines in her local library. Even though the book was branded a literary hoax, the lovely and realistic scenes and events depicted by the young lady caused the book to sell well. In 1953, a new edition of the *diary* was issued, with a lively and elucidating preface by King-Hall herself. The new edition was properly labeled fiction.

Sexual High Jinks. *Pleasure Was My Business*, by "Madame Sherry," as told to Robert Tralin, was a racy, bawdy house memoir of the 1950s. Madame Sherry, who reputedly ran The Best Little Whorehouse in Miami, featured in her memoirs a spicy, x-rated chapter on how King Farouk, the deposed monarch of Egypt, had "taken over" her Florida brothel for a whole week for one long sex orgy. Farouk promptly sued the author and the publisher for gross libel. "I have never, repeat never, set foot on the shores of the continent of North America," stated Farouk's rebuttal "hence I have never been in this madam's Miami establishment. Therefore, pay me." It was only the sudden death of Farouk that prevented the case from coming to trial and exposing Madam Sherry's tale as a hoax. The author's real name was Ruth Barnes.

Hoaxing Reverend. There is one literary hoax that defies explanation. The Reverend M. Carmichael edited and wrote an introduction to the autobiography of the Rev. John Williams Walsche, a missionary churchman in China during the latter part of the eighteenth century. The book, *The Life of John Williams Walsche*, edited [sic] by M. Carmichael, was published by Dutton in 1902. Reverend Walsche was non-existent. Why a respected cleric like Reverend Carmichael would have produced this literary hoax remains puzzling.

Poetic Justice. Poetry has not been immune from the literary hoax. In the nineteenth century, German scholars had an inordinate fascination with French literature. Pierre Louys, a French erotic novelist who was famous for his novel *Aphrodite*, was annoyed with the whole sycophantic German concept. In *Conque*, a French poetry review that he founded, Louys announced that he had translated the sixth-century Greek poetry of Bilitis into French. When *Chansons de Bilitis* was published, the Germans eagerly translated them into German. As they were excellent poems, remarkable in their imitation of Sappho's poetry, many editions and translations were published. In the United States, Argus Books published a beautiful illustrated edition of *Songs of Bilitis*.

Travel in Literary Hoaxes. Travel and exploration in fiction overlaps the literary genre. (*See* also Exploration and Travel Hoaxes, p. 45). After Columbus "discovered" the New World and Marco Polo opened up Asia, travel books burgeoned. Leading the pack of impostors was Jonathan Swift's (*See* Jonathan Swift's Hoaxes, p. 144) *Gulliver's Travels*, or as it was first titled, *Travels Into Several Remote Nations of the World, in four parts. By Lemuel Gulliver, First a Surgeon, and then a Captain of Several Ships.* At first Swift dared not put his name on the book as author. "I would anger the world," he decided prior to publication. So the book appeared as the original work of one Lemuel Gulliver. The publisher claimed that he had received the original manuscript "he knew not from whence, nor from whom, dropped in the dark, from a hackney-coach." One version of the story has a black-draped coach racing by the printer's shop, hurling a heavy and bulky package onto the sidewalk in front of the establishment, and speeding away in the night. A bewildered clerk ventured out and brought the mysterious package into the printing shop. The contents turned out to be Gulliver's travel log of an adventurer who visited strangely-governed lands, populated with preposterous people with ridiculous customs and manners. As travel books were then in vogue, the publisher decided to issue the book. It was only after it was published that the slow realization came that the peoples, governments, and customs portrayed in *Gulliver's Travels* were of their very own England and Ireland, and that the book was a marvelous satire on their own image.

The work of the man known as George Psalmanazar, another travel hoaxer, but this time with the real intent to deceive, is covered separately (*See* Exploration and Travel Hoaxes, p. 45).

Sir John Mandeville also made marvelous voyages—entirely of the imagination—that were starkly recorded in *The Marvelous Adventures of Sir John Mandeville. Being His Voyages and Travels.* His hair-raising tales of fabulous and ferocious beasts, along with hazardous flora—menacing plants that ate people—were more than enough to scare most budding adventurers.

Scottish Hoax. The Scotch have one outstanding literary hoax in their history, executed by a hoax-poet, who was so good that his poems are still read today. James Macpherson, a minor poet, returned from the Hebrides with fragments of poetry by ancient celtic bards, gathered from far away in the Highlands. He published them as the poems of Ossian. Suspicious of Scotsmen in general, and Macpherson in particular, lexicographer and writer Dr. Samuel Johnson personally made a trip to the Hebrides to verify Macpherson's story. According to the doctor, Macpherson's story could not be proven. Other investigators have since confirmed this. In spite of this, other Ossian titles (all "translated" by Macpherson) followed. Ossian was not just popular in the British Isles. American editions, including *The Poems of Ossian, The Son of Fingel,* were published by Thomas Long in Philadelphia. *Fingel* was a thick volume, some 500 pages. As late as 1931, Duke University's literary magazine wrote about "The Vogue of Ossian in America." The whole hoax was finally unravelled when, upon the death of Macpherson, a handwritten manuscript copy of one of the Ossian titles was found among Macpherson's effects.

Spectric School of Poetry. Another "school" of poetry that was a hoax was the Spectric School, popular in the years just prior to World War I. Witter Bynner, poet, essayist, and playwright, collaborated with fellow poet Arthur Ficke and thought up Spectra. In the spring of 1916 with the cooperation of Chicago publisher Mitchell Kennerly, *Spectra: A Book of Poetic Experiments* by Emanuel Morgan and Anne Knish was published. Bynner's pseudonym was Morgan and Ficke's was Knish. As poetry was fashionable among the intelligentsia at the time, the new school of poetry was warmly received and literary magazines praised the book and the new school of poetic expression. Problems arose when the press and the enthusiastic adherents of the Spectric style wanted to meet the authors.

Bynner and Ficke made up excuses as to why the two authors could not face an audience. The hoax continued unabated for a couple of years. More and more poetry of the Spectra School was turned out and the hoax took root. The hoax continued to live on even after the evening in Detroit in 1918 when, in the midst of Bynner's scheduled lecture, a member of the audience baited him about the legitimacy of it all. At that point, Bynner confessed the hoax. William J. Smith tells the story in his definitive title *The Spectra Hoax.*

"Blanket" Plagiarism. Plagiarism—the act of taking another's work and passing it off as one's own, without acknowledgement—can sometimes be classed as a literary hoax, when it is a case of *blanket* plagiarism, as with *The Portrait of a Lover,* a novel by J. Edward Harris published in hardcover by Lyle Stuart in 1969. That same year Grove Press issued an anonymous erotic paperback novel in their Venue Library series, called *The Alter of Venus.* Book dealer C. J. Scheiner noticed that the two books were identical, word for word. They were both typeset from one of the many anonymous pornographic typescripts that circulated in the 1930s.

More Hoaxing Preachers. *Marie Schweidler, The Amber Witch,* was supposedly by Abraham Schweidler, a hell-fire and brimstone preacher of the seventeenth century. The manuscript was "discovered" by another member of the cloth, Rev. Johann Meinhold, who had the book published in 1844 with enthusiastic prodding from his clerical elders. Later it was revealed that it was all the work of Meinhold, who wanted to show up the ignorance and haughty pomposity of his clerical contemporaries. The book was originally published in German, but when the English translation was issued in 1861 in England, Abraham Schweidler was still listed as the author, with Reverend Meinhold's son credited as the editor.

Backfiring Blank Page Hoax. Whimsical humorist H. Allen Smith's *The Complete Practical Joker,* published by Doubleday in 1975, was issued with one full page in the middle of the book left completely blank. It was intended as a joke, but the publisher and bookstores were swamped by angry book buyers, all demanding to have their "defective" copies of the book replaced with complete ones. Publisher William Morrow produced a reprint edition of the book in 1980 that did not include the blank page.

American Indian Poseur. The Education of Little Tree was purported to be an autobiography of an American Indian child growing up and was supposedly by Forrest Carter. The book was actually written by a hard-line racist and Ku Klux Klan member named Asa Carter, who was definitely not raised as an American Indian. It is not clear why the hoax was done, or where Carter obtained his intimate knowledge of the problems faced by Indian children in America.

Faux Alger Biography. Horatio Alger (1832–1899) authored dozens of popular books about how poor children overcame obstacles and became successful adults. In 1928, Herbert Mayes published the first full biography of Alger, entitled *Alger: A Biography Without a Hero*, published by Macy-Masius in New York. The work became the standard biographical source on Alger, who led a fairly eventful life. When questioned about his biography the author—a former magazine editor—always refused to discuss it. Over the years, writer William Henderson managed to pry a full confession of the literary hoax from Mayes. Mayes intended that the book be viewed as a piece of humor, and not a biography. However, the humor was lost on people, and the book was viewed as serious from the beginning. In fact, Mayes admitted that his book was not just partly fictional, "it was practically *all* fictional."

Giving the People What They Want. Occasionally, a book that does not really exist is created to meet a demand (*See* The Three Impostors, p. 89). In the case of *The Necronomicon*, demand was created by the fantasy writer H. P. Lovecraft. He documented and described the book (supposedly by Abdul Alhazred) so carefully that a group of Lovecraft fans decided in 1973 to produce the book as described. Their work was a 197-page supposed facsimile of the "Duriac Manuscript." It is written in Persian, specifically Farsi, an Iranian language although it is pure gibberish, preceded by a preface that explains the "history" of the manuscript. Lovecraft's own "history" of *The Necronomicon* was included in the preliminary matter to his *Beyond the Wall of Sleep*. There has since been an English version of the Farsi book, with as much claim to legitimacy as the first one.

Concocted Rejected Addresses. When the Drury Lane theatre in London was about to open in 1812, a contest was held for the best opening speech. So many written entries were received that the judges gave up, and simply commissioned a poem from Lord Byron to serve as the text. Many of the people who entered the contest were outraged. A book called *Rejected Addresses* appeared, supposedly containing all of the contest entries, including many from famous poets. They were all fakes, but were fine parodies of the style of those poets. Another publisher then published the *real* reject-

ed contest entries, under the title *Genuine Rejected Addresses.*

Sterne Letters. In 1779, a volume of letters by Lawrence Sterne, then recently dead, was published in London under the title *Letters Supposed to have Been Written by Yorick and Eliza*. In 1784, the publisher began advertising them as being by a friend of Sterne's named William Combe. Although some believe the letters were penned by Sterne, Lewis B. Curtis exposed the letters as Combe's, in 1935.

Angry Penguins. Another poetry hoax occurred in Australia. The literary review *Angry Penguins*, published in Adelaide, Australia, received some unsolicited poems in the mail in 1944. They were from a previously unknown poet named Ern Malley. The magazine's editor, Max Harris, was impressed and asked for additional poems and details of the poet's life. The poet's sister—who submitted the initial poems—replied with more poems and the sad news that her brother died recently of Graves disease at age twenty-five. Harris should have realized then that a hoax was afoot, as Graves disease (a thyroid hormone deficiency) is almost never fatal. Another clue was that "Malley's cow" was an Australian expression for a person who disappears without a trace. Harris published many of the poems and they were anthologized in several books. It was soon revealed, however, that the poems were by two army enlistees, Lt. James McAuley and Corp. Harold Stewart. The soldiers decided to see if modernism would tolerate "deliberately concocted nonsense" in the form of poetry. An twist on this story occurred when the police brought an action against *Angry Penguins* for publishing obscenity in several of the Ern Malley poems. Harris was tried and convicted; he was fined five pounds. The allegedly obscene material is nonsensical (e.g., "The swung torch scatters seeds/ In the unbelliferous dark").

Sir Arthur Conan Doyle Hoax. A literary hoax of a different sort occurred with the supposed bookplate of Sir Arthur Conan Doyle. The mark of ownership of a famous person often adds price and demand for a book. That may have motivated someone to design, print, and apply fake bookplates bearing the coat of arms of Sir Arthur Conan Doyle—creator of Sherlock Holmes—to several volumes. Examination of a number of large authentic collections of Doyle materials, as described by author Stanley Wertheim, have clearly shown that Doyle never used a bookplate. The bookplate seems to have originated with Doyle's son, who suggested what such a coat of arms of the Doyle family would look like. A few such plates were ordered by Julian Wolff, a Sherlockian scholar. The printer evidently printed more than were ordered, and the extra plates seem to have been innocently distributed to

Holmes collectors by Wolff. A few turned up in Doyle books.

Hitler's Doctor. A strange literary hoax was concocted by David George Plotkin (d.1965). Though he had never been to Germany, he wrote a book (under the name Dr. Kurt Krueger) entitled *I Was Hitler's Doctor.* The book was first published by Avalon Press in 1941, under the title *Inside Hitler.* Plotkin managed to recruit Upton Sinclair to write the prelude, and a real physician named K. Arvid Enlind to write the preface. The book was published by Samuel Roth, a notorious literary and publishing charlatan. Upton Sinclair was convinced the book was a genuine memoir, even though he claimed not to know the author personally. Perhaps the most peculiar item in the book is the long psychiatric profile that the author gives of Hitler, attributing his behavior to a series of Freudian incidents.

Arnold Bruce Levy

[Other Literary Hoaxes]

Sources:

Bales, Jack. "Herbert R. Mayes and Horatio Alger, Jr.; Or the Story of a Unique Literary Hoax." *Journal of Popular Culture* 8 no. 2 (1974): 317–19.

Bruns, Bill. "Naked Truth About the Great Novel Hoax." *Life* (August 22, 1969): 69–70.

Curtis, Lewis B. "Forged Letters of Laurence Stern." *Papers of the Modern Language Ass'n.* 50 (1935): 1076–106.

Farrer, J. A. *Literary Forgeries.* London: Longman, Green & Co., 1907.

Lehman, David. "The Ern Malley Hoax: Australia's 'National Poet'." *Shenandoah* 34 no. 4 (1983): 47–73.

McGrady, Mike. *Stranger Than Naked; Or, How to Write Dirty Books for Profit; A Manual.* New York: P. H. Wyden, 1970.

Paull, H. M. *Literary Ethics: A Study in the Growth of Literary Conscience.* Port Washington, NY: Kennikat Press, 1968. Reprint of 1928 edition.

Pullar, Philippa. *Frank Harris.* London: Hamish Hamilton, 1975.

Reid, Calvin. "Widow of 'Little Tree' Author Admits He Changed Identity." *Publishers Weekly* (October 25, 1991): 16–17.

Smith, William Jay. *The Spectra Hoax.* Middletown, CT: Wesleyan University Press, 1961.

"Timeless Tentmaker" [Omar Khayyam]. *MD* (May 1978): 111–16.

Wertheim, Stanley. "The Adventure of the Arthur Conan Doyle Bookplate." *Manuscripts* 34 no. 4 (Fall 1982): 279–89.

Whitehead, John. *This Solemn Mockery: The Art of Literary Forgery.* London: Arlington Books, 1973.

Medical Hoaxes

There have always been people willing to pay to relieve their illness. There have also been people who claim to be able to relieve that illness, "for a small fee." Although many remedies did not work, it is only when the purveyor of those remedies knew in advance that the treatment would not work that fraud has taken place. This section will consider only those who seemed to operate from motives other than purely financial ones.

In many cases, the motives of the promoters are difficult to decide. Nearly everyone viewed Dr. Andrew Ivy as a misguided, but sincere, scientist when he promoted the worthless cancer "cure" Krebiozen. He was eventually made to realize his mistake, but his career and reputation were ruined. No hoax was involved on Dr. Ivy's part, although it is unclear whether the two brothers who sold Dr. Ivy on the merits of Krebiozen were innocent.

There are literally thousands of medical remedies that did not or do not work. Many of these were mere money-making schemes, in which the maker and seller of the product knew they didn't work, and won't be discussed in this book.

For this section the list of medical frauds was pared down to those that involved only hoaxes. Products that are misbranded—that simply do not contain the agents, chemicals, or drugs that they claim to contain—will also not be covered here. Medical impostors are covered elsewhere (See Impostors, p. 105).

Aristotle's Masterpiece

Aristotle's Masterpiece is perhaps the longest-lived medical hoax. Its origins date to the Middle Ages and it has slowly evolved. Until the 1930s, the book was still in print.

The origins of what is usually called Aristotle's Masterpiece are obscure. It is certainly not by Aristotle, rather his name was used to add authority to a collection of sexological and folkloric ideas that would otherwise probably not have survived the Middle Ages. Scholars claimed that Aristotle's Masterpiece was one of the major sources of sexual "knowledge" for the working classes until well into the twentieth century. The book, published in more than 150 editions in English alone, evolved in content over the centuries as various hacks have added to it. The work is substantially different from period to period.

In its nineteenth-century version, the book is roughly divided into several parts. In its full development, these parts were entitled "The Masterpiece," "The Experienced Midwife" (which, in turn, had two parts: "A Guide to Childbearing Women," and "Proper and Safe Remedies for Curing All Those Distempers that Are Peculiar to the Female Sex and Especially Those Observations to Bearing of Children"), "Aristotle's Book of Problems," and "The Last Legacy." In earlier periods, some of these parts were missing or their titles altered. In addition, the contents of each section were often vastly different. A section called "Remarks on Physiognomy" was often included. The general emphasis remained on reproduction, however.

The contents were largely designed to inform couples how to have children. There was no information about contraception, even in the nineteenth-century editions. In addition, there was some information (almost all of it incorrect) about the cause of various male and female reproductive systems' disorders and diseases. The anatomy of the reproductive system was also covered, with much more emphasis on the female anatomy. Why there was an emphasis on female anatomy was not clear.

The sales of Aristotle's Masterpiece through the years indicated that a portion of the English-speaking population was both ignorant of sexual matters and interested in learning about them. It is impossible to know the effects the incorrect information found in any of the editions of the *Masterpiece* had. The contents are amusing from a modern vantage point, but fewer than 100 years ago this book was taken seriously by many people. They believed in the "humors" of phlegm, yellow bile, black bile, and blood, (when the four humors were unbalanced, disease was present) even though they were holdovers from the thinking of Hippocrates more than 2,000 years ago. Yet the humors were mentioned as though this was modern medical thinking. Other vestiges of an earlier time included the idea that deformed children—or "monsters" as they were referred to—were caused by something that the mother saw or thought about during her pregnancy.

Sources:

Beall, Otho T., Jr. "*Aristotle's Masterpiece* in America: A Landmark in the Folklore of Medicine." *William & Mary Quarterly* (3rd Series) 20 (1963): 207–22.

Blackman, Janet. "Popular Theories of Generation: The Evolution of Aristotle's Works, the Study of an Anachronism." in John Woodward and David Richards, eds. *Health Care and Popular Medicine in Nineteenth-Century England.* New York: Holmes & Meier, 1977: 56–88.

Lawn, Brian. *The Salernitan Questions: An Introduction to the History of Medieval and Renaissance Problem Literature.* Oxford: The Clarendon Press, 1963: 98–111.

Power, D'Arcy. "Aristotle's Masterpiece." in *The Foundations of Medical History.* Baltimore: Williams & Wilkins, 1931: 147–78.

Biorhythms

Biological rhythms are real; biorhythms are a hoax. Biological rhythms are the relatively large number of phenomena in the living world that display a regular cyclic behavior, most of which are tied to the twenty-four-hour rotation period of the earth. It is the light and dark cycle or the tidal cycle every twenty-four hours that seems to be the "synchronizer" for these "circadian" (about twenty-four-hour long) rhythms. Some examples are activity cycles, feeding cycles, and sleeping cycles.

Biorhythms seems to have originated in 1887 with Wilhelm Fliess, a German physician. He claimed that everyone was basically bisexual. Male characteristics (strength, courage, and endurance) were keyed to a cycle of twenty-three days. Female characteristics (sensitivity, intuition, love) were keyed to a twenty-eight-day cycle—but *not* the menstrual cycle. He claimed that every body cell had a cycle, and that it played a key

role in the peaks and valleys in vitality and mental and physical strength. Biorhythms even determined death dates.

This two-cycle explanation was expanded to include three cycles: physical, intellectual, and emotional. The addition of the third cycle was the work of Alfred Teltscher, an Austrian engineer, in the 1920s. Since the birthdate determined the start of these cycles, biorhythms were connected to astrology. This feature was added by Herman Swoboda around 1900.

The most widely read popularizer of biorhythms was Bernard Gittelson, who tried to piggyback biorhythms onto legitimate biological rhythms by purposely intermingling the two concepts into the same sentence in his books. For example, in *Bio-Rhythm*, there appeared the following sentence: "In man—the most complicated form of life—there are so many subtle, elaborate biological cycles that scientists have only begun to sketch in the nature of the larger cycles of human life that we call biorhythms."

Biorhythm theory says that there is a physical cycle, lasting twenty-three days, an emotional cycle lasting twenty-eight days, and finally an intellectual cycle lasting thirty-three days. All of these cycles start at "zero" at the moment of birth, and then follow an "S-shaped" sine curve in value. The emotional cycle reaches its peak in seven days, then crosses the zero line in another week. It then declines for a week to its minimum value, then rises again in another week. Thus, it has made a complete sine curve in twenty-eight days.

Biorhythm theory says that when a cycle is above the zero line (positive), the abilities governed by it are increased, and vice versa. Thus, a person can, on any given day, have one, two or all three curves positive, negative, or mixed. When all three curves are at their positive maximum, the person is at his or her peak of behavior. Similarly, when they are all at a minimum, it is probably best not to leave the house. When a cycle line is crossing the zero axis, it is "critical." This is when people are most prone to catastrophes in that particular dimension of life. Human disasters, the theory says, are much more likely to occur to a person who has more than one critical cycle on a given day. Biorhythms were introduced into the United States by George S. Thommen, a Swiss importer, around 1960.

Neither Thommen nor Gittelson is a scientist, and neither understands what constitutes valid scientific research. Instead, they rely on anecdotal evidence of people who had tragedies in their lives that occurred on days when more than one of their cycles were critical or minimal. Thus, airplane crashes occurred when a pilot's cycle was unfavorable. Gittelson comments that "The most convincing studies of biorhythm are those you can do for yourself . . . . try out the theory in your own life.'' (19–20).

In contrast, *biological* rhythms differ in length from individual to individual. They develop slowly during the first one to two years of life. They also vary in length somewhat within the same individual.

The studies that Fliess, Swoboda, and Teltscher claimed they did to validate biorhythm theory do not exist. Swoboda claimed that his eight trunks of research notes were lost when the Nazis invaded Vienna. Teltscher's research was never published. Fliess contributions to the idea of biorhythms consist of anecdotal stories taken from psychiatric interviews with patients. These were contained in rare (United States) books that were never translated from German. Fliess' other ''major'' contribution to knowledge consisted of the idea that all illnesses were controlled by centers in the nose. Almost any condition could be treated by operating on the patient's nose.

Nevertheless, several people attempted to test biorhythm theory by using published sports statistics. Knowing the athlete's birthdate, one could identify the biorhythm curves and compare them with performance. Studies involving Arnold Palmer's golf tournament victories were quoted as supporting biorhythm theory. The idea would be that Palmer's physical curve would peak on the day of a ''win,'' while his other curves would not be critical. A careful reexamination of the data (mentioned by author William Bainbridge Sims) showed that incorrect statistical tests were applied. *Few* of Palmer's wins were on days when his physical curve was *high*. Other studies of golfers' biorhythms on dates they won tournaments, showed that the results do not differ from those expected by chance. Similar results were obtained from a study of the pitchers of no-hit baseball games.

Both the theoretical underpinning and the practical scientific verification of biorhythm theory are lacking. Without those, biorhythms became just another pseudoscientific claim that people are willing to accept without the required evidence. Those pushing biorhythm calculators and books on a gullible public are guilty of making fraudulent claims. They are hoaxers of the public if they know that what they are saying has no factual justification.

Sources:

Bainbridge, William Sims. ''Biorhythms: Evaluating a Pseudoscience.'' *Skeptical Inquirer* (Spring/Summer 1978): 41–56.

Gittelson, Bernard. *Bio-Rhythm: A Personal Science.* New York: Warner Books, 1977.

Hines, Terence M. ''Biorhythm Theory: A Critical Review.'' *The Skeptical Inquirer* 3 no. 4 (summer 1979): 26–36.

Luce, Gay Gaer. *Body Time: Physiological Rhythms and Social Stress.* New York: Pantheon Books, 1971.

Palmer, John D. *An Introduction to Biological Rhythms.* New York: Academic Press, 1976.

Schadewald, Robert. ''Biorhythms: A Critical Look at Critical Days.'' *Fate* (Feb 1979): 75–80.

Fireproof People

In ancient Greek and Roman classics ''ordeal by fire'' was common. In the play *Antigone,* soldiers agreed to hold a red hot piece of iron or walk through a bed of burning coals to prove their innocence. Years later, after the legal system abandoned ''ordeal by fire,'' entertainers took up the same challenge to show that they could hold red hot objects or surround themselves with fire without injury.

Recently, firewalkers have offered courses in the United States that teach people how to increase their will power to overcome pain and fear (*See* Firewalking, p. 98).

Two different types of explanations for this demonstrated tolerance for heat are involved. Walking into a 400 degree oven carrying two raw steaks and emerging twenty minutes later with the steaks cooked, but the person still ''raw,'' *might* be a conjuring trick. This feat was one of the main features of several acts in the 1800s. At the same time, walking the length of a bed of hot coals in bare feet might *not* be a conjuring trick, for there is no deception involved. People *can* walk on beds of hot coals, and emerge unscathed (*See* Firewalking, p. 98). The person in the oven, however, never spent twenty unprotected minutes in a blazing inferno, even though it appeared that he did. This *was* deception.

Although many ''fireproof people'' effects were performed as a form of entertainment, other instances of apparent flameproofing are found in various native societies, where invulnerability to fire is a sign of high status. For example, among the Shona tribe in Southern Rhodesia in the 1950s, a tribal elder showed Frank Clements his disdain for Clements' Zippo lighter which could produce ''fire'' at will. The elder picked up a burning stick and licked the flame, finally quenching it between his hands. The point was simply that ''although you [Clements] can make fire at will, I [the elder] can handle it without damage.''

Investigating the acts that fireproof people performed in the past is difficult. No one performs these feats today, and one cannot take a trained observer to get an opinion about how it was done. Instead, statements of relatively naive observers—who did not know how to spot a magician's tricks or a charlatan's frauds—are the only means to investigate how the acts were performed. Worse still, often the only source of information is a poster advertising the fire king's act. These posters often contained more "hype" than truth, as their object was to draw in the audience with fantastic claims of the performer's abilities. In short, it is difficult to know exactly *what* feats were actually performed, much less to identify how they were performed.

Invulnerability to fire was occasionally used as part of the "performance" of spiritualist mediums and others who were not known primarily as fireproof people. Among the most famous of these was Daniel Dunglas Home, (1833–1886) perhaps the best physical medium who ever lived. Home, on more than twenty occasions reportedly picked up red-hot coals directly from the fireplace with his bare hands. He occasionally stirred the embers with his hand as well. Home could also transfer his fireproof qualities to others, as he gave others a red-hot coal to hold for several minutes without their hands being burned. Although it is still unclear how Home accomplished many of his feats, that does not necessarily mean that no trickery was involved. Several times trained observers saw him cheat, but it is true that Home was never publicly exposed while doing trickery.

Salves or solutions rubbed on the skin were supposedly able to provide protection from fire or heat. Among these solutions were those that contained "sulfuric ether" (sulfuric acid) or alum, repeatedly applied to the skin until it became thickened and insensitive. The idea seems logical, but thick skin would still burn—perhaps painlessly. It is a possible explanation for one or two cases of handling red-hot metal, but it seems unlikely that a regular performer could maintain an act based on this method. He or she couldn't continually grow or scar skin that quickly. The smell of burning flesh would also most likely drive the audience away. Finally, only a small portion of the body could be rendered insensitive so that would not explain how the tongue, lips, and often the entire body, in the oven performances, could be protected. Other chemicals mentioned in some sources were to be applied repeatedly as a paste that was left on. It is difficult, however, to see how a hand covered by many layers of paste would go undetected.

Simpler methods could be used to suggest the handling of hot metal. The performer could switch the hot metal for a cold piece at some point prior to handling it. One could also use a natural layer of moisture between the hot metal and the skin—the so-called Liedenfrost Effect—which may explain how red-hot metal can be touched to the tongue. The water layer on the tongue is vaporized by the heat, and turns into a series of small spheres of water that act as an insulator between the metal and the tongue. The effectiveness of this layer depends on brief contact.

When molten metal was poured over a part of the body without harm—a stunt done by performers of the nineteenth century—the metal used was an alloy known as Mallot's metal. It melts at a temperature lower than that of boiling water, and can be safely touched for short periods without burning the skin. Liquid mercury may also have been substituted, in some of these performances.

Fire eaters are still occasionally seen in carnivals. They seem to quench flaming torches in their mouths and blow smoke and flame without burning themselves. This is possible, but only after much practice and many burns. They take simple precautions to protect themselves from harm. For example, they must always breathe out when flame is in their mouth. Breathing in will draw smoke and flame into the lungs, with resulting damage. Simply closing their mouths will put out all flames from lack of oxygen. Saliva serves as a barrier for momentary protection against burns. They must use gasoline as a fuel and be careful not to breathe in the fumes. With those and a few other precautions, fire eating is a matter of care and practice.

The actual practice of firewalking goes back thousands of years. It was often an integral part of religious ceremonies and formed a kind of "proof" that the deities were protecting the firewalker. The courses that are offered around the country to enable people to have the confidence or ability to firewalk are largely hype.

Another form of immunity to fire was demonstrated by the famous spiritualist medium Daniel Dunglas Home (1833–1886), mentioned earlier in this section. Although fire immunity was only a small part of Home's repertoire, he demonstrated it a number of times. Perhaps his most convincing feat was in 1869, when he went to the fireplace at the home of Mr. S. C. Hall—where a seance was taking place—and removed, with bare hands, a large glowing coal from the fireplace. He then placed the coal on top of the head of Mr. Hall, who had long, white hair, and still suffered no burns. Home then drew Mr. Hall's hair over the coal, so that a red glow could be seen through the piled-up hair. After removing the coal, Home asked several of the bystanders to hold it or touch it. Several were burned. The source for this incident is cited as S. C. Hall's autobiography *Retropsect of a Long Life.* However, careful examination of this 600-page work, failed to find a single mention of either Home or of this incident, although Hall and Home were well-acquainted. In related demonstrations, Home allegedly put his head in a fireplace filled with glowing embers, and stirred the embers with his hand. He also held glowing coals in his hand without harm.

Among the most unusual effects he accomplished was the "transference" of his fire immunity to others. He would repeatedly pass his hand over another's and if he thought the person had enough "faith," he could pass the glowing coal to the person to hold in his or her own hand without injury. This transference is perhaps the most puzzling part of the whole phenomenon. Unusual as Home was, several elements of his seances were "suspicious." For instance, he often insisted that his audience not look directly at an effect. He also indulged in an almost constant patter, and moved incessantly about the room. Home also insisted that the lights be dimmed before his levitations, and suggested to his audience what they were about to see.

A larger, religious context surrounds the handling or swallowing of red hot coals, or handling hot metal. In Brazil, for example, as part of a religious rite, members of the Batuque cult burn gunpowder in the palms of their hands, and slowly pass the flames of candles along the skin of their arms and face. In the United States several southern Appalachian cults, handle both fire and poisonous snakes. Former members of the Church of God headquartered in Tennessee, are now part of independent Free Pentecostal Holiness churches. This rite stems from biblical verses used by these cult members. Among them are "When thou walkest through the fire, thou shalt not be burned; neither shall the flame kindle upon thee." (Isaiah 43:2), and "Faith . . . quenched the violence of fire" (Hebrews 11:33–34). Their rituals involve the use of soda bottles filled with kerosene with a twisted rag wick. The torches are passed slowly over the hands, feet, arms, or fingers, for up to ten seconds without visible agony. One firehandler supposedly let a "non-believer" pour kerosene on his socks and then let his socks be ignited. The socks were destroyed, but the man's feet were uninjured.

Explanations offered by these cult members may help to explain *many* of the phenomena of fire immunity. They claim that they either have complete faith in God's protective powers, or—more often—they become "anointed." This anointing is a special power or state, supposedly granted by God, which lasts only a short time and varies in intensity and duration. The anointed person can almost always tell he or she is in this state because they are euphoric and their arms get numb—much like when they "fall asleep." The flow of blood is cut off and the limbs feel cold, which would indicate diminished blood flow.

This information provides an answer, or partial answer, to how this sort of fire immunity is accom-

plished. It cannot be nervous system control, because the effects felt are not simply those of one part of the autonomic nervous system or the other. They seem mixed, indicating a *chemical* effect. The chemical to produce these effects has recently been discovered in the body. This chemical is β-Endorphin. Sometimes called the brain's own opiate, β-Endorphin produces euphoria and *immunity against pain*. β-Endorphin can be released during such ordinary but stimulating events as gambling, jogging, or dancing. The highly emotional state of anointing, which occurs after much singing, praying, testifying, and other religious furor, could surely trigger β-Endorphin release. This, in turn, could cause the immunity to pain and the euphoria also reported.

I. I. Chabert, who was born in France in 1792, was perhaps the best-known "fire king." He flourished from 1820–1833, doing many of his "fireproof" and "poisonproof" stunts. In 1826, he began performing the first of his oven feats, in which he entered an oven especially constructed on four pillars. There was a small opening for breathing and conversation. Chabert entered the red hot oven with a raw rumpsteak and a piece of raw mutton, and remained inside until both were well-done. He then emerged and joined the audience in eating both pieces of meat.

Chabert *was* apparently in the oven the entire time the meat cooked. He could be heard and seen through the small opening. The time elapsed may have been as long as thirty minutes, but could have been considerably reduced (perhaps to about fifteen minutes) through the use of bellows or forced air currents on the meat. How the oven was constructed is not known. It is not known if the fire under the oven was only glowing coals at the time he entered the oven. Further, it is not clear whether the entire bottom of the oven was open to the fire, or if only the center was. If so, Chabert could have put the meat to be cooked over the open part of the floor of the oven, while he stayed in a closed corner of the oven. The human body can withstand several minutes in 300 degree heat. Although staying in an oven this hot for fifteen minutes puts a great strain on the heart and circulation, it *can* be done. The idea postulated by some that Chabert donned an asbestos suit with a hood while in the oven, is possible but would not have been necessary.

"Fire queen" Josephine Girardelli performed various stunts with red hot metal, molten metal, and acid— and drank "boiling oil." Many of these effects can probably best be explained as sleight-of-hand and traditional magic, with no need to invoke bodily immunity to fire. Others who performed similar acts during the nineteenth century were Eugene Rivalli, J. A. B. Chylinski, and Mr. Richardson.

Some of the fire immunity phenomena are genuine, but not inexplicable by the laws of physics (e.g., firewalking); some are done with careful practice (e.g., fire eating); and others are due to a state in which the body becomes impervious to pain by means of natural chemicals (e.g., religious fire handling). There are also cases in which sleight-of-hand or trickery is probably involved (e.g., touching molten metal). There is also a residuum of effects that cannot be explained (e.g. the oven effects). The oven effects or other inexplicable effects (such as those of D. D. Home) may have been cases of fire immunity by the human body. It is possible that the fire kings did their oven effects through the application of sound knowledge of the capacity of the human body to resist heat. Home may have used any combination of these methods. There is little in the realm of fire immunity phenomena that can't be explained by natural methods. Most, if not all, of the more extravagant claims of fire immunity are simply hoaxes.

Sources:

Jay, Ricky. *Learned Pigs & Fireproof Women*. New York: Villard Books, 1986.

Kane, Steven M. "Holiness Ritual Fire Handling: Ethnographic and Psychophysiological Considerations." *Ethos*, 10 no. 4 (Winter 1982): 369–84.

Leikind, Bernard J. and William J. McCarthy. "An Investigation of Firewalking." *Skeptical Inquirer* 10 no. 1 (Fall 1985): 23–34.

Mannix, Dan. *Step Right Up!* New York: Harper & Brothers, 1950.

Pankrantz, Loren. "Fire Walking and the Persistence of Charlatans." *Perspectives in Biology and Medicine* 31 no. 2 (Winter 1988): 291–98.

"Goat Gland" Brinkley

John Romulus (later Richard) Brinkley (1885–1942) was an original kind of hoaxer. In his prime during the 1920s and 1930s, he was a small, dapper man with a gray goatee. Brinkley offered to revive the sexuality of old men by implanting male goat testes in them. The glands cost $750 a pair; the testes of a young goat cost $1,500 a pair. In sixteen years, Brinkley implanted more than 5,000 pairs of testes into men from all over the United States. He made several million dollars.

Brinkley's medical "degree" came from a diploma mill in Kansas City, named the Eclectic Medical University. Later he obtained a fraudulent certificate from the National University of Arts and Sciences in St. Louis, and then a diploma in medicine and surgery from the Royal University of Pavia in Italy. On the strength of these, he was admitted to practice in Arkansas and then used reciprocity agreements to become licensed in Kansas. He outsmarted the American Medical Association—which wanted him put out of business—the Herbert Hoover administration, and politicians in Kansas, where he ran for governor.

On April 1, 1930, Brinkley began his radio broadcasts over KFKB in Milford, Kansas. Brinkley was one of the first people to realize the power of radio advertising. He founded the first radio broadcasting station in Kansas in 1923. By 1930, it was one of the most powerful stations in the country. Brinkley talked each night except Sunday on the radio about "glandular troubles" and "male weakness," or impotence. He diagnosed the ailments of listeners who wrote in to him, developing a thriving mail order drug business. Among the other fare on KFKB was country music, farm features, college credit courses, and old-time religion. In 1930, the station was selected in a nationwide contest as the most popular in the United States.

Brinkley cemented political friendships by offering state politicians free air time. That was not enough to prevent the Kansas Medical Society—at the urging of the American Medical Association—from filing a complaint charging Brinkley with alcoholism, malpractice, and unprofessional conduct. The Federal Radio Commission (predecessor of the Federal Communications Commission) rejected the license renewal application of KFKB on the grounds that the content of the program was not serving the public interest. That same year (1930), the Kansas Medical Board revoked Brinkley's license to practice on the grounds that the goat gland operations were biologically useless.

Brinkley struck back with the announcement that he was running for governor of Kansas. Although it was too late to get his name printed on the ballot, he conducted a vigorous write-in campaign, promising old-age assistance and free school books. Although Brinkley did not win, he turned out such a sizable vote and was so popular that prevailing political wisdom said if he had been on the ballot he would have won the governorship. He ran twice more for governor, but his popularity was then on the wane and he again lost.

The state of Kansas succeeded in stripping Brinkley of his medical license, but the goat gland operations were still performed by other physicians at Brinkley's hospital. The operation consisted of implanting the testes—sometimes sliced into pieces—into the scrotum of the patient. Although Brinkley supposedly connected the blood supply and nerve supply to the implant, three surgeons who watched his work as official

John "Goat Gland" Brinkley.

Sources:

Branyan, Helen B. "Medical Charlatanism: The Goat Gland Wizard of Milford, Kansas." *Journal of Popular Culture,* 25 no. 1 (Summer 1991): 31–37.

Carson, Gerald. *The Roguish World of Doctor Brinkley.* New York: Rhinehart, 1960.

Clugston, William George. *Rascals in Democracy.* New York: R. R. Smith, 1940.

Mehling, Harold. *The Scandalous Scamps.* New York: Henry Holt & Co., 1959: 39–68.

witnesses during the license revocation hearing said that he did not connect the nerve supply. The nerves Brinkley said were involved did not exist in the scrotum area. Besides, nerves could not be "connected" in those days, even if they had been present.

Yet Brinkley had satisfied customers, many who testified on his behalf. Brinkley claimed that the operation was really recommended for "hypertrophic prostatitis," but there is virtually no possibility that it could have helped that condition, even if the goat glands had functioned actively.

After Brinkley's radio license was revoked, he moved to Del Rio, Texas, and broadcast over XER, in Mexico. This was one of the most powerful radio stations of the time and was immune from Federal Radio Commission action, since it was in Mexico. After Morris Fishbein of the American Medical Association declared Brinkley a quack, Brinkley sued for libel and lost when the court confirmed that he *was* a quack.

The end of Brinkley's career came when the U.S. Government put pressure on Mexico to reallocate their radio frequencies. Stations XER and XERA, its successor, were shut down in 1941. Brinkley's leg was amputated in 1942 because of complications from a blood clot and he died later that year from heart disease and further complications of the surgery.

Graham's Celestial Bed

James Graham was born in England in 1745. He was the son of a saddle maker, and studied medicine at the University of Edinburgh. Although it is not clear that he graduated, Graham went to America as a physician. He spent some time in Philadelphia and learned of Benjamin Franklin's electrical experiments. He then returned to England. In 1775, he settled in London, where he opened a practice devoted to diseases of the eye and ear. In May of 1779, Graham opened his "Temple of Health" on the Royal Terrace, London. This was an elaborately furnished house. The rooms were full of exquisitely decorated and cleverly constructed quasi-medical devices. There was an "electrical throne," made of glass columns on gold bases. These were connected by brass rods to an electrical conductor. The person making contact with the rods received a jolt of electricity,—allegedly for health reasons.

Presiding over the Temple was Emma Lyon, later Lady Hamilton. She was immersed, at least part of the time, in a special healing mud up to her shoulders. Those who attended the Temple were promised "at least a hundred years of good health." Graham did not live long enough to have to pay off on his guarantees. He died in 1794, less than fifty years old.

The major attraction of the Temple was the Celestial Bed. This bed was twelve feet by nine feet, supported by pillars of glass, and insulated from the ground. The headboard was electrified ("it sparkled with electrical fire"), and the saying "Be fruitful. Multiply and Replenish the Earth." was written on it. The bed was tilted and the mattress filled with stallion's hair. Music—"the celestial sounds of flutes, oboes, and kettle-drums" according to the advertisement—accompanied anyone who chose to rent the bed for the night for lovemaking and procreation. The fee was anywhere from fifty pounds to several hundred pounds, depending on the means of the renter. The bed, it was said, cost Graham 10,000 pounds to build and decorate with gilt, silk, and statuary. A successful "blessing with progeny" was promised to those who made love on the bed.

Although the initial fees for using the bed dropped to as low as twenty-five pounds, eventually the public became bored and the Temple closed in 1784.

Graham then turned to burying people up to their necks in warm earth, but this did not turn out to be popular. Later, he became a religious fanatic of sorts, sinking into poverty, ill health, and according to some accounts, insanity.

Sources:

Bettany, George Thomas. "James Graham." in *Dictionary of National Biography*, Oxford, UK: Oxford University Press, 1921–1922, Vol. 8: 323–26.

Jameson, Eric. *The Natural History of Quackery*. Springfield, IL: Charles C. Thomas, 1981, pages 112–32.

Maple, Eric. *Magic, Medicine and Quackery*. New York: A. S. Barnes & Co, 1968: 117–19.

Mary Toft and the Rabbit Babies

In 1726, English residents were discussing the remarkable case of Mary Toft, who allegedly gave birth to a litter of rabbits. Toft, of Godalming, England had recently miscarried after previously having three children. During that pregnancy—at five weeks—she craved cooked rabbit. She chased several, but could not catch them. She dreamed there were two rabbits in her lap. A month after her miscarriage, she sent for surgeon John Howard, who had also been a midwife for thirty years. He was astonished as Toft delivered a rabbit, and then eight more over the course of several days. Howard swore he could feel the first rabbit in the uterus, and then several others "jumping" in her womb. The rabbits were all born dead, without fur or skin.

Howard began to write to other midwives, surgeons, and obstetricians around the country, telling them of this astounding case. Soon, several prominent people visited, including Nathanael St. Andre—surgeon-anatomist to King George I, and later Sir Richard Manningham—the foremost obstetrician in London. St. Andre pronounced the phenomenon genuine, even though a small piece of lung from one of the newly-delivered rabbits floated when placed in water. This indicated that the donor of the lung tissue had breathed air prior to its demise, something that couldn't have happened inside a human or rabbit uterus. Also suspect was the fact that Toft's cervix was not dilated. This meant that the rabbits could not have passed from her uterus into her vagina. The only proper conclusion that could have been drawn from this data was that the rabbit carcasses had somehow been introduced into Mary's vagina.

Sir Richard Manningham was not fooled, however. He pronounced the first item Toft delivered in *his* presence for there were several deliveries, to be a piece of hog bladder. Sir Richard stated that he would not be satisfied until he actually delivered a rabbit from Toft's uterus himself. St. Andre hastily published his findings—in support of the authenticity of the births—in December of 1726, while Toft was still under observation—and suspicion.

The matter began to unravel when a porter at Toft's lodging confessed that he was sent secretly to procure a rabbit for Mary. Others came forward, saying they had sold Toft's husband Joshua a number of rabbits over the past several weeks. Sir Richard finally told Mary that she would either have to confess to fraud or he would be forced to surgically open her uterus. The next morning, Toft confessed.

She managed to slip the first rabbit into her uterus (still soft from her recent pregnacy and miscarriage), but the insertion was so painful that all of the other rabbits were merely inserted into the vagina. Her false labor pains were most likely due to the womb's irritation from the inserted material.

Toft was imprisoned to await trial for fraud. St. Andre was ridiculed in the press and in pamphlets for his incompetence. Further suspicious details were that no umbilical cords, bloody fluid, or placenta was produced along with any of the rabbit "births." Eventually, Toft was released from prison without trial. She returned to Godalming, but in 1740 was again sent to prison for receiving stolen goods. She died in 1763. Both John Howard and Nathanael St. Andre were ruined as medical practitioners, and were not heard from again, although St. Andre promised to publish a second pamphlet revealing his knowledge of the fraud all along. It was never published. The public finally learned, too, that human beings can only give birth to other human beings.

Sources:

Manningham, Richard. *An Exact Diary of What Was Observ'd During a Close Attendance Upon Mary Toft . . .* London: J. Roberts, 1726.

Seligman, S. A. "Mary Toft—The Rabbit Breeder." *Medical History* 5 (1961): 349–60.

St. Andre, Nathanael. *A Short Narrative of an Extraordinary Delivery of Rabbits Perform'd by Mr. John Howard, Surgeon at Guilford.* London: J. Clarke, 1726.

Wall, L. Lewis. "The Strange Case of Mary Toft (Who Was Delivered of Sixteen Rabbits and a Tabby Cat in 1726)." *Medical Heritage* 1 (1985): 199–212.

Munchausen's Syndrome

Some people (admittedly mentally ill) thrive on being admitted to the hospital and even to having unnecessary surgery. These people have been said to suffer from "Munchausen's Syndrome," a disorder characterized by a chronic desire for unnecessary hospital or surgical intervention. The disorder is named after the semi-fictitious Baron Munchausen, who really lived, although the book of his purported adventures was a work of fiction. The fictional Baron was famous for dramatically lying about his adventures. Similarly, sufferers of the syndrome named for him are famous for lying—in a dramatic way—about their medical condition. The name was given to the syndrome by R. Asher in a 1951 *Lancet* article.

People who have Munchausen's Syndrome often come to the emergency room of the hospital with what appear to be genuine emergency symptoms. They often have many scars indicating previous surgeries. The patients tend to be isolated socially, with no close family ties or friends. They usually leave the hospital early—against medical advice—and without paying their bills.

The psychopathology of those suffering from the syndrome remains unclear. It may represent the coincidence of surgical addiction, malingering, self-mutilation, and vagrancy. Or, these patients may simply enjoy pity in place of love. However, guilt prevents them from accepting the pity. It has also been theorized that the surgeon may represent a parent substitute.

The hospital admissions of many Munchausen's Syndrome patients range to more than 100 apiece. The condition is rather rare, with perhaps 200 known cases through 1990. Author Loren Pankratz noted that these admissions followed a pattern. The patients usually used the same symptoms as in their previous hospitalization, but added a minor additional symptom. They were familiar with medical terminology and hospital procedures, which helped them present a convincing case. Many were also drug abusers who relied upon deceived physicians for their supply of the prescription drugs.

Many Munchausen patients *do* have some underlying medical problems. Others have faked their conditions by mixing blood into their urine specimens, injuring themselves—including lacerations and broken bones,—or producing fevers by injecting pyrogenic substances. Recently, there have even been reports of "Munchausen's Syndrome By Proxy," in which a parent hurts his or her children in order to get attention, often by medical personnel. Other cases of this sort involve the parent contaminating a child's urine speci-

BARON MUNCHAUSEN's
N A R R A T I V E
OF HIS
MARVELLOUS TRAVELS
AND
C A M P A I G N S
IN
R U S S I A.
HUMBLY DEDICATED AND RECOMMENDED
TO
COUNTRY GENTLEMEN;
AND, IF THEY PLEASE,
TO BE REPEATED AS THEIR OWN, AFTER A HUNT
AT HORSE RACES, IN WATERING-PLACES, AND
OTHER SUCH POLITE ASSEMBLIES; ROUND THE
BOTTLE AND FIRE-SIDE.

OXFORD:
Printed for the EDITOR, and fold by the Bookfellers there and at Cambridge, alfo in London by the Bookfellers of Piccadilly, the Royal Exchange, and M. SMITH, at No. 46, in Fleet-ftreet.—And in Dublin by P. BYRNE, No. 108, Grafton-ftreet.
MDCCLXXXVI.
FIRST ISSUE OF BARON MUNCHAUSEN'S TRAVELS (*enlarged*)

First edition title page of *Baron Munchausen's Travels*.

men so that a diagnosis of a serious illness will be made. Often the children involved are infants or toddlers, therefore too young to tell of their own symptoms or lack of symptoms.

Munchausen's Syndrome has recently been renamed "Chronic Factitious Illness," but the old name has also remained popular.

Sources:

Ireland, Patricia, Joseph D. Sapira, and Bryce Templeton. "Munchausen's Syndrome: Review and Report of a Case." *American Journal of Medicine* 43 (1967): 579–92.

Kantowitz, Barbara and Karen Springen. "Parental Indiscretion." *Newsweek* (April 22, 1991): 64.

Pankratz, Loren. "A Review of the Munchausen Syndrome." *Clinical Psychology Review* 1 (1981): 65–78.

Sakula, Alex. "Munchausen: Fact and Fiction." *Journal of the Royal College of Physicians* 12 no. 3 (1978): 286–92.

Spiro, Herzl R. "Chronic Factitious Illness: Munchausen's Syndrome." *Archives of General Psychiatry* 18 (1968): 569–79.

Psychic Surgery

Psychic surgery is the process by which the practitioner rubs the part of the body that he claims is diseased. The practitioner then reaches through the skin with his bare hands—to the accompaniment of much blood—to remove tissue claimed to be tumorous. The "wound" then apparently heals instantly, without leaving a scar. The patient is sent home, seemingly cured and often poorer.

To his victims the psychic surgeon appears to remove tissue and blood appears to flow without use of a scalpel. An observation by trained magicians of both the actual "operation" and of films of the operation, revealed that the entire procedure is sleight-of-hand. Magician James Randi has perfected his own performance of psychic surgery to such an extent that he is indistinguishable from the psychic surgeons themselves in his methods. Yet Randi admits that it is all a trick, and has revealed how it is done.

The secret of psychic surgery lies in careful advance preparation. First, a false "thumb tip" must be bought at a magic supply house. This is a rubber false finger, bigger and longer than a person's own thumb, that fits over the real thumb. Also, animal tissue and chicken, pig, or cow blood must be procured at a butcher's. If it is a fatty tumor chicken fat and sinew are used. The tissue and the blood are placed inside the hollow thumb tip. The thumb tip is slipped on when various gauze bandages (used to cleanse the area) are picked up. The thumb tip is then squeezed for a flow of blood. The tip is removed to the inside of one hand. When the tissue needs to be produced, it is squeezed out of the open end of the thumb tip. Practice makes the movements virtually undetectable to the uninitiated.

Often, when working on a heavy person's abdomen, the psychic surgeon bends his fingers under so it appears his hands are actually inside the patient's body. The thumb tip is disposed of in the soiled and bloody gauze from the "operation." Although this prank may seem unbelievable, people are fooled. Some have refused to see a regular physician to treat a real tumor until it is so advanced that it is no longer operable.

There have been a number of well-known psychic surgeons, and a number of locales where they flourished. The most popular locales for psychic surgery are the Philippines (where it is a multi-million dollar a year industry), and Brazil. The best known psychic surgeons were "Arigo," whose real name was Josè Pedro de Freitas, and Antonio Agpaoa, of the Philippines. These men treated several hundred people.

Author James Randi followed up on some of the people who were treated by psychic surgeons. Additional follow-up work on them was done by Granada Television, which made a film for British television a number of years ago about psychic surgery in the Philippines. Virtually all of the patients died within a year or two of their visit to the psychic surgeons.

Sources:

Christopher, Milbourne. *Mediums, Mystics & the Occult.* New York: Thomas Y. Crowell, 1975: 52–65.

Fuller, John G. *Arigo: Surgeon of the Rusty Knife.* New York: Thomas Y. Crowell Co., 1974.

Randi, James. *Flim-Flam!: The Truth About Unicorns, Parapsychology and Other Delusions.* New York: Lippincott & Crowell, 1980: 173–88.

Valentine, Tim. *Psychic Surgery.* Chicago: Henry Regnery Co., 1973.

Other Medical Hoaxes

Smoking Banana Peels. One hoax that enjoyed a brief popularity during the 1960s involved the idea that smoking the inside lining of banana peels would produce a high similar to that obtained by LSD. An analysis of the dried scrapings from the inner portion of the peels showed that it contained nothing but non-hallucinogenic material. The scrapings, known as "bananadine" or "mellow yellow," were nevertheless reported to have produced hallucinations. In those cases, however, the material was smoked in a group setting with psychedelic lighting. A team of scientists from New York University—after interviewing fifty people who claimed to have smoked the scrapings—found that the effects noted were psychological, not pharmacological. Evidently the story of the alleged psychedelic effects was fabricated to "bait" authorities.

LSD Star Tattoos. Another drug-related hoax had to do with the warnings passed out at elementary and high schools in the United States that "tattoos" or comic strip cartoons, sometimes in the form of "Blue Stars" on paper, were laced with LSD. The flyers claimed that LSD could be absorbed through the skin, especially if any of the tattoos were applied. The flyers have appeared for more than twenty years, all over the country. They *appear* to be sincere attempts by frightened people to warn others of potential danger. However, the federal Drug Enforcement Administration says the warnings are a hoax—a kind of hysteria that was based upon "microdots" of LSD that existed briefly in the mid-1970s. Microdots were ingested, however, and not absorbed through the skin. The Drug Enforcement Administration says that it has never encountered "Blue

Star"—or any other brand—tattoos containing LSD absorbable through the skin.

The Self-Abuse Hoax. It is difficult to know the origins of this hoax—whether it was hysteria induced by misinformation or there were darker perhaps religious motives. In the eighteenth and nineteenth centuries, the idea that masturbation led to insanity, feeble-mindedness, hair growth on the palms, acne, and worse was quite common. These were not just old wives' tales, they were incorporated into the advice given by recognized physicians.

One of the most vocal opponents of masturbation was Samuel Auguste David Tissot (1728–1797), a Swiss physician. Tissot's book, *Onanism: Or, a Treatise Upon the Disorders Produced by Masturbation,* enjoyed a number of editions in French, then was translated into English. The text is amusing today, but it was once taken seriously. Tissot claimed that the loss of an ounce of "seminal liquor" weakened the male human as if forty ounces of blood were lost. Of course, an ounce of semen is more than is ever "lost" at once.

Tissot referred to Hippocrates to quote the disorder called "tabes dorsalis" (now used to refer to one of the symptoms of late syphilis), which he said was a disorder affecting "young married people and those of a lascivious disposition." The disorder caused them to "shed a great quantity of thin seminal liquor" with each urination. The young people were, Hippocrates added, "incapable of procreation and they frequently dreamed of the act of coition." Eventually, they would have "a violent fever (lypiria) that terminates their days."

Tissot quotes Aetius, who states that too great a discharge of the semen produces young people who "have the air and appearance of old age; they become pale, effeminate, benumbed, lazy, base, stupid, and even imbecile; their bodies become bent, their legs are no longer able to carry them; they have an utter distaste for every thing, are totally incapacitated, and many become paralytic."

Tissot's reaching back to ancient medical texts—a common practice hundreds of years earlier, but not at the time Tissot wrote—indicates that he knew he was not being honest with his readers.

AIDS Hoaxes. One AIDS hoax involved the report, originated by Donna Spence, an employee of the Ark-Tex (Arkansas and Texas) Council of Governments, that an unusually high number of students had AIDS at a northeastern Texas high school. She made the statement in an application for a monetary grant to do AIDS counseling. The school was later identified as the Rivercrest High School in Bogata, Texas. A high rate of AIDS was not found in the school.

Another AIDS hoax was the brief and scary one invented by Natasha Johnigan, who finally admitted that she wrote the letter to *Ebony* magazine, signed "C. J." that was purportedly from a woman in the Dallas, Texas area. The woman claimed she caught AIDS from a man and was intentionally spreading it. People claiming to be "C. J." called a Dallas radio station to explain why they were spreading the disease as a sort of "revenge" on men. It turns out that Natasha Johnigan, who did *not* call the radio stations (as best as can be determined), was a fifteen-year-old high school sophomore. She said her aim was to make people more aware of the disease.

The Baby Parts Hoax. According to Todd Leventhal of the U.S. Information Agency, a false story has been spread all over the world since January of 1987, that babies are being raised on "farms" in certain third world countries to provide organs for organ transplants in the United States. He points out that several international investigations have shown that there is no basis for this story. In fact, it would be virtually impossible to obtain, or use secretly obtained, organs in any American transplantation operation.

Lost Manhood Restored Hoaxes. The inability to have an erection (impotence) is one of the conditions most frequently "treated" by medical hoaxers and quacks. Only *devices* that supposedly cure this condition will be addressed here; the various medications and treatments will not. One of the most popular gadgets allegedly to restore lost manhood was the electrical belt. One version was immersed in vinegar before use—reportedly to start the electricity flowing. The belt was recommended for "female problems" (gynecological problems) as well as male ones. (For surgical approaches to impotency, *see* Goat Gland Brinkley, p. 164.)

Use of testimonials was important to the success of these devices. It is not clear, however, whether the testimonials were obtained by paying people for the use of their names, or whether the testimonials were simply made up, including the names of the people giving them. Probably some of each occurred.

Aphrodisiacs. The idea that some chemical or natural product will improve the sex drive—whether by enhancing sexual performance or making the individuals more desirous of sex—is alluring. People have searched for aphrodisiacs for thousands of years, often making claims for such an effect in a food or plant because of its shape, taste, or smell. Unfortunately, all such claims have proven false. The smell of perfume may make a person feel romantic, but that is different from the biological stimulatory effect claimed for an aphrodisiac.

Several substances do affect sexual function or desire, but they are deceiving. For example, "Spanish Fly" or Canthrides is a powerful irritant concentrated in the urinary system, where it causes dangerous blistering of the membranes. This produces an "itch," which seems like sexual arousal, but seriously damages the tissues. It should never be used. Yohimbine possibly increases the flow of blood to the penis, thereby helping achieve and maintain an erection, but has no effect on desire. Only sex hormones affect desire and the physiological readiness of the sexual organs. So far, the claims of people to have true aphrodisiacs for sale are hoaxes.

Sources:

Adler, Jerry and Peter Annin. "A Hard Lesson or a Hoax?" *Newsweek* (March 2, 1992): 77.

"Alarming in Texas." *New York Times* (October 27, 1991): E7. Armstrong, David and Elizabeth Metzger Armstrong. *The Great American Medicine Show.* New York: Prentice Hall, 1991.

"The Big Banana Hoax." *Science Digest* 63 (Feb 1968): 62–63.

Cramp, Arthur J., ed. *Nostrums and Quackery.* Vol. 1 (1911); Vol. 2 (1921); Vol. 3 (1936). Chicago: American Medical Association.

Holbrook, Stewart. *The Golden Age of Quackery.* New York: Macmillan, 1959.

Kantrowitz, Barbara. "Anatomy of a Drug Scare: A Phony LSD Warning?" *Newsweek* 108 no. 21 (Nov 24, 1986): 85.

Leventhal, Todd. "Traffic In Baby Parts Has No Factual Basis." *New York Times* (February 26, 1992) A20.

McNamara, Brooks. *Step Right Up.* New York: Doubleday, 1976.

Taberner, P. V. *Aphrodisiacs: The Science and the Myth.* Philadelphia: University of Pennsylvania Press, 1985.

"Texas Health Officials Unable to Verify School HIV Report." *New York Times* (February 27, 1992): A20.

Tissot, [S. A. D.]. *Onanism: Or, a Treatise Upon the Disorders Produced by Masturbation: Or, the Dangerous Effects of Secret and Excessive Venery.* London: Printed for A. Hume, 1766.

Young, James Harvey. *The Medical Messiahs: A Social History of Health Quackery in Twentieth Century America.* Princeton, NJ: Princeton University Press, 1967.

Military Hoaxes

One of the ingredients in a successful military campaign is deception of the enemy. Espionage, regarded as an essential part of a military operation, consists largely of deception. Acts of espionage could be viewed as hoaxes. Since espionage is a broad category, the hoaxes here will be confined to those espionage operations that involved an extensive campaign of deception. Similarly, only extensive military hoaxes will be covered here.

The Angels of Mons

The Angels of Mons story thrilled readers during World War I. The British Expeditionary Force, outnumbered by more than two to one, tried to escape from the German First Army. On August 26, 1914, the third day of the British retreat near Mons, Belgium, the British found themselves almost completely surrounded by the Germans. While waiting for certain annihilation, a shimmering mirage rose over the enemy lines. Tall, winged figures appeared. They distracted and slowed the Germans enough that the British were able to escape. Legend has it that these winged figures appeared to be angelic archers. However, the story did not appear until September 29, when British journalist Arthur Machen published "The Bowmen" in the London *Evening News*.

According to this story, a soldier at Mons murmured a Latin motto—"May St. George be a present help to the English"—as he waited in the treacherous situation. He felt an electric shock and heard shouts of "St. George! St. George!" He then saw in the air a "sort of shining thing," which soon became the figure of St. George in full armor, flanked by an army of bowmen. This was a scene out of the legendary Battle of Crecy in 1346, or Agincourt in 1415. The phantom army rained arrows on the Germans as the British made their escape.

Machen stated that his story was fantasy, and the idea for it came to him while in church listening to a sermon. People wrote to him from throughout Britain, stating that they received letters from soldiers at Mons who told them of the same phantom bowmen. It was rumored that letters were received long before Machen's story was published, so Machen was asked to issue his story as a separate pamphlet, with an introduction explaining his exact authorities for the incident. He refused, *reiterating* that the story was fiction. The *Occult Review* published a statement from a lance corporal—as told through a Red Cross nurse—indicating that he saw in the sky three shapes that appeared to be soldiers. A theory that Machen had telepathically received his idea for the story from the mind of a dying soldier at Mons was suggested.

Phyllis Campbell, the Red Cross nurse, was largely responsible for turning Machen's story into alleged fact. She had been in France as a war nurse. She expanded on the stories in circulation, claiming that the French soldiers saw a figure in the sky that had been Joan of Arc in full battle armor. She also claimed that St. Michael frequently appeared to soldiers on the Russian front. When challenged by Arthur Machen to produce evidence for her claims, she said that the soldiers involved were forbidden to talk about what they saw. This was highly suspect. She talked of writing a book giving all of the evidence, but she never did. Her motivation was apparently a fanatical type of patriotism.

The reason for the successful British retreat from Mons remains a partial mystery, however. There were 160,000 German soldiers, with 600 heavy guns facing 70,000 exhausted British soldiers with only 300 guns. Yet, 56,000 British escaped. Perhaps, as has been suggested, the Germans were the ones who were really exhausted.

There are also a couple mundane explanations for the British escape. The first is that the British had accurate riflemen, who made it seem that they were using machine guns. The other is that the British soldiers had an efficient entrenching tool that allowed them to dig protective earthworks quickly.

Sources:

Brown, Raymond Lemmont. *The Phantom Soldiers*. New York: Drake Publishers, 1975: 31–32.

Harris, Melvin. *Sorry—You've Been Duped*. London: Weidenfeld and Nicholson, 1986: 80–93, 185–91.

Machen, Arthur. *The Angels of Mons: The Bowman and Other Legends*. New York: G. P. Putnam's Sons, 1915.

H. M. S. Dreadnought

In 1910, the British navy was a source of intense pride to Englishmen. The Channel Fleet (or Home Fleet) was assembled for review at Weymouth. The admiral of the fleet was on the flagship *Dreadnought*. Horace de Vere Cole, a prominent prankster of the period, decided to pull a hoax on the entire British fleet. He enlisted the cooperation of naturalist Anthony Buxton, the artist Duncan Grant, brother and sister Adrian and Virginia Stephen (later known as Virginia Woolf), and Guy Ridley, the son of a judge. Four of the fellow pranksters became Ethiopian royalty, dressed in blackface and African robes. Buxton portrayed the emperor. Cole played Herbert Cholmondley of the Foreign Office, dressed in top hat and tails.

One February morning in 1910 they went in costume to Paddington Station in London to catch a train for Weymouth. When the stationmaster at Paddington was hastily informed that royalty was present, he arranged an impromptu reception on the platform.

While the group was on the train, an unidentified additional conspirator sent off a telegram to the admiral of the fleet at Weymouth, informing him that the party was enroute. He was asked to "kindly make all arrangements to receive them." The telegram was signed by the head of the British Foreign Office. The real head did not learn of the forgery until many days later. When the train reached Weymouth, the "royal" party descended to find a red carpet welcome, complete with escort and car. They were taken to a special launch in the harbor and then out to the flagship *Dreadnought*.

Once on board the *Dreadnought*, the party was received by Admiral Sir William May. They inspected a marine guard and toured the ship. Adrian Stephen, who did most of the talking for the Ethiopians, was at first puzzled by what he should use for the Ethiopian

The Dreadnought hoaxers.

language, which he did not speak. He finally decided to quote from memory long passages from Virgil's *Aeneid*, mispronouncing the Latin beyond recognition. When he ran out of Virgil, he switched to mispronounced Greek from Homer. The other Ethiopians limited themselves to loud exclamations of "bunga, bunga" at everything they saw.

A light rain began to fall, signaling a possible disaster. The blackface makeup and attached mustaches threatened to come off. When it was suggested to the Captain that everyone would be more comfortable inside, the Captain fortunately agreed. When the Ethiopians left the ship, a band broke into the national anthem of Zanzibar, as they had been unable to find the music for the Ethiopian national anthem.

Once back on shore, the Ethiopians boarded another train. Herbert Cholmondley (Cole) told the railroad personnel that the only way the Ethiopians would eat is if they were served by people wearing white gloves. When the train stopped at Reading, several people rushed out to find a store that sold white gloves. That accomplished, the Ethiopians were served dinner. In London they paused for a group photograph, then washed off their makeup and returned their rented costumes.

Cole, unable to keep the affair a secret, went to the London newspapers. The group photograph and the story of the hoax appeared in several newspapers. No real names of the hoaxers were used; they were, however, revealed in author Adrian Stephen's 1936 title, *The "Dreadnought" Hoax*. As a result, several groups, among them Scotland Yard and the Admiralty, talked of launching an investigation. When it was pointed out that the most serious crime committed by the group was sending a telegram under a false name, the investigations were dropped.

Sources:

Highet, Gilbert. "The Art of the Hoax." *Horizon* 3 no. 3 (January 1961): 66–72.

Hone, Joseph. "The Serious Art of Hoaxing." *Living Age,* December 1940, pages 365–68.

Stephen, Adrian. *The "Dreadnought" Hoax.* London: Leonard and Virginia Woolf at the Hogarth Press, 1936.

John Paul Jones and the American Navy

John Paul Jones (1717–1792) is usually given credit for founding the United States Navy. This misplaced credit is founded upon a set of spurious documents by Augustus C. Buell, a Jones biographer.

John Paul Jones, whose birth name was simply John Paul, was born in Scotland. Drawn at an early age to the sea, he became an apprentice seaman at age twelve. For bringing a merchant ship in safely to port after both the captain and first mate died, he was given ten percent of the value of the cargo, plus command of a ship. After a difficult period as a captain, he found himself in America at the beginning of the Revolutionary War, unemployed. This was when he added "Jones" as his new last name. Jones obtained a position as an officer aboard the *Alfred*—the first naval ship bought by Congress—by means of a political acquaintance with a congressman. Later, he was given command of the *Providence*, where he compiled a distinguished record.

Promotion to captain and command of the sloop *Ranger* followed. Jones was sent to France. On his return trip to the United States, he managed to capture the British sloop *Drake,* with many prisoners. Upon his return to France with seven "kills" and many prisoners to his credit, Jones was hailed a hero. On a journey around the British Isles, Jones captured seventeen ships, then defeated the *Serapis* in a notable engagement. On another return trip to America, Jones was blocked by political rivalries from his promotion to admiral, but was given command of the *America,* the largest ship in the Navy. This ship, then under construction, was eventually turned over to the French, without Jones ever taking command. Jones was awarded a gold medal by Congress. He then accepted an offer from Catherine the Great to serve in the Russian navy. His ideas for combat against the Turks were largely undercut by a jealous French adventurer. Jones spent the last two years of his life in Paris, where he was quite ill. His body, buried in a French cemetery that was eventually overbuilt by houses, was finally shipped back to the United States in 1905. In 1913, his remains were buried

John Paul Jones.

in a specially constructed tomb at the U.S. Naval Academy in Annapolis, Maryland.

Augustus C. Buell was called a "fraudulent historian" by author Milton Hamilton, among others. Samuel Eliot Morison, the author of the latest biography of Jones, devotes several pages to a list of Buell's false statements about Jones. Buell was responsible for the misinformation about Jones' role in the formation of the United States Navy (among other frauds), so Buell is the hoaxer.

Buell's statements about his own background contain a number of falsehoods. He claimed to have ancestors who worked for, or knew personally, all of the subjects of his biographies. Buell wrote biographies of Jones, Sir William Johnson, William Penn, and Andrew Jackson.

All of these contain statements drawn from what appear to be sources manufactured for the occasion by Buell. He invented letters, journal entries, books (usually described as quite rare), and whole archives. He thanked the Librarian of Congress for making materials available, while Morison states that he never visited that library.

Buell's forgeries go back to his first publication, a book of his memoirs of the Civil War. Buell claims to have been a cannoneer at Gettysburg and elsewhere.

His vivid recollections of that battle (published in 1890 as *The Cannoneer*) were quoted in other anthologies of Civil War writings. The official records of Buell's military service found in the Adjutant General's office in Albany, New York, show that he was not even in the service until six weeks *after* the Battle of Gettysburg. He was never a cannoneer and was not at the battles in which he claims he participated.

Author Anna De Koven stated in the first exposé of Buell's biography of John Paul Jones in 1906, that the

> book is based upon a bare framework of truth, . . . but is padded with inventions of clever construction and unparalleled audacity. It contains reports of imaginary committees in Congress, invented letters from Washington, Franklin and Hewes, false letters and imaginary journals of Jones himself, false entries in the diaries of well-known persons such as Gouverneur Morris and the Duchesse d'Orleans, and quotations from others which existed only in Col.[!] Buell's imagination . . . The bibliography . . . is a masterpiece of invention, and is so shortsighted in its careless untruthfulness as to raise suspicion of the author's mental responsibility.

Scholars' reactions to Buell's biographies ranged from praise at his new "discoveries," to a conclusion that Buell located material that was no longer available. Librarians and archivists knew that scholars' requests to look at materials that Buell had supposedly found in their libraries usually led to no material. Buell's statements his ancestor had worked with or been related to the subject of his biography provided a clever "out" in concluding that there must be a private family archive that Buell consulted. There was no such archive.

Morison says of Buell:

> He found it easier to write Jones' letters himself than to use the genuine ones in the Library of Congress, which he never visited. How, then, did Buell acquire such a high reputation? He was a clever dog, wrote good salty prose and supported his statements by references to mythical sources and fictitious books, which gave his work an air of scholarly authenticity. Any librarian . . . will do a service to posterity by reclassifying as fiction Buell's book [on Jones], and the other three mentioned. . . .

Sources:

Buell, Augustus C. *Paul Jones, Founder of the American Navy, A History.* 2 vols. New York: Charles Scribner's Sons, 1900.

De Koven, Anna F. *The Life and Letters of John Paul Jones.* 2 vols. New York: Charles Scribner's Sons, 1913.

De Koven, Mrs. [Anna] Reginald. "A Fictitious Paul Jones Masquerading as the Real." *New York Times* (June 10, 1906) Section 3: 1–2.

Hamilton, Milton W. "Augustus C. Buell, Fraudulent Historian." *Pennsylvania Magazine of History and Biography* 80 (1956): 478–92.

Morison, Samuel Eliot. *John Paul Jones: a Sailor's Biography*, Boston: Little, Brown & Co., 1959: 425–28.

Paullin, Charles Oscar. "When Was Our Navy Founded? A Criticism of Augustus C. Buell's 'Paul Jones, Founder of the American Navy.'" *Proceedings of the U.S. Naval Institute* 36 no. 1 (March 1910): 255–67.

The Man Who Never Was

War produces some ingenious deceptions and hoaxes, usually in the realm of espionage or covert operations. "The Man Who Never Was" is the name given to one of the most complex and clever military impostures ever devised. Under the guidance of Ewen Montague, it succeeded in fooling the Germans almost completely. The idea was to deflect Hitler and Mussolini's attention from the upcoming allied invasion of Italy, which was to start in Sicily. The object was to make the Germans think that the invasion would take place from Greece and Sardinia, not Sicily.

The deception began with the search for a body. It had to be a body that died of drowning or pneumonia, and that body had to be available for use by British Military Intelligence. A long search *did* produce just such a body, whose owner had died of pneumonia after exposure. Permission to use the body was obtained and it was stored in refrigeration.

The plan was called "Operation Mincemeat." The body would wash ashore at Huelva, Spain, as there were active German agents among the Spanish located there. The plan was for the body—dressed in a British Marine Officer's uniform and carrying appropriate ID—to have a briefcase chained to him. The briefcase would contain information leading the Germans to think the invasion would be from Greece and Sardinia, with Sicily given as a red herring to throw the Germans off. The body would appear to have come from a ditched airplane and would be accompanied by a life raft. Great care went into the fabrication of the papers, and the back-up materials that would convince the Germans that this was a real courier who had inadvertently drowned.

Since dropping the body from an airplane might damage it, a submarine was used to release the body into the water. A torpedo-shaped canister was built for the body, which would then release it when opened.

Ewen Montague, deviser of The Man Who Never Was.

The canister contained dry ice to drive out the oxygen that would speed up the body's decomposition.

Accompanying the body—which was given the name Major William Martin—were letters of transfer from various generals. According to the letters, Martin was being sent to North Africa because of his expertise of amphibious barges. There were also several letters from his fiancée, Pam, and from his father. Also enclosed were an unpaid bill for an engagement ring; a notice that his lodging bill was overdue; and the proofs for a military publication, with a letter to General Dwight Eisenhower, requesting that he write the preface to the American edition. Of course, there were also the secret letters that disclosed that the real attack would come from Sardinia and Greece, not Sicily.

After much difficulty (especially in getting the boots on the corpse's feet), the container with the body and the briefcase was loaded aboard the submarine *Seraph*. It proceeded to a site off the Spanish coast near Huelva, where the body was removed from the canister and "launched" towards shore. Several days later, a radio signal was received from the naval attaché in Madrid that Major Martin's body had been recovered off Huelva. Strong requests for the return of all papers carried by Martin were made through Spanish diplomatic channels. Eventually everything was returned. Tests showed that the letters had been opened and

resealed. "Major Martin" was buried in Spain, and his name and those of his plane's crew were added to the list of casualties for the week.

As was expected, the information in the secret letters was sent to Berlin, where the German intelligence service believed it. As Churchill was told in a cablegram, "Mincemeat [was] swallowed whole."

When the allies *did* invade Sicily, they found it lightly defended; most of the defenses that *were* there had been relocated to the northern end of the island. The ally attack came at the southern end. After the war, an examination of captured German naval intelligence files turned up a German translation of the secret letters carried by Major Martin which told of the real targets as Greece and Sardinia. The translations were initialled as having been read by Admiral Doenitz, commander-in-chief of the German navy. The German intelligence staff indicated it believed the contents to be authentic. Doenitz met with Hitler about that time, and it is known that Hitler did not think an allied attack would be made first against Sicily. General Rommel was sent from Italy to Greece to take charge of operations there, so it appears that the Nazis were expecting an allied attack on Greece. Operation Mincemeat was a success and remains a classic military hoax.

Sources:

Cooper, A. Duff. *Operation Heartbreak.* New York: Viking Press, 1950.

Montagu, Ewen. *Beyond Top Secret U.* London: P. Davies, 1977.

———. *The Man Who Never Was.* London: Evans Brothers, 1953.

The Miraculous Bullet

The American Civil War has been the source of many unusual stories. One particularly unusual story was first reported by Dr. LeGrand G. Capers in the *American Medical Weekly* in 1874.

Although this was nine years after the Civil War ended, Capers had been a Confederate Army surgeon during the war and he submitted his account of this incident anonymously to the magazine. The magazine's editor, Dr. E. S. Gaillard, recognized Capers' handwriting, and decided to print his name on the article. Apparently Capers had been professor of anatomy at the New Orleans School of Medicine and a founder of the Confederate Medical Department. The editor was a southern physician, who *could* have had past contact with Capers. Although it is not clear that Capers was asked permission, the article does contain his name. That his handwriting was recognized by the editor is not so farfetched as may at first be thought.

According to the story, at an unidentified battle site in Virginia in May of 1863, an unidentified young soldier was hit in the leg by a "minnie ball." This was a ball-shaped bullet, today called a musketball. The bullet passed through the soldier's testicle before continuing out of his body. The bullet finally lodged in the abdomen of a seventeen-year-old girl who lived near the battlefield. To her great surprise, she delivered an eight-pound baby boy nine months later, although she claimed to be a virgin. Three weeks after the birth, Dr. Capers was again called, this time to examine the baby. The grandmother suspected something was wrong with the baby's genitals. After Dr. Capers felt a lump in the scrotum, he extracted a battered minnie ball. He reasoned that the bullet carried some of the soldier's sperm on it, then penetrated the ovary and impregnated the young girl. The symptoms of the pregnancy were first thought to be some sort of reaction to the abdominal wound. The soldier and the girl were eventually married and had additional children "by a more conventional method."

Dr. Gaillard evidently thought that Capers was hoaxing the medical community. Gaillard and James O. Breedon, Civil War medical historian believed the story a hoax, but for different reasons. Both felt that the anonymous submission of the article was a sign of fraudulence. Gaillard felt that people were not willing victims, but were "willing to allow the author some fun. Breedon felt that Capers "was indeed poking fun, but justifiably and commendably so, at the veritable flood of highly embellished, often spurious, personal reminiscences of wartime service and accomplishments that was [sic] inundating the land . . . ."

The story was both physiologically and logically impossible and the fact that the bullet was found in the scrotum of the baby marks the story as demonstrably false. This piece reduces the story to an impossibility. Embryology reveals that the scrotum is formed in the fetus from the two undifferentiated "lips" that in a female form the labia majora. They fuse in a male. The chances of them fusing around a bullet are remote. This part of the story seems to be a "moral fable," and marks the entire story as a hoax. Gould and Pyle, in their definitive *Anomalies and Curiosities of Medicine*, concur.

Sources:

Breeden, James O. "'The Case of the Miraculous Bullet' Revisited." *Military Affairs* 45 no. 1 (February 1981): 23–26.

Capers, LeGrand G. "Attention Gynecologists!—Notes from the Diary of a Field and Hospital Surgeon, C. S. A." *American Medical Weekly* 1 (1874): 233–34.

Gaillard, E. S. "Miscellaneous." *American Medical Weekly* 1 (1874): 263–64.

Gould, George M. and Walter L. Pyle. *Anomalies and Curiosities of Medicine.* Philadephia: W. B. Saunders, 1900: 44–45, note.

Napolitani, F. Donald. "The Case of the Miraculous Bullet." *American Heritage* 23 no. 1 (December 1971): 99.

The Philadelphia Experiment

This is an outrageous and profitable military hoax. In their book *The Philadelphia Experiment*, William L. Moore and Charles Berlitz report that in 1943, during World War II, the United States Navy experimented at the Philadelphia Navy Yard with a device that used "electronic force fields" to make a battleship invisible. The experiment succeeded and the ship was made invisible and teleported in seconds to Norfolk, Virginia and back. The vessel was identified as either DE-173 or DE-168, a destroyer escort, possibly named the *Eldridge*. Unfortunately, the experiment produced ill effects upon the crew. As a result, the Navy abandoned further research of this sort, classified the entire project above top secret, and denied that the incident ever happened. That is the story told by Moore and Berlitz.

Berlitz mentioned the disappearing boat in his 1974 book *The Bermuda Triangle*. There the information was attributed to Morris K. Jessup and Carlos Allende (also known as Carl M. Allen, his birth name). Jessup learned of the Philadelphia Experiment from Allende, who claimed he witnessed the disappearance from the deck of the *S. S. Andrew Furuseth* which at the time was right next to the one that disappeared. That ship was a Matson Lines Liberty Ship, used by the Navy.

Allende had written a letter to physicist Morris K. Jessup in 1956. In that letter Allende scolded Jessup for continuing his research into unified field theory (UFT). Allende claimed that this was a dangerous area for research because of the 1943 U.S. Navy Philadelphia Experiment. He claimed that most of the crewmen on board that ship had gone mad, but Allende gave no more details. Jessup replied, asking of evidence for Allende's story. Allende said he had no exact dates and he could not remember names of the crew. He suggested hypnosis to try to jog his memory; Jessup let the matter drop.

A year later, while Jessup was visiting the Office of Naval Research (ONR), he was shown an ONR copy of his own paperback book, *The Case for the UFO*. It was heavily annotated, supposedly by three different people, each using a different colored ink. These people were referred to as "Mr. A," "Mr. B," and "Jemi." Jessup recognized Allende's peculiar spelling and capitalization. The annotations were purported to be those of extraterrestrials. They "explained" UFT, levitation, gravity and telepathy, among other things.

The Varo Corporation—which did military research under contract—reproduced a number of copies of the annotated version of the Jessup book. On April 20, 1956, Jessup committed suicide.

In 1969, the Aerial Phenomena Research Organization (APRO) in Tucson, Arizona, reported in its *Bulletin* that Allende had dropped into its headquarters and confessed that the Varo edition annotations were a hoax. Allende admitted that he wrote all three sets of annotations himself for the purpose of scaring Jessup away from further UFT research.

Allende was born in Springdale, Pennsylvania on May 31, 1925. He was considered a brilliant but lazy child, and was a practical joker. He never held a job for long or pursued a career. His propensity for deception may provide the answer to the question of the genuineness of the Philadelphia Experiment.

It looks as though this was Allende's hoax. The "facts" as stated by Allende practically prove the incident to be a hoax. Top secret Navy projects would not be conducted in public during wartime. The presence of the *Andrew Furuseth* right next to the *Eldridge* would seem unlikely too, especially since the *Furuseth* was filled with sailors who did not have secret clearances. Subjecting a ship's crew to strong "force fields" would also be reckless and irrational.

However, there is an even stronger reason to believe that the entire Philadelphia Experiment story was a hoax. Author Paul Begg found the records of the *Andrew Furuseth* for 1943. Moore and Berlitz said that these records did not exist. The records showed that Carl M. Allen *was* a sailor on the *Furuseth* during 1943, however, the ship was docked from the fourth to the twenty-fifth of October in a location far from the *Eldridge*. During the rest of the month, the *Furuseth* was at sea far from the *Eldridge*. Therefore, the two ships were never close together during the month of October, 1943, when Allende says the disappearance of the *Eldridge* was visible from the deck of the *Furuseth*. This makes quite a strong case against Allende.

Allende's brother Randolph told journalist Robert Goerman that an interview with Carl face to face would not produce an admission of a hoax. He would keep changing his story to cover any discrepancies that might be uncovered—one of the cardinal signs of deception.

Moore and Berlitz's book was a bestseller, and a movie was made from the book in 1984 starring Nancy Allen and Michael Pare. The plot of the book was changed considerably in the movie, which did not fare well at the box office.

Sources:

Begg, Paul. "Immaterial Evidence." in *The Unexplained*. Peter Brooksmith, ed. London: Marshall Cavendish, 1985: 1206–10.

Goerman, Robert A. "Alias Carlos Allende." *Fate* (October 1980): 69–75.

[Lorenzen, Bill and Coral]. "Allende Letters a Hoax." *A. P. R. O. Bulletin* (July/August 1969): 1, 3.

Moore, William L. and Charles Berlitz. *The Philadelphia Experiment*. New York: Grosset & Dunlap, 1979.

Steiger, Brad and Joan Whritenour. *New UFO Breakthrough: The Allende Affair*. New York: Award Books, 1968.

Other Military Hoaxes

The Trojan Horse Hoax. One the most famous hoaxes of all time may merely be fiction. The Trojan horse, was a large wooden horse filled with Greek soldiers that was left as a "gift" outside the gates of Troy. One soldier outside the horse announced the gift as a peace offering, and saw that it was taken inside the locked gates of the city. At night, soldiers from inside the horse came out and opened the gates of Troy from the inside for the invading Greek army. Troy fell as a result. However, the story exists solely within Homer's *Odyssey*. The *Odyssey* is based to some extent upon real history, but it is built upon popular tales passed down through the oral tradition, which may or may not be true. No confirmation of the hollow Trojan Horse from contemporary sources has been found. However, in Dictys of Crete's *A Journal of the Trojan War*, there is mention of a Trojan horse as a solid, large gift, too big to fit through the gates of Troy, which caused the Trojans to tear down their own gates to get the horse inside. Further, there *was* a city of Troy and it was conquered in about 1250 B.C. According to Homer, Odysseus—hero of *The Odyssey*—conceived the idea of the wooden horse, and a craftsman named Epeios built it. According to the tale there was room inside the horse for thirty men and their weapons. Although this hoax remains a masterpiece of military deception, its historical occurrence remains to be proven.

The Nazi Astrology Hoax. Often the two conflicting sides in a war see the same events differently. In the case of this World War II hoax, two different printed records existed, one telling of the event from the Allied side, the other from the Nazi side. It is hard to know which is more accurate, so *both* sides will be presented. Both sides agree that a hoax was perpetrated, but the degree of its success varies. The Allies say the Nazis were fooled. The Nazis say they saw right through the hoax and were not fooled.

The hoax depended upon the fact that Heinrich Himmler, Nazi head of the S. S. State Police, was a strong believer in astrology. A German astrological magazine, *Der Zenit* was published until 1938 when its former editor was arrested and sent to a concentration camp. The British persuaded Louis de Wohl, a professional astrologer, to work for their "Political Warfare Executive," the top-secret "dirty tricks" branch of military intelligence. De Wohl was to prepare a couple of new issues of *Der Zenit*, "predicting" battle results on the basis of astrology. The results would be accurate because they were made *after* the battles were already fought. The issues of the magazine would then be back-dated and smuggled into Germany. There they would "fall" into S. S. hands and get Himmler's attention. The idea was to convince the German military that this astrological magazine could accurately predict the results of military campaigns. In subsequent issues, ominous astrological information would be for certain generals included in the magazine. The allies hoped to successfully demoralize the generals who believed in astrology.

Author Wilhelm Wulff reports that the Nazis tell a somewhat different version. They claim that a crate of the bogus issue(s) of *Der Zenit* was confiscated at the town of Stettin, Germany after having been smuggled in from Sweden. It was immediately apparent to the Gestapo that this was a British hoax, although cleverly done. The Nazis, especially Joseph Goebbels, were not above using the occult in their own sort of military hoax. Goebbels had a new "translation" of Nostradamus' works (*See* Nostradamus's Predictions, p. 86) made in which Nostradamus predicted a German victory in World War II.

Captain William Voight. William Voight, (d. 1914) was a shoemaker and ex-convict. In 1906, he took all his money and bought a captain's uniform he saw in the window of a shop. He then took a train from Berlin to the small town of Kopenick, Germany. As "Captain" Voight got off the train, he commandeered some soldiers who were marching nearby. They marched to the town hall, where Voight placed a soldier at each entrance, instructing them to keep anyone from entering or leaving while he was inside. Voight then went to the office of the burgomeister (mayor) Lagerhans, and placed him under arrest. Lagerhans protested, but was told that the authorities in Berlin would explain everything to him. When Lagerhans' wife and the chief of police entered the office, the chief was told to station his men in the town square to prevent any disturbances. Voight then went to the town treasurer's office and arrested him as well. Before he was taken away, the treasurer was told to "fix his books" and turn over all the money he had on hand. He protested that only the burgomeister could order that. When the treasurer was informed that the burgomeister was under arrest, the treasurer turned over about 4,000 marks ($300) to Voight. Two closed carriages were ordered, and the burgomeister, his wife, and the treasurer were driven off to Berlin military headquarters. The Captain ordered the rest of his men to return to their barracks and he disappeared. At military headquarters, the burgomeister and the treasurer were passed from one official to another. When they reached the Berlin Police Chief's office, and the office of the Adjutant-General, the hoax was discovered.

When the press heard of the hoax it made much of the fact that anyone in a uniform seemed to be obeyed by all. Voight was caught nine days later. The judge at his trial gave him the minimum sentence of four years in jail, but it was then reduced to twenty months by the kaiser himself, who was evidently amused by the incident. When Voight was released, he was famous. He made a living in Vaudeville, telling the story of his escapade to audiences.

The Army Base Take-Over. Captain Alan E. Goetsch first appeared in uniform at Fort Rucker in Alabama on March 7, 1985. He had a military ID, and told people he was on an assignment from the Central Intelligence Agency (CIA). For the next month, he had full freedom on the base. He fed and housed two men he brought in from California, supposedly to assist him in his work. He befriended a number of officers and went on several parachute jumps.

Goetsch was not a soldier, but a con man. On April 10, 1985, he was arrested by the Federal Bureau of Investigation (FBI) and charged with impersonating a military officer. Although a spokesman for Fort Rucker said that Goetsch did not have access to classified material, what he *did* remains a mystery.

Although Fort Rucker is an open base—meaning that virtually anyone could buy an officer's uniform and get on the base—the orders that Goetsch had, marked "Top Secret," were forged. The orders evidently enabled him to obtain his military ID at Fort Benning in Georgia. In jail, Goetsch continued to insist that he was really a captain and *had* orders from the CIA. In the living room of his rented home, he set up his "headquarters," including several computers, a shredding machine, and several telephones. Here his wife heard him calling military and government officials, including senators and generals.

Goetsch's real military record showed that he served two years in the army, leaving in 1972 with the rank of sergeant. He spent his service in the United

States. He had a record of arrests for passing bad checks and for impersonating an emergency medical technician. Nearly everyone at Fort Rucker believed he was genuine and helped him on his "missions," which involved either rounding up military supplies for overseas operations, or helping to find soldiers still missing in Laos. Neither was a real operation, and Goetsch was not legitimate. Still, little about this hoax has been revealed.

Battlefield Decoys. The use of fake tanks, planes, and artillery pieces on open fields—usually not at an active battle site—reached its peak in World War II. The object was to cause the enemy to overestimate the strength of its opponents' forces. It also drew enemy fire, and wasted their ammunition, forces, and time in fighting a harmless target.

In Operation Quicksilver during World War II, elements of deception involving decoys were used. As author Michael Dewar explains it, dummy Sherman Tanks—inflatable rubber items by Dunlop Rubber Company—were employed. These and an entire dummy fuel installation, a dummy landing craft made of plywood, and dummy guns and vehicles were scattered throughout the woods and fields of Kent and Essex in England. Whole airfields were filled with dummy airplanes. The idea was to fool the Germans into thinking that the invasion on D-day would be near Le Havre, and not at Normandy. This was only part of a large scale effort to delude Hitler into thinking the allied invasion would be somewhere other than Normandy.

Sources:

Dewar, Michael. *The Art of Deception in Warfare.* Newton Abbot, UK: David & Charles, 1989.

Frazer, R. M., Jr. *The Trojan War: The Chronicles of Dictys of Crete and Dares the Phrygian.* Bloomington, IN: Indiana University Press, 1966: 112–13.

Painton, Priscilla and Scot Thurston. "Con Man Had Run of Entire Army Base." *Atlanta Constitution* (April 20, 1985) "Weekend" section: 1, 13.

Sklar, Dusty. *The Nazis and the Occult.* New York: Dorset Press, 1977.

Wulff, Wilhelm. *Zodiac and Swastika: How Astrology Guided Hitler's Germany.* New York: Coward, McCann & Geoghegan, 1973.

Photographic Hoaxes

Photography is basically a matter of artistic taste and talent, optics, chemistry, and—lately—electronics. Because so few people understand the science behind photography, they are easily fooled with photographs, especially if they believe that the camera cannot lie. Perhaps cameras do not lie, but photographers may, and that makes photography one of the richest sources of hoaxes.

The first recorded photographic hoax is credited to the French photographic pioneer Hippolye Bayard in 1840, only a year or two after the first known photographs. Bayard, in an effort to convince the French government that his new photographic process was different from that of rival Daguerre, posed for a picture while pretending that he was drowned. The picture, called "Self-Portrait of a Drowned Man," was intended to convince the French government that they should look again at his process. The government was not impressed.

The entire field of spirit photography, popular between 1860 and 1920, is covered later in this section (See Spirit Photography, p. 183). The famous Cottingley fairy photographs also follow, along with the "thoughtographs" of Ted Serios, which were claimed to be images made by a man's mind directly on film. Finally, the field of Kirlian photography has its own article (See Kirlian Photography, p. 183). Other photographic hoaxes involved UFO sightings, (See UFO Hoaxes, p. 267) and strange creatures (See Sea Serpent and Lake Monster Hoaxes, p. 264; Bigfoot Hoaxes, p. 245; and Plant and Animal Hoaxes, p. 259).

The Cottingley Fairies

In 1920, Sir Arthur Conan Doyle, best known for his Sherlock Holmes mysteries and his defense of spiritualism, wrote an article in *Strand* magazine stating that real fairies had finally been photographed by two young ladies in Bradford, England. The fairies were photographed in Cottingley Glen by Frances Griffiths (then aged ten) and Elsie Wright (then aged 16) in July and September of 1917. There were five photographs in total, the last three made in 1920, at the insistence of Edward Gardner, leader of one of the branches of the Theosophical Society in England.

Nothing much had been done with the photographs until Elsie's mother happened to show them to Gardner. He was impressed, and had local photographic "expert" Snelling, look at the photographs, which had glass plate negatives, then common. He pronounced them unretouched authentics. As it turned out, he was wrong on both counts. Even if the negatives were *not* retouched, they could still be unauthentic.

When Gardner gave Arthur Conan Doyle the photographs, Doyle had Kodak in England look at the negatives. Kodak's experts said that they could not find "any evidence of superimposition, or other tricks." Kodak said that they could duplicate the photographs using all the sophisticated equipment available to them, but did not think trickery was used in the film or in the scene photographed. Although Elsie was employed at a photographer's shop, she allegedly only worked at the counter. Later it was shown that she specialized in retouching photographs, but the fairies were not introduced into the photographs by retouching.

The first photograph shows Frances with four dancing fairies in the foreground. The second shows Elsie with a "gnome." A third photo shows Frances with a single leaping fairy, and the fourth shows Elsie being offered a posy by a fairy. The last photo shows several fairies in their "sunbath," with no humans present. The first two photos were made several years before the last three.

A man named Geoffrey Hodson was sent to observe the fairies with the girls, as they claimed that

Frances Griffiths and the Cottingley fairies.

Cottingley photograph of Elsie Wright and fairy.

Cottingley Glen was a regular fairy site. Hodson claimed that they all saw fairies, although at that (August 1921) visit they were unable to take additional photographs of the fairies. Of course, Doyle's book strongly supported the authenticity of the photographs. Their authenticity went unchallenged until Brian Coe at Kodak in London reexamined the negatives in 1978 for the British Broadcasting Corporation (BBC) when they were doing a program on the fairies. His examination showed a number of curious facts.

First, although it was claimed that the first two photos were made with a "Midge" camera, the plate for number two would not fit into a Midge camera. The first photo's technical information, as given by Elsie, was incorrect. The light was subdued, and the emulsion on the film could not work without at least a 1 to 2 second exposure, instead of the 1/50 of a second Elsie claimed was used. This means that the time was long enough for the fairy's wings to have beaten several times (1/50 of a second would have been fast enough to make them appear still). Yet the wings are not blurry. Which means they did not beat during that two seconds or so. Yet the waterfall in the background is blurry, since it was moving during the two seconds.

Computer analysis of the fairies in photos one, three and four, showed that the fairy figures were two-dimensional, not three-dimensional. Fred Gettings discovered in 1978 that the fairy figures in the first photo looked a great deal like the dancing figures found in a children's book called *Princess Mary's Gift Book*, published in 1915. With the addition of wings and a few other small items, they could pass as duplicates.

Still, the girls—now women—refused to admit they faked the photos. As late as 1975, they held to their authenticity. In 1981, with Frances aged 74 and Elsie 80,

Frances finally told Joe Cooper—who supported them for years, while trying to get at the truth—that they used hatpins to support the fairy figures. They insisted to the end, however, that the fifth photo was not faked in any way. Author James Randi claimed, however, that he and Brian Coe detected signs that the photo was a double exposure, perhaps unintentional. It appears to employ cutouts as well. Frances admitted that they used *Princess Mary's Gift Book* as the source of some of the fairy cutouts. So, the work of two school girls who didn't expect to fool anyone wound up fooling much of the world for many years. Although it was probably intended as a prank, it became a classic photographic hoax.

Sources:

Clark, Jerome. "The Cottingley Fairies: The Last Word." *Fate* (November 1978) 68–71.

Cooper, Joe. *The Case of the Cottingley Fairies*. London: Robert Hale, 1990.

Doyle, Arthur Conan. *The Coming of the Fairies*. New York: George H. Doran, 1922.

Gardner, Edward L. *Fairies: The Cottingley Fairies and Their Sequel*, 3rd ed. London: Theosophical Publishing House, 1957.

Gettings, Fred. *Ghosts in Photographs: The Extraordinary Story of Spirit Photography*. New York: Harmony Books, 1978.

Randi, James.*Flim-Flam: The Truth About Unicorns, Parapsychology, and Other Delusions*. New York: Lippincott & Crowell, 1980: 12–41.

Shaeffer, Robert. "The Cottingley Fairies: A Hoax?" *Fate* (June 1978): 76–83.

Kirlian Photography

Kirlian photography was named after Semyon and Valentina Kirlian, Russian engineers who first noticed the effect in 1939. Although they considered this a new discovery, the phenomenon was known previously and called corona discharge photography. Certainly the Kirlians popularized the subject. Kirlian photography consists of taking a photograph without outside light or a real camera. A high voltage (but low amperage) electric current is placed in close contact with the object to be photographed. The photographic film, usually on a set of rollers between two light-proof chambers, is exposed to the object in its electrified state (in darkness) for a second or two. The film is then developed normally producing an image of the object surrounded by electric "coronas" or spikes of electricity.

The idea soon became popular that Kirlian photography measured the "aura" around objects, and measured health, happiness, or some psychological dimension. Many amateurs began producing Kirlian photographs, often under uncontrolled conditions. As a result they produced pictures that they were unable to interpret correctly.

Author Richard Szumanski found that an entirely different "aura" was pictured on the film, depending upon the *angle* at which a photographed finger touched the film. The amount of finger surface that touched *and the pressure used* was the determinant of the size of the "aura." He overcame this problem by redesigning the electrode with the film so that it could be lowered down onto the subject to be photographed, making the pressure a constant. He found no more mysterious unexplainable changes in "auras."

Although Kirlian photography claimed to predict the well-being or health of the objects photographed by means of the size or intensity of their aura, the fact that mechanical, non-living things such as coins, water, and gears have auras refutes this claim. The aura, although a real phenomenon, actually represents the discharge of the electric field into the surrounding air (i.e., a corona).

Another theory claims that the sharpness of the boundary between objects next to each other on a Kirlian photograph indicates the incompatibility between the objects. The sharper the boundary, the more incompatible. Since two fingers of the same individual show a high incompatibility in many cases, this is unlikely.

It is also claimed that missing parts of a leaf or salamander's tail will show up on a Kirlian photograph. This does not happen routinely and authors Watkins and Bickel were unable to reproduce this effect.

Scientists John Pehek and his co-authors discovered the "dirty little secret" about Kirlian photography. It is not the health, mood, or attitude of a subject of a Kirlian photograph that determines the size and shape of its image. Rather, it is the amount of moisture. The corona images obtained from dry fingers were quite similar to those obtained from dry inanimate objects. The amount of moisture present also influenced the color of the corona.

Kirlian photography is a hoax. It has nothing to do with the health, vitality, or mood of a subject photographed. The so-called aura is merely an effect produced by high-voltage electricity and moisture.

Sources:

Krippner, Stanley and Daniel Rubin, eds. *The Energies of Consciousness.* New York: Gordon & Breach, 1975.

———. *The Kirlian Aura: Photographing the Galaxies of Life.* Garden City, NY: Anchor Books, 1974.

Pehek, John O., Harry J. Kyler, and David L. Faust. "Image Modulation in Corona Discharge Photography." *Science* 194 (Oct 15 1976): 263–70.

Szumanki, Richard. "A New Hard Look at Kirlian Photography: Has It Lost Its Halo?" *Fate* Part I (Jan 1976) 30–38; Part II (Feb 1976): 78–85.

Watkins, Arleen J. and William S. Bickell. "A Study of the Kirlian Effect." *The Skeptical Inquirer* 10 (Spring 1986): 244–57.

Spirit Photography

The presence of spirit "extras" on photographs was primarily a nineteenth century phenomenon. It

Nineteenth-century spirit photograph.

Another example of a spirit photograph.

started with William Mumler, a Boston photographer, who made his first spirit photograph in 1862. The last known spirit photographer of any renown was John Myers, who was active in the early 1930s. However, by about 1920, spirit photography had tapered off due to an increasingly sophisticated public understanding of how photography works and the movement from glass plates and film in single-plate carriers to gelatin-based film in rolls. These elements made it much more difficult to produce convincing "spirits" on the photographs.

In the spirit photographs of the nineteenth century, most of the "spirits" are either quite faint, or else they are heavily draped or veiled. In both cases no clear identification of the spirit can be made. In many ways this was advantageous to the photographer because an ambiguous image could be seen as a long dead relative by different people, each projecting their hopes into the image. In the few cases in which the "spirit" was clearly identifiable, a careful study made by author Fred Barlow that showed that the image was identical with that of a known photograph of the "spirit" when alive.

Perhaps the most famous spirit photographer was William Hope, who did most of his work after 1908 in England. He was exposed in 1920 by Bush, in 1922 by psychic investigator Harry Price, and finally in 1933 by Barlow. Hope bounced back after each investigation.

The three exposures were summarized by Barlow. He mentioned that Price caught Hope doing a film plate substitution. His extras were from known photographic images. There was evidence of double exposures on his negatives and his images could have been produced by normal means. Many of the images looked like they were cut out of magazines. In short, Hope was a fraud. Other spirit photographers, including Hudson, Mumler, and Boursnell, were also proven as fakes.

Spirit photography appealed to those seeking evidence that their loved ones had survived death. This type of photography, however, could not survive improvements in the field, and died from lack of technical expertise that became necessary to fool more sophisticated patrons.

Sources:

Barlow, Fred and W. Rampling-Rose. "Report of an Investigation into Spirit Photography." *Proceedings of the Society for Psychical Research* 41 (1933): 121–38.

Edmunds, Simeon. *Spirit Photography*. London: Society for Psychical Research, 1965.

Gettings, Fred. *Ghosts in Photographs: The Extraordinary Story of Spirit Photography*. New York: Harmony Books, 1978.

Permutt, Cyril. *Photographing the Spirit World: Images from Beyond the Spectrum.* Wellingborough, England: Aquarian Press, 1988.

Sidgwick, Mrs. Henry [Eleanor]. "On Spirit Photographs, a Reply to Mr. A. R. Wallace." *Proceedings of the Society for Psychical Research* 8 (1891): 268–89.

Ted Serios and Thoughtography

Ted Serios and his mentor, psychiatrist Jule Eisenbud, believed that a person could transmit the thoughts or images in his mind directly to photographic film. Serios, an often unemployed Chicago bellhop, had at least one book written about his abilities. This was Eisenbud's *The World of Ted Serios.* In it are about 150 examples of film images made by Serios without the camera being aimed at the object photographed. Serios' used the Polaroid camera, so many of the usual objections that raised about tampering with film or switching it during development, are not relevant.

A two-part study by Charles Reynolds and David B. Eisendrath, Jr. appeared in *Popular Photography* magazine in 1967. Here, Serios' work was reviewed by skilled photographers who were also magicians. These investigators noted that the so-called "gizmo" that Serios placed up against the camera lens to "concentrate his thoughts" could well have contained a small lens or film system. The gizmo was a paper or cardboard tube, similar to a toilet paper roll, which was always empty when examined. However, a few times the photographer/magicians observed what might have been a sleight-of-hand maneuver, just before and after a successful image was produced on the film. This could have been to move the lens/film system into and out of the gizmo.

The Polaroid camera was set on infinite focus. When magicians—and later James Randi—experimented with lens/film systems, they found that they could obtain an image on the Polaroid film that looked quite a bit like Serios' images by using an inner tube of one inch in length, by inch in diameter. At one end of the tube was a positive lens with a focal length one inch. At the other end of the tube was a film transparency of the object to be obtained on the Polaroid film. Light was allowed to pass through this transparency as the lens end was held virtually touching the Polaroid camera's lens. This device *may* explain how Serios did his images. The control exercised over Serios during the trials in which he was able to produce images (mostly supervised by Jule Eisenbud) was inadequate for solid scientific research. When Serios was more tightly controlled, he was unable to produce any images.

Serios lost interest in making thoughtographs and Eisenbud lost interest in defending Serios. In the absence of carefully controlled tests, the use of the lens/film system was the best explanation of how the images got on the film.

Sources:

Eisenbud, Jule. *The World of Ted Serios.* New York: William Morrow, 1967.

Randi, James. *Flim-Flam! The Truth About Unicorns, Parapsychology and Other Delusions.* New York: Lippincott & Crowell, 1980: 222–28.

Reynolds, Charles and David B. Eisendrath. "An Amazing Weekend With the Amazing Ted Serios." *Popular Photography* (October 1967): 81–87, 131–41, 158.

Welch, Paul. "A Man Who Thinks Pictures." *Life* 63 (Sept 22, 1967): 112–14.

Other Photographic Hoaxes

The Gettysburg Battlefield Photograph. Alexander Gardner's photograph of a Union Soldier who had fallen at Gettysburg was printed in *Harper's Weekly* magazine in 1865 as a hand-engraved copy. In order to "spice up" the photograph, more bodies, a smashed cart and stormy sky from other photographs were added. Gardner used this same original photograph to pull a hoax of his own. He moved the body of the fallen Union soldier to another different location, arranged his gun differently, and identified him as a fallen Confederate soldier for a different photograph.

World War I Aerial Photographs. In 1933, an anonymous book ("By a Flying Corps Pilot") was published in London. The book's title was *Death in the Air: The War Diary and Photographs of a Flying Corps Pilot.* This book contained dramatic photographs of aerial combat during World War I. There were photos of dogfights taken from one of the planes in the air. There where photos of planes being shot down in flames. In short, these were unparalleled wartime aerial action photos. The anonymous author claimed that he took the pictures using a captured German camera from a downed aircraft. The pilot rigged the camera to the wing of *his* plane, and controlled it with his machine gun trigger. When the gun went off, the shutter clicked once with the first shot.

Since it was strictly forbidden in the Royal Air Force to take unofficial combat photos, the photographer's name was not made public, all identifying numbers were removed from the photographs of the planes,

"New Yalta Conference," an example of an electronic composite photograph.

and more than twelve years passed before the photos were shown publicly. The photographer had supposedly been killed in combat in the meantime.

It was the number of photographs (only one could be taken per mission) that made some fellow pilots suspicious. The photos in this book were displayed in exhibitions in New York and Philadephia, where they were identified as having come from the "Cockburn-Lange Collection." Mrs. Cockburn-Lange, a reclusive woman, would not publicly vouch for their authenticity. World War II brought gradual obscurity to the photographs.

In 1984, the original negatives of the photos were identified in a collection of material donated to the Smithsonian by John W. Charlton. Most of the materials belonged to his friend, Wesley David Archer, husband of Mrs. "Cockburn-Lange." She was neither

"Cockburn-Lange," nor British. Archer once worked as a model maker in the film industry. He crafted the close-up photographs of air combat by posing carefully-made model planes, photographing them, and then superimposing them upon backgrounds. Traces of the wires holding the planes up were eventually detected.

Composite Photographs. In the 1880s, composite photographic scenes were in demand. These were put together with four or five photographic figures, each cut out from a separate original. The images were pasted down on a background scene and rephotographed. Ralph W. Robinson was one of the pioneers in this technique, which was a hoax because it used conscious deception to produce a scene which never, in reality, occurred.

The art of composite photography has advanced greatly in the past few years; a photograph can now be crafted from electronically disassembled "bits" ("pixels") made from images taken from various photographs.

Wisconsin State Capitol dome collapses.

Hitler baby picture hoax.

Once the components have been broken into pixels, they can be manipulated into position either singly or as a group. A computer mouse or a light pen can do what an airbrush used to do, namely erase lines and areas. The erased areas can be filled in with pixels "imported" from another area.

The electronic process makes it virtually impossible—no matter how powerful a magnifier is used to examine the finished print—to detect the joining of images. The photograph of the Yalta Conference with Sylvester Stallone and Groucho Marx in attendance, is an example of a state-of-the-art composite photo done electronically. For less than $200, an amateur can buy a scanner to go with software and a personal computer to do pixel work.

Houdini's Flying Hoax. Few people realize that magician Harry Houdini (1874–1926) made several silent movies. He starred in these adventure films and performed most of his own stunts, including rather dangerous ones. In 1919, Houdini was promoting his latest film, *The Grim Game.* Houdini's character in the film was to attempt to transfer from one airplane to another in flight. The character was to jump from a rope dangling from one airplane into another plane flying below. Allegedly, the stunt failed during the filming and the two planes collided unexpectedly. They locked together and plunged toward the ground. Houdini

thought he would be killed, but the planes separated and glided to earth, although both were badly smashed upon impact.

Houdini did not tell the precise truth here. The man hanging from the rope was airman Robert E. Kennedy, not Houdini. Houdini was willing to do the stunt, but director Irvin Willat would not allow it. Willat did not want to risk his star's life. Kennedy was selected as the stuntman. On May 31, 1919, he confidently climbed out of the plane over Santa Monica beach. The unexpected mishap, collision and crash landing were filmed by the director and included in the final film. Although Houdini was not in either plane, he went around promoting the film with the offer of $1,000 to "anyone who can prove that the aeroplane [sic] crash in the movie is not genuine!" No one could collect and Houdini hoaxed people into believing that he was hanging from the rope during the crash.

Wisconsin State Capitol Dome Collapse. On April 1, 1933 (*See* April Fool's Day Hoaxes, p. 9), the Madison, Wisconsin, *Capital Times* reported that a gigantic series of explosions had blown the $8 million state capitol building's dome off. A photograph of the Capitol minus its dome—which lay nearby—was featured. The alleged suggestion was that " . . . large quantities of gas, generated through many weeks of verbose debate in the Senate and Assembly chambers, had in some way been ignited, causing the first blast." The last paragraph stated "April Fool."

Adolf Hitler's Baby Picture. In 1938, Acme Newspictures released a set of two photos that partially explained the origin of a supposed baby picture of Adolf Hitler that had been circulating widely since 1933. The picture, which showed a heavy, scowling baby, was actually a retouched photograph of John May Warren, then living in Lakewood, Ohio. He was two years old at the time of the photograph. His mother recognized the supposed Hitler photograph as her son's—minus his baby cap, and subjected to a retouch of that made the baby's expression much more menacing than it had been. The retouched photograph originated in Austria, but how it got there and who retouched it has never been discovered.

Sources:

Browne, Malcolm W. "Computer as an Accessory to Photo Fakery." *New York Times* (July 24, 1991): A6.

"Dome Topples Off Statehouse." Madison, WI *Capital Times* (April 1, 1933): 1.

Fielding, Raymond. *The Technique of Special Effects Cinematography*, 4th ed. London: Focus Press, 1985.

Goldsmith, Arthur. "Photos Always Lied." *Popular Photography* (November 1991): 68–75.

Park, Edwards. "The Greatest Aerial Warfare Photos Go Down in Flames." *Smithsonian Magazine* 15 no. 10 (January 1985): 102–8. Ronnie, Art. "Houdini's High-Flying Hoax." *American Heritage* 23 no. 3 (1972): 106–9.

Rosenbaum, Naomi. *A World History of Photography.* New York: Abbeville Press, 1984.

Smith, Thomas G. *Industrial Light & Magic: The Art of Special Effects.* New York: Ballantine Books, 1986.

Political Hoaxes

Many hoaxes have a political motive, but are not political in content. Some are intended to embarrass a politician or to make political capital out of a given situation. Some are intended to advance or diminish a country's prestige in the eyes of other countries. Still others are intended to enhance or tear down the reputation of dead political figures.

The Communist Rules for Revolution

A set of ten "rules," *The Communist Rules for Revolution*—written as official Communist policy—have been repeatedly reproduced, especially in right-wing publications during the past fifty years. The rules had supposedly been "captured" in Düsseldorf, Germany in 1919 by the Allied Forces.

This is one version of the *Rules*, as given by Brunvand:

1) Corrupt the young. Get them away from religion. Get them interested in sex. Make them superficial. Destroy their ruggedness.

2) Get control of all means of publicity.

3) Get people's minds off their government by focusing their attention on athletics, sexy books and plays, and other trivialities.

4) Divide the people into hostile groups by constantly harping on controversial matters of no importance.

5) Destroy the people's faith in their natural leaders by holding the latter up to contempt, ridicule and obloquy.

6) Always preach true democracy, but seize power as fast and as ruthlessly as possible.

7) By encouraging government extravagance, destroy its credit and produce fear of inflation with rising prices and general discontent.

8) Foment unnecessary strikes in vital industries, encourage civil disorders, and foster a lenient and soft attitude on the part of government toward such disorders.

9) By specious argument cause the breakdown of the old moral virtues, honesty, sobriety, continence, faith in the pledged word, ruggedness.

10) Cause the registration of all firearms on some pretext, with a view to confiscating them and leaving the population helpless.

In 1981 *Chicago Tribune* columnist Bob Greene was tired of receiving copies of the *Rules*. He decided to investigate their authenticity. Greene contacted a number of historians and scholars who were experts on Communism and Soviet history. They all said that the *Rules* were fakes and never existed as Communist policy. They were not composed by the early Communists in 1919. Rather, the experts felt that they were a modern construction (c. 1950).

Prof. Davis Joravsky of Northwestern University—one of the scholars consulted by Greene—stated that "the Rules are an obvious fabrication. They are not Communist in their origin." He stated that many of the rules were *contrary* to true Communist beliefs. Prof. Jeffrey Brooks at the University of Chicago agreed that the *Rules* were "impossible and improbable" as Communist policy. Arcadius Kahan, a professor of economics and history at the University of Chicago, said a person would have to be "an idiot" to believe that the *Rules* were published or written by the Communists. He added that the very idea that a "Master Plan," such as the *Rules*, could be kept in use for fifty to sixty years was naive. There was also a search made of the U.S.

National Archives, which failed to turn up a copy of the *Rules* as an authentic captured document. The conclusion is that *The Communist Rules for Revolution* were a hoax.

Sources:

Brunvand, Jan Harold. *The Mexican Pet: More "New" Urban Legends and Some Old Favorites.* New York: W. W. Norton & Co., 1986: 108–09.

Greene, Bob. "A Communist Master Plan? The Plot Thins." *Chicago Tribune* (March 23, 1981) section 2: 1.

Kominsky, Morris. *The Hoaxers: Plain Liars, Fancy Liars, and Damned Liars.* Boston: Branden Press, 1970: 600–05.

The Diary of a Public Man

Rarely does an autobiography open itself up to charges of being a hoax (*See* Howard Hughes' Autobiography, p. 72 and the Hitler Diaries, p. 68 for exceptions). In the case of *The Diary of a Public Man,* the controversy continues, but it is most likely a hoax. The *Diary* first appeared as a series of anonymous articles in the magazine the *North American Review* in 1879.

The articles purported to be the diary of a man who moved in the top circles of Washington in the Civil War period. He knew Lincoln, Seward, and most of the other political leaders of the day and his diary cast light on the inner politics of the day for which there is no other source. The author of the article is still in question. Many attempts have been made to discover this from facts in the articles. Author Frank Anderson in particular has devoted much effort to identifying who was in Washington or New York on the days that the author of the work says he was there and who met with Lincoln or Seward on the days the author says he did. Unfortunately, no one was identified who did everything and was everywhere claimed.

Although Anderson concluded that lobbyist Sam Ward was the author, he also concluded that at least *some* of the *Diary* was fiction. Ward could not have been in all of the places at all of the times stated by the author. However, author Roy Lokken states that Anderson was premature in concluding that no person could have met the requirements outlined by the "facts" in the *Diary.*

Evelyn Page feels that the *Diary* was a work of fiction. Page indicates that the framework of the four parts of the *Diary* is literary and not "colloquial," as it would be if it were a record of actual conversations and events. Page feels that Allen Thorndike Rice, editor of

the *North American Review* at the time of the *Diary* publication, would not accept an anonymous contribution from an unknown contributor that was purported to be factual. Rice supposedly knew the identity of the author but never revealed it.

Page makes a case for the authorship of Henry Adams (1838–1918), author and historian. Adams was in Washington at the appropriate time. He was the son of U.S. ambassador to England, Charles Francis Adams and wrote about his time in Washington in a series of journalistic pieces. She feels that the style revealed by Adams in his earlier writings was more developed in the *Diary,* but similar. However, she offers no specific examples of stylistic similarities. Henry Adams does not seem a definitive candidate.

Anderson provides subtle clues that the *Diary* might be entirely fictional. He tells of examining Lord Lyons' (the British ambassador to the United States in 1861) papers for the date at which the diarist claims he met with Lyons to discuss "those vexatious people in Barbadoes [sic] and Antigua." Nothing on this matter was found, nor any real clue as to who the diarist might be. Among the individuals whom Anderson investigated as the possible author of the *Diary* were Sam Ward, Thurlow Weed, Amos Kendall, Henry Wikoff, Charles Edward Stuart, D. H. Strothers, Joseph C. G. Kennedy, Horatio King, John Van Buren, Jacob Collamer, Henry S. Sanford, and John W. Forney. None of these people meet all of the eighteen criteria that Anderson had established as necessary for the diarist. As a result, Anderson discarded some of the criteria, leaving him with thirteen. Still, nobody quite fits even the thirteen criteria. This eventually led Anderson to state that some of the *Diary* must be fiction. Hiram Barney, the only person mentioned in the *Diary* who was still alive when Anderson investigated, firmly denied that the incident involving him mentioned in the *Diary* had occurred. This adds to the possibility that the work is a piece of fiction.

The solution to who wrote *The Diary of a Public Man* has not been solved. It appears to have elements of a hoax, especially if it is a work of fiction. If it is an actual diary, written as true by someone who was where the diary states at the times stated, then perhaps the diarist has a faulty memory.

Sources:

Anderson, Frank Maloy. *The Mystery of "A Public Man."* Minneapolis: University of Minnesota Press, 1948.

"The Diary of a Public Man: Unpublished Passages of the Secret History of the American Civil War." *North American Review* 129 (August, September, October,

November 1879): 125–40, 259–73, 375–88, 484–96.
Reprinted in the back of Anderson's book as well.

Lokken, Roy N. "Has the Mystery of 'A Public Man'
Been Solved?" *Mississippi Valley Historical Review* 40
(December 1953): 419–40.

Page, Evelyn. "The Diary and the Public Man." *New
England Quarterly* 22 (June 1949): 147–72.

Other Political Hoaxes

Abraham Lincoln Hoaxes. Abraham Lincoln's (1809–
1865) signature and documents have been widely forged,
but there are also a number of other hoaxes involving
Lincoln. During the 1880s a collection of Lincoln speeches
was published containing material never spoken or
written by Lincoln. For instance, he allegedly said

> I see in the near future a crisis that unnerves me, and
> causes me to tremble for the safety of my country. As a
> result of war, corporations have been enthroned and an
> era of corruption in high places will follow, and the
> money power of the country will endeavor to prolong
> its reign by working upon the prejudices of the people
> until all the wealth is aggregated in a few hands and the
> republic is destroyed.

Lincoln never said this.

Spurious quotes have been used to suggest that
Lincoln favored a high tariff. Lincoln was also made to
appear in favor of Italian unification, although he never
addressed the issue. An 1896 issue of *McClure's Magazine* (7:319–31) published what it called "Lincoln's Lost
Speech," supposedly delivered at the Republican State
Convention in Bloomington, Illinois in 1856. Since no
one wrote the speech down, its text was thought lost. In
1930, Lincoln students, after studying the style of the
speech carefully, concluded that the speech was a fake.
The original text was never found.

Original copies of newspapers published on the
day after Lincoln's assassination are scarce. Reprint
facsimiles are common especially of the April 15, 1865
issue of the *New York Herald*. Photographic fakes of
Lincoln, sometimes as a "spirit," (See Photographic
Hoaxes, p. 181) are common as well. The photograph of
John C. Calhoun's body with Lincoln's head grafted on
it is still common in public school classrooms.

The Bixby letter was supposedly written by Lincoln to a widow who lost five sons in the Civil War. The
letter itself may have been written by Lincoln's secretary, John Hay, in the *mistaken* belief that Bixby lost five
sons (it was actually only two sons). In any case,
Lincoln does not appear to have written the letter, even

though a copy of it exists in what appears to be in his
handwriting. Hay was expert in imitating Lincoln's
writing, and the original of the letter has never been
found.

In 1928 and 1929, the *Atlantic Monthly* published
in a set of love letters supposedly written by Lincoln to
Ann Rutledge. The letters were overwhelmingly described as fakes by Lincoln scholars and publication
was discontinued by the magazine.

Report From Iron Mountain. In 1967, a book was published in New York entitled *Report From Iron Mountain
on the Possibility and Desirability of Peace.* The introduction was by Leonard C. Lewin. He claimed that the
report was secretly compiled by fifteen experts—gathered together by some branch of the United States
government—who had been meeting secretly for two
years to prepare the report. "John Doe," one of the
pseudonymous experts, had decided to release the
report to the public.

The subject of the report was whether long-term
peace was possible, given the economic situation of the
world. The answer, the report said, was no. War was
needed regularly to keep world economies function-
ing. People immediately, smelled a hoax. The review in
the *New York Times* on November 20, 1967 by Eliot
Fremont-Smith called the book a hoax, although he
could neither prove it to be a hoax nor identify the
hoaxer.

Fremont-Smith thought the book was the work
of either economists John Kenneth Galbraith, Kenneth
Boulding, or Leonard C. Lewin. Suspicion fell on Lewin
because he wrote the introduction and authored a book
of political satire. In addition, Lewin reviewed Herman
Kahn's book *The Year 2000*, which was exactly the sort
of work that the report parodied, even setting "Iron
Mountain" right near Kahn's Hudson Institute.

The evidence in favor of Galbraith points to the
fact that he reviewed the book under a pseudonym for
Book World. Both *New York Times* reviewers favor Lewin
as the author and in the absence of any definitive
evidence, perhaps that conclusion should be tentative-
ly accepted.

Dick Tuck's Hoaxes. Since prankster Dick Tuck's hoaxes
have been exclusively in the realm of politics, he is
included here. Tuck, perhaps best known for his pranks
against Richard Nixon, denied that the hoax most
people think of as his best was ever done by him—
although he wishes he *had* done it. That hoax involved
wearing a train conductor's uniform to motion a train—
on which Richard Nixon was speaking from the rear
platform—out of the station. The train supposedly

departed while Nixon was still talking. On an audiotape made by Tuck, he denies having anything to do with this incident, which may never have occurred as it is not documented.

Tuck was involved in other hoaxes. He introduced Nixon at a college rally, but in setting up the rally, he obtained a 4,000-seat auditorium, knowing only a few people would attend. There were forty. He then announced he was going to wait for more people to show up. In the waiting period, ten more people left and none arrived. He asked all kinds of questions aloud to Nixon in his introduction attempting to stall the start of Nixon's talk. Finally, he said "Richard Nixon will now speak on the World Monetary Fund." Nixon who never intended to speak on the World Monetary Fund, was stunned, and speechless for a while.

When Nixon was running with Eisenhower for reelection as Vice President, the Republican Convention was held in San Francisco. Tuck found that the main route taken by many garbage trucks going to the city dump was right by the convention center. He had posters applied to each garbage truck that said "Dump Nixon."

During the 1962 Nixon/Kennedy race, Tuck had a woman approach Nixon as he descended from an airplane the day after the first debate with Kennedy. She kissed Nixon on the cheek and said "That's all right, Mr. Nixon. He beat you last night, but you'll win next time." Nixon was shattered for about five minutes before he managed to compose himself.

The Sentry Box Hoax. When the Soviet Consulate on East 91st Street in New York City was abandoned in 1980 at the request of the State Department, the functions formerly housed there were moved to other offices. The empty building was eventually left unguarded by the New York City police department. Then, on December 11, 1981, Sergeant Joseph Gillan of the 23rd Precinct (in whose domain the former Consulate building lay) took a call from Officer Cowans of Patrol Borough Manhattan North. This was the command center for northern Manhattan. Because of the current crisis in Poland, Cowans said, Inspector Whitmore of police intelligence was ordering a permanent sentry box and officer to be stationed outside the consulate until further notice. Accordingly, a policeman was placed in a sentry box twenty-four-hours-a-day from December 12, 1981 through May 17, 1982.

The residents of East 91st Street appreciated the presence of police on the street, but nothing much happened at the consulate. Then in mid-May of 1982 a van containing stereo equipment and belonging to the Russians was burglarized. Since diplomats were the

victims, the intelligence division was notified and told that the incident occurred near the sentry booth. "What booth?" asked an intelligence officer. The 23rd Precinct checked and found no Officer Cowans in Manhattan North and no Inspector Whitmore in Intelligence existed. The entire order for the booth and police guard was a hoax, but no one has been identified as the perpetrator.

The Tanaka Memorial. The *Tanaka Memorial* was supposedly written by Baron Giichi Tanaka (1863–1929), when he was the Japanese Premier. The work was sent to the Emperor of Japan on July 25, 1927. It came about as a result of the Manchurian situation. Few far eastern experts were surprised at the contents which were soon leaked to the public, because they were similar to rumors that had circulated among the Japanese for 200 years. The *Memorial* tells of Japan's aims in Manchuria and in China generally. It is basically an outline of the imperialist aims of Japan in spreading its empire into the rest of Asia.

The *Memorial* was reprinted in a number of languages and widely distributed. Its authenticity was vigorously denied by the Japanese at the time, but was not doubted by most other countries. Author John Stephan has shown, however, that the document both is formulated in a tone that no Japanese—even the premier—would use in a document sent to the Emperor, that the *Memorial* contained a number of factual errors that Tanaka would never have made. In short, the *Memorial* was a hoax.

One error was the statement in the *Memorial* that Manchuria's and Mongolia's combined area was 74,000 square miles. In fact, it is 1,000,000 square miles. Japan's total financial investment in Manchuria was given as 440,000 yen. Actually, it was two billion yen. The Chinese were referred to as the only trading partners of Japan, when actually they comprised about one-quarter of the trade done by Japan at the time. Tanaka recalls a 1922 attempt on his life as occurring while he was en route back to Japan—through Shanghai—from a trip to America and Europe. Actually, he had never been to the United States or Europe after 1914. He was actually returning from a trip to the Philippines. All of these facts were known to Tanaka, so it is unlikely that he had any role in the composition of the *Memoir*. Rather, the role of the Chinese government (with possible Japanese help) in the construction of the forgery seems likely. Although the true culprits have never been identified, scholarly opinion favors the *Tanaka Memorial* a political hoax.

The Stringfellow Hoax. Douglas R. Stringfellow was a genuine war hero, elected to the U.S. House of Representatives in 1952, as a Republican from Utah. He had served one term, and was running for reelection when his fake background caught up to him.

Although Stringfellow claimed to be a paraplegic as a result of war injuries, investigation into his war record by Democratic opponents showed that, although he was injured in a mine explosion while on a routine mission in France, his story of working for the Office of Strategic Services (OSS), and being captured and tortured in Belsen prison, was a lie. Stringfellow was not a paraplegic as claimed, in fact he walked with the aid of a cane. He also falsely claimed that he rescued German scientist Otto Hahn from behind German lines. Stringfellow claimed a religious experience while lying gravely wounded. He went around the state of Utah, with Mormon blessing, giving what amounted to sermons about his experience. His approximately 1,000 speeches, none of them written down, contained so much variation in the "facts" that it was difficult to know what was true. He supposedly attended Ohio State University and the University of Cincinnati, but neither had record of him. He said he received the Silver Star medal, but he hadn't. His past was riddled with lies.

When the Mormon Church found out about his background, its president David McKay, ordered him to make a public confession and to drop his bid for reelection. Stringfellow *did* appear on television that evening. His confession was cleverly worded to arouse public sympathy for him. He then went on a public speaking tour, which was a failure. Stringfellow finally wound up back in radio announcing, where he had previously worked. He used a pseudonym and worked on a number of Utah stations.

Qaddafi's Fake Assassination. Libyan leader Muammar Qaddafi apparently has a tendency to do away with his rivals. Therefore, it was no surprise when word got out in November of 1984 that Abdul Hamid Bakkush, the Prime Minister overthrown by Qaddafi in 1969, was on the "hit list." Bakkush lived in Cairo in 1984 and the Egyptian government decided to protect him by faking his assassination. Photographs were made of a seemingly dead Bakkush covered with blood and lying in a pool of blood. They were sent to Libya by Egyptian intelligence agents. Libya then announced publicly that Bakkush was killed by Libyan "suicide squads." Egypt announced the next day that it had hoaxed Libya and that Bakkush was still alive. They also announced that four members of a Libyan assassination team were under arrest. The team's two Britons and two Maltese had hired Egyptian collaborators who turned out to have been undercover agents.

The Parnell Libel. Charles Stewart Parnell (1846–1891), the Irish leader, was the victim of a hoax intended to discredit him. The London *Times* published a series of articles in 1887 entitled "Parnellism and Crime." In the April 18 article the text of letters supposedly written by Parnell appeared, expressing his pleasure at the Dublin murder of Lord Frederick Cavendish, the newly-appointed British Secretary for Ireland. The letters were taken as genuine, despite Parnell's denials. Lord Salisbury, the British Prime Minister, denounced British Prime Minister Gladstone for his friendship with Parnell.

During a libel suit brought by a former member of Parliament against the *Times* for the letters, Parnell's reputation was further damaged by a new set of letters, presented in court. Parnell then requested a select committee to look into the authenticity of both sets of letters. The House of Commons finally agreed to appoint a commission of judges to the matter. In the court, Parnell produced Richard Piggott, who was shown to have been responsible for the letters getting to the *Times.* Piggott revealed under examination that he made the same errors of spelling as the author of the letters. Eight days later, Piggott committed suicide after submitting a signed confession that he wrote the letters. Parnell received a settlement of 5,000 pounds from the *Times.*

Soviet-Related Hoaxes. A number of books purporting to tell the inside story of the Soviet Union at high political levels have appeared on the market. Some of these are complete hoaxes. Among the hoaxes was the 1952 *My Uncle Joe* [Stalin], by Budu Savanidze. The book was supposedly by Stalin's nephew (his brother-in-law's son) John Reed Savanidze, but he was never called "Budu." The book tries to portray Stalin as a nice human being—perhaps motivated by a campaign, shared by the other books mentioned here, to "humanize" Stalin. Another fake was *I Was Stalin's Bodyguard* by Achmed Amba, a fictitious Turkish creation. Amba packed more exciting adventures into one lifetime than is humanly possible, especially when many of them occurred simultaneously in different places. A third similar fake was the secret diary of Maxim Litvinov, the Soviet Foreign Minister. Published as *Notes For a Journal* (1955), it was not written by Litvinov at all. The manuscript was smuggled out of Russia as a microfilm of a typewritten manuscript, with no handwritten corrections. It contains mostly descriptions of trivial events, with nothing about the important events with which Litvinov was involved. Parts seem to be rewrites of a book by Grigory Bessedovsky, *Revelations of a Soviet Diplomat.*

The Miscegenation Hoax. In 1863, three young newspaper reporters for the New York *World* devised a complex political hoax, which embarrassed the Republican Party. They were determined to publish something about race mixing, then a hot topic. They decided that "amalgamation," the term used for this, was undesirable and invented a new word for interracial mixing "miscegenation," which was the title they used for their pamphlet. To lend their work scientific authenticity, they obtained a book by anthropologist James Cowles Prichard, *The Natural History of Man* (1843), and used the names of the authorities he quoted. By doing so, they cited a number of arguments in favor of miscegenation.

Before the pamphlet was published, proof copies were sent to prominent abolitionists and reformers in the country. Enclosed was a circular asking for their opinions before the work was published. Many prominent people wrote, praising the pamphlet. Then, an article was inserted in the Philadelphia *Inquirer*, stating that "a charming and accomplished young mulatto girl was about to publish a book on the subject of the blending of the races, in which she took the affirmative view." Nearly every newspaper in the country reprinted the article. When the pamphlet was published in 1864, copies were sent to leading newspapers and magazines. Many reviews, mostly favorable, were published.

The booklet was brought to the attention of Samuel Sullivan Cox of Ohio in the U.S. House of Representatives who made a speech about miscegenation and he was answered by several other representatives. Attempts to get President Lincoln to comment failed. The New York *Tribune* began attacking the Republicans on the grounds that they were in favor of miscegenation. The book went through several editions before fading into obscurity. It *had* succeeded in embarrassing the Republicans.

Sources:

Barnum, P. T. "The Miscegenation Hoax." *Humbugs of the World.* Detroit: Singing Tree Press, 1970 (reprint): 204–11.

"Cairo Fakes Pictures and Foils Libyan Death Plot." *New York Times* (November 18, 1984): 1, 13.

Farber, M. A. "The Hoax of the Sentry Catches Police Off Guard." *New York Times* (May 18, 1982): B1, B9.

Goodman Croly, David. *Miscegenation: The Theory of the Blending of the Races, Applied to the American White Man and Negro.* New York: H. Dexter, Hamilton & Co., 1864.

Jonas, Frank H. *The Story of a Political Hoax.* Salt Lake City: Institute of Government, University of Utah, 1966.

[Lee, Sidney]. "Charles Stewart Parnell." In *Dictionary of National Biography.* Edited by Lee and Sidney. Oxford: Oxford University Press, 1921.

[Lewin, Leonard C.?]. *Report From Iron Mountain on the Possibility and Desirability of Peace.* New York: Dial Press, 1967. Reviewed in the *New York Times* (November 20, 1967): 45; and (November 27, 1967) Section VII: 70–71.

"Libya Says Its Squads Killed Ex-Prime Minister." *New York Times* (November 17, 1984): 5.

Luthin, Reinhard H. "Fakes and Frauds in Lincoln Literature." *Saturday Review* (February 14, 1959): 15–16, 54.

Stephan, John J. "The Tanaka Memorial (1927): Authentic or Spurious?" *Modern Asian Studies* 7 no. 4 (1973): 733–45.

Tuck, Dick. *An Evening With Dick Tuck: The Confessions of a Political Prankster.* [audiotape] North Hollywood, CA: Center for Cassette Studies, 1973.

Wolfe, Bertram D. "Adventures in Forged Sovietica." *New Leader* (July 25, 1955): 13–14; (August 1, 1955): 11–14; (August 8, 1955): 21–22.

Psychology Hoaxes

The psychology hoaxes category includes parapsychology, occult psychology and related areas. While many would claim that all parapsychological phenomena fall into the hoax category, this is not assumed here. Only those incidents involving deliberate deception will be included. Since all conjuring requires use of the psychology of deception in order to succeed, and is not a case of unsuspected deception, conjuring will not be included.

Bridey Murphy and Past Lives

In 1956, one of the bestselling books of the year was *The Search for Bridey Murphy*, by Morey Bernstein. The book was about an amateur hypnotist (Bernstein) and an Irish woman from the early nineteenth century (Murphy) whom he uncovered when he "regressed" a woman he called Ruth Simmons backwards in time under hypnosis. Although this was not the first time that a person had been regressed past birth under hypnosis, it was well-publicized and captured much attention.

The hypnosis of Ruth Simmons, whose real name was later revealed as Virginia Tighe, took place in Pueblo, Colorado. It was not until *Denver Post* reporter William J. Barker wrote several articles about the story for his newspaper's Sunday magazine section, that the story became well-known. The public responded with enthusiasm, as the story suggested that it was possible to survive death.

Eventually, Doubleday offered a publishing contract to Bernstein and a bestseller was born. At the same time, the *Chicago Daily News* obtained rights to republish parts of the book. The arch-rival *Chicago American* decided to employ a number of its reporters to carefully check out the story. They discovered that the real name of the woman was Virginia Tighe, and that she spent much of her youth in Chicago. This made investigation much easier and it soon bore important results.

Under hypnosis, the following information was volunteered by Virginia Tighe in response to Morey Bernstein's request that she remember what happened to her before her birth. She said that she was born as Bridget ("Bridey") Kathleen Murphy in 1798 in Cork, Ireland. Her father was a Protestant barrister named Duncan Murphy and her mother was named Kathleen. She also had a brother named Duncan Blaine Murphy. They lived right outside Cork, in an area she called "The Meadows." At age twenty she married Sean Brian Joseph MacCarthy, the son of another Cork barrister. Her husband's family was Catholic. They had two wedding ceremonies—one Protestant and one Catholic—the latter performed by Fr. Joseph John Gorman at St. Theresa's Church in Belfast. They set up housekeeping in a cottage on Dooley Road in Belfast. Bridey's brother married Aimee Strayne, the daughter of Bridey's school mistress. Her brother and Aimee stayed in Cork and had children. Bridey and her husband had none. Her husband was a barrister, who taught at the law school at Queen's University in Belfast. He also wrote about the law in the *Belfast News-Letter*. Bridey died in 1864 at age 66. She also mentioned being punished when about four years old for scratching the paint off of her metal bed, and being read to as a child from two books, *The Green Bay* and one about the sorrows of Dierdre.

Some of the facts here were susceptible to verification. The *Denver Post* sent William Barker over to Ireland for three weeks to check on the story. He was not an experienced genealogist or historical researcher and did not uncover much in support or contradiction of Bridey's story. However, he failed to realize that *not* finding her husband's name among those listed as barristers weakened her story, as the lists of barristers were accurate and complete for this period. Barker tried to explain the absence of his name by saying that Bridey exaggerated and her husband probably was not a barrister, but only a bookkeeper. If she lied under hypnosis about her husband's occupation, she could easily have lied about being Bridey Murphy in a past life.

The story here becomes quite complicated. As mentioned, the rival newspaper to the *Chicago Daily News,* namely the *Chicago American,* came out with the results of its investigation. They said that Virginia Tighe had an aunt born in Ireland, who told her many stories about Ireland when Virginia was a child in Chicago. Reports said that across the street from Virginia's childhood home, lived a woman named Bridie Murphy Corkell, also from Ireland, who also told Virginia stories about Ireland. *Life* magazine picked up this news and published it as the solution to the problem. Other newspaper stories questioning the *American* article were ignored by *Life.*

William Barker responded to statements made by the *American* and *Life* in a chapter added to the paperback edition of Bernstein's book. In it he provided a few points of support for Bridey's story (e.g., the existence of two grocers called Farr and Carrigan in Belfast). It is difficult to understand how she found the names of two obscure grocers who only flourished for a few years in the mid-1800s. She was unable to 1) speak any Gaelic; 2) tell where she was buried, although she said she witnessed her own funeral; or 3) tell about anything that existed in directories or atlases of the time (e.g., publications showed no St. Theresa's Church, Dooley Road, Mrs. Strayne's Day School, MacCarthy family of barristers, metal beds in Ireland in 1802, Fr. Joseph John Gorman, and no book called *The Green Bay*).

Although Morey Bernstein was completely honest and sincere in his hypnotic work, there is still a distinct possibility of "a hoax," although it is difficult to demonstrate exactly who was the hoaxer. If Mrs. Tighe's "recollections" were only forgotten memories of childhood stories, the entire Bridey Murphy case may be nothing more than a hypnotized person trying to please the hypnotist. She might have pulled from any memories that satisfied what was requested by the hypnotist. It has been demonstrated that the mind can remember foreign languages not understood but heard once in childhood. Sentences in those languages can be repeated perfectly, even though not consciously known or ever spoken before. If the mind can do this, it can most likely remember stories heard in childhood, even if as an adult the source of those stories is no longer known. Historical facts can also be remembered, often from historical novels read years earlier. This may be the source of a few of the "facts" that confirmed Bridey's story.

In cases such as this, the burden of proof is upon the person who goes against readily observable facts. If the knowledge Virginia Tighe showed came from her memory of a previous life, then that assertion must be documented with myriad facts. William Barker was unable to do this. He came up with excuses *why* he couldn't document what "Bridey" said, but few facts. His excuses ranged from her poor spelling and pronunciation, to her empty bragging, to a failure of the documentary sources to list particular facts relevant to authenticating the story. Until more documentation exists, such as finding the Bridey Murphy MacCarthy graves, the whole incident should be considered unproved and *probably* a hoax.

Sources:

Bernstein, Morey. *The Search for Bridey Murphy.* New York: Avon Publishers, 1965. Revised edition.

Brean, Herbert. "Bridey Murphy Puts Nation in a Hypnotizzy." *Life* (March 19, 1956): 28–35. See also *Life* (June 25, 1956): 109.

Cohen, Daniel. *The Mysteries of Reincarnation.* New York: Dodd, Mead & Co., 1975.

Dingwall, Eric J. "The Woman Who Never Was." *Tomorrow* 4 no. 4 (Summer 1956): 6–15.

Kline, Milton V. *A Scientific Report on "The Search for Bridey Murphy".* New York: Julian Press, 1956.

Counting Horses

Horses that counted out answers to addition and subtraction problems posed by owners by tapping their hooves until the correct number was indicated were quite the rage around the turn of the century. There were also counting pigs, dogs, chickens, and geese. The most famous counting horse was "Clever Hans," a German horse belonging to Wilhelm van Osten.

Clever Hans was investigated by a commission of thirteen men, some of whom were scientists. They were to examine whether the owner and the trainer of Hans were in some way using "tricks" to get the horse to "count" or whether the horse was actually able to think. The commission did not say that Hans could think, yet they *did* exclude unintentional signs or signals being given to the horse that would produce the "counting." In part, their conclusion was based upon the character of the two men suspected and the fact that the commission could not detect any such signs. A circus manager gave the final determination of whether there were any voluntary signs or clues being given by the trainer to prompt the horse to start and stop tapping.

In October 1904, Oskar Pfungst and Mr. Schillings of the Psychological Institute in Berlin continued the investigation. It was soon discovered that Clever

Hans' performance decreased as the distance between him and his trainer increased. It was next discovered that the presence of blinders on the horse's eyes, which enabled him to only see straight ahead, greatly reduced his abilities to "count," especially if he could not see his trainer.

Pfungst decided the horse was being "cued" by the trainer. The horse was trained to raise his hoof and tap it in response to the number of large wooden pins placed in front of him. Hans was told —when there were three pins present—"Raise the foot! One, two, three!" His foot was then raised and lowered by van Osten three times. Eventually Hans learned that the word "three" should be responded to with three taps of his hoof. To teach the animal what appeared to be adding, van Osten taught Hans to understand the concept "and." To do this, a large cloth was held in front of the horse and this action became associated with the spoken word "and." Three pins were shown on the right, the cloth placed between the pins and the horse, the word "and" was said, and then two pins were shown on the left. Finally, the horse was able to tap for the first three pins three times, and then (after hearing the word "and") tap two times for the two pins on the left, running these all together to make five taps. All the time the horse was watching van Osten's face for relaxation, indicating he tapped enough. It should be noted that horses—and perhaps most domestic animals—can perceive subtle changes of emotion on human faces, or via human "body language."

Mr. van Osten claimed that Hans figured out the principles of multiplication by himself, but this is doubtful. Subtraction was taught by reversing the process used to teach addition.

Some tests were devised that showed that Hans could perform even if his trainer were not visible, but could be heard in the room. Also, Hans could take problems from a few other people he knew, even with his trainer not present. Perhaps the most amazing feat that the investigating commission saw Hans perform consisted of having the names of six members of the commission each written on six small blackboards. These six blackboards were suspended from six strings in front of the horse. One of the six men was pointed to by the trainer, and Hans would tap the blackboard with the man's name on it.

Further tests of Clever Hans revealed that he failed to perform correctly whenever the solution to the problem was unknown to any humans present. This immediately suggests that cuing occurred during those times when humans with a knowledge of the correct answer were present. It was also found that the horse could not interpret a written number or the actual objects (pins), *if* they could not also be seen by at least one human present. In other words, the horse could not read or count numbers unless a human present also knew the number. Again, cuing by the human was suggested.

The conclusion of Pfungst and his fellow investigators was that Clever Hans detected slight changes in body posture or body language on the part of humans. The horse was so familiar with van Osten, that the movements being read were undetectable by other observers.

Related to the counting horse phenomenon, is the question of whether apes can learn to communicate with humans using some sort of language. Investigators have suggested that apes cannot use language, which requires the use of a syntax or "grammar" in structuring responses into true sentences. Apes may use a few symbols from sign language and repeat them back to the humans while watching for a body language response by the humans.

Early 1970s work of Francine "Penny" Patterson with "Koko" and of Roger Fouts with "Washoe" have come under heavy attack by other scientists for their flaws in experimental design. The problem with the design of the experiments was the prevention of the ape from merely repeating back symbols while watching the experimenter for cues. Herbert Terrace did several years' worth of experiments with the chimp "Nim Chimpsky" before he was convinced that the chimp did not use real language. Terrace examined the *unedited* videotapes of Patterson and Fouts and saw what he thought was visible cuing. He noted that most of the ape's responses involved using the *same* symbols that the human just used. He also noted that the ape rarely initiated signing. The ape usually tried grabbing something he wanted first, then if that failed, used a sign. The ape also constantly interrupted humans, not trying for a two-way conversation.

Terrace caused a sensation when he described his conversion from believer to non-believer in a 1979 article. This article was largely responsible for the subsequent decision not to fund more ape language studies.

Several language theorists, such as Thomas Sebeok, have strongly maintained that apes are not capable of the use of language. The issue is quite complicated, as linguist Noam Chomsky points out in the Sebeok 1980 anthology, because teaching a pigeon (as can be done) to peck at four buttons—labelled "please," "give," "me," and "food," in that order—does not indicate that the bird has any conception of or ability to use language. The use of language requires more than the memorizing of vocabulary, or learning order, although both *are* essential parts of language use.

Although lack of funding for this type of research has minimized it, the issue is not yet settled. Evidence on videotape of an ape making up an original, clearly-signed response to a question that could not be answered *except* by understanding and responding in a syntactically correct way to the language used by the experimenter, would go far towards resolving this question. While no hoax was implied in past research, a possible element of deception exists.

Sources:

Gardner, Martin. *Science: Good, Bad and Bogus*. Buffalo, NY: Prometheus Books, 1981: 391–408.

Patterson, Francine "Penny". "Conversations With a Gorilla." *National Geographic Magazine* (October 1978): 438–65.

Pfungst, Oskar. *Clever Hans (the Horse of Mr. Van Osten): A Contribution to Experimental and Human Psychology*. New York: Holt, Rinehart and Winston, 1911.

Seboek, Thomas A. and Robert Rosenthal, eds. *The Clever Hans Phenomenon: Communication With Horses, Whales, Apes and People*. New York: The New York Academy of Sciences, 1981.

Seboek, Thomas A. and Donna Jean Umiker-Seboek, eds. *Speaking of Apes*. New York: Plenum Press, 1980.

Terrace, Herbert. *Nim*. New York: A. A. Knopf, 1979.

Terrace, Herbert, and others "Can an Ape Create a Sentence?" *Science*. 206 (November 23, 1979): 891–902.

Umiker-Seboek, Jean and Thomas A. Seboek. "Clever Hans and Smart Simians." *Anthropus* 76 (1981): 89–165.

Houdini's Return from the Dead

Magician Harry Houdini (born Ehrich Weiss, 1874–1926) was an expert on magic and sleight-of-hand. He was quite close to his mother and was greatly shaken when she died in 1913. He decided to see if there was truth to the idea that the spirit of his mother could be contacted through spiritualist mediums and soon saw that mediumship was fraudulent. The mediums who claimed that his mother's spirit was talking to him failed to observe the facts that his mother always called him "Ehrich" and that she spoke no English—only Hungarian and Yiddish. This angered him, especially since his expertise made it easy for *him* to spot the fraud, whereas others were not so fortunate. He therefore began a campaign to publicly challenge and expose fraudulent mediums. His crusade was probably largely responsible for the ongoing decline of physical mediumship.

While not at all convinced that the spirits of the dead could be contacted, Houdini still hedged his bets by working out a method by which he could demonstrate that his spirit survived, if indeed it did. Houdini figured that if *anyone* could escape the spirit world to make contact with the world of the living, he would be that person.

Accordingly, Houdini arranged with is wife Bess to use a signal or code that would show that he was really trying to contact her. This code was based upon an old vaudeville mentalism act they did together. The chances of anyone knowing this routine at the time of Houdini's unexpected death in 1926 was slim.

For several years Bess Houdini attended seances on the anniversary of Houdini's Halloween death. Each year there were no convincing results. In addition, a number of mediums contacted Bess, telling her that Houdini's spirit was trying to get in touch with her. In all of these cases, the spirit did not have the correct message. Bess offered $10,000 for the correct message, so there was much interest among mediums.

In 1929, the medium Arthur Ford, then pastor of the First Spiritualist Church of New York City, said to his congregation that Houdini's mother was trying to make contact. She wanted to relay the message "forgive" to Bess Houdini. Ford got in contact with Bess and she replied that "forgive" was indeed the message that Houdini had kept as their secret. Ford was incorrect, however, in stating that Houdini's mother had called him "Harry." Bess's response was misquoted in Ford's subsequent literature about the matter. Houdini's mother did not know the message in life. Actually, the "forgive" word had already been published in the *Brooklyn Eagle* newspaper about a year earlier. Ford's representatives could have picked up the "secret" message when they met with Bess while she was in the hospital, in a semi-delirious state, after suffering from both influenza and a bad fall.

A few days later Ford staged a seance in Mrs. Houdini's home. He then repeated, supposedly while in a trance, the entire coded part of the message, which was "Rosabelle, answer, tell, pray, answer, look, tell, answer, answer, tell." This was the mentalist's code for "believe," and it had *not* been previously published to her knowledge.

Mrs. Houdini had signed a statement written out for her while she was in the hospital and mentally hazy (her fall gave her a concussion, and the influenza a high fever). Ford admitted that Houdini had never been in

Harry Houdini.

contact with him since, directly or indirectly. Although Bess felt that only she and Houdini had known the code, the magician Joseph Dunninger pointed out that it was previously published on page 105 of Harold Kellock's biography of Houdini, *Houdini: His Life Story.*

As further evidence of the disordered condition of Mrs. Houdini's mind when she was in the hospital, she told reporters that there were three messages from Houdini (copies of what he was supposed to send from the spirit world) locked in her safe deposit box. The other two messages were to Arthur Conan Doyle and Remigius Weiss. Both of those men denied that Houdini had promised them a message from the spirit world. Although Bess said that she would reveal the messages as soon as she got better, she never did, and her attorney said there *were* no messages in her safe deposit box. The word Rosabelle, which was an early pet name for Bess, was engraved inside her wedding ring. She had showed it to many people. Bess also later said that she was not certain what the exact message from Houdini was to be, but only that it would be a ten-word message given in their mentalist's code. Ford later admitted to reporter Rea Jaure that he had obtained the code from Mrs. Houdini previously. Bess denied this. She did, however, later avow many times that no one had yet produced the desired message from Houdini. Houdini had said that anyone could talk to the dead, but the dead don't answer.

Sources:

Christopher, Milbourne. *Houdini: The Untold Story.* New York: Thomas Y. Crowell, 1969.

———. *Mediums, Mystics & The Occult.* New York: Thomas Y. Crowell, 1975: 122–45.

Churchill, Edward. "Houdini Message a Big Hoax." *New York Graphic* (January 10, 1929): 1.

Gresham, William Lindsay. *Houdini: The Man Who Walked Through Walls.* New York: Holt, Rinehart and Winston, 1959.

Kellock, Harold. *Houdini, His Life Story.* New York: Harcourt, Brace & Co., 1928.

Hysterical Epidemics

The hysterical epidemic is an outgrowth of the mob psychology phenomenon. An hysterical epidemic is a mass wave of illness or other trouble that occurs in an area without an infectious physical or toxic cause present. In such cases, the conclusion of epidemiologists is that no physical causes were present, only psychological causes.

Not all instances of hysterical epidemics manifest themselves as physical illness. There can be a rash of sightings of a "monster," or a rash of apparently damaged windshields. In addition, the "diagnosis" that the causes are hysterical is usually a default diagnosis—the one left after all others have been examined and either ruled out or ruled too unlikely.

The earliest recorded hysterical epidemics are the so-called St. Vitus Dance epidemics in Europe in the fifteenth and sixteenth centuries. They were characterized in the small groups in which they occurred by convulsive movements and a state of ecstatic frenzy. This has been "explained" as a guilt reaction to the need for punishment for sin, which was fulfilled by mass episodes of uncontrolled hopping, dancing, and jumping. A similar series of episodes occurred in convents during the witch hunts between 1550 and 1650. In the United States, a similar phenomenon was the frenzies of the Jumpers, Barkers, and Shakers (religious groups that danced as part of worship), and perhaps elements of the Charismatic movement. Author François Sirois catalogued seventy-eight distinct outbreaks of epidemic hysteria, as he called it, between 1872 and 1972. This subject is included among the hoaxes because in order for it to spread, an hysterical epidemic must have an element of deception, since the purported cause of the contagion does not really exist. It is like a rumor spreading unchecked, despite the fact that many who spread it know it to be untrue.

Several examples of hysterical epidemics will be given in detail. These were the best documented or best reported. In all cases, there seems little doubt that there was no *physical* cause for these epidemics.

As gas is usually invisible and hard to detect, it is understandable that some cases of hysterical epidemics were claimed to have been caused by a gas that made people ill. The best known instance of this is the phantom anesthetist of Mattoon, Illinois. On September 1, 1944, a woman in Mattoon reported to the police that someone opened her bedroom window and sprayed her with a gas that paralyzed her legs and caused her to feel ill. The local paper reported the event and soon other cases were reported, all variations of the same theme. The night after the first "attack," a man reported that he woke up and retched, asking his wife if she had left the gas on. His wife was unable to walk for a while. Some other cases were then made public, including ones in which a tall, thin man was seen running away from the house where the "gassing" occurred. About twenty-five instances were reported in the twelve days the event lasted, after which reports stopped. During this time, the local papers, as well as some state and national newspapers gave the incident heavy coverage. Citizens in Mattoon armed themselves and stood guard or actively searched for what the media had speculated was a gasser. No one was caught.

The symptoms of an attack were usually nausea and vomiting, palpitations, leg paralysis, dryness of the mouth, and sometimes burns about the mouth. Of the four people who saw a physician before the symptoms quickly disappeared, the diagnosis in all cases was "hysteria." It is unlikely that a person gassed citizens in their homes. The type of gas required would have had to be potent, stable, quick-acting, and selective, with no lasting aftereffects. It simply does not exist. It is highly unlikely that a "mad genius" working in his laboratory invented such a gas then went about Mattoon "testing" it. No motive seems to exist. No money was stolen and no "peeping" was done. The houses themselves were never entered. The symptoms here all seem to point clearly in the direction of an hysterical epidemic, fueled by the local press. There are other cases of gas as the cause of hysterical epidemics.

Perhaps the most bizarre sort of hysterical epidemic is that which deals with what has been called "koro." Koro is a psychiatric condition in which males think—in a contagious sort of way—that their penises are shrinking and disappearing inside their abdomen. In a few cases, women are affected, fearing that their breasts are shrinking and disappearing. There are published reports of cases of koro in West Bengal, India, Thailand, and French Canada.

Another rather strange outbreak was reported by author Norman Jacobs. He was in Taipei in 1956, when there was an epidemic of child slashings, or so it appeared. Children from six months to eight years of age were involved. The slashings occurred on the street, while the child was waiting, walking, or being carried. The number of cases varied from eight to more than thirty, depending upon the source. No one saw the slashings inflicted, but many had of ideas as to why they were done. These ideas varied from covering a robbery to a blood ritual to an attempt to bring good luck to the perpetrator.

The police did a thorough investigation. The press was involved with many stories about the slashings. It soon came to light that some of the cuts were not inflicted by a razor, as originally thought. A number of cases dissolved into hoaxes when the victims were questioned by the police. Other people involved were fined for filing false police reports. Of the twenty-one cases reported, thirteen were quickly proven false (not due to razor cuts inflicted by an unknown slasher). Later, a statement was issued that all twenty-one reported cases were proven false.

Author Edgar Schuler reported that there was an outbreak of hysterical leg twitchings among the high school students of Bellevue, Louisiana in 1939. There were only about seven cases in all, but they spread in a pattern typical of an hysterical epidemic.

A different sort of an epidemic occurred in the Seattle, Washington area in 1954. On March 23, the Seattle newspapers began carrying news of a number of strange damage reports about car windshields that were "pitted." On April 14, there were reports of windshield damage at a town about forty-five miles from Seattle. Between April 14 and 15, there were 272 reports to the police, involving more than 3,000 vehicles. The reports usually involved pitting marks that grew into bubbles about the size of a thumbnail in the glass. Many ideas, from nuclear fallout to sandflea eggs hatching in the glass, were put forth. It was also suggested that perhaps people were looking *at* their windshields, instead of just *through* them for the first time, thereby noticing little bits of damage that had accumulated for quite some time. A chemist at the University of Washington was assigned to investigate and write a report. He said that there was no evidence of pitting that couldn't be explained by ordinary road exposure. The mysterious little black spheres noticed on many windshields turned out to be bits of coal common in the Seattle air that were not burned thoroughly. They could not have been responsible for the pitting. Eventually, the furor died down and the cause became accepted as simply the noticing of ordinary road effects upon the windshield.

The form of an hysterical epidemic can vary widely. The lack of an identifiable cause is common in all these contagions, and the data are such that no cause can even be suggested, other than an hysterical one. The amount of conscious deception in any particular hysterical epidemic may vary from none to a considerable amount, but the element of deception *is* there.

Sources:

Clark, Jerome and Loren Coleman. "The Mad Gasser of Mattoon." *Fate* (February 1972): 38–47.

Jacobs, Norman. "The Phantom Slasher of Taipei: Mass Hysteria in a Non-Western Society." *Social Problems* 12 (1965): 318–28.

Johnson, Donald M. "The 'Phantom Anesthetist' of Mattoon: A Field Study of Mass Hysteria." *Journal of Abnormal and Social Psychology* 40 (1945): 175–86.

Kerckhoff, Alan C. and Kurt W. Back. *The June Bug: A Study of Hysterical Contagion.* New York: Appleton-Century-Crofts, 1968.

Medalia, Nahum Z. and Otto N. Larsen. "Diffusion and Belief in a Collective Delusion: The Seattle Windshield Pitting Epidemic." *American Sociological Review* 23 (1958): 180–86.

Schuler, Edgar A. and Vernon J. Parenton. "A Recent Epidemic of Hysteria in a Louisiana High School." *Journal of Social Psychology* 17 (1943): 221–35.

Sirois, Francois. *Epidemic Hysteria.* Published as Supplementum 252 to *Acta Psychiatrica Scandinavica.* Copenhagen: Munksgaard, 1974.

Poltergeist Hoaxes

Typified by disturbances involving rapping sounds, thrown objects, broken dishes, and similar acts of mischief, poltergeist (German for "noisy spirit") activity is attributed to a variety of causes. Believers in the reality of the phenomenon usually equate it with ghostly manifestations or attribute it to psychokinesis (supposedly a mind-over-matter form of ESP). On the other hand, when skeptics have ruled out naturalistic explanations (like chimney drafts), they suspect the occurrences of being hoaxes.

In fact, paranormal explanations continue to have only a hypothetical basis in the case of poltergeists. In case after case, this type of disturbance has been traced to the mischief of adolescents. For example, in 1772 in Stockton, Surrey, England, an outbreak of strange happenings at the home of an elderly widow included a row of plates crashing from a shelf, an egg sailing across the kitchen and breaking on a cat's head, and objects—such as a cask of beer in the cellar—being overturned. Later, a young maid who was suspected of causing the disturbances confessed to a clergyman that she had yanked a hidden wire to dislodge the plates, pelted the cat with the egg, and secretly performed the other acts attributed to mysterious forces.

More recent cases have similar explanations. An outbreak of mysterious blazes in an Alabama home in 1959 ended with the confession of a nine-year-old boy. He had wanted his family to return to the city from which they had moved. In 1974, near Los Angeles, a rash of flying-object disturbances ceased when a thirteen-year-old girl was seen kicking an object; she then claimed the poltergeist was responsible. She was reported to having "deep hostilities." In 1984, after a poltergeist overturned furniture, smashed picture frames, and caused other mischief in a Columbus, Ohio, household the family's adopted fourteen-year-old daughter was caught on film and videotape in the act of toppling a lamp and performing similar acts. She was described as "hyperactive and emotionally disturbed."

Especially clear proof of such hoaxing was shown on a 1970s episode of the TV series "Arthur C. Clarke's Mysterious World." A hidden camera left in a little girl's room during an outbreak of disturbances recorded her slipping from bed, breaking an object, then rushing back to pull the bed covers over her and to call for her mother to come witness what the "poltergeist" had done.

In addition to hoaxes and natural forces, however, there would appear to be at least one other explanation for some poltergeist disturbances. An eleven-year-old girl, while admitting she was responsible for one outbreak, nevertheless stated "I didn't throw all those things. People just imagined some of them."

Joe Nickell

Sources:

Christopher, Milbourne. *ESP, Seers and Psychics.* New York: Thomas Y. Crowell, 1970: 142–63.

Gauld, Alan & A. D. Cornell. *Poltergeists.* London: Routledge & Kegan Paul, 1979.

Randi, James. "The Columbus Poltergeist Case." *Skeptical Inquirer* 9 no. 3 (Spring 1985): 221–35.

Rogo, D. Scott. *On the Track of the Poltergeist.* Englewood Cliffs, NJ: Prentice-Hall, 1986.

Project Alpha

Magicians have long known that highly educated people are not necessarily good observers of tricksters. In such fields as spiritualism and in some areas of parapsychology there is a long history of conjurors and other frauds. The skills of a person trained in magic and conjuring are helpful—and perhaps essential—in order to be aware of such trickery. The conjuror James Randi urged parapsychologists to seek the advice of a magician in designing their experiments, and also to have a magician present when demonstrations or tests of supposed paranormal powers were being done. Randi's advice was roundly ignored by leading parapsychologists.

To illustrate the ease with which a conjuror can fool a parapsychologist, Randi set up an elaborate hoax, which he called "Project Alpha." Two young magician friends of Randi's, Steve Shaw and Michael Edwards, were recruited. They appeared at the McDonnell Laboratory for Psychical Research at Washington University in St. Louis, Missouri. This research center was funded by a large grant from wealthy aircraft manufacturer James S. McDonnell, chairman of McDonnell-Douglas Aircraft. Randi also hoped to test whether the problem with parapsychological research was a lack of funding, or whether it would be sloppily conducted even *if* adequate funding were available. McDonnell Labs had adequate funding.

One of the principal investigators at McDonnell Labs was physicist Peter Phillips. Supposedly, Randi approached him and urged him to use magicians in designing his experiments. Phillips agreed, even earning the "Straight Spoon Award" given by Randi for good experimental design. When the two young magicians were tested for metal-bending psychic ability by Phillips using the tightened protocols of experimental design the metal-bending phenomena disappeared. What happened next is not clear. Somehow the young magicians fooled at least some of the staff at McDonnell Labs for more than two years. Many of the staff there thought they had genuine psychic abilities, especially psychokinetic abilities to bend metal with their minds. How this relates timewise to the stricter experimental controls is unclear and in dispute. The tightened protocol *could* have been conveniently loosened to suit the desired results of the tests. Also in dispute is the question of whether Randi told the two young magicians to admit they were frauds if they were asked. Randi and the two magicians claim that they were never asked if they were frauds—but admit that they were. McDonnell Lab staff said they *were* asked and lied.

Some of the methods used by magicians Shaw and Edwards to produce the phenomena follow. When more than one metal test object to be bent was present (Randi warned against this), and the objects were tagged with a paper tag attached by a string loop (again contrary to Randi's advice), Shaw and Edwards simply switched the tags after the objects were measured and substituted similar objects, already bent. When they were presented with an envelope "sealed" by staples that contained a drawing they were supposed to guess by telepathy, they simply removed the staples, peeked at the drawing, and then replaced the staples in their original holes. They also managed to "blow" fuses prematurely by simply reinserting a blown fuse in its holder. The circuit used did not immediately indicate a blown fuse, but when it did, it was because these were already-blown fuses.

When word was leaked by Randi himself that the tests were suspect, Phillips wrote to Randi to ask for assistance (according to Randi). Randi sent him a video-tape revealing how the metal bending trickery was done. Phillips sent Randi—at Randi's request—a videotape of the two young magicians at work bending metal in the lab. Phillips had the two tapes formally viewed at a Parapsychology Association meeting, to the consternation of many of his colleagues. Again according to Randi, Phillips then instituted strict controls on Shaw and Edwards and the phenomena stopped.

At other labs where the young magicians were tested, the controls remained weak, so their phenomena continued. Another example of the trickery they used on these occasions occurred when each was given a cheap digital watch—permanently sealed and with no control knobs. They were asked to alter the time display. Edwards simply put the watch inside his sandwich, microwaved it, and the watch's readout was drastically altered.

When Randi finally went public with his disclosures in a press conference held by *Discover* magazine, parapsychologists were embarrassed. Shaw and Edwards had spent more than 120 hours being tested at McDonnell Labs, over a period of more than three years. Of all the people that the laboratory had tested, only Shaw and Edwards were considered to have genuine psychic ability, according to Phillips himself. Many of the methods used by the magicians were revealed at that time. Surprisingly, there has been no movement toward using magicians in evaluating parapsychological research protocol design. The McDonnell Lab's grant was not renewed, however, and they have since closed down. It is not clear exactly what role Randi's hoax played in all of this.

In 1983, James Randi was himself hoaxed about spoon bending by Dennis Stillings. Stillings issued two copies of a fake newsletter and distributed them to Steve Shaw and Mike Edwards, the two magician subjects in Randi's Project Alpha. The newsletter announced that the Medtronic Corporation, a Minneapolis manufacturer of pacemakers, awarded Stillings $217,000 to study spoon bending. Randi obtained this information from the two magicians. He subsequently awarded his "Uri Award" to the Medtronic Corporation for the most foolish project funded during the past year. Stillings had hoaxed Randi, as there was no truth to the funding at all.

Sources:

Broad, William J. "Magician's Effort to Debunk Scientists Raises Ethical Issues." *New York Times* (February 15, 1983): 19, 21.

Collins, Harry. "Magicians in the Laboratory: A New Role to Play." *New Scientist* (June 30, 1983): 929–31.

Randi, James. "The Project Alpha Experiment." *The Skeptical Inquirer* Part I: 7 no. 4 (Summer 1983): 24–35; Part II 8 no. 1 (Fall 1983): 36–45.

"Skeptical Eye: Psychic Abscam." *Discover* (March 1983): 10, 13.

Truzzi, Marcello. "Reflections on 'Project Alpha': Scientific Experiment or Conjuror's Illusion?" *Zetetic Scholar* 12/13 (1987): 73–98.

The Soal and Levy Hoaxes

Dr. S. G. Soal and Dr. Walter J. Levy were parapsychologists. They both did experiments that seemed to indicate statistical support for the presence of extrasensory perception (ESP) in guessing experimental target shapes. Their results formed temporarily impressive documentation for the existence of ESP.

Dr. Levy's deception was uncovered in 1974. The work had been done at the Institute for Parapsychology in Durham, North Carolina, under the directorship of Dr. J. B. Rhine. Levy's experiments indicated that mice possessed ESP. What Levy—and the whole field of parapsychology—had been looking for was a *repeatable* experiment demonstrating ESP.

Levy had recently finished medical school and was drawn to parapsychological research rather than medicine. Instead of taking an internship, he moved to Durham to join the institute. Levy's research investigated the precognitive abilities of mice to jump or run faster to avoid an electric shock that they knew was coming, but did not know when or where. He was also interested in whether chicken embryos could psychokineticly increase the amount of time a heat lamp, supplying them with warmth, was turned on. Between 1969 and 1974, Levy authored twenty studies. Rhine, impressed with Levy's energy, made him director of the institute in 1973.

In 1973, rumors began circulating that Levy misrepresented or falsified data. No hard evidence to back up these suspicions was available until the summer of 1974. Levy was then observed to be "hanging around" the computer during an experiment. This was odd since the equipment was fully automated and required no attention during the experiment. Curiously, the results of *this* experiment were highly significant. Laboratory workers decided to lay a trap for Levy. They installed a second set of wires that went around Levy's point of manipulation. In that way, if different results were obtained from the two different sets of wires, that would show that Levy had manipulated one set of data. A hidden observer *did* indeed see Levy manipulate the equipment so that a string of "hits" would be registered. The second set of data showed only chance scoring.

The workers approached Mrs. Rhine with the information who took it to her husband. Rhine immediately confronted Levy with the evidence of fraud and Levy confessed. However, Levy insisted that his only fraud was during the recent experiments, blaming "overwork." He was fired shortly thereafter.

As a result of this, Levy's previous research also came under review. It soon became apparent that Levy's fraud had been extensive. James Terry, who had collaborated with Levy in some of the early work, was alarmed by these developments. He contacted Rhine and urged that *all* the work he had done with Levy be repeated. Rhine agreed. When Terry came to Rhine with the results of the first set of attempted replications (which showed no significant evidence of ESP), Rhine refused to let them be published. Rhine also refused to allow Terry to publish his negative results of the whole series of attempted replications. Terry finally went over Rhine's head to the president of the Parapsychological Association, Dr. Charles Honorton. In spite of Rhine's withdrawal of the results, Honorton allowed Terry to report them at an association annual meeting.

Author Scott Rogo thought that Levy's deception was due to a character flaw, compounded by overwork, and Rhine's attitude that the only "good" parapsychologist was one who obtained positive experimental results.

Dr. S. G. Soal had set out to try to replicate the work of J. B. Rhine in his card-guessing experiments. Starting in 1934, Soal tested 160 people, during 57,000 telepathy trials and 70,000 clairvoyance trials. He *failed* to show any significant presence of ESP. Soal was therefore startled when he discovered that participants seemed to correctly "guess" the card immediately *after* or *before* the correct card to be guessed. Soal also noted that a man named Basil Shackleton had shown scoring significantly *above* chance if the results were analyzed for one card before or one card after the intended target, but only *at chance* if the results were analyzed in the regular way.

Shackleton, a professional photographer, was sought out by Soal for further experimentation in 1940. Gloria Stewart, a subject who had also shown the same significant tendency on the previous and subsequent guesses, was also retested. Soal's significant results with these two subjects were reported in 1943, and repeated in summary form in 1954. Soal had done some 12,000 trials with Shackleton and 50,000 trials with Stewart in this new set of experiments.

In 1946, Shackleton moved to South Africa, where he lived until his death in 1978. The 1940s trials with Stewart and Shackleton are of interest in the following case.

The experiment consisted of five cards with a picture of an animal (lion, elephant, giraffe, pelican, or zebra) on their faces, placed face down in front of the subject. One number from one to five would be displayed, and the subject was required to guess which animal was pictured on the card bearing that number.

Several years later, a witness at some of the trials, Gretl Albert, said that she had seen Soal alter some of the responses in ink while the experiment was being run. Soal denied this and an examination of some of the score sheets—some were supposedly lost—did not reveal any obvious alterations. Nevertheless, a computer examination of the numbers supposedly used to randomize the trials did not match any table of random numbers that was tested. Computer examination of other aspects of Soal's results showed more irregularities. Most of the definitive irregularities were presented by statistician Betty Marwick.

Finally, the Soal's defenders concluded that at least some of the data was manipulated. It is unclear *how* Soal manipulated the data, or even if he did it consciously. Reluctantly, Soal's card-guessing data have been discredited and are no longer considered evidence for ESP, even by parapsychologists.

Sources:

Marwick, Betty. "The Establishment of Data Manipulation in the Soal-Shackleton Experiments." In *A Skeptic's Handbook of Parapsychology*. Edited by Paul Kurtz. Buffalo, NY: Prometheus Books, 1985: 287–311.

———. "The Soal-Goldney Experiments With Basil Shackleton: New Evidence of Data Manipulation." *Proceedings of the Society for Psychical Research* 56 no. 211 (1978): 250–81.

Rhine, J. B. "A New Case of Experimenter Unreliability." *Journal of Parapsychology* 38 (1974): 215–225.

———. "Second Report on a Case of Experimenter Fraud." *Journal of Parapsychology* 39 (1975): 306–25.

Rogo, D. Scott. "J. B. Rhine and the Levy Scandal." In *A Skeptic's Handbook of Parapsychology*. Edited by Paul Kurtz. Buffalo, NY: Prometheus Books, 1985: 313–26.

Scott, Christopher and Philip Haskell. "Fresh Light on the Shackleton Experiments." *Proceedings of the Society for Psychical Research* 56 no. 209 (1974): 43–72. See also papers by K. M. Goldney (73–84), C. W. K. Mundle (85–87), Robert H. Thouless (88–92), John Beloff (93–96), J. G. Pratt (97–111), M. R. Barrington (112–16), Ian Stevenson (117–129), and J. R. Smythies (130–31) in the same issue.

Spiritualistic Hoaxes

Most people who have made a serious study of spiritualism agree that it is basically a religion. This religion holds that human personality survives death and that specific spirit personalities can be contacted by humans by means of mediums. This article will not be a critique of the tenets of spiritualism, but an examination of demonstrated cases where fraud and hoax perpetrated within spiritualism.

A number of physical and psychological conditions at a seance set a convenient stage for the hoaxer. First, many seances are held in the dark, where it is relatively easy to deceive the senses. Second, many of the people at a seance have recently lost someone whom they desire to contact. They want to believe. Even exposures of fraud don't stop these true believers. Third, mediums make money when they produce phenomena, providing the less scrupulous with ample incentive to deceive.

A number of former professional mediums (including M. Lamar Keene) have explained how they performed their deceptions. Some have feared the wrath of other mediums after their exposures. Many of the techniques of fraudulent mediums are the same ones used by professional mentalists and magicians. The major difference is that mentalists and magicians reveal that they fool people for entertainment. The mediums report the opposite—that they are *not* fooling, but authentic. This is what separates the unethical from the ethical, the hoaxer from the entertainer.

Perhaps the most widely known trick of mediums is to read and answer questions submitted by the audience in sealed envelopes. This is called "billet reading" and is a complete trick. The first question is made up by the performer or a confederate. When that question is asked and answered, the first envelope is opened to "verify" the performer's accuracy. That first envelope actually contains the first question submitted by the audience. The performer then reads that question to himself or herself and answers it as the second sealed envelope is picked up. Thus, the performer is always "one ahead" of the audience.

Another method of billet reading does not require that the question cards be removed from the envelope. Merely holding the envelope up to a strong light makes most envelopes transparent enough to enable the question to be read. Applying lighter fluid to the outside of the envelope also makes it transparent until the fluid quickly evaporates.

Another common trick used in seances, is when all of the participants are seated around a table holding hands and/or touching feet. The medium can usually get at least one hand and one foot free to use to create other phenomena. The medium works his own hands close together, and then uses the palm of one hand to touch one person's hand and the fingers of the same hand to make contact with the person on his other side. The medium's foot can be removed from the shoe if a metal plate in the toe of the shoe holds its place, making it feel that the foot is still in the shoe. The person next to the medium must have his foot *on top of* the toe of the shoe from which the medium wants to remove his foot.

Mediums also use metal trumpets to represent a loved one's voice. The trumpet is put against the ear of the "victim." The trumpet can also be expanded from one foot to four feet long by use of a telescoping mechanism. The audience often doesn't understand how far it can reach. Telescoping "reaching rods" (small collapsible rods that expand from about six inches long to three feet or more; they have a cap or fastener at the end) are also employed in the dark.

One strange phenomena of spiritualism, once popular, was the production of ectoplasm. This was a white substance that appeared to ooze from various openings of the medium's body. It was usually made of gauze, chiffon, or cheesecloth, often soaked or treated with various substances. Medium Helen Duncan was able to swallow and regurgitate large amounts of this. Apparently others produced it from more personal orifices, but the exact details are unknown. Keene reveals a method for materializing a full figure of ectoplasm. With the lights off and only a single red darkroom bulb lit, the medium—clad entirely in black and therefore invisible—unrolls a ball of white chiffon onto the middle of the floor. He then manipulates it until it envelops his body. It appears to the audience as though shimmering tendrils of ectoplasm eventually coalesce into a fully materialized spirit. The spirit can be dematerialized by reversing the process, and can be made to fade away or seem to disappear into the floor.

What convinces many attendees at seances is the amount of personal information that many mediums seem to have about each participant. How they get the information is amazing, but it is not from "spirits." Rather, the information is provided by the participants themselves. Attendees' purses are looked into while they aren't watching. A pocket may be picked, the items returned after review. Sometimes small objects are removed from the purses and kept, to be returned later "by the spirits." For regular attendees, a card file is kept about the names of relatives, whether they are alive or dead, and significant interests or events in the person's life. A nationwide card file exists for some people, and can be accessed by several professional mediums.

"Apports" are objects that suddenly appear in the seance room as if they were carried into that room by spirits. Apports actually get into the room either by being carried in by confederates or the medium conceals them and brings them in himself. Often the objects were stolen from the victim on an earlier occasion.

A 1983 exposure of hoaxed apports by medium Paul McElhoney was reported by author Jerome Clark. McElhoney produced purported flowers and other objects. He was searched before the seances, but nothing incriminating was found. He did carry a large tape recorder with him into the seance room, with its battery compartment sealed with black tape. This was not searched. After many successful seances, one of the attendees became suspicious and opened the sealed battery compartment of the tape recorder while the medium was out of the room. It was full of flowers and other objects. A trap was laid for the medium, and he was caught red-handed in the middle of a seance with the tape recorder back open and his pockets full of flowers. One flower was still in the battery compartment. The medium fled, leaving his tape recorder behind.

Levitations are complex (*See* Levitation, p. 254), but one simple way in which a levitation of a person seated in a chair can be accomplished is by the use of two black-clad assistants who sneak into the seance room in the dark and simply lift the chair by its lower legs. They are virtually undetectable by the victim in the dark.

Spiritualism's first effect was rapping noises heard on the furniture and supposedly produced by spirits desiring to communicate with living people. The three Fox sisters were the founders of spiritualism, and they invented this phenomenon. Years later, Kate Fox admitted that she produced the noise by snapping her big toe. When this is done against a piece of heavy furniture, quite a loud rap can be produced.

Musical instruments that seem to play by themselves are another feature of some seances. There are a number of ways in which this can be done. Taped music can be played along with one live player to make an apparent duet. A music box can produce some effects similar to musical instruments. The use of a harmonica concealed in the mouth can imitate some instruments. In addition, there are specially-manufactured trick instruments, available from magic dealers, that really *do* play themselves.

Table "turning," or the movement or lifting of furniture without apparent human assistance, is discussed in the "Levitation" article. Briefly, there are devices that strap to the arm that can be used to make a table, even a heavy one, rise into the air.

Slate writing was a feature of nineteenth century seances. Messages "from the spirits" were found written in chalk on the inside of two slates sealed together. They appeared blank when sealed together at the beginning of the seance. There are several methods that can be used to produce writing between sealed slates. A number of mediums who specialized in these effects (such as Henry Slade) have been exposed as sleight-of-hand artists in the past and discredited.

In the nineteenth century there were a number of mediums who allowed themselves to be bound with rope or immobilized in some other way in their "cabinet," behind curtains, before any phenomena occurred. If the medium did not get out of his or her bonds, no phenomena occurred or a confederate produced the phenomena. The longer the piece of rope used, generally the easier it is to get out of it. The most difficult tie is with a series of short pieces of string, as Houdini demonstrated when he tied up one Italian medium in that way. All the medium could do was to say "Spooks a no come!" By flexing muscles *while* being tied it is always possible to get a little slack in the rope. Slipping it off takes some experience and work, but is not that difficult. It is more difficult to get the ropes back on in a way that looks like the original tying.

"Cold reading," if performed by an expert, is truly impressive. Cold reading is the art of using the information unwittingly given by the "victim" in pronouncements made by the medium. Most victims are not aware of how much information they are giving. A tape recording of the exchange with the medium would reveal exactly what was told by the victim to the medium. The most amazing facts can be "revealed" by a clever medium or mentalist, creating the impression that he or she has great psychic powers, when in fact everything came originally from the victim, with a few deductions from that information by the medium.

Sources:

Abbott, David P. *Behind the Scenes With the Mediums.* Chicago: Open Court Publishing Co., 1907.

Christopher, Milbourne. *Mediums, Mystics & the Occult.* New York: Thomas Y. Crowell, 1975.

Clark, Jerome. "Scandal in the Spirit World." *Fate* 36 no. 11 (November 1983): 63–67.

Evans, Henry Ridgley. *The Spirit World Unmasked.* Chicago: Laird & Lee, [c.1908].

Keene, M. Lamar. *The Psychic Mafia.* New York: St. Martin's Press, 1976.

Oppenheim, Janet. *The Other World: Spiritualism and Psychical Research in England, 1850–1914.* Cambridge, England: Cambridge University Press, 1985.

Revelations of a Spirit Medium. London: Kegan Paul Trench, Trubner, 1922 [facsimile ed.].

Other Psychology Hoaxes

The Tamara Rand Hoax. The so-called psychic Tamara Rand claimed that she predicted the March 30, 1981 assassination attempt on Ronald Reagan on a TV show in January. Rand said that she had a videotape of her prediction on the KNTV show "Dick Maurice and Company," aired in Las Vegas on January 6. Her prediction was that she saw President Reagan shot in the chest at the end of March or early April by a young, fair-haired man acting alone. He would be from a wealthy family and have the initials "J. H."

The tape was broadcast on the NBC "Today" show and on ABC's "Good Morning America" on April 2, 1981. Careful checking by an Associated Press reporter revealed that the tape had actually been made in the Las Vegas studios of KNTV on March 31, one day *after* the shooting. Although Rand appeared in early January, as stated on Dick Maurice's show, she had not made the prediction then. Rand put on the same dress she was wearing in the January taping and—with the assistance of Dick Maurice—tried to restage the appearance, this time inserting the assassination prediction. Her hoax was undone when an investigator noted that she wore different rings on her fingers on the "prediction" segment than she wore on the rest of the show. Also, the microphones were in slightly different positions. When confronted with the evidence, Dick Maurice admitted the hoax and was suspended from his show. Tamara Rand also subsequently confessed. Maurice said that the whole thing was done to advance Rand's career. It took some prodding of the TV networks to get them to retract their stories about the prediction, but eventually both ABC and NBC did so. NBC even devoted a subsequent segment to the hoax.

Edgar Borgatta's Hoax. An issue of *Psychological Review* (v. 61, iss. 5, 1954) carried an article by Edgar F. Borgatta entitled "Sidesteps Toward a Nonspecial Theory." This is one of the few instances in which a scholarly journal published a purportedly scholarly article, that was a hoax from beginning to end. The article and title are nonsensical. Although the article sounded serious, it raised concepts such as "mammary envy," trauma of the infant upon the loss of its umbilical cord, and "digital gratification." It was never made clear whether the journal knowingly played along with the hoax, or whether they were tricked which seems unlikely.

Near Death Experiences. This is a case of willing something to be true to the extent of employing deception to make it *appear* true, rather than a true, deceptive hoax. Nevertheless, because of its popularity and pervasiveness, it is included here. The Near Death Experience (NDE) is fairly common among people who suffer from a cessation of respiration or heartbeat. These people are *near* death. Once out of this state they often (of the time) report having seen a tunnel of light, and experiencing a feeling of great calm. Sometimes these people have an out-of-body experience (OBE), seeing their own body lying on the operating table below them. Other times there is a review of their life and sometimes a near encounter with a "being of light." Finally, there is a return to the body.

The confusion occurs because of the previously imprecise definition of death. Legally and medically, most of the United States have adopted the cessation of electrical activity in the brain as the *definitive* criterion of death. No one whose brain's electrical activity has ceased for more than a few seconds has *ever* been revived. On the other hand, many have been revived from cessation of heartbeat and breathing. So many have recovered from this that it led to a change in the criteria of death.

The deception is further perpetrated by those looking for scientific support for their religious beliefs. The idea that humans survive death has always been attractive. If some evidence for this survival could be drawn from the NDE, it would be a powerful tool in the hands of religious zealots. Some of Raymond Moody's popular anecdotes about NDEs have been used in this way, by Moody and others. Actually the NDE sheds no light *for* or *against* the survival of death, since no one having an NDE has actually been dead.

The House of Blood. An article in a number of newspapers in the summer of 1987, reported on a house in Atlanta—occupied by a couple of elderly people—that was oozing blood through the walls, ceilings, and floors. The blood was reportedly human. Surprisingly, no follow-up story was printed. An investigation by Bob Grove showed that the initial reports were blown out of proportion. Several squirts of blood, such as might be found if a single intravenous bag of blood was squeezed a few times, were found in several rooms of the house. The blood did not match the type of either of the elderly occupants of the house. The blood *probably* came from another member of the family, who was undergoing kidney dialysis, and who probably obtained either blood at the dialysis center or else squirted some of his or her own blood from the blood vessel to which the dialysis tubing was connected. The case was "closed" by the police. A combination of police and media "hype," plus a desire to believe in paranormal phenomena produced this report.

Sources:

Borgatta, Edgar F. "Sidesteps Toward a Nonspecial Theory." *Psychological Review* 61 no. 5 (1954): 343–52.

Frazier, Kendrick and James Randi. "Prediction After the Fact: Lessons of the Tamara Rand Hoax." *Skeptical Inquirer* 6 (Fall 1981): 4–7.

Grove, Bob. "Atlanta's 'Infamous House of Blood' Case Closed." *Skeptical Inquirer* 13 no. 3 (Spring 1989): 248–49.

Randi, James. "The Psychology of Conjuring." *Technology Review* (January 1978): 56–63.

Stein, Gordon. "Does the Near Death Experience Give Proof of an Afterlife?" *American Rationalist* (March/April 1983): 84–88.

"TV Host, Psychic Admit Reagan Hoax." *Chicago Tribune* (April 6, 1981): 1, 4.

Public Relations Hoaxes

This section is reserved for hoaxes executed to gain publicity. It also includes people who specialized in perpetuating hoaxes for publicity (See Jim Moran's Hoaxes, p. 213). Many of these hoaxes merge gradually with practical jokes; the demarcation between the two is far from clear.

Alan Abel's Hoaxes

Alan Abel (b. 1930) is probably the king of living American hoaxers. He seems to delight in the completion of a perfectly executed hoax. His hoaxes are never harmful—except perhaps to ego—and never involve cheating people out of money. Abel views hoaxes as a teaching tool and a form of public entertainment. They show people how easily they can be fooled. This knowledge makes them more cautious in the future, he implies. Although the experience is humbling it hopefully makes the individual more realistic about the limitations of individual perceptions. According to Abel, another valuable function of media hoaxes, is they deflate the pomposity and redress the insensitivity that the media often exhibits.

Abel first became aware of some of the simple deceptions that people would cheerfully accept when he watched how his father—who owned a small-town variety store—was able to make slow-moving merchandise sell. For example, by placing a sign in front of a box of the slow seller saying "Absolutely only one to a customer," the items quickly sold.

Perhaps Abel's most famous hoax was the establishment of SINA, the Society for Indecency to Naked Animals. This organization claimed that having naked animals around us was grossly indecent, and that horses, dogs, and other domestic animals should be clothed about their "privates" for moral reasons. The unemployed actor Buck Henry was used as the spokesperson for SINA. Henry appeared on a number

Alan Abel.

of national TV talk shows; in almost all cases, the host took SINA seriously. Even the name should have trou-

"Idi Amin's wedding."

bled some. It was the "Society *for* Indecency to Naked Animals." How does a person become indecent towards naked animals? The public was told that their moral standards were being lowered by having to see the privates of naked animals.

Another hoax involved the staged wedding of Idi Amin, just after the former Ugandan dictator was expelled from his country. Abel thought it would be newsworthy if Amin married a white Anglo-Saxon Protestant (WASP) American woman in order to become an American citizen. A wire was sent to the New York media by an Abel confederate in Johannesburg stating that the wedding would take place at the Plaza Hotel in New York. Over 150 reporters showed up. Abel found an Idi Amin look-alike and used an eighteen-year-old actress to play his bride. Uniformed Pinkerton (private security) guards surrounded the bride and groom, preventing even the Federal Bureau of Investigation (FBI) and Immigration and Naturalization Service (INS) agents from getting close to him. The bride and groom argued during the entire service.

Another notable Abel hoax was the School for Panhandlers run by Omar the Beggar. Omar (really Abel in a hood to conceal his identity) was a former executive who lost his job. He discovered that a well-dressed panhandler could make several hundred dollars a day on the streets of New York. This was in 1977, before the large influx of homeless people to the streets. Omar decided that some of his techniques were so good and original that he could teach them to others. Accordingly, Omar opened a School for Panhandlers. All of this was pure fantasy and a hoax. Nevertheless, Omar appeared on a number of TV and radio talk shows, plugging his school, and a book on panhandling. The book, was another hoax, containing the life histories of many of the successful graduates of Omar's school.

One of Abel's early hoaxes occurred when he was still an undergraduate student at Ohio State University. As the person in charge of booking performers for a jazz series, he secured a verbal agreement with the drummer's manager to have Gene Krupa perform at the University after he finished a performance at nearby Buckeye Lake Park. The day before the scheduled performance, Abel called Krupa's manager at the lake. Krupa had an important meeting the next day, the manager said, and would not come. Abel would be left with a sold-out house and no Krupa. Abel decided to insure that Krupa appeared. He checked to make sure that there was no important meeting. He then had "Gene Krupa Day at OSU" banners made up. He assembled a dozen convertibles and six attractive co-eds, plus musicians and drivers. The entourage left as a convoy for Buckeye Lake. Krupa was carried out to the waiting cars by the coeds, rather groggy. The cars went back to the university. There, Abel had a hard time persuading Krupa to perform, but he finally succeeded in doing so. He went on as planned, but would only lecture and answer questions until the audience demanded a drum solo. Krupa's own band had followed him to the university and they were in place on stage. Krupa finally agreed and a concert followed. Abel said that Krupa offered him a job managing his band, but Abel wanted a college degree, so refused. Reportedly whenever Krupa saw Abel in later years, he looked around for the coeds, but they weren't there.

Alan Abel ventured into political hoaxes a few times. The most notable was the "Yetta Bronstein for President"—and after that, Mayor of New York City—campaign. Yetta, a Bronx housewife played to perfection by Abel's wife, including a Yiddish accent, promised such things as lowering the voting age to eighteen to give juvenile delinquents something to do; seizing Russians' baggage if they didn't pay their United Nations bill; and staffing her cabinet only with people who learned to live with failure. She promised "a Jewish mother in the White House." Her folksy responses to reporters' questions made good copy, even if it was fairly clear that Mrs. Bronstein was not a real contender for the nomination. A number of parades and rallies were held for Yetta, although she did not get nominated. The stage *was* set, however, for her subsequent candidacy for Mayor of New York City. She ran against John Lindsay and Abe Beame in 1965. Again, her folksy answers to reporters' questions earned her a good deal of press and media coverage. She promised "low rent, plenty of hot water and occasional taxes." A flyer offering a $50 reward for information leading to the whereabouts of Mrs. Bronstein was distributed at one point. People who called the phone number on the flyer got a recorded message from Yetta saying, "I've been found." Mrs. Bronstein lost again, but ran again for President in 1968, and was the only candidate to march in the parade in honor of Israel's twentieth anniversary. The hoax began to wear thin, however, the campaign was still publicized in the national media. She urged sex education, but stipulated, "let's make it very *boring*".

A worldwide hoax that Abel claims was his, but for which he has not yet taken public credit, was the incredible story of the "extraterrestrial" seen by a number of Russian school children in the city of Voronezh. The children correctly swore that they saw a tall, three-eyed creature in a local park. The "nine-foot-tall" creature was actually an actor dressed in aluminum foil garments. Although the story was embellished in the retelling, Abel claims to have shipped the materials to Russia and masterminded the hoax from the United States.

Another Abel hoax was the story that a single young New Yorker won the $35 million New York Lotto jackpot in January of 1990. It made the front page of the *New York Post* and the exposure made the front page of the *New York Daily News*. Perhaps Abel also planted his own obituary in the *New York Times*. This was supposedly the only fake obituary ever printed in the *Times* and the paper was sheepish when it had to publish a retraction later. The obituary appeared on January 2, 1980, and took a great deal of planning to accomplish. The *Times* checked with the funeral home and several other places, but precautions were made for this.

Abel claims that the executive editor of the *Times* was so mad at being taken by Abel that he swore they would never mention his name again in their paper. They were not able to keep their vow, as the lotto hoax was duly reported, along with Abel's name.

The hoaxing career of Alan Abel is by no means over. Although a natural death claimed the life of one man who often funded the thousands of dollars needed to perpetuate Abel's hoaxes, Abel may strike again at any time.

Sources:

Abel, Alan. *The Confessions of a Hoaxer*. New York: Macmillan, 1970.

———. *The Great American Hoax*. New York: Trident Press, 1966.

———. *How to Thrive on Rejection: A Manual for Survival*. New York: Dembner Books, 1984.

———. "Omar the Beggar." *The Panhandler's Handbook*. New York: Zebra Books, 1977.

Ball, Edward. "$35 M[illion and She's Single." *New York Post* (January 8, 1990): 1.

Blau, Eleanor. "Rare Thrill for Tass: Joshing Over Its U.F.O. Report." *New York Times* (October 12, 1989): A18.

Fein, Esther B. "Hot News From Tass: Tourists From Space." *New York Times* (October 10, 1989): A1, 10.

———. "U.F.O. Landing Is Fact, Not Fantasy, Russians Insist." *New York Times* (October, 1989): A6.

(REsearch Editors). *Pranks.* San Francisco: REsearch, 1987: 103–09.

Harry Reichenbach's Hoaxes

Although Harry Reichenbach (1882–1931) is virtually unknown today, he was the first Hollywood press agent and public relations man to the stars. He created the occupation that lives on after him. Among his clients were Rudolph Valentino, Gloria Swanson, Charlie Chaplin, and Pola Negri. He also handled publicity for Florenz Ziegfeld and Metro-Goldwyn pictures.

Reichenbach originated the publicity stunt—a harmless kind of hoax—in America. In his early teens he ran away from home to join a circus. There he soon became one of the barkers who announced the sideshow attractions.

He wound up in Hollywood, hired by the fledgling Metro Pictures Company, predecessor of MGM. Although Metro had several films in production, it had not yet released one. Theatres and the public were getting worried that the company might go bankrupt. Reichenbach managed to get the company awarded the gold medal from the International Exposition at Los Angeles for "best productions of the year," although not a single film was released. Everybody was impressed and relieved.

He was given the task of publicizing the first Tarzan of the Apes movie, a sad affair that was badly produced. He had all of the foliage from the movie set sent from California to New York, where it was installed in the lobby of the movie theater he rented. Reichenbach dressed a orangutan in a tuxedo, called him Prince Charley, and had the ape make an appearance in the lobby of the fashionable Knickerbocker Hotel. It was filled with New York society people who panicked; the ape was arrested. A judge, getting no response to his questions to the ape, suspended charges of disorderly conduct on the condition that the ape not dress up and stay out of hotel lobbies in the future. All of this made the front page in the local papers, and filled the theater showing the Tarzan picture.

The second Tarzan picture was an unpublicized flop and film producer and MGM executive Samuel

Goldwyn didn't want the third one, "The Return of Tarzan," to have a similar reception. Goldwyn gave Reichenbach the job of publicizing it. Reichenbach—disguised as an eccentric music professor—registered at the Hotel Belleclaire, requesting a room on a lower floor. The professor did this because he planned to have his piano hoisted up to his room by a block and tackle. The crate that allegedly held the piano actually contained a live (tame) lion. When room service came to take his order, Harry requested fifteen pounds of raw meat for his lion. Soon the police arrived with drawn guns. Harry convinced them the lion was tame by putting his head in its mouth. He told the reporters that arrived that his name was T. R. Zann, and that he was sailing for Africa next week, along with his pet. Every morning newspaper in New York covered the story of T(a). R. Zann and his lion. It was only the next week, when the ads for the movie "The Return of Tarzan" ran, that the hoax became clear.

Around 1905, a small art shop in New York City printed 2,000 copies of a lithograph of a nude woman bathing in a small pond. They asked ten cents for each print but no one was buying. Reichenbach was hired to dispose of them. He put a copy in the window of the shop, hired a few youngsters to stand around outside and gawk at it, then phoned Anthony Comstock, head of the anti-vice society, to complain that the children were being corrupted by the art. Comstock took a look, became outraged, and ordered the shopkeeper to remove the picture. The shopkeeper refused and Comstock went to the courts. The resulting publicity caused the picture, titled "September Morn," to sell seven *million* copies at one dollar each. Reichenbach received $45 for his work.

According to Reichenbach, and unconfirmed elsewhere, he went first to Argentina and then to Uruguay to work on election campaigns. In Argentina, the editor of a large newspaper directed Reichenbach to write an article aimed at discrediting the vice president of the country's presidential ambitions. The article backfired, Reichenbach had to leave the country, and the editor was fired. The vice president was twice elected president. Reichenbach went to Uruguay, where he was hired by the editor of the major newspaper in Montevideo, Dr. Crispo, to rile the voters into demanding a presidential election. Elections had not been conducted in many years and only the sitting president could call one. He was corrupt and would not do so. Reichenbach wrote a series of articles that so inflamed the voters that a new election was called (in which several times the whole country's population voted), and Dr. Crispo was elected president. He promptly ordered Reichenbach to leave the country, saying that if he could fix one election, he could just as easily be hired by the opposition to have Crispo removed from office.

During World War I, Reichenbach was asked to go to England and Italy to help direct the propaganda forces of the Allies. He invented a flyer that was distributed by the tens of millions over enemy trenches, promising every private that if he surrendered he would be treated like an officer, including twenty-four sheets of toilet paper per day. Hundreds—perhaps thousands—of German soldiers surrendered. Any German soldier caught picking up one of the flyers was shot on sight.

Reichenbach worked diligently to promote the films and careers of early silent movie stars. Although Reichenbach tried to salvage their careers, many could not make the transition to the "talkies" because of their voices or inability to use them well. Harry did not last far into the era of sound pictures; he died rather unexpectedly of cancer in 1931, at the age of forty-nine. Although a number of his activities did not amount to hoaxes, some definitely did. One hoax that did not work involved teaching blacks from Harlem to dance an African dance and portray cannibals to publicize a film about cannibals in Africa. The blacks became scared when they saw the skeletons that Harry had hung around the deserted house in which they were supposed to perform their rituals. They ran away and the hoax was ruined. No publicity resulted; he had mistakenly forgot to remove the tags from the big toes of each skeleton that said "Property of Fordam Hospital." The police were not impressed.

Sources:

"Final Tributes Paid to H. L. Reichenbach." *New York Times* (July 10, 1931): 26.

"H.L. Reichenbach, Press Agent, Dead." *New York Times* (July 4, 1931): 13.

Hynd, Alan. *Professors of Perfidy*. New York: A. S. Barnes & Co., 1963: 40–88.

Reichenbach, Harry and David Freedman. *Phantom Fame: The Anatomy of Ballyhoo*. New York: Simon & Schuster, 1931.

Jim Moran's Hoaxes

James Sterling Moran (b. 1909) was one of the most original public relations men in the business. He specialized in book and movie publicity and often succeeded in obtaining widespread media coverage at little personal expense. His clients, however, were charged plenty. While many of Moran's activities could be called "stunts," they could also be hoaxes with rather harmless intentions.

Moran loved to perform the difficult, impossible, or inadvisable. For instance, he went to Alaska and sold a refrigerator to an Eskimo. He changed horses in the middle of a stream. He searched through an entire haystack—for eighty-two hours—before he found the needle placed in it. He restaged a small part of the Battle of Bunker Hill, using nearsighted, farsighted, cross-eyed, and normal men. His point was to illustrate the stupidity of the expression "Don't fire until you see the whites of their eyes." He brought a real bull into an expensive china shop on Fifth Avenue in New York City. The bull did not break anything, but Moran's client, bandleader Fred Waring, backed into a small table, breaking a few items.

The California and Florida tourist bureaus took interest in his project to uncover half his body to the sun in Florida, then expose the other half for the same time in California. He wanted to compare the two tans. Another time he colored a cow purple with harmless dye and brought the cow to Gelett Burgess, who wrote the poem "I Never Saw a Purple Cow." Another time he conspicuously "read" a book containing only blank pages throughout a train trip from Chicago to Los Angeles. The other passengers thought him strange. To advertise the movie "The Egg and I," he hatched an ostrich egg by sitting on it for nineteen days in public. He gave his new "son" to a zoo.

At an annual meeting of magicians, he unveiled a new trick. A sealed carton of decks of playing cards was opened by a randomly selected member of the audience. Another picked out a deck. A third opened the deck, a fourth cut it, and a fifth removed a card without showing it to Moran. "It is the six of diamonds," he called out. He was wrong. "If it *had* been the six of diamonds, those bastards would *still* be talking about it," he said later.

His scheme to publicize sunglasses did not work. He had six homing pigeons fitted with clear glasses and six with miniature pairs of his client's sunglasses. His plan was to release them on a sunny day to see if the ones with the sunglasses were more successful in finding their way home. A powerful radio antenna confused the birds, and *all* were lost.

Perhaps his best-known hoax involved publicity for the movie "The Mouse That Roared," in which the tiny country The Grand Duchy of Fenwick declares war upon the United States in order to get foreign aid when Fenwick is defeated. Moran acted the role of the ambassador of the Grand Duchy of Fenwick to the United States in Washington. He had an appropriate uniform, fake diplomatic license plates on his car, and hosted a diplomatic ball to which many of the ambassadors in the nation's capital came.

Another stunt that went wrong was Moran's idea to loft midgets into the air by means of kites. These kites would carry the midgets near the windows of office buildings, thus allowing their advertising slogans to be seen. After experimenting, and finding a kite that could carry the midgets, he had the midgets insured by Lloyd's of London. On the day he was to launch the kites from New York's Central Park, his plan was halted by a policemen who said that the midgets might fall and injure someone on the ground. The launching was scrapped.

Sources:

Fuhrman, Candice Jacobson. *Publicity Stunt!* San Francisco: Chronicle Books, 1989: 47–50, 90–91, 122–23.

Gehman, Richard. "The Little World of Jim Moran." *Playboy* (September 1981): 68–69, 123–29.

Paar, Jack. *I Kid You Not.* Boston: Little, Brown & Co., 1960: 175–84.

Smith, H. Allen. *Lost In the Horse Latitudes.* Garden City, NY: Doubleday, Doran & Co., 1944: 56–64.

———. *Low Man on a Totem Pole.* Garden City, NY: Doubleday, Doran & Co., 1941: 130–44.

Lord Kitchener's Coffin

In 1926, a forthcoming movie about Lord Horatio Herbert Kitchener (1850–1916), British military hero, inspired a British press agent to announce that Lord Kitchener's body had been found in Norway. In 1916, Kitchener was lost at sea when the cruiser *Hampshire* hit a mine and sunk off the coast of Norway. The press agent announced that Kitchener's body was being shipped back to England in a coffin for burial. At the same time, a memorial service was being conducted and a statue of Kitchener was being unveiled on the tenth anniversary of his death.

When the boat bearing the coffin arrived in England on August 8, 1926, the coffin was opened at Lambeth Mortuary by the police and a coroner. It was empty. The Norwegian government told the British that, as far as they knew, no permit to open a grave had been issued, no grave had been unearthed and opened, and no body found in Norway. Since the Norwegian government needs to give its permission before a grave can be opened, this was viewed as strong evidence against the authenticity of the story. The coffin itself turned out to have been made in England, which was odd for a coffin supposedly obtained in Norway by the Norwegian government. It was later shown that the coffin never left England.

The press agent, who called himself "Frank Power," but whose real name was Arthur Vectis Freeman,

Lord Kitchener.

had reported that Kitchener's grave was found in a Norwegian cemetery.

Actually, Power had purchased the coffin early in 1926, and it had remained in storage until July 27, when it was ordered shipped (empty) to Newcastle, England. When Mr. Power returned from Norway, he had the coffin shipped to him in London. When he was in Norway, Power had ordered a coffin from a mortuary there, arranged a mock funeral during which the coffin was covered with a Union Jack, and the ceremony filmed. The coffin was taken to a dock and put on a steamer for Bergen, Norway. It was subsequently removed and returned to the undertaker from whom Power had borrowed it.

This whole incident caused the British Admiralty to finally issue an overdue report about the secret mission to Russia that Lord Kitchener had been on when his ship was sunk. Power insisted that the body had been stolen from the coffin, but few believed him. Few people went to see Power's unsuccessful movie.

Sources:

"Home Office and Mr. Power: Kitchener Allegations Refuted." *Times of London* (September 10, 1926): 9.

"The Lord Kitchener Body Myth." *Times of London* (November 16, 1926): 5.

"Lord Kitchener: Coffin Removed by Scotland Yard." *Times of London* (August 16, 1926): 12.

"Lord Kitchener: an Empty Coffin Opened." *Times of London* (August 17, 1926): 12.

Maurice, Frederick Burton. "Horatio Herbert Kitchener." *Dictionary of National Biography, 1912–1921.* Oxford: Oxford University Press, 1927: 306–14.

Other Public Relations Hoaxes

Hugh Troy's Hoaxes. Hugh Troy (1906–1964) was perhaps the United States' most innovative practical joker and minor hoaxer. He viewed his hoaxes purely as entertainment, combined with a bit of one-upmanship. Troy was born in Ithaca, New York, and attended Cornell University. While at Cornell he performed his first major hoax. Prior to this, he had done little besides placing a sign saying "Jesus Saves" outside a local savings bank and wiring apples into his neighbor's cherry tree.

Troy noticed a wastebasket made from a rhinoceros' foot in a friend's house. Waiting for a new snowfall, he borrowed the foot and carefully used it (supported by a rope and filled with weights) to make a series of footprints leading across the campus to a frozen reservoir. The footprints then led across the ice to a large hole. The zoology department was called in to identify the strange footprints. They said they were definitely made by a rhinoceros. Ithaca residents complained that their water tasted of rhinoceros. These complaints stopped once Troy revealed how the footprints were made.

While at Cornell, Troy studied architecture. One of his professors chronically complained about the weakness of the ceiling in the classroom. One day, while the classroom was unoccupied, Troy and friends put a ladder up to the ceiling and painted a large black hole on it. They piled debris on the floor under the "hole." When the professor came into the classroom, he took one look, fled to notify the authorities. While he was gone, Troy and friends removed the black paint and the debris. When the professor returned with the head of buildings and grounds for the University, the professor was angry and thoroughly embarrassed.

One of Troy's classic hoaxes was done in New York City. It was modelled after a hoax done by William Horace De Vere Cole (*See* H. M. S. Dreadnought, p. 172). Five men dressed in overalls roped off a section of Fifth Avenue, hung out "Men Working" signs, and began to tear up the pavement. By lunchtime they had made quite a large hole. The workmen dined at the restaurant of a fashionable hotel nearby, much to the other diners' disgust. Troy told the waiter that this was a "gag" done by the manager. After lunch, the hole was further enlarged; red lanterns, signs, and rope installed; and the hole abandoned. Although city officials discovered the hoax the next day, they never were able to identify the perpetrators.

Another Troy hoax took place in New York City's Central Park. Troy purchased a park bench exactly like those found in Central Park, and placed it in the park near some other benches. He and a friend sat down on the bench. When they saw a policeman walk by, they picked up their bench and departed. The policeman stopped them and took them in for attempting to steal city property. Once at the police station, Troy produced his bill of sale for the bench and was released. They repeated this hoax several times until the police caught on.

A slightly grislier hoax was Troy's contribution to an exhibit of Vincent Van Gogh's work at the Museum of Modern Art in New York in 1935. Troy made a replica of a human ear out of chipped beef and mounted it in a blue velvet display case. A small card, was attached explaining that this was the ear that Van Gogh cut off and sent to his mistress. Troy placed the "ear" on a table in the exhibit gallery; it attracted the largest crowd in the exhibit.

The vast majority of Troy's hoaxes and pranks were not nasty. One exception occurred when he became annoyed at the manager of a Greenwich Village movie theater. Troy released a large jar filled with moths inside the theater. The moths flew directly to the light coming from the movie projector, casting large images on the screen.

During World War II, "Captain Troy" originated the "flypaper report." He began sending reports to the Pentagon on the number of flies killed by different types of flypaper hung in the company's mess hall. Soon, the Pentagon was asking other units where their flypaper reports were.

The Bunny Burger Hoax. The satirical magazine *Spy* has tried a number of hoaxes. The only one that qualifies for inclusion here is the Bunny Burger Hoax. The magazine was trying to prove that, using sophisticated marketing techniques, "people can be sold anything, whether they want it or not." What was really proven was that public relations firms think that's true, but not the general public.

The idea was to start a chain of fast food hamburger restaurants that used rabbit meat for the hamburgers. The burgers would be accompanied by salads and french fried carrots. Diners would have the opportunity to select their own bunny for grinding into hamburger.

Obviously, the whole idea was likely to be met with horror and disgust. *That* was part of the hoax. The hoaxers' aim was to see if national public relations firms would be willing to work on this account and whether they thought the restaurants could be commercially successful. Fake prospectuses and a twenty-four-page business plan were made up before contacting the public relations firms. The firms were told that as a part of the initial phase, there would be twenty-six restaurants in New York, Ohio, Massachusetts, and New Jersey, and four in Ontario. All nine of the public relations firms contacted were interested in working on the account. The public relations firms suggested the use of focus groups—small groups of typical consumers, who are presented with various ideas about projects and asked for their reactions. The focus groups were unanimous in their revulsion.

A trial restaurant was opened in a New Jersey mall. Ground turkey meat was used for the hamburgers. Although many people tried at least a bite of the burgers, there was little enthusiasm and much revulsion. "It's like eating your pet" was the general reaction. The reluctant conclusion was that the concept would not work, except among public relation firms.

Sources:

Aaron, Andy and Joe Queenan. "Let Them Eat Bunnies." *Spy* (April 1992): 56–62.

Smith, H. Allen. *The Compleat Practical Joker.* New York: Doubleday & Co., 1953: 102–03, 134–51.

Troy, Con. *Laugh With Hugh Troy, World's Greatest Practical Joker.* Wyomissing, PA: Trojan Books, 1983.

Religion Hoaxes

This section will concentrate on religious areas that purport to supply facts, but instead knowingly and consciously deceive people into believing the truth of demonstrably false ideas. The motivation for doing so can range from the financial to the pious.

The Archko Volume

Little is mentioned in the New Testament about the personal life of Jesus yet there is a demand for information about his childhood, youth, and family. Many manuscripts and other ancient writings have been lost, so it is inevitable that some of this lost material may be found. This is the premise that supports several hoaxes involving the life of Jesus.

The Archko Volume was the name given to the translated set of letters or reports about Jesus that German scholar H. C. Whydaman supposedly found in the Vatican Library. After his discovery Whydaman was stranded in a snowstorm in Missouri in 1856. During that time he spent several days at the home of Rev. William D. Mahan, whom he told about the materials in the Vatican Library. Mahan paid to have the items retrieved by Father Freelinhusen, the curator of the Vatican Library. The materials were then translated and eventually published as The Archko Volume in 1886.

The book consisted of eleven chapters, each a letter or report submitted to Rome by someone in ancient Israel. The book includes Valleus' notes of Pontius Pilate's report to Caesar on the arrest, trial, and crucifixion of Jesus; Caiaphas' report to the Sanhedrim concerning the resurrection of Jesus; Jonathan's interview with the Bethlehem shepherds; and Gamaliel's interview with Joseph and Mary. If genuine, this would be quite an historical find. Unfortunately, it's a hoax.

The book remains a constant seller since its publication. It is still in print, despite the near unanimous criticism by New Testament scholars that it is an obvious forgery.

Mahan was a Presbyterian minister in Missouri who became a hotel keeper during his last years. He admitted that he fabricated the materials, but claimed that they did good, so it was justified—the so-called "pious fraud" defense. The composition of the work was in three stages. The first was A Correct Transcript of Pilate's Court, copyrighted in 1878, and published as a pamphlet in 1879. This work contained the story of the stranded Whydaman. Careful searches for the existence of Whydaman and Freelinhusen have revealed no one of those names in the positions they were supposed to occupy.

The pamphlet went through a number of editions, even though it was obvious, as author Edgar Goodspeed has pointed out, that "The whole work is a weak, crude fancy, a jumble of high-sounding but meaningless words, and hardly worth serious criticism. It is difficult to see how it could have deceived anyone."

Nevertheless, many people were deceived. In 1884 Mr. Mahan published a volume of nine similar works with the general title The Archeological and Historical Writings of the Sanhedrin and Talmuds of the Jews, Translated from the Ancient Parchments and Scrolls at Constantinople and the Vatican at Rome. In this volume, the help of two "great scholars" (otherwise unknown), named Dr. Twyman and Dr. McIntosh, is acknowledged. They were able to add about 1,200 words to the first pamphlet work (supposedly accurately translated for Mahan). Again, the contents are marred by elementary errors, obvious to any scholar of the ancient world. One of the chapters is an interview by Eli with the Magi. Unfortunately, several pages of this were copied verbatim from the novel Ben Hur. Mahan accidentally omitted a line from the novel, resulting in an incomprehensible sentence. This chapter is omitted from the recent editions of *The Archko Volume.*

Charges of plagiarism and falsehood were filed against Reverend Mahan by the Lebanon, Missouri presbytery in September of 1885. Among the witnesses consulted for the trial was Gen. Lew Wallace, the author of *Ben Hur,* who was also with the United States legation at Constantinople when Reverend Mahan claimed he was there. No one connected with the legation could remember any such visit. In fact, Mahan had never been out of the Midwest in his life. Wallace even went to the library in the mosque of St. Sophia, where Mahan claimed that he and "Dr. McIntosh" discovered the manuscript of Eli. The librarian did not recall Mahan or McIntosh and had no such manuscript in the library.

As a result, Mahan was found guilty of falsehood and of plagiarism. He was suspended from the ministry for one year. He also promised to withdraw the book from circulation. However, it was reprinted several times during the next few years. In 1896, the library at St. Sophia was examined again. No such manuscripts that Mahan claimed to have seen were found. Yet the book was reprinted and reprinted, deceiving a great many people along the way. It is still in print.

Sources:

Anderson, Richard Lloyd. "The Fraudulent Archko Volume." *Brigham Young University Studies* 15 no. 1 (Autumn 1974): 43–64.

Goodspeed, Edgar J. "Pilate's Court and the Archko Volume." *Strange New Gospels.* Chicago: University of Chicago Press, 1931: 42–62.

Mahan, William D. *The Archko Volume.* New Canaan, CT: Keats Publishing, 1975.

The C. S. Lewis Hoax

Clive Staples Lewis (1898–1963) was a British author, popular theologian, and fantasist. In 1988, Kathryn Stillwell Lindskoog published a book entitled *The C. S. Lewis Hoax,* in which she tried to make the case that Lewis' book *The Dark Tower* was not by Lewis at all. She also claimed that there were other minor hoaxes in Lewis' life.

The major problem with Lindskoog's charges had to do with C. S. Lewis' handwriting and the role of his self-proclaimed secretary and literary executor, Walter Hooper. Hooper, an American trained as an Anglican priest, had a background that changed so frequently in his writings and speeches that it is difficult to know where the truth lies. It is clear that Hooper

edited and released a large number of Lewis's works posthumously. Determining exactly which works were those of Lewis is complicated by two facts; Hooper learned to imitate Lewis' handwriting and signature precisely, and Hooper had access to Lewis' papers, published and unpublished.

It is not possible in this article to untangle the truth about Lewis' work or to determine the truth about Hooper's claims. Rather, Lindskoog's charges and some responses to them will be mentioned. That Lindskoog makes a charge that cannot be refuted does not mean that the charge is true.

Hooper, much as C. S. Lewis' brother Warren feared, gradually moved into the C. S. Lewis home and into the business of controlling the publishing of Lewis's materials. Warren Lewis objected strongly to the publisher that Hooper not be involved in the writing of the official C. S. Lewis biography. Warren was assured that only Roger Lancelyn Green would write it, with *some* materials supplied by Hooper. However, Hooper was able to delay the publication of the official biography (*C. S. Lewis: A Biography*) until Warren Lewis was dead. Of course, Hooper became co-author of the book, and used the opportunity to enshrine the way he wished to be thought of in relation to Lewis. Old stories of how Hooper was Lewis' secretary for the last years of his life (impossible, according to both Lindskoog and independent fact), and others, were retold. Warren Lewis did write what he viewed as the truth about Walter Hooper in his diary. Warren then willed the diary to Wheaton College in Illinois, where many of Lewis's papers outside the control of Walter Hooper are located. When excerpts from the diary were finally published in 1982, as *Brothers and Friends,* there was no mention of Walter Hooper.

Another hoax mentioned by Lindskoog was the bonfire incident. Supposedly, after C. S. Lewis's death, his brother Warren tried to clean out the family home and made a huge bonfire for refuse. Into this fire went many of Lewis's papers. It was only the sudden, unexpected appearance of Walter Hooper that spared many of the papers. A subsequent letter from a physical chemist at Oxford claimed that his new test of soil could detect traces of a large fire for many years afterward. It was performed on the soil from around Lewis' home. The chemist claimed that no bonfire had been made on the land for more than 800 years. In other words, the bonfire story was a hoax. The chemist was Anthony Marchington, an undergraduate at Oxford, who had lived in the Lewis household. The eminent scientist with whom he was working turned out to be another undergraduate. In short, the whole story of the failure to find traces of a bonfire was probably a hoax. It is difficult to know what to believe about the bonfire incident.

As to *The Dark Tower,* again there are difficulties in trying to reach the truth. Although author A. N. Wilson stated that the manuscript of this work, now at Oxford University's Bodleian Library, is in Lewis' handwriting, the style—as Lindskoog points out—is rather un-Lewisian. The manuscript was "discovered" among the Lewis papers supposedly rescued from the bonfire by Hooper, and did not become publicly acknowledged as existing until 1975, with publication in 1977. By then Hooper had mastered Lewis' handwriting, so the matter is further complicated. *The Dark Tower* is either second-rate Lewis, or not by Lewis at all.

There are other authorship questions dealing with many of C. S. Lewis's works, among them *The King's Ring.* Many parts of works purportedly by Lewis are simply not written in his distinctive style. An explanation for that has not been discovered. A vast tangle of possible hoaxes exist in the writings and life of C. S. Lewis.

Sources:

Frame, Randy. "A Hoax Observed." *Christianity Today* 33 (June 16, 1989): 64–65.

Griffin, William. *Clive Staples Lewis: A Dramatic Life.* San Francisco: Harper & Row, 1986.

Lindskoog, Kathryn. *The C. S. Lewis Hoax.* Portland, OR: Multnomah, 1988.

Wilson, A(ndrew) N(orman). "C. S. Lewis, Sins and All." *New York Times Book Review* (December 24, 1989): 1, 26–27.

———. *C. S. Lewis: A Biography.* New York: W. W. Norton, 1990.

Faith Healing

It is not asserted here that the human body cannot heal itself spontaneously by means unknown. In fact, it can. Whether anything supernatural is involved is also not a concern at this point. A hoax *is* involved, however, when anyone purporting to be a faith healer uses conscious deception to accomplish the *illusion* of faith healing. A number of so-called faith healers have been caught and exposed in recent years.

James Randi (in his book *The Faith Healers*) lists the following five criteria that should be used to determine whether the disappearance of a given disease or condition was a true faith healing: 1) The disease involved must not be normally self-limiting (normally cures itself after a given period of time), 2) The recovery must be complete, 3) The recovery must take place in the absence of any medical treatment that might normally be expected to affect the disease, 4) Adequate

medical opinion that the disease was present *before* the application of the "miracle" must be present, and 5) Adequate medical opinion must verify that the disease is not present *after* the application of the healing.

When James Randi and others decided to investigate faith healers in 1985 and 1986, they decided to limit their study to those who appeared to be doing some form of mentalism. That is, they were possibly employing the techniques that mentalists who do entertainment similar to magicians might use. Among the features that might form a mentalist's routine was what is called on the revival circuit "calling out." This is the practice of approaching a person in the audience by name (although there is no way the healer supposedly could have known the name) and telling them the medical problem that affects them. The person's address, the name(s) of the doctor(s) who treated the condition, and other personal details are often added. The faith healer claims that he obtained this information "from God" or "from Dr. Jesus." Among the faith healers who employed this technique, the two best-known are W. V. Grant and Peter Popoff. Accordingly, these two were the main focus of the investigation conducted by the Committee for the Scientific Examination of Religion, with the assistance of James Randi.

This investigation—discussed in detail in two issues of the magazine *Free Inquiry,* and in Randi's book—consisted of attending many sessions of the faith healer's meetings, often using audience plants who claimed to suffer from various illnesses as persons to be healed. An attempt was also made to trace the long-term results of supposed cures for those attending the faith healing services.

Their investigation of W. V. Grant produced details about his life and his methods. Grant falsely claims that he was a star football player in high school, who received seventy-seven NCAA football scholarship offers. His high school coach says he did not receive one. Grant claims to have gone to the University of California, Los Angeles (they have no record of him) and to have received a "Doctor of Divinity" degree from "Midstates Bible College" in Iowa. Neither the Iowa Department of Public Instruction, the American Association of Bible Colleges, nor the Association of Theological Schools has any record of the school's existence.

A follow-up investigation was conducted on one man whom Grant claimed was cured by "closed heart surgery" performed upon him by "Dr. Jesus" after six physicians (all named by Grant) scheduled him for open heart surgery in Georgia. Because of the specificity of the information, an investigation was undertaken in Georgia by a physician practicing there. None of the six physicians mentioned was listed in any of the registers of Georgia physicians. One hospital mentioned had no record of the patient and never performed open heart surgery there. Several other cases investigated by the Committee revealed that people who were claimed to be cured (in one case of a blind eye, in another of diabetes, and in a third of total blindness) still suffered from conditions after they were pronounced "cured" by Grant. Their images were used in his magazine as among the many miracle healings under his auspices.

As far as the "calling out" phenomenon goes, the committee found that if people went early to one of his rallies, they would be assured of an aisle seat where Grant could talk to them during the service. Many people went early for this reason. These early arrivers were approached by Grant, dressed casually, and asked for their name, the name of their physician, and their illness. The pretense for asking this information was so that Grant could decide who would be approached to be healed. How did Grant remember all the information given him by the perhaps twenty people who were approached to be healed? Grant also instructed all those on his mailing list in the particular area he was visiting to come early and bring their "special offering envelopes" to hand to him personally. As each person came up to the stage to hand Grant his or her envelope (which had the person's name on the front), he would fixedly stare at them for a second or two. This, Randi recognized, was the way people who use a mnemonic system, remember a long list of names and faces. After receiving the envelopes, Grant would retire backstage, where he could open the envelopes, see the people's addresses, and read their "healing cards," stating what they were hoping to be healed of that night. The rest was all memorization, although Grant made his job easier by making notes that he concealed in his Bible.

The people who were in wheelchairs at each Grant meeting were able to rise out of their wheelchairs and walk (even push Grant around in their wheelchair) after they were "healed." The explanation is simple. Grant's organization supplied most of the wheelchairs and asked people who *walked* into the auditorium, but who were in need of some type of healing, to sit in the wheelchairs. These wheelchairs were then pushed towards the *front* of the auditorium. People who came in their *own* wheelchairs (and were presumably unable to walk), were placed at the *rear* of the auditorium and never approached by Grant to be healed. Randi was able to get some of Grant's "crib sheets" in the garbage, thrown out after one of the services. There were letters from those "healed," giving all the details of their illnesses. On one of his crib sheets was the following: "Anthony—deaf in both ears, and bladder and tumors. Connie—pain in left eye and left jaw, thyroid and arthritis. Digestive problems. Bernadette—psoriasis,

arthritis. Michael—deaf in left ear. Syl—high blood pressure."

Grant's performances were acts similar to mentalists' acts. Any "healings," if they occurred were in spite of what he did, not because of it. Since Randi's exposure of Grant, Grant has largely lost his television audience and has experienced at least a temporary decline in contributions.

The other faith healer investigated by the committee was Peter Popoff. What the committee found after extensive investigation was alarming. By attending a number of Popoff's services it was clear that he did not associate with his audience before the service. He did not refer to crib notes, yet Popoff was able to do a smooth "calling out" performance. He seemed to know people's names, illnesses, and physician's names without prior information. It was only when one of the committee members managed to get close enough to Popoff during a service to look in his ear, that the mystery began to be solved. Popoff wore a tiny hearing aid in his ear. At a subsequent service, an electronics whiz working for the committee managed to sneak an electronic scanner into the auditorium. A search of frequencies in use in the immediate area soon located a transmitter on 39.17 megahertz that was carrying the voice of Popoff's wife backstage into Popoff's ear. She was reading off information about the various audience members that she had obtained before the service by having them fill out "prayer cards." All of the transmissions from Elizabeth Popoff to Peter Popoff were recorded and some were later played by James Randi on the Johnny Carson Tonight Show. Popoff later declared bankruptcy after his services were cancelled by many TV stations. He has come back again in a limited way, but perhaps without the "hearing aid." The 1992 movie "Leap of Faith," starring Steve Martin, is loosely based upon these incidents.

Sources:

Koromvokis, Lygeri. "Faith Healers in the Laboratory." *Science Digest* (May 1982): 88–92, 95.

Kurtz, Paul. "Does Faith-Healing Work?" *Free Inquiry* 6 no. 2 (Spring 1986): 30–36.

Nolen, William. *Healing: A Doctor in Search of a Miracle.* New York: Random House, 1974.

Randi, James. "'Be Healed in the Name of God!': An Exposé of the Reverend W. V. Grant." *Free Inquiry* (Spring 1986): 8–19.

———. *The Faith Healers.* Buffalo, NY: Prometheus Books, 1989.

———. "Peter Popoff Reaches Heaven Via 39.17 Megahertz." *Free Inquiry* 6 no. 3 (Summer 1986): 6–9.

Léo Taxil, the Freemasons, and the Catholic Church

The Roman Catholic Church has publicly voiced strong opposition to secret societies such as the Freemasons. In fact, they have forbidden Catholics, under pain of excommunication, from joining the Freemasons. However, the church does have a somewhat similar organization for Catholics, the Knights of Columbus.

The following hoax involving the Freemasons was perhaps the most elaborate hoax ever devised. Gabriel Jogand-Pages (1854–1907), a French journalist, had an intense hatred for both the clergy (and therefore the Roman Catholic Church) and of secret societies, such as the Freemasons. He decided to devise an immense scheme (with the help of several unknown others) that would discredit both the Catholic Church and the Freemasons in the minds of all Frenchmen, and mightily embarrass both. For his scheme, Jogand-Pages used the name Léo Taxil.

The central idea Léo Taxil had was to insinuate (with manufactured, but believable "evidence") that the Catholic Church *secretly sponsored* the Freemasons and that the Freemasons were Satanists. Thus, the Catholic Church was secretly a Satanist organization! This set of lies was too much for anyone to accept easily, so Taxil went to great lengths to make up imaginary people and to have them confess to their actual "experiences" *inside the Freemason leadership.* There were a number of long and detailed works about the Freemasons, issued under various pseudonyms, but mostly all by Taxil himself.

The most important of these characters was Miss Diana Jean- Marie-Raphaelle Vaughan, henceforth called Diana Vaughan. She was supposedly descended from Henry Vaughan, who was the head of the Rose-Croix (the Rosicrucians, a religion in the Ancient Wisdom Family that employed a system of occult sexuality). Henry Vaughan had supposedly signed a pact with Satan on March 25, 1645, that assured that Vaughan would have thirty-three years in which to propagate Satanism. He went to the New World in 1646, and had a child with an American Indian woman. This child was named Diana, and was the direct ancestor of the above Diana Vaughan. Vaughan's father had founded in Louisville, Kentucky, "le Grand Triangle des Onze-Sept" (the Great Triangle of September 11th), a super-secret organization, with 3,000 members.

Albert Pike.

In 1889, Diana Vaughan officially presented her fiancee—the demon Asmodeus—to the Sanctum Regnum (Ruling Council) of the Great Triangle. At least that is what Léo Taxil had Vaughan say in her autobiography *Memoires d'une Ex-Palladiste.* Supposedly, Vaughan had the help of Dr. C. Hacks and Dr. Bataille in writing a major exposure of the Satanist aspect of Freemasonry in the book *Le Diable au XIXe Siecle,* purportedly by Dr. Bataille (actually Gabriel Jogand-Pages.) It is unclear whether Dr. Charles Hacks was actually involved in the writing of any of this book.

Actual charges were made by Léo Taxil, Diana Vaughan, and Dr. Bataille against the Freemasons (and hence against the Church). In the book *Le Diable au XIXe Siecle,* purportedly by Dr. Bataille, the following are among the myriad charges by the author.

First, the particular division of the Freemasons involved is the one founded at Charleston (South Carolina) by Albert Pike. The group is called by Taxil both the Re-Theurgistes Optimates and the Palladists. They followed ceremonies composed by Albert Pike. A number of their hymns are given in *La Restauration du Paganisme,* translated by Vaughan from the English of Albert Pike. Pike's photograph is reproduced in that book and in the *Memoires.* Diana Vaughan's photograph is in the *Memoires* (p. 81); she is dressed as "Inspectress General of the Palladium." Allegedly, the group worshiped Satan and actively wished for the triumph of Satan over Christianity. Dr. Bataille was told by members of the sect that they often felt they were in the presence of Lucifer himself.

The existence of Vaughan herself was publicly questioned by some Germans, and they conducted a meeting on September 29, 1896 to examine this question. Léo Taxil was there, and in response to proof of the deconversion of Vaughan from Freemasonry, he said that he had the proof right in his pocket, but that he could not show it to them for fear of endangering Vaughan's life. All he could do at present, Taxil said, was to communicate with a certain bishop in Rome and have him get the necessary agreements with the permission of the Pope! Bishop Lazzareschi was chosen to receive the request; Taxil sent him a letter. Some months later he declared that Taxil's request was refused. The length of time the bishop took before responding was viewed by Taxil and his followers as an indication that the Church's honor was at stake.

At the congress of the Anti-Masonic Union (founded by Taxil), held soon thereafter, the president of the union announced that the inquiry into Vaughan's existence had been abandoned. A special commission had been set up see to all matters concerning her.

Meanwhile, other Catholic publications throughout Europe were beginning to denounce Léo Taxil as the inventor of a myth. The Vatican, however, would not admit that it had been fooled. The Pope's chaplain and secretary to Cardinal Parocchi wrote to Diana Vaughan in October of 1896 that she had been correct in what she said about the Freemasons, that she existed, and that her conversion from Freemasonry was sincere.

Occult history expert Arthur Waite published a book in 1896, called *Devil-Worship in France*, which gives Dr. Bataille's and Diana Vaughan's charges against the Freemasons in English, and then shows that *both* Bataille and Vaughan are mistaken in virtually everything they say.

Other publications were increasingly becoming suspicious of the whole affair. Accordingly, on February 25, 1897 Léo Taxil had Diana Vaughan announce a press conference to be held on April 19. Only the press was invited, but many publications from around the world sent their reporters. Taxil promised that a summary of what was said at the press conference would be printed in his publications and that Diana Vaughan would then go on a worldwide speaking tour.

In the *Memoires* of April 15, just four days before the press conference, it was announced that Diana had to go to Louisville, Kentucky to close a chapter of the Triangle of September 11th. His concern for her safety

Léo Taxil.

seems to have disappeared. Accordingly, at the April 19 press conference only Léo Taxil himself appeared. H. C. Lea says that Taxil's speech cannot be equaled for effrontery and cynicism in all of literature. Taxil stated that the Palladium was dead, and that he—its father—had killed it. The person who had played the role of Diana Vaughan when needed, had only been his typist. However, he said that the church was responsible for the writings about Freemasonry issued under his name, Dr. Bataille's, and Diana Vaughan's! The church was trying to convince the faithful that Freemasonry was Satanic in an attempt to keep the faithful as church members. Taxil kept up his hoax, weaving it even more elaborately, in front of his cursing and hostile audience. Taxil was finally led out of the room under police protection and went peacefully to a nearby cafe.

Although the anti-Freemasonry movement faded away after Taxil dropped it, there were still those who believed that Diana Vaughan was real and that she had been telling the truth. Strangely, none of the books of Léo Taxil, "Diana Vaughan," or "Dr. Bataille" was ever put on the Index of Prohibited Books that Catholics cannot read without special permission. The church never admitted that it had been hoaxed, although it was quick to point out that Taxil had not been honest.

Léo Taxil played another hoax upon the Catholic Church in 1886, when he published his autobiography, entitled *Confessions of an Ex-Freethinker* (in its translated title, although it was never published in English). In this book, Taxil explains how he converted from a non-believer to a Catholic. In fact, Taxil remained both a freethinker and a staunch anti-Catholic.

Sources:

NOTE: Little has been written in English about this hoax. Therefore most of the references are in French or Italian. There is a half-page, rather inaccurate, summary of the hoax in Solomon Reinach's *Orpheus: A History of Religions.* New York: Horace Liveright, 1930, p 425–26. There is also a misleading summary on pages 98–100 of Curtis MacDougall's *Hoaxes.*

Bataille, Dr. [Léo Taxil]. *Le Diable au XIXe Siecle.* Paris: Delhomme et Briguet, [c.1893].

Jastrow, Joseph. *Error and Eccentricity in Human Belief.* New York: Dover Publications, 1962: 26–34.

Lea, Henry Charles. *Léo Taxil, Diana Vaughan et l'Eglise Romaine.* Paris: Societe Nouvelle de Librarie et d'Edition, 1901.

Taxil, Léo. *Confessioni di un Ex-Libero-Pensatore.* Florence, Italy: Tipografia Editrice di A. Ciardi, 1887.

Vaughan, Diana [Léo Taxil]. *La Restauration du Paganisme.* "Written by Albert Pike, translation by Diana Vaughan." Paris: A. Pierret, [c. 1896].

———. [Léo Taxil]. *Memoires d'une Ex-Palladiste.* A Monthly Publication. Paris: A. Pierret, 1895–1897.

Waite, Arthur Edward. *Devil-Worship in France.* London: George Redway, 1896.

The Mahatma Hoax

Helena Petrovna von Hahn Blavatsky (1831–1891), known widely as "Madame Blavatsky," was the found-er of the religion Theosophy. Blavatsky's life was ob-scured by lies. She was in fact born into a wealthy aristocratic family in Ekaterinoslav, Russia in 1831. Her mother was from the Dolgorukuv family, while her father was Peter Alexeyeivich von Hahn, a captain in the Russian horse artillery. When Helena married the Russian provincial vice-Governor Nikifer Blavatsky—mostly because her family was opposed—he was thirty-nine and she was eighteen. In later years, Helena exaggerated her husband's age at the time of their marriage. The marriage lasted three stormy months, and was notable only in that it provided her with the last name she would use for the rest of her life.

Madame Blavatsky claimed to have spent years living in Tibet and India while absorbing the wisdom of

Madame Helena Blavatsky.

the East. Although she did study the occult, her travels during this period (1850–70) are dubious.

In 1842, Edward Bulwer-Lytton had written a novel named *Zanoni.* Madame Blavatsky's Mahatmas (wise ascended masters) may have been modeled upon the title character Zanoni who is a rich, handsome, ageless Indian member of a mysterious brotherhood. While she was organizing the Theosophical Society and writing her two major works, *Isis Unveiled* and *The Secret Doctrine,* Madame Blavatsky studied occult works. As part of her claimed "enlightenment," she said that she was in contact with two "Ascended Masters," who communicated with her by means of letters they dropped ("precipitated") through the ceiling. This contact with the Mahatmas, was a sign that Madame and, the Theosophical Society, were in touch with higher sourc-es of truth. The Eastern Sages she contacted had the power of mind over matter in their letter dropping. In 1879, Madame Blavatsky went to India to try to find "her" masters, but was stumped by the necessity to master the Hindi language.

The first Mahatma letter was found on the desk of Alfred Sinnett in October of 1879. It was in response to two letters that he wrote to "Unknown Brother." He gave the letters to Madame for "delivery." The first response Sinnett received was a detailed explanation of why the world wasn't ready to receive miraculous replies from spirits. It was signed "Koot Hoomi Lal Singh" in a different script from the rest of the letter. A second letter from Koot Hoomi rejected Sinnett's pleas to communicate without the use of Madame Blavatsky as an intermediary. Three other brief notes appeared on Sinnet's pillow and beside his dinner plate.

During the next few weeks Blavatsky worked out a way to give Sinnett unassailable proof of Koot Hoomi's existence. She worked out a system of telegraphed responses from a distant city in reply to a letter that Sinnett would give Madame. It was arranged so that the response would arrive from the distant city—handwritten—two hours after Sinnet's letter was given to Madame. It did manage to convince Sinnett that some supernormal means were at work. Meanwhile, Madame Blavatsky had plenty of time to write a number of additional Mahatma letters. Eventually, there were 120 letters supposedly written by the Mahatmas between 1880 and 1884. The letters, obviously written by Madame Blavatsky, served as a means for her to present an occult religious philosophy that would not have succeeded if she had claimed to have been its author.

There were flaws in Blavatsky's work. Koot Hoomi, for example, claimed to have been an Indian (not a Tibetan) who studied in Germany. Yet he did not speak German, Hindi, or Punjabi. He spoke French and English, but wrote them using the overlined characteristic of Russians who write in English or French. The other Mahatma, Master Morya, had a weakness for pipe smoking, something that was strictly forbidden (as was all smoking) in Tibet. Both these Masters supposedly lived in Tibet. Other inconsistencies obvious now, were not enough to alert Sinnett that he was being hoaxed.

Annie Besant, once a materialist and co-leader of England's atheists with Charles Bradlaugh for ten years, was also won over to Theosophy by Madame Blavatsky. Besant became the leader of the movement after Blavatsky died in 1891. When questioned about the Mahatma letters, Besant said on December 23, 1894, that she could not believe Madame Blavatsky was guilty of fraud. She added that, although the letters were undoubtedly a fraud, the existence of the Mahatmas themselves was beyond question. Besant avoided the contradiction about Madame's fraudulence by claiming that William Q. Judge, a vice president of the Theosophical Society, forged the letters. Evidence is now unavailable to support the charges against Judge.

When Blavatsky settled at Madras, India for the last few years of her life, she had a special "Occult Room" built in her house. It was designed to help receive letters from the Mahatmas. To facilitate this was a cedarwood cupboard built against one wall. This cupboard had several sliding panels in the back. Placed as it was against the bricked-up former doorway leading from the Occult Room to another room, it hid the small opening left in the bricks. The opening allowed someone in the adjoining room to reach through the wall, open the sliding panel, and insert a letter (or something else) into the closed cupboard. Letters from the Mahatmas made their regular appearance in this cupboard. The fact that the cupboard hung halfway up the wall, suspended from the ceiling by heavy wires, completed the illusion. The hole in the wall was discovered after Madame Blavatsky moved from the house.

Although the Mathama letters were only a small part of Theosophy, it does seem that *this* part of the Theosophical offering was an indisputable hoax.

Sources:

Garrett, Edmund. *Isis Very Much Unveiled, Being the Story of the Great Mahatma Hoax.* London: Westminster Gazette, [c. 1894].

Meade, Marion. *Madame Blavatsky: The Woman Behind the Myth.* New York: G. P. Putnam's Sons, 1980.

Symonds, John. *The Lady With the Magic Eyes: Madame Blavatsky— Medium and Magician.* New York: Thomas Yoseloff, 1959.

Maria Monk

In the late 1830s, the northeastern United States was victim of a hoax that involved a young lady named Maria Monk and her purported disclosures of the scandalous doings in the Hotel Dieu convent in Montreal. Miss Monk claimed in person, and in her book *Awful Disclosures* to have spent more than a year as a novice in the Hotel Dieu. She said that the nuns at the convent were dissolute, and had sexual relations with priests who entered the convent through a secret tunnel from their seminary. Any babies born as a result of these escapades were baptized, then killed and dumped in a lime pit in the basement of the convent.

Maria Monk claimed she was in the Hotel Dieu for two years as a Black Nun (after taking her vows). Before that she was in the convent as a novice for about five years. She left when she became pregnant by a priest and couldn't bear the thought of her child being killed. Maria Monk's charges were serious and aroused public indignation when her book was first published in 1836. An immediate investigation of the convent was called for by leading Protestants in New York and Montreal. At the time, great anti-Catholic movement was taking hold in the United States. It culminated in 1834 with the burning of the Ursuline Convent in Charlestown, Massachusetts, where a number of Protestant young ladies were supposedly being held against their will. Although the Bishop of Montreal had at first ignored calls to have an impartial investigation made

Maria Monk.

William Leete Stone.

of the convent at Hotel Dieu, the clamor was now so loud from outside of Montreal that he finally agreed. Several Protestant clergy did an investigation, pronouncing Maria Monk a fraud, but these clergy were accused by the U.S. Protestants of being Jesuits in disguise.

When William Leete Stone, a New York newspaper editor, asked the bishop for permission to investigate the convent with a team of Protestants, his request was granted. In October of 1836 (Monk's book had only been published in January) Stone and his team (consisting of A. Frothington, President of the Bank of Montreal, and Duncan Fisher, an attorney) investigated the convent. They were shown around the convent by Sister Beckwith, one of the sisters who spoke English. When the contents of Maria Monk's book were mentioned to Sister Beckwith, she said that she had not read the book, but heard about it. Although Sister Beckwith had been in the Hotel Dieu convent for ten years, she never encountered Miss Monk and stated that Maria Monk had never been a novice there during the time the book indicated. Interestingly, Sister Beckwith left the convent shortly after this, reportedly quite upset about the situation. She returned to the convent years later and died there.

Colonel Stone walked around the most accessible parts of the convent with Maria Monk's book in his hand. He found little correspondence between the physical layout of the inside of the convent (she described the *outside* of the Hotel Dieu correctly), and what Maria had written about it. After seeing the more accessible areas, such as the hospital, Stone asked to see the nuns' rooms and the basement areas. He was refused permission and returned to New York City. He did note that if a tunnel was present, as Maria described, it would run right under the huge new Notre Dame Cathedral. He mused that digging the foundation for the Cathedral would have certainly uncovered any such tunnel.

Stone wrote to the Bishop of Montreal to ask permission to visit the "off limits" parts of the convent. He received support in his quest from some of the bishop's staff. Finally, permission was granted. Colonel Stone, Mrs. Stone, and Mr. Frothington were admitted, along with a Mr. Shepherd of Richmond, Virginia, who had obtained permission separately. A man named Reverend Clary, who had previously applied to search the premises in the company of Maria Monk herself, and had been refused, was also to join the group (without Maria). At the last moment, he declined to go.

Stone made it clear that he wanted to see every room, and to make a thorough inspection from basement to attic. He had a copy of the latest edition of Maria Monk's book, this one containing a plan of the inside of the nun's quarters at the convent. Colonel

Stone was assured of full cooperation by the staff. He looked carefully behind trap doors and tested the mortar with an iron-tipped cane to make sure it was not recently poured. He found no recent changes in the architecture and a different layout from that pictured by Miss Monk. As Stone said, "But so far as regards the whole interior, neither I nor my companions could discover from the [Maria Monk] drawings, the least evidence that the author had ever been within the walls of the cloister." (*A Refutation of the Fabulous History of the Arch Impostor Maria Monk*, p. 30).

The story did not end here. Another escaped nun, Sister Frances Patrick, came forward and claimed to have known Maria in the convent. It was apparent under questioning that Sister Frances had not prepared herself. *She* clearly had never been in the Hotel Dieu convent. Therefore, her support for Maria Monk raised more questions than it answered, especially since Maria had embraced Frances and claimed to have known her in the convent as well.

Meanwhile, Maria added new revelations to her story. She gave birth to a girl, then claimed her daughter was abducted by six priests and taken to Philadelphia. Maria had escaped and sought refuge with Dr. W. W. Sleigh. He was at first taken in by her story, but later wrote a pamphlet claiming Maria was a hoax. Maria also wrote a sequel to her *Awful Disclosures*, taking up her adventures from the point at which she escaped from the convent. Her companion in all this (acting as a sort of manager) was W. K. Hoyt, a Canadian Protestant clergyman and strong anti-Catholic. Some claimed he was the real father of Maria's child. Another candidate was her apparent lover, John J. Slocum.

Charges were made that *Awful Disclosures* was ghostwritten by Hoyt, Slocum, or by Theodore Dwight. The latter was the nephew of Timothy Dwight, theologian and president of Yale College. In any event, Maria and Hoyt would later sue Dwight and Slocum for appropriating the profits from her book. The case was lost by Maria and Hoyt.

Frances Patrick (sometimes called Frances Partridge) was finally denounced as an impostor in the pages of the *Protestant Vindicator*, the New York newspaper that had first broken the Maria Monk story months before her book was published. Little was heard of Maria Monk after 1837. She died in prison on Welfare Island, New York City, in 1849. She was arrested for picking the pocket of a man who had evidently paid her for sex. It was previously rumored that Maria had been a prostitute in Montreal and had really spent her "convent years" in the Magdalen Asylum for wayward girls. There is evidence both for and against this. Meanwhile, Maria Monk's *Awful Disclosures* remained in print until well into the twentieth century. It had supposedly sold more than 300,000 copies by the 1920s and was still going strong forty years later.

Sources:

The literature on Maria Monk is both vast and difficult to find. Most of the material consists of privately published pamphlets, many of which have survived in only a few copies. The list that follows represents some of the more useful material.

Awful Exposure of the Atrocious Plot Formed by Certain Individuals Against the Clergy and Nuns of Lower Canada, Through the Intervention of Maria Monk. New York: Printed for Jones & Co. of Montreal, 1836.

"Awful Disclosures of Maria Monk." *Dublin Review* 1 no. 1 (May 1836): 151–74.

Billington, Ray Allen. *The Protestant Crusade, 1800–1860: A Study of the Origins of American Nativism.* New York: Macmillan Co., 1958: 98–117.

Monk, Maria. *Awful Disclosures of Maria Monk.* New York: Howe & Bates, 1836.

Stone, William Leete. *A Refutation of the Fabulous History of the Arch-Impostor Maria Monk, Being the Result of a Minute and Searching Inquiry by William L. Stone, Esq. of New York, To Which are Added Other Interesting Testimonies.* N.P., 1836.

Thompson, Ralph. "The Maria Monk Affair." *The Colophon* Part 17 no. 6 (1934).

Mother Shipton's Prophecies

So-called prophets have written or said things that later came true. Many times careful investigation showed the "prophecies" were made *after* the events they supposedly predicted. Ursula Sonthiel Shipton, popularly known as Mother Shipton, is one such prophet. Her best-known prophetic verse was the couplet

The world to an end shall come,
In eighteen hundred and eighty one.

She was clearly wrong in this prophecy, but some of her other predictions remain more impressive. The earlier part of the verses quoted above read:

Carriages without horses shall goe,
And accidents fill the world with woe.
Around the world thoughts shall fly
In the twinkling of an eye. . . .
Under water men shall walk,
Shall ride, shall sleep and talk;
In the air men shall be seen,
In white, in black and in green. . . .
Iron in the water shall float,
As easy as a wooden boat; . . . .
A house of glass shall come to pass,

In England, but alas! . . . .

The above verses were supposedly composed and published in 1448 and republished in 1461, while Shipton lived from 1488 to 1561, so the publication and republication of her verses occurred *before* she was born! The earliest extant edition of Mother Shipton's works is from 1641, and the earliest with biographical information is a 1684 edition edited by Richard Head. Head, who used only his initials in the 1684 edition, says in the biographical section of the book that Agatha Shipton lived in 1486 in a place called "Naseborough" in Yorkshire. She made a pact with the devil and he fathered her child, Mother Shipton. The believable facts were controverted by statements, by S. Baker in his 1797 edition of Mother Shipton (London: Denley), that Sonthiel was Mother Shipton's maiden name and she married Toby Shipton when she was twenty-four years old. Baker added that she was "larger than common, her body crooked, her face frightful; but her understanding extraordinary." Head stated that Mother Shipton was born extremely ugly

of an indifferent height, but very morose and big boned, her head very long, with very great goggling, but sharp and fiery Eyes, her Nose of an incredible and unproportionate length, having in it many crooks and turnings, adorned with many strange Pimples of diverse colours, as Red, Blew, [sic] and mixt, which like Vapours of Brimstone gave such a lustre of the Night, that one of them confessed several times in my hearing, that her nurse needed no other light to assist her in the performance of her duty . . .

This section goes on to describe what must have been the ugliest human baby ever born. As she grew up, her father the devil visited her regularly in the form of various animals. She was highly precocious at school and began telling fortunes, as well as predicting the future.

The 1641 first extant edition of Mother Shipton has the prophecies in prose, not verse. This edition included the statement that Cardinal Wolsey (d. 1530) should never go to York, but that he would see it. Wolsey was on his way to York in 1530. He climbed to the top of a nearby tower, and saw York in the distance. At that point, he received a message from King Henry VIII, summoning him back to London. Wolsey died on the way to London. In other words, Mother Shipton's prophecy was exactly correct. However, the first record of the prophecy is from 1641, long after 1530 when the prophesied event occurred.

The 1645 edition, *A Collection of Ancient and Moderne Prophesies* edited by William Lilly, contains prophecies by Mother Shipton, all of which had already been fulfilled. In other words, the verses quoted above, all of which predict technology of the nineteenth century, are

not present in the book. These verses appeared first in an edition of Mother Shipton published in 1862, and edited by Charles Hindley. Mr. Hindley admitted in a letter to the editors of *Notes and Queries* in 1873 (4th Series, XI, 355) that he fabricated the entire set of verses quoted above, and more. These verses were reproduced in many subsequent editions of Mother Shipton. Hindley dated his verses from the 1500s. In addition, author William Harrison has shown that Richard Head made up almost all of the so-called "facts" of Mother Shipton's life. It is now doubted whether she ever existed. The 1641 edition appears to have been the first ever published, so that would mean that Mother Shipton's words, if she did exist, were not published until more than eighty years after she died. Before that they *may* have been an oral tradition in Yorkshire. Or, they may have been composed by someone else just before 1641. In either situation, the events supposedly prophesied by Mother Shipton had already occurred. The other modern events were added by Hindley in 1862.

Mother Shipton was a hoax on several levels, with a fake biography, post-dated prophecies by at least two different hoaxers, and much copying to conceal the facts.

Sources:

Harrison, William H. *Mother Shipton Investigated.* London: W. H. Harrison, 1881. Reprinted by Norwood Editions, (Norwood, PA), 1976.

Hering, Daniel W. *Foibles and Fallacies of Science.* New York: D. Van Nostrand & Co., 1924: 213–18.

Shipton, Ursula. *The Strange and Wonderful History of Mother Shipton.* London: Printed for E. Pearson by J. Davy, 1870.

Noah's Ark

Whether the Old Testament version of the Flood and Noah's Ark, as described in the book of Genesis, really happened is uncertain. Perhaps the story was based on some earlier stories that—in turn—had an historical basis. Regardless, it is not necessary to believe that the Bible is literally true in order to hold that there *might* be a true historical event behind the Flood and Noah's Ark stories. Here it is presumed that a true series of events *was* behind the Bible stories, but not that they *had* to be true because they were in the Bible. This section will investigate any archeological, geological, or historical data that could be used to support the idea of the Flood or the Ark. The possible hoax element comes from claims to have found the Ark when it would have been impossible for there to have been an Ark on Mt. Ararat.

There are three major questions that must be asked in any investigation of the Noah's Ark problem: 1) was there a universal (worldwide) flood? 2) was it theoretically or technically possible for an ark to be built in ancient times that would hold at least two of all land-dwelling species, and 3) does evidence clearly indicate where this Ark landed after the flood? Each of these problems will be addressed in turn. If the answer to the first two is "no," the case for Noah's Ark is doomed. This article will start with the third question first.

Does evidence clearly indicate where the Ark landed after the flood?

The Bible and other sources do not reveal exactly where the Ark was supposed to have landed, assuming that there was a universal flood and an ark built to survive it. A careful reading of the Bible text (Genesis 8:4) says that the Ark " . . . rested in the seventh month on the seventeenth day of the month, upon the mountains of Ararat." Notice that the text does not say "Mount Ararat," but the *mountains* of Ararat. The text describes an entire mountain range—not simply a single mountain.

The mountain now called Ararat is two mountains, Little Ararat and Great Ararat. Great Ararat is the tallest mountain in the area at 16,900 feet. It is in Turkey, right on the border of Armenia and Iran. The sister peak, Little Ararat, is 12,900 feet tall and joined to Great Ararat by a rock "saddle." This saddle is from 7,000 to 8,000 feet high. "Ararat" is an ancient name for an extensive area, later called Urartu, then the country Armenia. Still later, Ararat referred to a small northern district in Armenia. The mountain called Mount Ararat today was not called that by the Armenians who lived there until about the eleventh century A.D. The fact that Great Ararat is the tallest mountain in the region makes it a tempting site for a landing of an Ark.

Other early traditions about where the Ark landed exist. Traditionalists place the date of the landing in about 2,345 B.C. Between this time and the writing of the Genesis account was a period of 1,300 years.

In the Koran, the story of the Ark is told with somewhat similar details. However, in the Koran, the Ark landed upon "al-Judi." This has generally been interpreted to mean a mountain in the southeastern corner of Turkey now called Cilo Dagi—a mountain more than 13,000 feet high. Although the mountain is the highest mountain on the border of Armenia and Mesopotamia, its common name of "Mount Judi" derives from the association with the statement in the Koran, and not the other way around. The remains of the Ark are to be found at Carrhae, according to the

historian Josephus. Carrhae refers to the ancient city of Haran in Turkey, near the Syrian border.

In the third century B.C., the Babylonians located the Ark's landing site as the Gordyaean or Kurdish mountains. The Jewish book of Jubilees, written around 200 B.C., says that the Ark landed on the peak in the Ararat mountain known as Lubar. The location of this peak is unknown. In Nicolaus of Damascus's writings, as quoted by Josephus, the Ark is said to have landed upon a great mountain named Baris. Again, the location of this mountain is unknown. Later, the Greeks spoke of the Ark as having landed at Mount Parnassas in central Greece.

The earliest Christian mention of the Ark occurs in Theophilus', the bishop of Antioch's, writings. In about 180 A.D. he mentioned that the Ark landed "in the Arabian mountains." Sextus Julius Africanus says that the Ark landed in "Parthia," which is now in Iran. This confusion occurred because "the mountains of Ararat," as mentioned in Genesis, was an unknown location to people of the period. By the fourth century, scholars agreed (but not the local residents, as mentioned) that Mount Ararat referred to the mountain called Agri Dagi in Turkish, or Mount Massis in Armenian. This consensus was probably arrived at simply because Agri Dagi is the tallest mountain in the region. Thus, one can see that what is now called Mount Ararat is really a late choice for the site of Noah's landing.

The Judeo-Christian tradition having settled upon Mount Ararat as their late and final choice for the resting place of the Ark, there began a period of vast indifference about its location on the mountain. Several people inquired locally about the site, but were usually told that the mountain was so tall and dangerous that it was impossible to climb to the Ark. There was some truth to this claim, as the mountain *is* difficult to climb. In Mandeville's *Travels*—a work renowned for its inaccuracy—the author says that the remains of the Ark could be seen on the mountain during clear weather. During the seventeenth century, several monks lived as hermits on the mountain's lower parts.

Finally, in 1829, explorer J. J. Friedrich Parrot climbed to the top of Ararat. Although he believed in Noah's Ark, he failed to find it on Ararat. His conclusion was that it must be under the ice covering the summit. Scientist D. W. H. Abich was the first to climb the eastern peak of Ararat in 1845. Although he was not looking for the Ark, he found no sign of it on his journey. In 1850, some sixty Russian soldiers climbed the mountain, but found no Ark. In 1876 James Bryce from Oxford University climbed Great Ararat and found a stick four feet long. He thought it must be from the Ark, but offered no evidence for his claim. John Joseph Nouri, a churchman from India, tried unsuccessfully three times to climb Ararat. Finally, he claimed he succeeded and saw the Ark. He also claimed to have gone inside the boat and taken measurements. Those measurements coincided precisely with those given in Genesis. Several other people climbed Ararat before the 1930s. None found the Ark.

During the 1940s, a number of claims to have seen the Ark were made. An unnamed Kurdish farmer said he saw the prow of a ship protruding from a canyon on the mountain. In 1953 George Jefferson Greene, an American mining engineer, said that he took a number of photographs of the Ark from a helicopter. He showed these pictures to several people in an attempt to get them interested in financing a new expedition to Ararat, but he was unsuccessful. Although his photographs have since disappeared without a trace, they were probably not too impressive or the response would have been better. A sketch made from memory years later by someone who saw the photos, shows a side and end view of an object on a ledge. The object appears laminated. Many false stories—some later retracted or disowned even by Fundamentalists—had a large Russian expedition finding the Ark in about 1917. Supposedly they carried a report back to the Czar—right in the middle of the Russian Revolution, after he was deposed—and he organized a further expedition. All traces of the report supposedly vanished during the next few years of war. The story seems apocryphal, as does one about three atheist scientists who stumbled upon the Ark. They supposedly were so angered by its existence that they tried to destroy it, then swore an oath never to tell anyone. The documentation for this story is weak. Aaron Smith, a clergyman from North Carolina, searched in vain for the Ark in 1949, even though he claimed to have had a divine revelation telling him exactly where it was located. In 1949, two Turkish journalists claimed that they found the Ark on Mount Judi, not Ararat. In 1952 was the first trip of the founder of modern "Arkology," Fernand Navarra.

Navarra was a wealthy French industrialist who was convinced he found the Ark. He brought down several samples of wood. The laboratory where he had the wood analyzed said that it was 5,000 years old. Unfortunately, they had not used radiometric tests. When several laboratories did more accurate tests, they found that the wood dated from about 800 A.D. It was undoubtedly from a monk's shrine built as a monument on the mountain. Navarra returned to Ararat in 1955. Again, he claimed that he found the Ark, this time at the bottom of a crevasse. However, when he reached the spot where he believed it was, he was mistaken.

In 1960, *Life* magazine published a photo of a depression on a mountain in the area that appeared to be shaped like a ship. This was discovered from an aerial photograph. When an expedition reached the site (which was on a mountain twenty miles from Ararat), they found only a grassy mound surrounded by an earthen rim twenty feet high. It was a natural formation, created by a recent landslide. Other, more recent expeditions found nothing of note, although David Fashold claims to have found metal nails at the site. No good photographs of the Ark supposedly exist at present.

Was it theoretically or technically possible for an Ark to be built in ancient times that would hold at least two of all land-dwelling species?

Genesis 6:14-15 gives the dimensions that God wanted the Ark to be. These dimensions are 300 cubits by fifty cubits by thirty cubits. This translates to 450 feet long, seventy-five feet wide and forty-five feet high, for a total of 1,518,750 cubic feet of volume. This must be decreased by the space occupied by any interior structures, including the flooring for the three floors and the walls. A normal architectural figure for these is a thirty percent reduction for internal structures. This leaves 1,063,125 cubic feet, not including items such as cages, living quarters for humans, and food and waste storage areas.

A length of 450 feet would make the Ark slightly less than one-half of the length of the Queen Elizabeth II ocean liner. As of 1845 the largest ship in the world was the iron-hulled *Great Britain* at 322 feet. The largest wooden boat of modern times was the *Rochambeau* (formerly the *Dunderberg*), built in 1867, at 377 feet. Iron strapping holds its hull together. It is well known to ship architects that the maximum practical length of an all-wood ship is 300 feet. If it is any longer than that, warping and stresses will make the hull leak unless it is strapped with iron.

"Gopher wood" is the material from which God tells Noah to build the Ark. Even in the earliest texts, the term "Gopher wood," which only occurs once in the Bible, is obscure. Most assume it refers to wood from the conifer or cypress family. Another school of thought holds that the etymology of the word comes from the Hebrew "kofer," which means a kind of boat made from a closely woven "basketwork" type of materials. The matter is still unsettled today.

In the Bible, God instructs Noah to cover the entire outside of the Ark with pitch. Pitch is a sticky tar made from petroleum products and used today to seal roads and roofs. Unfortunately, pitch is produced by applying tons of pressure upon long-dead plant and animal matter. At the time of the Ark, life on the earth had existed (according to the Bible) for only about 1,700 years at most. Arkologists say that all oil and coal now known were produced by the pressure of the flood waters on plants and animals that died in the flood.

That pressure allowed the formation to proceed quickly (i.e., in the 4,000 years since the flood). Unfortunately, this does not explain how Noah got the large quantities of pitch he needed *before* the flood.

More than 923,000 animal species are known today, plus a possible 500,000 species not yet discovered by mankind. This totals 1,423,000 species. When the 200,000 species now known to be extinct, including dinosaurs, is added in, the total species equals 1,623,000— at two of each species, 3,246,000 individual animals. Genesis says that two of each unclean animal, seven pair of each clean one, and seven pair of each fowl were taken on board. Since it is unclear what was meant by a clean or unclean animal, the extra six pair (12) of each fowl of the air will only be considered. More than 8,590 species of bird are known. At 12 additional individuals of each bird, 103,080 animals are added for a total of 3,349,080 creatures.

With 1,063,125 cubic feet of space on the Ark, each of the 3,349,080 creatures would get exactly .356 cubic feet of space, not including cage space, food space, waste space, plant space or human space. This means a maximum of about one-third of a cubic foot per animal (i.e., 12″ x 12″ x 4″ per animal). There also had to be space for food (Genesis 6:21) at least, and waste had to be allowed for—at least temporarily—the flood lasted 371 days.

Since most plants would also not survive submersion under deep brackish water for a year, all of them would also have to be included on the Ark. There are about 420,000 known species of plants. Some plants could be taken as seeds, but many plants do not reproduce by seeds, so would have to be taken as adult plants. The plants would take up some additional space, but it is impossible to know exactly how much. Many animals (e.g., the hippopotamus, seals, and manatees) would require large tanks of fresh water as well.

There are other serious problems with the account of the animals to be taken on the Ark as given in Genesis. Arkologists claim that only two of each "kind" or "baramin" (not "species") were taken aboard the Ark. Thus, there were only two of the "dog/wolf kind," and not two of each species of canine family members. This greatly reduces the number of animals that taken aboard the Ark. However, if this was so, then only one of each kind of animal could have existed before the flood, since God told Noah to take two of "every living thing" onto the Ark. If only a generalized "kind" existed before the flood, it means that all present species of the canine family, for example, seen today have *evolved* since the flood. In that case, fossils should be found only of a generalized canine or equine kind from before the flood or immediately after the

flood. They are the only creatures that have had time to fossilize so far. However, no such fossils have been found. There are many species of equine, and canine, and feline fossils.

Arkologists have suggested that many of the space problems on the Ark could have been solved by taking only the eggs of those species (dinosaurs, reptiles, fish, amphibians, and birds) that reproduce by eggs. This theory does not work because the birds were specifically stated to be taken by God as "fowl of the air." Further, the sex of an individual cannot be determined by a examination of the outside of the egg. Therefore, *many* eggs would have to be taken on board. Also, the flood lasted for more than one year. Almost no creature has an incubation period for its eggs that lasts that long. All of the eggs would have hatched on board the Ark. A newly hatched animal requires a great deal of careful care, and the absence of the parents of the hatchlings would place an additional burden on the people caring for the young. The problems of fish and amphibian eggs, which hatch in water, are staggering. They are food for many species of fish, birds, and reptiles. They would have to be watched constantly, or kept in individual tanks.

No thought was given in the Genesis account to the survival of fish, amphibians, and aquatic mammals. These are assumed to be able to survive in the flood waters. However, this would not be the case. The change in salinity that would occur quickly during a flood would kill nearly all fish (both freshwater and saltwater), except for a few deep bottom dwellers, who might survive. Fresh water fish, amphibians, and mammals would have to be put in tanks of fresh water. The rapid saturation of land masses during the flood would wash great quantities of soil into the oceans. The result would be a murky, muddy, brackish water in which almost nothing could survive for a year. All plants would die, even saltwater plants. They could not get sunlight through the murky water, whose changed salinity would probably kill them even before lack of sunlight would. As mentioned earlier, plant *seeds* could have been taken on the Ark, but they would have to be gathered from all over the world, and many plants don't reproduce by seeds, including a number of large ones. Someone would have had to *dig up* two of each of these plants and carry them to the Ark.

Many parasites and infectious micro-organisms cannot survive outside of their host animals or humans. That means that for these creatures to survive, they must have infested/infected their hosts while they were on the Ark. For example, both of the horses on the Ark must have been infested with all the horse parasites and viruses. At the same time, neither could die during the year on the Ark, for loss of a male and female would discontinue the species. A number of human venereal disease bacteria (as well as other disease organisms) cannot survive outside of human beings. Therefore, Noah and his family must have been infected with syphilis, smallpox, tapeworms, gonorrhea, and leprosy at a minimum. Yet, they survived and functioned for more than a year on the Ark in spite of this.

To gather the species at the Ark site for loading, the animals had to walk or swim (or both) from their natural geographical habitats. Many came from places such as Australia and the mid-Pacific islands. Many of these species can't swim across an ocean. Others can't live for long outside of the water. Some arkologists have said, that the continents were all still connected at that point. The animals who live in deserts and those who live in swamps would still have to cross thousands of miles of inhospitable environment.

To feed the animals and dispose of their wastes would be impossible for 100 humans, much less for the eight on the Ark. Food and water would have to be changed, droppings removed, as in zoos today. Many animals, especially birds, must eat constantly throughout the day. Others require fresh meat (or live prey) each day.

A single elephant can produce forty tons of manure in a year. Dinosaurs probably produced even more. All the manure would have to be removed from the Ark often, or it would form a breeding place for bacteria and a source of unbearable fumes. Marine species must have their water oxygenated and wastes removed from it frequently. Fresh water dwellers must have their fresh water replaced at frequent intervals. Plants must be both watered and exposed to sunlight each day.

Many animals have special requirements for light, temperature, and humidity. They require special perches, stalls, floors, atmospheres, and wading areas. If they do not get what they need for more than a few days, they die. They could not have had these needs met on the Ark. Arkologists suggested that all of the animals simply hibernated. This could not be true because only a few species employ hibernation. Those that hibernate lose so much fat and muscle weight during hibernation that they nearly die. No animal hibernates for more than a full year (usually only during part of the winter), so the few species that hibernate would be awake for most of the voyage.

The eight people on the Ark included Noah's three sons. These eight are supposed to be the ancestors of all humans now alive. However, the three sons had the same gene pool. That leaves five people from outside that pool. Of those, Noah and his wife shared half of the same gene pool as their sons. That leaves only the three wives of the sons as the source of all the racial diversity and physical distinctions now found in the human race.

The entire pre-flood world was supposedly destroyed in the flood. All humans and all human civilization was destroyed. Yet not one of these pre-flood civilizations has ever been discovered by archaeologists.

When on the top of a mountain, all the animals had to disembark and climb down the mountain, swim the seas, and walk across continents to get back to their pre-flood habitats. At the same time, there was nothing for them to eat, as all plant and animal life not on the Ark had been destroyed.

The plants—or their seeds—stored in the Ark had to be redistributed all over the world in their proper habitats. Both the seeds and the plants had to be replanted in the proper type of soil, tended so they would grow, and made safe from animals that would eat them. All this had to be done by eight people.

Was there a universal flood?

Whether or not there is evidence for a worldwide flood is the most critical question in all of arkology, as if there was no worldwide flood, the whole problem of Noah's Ark becomes moot. In order to investigate this question, one must draw on the resources of several different disciplines, among them geology, archeology, folklore studies, history, anthropology, mythology, and comparative religion.

There *is* a tradition of a big flood in the folklore of many cultures. Among the cultures for which exist extensive records, and which do *not* have a tradition of a large flood, are the Egyptians. This fact is puzzling because the flood, even if it occurred, even locally, would surely have affected the nearby Egyptians.

Archaeological excavations in Palestine and Syria have not revealed any signs of a flood. There are remains of settlements in the Jericho area that date back to the Stone Age (8000 B.C.). In ancient Mesopotamia there are definite signs of a flood in *some* areas but it seems to have been a local flood.

While it is true that there are flood stories in many cultures, the stories vary considerably in content. A number of flood stories are older than the Genesis version. The most ancient of these versions found so far is the Sumerian flood tablet, found at the site of the ancient city of Nippur, now in modern Iraq. The tablet was found in the year 1872, but first published in English translation in 1914. The tablet seems to be from about 1600 B.C. The story itself was probably motivated to support the authority of kings and priests, as well as to promote divine laws.

The Babylonian story of the flood involves the hero Xisuthus, who performs the same role as Noah. An earlier Babylonian text, the Gilgamesh Epic, tells the story of Utnapishtim, the equivalent of Noah. He was secretly warned by the god Ea that the other gods were sending a flood to destroy mankind. Utnapishtim is urged to build a ship, which he does, sealing it with bitumen. He also took provisions, his family, and animals. He took along a number of skilled craftsmen as well. The flood came, lasting seven days. After twelve days, his ark landed on a mountain. Utnapishtim sent out a dove, then a swallow. Both returned. Finally, he sent out a raven, which did not return. He then made a sacrifice to the gods. Note the similarity to the Noah story in Genesis 7 and 8.

Both the Babylonian and the biblical versions of the flood story seem to have a common origin in the Sumerian flood story (c. 3000 B.C.). The hero here is called Zinsuddu or Ziusudra. The Hebrew origins of the flood story go back to about 1000 B.C., when it was probably written down for the first time. The Hebrews borrowed the story from their neighbors in Mesopotamia, the Hurrians. The Greeks eventually picked up the flood story, modifying it to include Zeus as the god who ordered the flood, Deucalion in the Noah role, and Mount Parnassus as the landing site for the Ark.

The biblical account of the flood is well known. What is not so well known is the fact that the story has been pieced together from two different accounts, imperfectly edited. These two versions are known as the "J" or Jehovist source, and the "P" or Priestly source. The two accounts have some areas of agreement and some differences. For example, God is called "the Lord" only in the J source. The distinction between clean and unclean animals is made only in the J source. The J source also does not mention any landing site for the Ark. The P source alone gives the details of the Ark's construction.

It is now time to consider the evidence of *geology* for the occurrence of the flood. Floods leave traces in the column of materials that settle at the bottom of lakes and oceans, and are deposited on dry land. An example would be the presence of sea shells in the geologic column buried under a mountain. Shells are evidence that the area was once under the ocean, but they are not evidence of a major flood. Because the surface of the earth is always shifting, mountains are thrust up due to tectonic plates that form parts of the surface of the earth. Areas of ocean are cut off from the rest of the ocean and may dry up. Sometimes the salt from the ocean remains (as in the Bonneville Salt Flats in Utah); at other times it is washed away by rainfall.

A genuine flood that did not last more than a year would leave some sedimentary deposits in a narrow band at the same level (representing the same date of occurrence) in all areas in which the flood occurred. Therefore, a truly worldwide flood would leave a single band of sediment at the same level in all the geologic columns of areas that had been dry land before the flood. Some additional sediment would also show up in the columns under the areas that had been ocean at the time of the flood, but it could be difficult to distinguish these deposits from those occurring naturally without a flood. The absence of a worldwide band of sediment like this is strong evidence that a worldwide flood never occurred. There *is* strong evidence of many local floods, however.

Other problems with the mechanics of a universal flood include the lack of a source for so much water. If all the ice in the North and South Polar regions melted, it would only raise the level of the oceans about thirty feet. Noah's flood needed enough water to cover a mountain 17,000 feet high completely. The amount of water in the clouds has evaporated from the earth. Not enough water is present in any known subterranean sources either. The opposite problem—namely where all the water went after the flood ended—is another consideration to the validity of the flood.

Almost no historic, geologic, or folkloric evidence for a worldwide flood is left. If this is so, what accounts for the widespread stories of a flood in the folklore of so many cultures? The answer lies in the lack of communication between people in ancient times. Their world was limited to the areas they could reach by travel. A flood covering all the land area they knew would seem to be worldwide. A worldwide flood seemed even more plausible to them when travellers from distant lands also told stories of large floods in their past. It might have been a different local flood at a different time, but it would soon be blended together as evidence of a worldwide cataclysm.

The Noah's Ark story collapses of its own weight. The major objections are that 1) it doesn't agree with the evidence of geology, 2) it is impossible from a consideration of the space requirements on the Ark, the number of animals involved, etc., 3) it doesn't explain the present diversity and distribution of human races or animal species, 4) it rests on a foundation of similar tales from other cultures that are older than the Hebrew one, and 5) it is found in a context, in the early parts of Genesis, along with other materials that seem to be a part of a folkloric and not a scientific explanation of the origin of life on the earth.

The failure of recent expeditions to Mount Ararat to search for the Ark are understandable. The searchers should not have looked for a real Ark in that location in the first place. Science does not operate by insisting that a fixed body of knowledge has to be accurate, and therefore an Ark must be on Mount Ararat. Rather, it looks at the evidence for the possibility of a worldwide flood, the construction of an Ark, and the loading of it with two or more of each species of animal (and maybe plant), to see if it could really be true. The probability is extremely small. The stories of having found the Ark are almost certainly hoaxes.

Sources:

Bailey, Lloyd R. *Noah: The Person and the Story in History and Tradition.* Columbia, SC: University of South Carolina Press, 1989.

Bright, John. "Has Archeology Found Evidence of the Flood?" *The Biblical Archeologist* 5 (1942): 55–61.

Fasold, David. *The Ark of Noah.* New York: Wynwood Press, 1988.

Moore, Robert A. "The Impossible Voyage of Noah's Ark." *Creation/Evolution* no.11 (Winter 1983): 1–43.

Teeple, Howard M. *The Noah's Ark Nonsense.* Evanston, IL: Religion and Ethics Institute, 1978.

Notovitch and the Unknown Life of Jesus Christ

An announcement was made in a number of 1926 newspapers that a manuscript—found in a monastery in Tibet in 1887 but not previously revealed—contained the previously lost *Life of Saint Issa, Best Loved of the Sons of Men.* The life of this "saint" was of interest because St. Issa was an Asian term for Jesus of Nazareth. What was purportedly found was a biography covering the "lost years" of Jesus' life—from his birth to about age thirty. The manuscript was discovered in 1887 and first published in French in 1894. It was therefore not—as the 1926 newspaper accounts said—unreported until then. The French version was entitled *La Vie Inconnu de Jesus Christ.*

The author of the French version was adventurer Nicolas Notovitch (18580–?) who claimed to have suffered a broken leg at the Convent of Himis in Tibet and to have spent several weeks there recuperating. While he was recovering, Notovitch convinced the Chief Lama to read the manuscript of *The Life of Saint Issa* to him, using an interpreter. The book was written in Tibetan; it had supposedly been translated from the Pali.

The book begins with an account of the Jews in Egypt, their deliverance by Moses, and their conquest by the Romans. An account is given of the Incarnation of Jesus and of his youth until the age of thirteen. At that time, Issa [Jesus] left home to go to India. Issa

studied Buddhism, was welcomed by the Jains, and finally spent six years studying the Vedas. Issa also taught people of all castes. The Brahmins opposed this and Issa denounced them and their sacred books. Issa fled to the Buddhists, among whom he also spent six years. He then learned Pali and visited Persia, where he preached to the Zoroastrians. At age twenty-nine, Issa returned to Jerusalem and began his ministry there.

There are many problems with the text. It shows knowledge by the writer of the contents of the Gospels of John and Luke, yet *The Life of Issa* purports to have been written within three to four years of Jesus' death—from the testimony of eyewitnesses. It was forty years or more after Jesus' death before Luke or John was written down. Other events mentioned appear to come from Acts and Romans in the New Testament. That would place the composition of *The Life of Issa* well into the second century, at the earliest.

The book also presents a colorless and unobjectionable version of morality. It is devoid, according to author Edgar Goodspeed, of insight and genius. The two volumes the Lama read to Notovitch at the convent were said to have been compiled from various copies in libraries at Lhasa, India, and Nepal. Although Notovitch made notes from the dictated translation, there was no attempt at a scholarly translation.

Famous orientalist F. Max Mueller points out that *The Life of Issa* does not appear in the great catalogs of the Tibetan literature. Mueller says that either the Buddhist monks deceived Notovitch or Notovitch was the deceiver. Mueller received a letter from an Englishwoman visiting Tibet in 1894, who stated that she visited the Himis monastery and asked about the Russian (Notovitch) who broke his leg and recovered there. The lamas stated that no such person had been there, and denied that they had a manuscript *Life of Issa.*

It therefore appears that *The Life of Issa* is Notovitch's creation. In fact, Notovitch states in the preface that there is no longer a manuscript of *The Life* in monastic libraries in Tibet or India. He doesn't say what happened to it, but *does* say that the Vatican Library possesses sixty-three complete or incomplete versions of the Issa manuscript. No independent student of Vatican manuscripts has reported the existence of even one of these.

Apparently, Notovitch *was* treated for a toothache at Leh Hospital in Tibet. When author Archibald Douglas read parts of Notovitch's book to the Chief Lama at Himis, he said with indignation, "Lies, lies, lies, nothing but lies."

It appears that *The Unknown Life of Jesus Christ* is a hoax, probably perpetrated by Nicolas Notovitch himself. It continues to be printed in new editions, and is still passed off as genuine.

Sources:

Douglas, J. Archibald. "The Chief Lama of Himis on the Alleged 'Unknown Life of Christ'." *Nineteenth Century* 39 (1896): 667–78.

Goodspeed, Edgar J. *Strange New Gospels.* Chicago: University of Chicago Press, 1931: 10–24.

Mueller, F. Max. "The Alleged Sojourn of Christ in India." *Nineteenth Century* 36 (1894): 515.

Notovitch, Nicolas. *The Unknown Life of Jesus Christ.* Santa Monica, CA: Leaves of Healing Publications, 1980.

Pope Joan

There was a tradition that held that the pope known as John VIII was really a woman. This pope was supposedly in office for two years, five months and four days, between the years 853 and 855 A.D. Before his elevation John VIII was probably called John Anglicus ("English John"—a name added by the church), because in those days popes did not change their given name.

Several sources cite the first mention of a Pope Joan in about the middle of the thirteenth century, about 350 years after her alleged reign. There was certainly no printing in those days, but there are many manuscripts. This first reference is in the *Chronicle of Metz*, as follows:

> Query: With regard to a certain pope—or rather popess, because she was a woman who pretended to be a man. By his excellent abilities having been appointed notary at the papal court he became Cardinal and eventually Pope. On a certain day, when he was riding, he gave birth to a child, and straightaway in accordance with Roman justice his feet were tied together and he was dragged for half a league at a horse's tail while the people stoned him. At the place where he expired, he was buried, and an inscription was set up: PETRE PATER PATRUM PAPISSE PRODITO PARTUM. [This Peter, the father of fathers, gave birth to a child]. Under him was instituted the fast of the Ember Days, and it is called the popess's fast.

The next known reference to Pope Joan is in the *Chronicon Pontificum et Imperatorum* of Martinus Polonus (Martin of Troppau), about fifty years later. It says:

> After the aforesaid Leo, John, an Englishman by descent, who came from Mainz, held the see two years, five months and four days, and the pontificate was vacant one month. He died at Rome. He, it is asserted, was a woman. And having been taken by her lover to

Athens in man's clothes, she made such progress in various sciences that there was nobody equal to her. So that afterwards lecturing on the Trivium at Rome she had great masters for her disciples and hearers. And forasmuch as she was in great esteem in the city, both for her life and her learning, she was unanimously elected pope. But while pope she became pregnant by the person with whom she was intimate. But not knowing the time of her delivery, while going from St. Peter's to the Lateran, being taken in labour, she brought forth a child between the Coliseum and St. Clement's church. And afterwards dying she was, it is said, buried in that place. And because Lord Pope always turns aside from that way, there are some who are fully persuaded that it is done in detestation of the fact. Nor is she put in the Catalogue of the Holy Popes, as well on account of her female sex as on account of the shameful nature of the episode.

There are a few general mentions of Pope Joan *before* the thirteenth century. The *Liber Pontificalis* or *Gesta Pontificarum Romanorum*, supposedly in part by Anastasius Bibiothecarius (d. 886 A.D.), lists Pope Joan. Sigebert (d. 1112) wrote his *Chronographia*, which lists Pope Joan. Otto of Freising (d. 1158) also includes Pope Joan in his *Chronicon*. Gervase of Tillbury, in his *Otia Imperialia* (c. 1211), tells of Joan in almost the same words as Martin of Troppau did in his *Chronicon Pontificarum et Imperatorium* (1278).

Defenders of the mythical status of Pope Joan respond to the early appearance of her name in the lists of popes by saying that the name is present only in *some* manuscript copies, and therefore was added later. Author Horace Mann offers a strong piece of evidence against Joan when he points out that there are coins in existence that picture Pope Benedict III and the emperor Lothaire together on the same coin. Pope Leo IV, Benedict's predecessor, died on July 17, 855 and Lothaire on September 28, 855. Therefore *if Benedict was pope at the time of the coin*, and Lothaire was emperor, this must have been between July 17 and September 28, 855, as that was the only time both were alive as pope and emperor, respectively. That left no time period between 853 and 855 when Joan could have been pope. The only explanation here would be that the date of Leo IV's death could have been altered later from 853 to 855.

Author Robert Ware provides excerpts from *many* "Romish" (Catholic) sources, dating from as early as 937 A.D., that not only mention but give descriptive information about Pope Joan. He lists forty-five sources from before the year 1500. Most importantly, six of them are from before the middle of the thirteenth century (1250 A.D.), the date at which modern Catholic authorities say was the first detailed mention of Pope Joan.

Among the sources listed before 1250 are Litprandus in his *Trithemium* (937 A.D.); Marianus Scotus in his

Philippum Morney & Baronius (1074 A.D.); Sigibert in his *Chronographia* (1100 A.D., already mentioned); Otho in his *Frizingensis* (1145 A.D.); Gothfridus Viturbiensis in his *Chronicles* (1186 A.D.); and Roger Hoveden in his *Historiae Angletere* (1214 A.D.).

The Roman Catholic Church's response to this has changed over the years. At first, the church seemed to accept the reality of Pope Joan. However, during the Reformation in the sixteenth century, the official position of the church shifted towards a denial of the historicity of Pope Joan. The church's recent position has been summarized by J. B. Alzog as follows:

> Some of the manuscripts of Anastasius the Librarian, a writer of the ninth century, do not contain it [mention of Pope Joan], while it is introduced into others from the works of Martinus Polonus. Neither is it to be found in the oldest manuscripts of this author—quite the contrary; for in them the opening words of the life of Benedict run as follows: 'Immediately after the death of Leo IV, Benedict was unanimously chosen to succeed him.'
>
> Moreover, the short passage relating to this affair, contained in the works of Marianus Scotus (A.D. 1806) and of Sigebert of Gemblours (A.D. 1112) is by no means authentic, for ... it is to be found only in the older printed editions of the writings of these authors, and not in the manuscript copies. That this tale is a fiction is evident from the account given of it in Martinus Polonus, the first writer to mention it, who represents the pseudo pope as residing at the Vatican, whereas it was well known that, until the eleventh century, the Popes uniformly resided at the Lateran Palace.
>
> Moreover, it has been proven to a demonstration that Matinus Polonus himself was entirely ignorant of the fable, and that it was introduced into his chronicle between the years 1278 and 1312.

Because of the ancient nature and unknown reliability of the sources, it appears that no definitive answer can be given to the question of whether Pope Joan was an historical character. It would appear that in either case, however, some sort of hoax is involved. If Joan is authentic, then the church has been hoaxing by denying her historicity. If Joan is a fable, then the people who insist on her authenticity are the hoaxers.

Sources:

Alzog, John B. *History of the Church.* Vol. 2. New York: Benziger Brothers, 1912: 266.

Mann, Horace K. *The Lives of the Popes in the Early Middle Ages.* Vols. 2, 3. St. Louis: B. Herder, 1906: 328 (v.2); 263 (v.3).

Olsen, Chris. *Pope Joan: A Riddle of the Dark Ages.* St. Louis: Rationalist Publications, [c. 1960].

Rhoidis, Emmanuel. *Pope Joan (The Female Pope): An Historical Study.* London: George Redway, 1886.

Thurston, Herbert. *No Popery: Chapters on Anti-Papal Prejudice.* London: Longmans Green & Co., 1930: 91–99.

[Ware, Robert]. *Pope Joan: Or, An Account Collected out of the Romish Authors, Proved to be of the Clergy and Members of that Church, Before Luther Left Her Doctrine; and Also of Romish Authors Since Luther Departed from Rome; Testifying that there was a She-Pope, who sate [sic] in that See, and Ruled the Same.* London: William Miller, 1689.

Wood, Clement. *The Woman Who Was Pope: A Biography of Pope Joan, 853–855 A.D.* New York: William Faro, 1931.

Relic Hoaxes

In the sensitive area of religious relics, a hoax will be defined—as with the rest of the book—as a conscious attempt to deceive. An obvious example is the supposed relic of St. Peter's brain that turned out to be a piece of pumice stone. Most of the time it will be quite difficult—if not impossible—to identify the actual hoaxer.

If not the most famous and important, certainly the most widespread relics of Christianity, are pieces of the true cross. The cross upon which Jesus was supposedly crucified had disappeared until at least the year 326 A.D. In that year, Helena—Constantine the Great's mother—on a pilgrimage to the Holy Land, was led to a spot where the true cross was supposedly buried by a Jew in accordance with tradition. When the ground at that spot was dug up, three crosses were found. Helena supposedly distinguished which cross was Jesus' by having a corpse laid upon each of the crosses. A body came to life immediately when placed upon Jesus' cross. Even if this story were true, there was a gap of 300 years—with no Christian tradition as to the location of the true cross—before anything purporting to be the true cross was found. Add to this the unlikeliness of the three crosses being buried together, and the wood surviving in the ground for 300 years.

Helena was the first Christian empress and accordingly, all sorts of amazing relics were brought to her for purchase. Among these were the nails with which Jesus had been fastened to the cross and the crown of thorns. The location of the sepulcher where Jesus had been buried was also brought to her attention. When doubt was expressed about the long survival of the true cross, a story was made up that it had first been found within a few years of the actual crucifixion by the wife of Roman ruler Claudius, but that she had reburied it on the spot at which she discovered it. At present, enough pieces of wood supposedly exist from the true cross that a good-sized ship could be built from them.

Although the number of nails used to fasten Jesus to the cross was originally stated to be three or four, so many nails have been "identified" that one source says fourteen nails were used to fasten Jesus, because that's how many have now been found.

At a temple at Kandy, Sri Lanka, is a relic of Buddha's tooth. However, the original tooth was publicly destroyed by Portuguese Christians several hundred years ago. What is on exhibit now as the Buddha's tooth appears to be a tiger tooth.

A highly dubious Hindu relic is the big toe of the left foot of the goddess Sati (Siva's wife). Sati is an entirely mythological being.

About 300 years after their deaths, the previously unknown tombs of St. Andrew, St. Luke, and St. Timothy were "found," and the bodies therein taken back to Constantinople. Samuel of the Old Testament was supposedly found and disinterred in the fourth century. His body was also taken back to Constantinople. St. Stephen's body was disinterred and taken on a long journey, with several intermediate stopping places. At Minorca, his relics were credited with converting 540 Jews to Christianity, helped no doubt by the burning of their synagogue and the driving of the Jews to probable starvation among the rocks.

The story given of the origin of the many vials of "milk" from the Virgin Mary—now venerated as relics—is worth noting. It is questionable how any woman's milk could be collected in a vial, especially during the period in which Mary lived. According to the story, during a flight to escape the massacre of innocents, Mary, Joseph, and Jesus the infant hid in a cave. Joseph thought their hiding place had been discovered and took Jesus with him, leaving Mary behind (why is not stated). Mary, nursing, but not having Jesus around, relieved the pressure in her breasts by squeezing the milk into a hole in a stone. One of the shepherds found the milk and "bottled" it.

The worship of Mary began in the fifth century. That is also when attempts to collect her relics were first made. Her tomb was "discovered" at Ephesus, then at Jerusalem. Finally, it was decided that the tomb in Jerusalem was empty because Mary had ascended bodily with Jesus into heaven. That is why there are no relics of the Virgin Mary that were actually a part of her body.

However, the clothing of the Virgin Mary was "discovered" around 620 A.D. in Thrace, unexplained. Pope Gregory V (who reigned from 996 to 999 A.D.) said

that he had found Mary's wedding ring in Chiusa, Italy. The fact that first century Jews did not wear wedding rings seemed irrelevant. Many churches also had samples of the Virgin Mary's clothing—including her girdles—among their relics.

Among other dubious relics are the plate from which the lamb was served during the Last Supper, the stone upon which Mohammed (or Jesus, or Mary) stood while ascending to heaven, the blood of Jesus, the foreskins (there are many) of Jesus, letters from Jesus (now lost), descriptions of Jesus from life, clothing of Jesus, portraits of the apostles and the Shroud of Turin (*See* Shroud of Turin, p. 240). Pieces of wood from Noah's Ark (*See* Noah's Ark, p. 227) abound as well.

Sources:

Bentley, James. *Restless Bones: The Story of Relics.* London: Constable, 1985.

Calvin, John. *A Treatise on Relics.* Edinburgh: Johnstone, Hunter & Co., [c.1854].

Rhys, Jocelyn. *The Reliquary: A Collection of Relics.* New York: Freethought Press Association, 1931.

Samuel Butler's *The Fair Haven*

The Fair Haven, by Samuel Butler (1835–1902), is one of his lesser-known works. Butler is perhaps best remembered for *The Way of All Flesh* and for his utopian novel *Erewhon*. However, *The Fair Haven,* first published in 1873, was a literary and religious hoax. The book purported to be by "the late John Pickard Owen, edited by William Bickersteth Owen, with a memoir of the author." It also proclaimed itself in its subtitle "A work in defence of the miraculous element in our Lord's ministry upon earth, both as against Rationalistic impugners and certain orthodox defenders."

The book opened with a memoir of the imaginary "late John Pickard Owen," (a biographical sketch of Owen, treating his mental evolution from believer to non-believer and back again) seventy pages long, that presented a pathway from belief to unbelief and back. The Reverend Owen used the book to present a number of discrepancies in the accounts of Jesus' death and resurrection in the Gospels. At the close of the memoir, passages from Reverend J. P. Owen's manuscripts, written during his period of unbelief, are quoted. They tend to drown out the believing tone of the text itself. In fact, they have been compared by author Lee Holt with the true feelings of Samuel Butler about Christianity, which appear in *The Note-Books of Samuel Butler*.

The text of *The Fair Haven* builds a gradual case against literal faith in the Bible, while the author simultaneously repeats that he is building up to an argument that will restore that faith. That argument concludes that one must believe in spite of the unbelievability of it all. This may explain why in the memoir, Rev. John Pickard Owen fell into a state of insanity before he died.

Although some readers of the book, when it was first published, thought that it was a sincere defense of the Christian faith, most saw that it was a satire upon that faith. This was made clear when Butler wrote a preface to the second printing of the book, in which he finally identified himself as the author. In that preface, Butler apologized for having used a pseudonym, and reported that he received no complaints about his treatment of the Gospels. This is rather hard to believe, since many people were reportedly offended, although mostly *after* Butler revealed that the book was a satire.

Although *The Fair Haven* is no longer read by many people, it does serve as a rare example of a book-length satire of religion by a major writer.

Sources:

Bullett, Gerald. "Introduction" to the Thinker's Library edition of *The Fair Haven*. C. A. Watts & Co., 1938: vii–ix.

[Butler, Samuel]. *The Fair Haven*. London: Trubner, 1873.

————. *The Note-Books of Samuel Butler*. New York: E. P. Dutton, 1907.

Holt, Lee E. *Samuel Butler*. New York: Twayne, 1964.

Raby, Peter. *Samuel Butler: A Biography*. Iowa City, IA: University of Iowa Press, 1991.

Satanism Hoaxes

Whether or not Satan exists, or whether or not some people worship Satan, is not the concern here. The concern is whether cases existed claiming that there was evidence of Satan worship or of Satanic activities, when there really was not, and that this deception was conscious.

Perhaps the most blatant example of a Satanism hoax is the case of Lauren Stratford, whose real name is Laurel Rose Willson. She wrote a book called *Satan's Underground*, published by a Fundamentalist Christian publisher in 1988. The publisher claimed that it "checked" the authenticity of the work, identifying that 1) the author told the same story to several editors, 2) the publisher's staff was impressed with her sincerity, 3) they talked with "experts," who confirmed that such things do happen, and 4) they obtained character references from her supporters. This is an inadequate method of testing the truth of Stratford's story.

Journalists Gretchen and Bob Passantino and John Trott had little difficulty in discovering that "Lauren Stratford" was Laurel Rose Willson, a physician's daughter, and that her story was absolutely false. Many of the obvious possible witnesses to events in the book said that the journalists' questions were the first ones they had ever been asked about Laurel's claims by *anyone*.

Willson said in her book that she was an only child. She claimed that she was repeatedly raped and made to participate in child pornography and bestiality with her mother's assent. Willson claimed that she had three children before she was first married. All three were killed in the making of "snuff" (a pornographic film in which an actor is actually killed) films or in Satanic rituals, she said. She claimed to be frequently involved in Satanism, as a victim and as a member. Willson's statement that she was involved in a lesbian relationship with Mrs. McMartin of the pre-school legal case in California, was only one of the more outrageous and false claims that she made.

The journalists' investigation showed that—according to her husband—Willson was a virgin at the time of her marriage. She had no children, had not been raped, was not involved in any Satanic groups, had never been in child pornography, and was widely viewed as a rather religious "choir girl" type. The book *Satan's Underground* is missing dates, places, and names. Its details are so repulsive that someone would probably have to be predisposed to believe that depraved Satanists were everywhere in order to accept it as factual. Willson claimed that she was born illegitimately, adopted, and had no siblings. The facts were that she *was* adopted at birth by Dr. and Mrs. Frank C. Willson, who lived near Tacoma, Washington. She had an older sister. Both of her parents were devout Christians, and she grew up in a Christian home. When Willson was nine, her father left the home. She was musically gifted and given several musical opportunities, including voice, piano, and clarinet lessons. She also sang in a number of groups in high school. Willson ran away to live with her sister (who was then married) once.

In college (a Christian college), Willson told several people that she had been molested and that her mother had encouraged her to be a prostitute. Under counseling, Willson admitted that these statements were false and that she made them up to "impress" people. She attempted suicide shortly thereafter. Willson transferred colleges and moved to Southern California, near San Bernardino. She made several additional suicide attempts, all involving cutting her arms. Her stories of sexual abuse also grew and involved elements from her early childhood, during a period when—due to her pure nature—they could not have been true. Her behavior grew more bizarre and self-destructive, and she continued to cry out for attention and sympathy.

She finally married at the age of twenty-two. Her husband said that it took some time before they were able to consummate their marriage and that Willson was a virgin until then.

Willson composed and sang for the church semi-professionally. She also gave music lessons, but her mental and physical health deteriorated. She began to tell stories of her involvement with people who were abusing children in the Bakersfield, California area. The police found her stories "useless." Satanism began to surface more often in her stories. Willson had read the book *Stormie*, which told of a woman who had grown up through child abuse. Willson contacted the author; the trail of confusion and lies continued.

Journalists attempts to confirm any of the statements made in her book about abuse, Satanism, and pornography, failed. Willson herself was unable, or unwilling, to provide any confirmation. Numerous acquaintances said that Willson had never been pregnant during the period when she claimed to have had three children. Her story was conclusively disproven. When journalists approached her publisher to seek confirmation for the story, they explained their aforementioned method of "testing" the story. They removed the book from sale in 1990, although they would not admit any error in having originally published it. No efforts were made to inform the public of the book's questionable contents. Surprisingly, however, a secular publisher has taken over publication of the book.

Animal Mutilations. The spate of animal mutilations (mostly cattle and sheep) that occurred in the American West in the 1970s, was initially blamed on UFO visitors, then on Satanists. Cattle and other animals were found with what appeared to be surgically precise incisions on their dead bodies. Organs such as the genitals, eyes, and tongue had been removed. Careful investigation showed that the parts removed from the animals by the "mutilators" were the same ones that natural predators, especially insects, preferred. Apparently most police did not know how to determine what was "surgically precise." The predators' work was not all that precise, although not violent.

As author Robert Hicks has pointed out, much of what appears to the general public to be a widespread incidence of crimes committed by Satanic cults is really only a collection of unsolved crimes, including malicious mischief by teenagers, or younger children. One example is tipping over gravestones, which is virtually never committed by Satanists. As Hicks shows, a small group of police, whom he calls "cult cops," have been instructed at seminars conducted by other cult cops (sometimes Fundamentalist Christians). The attendees then become "instant experts," conducting their own seminars for other police. The trouble with these "experts" is that they are predisposed to believe that Satanists are everywhere and everyone's activities are suspect. They operate from a "guilty until proven innocent" system, rather than placing the burden of proof upon the person who makes the charge, where it legally belongs. As a result, much of the fear and blame for crime is placed on largely imaginary "Satanists," who of course are never caught; this relieves the police of much of their investigative duty. Media hype about widespread Satanic cults, often fueled by Fundamentalists and aided by misled police, has resulted in a diffuse kind of Satanism hoax. Sociologists of religion have examined a number of the issues about Satanism that concern police. They have concluded that the number of Satanists is small, that they rarely do anything publicly that the police would notice, and that they *are* a religion. The number of child sacrifices/murders Satanists supposedly commit each year, according to some police "experts" is more than the total number of known homicides in the United States. The concept defied sense and data. These Satanic acts are still widely believed by the public and sought out by the news media, anxious for a sensational-sounding story.

Sources:

Carlson, Shawn and Gerald Larue, eds. *Satanism In America.* El Cerrito, CA: Gaia Press, 1989.

Hicks, Robert D. *In Pursuit of Satan: The Police and the Occult.* Buffalo, NY: Prometheus Books, 1991.

Kagan, Daniel and Ian Summers. *Mute Evidence.* New York: Bantam Books, 1984.

Passantino, Gretchen, Bob Passantino, and Jon Trott. "Satan's Sideshow." *Cornerstone* 18 no. 90 (1990): 23–28.

Richardson, James T., Joel Best and David G. Bromley, eds. *The Satanism Scare.* New York: Aldine De Gruyter, 1991.

Stratford, Lauren [Laurel Rose Willson]. *Satan's Underground.* Eugene, OR: Harvest House Publishers, 1988.

The Secret Instructions of the Jesuits

Almost all Roman Catholic sources say that the *Secret Instructions of the Jesuits* is a hoax. However, many other religious history experts say it is not. The origins of the *Instructions* are so obscure and so little hard investigation has been done on their history, that it is difficult to know whether or not they are authentic. Because of this obscurity, the signs point to a *hoax*, but they are not definitive.

The facts, as best determined at this time, are as follows. A book—written in Latin—appeared with the imprint "Notobrigae" (Cracow, Poland) and the date 1612. It was titled *Monita Privata Societatis Jesu* (*The Secret Instructions of the Society of Jesus*). The place of publication and the date (probably really 1614) are apparently false. Author Martin Harney states that the book was by Jerome Zahorowski, who was dismissed from the Jesuits in 1613. Harney does not give his source for this information, but other sources repeat it. Zahorowski was dismissed for "indecent behavior," but no details are given. It appears that his home town was Gozdziec, Poland. Although Zahorowski evidently tried to sue his order over his dismissal, he did not proceed with the suit.

The Bishop of Cracow, Peter Tylicki, published—after an investigation done in 1615—a statement that the book was by Zahorowski. A Bishop's Tribunal in 1616 condemned the book and it was placed on the index of books forbidden for Catholics to read in 1621. The first attempt at a written refutation appears to have been made by Forer in his *Anatomia* in 1634.

The Secret Instructions was more commonly known later as *Monita Secreta*. It was first translated into English in 1658. The first mention of the work is in a manuscript version (seventeenth century) appended to a copy of *Formulae Diversarum Provisionum*, (Venice, 1596) in the British Library.

It was stressed in older literature about the *Monita* that the very existence of such a book should be concealed from everyone, including lower level Jesuits. If the book were discovered, it was to be denied as authentic. This situation makes some of the denials of the book's authenticity suspect. After all, the Jesuits are *supposed to* deny the authenticity of the *Monita*, if they *are* authentic.

The book itself is largely a manual of how to make people, mostly women, feel guilty so that they give large sums of money to the church—especially to the Jesuits. The use of the confessional as a weapon in financial extortion is stressed. Also covered are other ways to achieve wealth or power for the order.

Some evidence offered against the authenticity of the *Monita* is weak, while other evidence is stronger. A stronger argument is that personal letters from leading Jesuits of the time (i.e., 1600) to the rulers of Europe, give advice that is the opposite of that in the *Monita*. Since these letters were not known to anyone other than the sender and recipient until hundreds of years after the first publication of the *Monita*, the so-called secret instructions it contains about how to curry influence and political power in various countries must be false. If it were not false, Jesuit leaders would have obeyed those secret instructions, instead of doing the opposite.

Another strong argument against authenticity is given by author Johannes Reiber. He compares the instructions in the *Monita* with what are now known to be *real* instructions given to the members of the Jesuits. These instructions are from internal Jesuit documents that existed all along, but were not open to the public. Only one of these will be given here, but Reiber goes through many others, citing chapter and verse of both sets of instructions. The example of what to do with widows (get money from them by pressuring them to leave it to the order in their wills, as the *Monita* says), is contrasted with *Constitutionum* pars VI, 2, 6 of the written Jesuit rules, dealing with the use of pressure to leave money to the order. It is stated that although a Jesuit can suggest to a person on his deathbed that he make a will, it is strictly forbidden for a Jesuit to either write that will or to even be present when it is written. This is spelled out in "Provincial Rule 28."

It appears that most evidence is on the side of those who claim that the *Monita* is a hoax. Nothing has been produced in favor of its authenticity except that they were written by a former Jesuit. They appear to be the work of a disgruntled former member who was looking for revenge upon his former order. The *Monita* forms a Catholic parallel with the *Protocols of the Elders of Zion* (*See* Protocols of the Elders of Zion, p. 87), which makes similar claims as to the real intentions of the Jews. Both are evidently hoaxes.

Sources:

Duhr, Bernhard. *Jesuiten-Fabeln*. Freiburg [Germany]: Herderische Verlagshandlung, 1892: 45–66.

Harney, Martin P. *The Jesuits in History: The Society of Jesus Through Four Centuries*. New York: The America Press, 1941: 464–465.

Reiber, Johannes B. *Monita Secreta. Die geheimen Instruktionen der Jesuiten verglichen mit den amtlichen Quellen des Ordens*. Augsburg [Germany]: Litterar Institut von Dr. R. Huttler, 1892.

The Secret Instructions of the Jesuits. New York: Truth Seeker Co., [c. 1910].

Secret Instructions of the Jesuits. Printed Verbatim from the London Copy of 1725. To which is Prefaced an Historical Essay; With an Appendix of Notes, by the Editor of The Protestant. Princeton, NJ: J. & T. Simpson, 1831.

The Shroud of Turin

Although still believed by many to be the burial cloth of Jesus, and thus the most important relic in all of Christendom, the so-called Holy Shroud has been subjected to several scientific tests and proven to be a Medieval hoax and forgery.

The cloth, a fourteen-foot sheet of linen seeming to bear the imprints of a crucified man, first appeared in the mid-fourteenth century at the town of Lirey in north-central France. It was in the possession of a soldier of fortune named Geoffroy de Charny, who was unable, or unwilling, to say how he acquired the fabulous "relic."

Such relics were legion. There had been some forty cloths alleged to be the Holy Shroud, together with vials of Jesus' tears and his mother's milk, countless pieces of the True Cross, thorns from the Crown of Thorns, and other macabre fakes (*See* Relic Hoaxes, p. 235).

Perhaps it was not surprising, therefore, that soon after the "shroud" appeared at Lirey, a scandal was uncovered. According to a later report to Pope Clement, dated 1389, the cloth was exhibited by the dean of a church at Lirey, "And further to attract the multitude so that money might cunningly be wrung from them, pretended miracles were worked, certain men being hired to represent themselves as healed at the moment of the exhibition of the Shroud." Eventually, a bishop "discovered the fraud and how the said cloth had been cunningly painted, the truth being attested by the artist who had painted it." As a consequence, Pope Clement judged the cloth to be merely a painted representation, and forbade it to be advertised as genuine.

Nevertheless, after a century of scandal and controversy, in 1453, Margaret, the granddaughter of Geoffroy de Charny, gained possession of the shroud, toured with it, and eventually sold it to the Duke of Savoy. Although some of the shroud's defenders like to portray Margaret as a pious woman who "gave" the shroud to the Duke, he "gave" her in return the price of a castle and the revenues of an estate. For her actions, Margaret was excommunicated—a fact that seemed scarcely to trouble her—and she died in 1460.

The Savoys and their successors—who later became the Italian monarchy—exhibited the cloth as the Holy Shroud and represented it as having magical protective powers. These appear to have been quite limited, unfortunately, for in 1532 the cloth had to be rescued from a fire that destroyed the chapel that housed it. A bit of molten silver from the shroud's

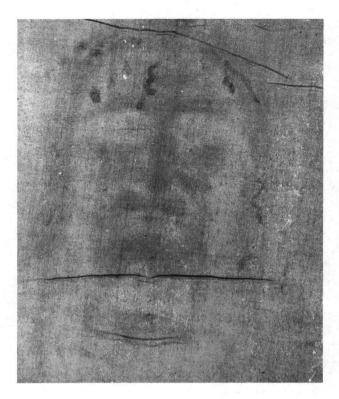

The Shroud of Turin face.

reliquary penetrated the cloth's many folds, resulting in the burn marks and subsequent patches that still flank the image.

The modern history of the shroud is characterized by a series of scientific tests, together with a number of pseudoscientific claims and speculations. For example, when the image was first photographed in 1898, it was discovered that its darks and lights were reversed. Proponents of the shroud's authenticity likened the image to a photographic *negative*, and portrayed it as a miraculous "photo" of Jesus. Actually, it is only approximately negative, since the hair and beard are in positive, and the quasi-negativity is easily duplicated by a simple artistic technique: taking a rubbing from a bas-relief.

When better photographs were made available in the 1930s, shroud enthusiasts like the French Catholic surgeon Pierre Barbet, began to insist that certain anatomical elements and realistic "blood" flows represented details beyond the knowledge and abilities of a Medieval forger. Skeptics countered that a footprint on the cloth was incompatible with the image of the leg that belonged to it; that the features were unnaturally elongated (like figures portrayed in French Gothic art!); that the hair fell as if the figure were upright, rather than recumbent; that the "blood" had failed to mat the hair; and that the flows were suspiciously picture-like

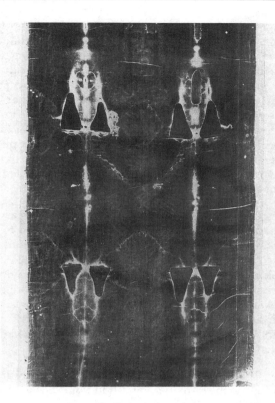

The Shroud of Turin.

and had remained *red*, unlike old blood that blackens over time.

The first physical tests of the shroud were carried out by an official, initially secret, commission in 1969–1976. The commission's existence was leaked to the press, denied by Turin church authorities, then finally admitted by them. They subsequently limited the availability of the commission's report, while freely circulating a *rebuttal*.

As one might expect from such actions, the commission's report was skeptical. Two experts questioned the provenance of the cloth and suggested it was an artistic work made by some imprinting technique (consistent with the rubbing method mentioned earlier). Two forensic serologists subjected "blood"-stained threads to extensive tests, but the "blood" failed all of them: standard preliminary tests, additional tests for hemoglobin, microscopic examination for blood corpuscles, and sophisticated instrumental analyses were performed. They reported the presence of reddish granules that would not even dissolve in the reagents, and another expert discovered what he believed were traces of paint.

A further examination of the cloth was carried out in 1978 by the Shroud of Turin Research Project (STURP). Unfortunately, STURP's leaders served on the executive council of the pro- authenticity Catholic Holy Shroud Guild, and many STURP scientists indicated their bias in favor of authenticity before ever examining the shroud. With one exception, STURP lacked essential expertise in identifying paint pigments or otherwise detecting art forgeries.

The exception was world-famous microanalyst Walter McCrone. He performed a "blind" microscopic study of samples taken from the shroud, finding significant amounts of the pigment red ocher (red iron oxide) on image areas, but not on off-image ones. He identified the "blood" as tempera paint containing both red ocher and another pigment, vermillion, and confirmed the identification by microchemical and instrumental analyses. Unfortunately, STURP refused to sanction McCrone's report for publication and held him to a "covenent not to disclose." After this expired, he published his reports, complete with color photomicrographs of the paint globules and pigment particles.

McCrone, who says he was "drummed out" of STURP, was replaced by two scientists, John Heller and Alan Adler, who soon claimed that McCrone's findings, as well as those of the commission scientists, were in error, and that they had "identified" the presence of blood on the shroud. Actually, neither Heller nor Adler was a forensic serologist, nor a pigment expert, raising the question of why they were selected to perform the analyses. Heller conceded that McCrone "had over two decades of experience with this kind of problem and a worldwide reputation. Adler and I, on the other hand, had never before tackled anything remotely like an artistic forgery."

Forensic analyst John F. Fischer reviewed Heller and Adler's claims and observed that none of their tests was specific for blood, that their approach—an attempt to add together individual aspects, such as the presence of iron and protein—was not a forensically acceptable means of identifying blood, and that similar results might be obtained from tempera paint. In a presentation to the International Association for Identification, (an organization of police officials and individuals engaged in forensic sciences, investigation, and scientific crime detection work) Fischer also observed that spectral analyses of the "blood" were fundamentally inconsistent with genuine blood.

Tests that were ultimately devastating to any claims of authenticity involved radiocarbon dating of small swatches cut from the shroud. Three laboratories—at Oxford, England, Zurich, Switzerland, and Arizona—used accelerator mass spectroscopy to perform the analyses, obtaining dates in impressively close agreement. The age span was circa A.D. 1260–

1390, the median age being consistent with the date of the forger's confession. Control tests run on a variety of swatches from ancient cloths of known dates underscored the accuracy of the radiocarbon results.

Based on the sheer amount of scientific effort expended on its behalf, the "shroud" might well be regarded as the greatest hoax in history. The deceptive power of this cloth—which never held a body—and which dates from some thirteen centuries after the death of Jesus continues. Shroud proponents are now attacking the carbon dating on a variety of grounds, some suggesting that radiant energy from Jesus' resurrection altered the carbon ratio and thus the apparent age of the cloth!

Joe Nickell

Sources:

Browne, Malcolm W. "How Carbon 14 Was Used to Fix Date of Shroud." *New York Times* (October 14, 1988): 10.

Damon, Paul, and others "Radiocarbon Dating of the Shroud of Turin." *Nature* 337 no. 16 (February 16, 1989): 611–15.

McCrone, Walter. "The Shroud of Turin: Blood or Artist's Pigment?" *Accounts of Chemical Research* 23 (March 1990): 77–83.

Nickell, Joe. *Inquest on the Shroud of Turin.* 2nd ed. Buffalo, NY: Prometheus Books, 1988.

Suro, Robert. "Church Says Shroud of Turin Isn't Authentic." *New York Times* (October 14, 1988): 1–6.

Wilson, Ian. *The Mysterious Shroud.* Garden City, NY: Doubleday, 1986.

Other Religion Hoaxes

The Blood Libel Hoax. The blood libel was a serious anti-semitic accusation. It is alleged that Jews kidnapped and killed Christian children in order to collect their blood for some ceremonial purpose. Supposed ceremonial uses for the blood range from it being mixed into the matzoh bread eaten at Passover, to rubbing the blood over the body. There was also the idea that the Jewish male's circumcision wound bled every month, like menstruation, and that the child's blood was a replacement for the lost blood. These accusations are ignorant, considering that blood sacrifices are expressly forbidden by the Torah.

During the Medieval and Renaissance period in European history, a number of blood libel charges were lodged against Jews and many were killed as a result. No proof that any Jew had actually killed any Christian child for its blood was ever offered. In fact, several extensive investigations on such charges were undertaken. In about 1240, Emperor Frederick II investigated and found that the whole blood libel idea was without any justification. Pope Innocent IV, in 1247, also pronounced the Jews innocent of the practice after an investigation. In 1759, Cardinal Gajanelli (later to be Pope Clement XIV), also found the blood libel idea false. None of these investigations stopped the popular idea that the Jews *did* steal Christian blood. The blood libel was a hoax and has never been substantiated in even a single case.

The Teachings of Carlos. In order to show how easy it was to make up a book of sayings that appeared to be wise, in 1988 the magician and exposer of fraudulent psychics James Randi produced a sixty-three-page booklet entitled *The Teachings of Carlos.* The sayings were supposedly "channeled" (accessed and expressed by someone who is convinced that the source is not their ordinary consciousness) through José Luis Alvarez from "Ascended Master" Carlos, who had passed to a higher plane of existence.

The text itself was a fair imitation of mystical wisdom, in the format of a question from "Seeker" and an answer from Carlos. For example:

Seeker: Where do we find perfect peace? Carlos: I will tell you. In the competitiveness of consciousness. Where there are people there's bound to be purity. With a person present, who can recognize the purity? Go to where there are many other people. They will all remind you of your decisions. All. It is the hunger called wisdom that means you have to continue doing it, forever. It is only beginning.

It is not clear how many people have been hoaxed by the booklet.

The Blood of St. Januarius. It is a "miracle" when three times a year the matter kept in a vial in Naples Cathedral—supposedly the blood of St. Januarius (died in 309 A.D.)—liquefies. In October of 1991, an Italian chemist named Luigi Garlaschelli announced that he duplicated the liquefaction of the "blood" using a phenomenon known as thixotropy. He mixed several simple chemicals, among them ferric chloride and sodium choride, which were easily obtainable at the time the blood was first annually exhibited in the eleventh century. While no analysis of the material inside the vial was allowed at the cathedral, the chemicals of Dr. Garlaschelli *looked* like blood, solidified like a blood clot, and liquefied like the material in the vial. Without an analysis of the material in the cathedral's vial it is still unknown whether the "miracle" was duplicated by chemical means. It is highly likely that this is the explanation for what has occurred. If the materials in the vial are *not* blood (or not the blood of St. Januarius,

See Relic Hoaxes, p. 235), then a hoax has been perpetrated.

George Washington's Prayer. Popular misconception exists about the religious beliefs of the Founding Fathers of the United States. Thomas Jefferson, George Washington, Benjamin Franklin, Thomas Paine, and James Madison were not Christians, but deists. Part of the misinformation about Washington's religious beliefs can be traced to a hoax. The hoax involved a supposed prayer of Washington's inscribed upon a plaque mounted next to Washington's former pew (while he was president) at St. Paul's Chapel in Washington, D.C. The date of the prayer is not indicated.

In fact, the prayer was manufactured from part of the text of a circular letter that Washington addressed to the governors of the thirteen states when he disbanded the army in 1783. The letter was addressed to the governors and not to God. By removing the opening words and substituting "divine language," the letter was fashioned into a prayer. As author Sherman Wakefield showed, about thirty-three percent of the "prayer" consisted of modifications to Washington's letter. Actually, Washington's original letter was written by his aide, David Cobb, although it probably contained Washington's sentiments.

Washington occasionally attended services at Christ Episcopal Church in Alexandria, Virginia before becoming president. He always refused to take communion and left the church before the communion service. When the clergyman in charge approached Washington about this, Washington responded by not attending church on Sundays since that was when communion was offered.

Hell in Siberia. In this hoax a 1980s report, widely believed by Fundamentalists, was released stating that scientists drilling through the earth in Siberia had literally drilled into Hell. Though Fundamentalists said the story came from a scientific journal, it turned out to be from a Finnish missionary newsletter. The newsletter picked the story up from a reader's letter to a Helsinki newspaper. Author Rich Buhler traced it back to a Christian newsletter from California. The story was that by lowering microphones down into the drill hole, which went nine miles into the earth, human voices wailing and screaming in torment could be heard. The temperature supposedly registered 2,000 degrees, but why the microphones didn't melt is not addressed. The story had miners running away in fright. There is not a grain of truth to the story.

Deathbed Conversions of Unbelievers. This hoax is more of a wish or hope than a fact, but false stories have been spread to make the hoax appear to have substance. One story said that many famous unbelievers, including Voltaire, Thomas Paine, Robert G. Ingersoll, Charles Bradlaugh, and Charles Darwin, all converted to Christianity on their deathbeds. Fortunately, there are eyewitness accounts of the deathbeds of Paine, Ingersoll, and Voltaire. None of them converted. In fact, there is no known case of an atheist or other non-believer converting on his or her deathbed. The so-called deathbed conversions did not occur.

A more serious charge was made in the case of Charles Darwin. It is claimed that he converted back to Christianity (he had once thought of becoming a clergyman) and expressed great regret for having come up with the Theory of Evolution (*See* Scientific Creationism, p. 263). According to author Pat Sloan, both of these stories are false. Darwin became less religious as he aged. He never regretted his scientific views and did not change them.

Joseph of Jerusalem. The Gospel of Joseph of Jerusalem is only one of many fake manuscripts purporting to be a missing part of the Bible. In 1927, Luigi Moccia, a municipal clerk from Cerignola, Italy, revealed to the world that he had a parchment manuscript of the Gospel of Joseph. The manuscript came from an old pilgrim, who just returned from Jerusalem. The original manuscript had allegedly been rescued by Helen, the mother of Constantine, and then was sent to the library at Alexandria. It was rescued from the burning library in 640 A.D. and disappeared until the pilgrim obtained it, although he would not reveal where he got it.

The manuscript is particularly notable as it says in its preface, "Fearful that this writing may be modified and destroyed by some of our opposers, I have left copies to our excellent brothers: Matthew of Capernium, Mark of Jerusalem, Luke of Antioch and John of Thesda." Therefore, the work purports to be a Fifth Gospel. As Goodspeed pointed out, the work is a definite fake. The language of the manuscript is Renaissance Greek, not ancient Greek. The parchment is also too modern. The text is a running together of the first four Gospels, with a few minor additions. The only conclusion is that the whole work is a hoax.

Sources:

Alvarez, José Luis [James Randi]. *The Teachings of Carlos.* [N. P.]: the author, 1988.

Buhler, Rich. "Scientists Discover Hell in Siberia." *Christianity Today* 34 no. 10 (July 16, 1990): 28–29.

Dundes, Alan, ed. *The Blood Libel Legend: A Casebook in Anti-Semitic Folklore.* Madison, WI: University of Wisconsin Press, 1991.

Garlaschelli, Luigi, Franco Ramaccini, and Sergio Della Sala. "Working Bloody Miracles." *Nature* 353 (October 10, 1991): 507.

Sloan, Pat. "Demythologizing Darwin." *The Humanist* (London), (April 1965): 106–10.

———. "The Myth of Darwin's Conversion." *The Humanist* (London), (March 1960): 70–72.

Stein, Gordon. "Deathbeds of Unbelievers." In *Encyclopedia of Unbelief.* Buffalo, NY: Prometheus Books, 1985: 129–31.

Wakefield, Sherman D. "Washington's Prayer." *Progressive World* 7 no. 6 (June 1953): 331–32.

Science Hoaxes

Fraud charges in science have been made against notable scientists such as Mendel, Galileo, Dalton, Ptolemy, and Newton. In most of these cases, the scientist was charged with some sort of "data smoothing," as results looked too good to be true. Still, this is a long way from a charge of fabricating their results. The charge of "hoax" is not appropriate in data-smoothing cases. Perhaps the poor knowledge of statistics that early scientists had (the field of statistics had not yet developed formally) was responsible for what appears to be—at worst—an inappropriate discarding of data outside a standard deviation or two from the mean. It seems reasonable to assume that this "smoothing" was not done to intentionally deceive.

An Account of a Meeting With Denizens of Another World

Rarely, a hoax becomes a "double" hoax, a hoax upon a hoax, or in the case of the book *An Account of a Meeting With Denizens of Another World*, (1871), a double hoax has deliberately been designed. This book purports to be the first printing (1979) of an 1871 Victorian Age manuscript. The Victorian manuscript, by William Robert Loosley, tells of an encounter he had with what would now be called extraterrestrials in High Wycombe, Buckinghamshire, England on October 3, 1871.

The book that first published the manuscript was edited and had a commentary by David Langford. It contained a photograph of Loosley with his wife and five children (all identified by name and year of birth). There is also a copy of a check from Lord Beaconsfield to Loosley, a photograph of the exterior of Loosley's furniture store in High Wycombe, and a photograph of Loosley's grave in Wycombe Cemetery. The dust jacket of the book has a close-up photograph of Loosley.

All of this is a hoax. The manuscript was written in the *1970s by David Langford*, not the 1870s by William Robert Loosley. Loosley was a *real* ancestor of Langford's wife. Langford admits all of this in his 1988 article in the *New Scientist*. He says that the project was actually made slightly less convincing as a hoax by a change of editors at the publishing company. The original plan was to include facsimiles of several pages of the original 1871 manuscript. The new editor viewed the book as a good science fiction *novel* and decided that the facsimiles were not needed. Unfortunately, the book does not mention anywhere that it is a novel or that Langford is the real author.

Although the book did not sell well, according to Langford publication set off a series of "Amazing UFO Proof" stories in sensationalistic newspapers and magazines. Nobody asked to look at the original manuscript. Langford says his "finest hour" came when he was attacked in print for "the excessive caution and skepticism of my commentary on Loosley's narrative." He confesses that "It is mildly depressing to have contributed another snippet of disinformation to the already over-large folklore, without even the compensation of getting rich. Apologies to all, including my bank manager."

Sources:

Langford, David. "Myths in the Making." *New Scientist* (May 26, 1988): 78.

Loosley, William Robert [David Langford]. *An Account of a Meeting With Denizens of Another World*. Newton Abbot, England: David & Charles, 1979. American edition: New York: St. Martin's Press, 1980.

Bigfoot Hoaxes

The existence of a large, hairy bipedal primate—known variously as Bigfoot, Sasquatch, the Yeti, Alma, the Abominable Snowman, or the Wildman—remains an unsolved mystery. Bigfoot reports have come from all over the United States and other countries. In the

United States, the description of what has been seen or found is fairly consistent. Usually, a visual sighting reports a seven- or eight-foot-tall creature, that walks upright on two feet. It is usually reported to have brownish-red fur (sometimes tan or black) and a foul odor. It is quite heavy, leaving deep, large footprints. There are reports of footprints—and plaster casts made from them—as well as hair samples, droppings ("scats"), recordings of vocalizations, and even a few films. Abroad, there are supposed scalps and hands of yetis, preserved in monasteries in Tibet. There are no skulls or skeletons.

All reports of such sightings are not hoaxes, quite the contrary. Many of these sightings are probably *not* hoaxes. However, as with UFOs (*See* UFO Hoaxes, p. 267), a number of sightings are definitely hoaxes. Fraudulent sightings muddy the waters for legitimate sightings, and they form an identifiable sub-group that does not irreparably damage the validity of the other sightings. Certainly some sightings not identified here as hoaxes may *be* hoaxes, but evidence about them is far from clear. What will be treated here are those bigfoot reports that can definitely be identified as hoaxes.

Footprints have been the most common evidence for bigfoot. In 1982, Rant Mullens, age eighty-six admitted that he had been making hoax bigfoot footprints in the Pacific Northwest for fifty years, using bigfoot "feet" carved from wood. A foot carved from wood, even if worn by a heavy man as a shoe, will not leave impressions on ground—snow is another matter—that are either deep enough or three-dimensional enough. A number of bigfoot authorities have said that they can recognize a footprint made by a carved piece of wood without any trouble. The plaster casts of footprints show three-dimensionality.

In 1978 or 1979, a pair of boots was found in Stone County, Arkansas that had pieces of rubber tire cut in the shape of large feet, attached to the soles. Again, experts said these would not fool them for long.

The supposed yeti scalp from the Tibetan monastery was borrowed for analysis by Edmund Hillary after much pleading with the Lamas. It was virtually a sacred relic to them. It was determined that the "scalp" was the shoulder skin and fur of a member of the rare goat antelope species known as serow.

On May 2, 1976, four witnesses said that they saw "a large hairy ape-like animal" carry off a twenty-three-year-old blonde woman (variously identified as Sherie Darvell, Cherie Darvell, and Sherry Nelson) from woods outside Eureka, California. The animal was said to be "smelly." The woman was a part of a television crew attempting to get film of bigfoot. This would be the first recorded abduction of a human

woman by a bigfoot, if true. The police began a search. Two days later she turned up outside a resort five miles from the site of her supposed abduction; the sheriff was not amused. He said that the woman was in good shape, did not smell bad, and was only missing a shoe. In response to reporters' questions, all the woman did was scream, according to newspaper reports. There was no follow-up article, so it is assumed the whole thing was a hoax staged for the cameras.

On May 24, 1975, the Superintendent of Police for Dibrugarh district in Assam, India announced that tribesmen in the area had captured a pair of "wildmen"—a male and a female. They were being shipped to the district headquarters at Tezu. The report apparently came from the Doom Dooma police station. Officers there said that their information came from reports out of Chowkhani, about fifty miles away. The Doom Dooma police, upon further checking were unable to find any confirmation for this story at all. It appears to have been a hoax.

The "Minnesota Iceman" was supposedly a bigfoot who was preserved in a block of ice. The Iceman was exhibited for years in a refrigerated case at small carnivals around the country. The Iceman would not be that significant—given the highly dubious nature of most carnival exhibits—except for the fact that word of the Iceman reached Bernard Heuvelmans, a biologist who is considered the father of cryptozoology—the study of unknown animals. He and biologist Ivan Sanderson visited the Iceman and spent two days examining the body through the ice. Heuvelmans—not an easy man to fool on a matter such as this—came away convinced that the Iceman was an authentic biological specimen, possibly a Neanderthal Man. John Napier, a primatologist, looked at the sketches and notes Heuvelmans made and concluded that, biologically, the Iceman was an impossible specimen. It was neither a bigfoot nor a Neanderthal.

The story that Iceman owner Frank Hansen gave about where he got the Iceman and why it appeared to have been shot through the eye also did not hold up. Several different stories were told with variant details. Gene Emery, science reporter for the *Providence* [RI] *Journal*, found that Howard Ball, a modelmaker for Disney Studios, confessed to his wife (widowed when Emery interviewed her) that he had made the Iceman at his studio in California. Hansen finally admitted to Emery that Ball had made an Iceman figure for him. It appears that the Iceman is a hoax, at least if the testimony of Mrs. Ball and Hansen can be believed.

"Jacko" was the name given to a small bigfoot that was supposedly captured in 1884 in British Columbia, Canada. The creature was four feet seven inches tall and weighed 127 pounds. Jacko might have been a chimpanzee, but clearly did not belong in the woods of Canada. In 1884, captive chimps were quite rare. The story was that Jacko was being held in the local jail. He was then to be sent in a cage by train to eastern Canada, but nothing further was ever reported about him. However, bigfoot investigator John Green found an article from another newspaper (the *Mainland Guardian* of July 9, 1884), that points out that the entire story—including the part that said that Jacko could be viewed at the Yale, British Columbia jail—was a complete hoax. The jailer there was particularly annoyed at having to fend off all the people who came to see the non-existent Jacko. Apparently the originator of the hoax was a reporter for the newspaper that ran the original story (the *Daily British Colonist* of July 4, 1884).

In September of 1976, four youths admitted that they had taken turns dressing up to resemble bigfoot and had made bigfoot "tracks" around Cashton, Wisconsin, using wooden attachments on their shoes. This hoax was complicated because at the same time and place other reports of bigfoot *not* produced by these hoaxers were made.

A man in a gorilla suit in Mission, British Columbia, perpetrated a bigfoot hoax on May 15, 1977, but the details are not clear. The suit was a rather poor imitation of what a bigfoot has been reported to look like.

Perhaps the most famous bigfoot report that has been called a hoax by many is the Roger Patterson film of a female bigfoot. This twelve-second, eight-mm film was made on October 20, 1967 near Bluff Creek in northern California. Patterson, on horseback, was riding through the deep woods, more than twenty-five miles from the nearest road. As he rounded a corner of the trail, he saw a female bigfoot with pendulous breasts. He leaped from his horse, got his movie camera from his saddlebags, and managed to take thirty feet of film before the creature disappeared into the woods. The film has been analyzed by all sorts of "experts." Their opinions range from "an obvious fake" to "definitely *not* a man in a monkey suit." Although one would think that a movie of a bigfoot in the woods would serve as one of the strongest pieces of evidence for bigfoot, the film has polarized its viewers into two camps, the hoaxers and the non-hoaxers. At this point in time, no conclusion can be firmly made about the Patterson film.

One peculiar scarcely reported incident that occurred in 1932 and resulted in tragic consequences was the killing of a "bigfoot" in upstate New York. A bigfoot was sighted in Hamilton County and a group of State Police and Conservation Officers were told that it was seen in the vicinity of an abandoned lumber camp. They formed a group, went to the camp, and spotted the bigfoot inside an old cabin. They called for it to come out, although it is unclear why they thought it would understand human language. The bigfoot jumped through a window of the cabin and ran away. It was spotted hiding behind a pile of lumber and ordered to come out, to which it responded—in English—"Leave me alone." The bigfoot then fired a shotgun blast at one of the policemen, wounding him. The police opened fire, killing the bigfoot. When the body was carefully examined, it was a 5' 6" black man, weighing about 160 pounds. He was wrapped almost completely in several layers of untanned bear and deer skins, including his feet. It was the layers of wrapping on the feet that gave the big footprint and that allowed the man to run quickly over the deep snow. The body was never identified, despite much effort, and was eventually buried in a pauper's grave.

Sources:

Bartholomew, Paul and Bob Bartholomew, William Brann, and Bruce Hallenbeck. *Monsters of the Northwoods: An In-Depth Investigation of Bigfoot in New York and Vermont.* [N.P.]: The Authors, 1992.

Bord, Janet and Colin. *The Bigfoot Casebook.* Harrisburg, PA: Stackpole Books, 1982.

———. *The Evidence for Bigfoot and Other Man-Beasts.* Wellingborough, UK: Aquarian Press, 1984.

Emery, C. Eugene, Jr. "News and Comment: Sasquatch-sicle: The Monster, the Model and the Myth." *Skeptical Inquirer* 6 no. 2 (Winter 1981–82): 2–4.

Green, John and Sabina W. Sanderson. "Alas, Poor Jacko." *Pursuit* 8 no. 1 (January 1975): 18–19.

Napier, John. *Bigfoot: The Yeti and Sasquatch in Myth and Reality.* New York: E. P. Dutton, 1973.

Sanderson, Ivan T. *Abominable Snowmen: Legend Come to Life.* Philadelphia: Chilton Company, 1961.

———. "The Missing Link." *Argosy* (May 1969): 23–31.

The Case of the Midwife Toad

Some scientific disputes lead to tragic consequences. One such dispute was the "Case of the Midwife Toad," as Arthur Koestler has titled his book about this case. In this instance, the accusation of fraud—perhaps unjustly—led to a suicidal tragedy.

The European midwife toad (*Alytes obstetricians*) lays its eggs on land. The eggs are sticky, and adhere to the male toad, who carries them until they hatch. Other toads that spawn in the water do not have sticky eggs. However, water-spawning male toads often have trouble mating with the wet, slippery females. Consequently the males develop a spiny black area on their forelimbs (called a nuptial pad), that helps them grasp the female during mating. Toads that mate on land do not need these pads and do not develop them. Researchers have wondered what would happen if the midwife toad was induced to spawn in water. Would subsequent generations—also raised in water—eventually develop nuptial pads? The scientist Paul Kammerer at the University of Vienna decided to find out. He had several generations of midwife toads mate in the water. Sure Some of the males developed nuptial pads. By the fifth generation, he claimed that all of the males had the pads. He preserved several male toads with the black pads, and published his results. He explained his results as a case of atavism, or reversion to an ancestral condition. Kammerer thought that this was evidence for the inheritance of acquired characteristics, but not proof that this could occur.

A swift response came from those who thought that Kammerer's results were suspect. Author William Bateson actually observed one of the preserved specimens that Kammerer brought with him to England. Bateson noted that the black "patch" did not have raised rough areas and it was located on the *palms* of the toad—not on the back of the front feet—where it would not be useful in holding the female from behind. When questioned by Bateson at the demonstration, Kammerer said that the pads *should* be on the palms. Also, Bateson's request of Hans Przibram—Kammerer's colleague at Vienna—for microscope slides of the pad region was refused.

Subsequent analysis of the blackened area of the supposed nuptial pad was made by G. Kingsley Noble. Noble and Przibram made *independent* gross and microscopic examinations of Kammerer's preserved pads and both concluded that the black in the "pad" was India ink. They chemically analyzed the pigment for confirmation.

The two investigators at first agreed to publish a joint paper on their findings, but they later disagreed and published separately. The disagreement was over whether the India ink was the *cause* of the pad or whether it was injected later into a pad already developed. Przibram said it had been injected later, while Noble thought it was the cause of the pad. A month after they published their results, Kammerer shot himself to death. He left a note for Przibram stating that an unknown person must have injected the ink.

The most influential work on the midwife toad controversy is Arthur Koestler's *The Case of the Midwife Toad*. This book, written by a layman, makes a case that Kammerer was an innocent dupe of someone else who, perhaps innocuously, injected ink into the pads with the aim of making them more visible.

In a letter Kammerer wrote a few days before his death he states that after reading Noble's article about the India ink, he reexamined his specimen in question and confirmed Noble's observations, that the "pads" resulted from the injected ink. In addition, he found India ink in several other specimens' pads. Writer Arthur Koestler, in contrast, would persuade his readers that the specimen demonstrated in England was genuine, with no India ink.

In Kammerer's estimation a more definitive experiment that could demonstrate the inheritance of acquired characteristics, was the one he performed later on the sea squirt, *Ciona*. He cut off the syphons—funnel-like organs that the animals use to feed—of several generations of squirts. Kammerer claimed that the syphons regrew longer than normal. Others, such as H. Munro Fox, failed to replicate his results.

Koestler's book favors evidence that exonerates Kammerer, while downplaying or ignoring evidence against him. Author Lester Aronson points this favoritism out in his article, giving many examples. One is that Koestler repeatedly charges that the scientific community has been irresponsible in not trying to repeat Kammerer's experiments. This charge is false, as H. Munro Fox tried to repeat some of Kammerer's work with *Ciona*, but was unsuccessful. Koestler also fails to state how the syphon experiment is different from Wiseman's attempt to see if acquired characteristics were inherited by cutting off the tails of mice for many generations. The next generation of mice was always born with tails. Kammerer attempts to distinguish between the mouse tail experiment and the syphon experiment, but his distinction is without merit.

Koestler's own hidden agenda may be that if Kammerer was right, then Lamark's idea that acquired characteristics can be inherited is strengthened. The Lamarkian idea supports to many ideas that foster parapsychology's theoretical basis. Kammerer was quite interested in the study of coincidences, as was Koestler. The acquired characteristics supports Jungian psychology, which also favors parapsychological ideas. Koestler left a great deal of money in his will to set up an endowed chair in parapsychology—now in operation at the University of Edinburgh. This theory is speculation as to Koestler's possible motive in distorting what happened in the case of Kammerer.

It is not known whether Kammerer injected the India ink, although this seems the most likely possibility. Why he might have done it is also unknown, but it may be that he was trying to bolster his philosophical ideas, even if the scientific evidence would not support them. Alternatively, one of his students may have acted without Kammerer's knowledge or approval.

Sources:

Aronson, Lester R. "The Case of *The Case of the Midwife Toad.*" *Behavior Genetics* 5 no. 2 (1975): 115–1025.

Bateson, William. "Dr. Kammerer's Alytes." *Nature* 111 (1923): 738–39.

Fox, H. Munro. "Note on Kammerer's Experiments with *Ciona* Concerning the Inheritance of an Acquired Character." *Journal of Genetics* 14 (1924): 89–91.

Koestler, Arthur. *The Case of the Midwife Toad.* New York: Random House, 1971.

Przibram, Hans. "The Nuptial Pad of Kammerer's Water-Bred Alytes." *Nature* 119 (1926): 635–36.

Crop Circle Hoaxes

Crop circles appear to be a relatively new phenomenon; the first modern crop circles were found in the British fields of Wiltshire in 1980. They have increased in frequency since then, with more than 300 being found in 1991 alone. In addition, crop circles have now been found in Canada, the United States, Japan and Australia, as well as in Germany.

A crop circle is usually a circular area of swirled, flattened crops, thirty-sixty feet across, sometimes more. Often smaller circles or lines radiating from the main circle or circles are found. The crops forming the circle are swept or combed down in either a clockwise or counter-clockwise direction, with stems unbroken. No signs of footprints, automobile, or tractor tracks leading into the circles are found. They are almost always made at night and discovered in daylight.

It should be mentioned that there were occasional anecdotal stories of crop circles found in England between 1930 and 1980. However, no photographs exist and they were not a common phenomenon. The "Mowing Devil" pamphlet of 1678 *may* be an early instance of a crop circle. From the description and picture of the "circle" on the cover of the pamphlet, it is possible that a crop circle is being described, although not accurately by today's standards. For example, the pamphlet says that the oats were "cut down," not bent down. Perhaps the circle was not observed closely or perhaps they *were* cut down. The effect is attributed to the devil—understandable for the time period. Author G. T. Meaden has made a compelling, but unsubstantiated suggestion, that many of the stone circles and round burial mounds of ancient England were built on the sites of former crop circles.

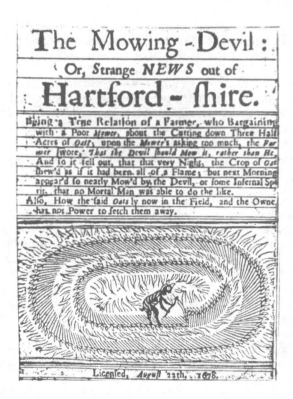

The "Mowing Devil" pamphlet of 1678.

While not *all*—or even most—crop circles are hoaxes, some certainly are. Since the origin of crop circles is presently unknown, it is impossible to say what percentage of the hundreds observed have been hoaxes. According to some crop circle experts—who may be biased in favor of authenticity—only a small percentage of crop circles are hoaxes. According to rumor, a hoaxed crop circle can be revealed by the lack of swirled crops in it. However, this is invalid. The British Broadcasting Corporation (BBC) film made of a tug-of-war team of six men hired to make a crop circle using only rope and a stake, clearly shows this. The team succeeded—including the swirled grass—in less than an hour. It seems that carefully trampled *green* crops do not break in the stem region, but simply press down in a swirled pattern when trampled with small footsteps. One of the major mysteries of crop circles turns out not to be a mystery at all.

Explanations offered for crop circles include that they are: 1) hoaxes by humans, 2) small whirlwinds, 3) UFO landing site marks, 4) plasma energy vortexes, and 5) an entirely new kind of energy with intelligence. Since no one has been able to make more than a few conclusive cases for any of these theories, there is no definitive explanation. Witnesses have claimed to have seen the formation of a crop circle from a distance. In some cases, a glowing ball of light was seen; in others, a loud humming noise was heard. Some have claimed to have seen much dust and debris swirling through the area immediately after the circle was formed, indicating a wind of some sort. Others have not noted this.

In the case of the crop circle found in Germany in the summer of 1991, the presence of a ouija board in the center of the circle has led most observers to conclude that it was man-made. This is suggested by the very presence of the ouija board, but it is possible that someone left a ouija board in the center of a naturally or supernaturally formed crop circle.

In August of 1991, a crop circle in the form of a Mandelbrot set—a complex mathematical design found in fractal mathematics— was discovered in a field near Cambridge, England. Suspicion immediately turned to hoaxers from the mathematics department of Cambridge University. However, as was pointed out in a week-long exchange of letters in the *New Scientist*, this assumption is flawed logically in that an alien intelligence could well use a pure mathematical function as a means of attempted communication, much as the United States decorated the space probe with a plaque showing a circle and the pi relationship to it. A writer also provided a method for easily constructing a Mandelbrot set (thought to be difficult to draw), using only a rope and stake.

In September of 1991, two men in their sixties, David Chorley and Doug Bower, claimed to be the hoaxers responsible for many of the British crop circles. Although the two men demonstrated that they could make a crop circle that could fool at least one expert, their claims soon came under scrutiny. They could not have been responsible for circles found in other countries of the world, including some in Canada found the day they confessed. It seemed unlikely that they could have made more than a few of the hundreds of circles found. It is possible that dozens of teams of hoaxers are at work, jointly and independently responsible for producing all of the crop circles. Somehow this seems unlikely. The mystery of the crop circles has yet to be solved.

Sources:

Chorost, Michael. *Circles of Note: A Reader's Guide to the Crop Circle Phenomenon.* San Antonio, TX: Dennis Stacey, [c. 1991].

Delgado, Pat and Colin Andrews. *Circular Evidence: A Detailed Investigation of the Flattened Swirled Crops Phenomenon.* Grand Rapids, MI: Phanes Press, 1989.

Fuller, Paul and Jenny Randles. *Controversy of the Circles.* London: BUFORA, [c. 1989].

Meaden, G. Terence. *The Goddess of the Stones.* London: Souvenir Press, 1991.

Noyes, Ralph, ed. *The Crop Circle Enigma.* Bath, UK: Gateway Books, 1990.

Skinner, Bob, and others "The Crop Circle Phenomenon." *Fortean Times* 90 no. 53 (Winter 1989): 32–57.

Darsee, Summerlin, and Research Fraud

Cases of true fraud in science—as opposed to honest experimental error or misinterpretation of results—are fairly rare. When fraud is uncovered, however, it often makes headlines. In addition, because science is self-policing and cumulative—with previous results built upon by later work—any fraud that goes undetected for long may have disastrous results when finally revealed. If a published paper is found to have been fraudulent, it has to be retracted publicly and all other research inspired by it must be redone.

With this in mind, the separate scientific fraud executed by William T. Summerlin and John Roland Darsee did considerable damage to biomedical research at the time. Several other fraudulent researchers added to the confusion in the 1970s and 1980s.

Darsee was a brilliant young physician, who was working at one of the hospitals affiliated with Harvard Medical School in Boston in 1981. He was known for his prodigious output of research papers. Although he obviously worked quite hard, many people wondered how he could be so productive with research that by its very nature was slow and meticulous. Darsee had received his M.D. from Indiana University. He was working on a determination of the viability of heart muscle after a heart attack. He found that much of the injured muscle could be restored to function.

One evening in May of 1981, Darsee was secretly observed by his suspicious lab coworkers forging raw data for an experiment that he was about to submit for publication. When asked by his supervisor for the raw data, he went into a laboratory and proceeded to create it. When confronted he confessed, but claimed that this was the only data he had ever faked. Darsee claimed that he had thrown away the original raw data accidentally. His colleagues were still suspicious, however. Darsee was stripped of his Harvard appointment, but was still allowed to continue working in the laboratory. Those who did not yet know of Darsee's fakery were informed of it.

After five uneventful months the National Institutes of Health (NIH) investigators (some funding had come from the NIH) began to suspect that the fraud might have been more widespread. Darsee had continued to contribute abstracts and papers after his fraud was discovered. In early December, a blue ribbon panel was formed at Harvard to look into the matter. It turned out that Darsee could not produce any raw data for studies he conducted after the supervision of his work was relaxed—about one year after he had arrived at the laboratory.

The blue ribbon panel's report absolved Harvard of any blame for letting Darsee continue his research in the lab for six months after his initial fraud was discovered. Two studies conducted during that six-month period contained data that were "highly suspect." Darsee was forced to resign from the Sloan laboratory.

Before he had gone to Harvard (but after medical school), Darsee was at Emory University. After Darsee's resignation, Emory opened an investigation of his work. In his five years there, he had authored ten papers and forty-five abstracts. The investigation showed that most of them were suspect and they were to be retracted. Two of the ten papers were allowed to stand, and only two of the forty-five abstracts. Darsee, had apparently put the names of Emory scientists on his abstracts as coauthors, without their knowledge. Apparently none of these "coauthors" objected, if they found out at all.

William T. Summerlin worked for Robert A. Good at the Sloan-Kettering Institute for Cancer Research in New York City in 1974. He had started with Good in 1971 while at the University of Minnesota. Summerlin had told journalists at a meeting of science writers that "after human skin is maintained in organ culture for four to six weeks, it becomes universally transplantable without rejection." It looked as if the major obstacle to transplantation had been overcome. Much of Summerlin's work involved the transplantation of rabbit corneas. His coworkers were suspicious of the supposedly transplanted rabbits, whose eyes looked perfect.

Summerlin produced two white mice with black patches on their skin that Summerlin told Good were areas of skin transplanted from black-skinned mice. Summerlin had inked the black patches on the mice with a felt-tip pen. A lab assistant noticed the fakery later and reported it to his superiors. Summerlin was immediately suspended from the laboratory. An investigation was set up by the president of Sloan-Kettering, Dr. Lewis Thomas. The investigating committee decided to terminate Dr. Summerlin's relationship with Sloan-Kettering. He was given a period of medical leave, with pay, so that he could recover from what was termed "exhaustion." Dr. Good was cleared of any role in the fraud. Summerlin claimed that he was forced to fraud because of the intense pressure on him to produce results that had been publicly announced already.

Yale University's College of Medicine was briefly marred by a scandal that involved faking research data by Vijay Soman, a researcher from India. Soman was working in the laboratory of scientist Philip Felig in 1979. Soman had "smoothed" the curve of many patients' results in a study of the insulin-binding ability of patients with anorexia nervosa. Perhaps worse, he had lifted phases and equations from a paper submitted by other scientists to Felig for review by the *New England Journal of Medicine*. A committee recommended Soman be fired and he returned to India.

Elias Alsabti, a Jordanian whose background is quite confusing due to his different tellings of it, was implicated in a serious case of scientific fraud in 1980. He was accused of pirating other scientists' published papers, changing the title and the authors, and submitting the papers to obscure foreign journals, where they were accepted for publication. He was forced to quit several positions as his research incompetence became clear to his supervisors. His present location is not known, but it is thought that he has left the United States.

John Long, at the Massachusetts General Hospital in Boston, was accused of faking his data. His research was on Hodgkin's disease, and he had supposedly established a line of cells from patients with the disease that was able to grow in tissue culture. Although the raw data was offered to doubters in a notebook, the data itself was entered fraudulently. When confronted with the apparently fake data in 1980, Long admitted creating it. Of his four lines of cultured cells, three turned out to be from the same individual, who did not have Hodgkin's disease. The fourth cell line was from a monkey. Although it is not known if the contamination was deliberate, Long should have been aware of it. Long resigned and took an unrelated job in another city.

Mark Spector was a different kind of hoaxer. He fabricated college degrees that he did not have and almost earned a doctorate at Cornell in 1981. He was known for his "golden hands" in the laboratory, because only he could get experiments to work. This should have aroused suspicion, but it did not for quite a while. His research was in the purification of a type of ATPase, the enzyme that pumps ions out of cells, converting ATP to ADP in the process. This is an important reaction in cellular metabolism and Spector apparently showed that cancer cells could not do the process well. His subsequent work provided a basis for a unified theory of cancer causation. Then, it was discovered that some of the radioactive bands that identified the separated-out enzymes were due to radioactive iodine that had been added to the mixture. No iodine should have been present, only radioactive phosphorous. When Spector's notebooks were inspected for raw data, they were full of data that had been written in, without printouts from the electronic equipment that was analyzing the samples. Spector did not receive his Ph.D., and his fraudulent B.A. and M.S. degrees were also revealed. He was dismissed from Cornell.

Sources:

Broad, William J. "Harvard Delays in Reporting Fraud." *Science* 215 (1982): 478–82.

———. "Report Absolves Harvard in Case of Fakery." *Science* 215 (1982): 874–76.

Broad, William and Nicholas Wade. *Betrayers of the Truth: Fraud and Deceit in the Halls of Science.* New York: Touchstone/Simon & Schuster, 1982.

Culliton, Barbara. "The Sloan-Kettering Affair: A Story Without a Hero." *Science* 184 (1974): 644–50.

Hixson, Joseph. *The Patchwork Mouse.* New York: Doubleday, 1976.

U.S. House of Representatives, 97th Congress. *Fraud in Biomedical Research.* Hearings before the Subcomitee on Investigations and Oversight of the Committee on Science and Technology, March 31–April 1, 1981. Washington, DC: United States Government Printing Office, 81: 14950.

The Great Moon Hoax

On August 21, 1835, a small notice appeared on page two of the New York *Sun* newspaper, then in its second year of publication. The item said "We have just learnt from an eminent publisher in this city [Edinburgh] that Sir John Hershel, at the Cape of Good Hope, has made some astronomical discoveries of the most wonderful description, by means of an immense telescope of an entirely new principle." Nothing more was heard of this until August 25. On that day, a page one story, entitled "Great Astronomical Discoveries" and extracted from the *Edinburgh Journal of Science* supplement, was published.

The first article was confined to a description of Hershel's new telescope. The article was dry and technical, but served to "authenticate" that the material was by Hershel. In the second article on the following day, spectacular discoveries were announced. The first of these was a lunar (moon) forest, followed by a lunar beach surrounding a sea. Also present were water birds, bisons, elk, and a kind of biped beaver. There were small zebras, pheasants, unicorns, and finally human beings with bat-like wings. These he called "Vespertilio-homo" (man-bat). They were about four feet tall, covered with short copper-colored hair, except on their faces, and had thin, membranous wings. These creatures were sentient in that they had buildings, use of fire, and some culture. Finally, in the sixth and final installment, another race of Vespertilio were

discovered that were "of infinitely greater personal beauty . . . scarcely less lovely than the general representations of angels by the more imaginative schools of painters."

The public was fascinated. Circulation shot up until the *Sun* because the largest-selling daily newspaper in the world. The articles were reprinted as booklets, and translations appeared in European languages. Most people believed the stories were true.

Several professors from Yale College came to the offices of the *Sun*. They wanted to see the actual copy of the supplement from which the articles were taken. They were directed across the street to a printing establishment, where the material was supposedly being set in type. At the printer, they were told that the foreman was not in and only he knew exactly where the supplement was, as it was not being typeset at that moment. The professors went away disappointed.

The *Journal of Commerce*, desiring to copy the article, sent one of its reporters to the *Sun*. This reporter happened to be a friend of journalist Richard Adams Locke, so he went to see him about permission to copy. Locke advised his friend that the article not be copied, and admitted that he had written it. The *Journal of Commerce* broke this news the next day.

The publisher of the New York *Herald*, rival James Gordon Bennett, saw the *Sun's* circulation improve as a result of the moon stories and struck back. The *Herald* had not published for several weeks, due to a fire in its plant. Bennett said that the moon story was a hoax, perpetrated by Richard Adams Locke. It mentioned that Locke was British and interested in astronomy and optics. Bennett correctly mentioned that the *Sun's* reports carried scientific inaccuracies and that the *Edinburgh Journal of Science* had not been published for several years. That meant that the original story could not have been reprinted from the journal's supplement.

Bennett invited Locke to use the *Herald's* columns to "tell the public frankly the whole secret history of his hoax. . . ." Locke responded at once, but not as Bennett expected. Locke wrote a letter to the *Herald* stating that he had no expertise in astronomy or optics. He could find no errors in the article, but *he* had not made those discoveries, the astronomer John Frederick William Hershel made them. That [Locke] had anything to do with a hoax was "too ridiculous to receive any further notice. . . ."

Bennett retreated. *If* the articles were hoaxes, he said, Locke would have been the one to write them. If they were genuine discoveries, Locke was the most likely person to know about them. The *Herald* then ran a burlesque of the whole series of moon hoax articles.

When Hershel was finally told of the stories about his "discoveries" that were being printed in New York, he was amused. He saw the interest people had in his work and was probably flattered, even if his discoveries were not nearly as wonderful as proclaimed.

Author Michael Crowe has stated that Locke's articles were not intended as a hoax, but as satire. Locke was supposedly trying to satirize the writings of Thomas Dick, who had published a number of articles suggesting that people on the earth build a giant signal to the people on the moon. As Crowe points out, Locke's attempt at satire (if that was *really* what it was) failed because he had underestimated public gullibility. People failed to see the satire in Locke's article. Dick himself was quite angry with Locke, reminding him that "all such attempts to deceive are violations of the laws of the Creator, who is the 'God of Truth' . . . and therefore, they who willingly and deliberately contrive such impositions ought to be ranked in the class of liars and deceivers." Crowe thinks that the point of Locke's satire was to show "That pitfalls await those who rashly pronounce on the ways of God."

Sources:

Crowe, Michael J. *The Extraterrestrial Life Debate, 1750–1900.* Cambridge, UK: Cambridge University Press, 1986: 202–15.

Evans, David S. "The Great Moon Hoax I" and "II." *Sky and Telescope* 62 (September 1981): 196–98 and 62 (October 1981): 308–11. See also issue of November 1981, pages 428–429 for related article by Michael J. Crowe.

[Locke, Richard Adams]. "Great Astronomical Discoveries." *The New York Sun* (August 25, 1835): 1–2.

Locke, Richard Adams. *The Moon Hoax: or a Discovery that the Moon Has a Vast Population of Human Beings.* New York: William Gowans, 1859. Reprint published by Gregg Press (Boston), 1975.

Price, George R. "The Day they Discovered Men on the Moon." *Popular Science* 173 (July 1958): 61–64.

The Jersey Devil

Sometimes the line between folklore and reality is blurred. For example, most people know that Pegasus, the winged-horse, was not a real creature but was part of folklore that is now called mythology. The Jersey Devil (sometimes called the Leeds Devil), while *now* recognized by most authorities as a folkloric creature, was promulgated as a real animal in 1909. In fact, there was nearly an hysterical epidemic (*See* Hysterical Epidemics, p. 199) of sightings of the creature.

Southeastern New Jersey has a large region known as "the Pine Barrens." It is about 1,700 square miles of sandy soil, pine trees (often stunted because of the poor soil), and empty space. Few people have lived there.

Legend has it that the Jersey Devil was born in 1735 when a woman named Mother Leeds—already the mother of twelve children—again found herself pregnant. She cursed her condition, saying out loud "I am tired of children! Let it be a devil!" Apparently this child was either born horribly deformed, or else born normal, but later took on a fiendish appearance. Mother Leeds kept it in the house, but it escaped. Other versions of this story have the child turning into a monster with a horse's head and hooves, bat wings, and a thick forked tail—right before the eyes of the startled midwife. All of this has the clear mark of folklore.

In 1740, a clergyman performed an exorcism on the Jersey Devil in the Pine Barrens, supposedly good for 100 years. In 1840, right on schedule, the Jersey Devil reappeared. This time it fed on chickens and sheep. There are several other stories of the Jersey Devil's origin; all stories are clearly folkloric. In January of 1909, the hoax elements of the Jersey Devil story occurred. The week of January 16 through 23 produced sightings of the Jersey Devil by thousands of people, or at least sightings of his footprints. The description of the creature was as a "jabberwock" (like Lewis Carroll's Jabberwocky) or a "kangaroo horse." As reports of the creature surfaced, schools and factories in the area closed, and people stayed behind locked doors. In the earliest reported sightings, the creature's descriptions are not similar. The creature is described as a luminous white cloud; an eagle; a winged and hopping bird but with a horrible cry; having the head of a ram; and having long, thin wings and short legs in front, with longer ones in the back.

Many footprints were found, often going over rooftops and other seemingly inaccessible places. The footprint resembled a horse's hoof. Perhaps the clearest sighting was made by Mr. and Mrs. Nelson Evans of Gloucester City. They saw the Jersey Devil cavorting on the roof of their shed for a full ten minutes. They described it as follows: "It was about three feet and a half high, with a head like a collie dog and a face like a horse. It had a long neck, wings about two feet long, and its back legs were like those of a crane, and it had horse's hooves. It walked on its back legs and held up two short front legs with paws on them."

During the nights of January 16–23, many chickens were found missing or dead. The Jersey Devil was blamed and said to be the cause of strange footprints found in the snow all over southern New Jersey and southeastern Pennsylvania. Fifty years later, one man

Philadelphia Evening Bulletin

The Jersey Devil.

in Salem admitted that he faked some of these footprints. Although there was much speculation in the newspapers about what the creature could really be, there was little agreement. In the desire to make money, some people claimed they had captured the creature and put it on exhibit at the Ninth and Arch Museum in Philadelphia at ten cents per view. The creature was a kangaroo fitted with wings and prodded to jump out towards the audience. After a week, the hysterical epidemic of sightings was over. Little was heard of actual sightings of the Jersey Devil after this, although there were a number of folkloric reports. It seems that the Jersey Devil has faded back into folklore, where it probably belonged all along.

Sources:

Jenkins, Patrick. "Jersey Devil Struggles for His Due in Face of Fiendish Development." *Newark Star-Ledger* (October 31, 1985): 61.

McCloy, James F. and Ray Miller, Jr. *The Jersey Devil.* Wallingford, PA: Middle Atlantic Press, 1976.

Skinner, Charles. *American Myths and Legends.* Philadelphia: J. B. Lippincott, 1903.

Sullivan, Jeremiah J. and James F. McCloy. "The Jersey Devil's Finest Hour." *New York Folklore Quarterly* 30 (September 1974): 231–38.

Levitation

Levitation acts—including people rising into the air unassisted, flying through the air horizontally, and climbing a rope into the air until they disappear from view are well witnessed, but seem to defy the laws of physics. Sometimes hundreds witness a supposed levitation, yet indisputable proof is provided that full audiences of these people were mistaken in what they saw, victims of trickery and deceit. At other times, only one witness was present, but the phenomena defy rational explanation. All types of people have claimed to have been levitated, from saints to spiritualists to Indian fakirs.

Some instances of levitation do not purport to be anything but fraud and entertainment. These include the stage illusionist's act of levitating a young lady. There are of variations on this type of performance and many ways of accomplishing the illusion as well. In the most common version of the trick, a young woman is brought on stage and put into a "trance." She is then allowed to lie down on a bed made of a board and two sawhorse-like supports. A piece of fabric drapes down over the edge of the board. One by one the supports are removed from under the board. Eventually, nothing apparently supports the board. Sometimes the board rises and falls on the magician's command. Sometimes no board exists, but the illusion is accomplished by the use of two chairs across which the lady lies. Sometimes the lady is entirely covered by a cloth and then vanishes from the levitated platform upon the command of the magician, only to reappear from the wings of the stage or from the audience. The variations seem endless.

Caution must be taken when explaining the means used to accomplish the trick. Myriad variations of the mechanism's design exist. Also, to reveal exactly how the trick works would destroy its entertainment value. In general, the principle involves a single strong support behind the platform upon which the woman lies. It is either fixed or mechanically portable, usually with a silent hydraulic system. Sometimes wires from above are used. In all cases the mechanism is cleverly hidden and the passes by hoops of metal or other devices around the table always just miss hitting the support. If the illusion is staged well, it can be convincing, even to the skeptic. Nevertheless, *this* form of levitation is admitted as trickery and therefore, not be considered any further.

Perhaps the most famous case of supposed levitation is the Indian Rope Trick. Rumors that this was a real event, but rarely performed, made a member of the British Magic Circle offer the sum of 500 pounds in March of 1919 to anyone who could perform the famous rope trick under carefully controlled conditions. Ads were placed in the *Times of India*, but no one accepted. The man who made the offer reluctantly concluded that the trick must be a myth. The purported trick was based on the following story. As reported—usually second or third hand—a Hindu fakir working outdoors in a level area would gather a crowd, then throw a long coiled rope up into the air. The rope would stay suspended vertically, with the top of the rope almost disappearing from view. The fakir would then tell his young assistant to climb up the rope. The assistant would do so, disappearing from view. The fakir would then call him several times to come down. There was no response. Growing angry, the fakir would seize a knife in his teeth and then climb up the rope after his assistant. Shortly thereafter, the sound of various parts of the assistant striking the ground would be heard and the limbs seen. Finally, the fakir would descend the rope, his clothes bloody. The various limbs of the assistant were gathered up into a pile (or sometimes placed into a basket), given a kick by the fakir, and miraculously reassembled into the live young assistant. The assistant arose or climbed from the basket and walked off unhurt. This was how the trick was reported, but never first hand.

The British magician who had no takers for his £500 offer may have been mistaken to conclude that the trick was a myth. He should have known that Hindu fakirs are often illiterate, even in their native language, and probably do not read the *Times of India*. It was not that the trick didn't exist, but perhaps it was that his offer was unknown to the people who mattered. One school of thought says that the Indian Rope Trick *does* exist, and although it is rarely performed because of the great difficulties and skills involved, the performed trick is not much different from the way in which it was described above. All that differs is that the trick is usually performed at dusk and in an area with small hills. The rope is usually thrown upwards several times before it remains upright. The rope also has a wooden ball containing several holes drilled through it, which is attached like a weight to the thrown end of the rope.

The secret of the Indian Rope Trick lies in carefully choosing the site and time of the performance, plus much advance preparation and skill in distracting the audience. A site must be picked that has two hills, one on either side of the flat area seating the audience. A long black wire is stretched from one hill to the other and pulled tightly at least thirty feet above the ground. The trick is always performed at dusk, so that the wire is invisible. Additional concealment of the wire comes from the fact that a number of electric lanterns—or bonfires long ago—were placed around the audience in a way that obscured a direct view upwards. The first few times that the wooden ball attached to the end of the rope is tossed into the air, nothing happens. The audience quickly loses interest, and begins to pay less

attention. Finally, the fakir attaches a metal hook through one of the holes in the wooden ball and throws the rope up to loop over the concealed wire. He makes sure it is secure, sometimes with the aid of two assistants at the ends of the wire on the small hills, and then sends the boy assistant up the rope. The long robes of the fakir conceal a body harness that contains the limbs of a shaved monkey and a realistic looking dummy head. When these parts have been thrown down after the fakir ascends the rope, the boy assistant fastens himself to the harness under the robes of the fakir and they descend with the boy concealed under the fakir's robes. Once back on the ground, the fakir's other assistants gather up the monkey parts. The boy slips out from under the fakir's robes while they are gather up the parts, takes his place in the basket, and the illusion is complete. Sometimes the rope is unfastened from the guy wire, sometimes the guy wire is released from its moorings, and sometimes the whole is "left in place temporarily." The great skill required to climb the rope, make the switches and divert the crowd's attention at the appropriate moments have made this trick so difficult that it is rarely performed. Usually members of one family perform it, having practiced for many years.

Another school of thought holds that the above description of how the trick was done was a hoax perpetrated by a journalist in 1888. Believers of this theory feel that an actual Indian Rope Trick never existed. The Indian Rope Trick is in either case a deceit. Other fakir levitation effects will be examined next. A few of these were witnessed by famous magician Harry Kellar on his trips to India in the 1870s and 1880s. He reported to see a fakir in Calcutta take three swords and bury their hilts six inches in the ground, with the points upward. They were positioned about eighteen inches apart. Another fakir laid down on the ground and was placed in a trance. His rigid body was lifted off the ground and placed on the swords. One sword was under the nape of the neck, another midway between the shoulders, and the third at the base of the spine. After a few minutes, the assistant dug down in the earth and uncovered the hilt of each sword, removing them entirely. The fakir was lying only on air, apparently supported by nothing. Two assistants then lifted the fakir's body and lowered it to the ground. Kellar was baffled at how the feat could have been performed outdoors, as it was, with an audience on all sides.

There is also a report—retold by Rickard, as was the Kellar incident—of a fakir who in 1829, working behind a blanket, managed to levitate from a lotus position. He wound up suspended only by a metal rod upon which he rested an arm, with his body about two feet off the ground (see Figure 1, p. 256). Rickard thinks the illusion *might* have been accomplished by means of an apparatus such as that pictured in Figure 2.

Modern claims of levitation have been made by members of the Transcendental Meditation Movement. They offer expensive courses that claim to allow a person to levitate a foot or so off the ground while in a full lotus position. In fact, they show photos of a small group of people each a few inches off the ground. However, a careful study of the photographs shows that the ground is heavily padded and the people appear to have hopped up into the air for a second or two. When questioned, the participants admitted hopping, but added that they felt with additional practice they could remain in the air for extended periods. No one has yet achieved this ability. It is hard to know whether they sincerely believe this or whether they have been taken in by an aggressive sales campaign for the "levitation lessons." At this point in time, no one has demonstrated true levitation from the lotus position.

The first of the possible unexplainable cases of supposed levitation have occurred in spiritualistic settings. Perhaps the most famous physical medium that ever lived was Daniel Dunglas Home 1833–1886. Although Home was occasionally seen in a fraud, as when he was seen taking his foot out of his shoe during a seance, he was either remarkably skillful in his deceptions or remarkably endowed with genuine powers. That he never charged for his seances, although he did accept gifts and hospitality, made many less anxious to expose him. Home frequently did levitations. He often appeared to be rising towards the ceiling in a semi-dark room. Most people knew he had risen because they felt his feet at the height of their faces. If they saw only his feet, then the supposed levitation had a neat explanation. Home simply removed his shoes from his feet and placed them on his hands. Then he needed only to move his shoe-clad hands about in the air in the vicinity of the participants' faces. They also often reported that his voice came from high up. This could be accomplished simply by standing on a chair before speaking. However, if the sitters could clearly see the rest of Home's body as he supposedly levitated, an entirely different situation exists, for which an explanation is difficult. Home often did not do his seances in the pitch dark that other mediums required, so observation of his whole body should have been possible. Suspiciously, Home did ask that lights be lowered whenever he was going to levitate.

Home also performed table levitations. In this case, an examination of the actual reports of such levitations occurring during Home's seances shows that the table rose, uniformly, when people were seated around it, joining hands on the table top. The table would then begin to rise, forcing the sitters to rise in order to maintain the circle of joined hands. If this were the case, how it was accomplished is simply explained.

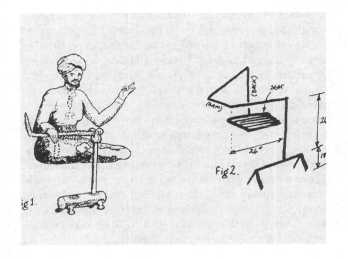

Levitating fakir.

An old medium's device consisting of a flat metal hook and straps fastens to the arm under a suit. When the hands are rested on a table, the hook can be engaged under the table top. When two people on the opposite sides of the same table—even a heavy table—have engaged their hooks, the table can be made to rise by having the two confederates make some comment that the table is rising, then get up themselves. This will lift the table with them and the others sitting around it will also have to rise, if it is made clear the importance of keeping the circle of hands unbroken. This is a fraudulent medium's way of doing this levitation and *may* have been employed by Home.

During levitation, Home has stated that he had a swollen and tingling feeling in his feet. He was generally lifted up perpendicularly. His arms became rigid and drawn above his head as if he were grasping some unseen power that was lifting him from the floor. He remained levitated for as long as four or five minutes. Home himself admitted that only one of his levitations occurred in daylight—in America, at the home of Ward Cheney in Connecticut in August of 1852. Yet, unless Home has confused two accounts, Mr. F. L. Burr, who reported this levitation, says that it occurred in "a darkened room." Why Home would claim it was in daylight (perhaps it *was* daylight outside) is not clear. However, he says one levitation did occur with four gaslights burning brightly.

In fact, the details are known of at least one 1859 levitation from the pen of a disinterested observer, J. G. Crawford, who reported that the room was almost dark. To that Home then exclaimed "I feel as if I were going to rise. I am getting up." As Crawford was only a few feet from Home, Crawford extended his hand towards him and felt the soles of both of his boots some three feet above the level of the floor. Crawford de-

Daniel Dunglas Home.

duced that Home had risen *from his voice*, according to his own account. In other words, Crawford did not actually see Home's body in the levitated state.

Additionally, there is the testimony of Mr. Jones of Peckham (not further identified), who was present at a Home levitation in 1860. He states that Home said "I am rising," but Jones could not see him in the darkness. They asked that Home come close to the window (it was dark outside), and when he did so, they saw

> his feet and a part of his legs resting or floating on the air like a feather, about six feet from the ground and three feet above the height of the table. He was then floated into the dark . . . I saw his head and face at the same height as before [it is not clear at what height], and as if floating on air instead of water. He then floated back [into the dark] and came down. Again, if Home were clever enough to know exactly what part of his body could be seen in the limited light, he could have presented only that part that would be visible in a horizontal position, by standing on a chair, for example, and bending forward or backward at the waist with his shoes on his hands.

Mrs. Lynn Linton's account of the same seance is curious in that she did not actually see Home float, but says that his voice gave her the indication that he was levitating as he moved about the room. She does claim to have seen the shadow of his body "on the mirror as he floated along near the ceiling." It could have been anything casting a shadow that she saw and not necessarily Home's body at the level of the shadow. Since the apparent height of Home's voice, plus the level at which his shoes were felt, seem to be largely responsible for the feeling among the audience that he had levitated, this may explain Home's spiritualistic levitations as deceptions.

Perhaps the most famous of Home's levitations was the one that occurred in the presence of Lord Adare, Lord Lindsay, and Captain Charles Wynne in December of 1868. As reported by Adare in his rare book *Experiences in Spiritualism With D. D. Home,* Home went into a trance, walked about the room, went into the next room, and opened the window. Lord Lindsay thought he knew what was going to happen and called out that the action was " . . . too fearful . . . He is going out of the window in the other room and coming in at this window." Lindsay later claimed he knew this through telepathic communication. Home then appeared at the outside of the window, opened it, and entered the room. He then asked Adare to close the window in the other room. When Adare went there to do so, he found it opened only about eighteen inches. Adare expressed amazement that Home could have exited through such a small opening. Home then showed him how he could do it by horizontally shooting through the window headfirst and returning in the same way.

The story is usually reported in this manner, with the additional information that the windows were eighty feet above the ground. A seven-foot-span was between the two windows, with only a four-inch-wide ledge between them. There was a wrought iron balcony outside each window as well. The seven-foot-measurement was between the two balcony edges.

An investigation of this event leaves several unresolved peculiarities. The first is that internal contradictions appear within the document describing the event, as well as between that document and several other shorter accounts of it. The date and location of the levitation have been misstated. The light from outside the window was bright says the author, but on the actual night of the levitation, there was a new moon. Furthermore, although the building in which this levitation occurred is no longer standing, there are photographs of it. These reveal that the two windows involved were only about thirty-five feet from the ground and the two balconies were about four feet apart. Either Home—who had plenty of time alone in the building to practice this feat—jumped from one balcony to the other or opened the window in one room, sneaked under cover of darkness from that room to the other window, stood on the *inside* ledge of the second window, and opened the window from the inside. Experiments have shown that in the dark it is hard to tell if someone is inside of a window or outside of it. Home could have faked this apparent levitation.

Home had a dominating relationship with the three men who were the witnesses, allowing them to accept his suggestions that he was levitating out one window and in the other. Two additional facts about the incident should raise question. Home consistently reported that he had no control over his levitations yet he told Adare and Lindsay that he was going out one window and in the other. If Home could not control his levitations, it would be dangerous to try floating out windows. Also, Home told everyone not to leave their seats and to remain in the one room while he went into the other. Perhaps they would have detected a fraud if they had not followed his instructions. There is no way to settle whether Home truly levitated on that night. The natural explanations of what may have happened no longer leave an inexplicable event that could only be real levitation.

In all fairness to the levitations of mediums, it must be pointed out that Home was not the only medium who claimed to be able to levitate, or who was seen levitating. Among the others were Stainton Moses, Mrs. Guppy, Eusapia Paladino, and Willy Schneider. Although they were sometimes levitated while sitting in a chair, their levitations were otherwise similar to Home's. The chair levitation is a special problem to explain rationally, as without a trained observer actually viewing it and examining the chair afterwards, it is not possible to give a definitive explanation of how it was done. Whether trickery was involved or not it is now impossible to determine.

The most perplexing of all claimed levitations are those of the saints Joseph of Cupertino and Teresa of Avila. These are not the only saints that supposedly levitated; in fact, more than 200 saints are reported to have levitated at least once in front of witnesses. The most recent of these was Marie-Francoise de Cinq Plaies, who died in 1791. Levitating saints have evidently become passé as there hasn't been one—other than sightings of the Virgin Mary—for about 200 years.

Perhaps one of the most famous levitating saint was Joseph of Cupertino (1603–1663). Forty recorded instances of Joseph levitating are recorded, including one time during which he flew up to the altar of the church from the pews, landing amidst flaming candles and being badly burned. The most impressive levitation reported for Joseph was when he supposedly flew seventy yards from a doorway to the top of a thirty-six-foot high cross that his group of friars was constructing. He then lifted the cross into the air and flew with it to the site to which it was to be moved. When evidence for these levitations is examined, however, it reveals that—as Butler in his *Lives of the Saints* even points out—these feats were not attested at the time by any eyewitnesses and were recorded only after his death. By then enough time had elapsed that events could be exaggerated and legends could arise. The problem with all testimony involving saints is that ulterior motives—including keeping and recruiting church members—were involved rather than mere historical fact. If Butler—a strong believer in the special qualities of the saints—could have his doubts about the accuracy of the

levitations reported about Joseph of Cupertino, perhaps skepticism is not altogether unjustified.

Saint Teresa of Avila—perhaps the best-known saint who levitated—also deserves mention. She was a specialist in vertical levitations, as opposed to the mostly horizontal ones of Joseph of Cupertino. Teresa (1515–1582) would likely be considered strange by anyone's standards. She was extremely ill much of her life and perfected the art of mystical rapture. It was while in one of these raptures that Teresa would occasionally levitate. As she describes the sensation in her autobiography, it came upon her without warning. She felt as if she were being carried up upon the wings of an eagle. Any attempt at resistance to the levitation was usually in vain and was also exhausting. It was usually best to just let it happen. Her hair would often stand on end during these raptures. A few times the nuns supposedly had to get Teresa down from a tree into which she had levitated. Again—although Teresa wrote her autobiography in which she claimed the power of levitation, or at least the fact of levitation—witnesses to her levitations came forth only many years later, during the investigations prior to her canonization.

Levitation and witchcraft were also connected. In the 1600s, levitation was looked on as a form of possession by the devil. In the 1657 case of Henry Jones, a twelve-year-old, his levitations were considered a sign that he was bewitched. Patrick Sandilands, a Scottish boy was also considered bewitched when he levitated in 1720. Mary London was actually tried for witchcraft, partly because her levitations often placed her on the roof of her house or so she claimed. Some poltergeist cases also involve reported levitation, usually of small children.

Traditionally, explanations for levitation have involved one or more of the following: divine grace (God recognizing special devotion in someone), the effects of demons or the devil, possession of some miraculous knowledge or "a word of power," electricity, magnetism or "odic" forces, a cantilever effect due to "pseudopods" that grew from the body and levered it up into the air, breathing exercises, or willpower. It is possible, that any of these forces might have been involved in a genuine levitation. A levitation is merely the overcoming of the force of gravity. Unfortunately, it is not understood at present exactly what the force of gravity is, and therefore it is not known how to overcome it (if it is even possible).

Since electricity and magnetism have dual, opposed aspects (north versus south poles, positive versus negative charges), it is theoretically possible for an object to repel another by the use of magnetism or electricity, similar to the way like charges repel each other. However, mass can only be in a positive direction when an object is not in space (where it can have no weight). Therefore, it is *theoretically* impossible, according to most physicists, for an anti-gravity device to ever be made on earth, since there *is* no "opposite" dimension from gravity. This theory, assumes that the laws of physics are correct. Additionally, it places an obstacle in the way of a possible explanation of some of the reported levitations.

Many levitators have said they did not understand what was happening to them, nor were they able to control the process in any meaningful way. This has not helped in the attempts to understand or control levitation. The lack of information leaves many questions as to the reliability of the witnesses to the saintly levitations, whether or not D. D. Home used trickery, and whether or not the reports of other spiritualists who supposedly levitated can be trusted. It is also possible that more than one phenomenon is present here calling for several different explanations. Without answers to these questions, it is difficult to explain levitation.

The only known photograph of a person actually levitating was the 1935 photo of the Brazilian medium Carlos Mirabelli, clad in a white lab coat, rising to what appears to be about six feet in the air in a room with his arms extended from his sides. This photo has recently been revealed as a fake. The original print was discovered showing that Mirabelli was standing on the top step of a ladder. The ladder was clumsily airbrushed out. The alterations are concealed on copies of the original by the flowered pattern on the wallpaper of the room.

Olivier Leroy, author of one of the few book-length studies of levitation, written in French, was extremely hesitant to draw any conclusions after nearly 400 pages of examining the phenomenon. Investigators can give up and accept the physics that indicates that anti-gravity is impossible on earth or they can work to produce clear cut levitations repeatedly under honest conditions. This may be impossible. At this point, it appears that all purported levitations are hoaxes of one sort or another.

Sources:

Clements, Warner. "Levitation: Some Phantasy and Some Physics." *Skeptical Inquirer* 13 no. 3 (Spring 1989): 289–95.

Hall, Trevor H. *The Enigma of D. D. Home: Medium or Fraud?* Buffalo, NY: Prometheus Books, 1984.

Keel, John. *Jadoo.* New York: Julian Messner, 1957: 142–56.

Leroy, Olivier. *La Levitation.* Paris: Librarie Valois, 1928.

Sea serpent skeleton.

Rickard, R. J. M. "Walking, Sitting and Lying on Air." *Fortean Times* no. 21 (1977): 16–24.

Stein, Gordon. "The Amazing Medium Mirabelli." *Fate* (March 1991): 86–95.

Plant and Animal Hoaxes

When the earth was not as thoroughly explored as it is now, professional biologists spent more time searching for new species of plants and animals. Enough is known now about genetics, evolution, and systematics to know when a suggested species is "impossible." It is clear that a mammal cannot crossbreed with a fish, so that the classical interpretation of a mermaid as half human and half fish is impossible. However, there was once quite a trade in making up new species by clever taxidermy, in which parts of one animal would be joined with those of another. Many of these examples of hoax species still exist, and recently, new ones have been discovered. This article will cover all such plant and animal hoaxes of note—including those that were illustrated but not presented as specimens, except bigfoot, the Loch Ness Monster, and other sea serpents which have had fraudulent instances, but may not be entirely hoaxes.

Stories of mermaids are widespread and appear throughout history. It is a common belief that many of these sightings may be explained by women-starved sailors seeing manatees or dugongs (sea cows) and mistaking them for women with fish tails. This is highly unlikely, as anyone who has ever seen a manatee or dugong would attest. Although mermaids have been reported in all the world's seas, the sea cow is only found in the ocean shallows along the coasts of East Africa, Australia, Southeast Asia, and Borneo. There are freshwater (river) species in Florida, Brazil, and Africa. It is doubtful if any sea cows ever lived in the

Mediterranean Sea, the source of the mermaid story. The seal or sea lion is another matter. It *does* bask on rocks, as many mermaids have been reported to do. It also "sings" after a fashion, while the sea cow is silent. Mermaids, too have often been reported to sing. A Scottish and Irish folk tradition has women being turned into seals by magic.

The origins of the mermaid story go back to the religious traditions of the Babylonians, at least. They had a triad of gods, one of whom was the fish-tailed god Oannes (or Ea). The Babylonians acquired this god from the Accadians (not Canadian), with an origin as far back as 5000 B.C. Besides ruling the waters, Oannes was the god of light and wisdom. He brought civilization to his people and he spoke. The existing picture of Oannes comes from only one surviving source, Berossus, a priest in Babylon. He claims that Oannes looked entirely like a fish, but the top "fish head" lifted up revealed a human upper body. He also had human feet, next to his fish tail. While all of this is quite different from the classic picture of a mermaid, it is perhaps a starting point. This story also contradicts a picture given of Oannes by Berossus. A sculpture of about 700 B.C. shows Oannes as a simple merman. This could be an evolution of the original Oannes concept, or else a different picture entirely of Oannes.

The *mermaid* seems to have arrived later than the merman. The mermaid is an old and widespread concept, however, included in the mythologies of China, Japan, India, and Greece. By the 1500s, the picture of the mermaid combing her hair while looking in a mirror—perched upon some rocks by the ocean—was known widely to the public. This concept may be a "humanization" of the fish-tailed god idea. Many sightings undoubtedly came because people *wanted* to believe in mermaids.

The earliest *manufactured* or hoax mermaids, are from the sixteenth century. The most famous of these mermaid "Jenny Hanivers,"—the term for the result when parts of different species are joined together by taxidermy—was the "1822 Mermaid." This was made by taking the upper half of an ape (orangutan, probably) and joining it skillfully to the lower two-thirds of a salmon. The teeth and jaws were those of a baboon. The entire object was about two feet ten inches long.

P. T. Barnum appears to have entered the mermaid game in 1842, with his "Fejee Mermaid." He bought the "1822 Mermaid" from the descendants of the original owner. It was exhibited successfully by Barnum for many years and is now in the Barnum Museum in Bridgeport, Connecticut, although in rather decrepit condition.

Quite a scare was felt by cryptozoologists in the 1980s when a number of reports of mermaids being

Artist's conception of a fabled mermaid.

seen, caught *and eaten* came from the Papua/New Guinea area. When an expedition was sent to the area, the natives were found to be using the word which translates as "dugong" (seacow) for the creature that they had captured and eaten. They identified the creature from pictures as well.

The unicorn has been made into a romantic, idyllic creature of the Middle Ages. Supposedly the only way to easily catch a unicorn was to have a virgin sit in an enclosure. The unicorn would then come and put its head into the virgin's lap, promptly falling asleep, allowing it to be seized. A unicorn's horn, ground up, was an antidote to all poisons. Parings from a "unicorn's" horn were sold at high prices for centuries. These were usually made from the "horn" (really tooth) of a narwhal, a rare type of small arctic whale.

The story of the dragon is complex. It is intimately involved in the mythology of many countries and covers the spectrum from being an evil, sinister, and frightening creature in the West, to being kindly and lovable in the Orient. Western dragons often lived in caves and guarded treasures. This led to the dragon being adopted as a warlike symbol on many shields and tools of war. It has been suggested that the dragon was a combination of a serpent, eagle-lion, and antelope-fish. It was probably originally a snake of some sort, but became more and more of a composite as time

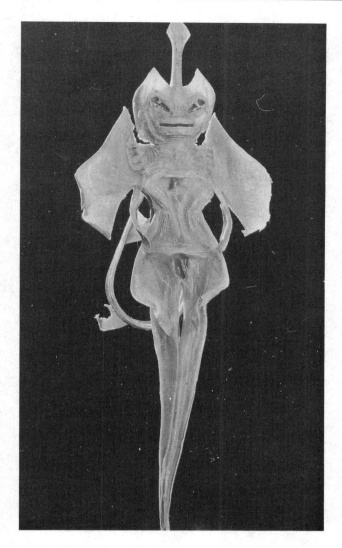

Example of a "Jenny Haniver," or, manufactured mermaid.

most of which was taken up by a neck and spine of more than fifty vertebrae. One of the people who viewed the fossil was Prof. Jeffries Wyman, an anatomist. He quickly realized that the skull of the creature was from a mammal, judging by the teeth. The vertebrae, he said, came from several different skeletons. Most of the bones were from a species of fossil whale that was only thirteen meters long.

Geese that were produced from the fruit of a tree, like apples, were a widely accepted idea in the Middle Ages. The fruit fell into the water and turned into barnacle geese. The story seems to have originated from the fact that the nests of these geese were never seen. That was because they nested in the far Arctic area. When explorers finally reached that region, they found plenty of barnacle goose nests.

The Nondescript was a human-like Jenny Haniver. It was made by skillful taxidermy from the head and shoulders of a Red Howler monkey. The bones of the skull were evidently removed and the skin stretched into a human-like appearance. It foiled some people for a while.

John Mandeville, a credulous fourteenth century travel book author and possible hoaxer himself, wrote about a "vegetable lamb" that grew to yield mutton and wool. This story was elaborated by Baron von Heberstein in the sixteenth century. The origins of this story are either in the cotton plant (for the "wool") or in an arborescent fern of the Cibotium species. Neither of these produces meat or wool, but may appear to do so.

The "Pig-Faced Lady" exhibited in the early 1800s consisted of a shaved bear, wearing white gloves. It was seated in a chair and clothed in a dress, shawl, and cap. It went by the name "Madame Stevens."

The Roc (or Rukh) was a supposedly enormous bird. It could lift an elephant and had eggs as big as a small building. It plays a role in *The Arabian Nights,* but it is fiction. Marco Polo seems to be responsible for spreading rumors about the real existence of such a bird on the Island of "Magaster" (probably Madagascar). Interestingly, there once *was* a gigantic bird on Madagascar. It was called Aepyonis, or the Elephant Bird. It disappeared about 300 years ago. The egg of the Elephant Bird was three feet long and its size proportional. Although it was large, it was nowhere near the size Marco Polo described. In addition, the Elephant Bird could not fly. It was simply too heavy. The Roc, as a flying bird, is simply impossible. The heaviest flying bird—the Albatross—weighs about thirty-five pounds. If a bird weighs much more than this, its wings would have to be so large that they could not be carried by the bird. This same problem explains why man cannot fly using bird wings.

passed. Medieval theology made the dragon into the symbol of the devil and the slayers of dragons into saints. Many small "dragon" specimens were fabricated from sting rays, whose "wings" were turned back to form the "wings" of the dragon. The "head" of the ray was also bent to make the nostrils appear to be eyes and the mouth to take on a fearsome appearance.

The basilisk was a lizard-like creature whose look was allegedly fatal. In other words, if the basilisk spied a person, he or she was as good as dead. It started out to be a highly venomous snake. Since it was the king of reptiles, it was often pictured with a crown on its head. In the Middle Ages, the creature gradually changed to one that was hatched by a toad from an egg laid by a seven-year-old cock.

In 1845, Albert C. Koch exhibited a large fossil skeleton in New York City which he claimed belonged to an extinct sea serpent. It was thirty-five meters long,

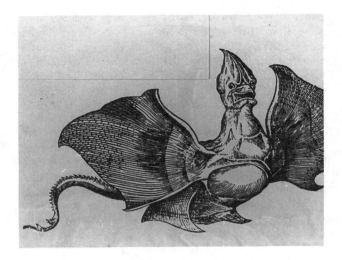

Another "Jenny Haniver."

The Upas tree came from stories of trees that produced a poisonous vapor that killed anyone who slept under them. The only source for something similar to this is a letter from a traveller to Madagascar named Liche, who spoke of a tree that intoxicated, then crushed its victims. This story may be to the fact that the sap of some trees *is* a deadly poison, used for arrow tips by some native tribes.

Sources:

Benwell, Gwen and Arthur Waugh. *Sea Enchantress: The Tale of the Mermaid and Her Kin.* London: Hutchinson, 1961.

Clair, Colin. *Unnatural History: An Illustrated Bestiary.* New York: Abelard-Schuman, 1967.

Dance, Peter. *Animal Fakes & Frauds.* Maidstone, England: Sampson Low, 1975.

Emboden, William A. *Bizarre Plants: Magical, Monstrous, Mythical.* New York: Macmillan, 1974.

Gudge, E. W. "Jenny Hanivers, Dragons and Basilisks in the Old Natural History Books and in Modern Times." *Scientific Monthly* 38 (June 1934): 511–23.

Rorvick and the Cloning of a Man

David Rorvik is a science journalist of some reputation. In 1978, he published a book called *In His Image: The Cloning of a Man.* The public was fascinated and largely accepting of his thesis that a human being had been successfully cloned. The scientific world was highly dubious, however. The scientists', reluctance was due to the fact that technology was not sufficiently advanced to produce a human clone and that Rorvik supplied inadequate documentation that human cloning had occurred.

In the book Rorvik tells how he received a telephone call from an elderly millionaire, whom he calls "Max." As Rorvik had been science editor of *Time,* Max knew of Rorvik's writings about human reproduction and cloning. The millionaire wanted to clone himself and was willing to pay millions of dollars to do it. Rorvik found a knowledgeable and willing scientist, whom he calls "Darwin," who was a gynecologist. They set up a laboratory in a tropical, possibly oriental, country where a ready supply of native women were to supply eggs and attempt to carry the embryo clone to term. A cell from Max's body had its nucleus transferred to an egg without a nucleus from the selected "mother." A young virgin—given the name "Sparrow" in the book—was selected and carried the embryo to term, delivering a boy in the United States. Max had his son and heir in a perfect clone of himself.

In 1978, J. B. Lippincott, the publisher of Rorvik's cloning book, was sued in federal court by a British scientist who claimed he was defamed in the book. Dr. J. Derek Bromhall sued because his name had been mentioned in the book as having developed the scientific basis for the cloning. This, led credence to the claim that the cloning had occurred. The suit asked the court to declare that the cloned boy depicted in the book was fictitious. Bromhall claimed that Rorvik quoted from his doctoral dissertation without authorization, which explored the *possibility* of human cloning.

The trouble with Rorvik's book was pointed out by Dr. Bromhall in 1978. In short, the problem was that Rorvik vaguely described the cloning process used, *and* it is *theoretically* impossible as Rorvik outlined it. Serious errors stemmed from Rorvik's misunderstanding of cloning research, as Bromhall pointed out.

More specifically, Bromhall noted that the difficulty involved in the successful cloning of a frog (done in the mid-1960s) is different than that of a human. The frog's egg is much larger and easier to work with. Rorvik claims that the donor egg was enucleated with the chemical Cytochalasin B. However, although this chemical *will* enucleate some cells, it will *not* enucleate an egg cell. Also, in order to introduce the new nucleus from Max's cell into the egg cell, the outer layer of the egg cell, called the "zona pellucida," would have to be stripped off. An egg cell stripped of its zona pellucida cannot survive implantation in a uterus. It *will* grow in a test tube, but will only produce colonies' of similar cells, *not* an embryo. Next, the idea of "serial transfers" of one nucleus to another in the developing human embryo—as Rorvik claims was done to speed up the success rate—cannot be done because only a colony of cells would exist. Rorvik claims that this problem was solved by the use of "biochemical breakthroughs." If this were true, these breakthroughs would solve most of the problems with tissue regeneration, cancer, and transplantation. They would entitle any scientist who came up with them an almost certain Nobel prize. It is considered next to impossible that a couple of scientists working in isolation in a small tropical lab could possibly have the equipment, technique, or knowledge to accomplish in one short period what thousands of scientists have been unsuccessfully trying to do for many years.

Logistical problems also complicated the experiment. Rorvik was trying to get information from Bromhall about his methods several months *after* he claims that the cloning had successfully been done. In addition, Rorvik's book was published by the *trade* division of Lippincott and *not* by the medical division. The medical division could have had outside experts review the manuscript. The trade division said that it merely went on Rorvik's reputation.

As a result of some of this evidence, and of the court's own experts, Judge John Fullam ruled the book "a fraud and a hoax." He said that the plaintiff had "finally and conclusively established" that "the cloning described in the book never took place" and that "all of the characters mentioned in the book, other than the defendant Rorvik, have and had no real existence." The case by Bromhall against Rorvik was settled out of court for an undisclosed sum in 1982. A part of the settlement agreement was an apology to Bromhall. Although Rorvik eventually said that the cloned boy had developed a "defect," perhaps leading to his death, it was too convenient a reason for not producing him. Although Max had agreed to blood tests, they were under such secret conditions that the results could not be tied with certainty to any particular individual. The only definitive test would have technicians draw blood from the two individuals—father and clone—in the same room at the same time to see if the blood was identical. This was never allowed.

It looks as though the whole matter was a hoax, despite Rorvik's rigorous attempts to deny it, especially in his interview with journalist Barbara Seaman. Nothing further has been heard about this matter for the past few years, so it was apparently closed without any further claims of a successful cloning.

Sources:

Broad, William J. "Saga of Boy Clone Ruled a Hoax." *Science* 211 (February 27, 1981): 902.

Bromhall, Derek. "The Great Cloning Hoax." *New Statesman* (June 2, 1978): 734–36.

"Publisher Lippincott Is Sued for $7 Million Over Cloning Book." *Wall Street Journal* (July 11, 1978): 37.

[Seaman, Barbara]. "Penthouse Interview: David Rorvik." *Penthouse* (June 1978): 93–98, 176–79.

"Suit Over Cloning Book Settled Out of Court." *Publishers Weekly* (April 23, 1982): 12–13.

Scientific Creationism

Scientific creationism has elements of religion, but also attempts scientific plausibility. Yet, the essential elements of a hoax—especially a conscious desire to deceive—are prevalent enough that it must be considered as a hoax, at least in the eyes of its leading figures. To the average creationist no elements of a hoax are present. Scientists who lead the movement *know* that what they say is contrary to the scientific evidence they purportedly use to judge its truth or falsehood.

The clearest example is a matter involving the Second Law of Thermodynamics. Simply put, the Second Law says that to maintain order in a closed system—one in which no energy enters or leaves the system—is not possible. The system will eventually run down and return to a disorganized, random state. This state of disorder is known as a state of high entropy. Since the Second Law is true, creationists say that evolution cannot occur on the earth. Evolution incrementally produces a more highly organized state than before. In a closed system like the earth evolution

Charles Darwin.

is not possible, the creationists say. Evolutionists, such as Charles Darwin, claim that earth is *not* a closed system. The earth receives all of its energy from outside its system, namely from the sunlight.

Therefore, the Second Law is being misapplied in this instance. Perhaps it applies to the Solar System as a whole, and indeed the sun's energy is running down and the sun is becoming more disorganized (e.g., its entropy is increasing). Creationists have been told over and over again in public debate and in written responses to their writings, that they are misusing the Second Law—that it is *not* violated by evolution—yet they continue to make this same charge. Unwillingness to accept this charge reveals conscious deception.

Evolutionary theory has the dinosaurs dying out about fifty million years ago, long before any type of human—including Neanderthals—was in existence. Evidence that dinosaurs and man coexisted would be a serious blow to evolutionary timetables. Therefore, the creationists were glad when the supposed footprints of dinosaurs and men were found together on what was once a muddy riverbank near Glen Rose, Texas.

Although evolutionists insisted that the footprints creationists called "human" were not, it was not until 1986 that paleontologist Glen Kuban made a careful study of the footprints. He found that what were called human footprints were really from a three-toed dinosaur. There had been some erosion of the footprints, but careful examination showed the other two toes had left a mark. The distance between prints was far different from that which a man would make. Still, the creationists say that dinosaurs and man coexisted, although they have withdrawn their film about the Glen Rose footprints.

With regard to the Bible's Flood—a concept crucial to creationist geology—it has been stated by both geologists and archaeologists that *no* evidence exists of a flood covering the entire landmass of the earth at once (*See* Noah's Ark, p. 227). Floods did occur that covered much of the Middle East (except Egypt).

The creationist problem lies in how the distribution of fossils was accomplished without the passage of millions of years. The creationists try to account for this by a combination of "hydraulic sorting," victim mobility, and natural habitat. They say that those animals living in the sea would be buried first, although it is difficult to understand why, since they would be at home in the water. Next, they say, would be the slow-moving amphibians and reptiles, then faster land animals, and finally man. In effect, the creationists are accepting the ordering of the geological column. A problem with *plant* fossils remains. Since no plant can run, flowering plants, which often are found near the

shore, should be low down in the strata. Yet, these were the last plants to evolve, according to the evolutionists, and they are not found in the lower strata.

The "hydraulic sorting" idea says that the weight and size—and therefore water resistance to gravity—of an animal should determine where it landed in the geological strata, if the strata were *all* laid down at the time of the Flood. This would mean that *large* trilobites, for example, should be in lower strata, and *small* ones in higher strata. Actually, this is the *reverse* of what is found. Although all of this has been pointed out to creationists in books, articles, and lectures, they continue to repeat their flood hypothesis.

The motivation of the creationists appears to be to assure and strengthen the faith of Fundamentalist Christians. To imply that science confirms the Bible is to place the strongest force for discovering "truth" behind the most important source of faith in the lives of Fundamentalists.

Sources:

Dolby, R.G.A. "Science and Pseudo-science: The Case of Creationism." *Zygon* 22 no. 2 (1987): 195–212.

Eve, Raymond A. and Francis B. Harrold. *The Creationist Movement in Modern America.* Boston: Twayne Publishers, 1991.

Lemonick, Michael B. "Defeat for Strict Creationists." *Time* (June 30, 1986): 75.

Pastner, Stephen and William Haviland. "Confronting the Creationists." *Northeastern Anthropological Association Occasional Proceedings* no. 1 (1982).

Schadewald, Robert. "Creationist Pseudoscience." *Skeptical Inquirer* 8 no. 1 (Fall 1983): 22–35.

Strahler, Arthur N. "Toward a Broader Perspective in the Evolutionist-Creationist Debate." *Journal of Geological Education* 31 (1983): 87–94.

Sea Serpent and Lake Monster Hoaxes

There have been hundreds of sightings by experienced sailors of what appeared to be sea serpents. There have also been many sightings of an apparently large creature in Loch Ness in Scotland, and in other large lakes all over the world. The existence or non-existence of large unknown fresh and salt water creatures is not something that will be considered or decided here. It is not being asserted that all such sightings are hoaxes. Rather, what will be examined here are a number of "sightings" that turned out to be, or most probably were, hoaxes.

It is always tempting for a skeptic to think that *all* sightings of something strange and unknown are hoaxes, but this "a priori" assumption of a hoax is always a dangerous and logically incorrect thing to do.

A number of Loch Ness "sightings" are accompanied by photographs. Hoaxes in photography (*See* Photographic Hoaxes, p. 181) have a long history. That is not to say that *all* the Loch Ness photos are hoaxes, but some definitely *are*. The most famous of all Loch Ness monster photos is perhaps the one called "The Surgeon's Photo." It was taken by British gynecologist Robert Kenneth Wilson in 1934. Wilson did not want his name associated with the photo, hence the "surgeon's photo" name. The photograph taken by Wilson shows what appears to be a neck and small head of some kind sticking out of the water, upon whose surface the wind has made small waves. A bit of what appears to be the back of the creature can also be seen breaking the water. Wilson never claimed that his photo showed the Loch Ness Monster, but only that he had photographed an object moving in Loch Ness. He shunned all publicity and all interviews about the photo.

The photograph was made with a quarter-plate camera with what was described by Wilson as a telephoto lens. Wilson claimed that at 7:30 A.M., probably on April 19th, he stopped on the road surrounding the loch at a point two or three miles on the Inverness side of Ivermoriston. At this point, the road is some 100 feet above the loch. While looking at the loch, he noticed a commotion about 200-300 yards out. Something raised what appeared to be its head out of the water. He ran back to his car nearby to get his camera, and managed to snap four pictures before the head disappeared below the water. Upon development, only two of the photographs showed anything. One was somewhat out of focus and over-exposed.

Campbell has done a thorough analysis of a recently discovered full original print of the best photo. The negative has been lost and the published versions were greatly cropped. Campbell's analysis shows that if the photo was taken from where Wilson says it was, the object shown is only 0.75 meters long (about 28"). Campbell concludes that the photo is of an otter (probably of his tail). There *are* otters in Loch Ness. In order for this to be of an otter (or of an object 28 inches long), however, one must conclude that the surgeon *knew* it was an otter or other small object, not "Nessie." This means that he was knowingly creating a hoax. While Wilson has never admitted doing so, his silence on the photograph could have covered his guilty knowledge that it was not what it seemed.

There is a well known drawing of what purports to be a sea serpent (really a sea monster, since it is not a

Loch Ness Monster fake.

"serpent") that was washed up on shore dead on one of the islands in the Orkneys, known as Stronsa in 1809. This carcass, was really the decomposing body of a basking shark, which had decomposed enough so that the lower jaw had fallen off. As a result, the "creature" appeared to have a long neck and a small head. Although this was not a hoax at first, the drawing, and later photographs of similarly decomposed basking sharks, was subsequently used in a number of books and articles without explaining that the creature had been identified as a basking shark.

Another hoax involving a sea monster was that of the American brig *Daphne* in 1848. The master of a ship called the *Mary Ann* reported that he encountered the *Daphne* just outside Lisbon harbor and was told by her crew that they had recently encountered a huge sea serpent at sea. They had repelled the creature with a charge of spike nails and scrap iron fired from a deck gun. The captain's letter was published in the *London Times,* but it was soon pointed out that the *Daphne* could not possibly have gotten from the latitude at which the serpent was encountered to Lisbon in 10 days, as stated, unless the sea serpent was towing her. It was then pointed out in another newspaper article that there was no such ship as the *Mary Ann* that had been in Glasgow recently, as its supposed captain had claimed. The whole story was evidently made up by a journalist.

Several lake "monsters" have subsequently been identified as large lake sturgeon, some 12-feet or more long. Although this was again not a hoax, the fact that the monster was identified as a perfectly known species, although unexpectedly large, has conveniently been forgotten by a number of writers who like to preserve mysteries where there really are none. This action is a hoax. Many other sea serpent and lake monster tales rest upon the word of a single "witness."

Since there is not confirming evidence, one cannot know whether the witness is being truthful or not.

Sources:

Binns, Ronald. *The Loch Ness Mystery Solved.* Buffalo, NY: Prometheus Books, 1984.

Campbell, Stewart. "The Surgeon's Monster Hoax." *British Journal of Photography* (April 20, 1984): 402–05, 410.

Heuvelmans, Bernard. "The Monsters of Loch Ness. By Roy Mackal." [book review]. *The Zetetic* (Fall/Winter 1977): 110–21.

Meurger, Michel and Claude Gagnon. *Lake Monster Traditions: A Cross-Cultural Analysis.* London: Fortean Tomes, 1988.

Oudemans, A.C. *The Great Sea Serpent.* Leiden, Netherlands: E.J. Brill, 1892.

Perry, James M. "Run for Your Life! That Thing Could be the Loch Ness Monster." *Wall Street Journal* (August 1, 1983): 1, 8.

Seeing Without Eyes

There have been many reports of people who could see without the apparent use of their eyes. Some of these have involved blindfolded people seeing an object or being able to successfully drive an automobile. Others involve an individual who can see or read with other parts of the body, such as the fingertips. This phenomenon has been investigated, and has long been a part of many mentalists' magic routines. The latter should suggest that the authenticity of this phenomenon is shaky.

Magicians have long known about and employed what is called the "nose peek." There was a Kashmiri magician named Kuda Bux who made a career of driving about the streets of many cities demonstrating his skills while being securely blindfolded. The blindfolding process consisted of the application of wads of dough over each eye, followed by the winding of yards of cloth around his head to form a sort of turban. In addition to being able to drive in this condition, Kuda Bux could read, describe objects held in front of him, and do math on a blackboard. The American mentalist Joseph Dunninger used silver dollars taped over each eye, then had adhesive tape applied crosswise to cover the eye socket. He could still identify objects held up in front of him.

The nose peek depends upon a small amount of light entering along the edge of the nose, no matter how well the eye is covered. In order to see well, blindfolded people who are using the nose peek have to tip the head slightly upwards, giving the appearance of sniffing. A sniffing posture is usually a dead giveaway of a nose peek being done, although the sniffing may occur several seconds or minutes before the "seeing" is done. All it takes is a "sniff" and memorization of whatever was seen until it is the appropriate time to reveal it. All of this is standard magical knowledge.

Among the unusual people who "performed," probably using the nose peek, was a boy who had lost one of his eyes. He made the revival circuit during the 1960s, showing the "miracle" of how he could read with his eyeless socket. Russian women have been quite active in eyeless vision acts, especially in distinguishing colors with the fingertips. Of course, it is a relatively simple matter to identify colors using the nose peek.

Author Martin Gardner has suggested a simple method of testing whether a person can *really* see without use of their eyes. No blindfold is necessary. The person's head is enclosed in a light-weight aluminum box that rests on padded shoulders. It can have holes on top for air. The metal must go under the chin and fit snugly around the neck. With this device in place, the nose peek is impossible. Another method might simply be to hold the object to be viewed above the head of the subject and to allow his or her fingers to touch the object, if it is claimed that viewing is being done with the fingertips. As long as the subject is not allowed to tip his or her head up, no nose peek is possible at this angle. Of course, none of the "researchers" doing this kind of work allowed either of these controls to be used. When tighter controls *were* used in one series of experiments, the phenomena decreased to chance levels.

Perhaps the best example of how *not* to conduct research on eyeless vision, or dermo-optical perception (DOP), as it is also called, lies in the work of French novelist Jules Romains. His work is summarized in his book *Eyeless Vision*, where every control that could have been used was not. The result demonstrates the existence of no phenomenon.

Sources:

"'Eyeless Vision' Unmasked." *Scientific American* 212 (March 1965): 57.

Gardner, Martin. "Dermo-optical Perception: A Peek Down the Nose." *Science* 151 (February 11, 1966): 654–57.

Robinson, Leonard Wallace. "We Have More than Five Senses." *New York Times Magazine* (March 15, 1964): 30–34, 106–08.

Romains, Jules. *Eyeless Vision*. New York: G. P. Putnam, 1924.

Rosenfeld, A. "Seeing Color With the Fingers." *Life* (June 12, 1964): 102–13.

UFO Hoaxes

Unidentified flying objects came into public consciousness in June of 1947, following private pilot Kenneth Arnold's June 24 sighting of nine fast-moving, disc-shaped objects streaking in formation over Mount Rainier, Washington. In a subsequent interview with a newspaper reporter, Arnold compared the discs' appearance and movement to saucers skipping across water. As similar sightings erupted over America, an anonymous headline writer coined the phrase "flying saucers." Nearly five decades and many thousands of reports later, the debate about the nature and meaning of the phenomenon, and even its very existence, continues with no resolution in sight.

In the early days of the controversy, skeptics presumed that hoaxes played a large role in UFO-reporting, but subsequent developments showed this was not the case. The overwhelming majority of witnesses are sincere; bogus reports, investigators agree, are more likely to result from misidentification than from conscious fabrication. The U.S. Air Force's Project Blue Book found that hoaxes comprised only slightly more than one percent of the reports in its files and many of these involved photographs.

Photographs have always been common in UFO hoaxes, because they are easy to perpetrate—usually no more than an airborne garbage lid is needed—and difficult to disprove. Only a handful of claimed UFO photographs have withstood rigorous analysis. In most instances, the bogus photographs probably do not merit characterization as a "hoax"; prank is a more apt description, since a significant number of these photographs were taken by teenage boys. Nonetheless, committed hoaxers have used fake photographs to enhance confidence schemes involving contacts with space people. These individuals are known as "contactees" and their large role in the history of UFO hoaxes will be reviewed presently. Except for their part in this subset of bogus UFO claims, photographic hoaxes will not be covered.

The Prehistory of UFO-hoaxing

Hoaxes that focus on unusual aerial phenomena predate the modern UFO age by decades. What may be the first such hoax was published in the March 29, 1880, issue of the Santa Fe Weekly New Mexican. The newspaper reported that late one evening residents of tiny Galisteo Junction, New Mexico, spotted a large, fish-

Manufactured photo of a supposed UFO.

shaped structure sailing overhead. They could hear its occupants making merry and at one point they dropped several items overboard. The recovered objects were a "magnificent flower, a slip of exceedingly fine silk-like paper," and a peculiar cup. Less than twenty-four hours later a young Chinese man showed up, examined the writing on the silk paper, and declared it to be a message from his fiance, who was aboard an airship on a maiden voyage from China to New York (New Mexican, April 7). No such voyage ever took place, but the story—probably a journalistic invention—foreshadows similar yarns that would appear in American newspapers in 1896 and 1897, when a wave of reports of mysterious "airships" inundated the country.

More remarkable because it sounds so modern is a story that came out of remote Dundy County, Nebraska, four years later. In early June of 1884, in a dispatch out of Benkelman, the *Nebraska Nugget* (a weekly published in Holdrege) reported that a band of cowboys had seen a blazing object plummet to earth. They moved close enough to it to see "fragments of cogwheels and other pieces of machinery lying on the ground . . . glowing with heat so intense as to scorch the grass for a long distance around each fragment." One witness who stood too close was badly burned and later lost his sight. As the cowboys retreated, they noticed that the "sand was fused to an unknown depth over a space of twenty feet wide by eighty feet long and the melted stuff was still bubbling and hissing." According to the newspaper, by evening local folk flocked to the scene to view the machine, which was still glowing. They found other pieces of the craft, which "seems to be about fifty or sixty feet long, cylindrical, and about ten or twelve feet in diameter."

When it reprinted the account in its June 8 issue, Lincoln's *Daily State Journal* remarked that if the story

Another UFO hoax.

were true, "this unusual object of wonder must be an air vessel belonging originally to some other planet." But two days later a dispatch from the same anonymous Benkelman correspondent related that the craft's remains had vanished in a rainstorm, "melted, dissolved by the water like a spoonful of salt." Decades later newspaper reporters, folklorists, local historians, and ufologists, tried unsuccessfully to uncover evidence that the story had some factual basis. Clearly the "incident" existed only in the imagination of the Benkelman correspondent whose name has been lost to history.

In the fall of 1896, residents of northern California began to report large, cylindrical flying objects that they likened to "airships." Aviation historians attested that they were not flying over America at that time. By late November, after these objects flew over Sacramento and San Francisco, the great airship scare commenced. It would not end until May of 1897, by which time reports were recorded from as far east as Ohio. While it is arguably true that a minority of alleged sightings were unexplained, it is undeniably true that a large number were hoaxes. The "airships" fell afoul of both widespread journalistic skepticism and a nineteenth-century tradition of folk humor that expressed the tallest of tales with the straightest of faces. From the point of view of newspaper editors, the airships were so obviously a preposterous notion that journalists had no particular obligation to report them seriously. Witnesses could be freely ridiculed and false reports, some written by the members of the press themselves, could be freely published.

Consider, for example, a story from the November 27, 1896, edition of the *Stockton Evening Mail*. Col. H. G. Shaw, a correspondent, "formerly of the Mail editorial staff," wrote that while on a trip associated with his duties as a representative of the Stockton, California, Commercial Association, he and a companion encountered "three strange beings . . . nearly or quite seven feet tall and very slender." Though generally humanlike, these presumed "inhabitants of Mars" had larger than normal eyes, were toothless, and were "without any sort of clothing." When Shaw attempted to communicate with them, they seemed not to understand him and responded with a "warbling" sound. He touched one of them and discovered that the being weighed less than an ounce. The creatures tried to haul him into an airship hovering nearby, but possessed neither the strength nor the weight to accomplish their aim. Shaw concluded his account by denouncing other airship tales as "clumsy fakes."

It is unlikely that any reader of the *Evening Mail* thought this story was anything other than a joke. Other newspapers, however, were reporting other kinds of stories that took their inspiration not from extraterrestrial motifs but from the widespread belief that the airships were the creation of a brilliant inventor or inventors who soon would announce to the world what they had accomplished. At least two California attorneys claimed to represent the inventor, who never materialized. Others said they had seen the airships land and talked with their pilots, whose lengthy discourses were "quoted" word for word in press accounts. In all but one set of cases, the names of the aeronauts varied, as did their stated objectives and their descriptions of an airship's mode of propulsion. Several reports from Texas in April of 1897 recount alleged encounters with an aeronaut named "Wilson," but the descriptions of his airship and even of his physical appearance differ from account to account.

Nonetheless hoaxes and jokes about extraterrestrial aeronauts continued into the 1897 phase of the airship saga. In Le Roy, Kansas, rancher Alex Hamilton swore in an affidavit that he, his son, and his hired hand had seen strange creatures in an airship steal one of his calves. First published in the Yates Center (Kansas) *Farmers Advocate* on April 23, Hamilton's account was backed by a statement from prominent citizens who declared that they had never known him to lie. The story was widely reprinted at the time, then revived in the UFO literature in the 1960s. In 1976, however, a statement was collected from an elderly Kansas woman who said she had been in the Hamilton house and heard Alex Hamilton boast to his wife about the story he and his friends—the signers of the statement and fellow members of the local liars' club—had made up. Other investigators found a brief item in the January 28, 1943, issue of an obscure Kansas weekly, the *Buffalo Enterprise*, consisting of an admission by former *Farmers Advocate* editor Ed Hudson that the tale was fiction and he had a role in concocting it. Later, folklorist

Thomas E. Bullard discovered an open confession by Hamilton himself in a letter to the editor of the *Atchison County Mail*, a Missouri newspaper. When asked about the alleged incident, Hamilton said, "I lied about it" (May 7, 1897, issue).

The other major hoax—revived, like Hamilton's, in the 1960s when reporters and ufologists reviewed 1897 newspapers looking for evidence of early UFO sightings—concerned the crash of a Martian spaceship in the tiny Wise County town of Aurora, Texas, on April 17. The story was related in one brief dispatch datelined Aurora and published in the *Dallas Morning News* on the April 19. Bylined S. E. Haydon, it stated that at 6 A.M. a low-flying airship plowed into Judge Proctor's windmill and exploded. In the wreckage were the remains of a "native of the planet Mars" who was to be buried "at noon tomorrow." There was no follow-up account and the same page of the *News* reported, as soberly as it did the Aurora tale, the testimony of a Farmersville "eye witness" who spotted "three men in the ship and . . . heard them singing 'Nearer My God to Thee.'"

Nonetheless, in June of 1966, when Frank Masquelette of the *Houston Post* rediscovered the Aurora account, a wave of excitement that would not crest until seven years later rose, and reporters, ufologists, and curiosity-seekers plagued Aurora's 300 residents for information about the Martian. In 1973, a treasure hunter claimed that his metal detector gave identical readings at the crash site and at a certain grave in the local cemetery. On one Sunday morning soon after, a crowd of angry, armed locals kept UFO enthusiast Hayden Hewes from digging up the grave. A few residents and former residents claimed to remember the incident. The issue of whether to dig up the grave divided the community. Those who opposed digging feared that the grave contained a victim of a turn-of-the-century spotted-fever epidemic and that an exhumation would bring the disease back. Soon the issue became moot when the district court blocked the effort.

Meanwhile, the metal—apparently planted at the site—turned out to be from a 1920s-era aluminum alloy used in cookware. Local historians pointed out that no histories of the Aurora area ever mentioned anything about the death of a Martian—surely a notable event if it had occurred. In fact, no record of the "incident" existed beyond the single *News* dispatch. Moreover, Judge Proctor did not own a windmill. The locals who said they "remembered" the event were either suffering from befogged memories or playing a joke on gullible inquirers. Other elderly residents emphatically insisted that Haydon's story was a hoax. Wise County historian Etta Pegues noted that in 1897 Aurora was in decline because of the disease epidemic, a devastating fire, and the boll weevil; perhaps, she

suggested, Haydon had made it up to draw attention to the town in an effort to revive its fortunes.

Hoaxing in the Early UFO Age

After the airship scare speculation about space visitors was limited to fringe occult groups (some of whose leaders claimed to get mediumistic messages from space people and departed human spirits) to a small band of followers of Charles Fort, a New York satirist and anomaly-collector who uncovered early reports of unusual aerial phenomena and theorized, not always entirely seriously, that these were vessels from other worlds. On occasions when newspapers took note of what subsequently would be thought of as UFO sightings, they were either likely to propose a prosaic explanation or to suggest that the witness had seen someone's secret aircraft. With no real audience to play to, hoaxers had little interest in telling tales or arranging stunts around the alien-visitor theme. After 1897, the next significant hoax would be perpetrated just days after Kenneth Arnold's sighting, and ironically, Arnold would be among its principal victims. Even so, he would be lucky—two other victims would die in the course of the investigation.

About three weeks after his June 24 sighting, Arnold was contacted by Ray Palmer, the Chicago editor of science-fiction magazines *Amazing Stories* and *Fantastic Adventures*, which regularly published material on "true mysteries," including what were suddenly being called flying saucers. Palmer wanted Arnold to write an article about his own sighting. In a follow-up letter he casually asked Arnold if he would look into a story he had heard from one Fred L. Crisman, who allegedly had recovered pieces of a flying saucer. Palmer did not mention it then, but this was not the first wild story he had heard from Crisman, who sometime earlier had written to claim that he had a gunfight in a cave with hostile alien creatures. Arnold did notice that Palmer didn't "seem to be real cranked up about whatever happened there."

Arnold flew to Tacoma, Washington, and interviewed Crisman and Harold Dahl. Dahl, who identified himself as a harbor patrolman, said that on June 21 he, his son, and two crew members had seen six doughnut-shaped objects east of Maury Island. One, apparently in trouble, spewed out two kinds of metal, one white and light, the other dark and "similar to lava rock." He said he had filmed the objects. The next day a mysterious stranger, who seemed to know everything about the incident, warned him not to discuss it further. But Dahl told Crisman, supposedly Dahl's superior in the harbor patrol, and Crisman went to the beach and collected samples. When Dahl showed Arnold one, he immediately recognized it as lava rock.

The following morning Crisman arrived in Dahl's company and, Arnold recalled, "definitely wanted to domineer [sic] the conversation . . . about the entire Maury Island incident." Hooked on the story, Arnold called a new friend, United Airlines pilot E. J. Smith, who on July 4 had experienced a much- publicized sighting. Smith flew up the next day and, with Arnold, interviewed the two men in his and Arnold's hotel room. That evening a local reporter called to say that someone had called his office and reported "verbatim" the secret discussions in their room. Arnold and Smith searched for microphones but found none.

The next morning Crisman and Dahl showed them samples of both the lava rock and the white metal. The latter was immediately identifiable, Arnold thought, as "ordinary aluminum which certain sections of all large military aircraft are made of." As if that were not suspicious enough, Dahl said he had given the UFO film to Crisman, who claimed to have "misplaced" it. Strangely, it still did not occur to Arnold that he was being hoaxed; to the contrary, he decided that he was involved with a story too big for him and Smith alone. He called Lt. Frank M. Brown, a military intelligence officer at Hamilton Field in California. Arnold knew Brown because he had investigated Arnold's sighting.

Brown, accompanied by Capt. William L. Davidson, flew up in a B-25 an hour or two later. As soon as Brown and Davidson saw the fragments, they lost interest, excusing themselves as politely as they could without hurting Arnold's feelings or indicating their true conclusions. They boarded their B-25, whose engine caught fire half an hour later. The resulting crash killed both officers. In flying-saucer folklore, the circumstances of their deaths would be depicted as mysterious. They would be characterized as two men who had died because they "knew too much about flying saucers."

In reality, as a follow-up Air Force investigation learned from Crisman and Dahl's confession, the story was a joke that had gotten out of hand. One of them had made the calls to the reporter's office. Embarrassed for Arnold, whose "investigation" had been well-intended but inept, the Air Force never officially informed Arnold of its findings, and for years afterwards he continued to believe the Air Force was covering up what it knew about the "Maury Island mystery." Later, in a memoir of his years at Project Blue Book, The Report on Unidentified Flying Objects (1956), Capt. Edward J. Ruppelt would call the affair the "dirtiest hoax in UFO history." Some, Palmer prominently among them, refused to accept the hoax explanation.

Another major hoax was chronicled—though not as a hoax—in a best-selling 1950 book, *Behind the Flying Saucers*. The author, a sincere but gullible *Variety* columnist named Frank Scully, wrote that in the late 1940s the U.S. government recovered the remains of three crashed spaceships and their small but humanlike Venusian occupants. Scully's sources, Silas Newton and Leo A. GeBauer (identified only as "Dr. Gee" in the book), were represented, respectively, as a prominent oil man and world-class scientific expert on magnetics.

Actually, Newton and GeBauer were life-long confidence artists (con men) who were seeking to peddle a bogus oil-detection device said to be based on technological secrets learned from the saucers. This fact did not come to light until investigative reporter J. P. Cahn wrote a devastating expose in the September 1952 issue of *True*. In the early 1980s, ufologist William L. Moore dug even deeper than Cahn had, finding among other things that Newton and GeBauer stole their hoax idea from another hoax, a claim made by B-movie producer Mikel Conrad that a 1949 science-fiction film of his, *The Flying Saucer*, contained actual scenes of a spaceship in government custody. Conrad even hired an actor to pose as an FBI agent and swear it was true. Press accounts of this small show-business controversy inspired Newton and GeBauer to give their swindle-in-the-making a UFO-age spin.

As with the Maury Island episode, a few diehards still argue that Scully/Newton/GeBauer's stories were true. In a 625-page book, *UFO Crash at Aztec* (1987), William S. Steinman and Wendelle C. Stevens contended that Scully and his associates had been the innocent victims of a smear campaign sponsored by sinister official agencies. Moore found, however, that Newton and GeBauer continued their confidence activities, and remained in and out of trouble with the law to the end of their days.

Aboard the Spaceships

On November 20, 1952, a new phase of popular fascination with flying saucers began when a Venusian "scoutcraft" landed in the southern California desert and George Adamski, a figure on California's occult scene for over two decades, communicated with its occupant. Three weeks later the scoutcraft flew low over Adamski's residence, and he was able to take clear pictures of it. These were not his first saucer pictures, by any means; he had been taking them for the past three years. But now that he had met with a space person, he was on his way to international occult celebrityhood.

In 1953 his fifty-four-page account of his experiences was appended to an already-completed book manuscript by Desmond Leslie (dealing mainly with spaceships in ancient history and mystical tradition) and published as *Flying Saucers Have Landed*. It proved an immensely popular and influential book, and in

1955, Adamski's byline appeared on *Inside the Space Ships* (ghostwritten by Charlotte Blodget); in it Adamski's meetings with Venusians, Martians, and Saturnians, along with his rides in their flying saucers, were recounted. In Adamski's rendition, the saucer people were benevolent "Space Brothers," spiritually and physically beautiful beings who were trying to stop warlike humans from destroying themselves with atomic weapons. Their "cosmic philosophy" was to critics, and even some admirers, indistinguishable from Theosophy—the movement that holds that there is basic truth in *all* religions—founded by Madame Blavatsky (*See* The Mahatma Hoax, p. 223).

To most people, including many ufologists, Adamski's claims seemed so absurd that it was hard to believe anyone could possibly take them seriously. Yet many people did and Adamski's followers vigorously defended him in books and newsletters. In May of 1959 he toured Europe and—to the consternation of the Dutch press, scientific community, and university students (who disrupted one of his lectures with jeers and flying fruit)—was granted an audience with Queen Juliana. That meeting took place, but Adamski's further assertion that he was summoned secretly to a conference with Pope John XXIII remains unverified.

Adamski's harshest critics were conservative ufologists who maintained that his extravagant tales contributed to the climate of ridicule surrounding genuine UFO reports. James W. Moseley, editor of *Saucer News*, prepared the single most damaging expose, based on interviews with individuals who had been around Adamski during the eventful period of November and December 1952. One of Moseley's informants, Jerrold Baker, claimed to have seen the model used in the scoutcraft photographs and to have heard a tape recording of Adamski and associates rehearsing what they were to say about the upcoming November 20 "contact."

Moseley could not resist the temptation to hoax the hoaxer. He and a friend, UFO and contactee publisher Gray Barker, secured copies of State Department stationery, with the department seal impressed on the paper. They wrote a letter, signed it "R. E. Straith, Cultural Exchange Committee," and addressed it to Adamski. "Straith" wrote that the "Department has on file a great deal of confirmatory evidence bearing out your own claims. . . . While certainly the Department cannot publicly confirm your experiences, it can, I believe, with propriety, encourage your work." The State Department immediately denied knowing anything of either Straith or his committee, but Adamski told his followers that after a "thorough investigation" he had learned both existed but were highly classified. Nonetheless one ufologist, Lonzo Dove, correctly surmised that the letter had been written on Barker's

typewriter; not knowing of Moseley's involvement, he naively tried to get his analysis printed in Moseley's magazine, but to no avail. Fearing legal retribution, Moseley did not confess the hoax until January of 1985, one month after Barker's death.

Many devoted followers deserted Adamski after he announced that he attended a meeting on Saturn in 1962. This was a bit much, but even harder to accept was his sudden involvement in psychic practices which he long had inveighed against. A trusted associate, C. A. Honey, parted company with Adamski when he caught him in questionable practices that were apparently designed to bilk the credulous with a for-profit operation on how to contact space people. Unable to accept the possibility that the scoffers were right all along, Adamski's followers insisted that Adamski must have fallen under evil extraterrestrial, demonic, or even CIA influence. He died on April 23, 1965.

In his wake many other flamboyant figures emerged, though none with Adamski's charisma or influence. These contactees, who included such figures as George Van Tassel, Daniel Fry, Orfeo Angelucci, Howard Menger, and Truman Bethurum, supported their colleagues and endorsed each other's claims. Although in a scathing review of contactee literature (*Fantastic Universe*, November 1957), ufologist Isabel Davis found so many contradictions in their respective cosmologies that she concluded they could not possibly believe each other. Their activities may have bordered on confidence crime, but remarkably few had serious run-ins with authorities.

Authorities did catch up to Reinhold Schmidt, whose interplanetary adventures began in November of 1957, when he met the occupants of a Saturnian spaceship near Kearney, Nebraska. Schmidt subsequently had many further contacts and rides aboard alien craft. At one point, as they flew over a California mountain range, the Saturnians revealed the locations of vast amounts of quartz crystal. Schmidt sought out investors in a mining venture, and in due course they suspected they had been duped. In an October 1961 trial in Oakland, a then obscure young astronomer named Carl Sagan testified that human life could not possibly exist on Saturn. A jury convicted Schmidt on two counts of grand theft and sentenced him to one to ten years in prison, and nothing was heard of him again. Until his legal misfortunes, he had achieved the status of a major figure in the contactee movement. His supporters charged that the government had railroaded him to ensure his silence.

The Adamski-style contactees—those who claimed event-level-reality experiences and offered spaceship photographs and other artifacts as "proof"—constituted a minority of space communicants even in the 1950s. The majority of contactees were well-meaning if naive recipients of "psychic" messages that manifested as voices in the head or through automatic writing (a form of mediumship in which one enters a disassociated state of consciousness and allows the hand to write without consciousness). The sincerity of these individuals seems beyond dispute. In one celebrated 1954 case, followers of the subject of a famous sociological study ("When Prophecy Fails," by Leon Festinger, Henry W. Riecken, and Stanley Schachter 1956), Dorothy Martin ("Marian Keach" in the book) left jobs and family and endured international ridicule to await geological catastrophe and deliverance by flying saucer. In an even more extreme case, channeler Gloria Lee starved to death in a Washington hotel room in 1962 while fasting for peace at the direction of a voice from Jupiter. Usually it was only when a contactee displayed physical evidence of his experiences that the issue of conscious fraud came up. If a person were unprepared to believe in the reality of Venusian scoutcraft, there seemed no alternative to the conclusion that pictures of one were faked.

Nonetheless, the motives of even some physical contactees were not always easy to read. Some may have engaged in flying- saucer hoaxing to attract an audience for sincerely held occult religious beliefs. No less than C. G. Jung, the eminent psychologist and philosopher, held Angelucci to be a genuine visionary. In *Flying Saucers: A Modern Myth of Things Seen in the Skies* (1959) Jung wrote that Angelucci's visions came "like a gift to the psychologist. The individuation process, the central problem of modern psychology, is plainly depicted in it in an unconscious, symbolic form . . . although the author with his somewhat primitive mentality has taken it quite literally as a concrete happening." Others who knew Angelucci were similarly impressed with his apparent commitment. Religious studies scholar Robert S. Ellwood, Jr., remarked on Angelucci's "charm, humility, and sincerity"; he represented, in Ellwood's view, the "religious wing of the UFO contactee movement at its best." To Davis, however, Angelucci was no more than a case of "vanity frustrated," and sociologist Rodney Stark, who knew Angelucci and other contactees in their heyday, deemed him no less cynical than the rest. In cases like these, only the contactees themselves knew what they really believed.

Physical contactees have largely disappeared from the scene, though in the 1970s Eduard ("Billy") Meier drew occult pilgrims from all over the world to his Swiss farm—site of frequent interactions with "cosmonauts" and "beamships" from the Pleiades star system. Meier took numerous photographs which were reproduced in books by American promoters along with hundreds of pages of Pleiadean philosophy. In 1987,

Atlantic Monthly Press released a sympathetic book on Meier's claims, Gary Kinder's *Light Years,* but Meier's supporters were hard-pressed to explain why a spacewoman in one of his photographs proved identical to a fashion model in a European magazine advertisement. Ufologist Kal Korff conducted an extensive investigation and found other discrepancies, detailed in his self-published (and hyperbolically titled) *The Meier Incident: The Most Infamous Hoax in Ufology* (1981).

A sensational but relatively short-lived contact hoax caused a sensation in the French press in late 1979. Two young peddlers from Cergy-Pontoise, a Paris suburb, told police that early in the morning of November 26 they had seen a glowing cloud envelope a car holding their friend and associate Frank Fontaine. The cloud turned into a cylindrical UFO shape and shot away, leaving an empty vehicle. Accounts of the disappearance received worldwide publicity, owing in part to the two "witnesses" energetic promotion of it. Fontaine reappeared a week later, and as his "memory" cleared, he "remembered" meeting extraterrestrials and getting messages from them.

Most French ufologists doubted the story from the start and investigators noted discrepancies in the participants' versions of events. They also found that the three young men were interested in UFOs, occultism, and science fiction. A neighbor who was looking outside at the time of the supposed abduction testified that nothing out of the ordinary had taken place; he had, however, seen two young men (presumably Fontaine and "witness" Jean-Pierre Prevost) get into a car and drive away.

In 1980, two books treated the incident as factual. One, *Cergy-Pontoise UFO Contacts* (in English translation), was written by science-fiction author Jimmy Guieu, who declared, "I hold a priori their story to be true." According to Guieu, the extraterrestrials were more interested in Prevost, who obligingly started channeling messages from Intelligences du Dehors (IDDs, or "Intelligences from Beyond"), than in Fontaine. Prevost had his own book out later that year. *The Truth About the Cergy-Pontoise Affair* recounted the author's newest space adventures and devoted many pages to IDD sermons about the sad state of the earth.

After trying and failing to establish a cultlike group around the IDD messages, Prevost finally confessed (in Le Parisien, July 7, 1983), "I confirm that the Cergy affair was a hoax from the beginning to the end. I am the only one to be held responsible. I organized and put together the whole story. . . . Frank Fontaine had spent the eight days of his disappearance in the apartment of a friend in Pontoise. I took him there and brought him back." By then Fontaine had fallen on hard times and was serving time in prison for robbery.

Before the contactee milieu is finished, one contact claim deserves note as a unique kind of hoax perpetrated for none of the usual reasons. After Adamski and Leslie's book proved immensely popular in England, another volume appeared, titled *Flying Saucer from Mars* (1954). In it author "Cedric Allingham" related that while vacationing in Scotland, he met a friendly visitor from the Red Planet. Though "Allingham's" story was hailed by the Adamski faithful as validation of their hero's truthfulness, "Allingham" proved peculiarly elusive, and it was eventually rumored that he died in a European tuberculosis asylum. In the 1980s, British ufologists looked into another rumor that "Allingham" was none other than space-science writer and television personality Patrick Moore, known as a vocal UFO scoffer. In spite of a body of circumstantial evidence pointing to him, Moore vehemently denied the charge. A Moore associate, Peter Davies, reported otherwise, saying he had helped Moore write the book so as to disguise the latter's distinctive literary style. According to Davies, Moore wanted to spoof Adamski and show up the credulity of those who believed him.

The "Mysterious" Carlos Allende

Among the most successful UFO- related hoaxes of all time was the creation of an eccentric drifter who sometimes used the name "Carlos Miguel Allende." Born in Springdale, Pennsylvania, on May 31, 1925, Carl Meredith Allen spent most of his life wandering the United States and Mexico, living (so his parents and siblings told Robert A. Goerman in *Fate*, October 1980) in a world of fantasy and invention. What rescued him from obscurity were three items: two letters to author Morris K. Jessup, and annotations in the paperback edition of Jessup's *The Case for the UFO* (1955).

Jessup received the first of the letters, forwarded to him from his publisher, in October of 1955, and the second the following January. Written in different colors of pen and pencil, spelled and punctuated erratically, they hinted that the correspondent, who identified himself as both Allen and Allende, knew all kinds of secrets about levitation and other matters. He alluded to an October 1943 experiment that resulted in

> complete invisibility of a ship, Destroyer type, and all of its crew, While at Sea . . . . Half of the officers [sic] and the crew of that Ship are at Present, Mad as Hatters . . . . The Experimental Ship Disappeared from its Philadelphia Dock and only a Very few Minutes Later appeared at its other Dock in the Norfolk, Newport News, Portsmouth area . . . . BUT the ship then, again, Disappeared And Went Back to its Philadelphia Dock in only a Very few Minutes or Less.

Jessup assumed Allende was a crank and thought nothing more about him until a year later, when an invitation arrived to come to the Office of Naval Re-

search (ONR) in Washington. There Jessup learned that in the summer of 1956 someone had mailed an annotated copy of *Case* to the ONR office. The annotations indicated that three persons (A, B, and Jemi), apparently Gypsies, were the authors; they intimated that they were privy to the secrets of the UFO beings (called "S-M's" and "L-M's") and knew of the former's hostility to the human race. For reasons that have never been explained (perhaps lack of exposure to crank mail), some of the junior officers were impressed sufficiently to study the annotations carefully. They wanted to know what Jessup thought. As he read them, noting among other things the reference to the invisibility experiment in Philadelphia, Jessup remarked that at least one of the writers was certainly Allende.

Intrigued, the authors arranged for a small printing of the book by the Varo Company of Garland, Texas, thereafter known in popular legend as the "Varo edition," and the letters. An unsigned introduction (written by ONR Special Projects Officer Cmdr. George W. Hoover and Capt. Sidney Sherby) explained, "Because of the importance which we attach to the possibility of discovering clues to the nature of gravity, no possible item, however disreputable from the point of view of classical science, should be overlooked."

On April 20, 1959, Jessup—distraught over a failed marriage and financial problems—committed suicide in a Florida park. The importance of the Allende letters and the Varo edition, already an object of wonder in some circles, was magnified accordingly. For years rumors circulated—even finding their way into print in small-circulation monographs such as Anna Lykins Genzlinger's *The Jessup Dimension* (1981)—that sinister government forces had murdered him because of what he had learned about the Philadelphia experiment and other matters hinted at in the Allende letters and the Varo edition.

The legend grew in the early 1960s with the publication of Borderland Sciences Research Associates' *M. K. Jessup and the Allende Letters* (1962) and Gray Barker's *The Strange Case of Dr. M. K. Jessup* (1963). Mass-circulation books such as Vincent Gaddis' *Invisible Horizons* (1965) and Ivan T. Sanderson's *Uninvited Visitors* (1967) picked up the story. In 1968, a cover blurb on Brad Steiger and Joan Whritenour's *New UFO Breakthrough* declared, "Our concept and understanding of flying saucers are totally wrong! So say the bizarre and terrifying ALLENDE LETTERS." The last two words were in the same size type as the title of the book beneath them. That same year Steiger and Whritenour put together a magazine-format anthology, *The Allende Letters*. In 1974, Charles Berlitz's huge bestseller *The Bermuda Triangle* took the tale to a large popular audience that had never heard of it before, and Berlitz's associate William L. Moore's *The Philadelphia Experi-*

ment (1979) reported the story as well as "evidence" and rumors in considerable detail. A science-fiction film of the same name, starring Michael Pare and Nancy Allen, was released by New World Pictures in 1984.

Ironically, Allen had owned up to the hoax years earlier. In 1969, he called on a Tucson couple, Jim and Coral Lorenzen, directors of the Aerial Phenomena Research Organization (A.P.R.O.). As with other conservative ufologists, the Lorenzens had never taken the "Allende" affair seriously and were barely interested in talking with the "mysterious" and "legendary" figure, whom they regarded simply as a self-important pest. Allen admitted to them that he alone had annotated the Varo edition. In a written statement he related that his claims in the book were "false . . . the crazyest [sic] pack of lies I ever wrote." Allen's confession was reported in the July/August 1969 issue of the *A.P.R.O. Bulletin*. Later Allen retracted the confession, helping to keep the "mystery" alive for those who wanted to believe.

For the doubters, however, all that remained to be answered was the question of who Allen was, and those answers came in a 1980 *Fate* article by Robert Goerman, who learned to his surprise that he had known Allen's parents all his life. Their black-sheep son was not someone they often discussed, they told their neighbor. They showed Goerman letters in which Carl, whom they called a "master leg-puller," bragged of his role in creating a modern legend. Carl's brother Randolph said, "He has a fantastic mind. But so far as I know, he's never really used it, never worked anywhere long enough to collect severance pay. . . . He reads continually, but the information gets all twisted somehow." Carl Allen is said to have died sometime in the 1980s.

Flying Saucer to the Moon

In 1957, in what was destined to be one of the most brazen confidence swindles in UFO history, Otis T. Carr announced, "I have invented a fourth dimensional space vehicle," shaped like a flying saucer and powered by a "revolutionary Utron Electric Accumulator . . . operating in unison with the free energy of the universe." Carr, a youthful hotel clerk in New York City, claimed to have befriended the elderly electrical scientist Nikola Tesla. Tesla had confided secrets for which he considered the human race unprepared, and now Carr, his pupil, was about to unleash them on the world.

Carr set up OTC Enterprises in Baltimore in 1955 and secured funding from a prominent businessman in the city. He also hired a skilled promotion man, Norman Evans Colton, who sent out a slew of "information bulletins" to investors and inquirers. The bulletins "explained" the flying saucer mechanics in sentences like these:

> Mount this whole rotating body, with its spindle, on another platform and rotate this platform on a spindle[;] then, if the counter-rotation is greater than the initial forward rotation of the body, a dip-needle on the second platform will point down while the first dip-needle points up, indicating the complete relativity of polarity. When the exact counter-rotation matches the forward rotation, the body loses its polarity entirely and immediately becomes activated by free-energy (tensor stresses in space) and acts as an independent force.

Investors who assumed Carr (who declared himself a greater scientist than Einstein) and Colton knew what they were talking about gave thousands of dollars, in spite of the duo's frequent public gaffes. On Long John Nebel's WOR radio show in June of 1958, Carr remarked that he could not "even begin to enumerate" Tesla's wonderful discoveries, but when a skeptical fellow guest urged him to "enumerate just one or two of them," Carr could only mutter, "That's funny—I cannot remember even one." Nor, when challenged to do so, could Carr recite even one of Newton's three laws of motion, leading Colton to interject that memorizing such things "verbatim" was a "waste of time."

Carr did much of his money-hunting on the contactee circuit, usually in the company of Margaret Storm (author of an occult "biography" of Tesla), contactee Wayne Sulo Aho, and Warren Goetz, who came into the world after a flying saucer materialized him on his mother's lap. Carr managed to garner respectful press attention as he discussed his plans to construct the OTC-X1, a craft forty-five feet in diameter and fifteen feet high, for $20,000,000.

Late in 1958, OTC Enterprises relocated to Oklahoma City, where Carr had found some particularly enthusiastic and well-heeled benefactors. Now he was announcing that on December 7, 1959, he would pilot the OTC-X1 from the earth to the moon and back. Meanwhile, on Sunday, April 19, a six-foot prototype would make its maiden flight from an Oklahoma City amusement park at three o'clock in the afternoon.

Though hordes of journalists, curiosity-seekers, and contactees (one of whom averred that "Captain Karnu" and his five invisible spaceships were monitoring the proceedings) converged on the site, the test was delayed for three days. There had been a "mercury leak," it was explained. Meanwhile Carr, having come down with a sudden throat ailment, was confined to an area hospital and safely removed from the scene. Three days later the test was called off entirely. Nebel, who had flown down from New York, demanded entry into the factory where the OTC-X1 was stored; he caught a brief glimpse of what looked like a jumble of unconnected parts and wires which bore no particular resemblance to an aircraft. The parts and wires, in any case, soon were destroyed in a mysterious fire.

On May 4, in the county courthouse in Oklahoma City, Carr repeatedly took the fifth amendment when asked to answer questions about stock sales to three wealthy local businessmen. Two weeks later Carr, Colton, Aho, and Lari Kendrick (the OTC Enterprises salesman who had brought Carr to the city) were charged with illegal stock sales. In Colton's case, the charges were leveled in absentia; having fled the state, he was unfindable. On November 19, Carr was fined $5,000 on a single charge, but the once-mighty OTC Enterprises had only $1.71 left in its checking account. Carr was sent to jail to work off the fine at a dollar a day. He faded from the scene, to die years later in a Pittsburgh slum.

For his part, Colton tried to revive OTC Enterprises until the New York state attorney general stepped in to stop him. Undaunted, Colton created something called the Millennium Agency and solicited orders for "free energy machines . . . operated entirely by environmental gravitic forces" which would "draw electricity from the atmosphere without the use of any fuel." Nothing came of the scheme.

Tomato Man, EBEs, and Others

For nearly three decades memories of the Scully hoax discouraged ufologists from paying attention to recurrent rumors about crashes of UFOs in the Southwestern United States in the late 1940s and early 1950s. But in the late 1970s ufologist Leonard H. Stringfield, who had been quietly collecting reports and rumors of such events, urged his colleagues to reconsider the matter. One consequence was a rash of bizarre hoaxes.

Among the most amusing—as well as the most ghoulish—was one centered on photographs of what purported to be the remains of an alien being amid flying-saucer wreckage. The photographs came to light through a Maryland man named Williard McIntyre, who had already established a reputation among UFO buffs as a man with a creative imagination. McIntyre said the pictures had been slipped to him from a secret source, a man who on July 7, 1948, had been flown to a Mexican site near Laredo, Texas, to record the crash. Later, when he was about to leave the service, he made duplicate negatives and took them from his office.

In November of 1980, the Coalition of Concerned Ufologists (McIntyre was a member) put out a monograph, *Alien Body Photos: An Updated Report*, on its

"investigation." The other members of the Coalition were not given access to McIntyre's alleged source, but they vehemently rejected a suggestion by another ufologist that the figure in the picture was a rhesus monkey killed in a rocket experiment. The coalition suggested this critic and other skeptics in the UFO community were part of a "plot," motivated by petty jealousy, to discredit this important item of UFO evidence.

Soon enough, however, one of the coalition members, Charles J. Wilhelm, could no longer contain his reservations. Stung by ridicule from other ufologists, who were calling the figure in the pictures "tomato man" because the helmet on his head bore resemblance to that fruit, Wilhelm went on to write his own monograph, *An Investigative Report Into the Alledged* [sic] *Alien Body Photos* (1982), based on a rather more thorough investigation than the coalition had conducted. Wilhelm determined that every detail in the story was fictitious, as was Williard McIntyre's "source." The photographs depicted the dead pilot of a small plane—his aviator glasses were visible not far from the body—and were not taken in the Southwest, but in an Eastern state, and more recently than 1948.

Another crashed-saucer tale surfaced in the tape-recorded testimony of "A. K.," one of UFO investigator Stringfield's original informants, who delivered a dramatic account of his encounter with a crashed saucer in the mid-1960s. Citing it as an example of the kind of information he was receiving, Stringfield played the tape in the course of a widely publicized lecture on "retrievals of the third kind" to the 1978 convention of the Mutual UFO Network (MUFON). A. K. claimed to have stood guard at a crash site near Fort Riley, Kansas.

Though Stringfield was inclined to take him at his word, another investigator, ufologist W. Todd Zechel, learned that A. K. was not only a knowledgeable UFO buff, but a man with a gift for melodramatic storytelling. Zechel phoned Gen. Jonathan O. Seaman, whom A. K. identified as the officer who led the recovery operation, and posed as a frightened former Fort Riley noncommissioned officer who was now being pressured to talk about the flying saucer he had guarded. The general said in a kindly voice, "If you think it happened and want to talk about it, go ahead." Meanwhile A. K. was busily promoting his tale on radio shows and in tabloid newspapers.

As fascination with crashed-saucer stories mounted, another earlier rumor was given renewed life: that the United States not only had access to alien hardware but was in direct contact with extraterrestrial intelligences. In England's January/February 1956 issue of *Flying Saucer Review* was a piece by an unnamed "special correspondent" who had spoken, he said, with a "highly placed American who was in touch with Air Force Intelligence and in a position to know the facts about flying saucers." From communications with the aliens the government learned that the purpose of the visitation was "completely friendly." Open contact would occur once the space people learned how to breathe the "heavily oxygenated atmosphere of this Earth."

Nine years later, the magazine identified the correspondent as "Rolf Alexander, M.D." and his informant as American general and diplomat George C. Marshall. Though *Flying Saucer Review* characterized Alexander as a prominent medical scientist, "Alexander" was the pseudonym of Allan Alexander Stirling, a New Zealand seaman who in 1920 jumped ship, entered the United States illegally, and concocted a fictitious biography and professional history to help him promote quack health schemes. Stirling's career was interrupted by occasional prison sentences for, among other things, mail fraud and grand embezzlement. Stirling also claimed the power to break up clouds through psychokinesis.

Far more puzzling was a series of events that began in 1973, when two Los Angeles documentary filmmakers, Robert Emenegger and Allan Sandler, were invited to Norton Air Force Base in California. In a meeting with the head of the base's Air Force Office of Special Investigations (AFOSI) and the audiovisual director, Paul Shartle, they discussed the possibility of making films about newly declassified Air Force projects. Emenegger and Sandler were told, to their considerable surprise, that in May of 1971 a UFO landed at Holloman Air Force Base, New Mexico, that the event had been filmed, and that the alien occupants had met with scientists and military officers. They were promised access to 3200 feet of the film, but after a complicated series of events they were refused permission. In 1988, on national television, Shartle would confirm the existence of the film, which he said he had seen. The aliens in it "were human size. They had an odd, gray complexion and a pronounced nose. They wore tight-fitting jump suits [and] thin headdresses that appeared to be communication devices, and in their hands they held a 'translator.' A Holloman base commander and other Air Force officers went out to meet them."

Thus began a complex, convoluted series of extraordinary claims that spanned all of the 1980s and gave every indication of being a counterintelligence operation, conducted for inscrutable purposes and designed to lend credence to rumors of government-extraterrestrial contacts. In some instances the stories were directly traceable to individuals in the AFOSI office at Kirtland Air Force Base, Albuquerque. They were spread via direct meetings with ufologists and journalists and through the circulation of official-look-ing documents, some of which contended that an organization called "Majestic-12" or MJ-12 directed government UFO policy and that the Air Force's highly classified "Project Aquarius" did the field work, which included recovery of crashed spacecraft.

One allegation was that in 1949, an alien survived a crash and was housed at Los Alamos, New Mexico, until its death from unknown causes in 1952. The humanoid was given the name "EBE" (ee-buh), short for "extraterrestrial biological entity," a phrase that in its plural form denotes all UFO intelligences, in official parlance. Nine extraterrestrial races visited the earth, and some played active roles in human evolution and cultural development. Some well-placed agents within the cover-up wanted it to end; others wanted it to continue. The former were leaking the story to the public through selected individuals. Their faces shaded and voices altered, two alleged cover-up insiders, "Falcon" and "Condor," told their stories on a nationally syndicated television show, "UFO Cover-up . . . Live," revealing that the EBEs liked strawberry ice cream—a detail that hardly made credible an already incredible body of claims.

There is no independent evidence to support any of these tales. Yet the tellers' motives are murky, and many unanswered questions remain. The Holloman film does seem to exist, though it does not necessarily depict what it purports to; presumably the EBEs are actors in masks. It may take a Congressional investigation to find out what really happened.

As these strange stories circulated through the UFO community and the larger public, other, more conventional kinds of hoaxers came forward with their own elaborations. They linked the stories to political conspiracy theories of the far (even neofascist) right and claimed as their authority secret documents they had seen while occupying sensitive positions in the military. Skeptical ufologists who looked into these individuals' backgrounds found that their military histories were considerably exaggerated, as were other assertions about their access to classified installations and materials. Nonetheless some of these men attracted huge paying audiences to lectures where books, videos, and tapes were hawked.

The tales seemed to grow with every telling. According to spokesmen for what wags have called the "dark side hypothesis," a sinister "secret government" (consisting of the CIA, the National Security Agency, and the Council on Foreign Relations) runs the United States and murders all those, everyone from cabinet members to Presidents (such as John F. Kennedy, who threatened to blow the whistle), who get in their way. They operate in collaboration with a Geneva-based international secret society, the Bilderbergers and the Trilateral Commission. Trilateral insignia are worn by "His Omnipotent Highness Krlll" (pronounced Krill), the Betelguese ambassador with whom President Eisenhower signed the first human-EBE treaty. The treaty allowed the EBEs to abduct human beings long as the latter were returned unharmed, while the earth's secret rulers were given the secrets of EBE technology. The EBEs violated the treaty by killing and mutilating some abductees.

Additional tales reveal that in an effort to deal with the alien menace without letting the rest of the human race know what was happening, America's secret government needed to raise vast sums of money quickly. Thus, it entered the drug trade, putting a Texas oil company president, George Bush, in charge of the enterprise. It also decided the population numbers had to be reduced, so deadly diseases including AIDS were introduced. It developed a space program, in cooperation with the Soviet Union, and by the early 1960s human beings thrived in colonies on the moon and Mars. One day less fortunate citizens will be taken to the colonies to work as slave laborers after society has been destabilized, and martial law and concentration camps set up. One aspect of the master plan is the enacting of gun-control laws so that criminals (some trained by the CIA) will have free reign to terrorize ordinary Americans. All the while, in vast underground tunnels in the Southwest, evil human and alien scientists stir enormous vats in which soulless android slaves are being created to replace inconveniently sentient human beings. Moreover, through the development of time travel, the rulers learned that the anti-Christ would be revealed in 1995, the same year World War III would occur; Christ himself would return in 2011.

What this scenario lacked in logic, coherence, or supporting evidence of the slightest sort, it made up for in delirious paranoia that rendered all previous UFO conspiracy theories wan in comparison, and appealed to the legions of the terminally frightened. The dark-side movement peaked in 1989 as its promoters' rhetorical and personal excesses became too much for all but a hardy band of credophiles. The benign, optimistic cosmic vision of Adamski and his colleagues had been filtered through Watergate, the Vietnam war era, and other shattering national traumas and become a terrifying nightmare in which any evil, terrestrial and extra-terrestrial, was imaginable.

Dreamland

In dark-side theorizing, as well as more restrained crash-saucer speculation, Area 51, located in a corner of the Nevada Test Site and sometimes called "Dreamland," is said to be the place where work on the secrets of UFO technology is conducted. In fact, such suspicions are part of the common folklore of the Southwest and have been remarked on in newspaper and magazine articles on the facility.

On November 11 and 13, 1989, Las Vegas' KLAS-TV, an ABC affiliate, carried an astonishing story on its evening news show, the result of a one and one-half year investigation by reporter George Knapp. The subject was one Robert Lazar, who claimed to have been employed at Area 51 in a location designated S-4. The Navy, Lazar related, hired him to study some classified technical papers on advanced propulsion systems. Lazar told Knapp that he was startled to read of systems far in advance of anything conventional physics could have conceived. "The power source is an antimatter reactor," he said.

The walls of the work areas displayed posters showing a disc ascending from the ground. The caption read, "They're here." In due course, Lazar was taken into a hangar where he saw a disc. Though instructed to walk by the vehicle and not look directly at it, he touched it briefly as he passed it. Later he saw the object in flight and was also allowed to view eight other craft in connecting hangars separated by large bay doors. Each had a distinctive appearance, but all were disc-shaped.

His superiors told him nothing about the nature of these craft or the circumstances of their recovery. Once, however, when he looked inside one, he saw "it had really some [small] chairs" as if its pilots were of shorter-than-human stature. That caused things, he said, "to click together just all too fast." After observing the discs in the air, he was convinced that no terrestrial technology could have accomplished what he was seeing. But what clinched matters for him was his discovery that a substance unknown to earthly science, element 115, played a major role in the development of the gravity-harnessing technology.

In the course of his investigation, Knapp interviewed a "technician in a highly sensitive position" and was told it was "common knowledge among those with high-security clearances that recovered alien discs are stored at the Nevada Test Site." Still, Knapp conceded, "Checking out Lazar's credentials proved to be a difficult task." He was unable to secure documentation to support Lazar's assertions about his professional and educational background, and polygraph examinations yielded inconclusive results. Even so, Knapp thought he was probably telling the truth.

For a short time Lazar was an international UFO celebrity, promoted by dark-sider John Lear (whom he had approached first) and reporter Knapp, who put together a follow-up television special. But as supporting evidence remained elusive and Lazar grew ever more evasive about key issues, doubts multiplied even among those who initially heard him out. In April of 1990, Las Vegas police arrested Lazar for his involvement in the operation of a house of prostitution, though by August plea-bargaining had reduced the charges to a single felony, pandering for which he was sentenced to three years' probation, 150 hours of community service, and psychotherapy.

Lazar has not confessed to making up the story about the alien discs in Area 51. Those who have met him say he has a somewhat enigmatic personality. His purpose in promoting the yarn is unclear. What seems much clearer is that the story was inspired by popular Area 51 rumors and by Lazar's exposure to dark-side lore through his friendship with Lear. It also appears certain that as crashed-saucer legends continue to command audiences and television slots, Lazar will not be the last of his kind.

Jerome Clark

Sources:

Cameron, Grant R., T. Scott Crain, and Chris Rutkowski. "In the Land of Dreams." *International UFO Reporter* 15 no. 5 (September/October 1990): 4–8.

Clark, Jerome. *The Emergence of a Phenomenon: The UFO Encyclopedia*, Volume 2. Detroit, MI: Apogee Books, 1992.

———. *UFOs in the 1980s: The UFO Encyclopedia*, Volume 1. Detroit, MI: Apogee Books, 1990.

Cohen, Daniel. *The Great Airship Mystery: A UFO of the 1890s.* New York: Dodd, Mead, 1981.

Ellis, Bill. "The US-EBE 'Secret Treaty': Folklorists Should Be Appalled." *Foaftale News* 17 (March 1990): 6–8.

Flammonde, Paris. *The Age of Flying Saucers: Notes on a Projected History of Unidentified Flying Objects.* New York: Hawthorn Books, 1971.

Moore, William L. "Crashed Saucers: Evidence in Search of Proof." In *MUFON 1985 UFO Symposium Proceedings.* Edited by Walter H. Andrus, Jr., and Richard H. Hall. Seguin, TX: Mutual UFO Network, 1985: 130–79.

Nebel, Long John. *The Way Out World.* Englewood Cliffs, NJ: Prentice-Hall, 1961.

Other Science Hoaxes

The German Rocket Hoax. On November 5, 1933, the *Sunday Referee*, a London newspaper, printed what it claimed was an "exclusive report" of a secret rocket flight that had occurred a week before at the island of Ruegen in the Baltic Sea. This would have been the first manned rocket flight in history. The story said that Otto Fischer had been rocketed to a height of 32,000 feet by the German War Ministry, before the rocket parachuted back to earth with him inside. The parachute had deployed when the rocket started descending. The whole flight had lasted just over ten minutes. Fischer had evidently made the flight while *standing* inside the rocket. He was white and shaken upon landing, but was otherwise unharmed by the flight. The article was signed by "Special Correspondent, Ruegen." The other London newspapers began an investigation, but their correspondents failed to confirm the story. However, a number of Swiss and French newspapers reprinted the story without checking the facts. Author Willy Ley investigated the existence of a rocket enthusiast named Fischer at that time, and failed to find one. Serious errors in the story also show it to be a hoax.

The Comet-Seeker Hoax. Famous astronomers have been targets—or at least the vehicle—of hoaxes before (*See* Great Moon Hoax, p. 252), but in this case, the great astronomer could not deny the truth of the hoax, no matter how hard he tried. It seems that Professor E. E. Barnard—a noted discoverer of comets of the Lick Observatory, read an article in the *San Francisco Examiner* of March 8, 1891, referring to an invention of his. This invention was a device made of a selenium cell, which was attached to an automatically moving telescope. When the telescope registered an unusual light source, such as a comet, it locked onto it and sounded an alarm in the astronomer's office. This invention was needed, as the drudgery of constantly scanning the heavens was an activity that many astronomers wished could be avoided. Yet, such a device could not have worked then and still is not practical 100 years later.

Barnard had nothing to do with the article and had not invented any such device. The article was written by a ficticious astronomer, "Collis H. Barton." The editors of the newspaper were told in advance by the perpetrator of this hoax that Professor Barnard would deny its truth. Barnard's angry letters of denial were ignored by the newspaper. Several years later, on February 5, 1893, the *Examiner* noted that it was contrite at having fooled the public into thinking that Barnard had invented such a device. The paper wished him "all the new moons and comets that may be necessary to his happiness." The real hoaxer remains undiscovered, although Barnard always thought it was Prof. James E. Keeler.

The Missing Day. A story was told—most publicly by TV evangelist Jimmy Swaggert—that some modern computer scientists who were working for National Aeronautics and Space Administration (NASA) ran into trouble when plotting the past positions of the planets through time. About twenty-four hours of time was unaccounted for in their calculations. When the scientists surmised that this must be the day God made the sun stand still for Joshua (Joshua 10: 12–13), the calculations came out correctly. The incident showed that modern science confirmed the accuracy of the Bible.

However, careful investigation by author Tom McIver showed that this whole story was a hoax, made up by a Fundamentalist engineer who was a former consultant to NASA. He used the story whenever "witnessing" in front of groups about "how science is proving the preposterous things in the Bible are true." He claimed that because the story produced converts to Christianity, it must be true!

The Soviet Space Program. There is a good deal of controversy about whether the *early* Soviet space program—including the first walk in space by Colonel Leonov—was actually a photographic hoax or a real space event. The strange thing about the "walk" was the film of the event released to the United States by the Soviets. This was the first walk in space by a human (1965), and therefore, if it was fake, the Russians had little guidance about how a body would react to floating in space.

When a number of American photography experts viewed the film *after* an American had walked in space (Ed White of Gemini-4), they noticed a number of details that seemed wrong, based on White's walk. For example, White had trouble keeping his legs together in zero gravity. The Russian did not, but stated that his space suit was not rigid. In addition to this, there was a shot of Leonov emerging from the hatch of the spacecraft. This shot could only have been filmed from *outside* the spacecraft, yet there was no one outside to film it. Only Leonov walked outside; his copilot remained inside. The film also never showed all of Leonov's body floating in space at any time. This seems odd, unless it was done to conceal supporting wires. A still photo shows what appear to be bubbles, indicating that the sequence was shot *underwater*, rather than in space. The film, although supposedly shot in color, appears to be blue and white (similar to black and white). Why this is so is not clear, unless it is to hide double exposures.

Ed White wore a faceplate that filtered out ninety percent of harmful ultraviolet rays and allowed him to see without the sun's bright glare. As a result, one could not see his face clearly through the faceplate. Yet, Leonov's face was clearly visible as if he did not need to have the harmful radiation filtered out. Author Lloyd Mahan claims that the lifeline connecting the astronaut to the ship shows sharp bends in the Soviet film. The American's lifeline shows a smooth loop. The difference indicates that perhaps one was not filmed in zero gravity. In addition, none of the still photographs provided by the Soviets was contained in the motion picture film provided. The still photos may have been shot in a tank of water, as mentioned, and not in space.

This possible faking of the first walk in space and perhaps of some other early Soviet space feats, does not cast doubt on the later Soviet space missions, which did occur in the 1970s and 1980s. Mahan feels that many of the earlier Soviet space flights were actually *unmanned*, even though the Soviets claimed they were manned. The few voice transmissions from those spacecraft in orbit, which were general "greetings" messages, may have been tape recordings. The lack of reception of these messages and their general content (nothing was transmitted about the data or activities of the mission), tend to support his conclusions.

The Orgueil Meteorite. Imagine the surprise of scientists when they closely examined a meteorite that had fallen at Peillerot, France on May 14, 1864, as a part of the Orgueil meteor shower. According to the museum records at Montauban, France, this thirty-four-gram meteorite was stored in a sealed glass display jar from 1864 until 1962, when it was examined by scientists. They found plant fragments, seed capsules, and coal fragments. Some of the plants were identified as from the area in France where the meteorite was found. The meteorite either gave evidence of life on other planets, or the plant fragments were an earthly contaminant, or it was a deliberate hoax. Amino acids were also found in the meteorite which showed the presence of collagen. Collagen is a major constituent of a number of glues and gelatins and is of animal origin. The conclusion was that the meteorite had been deliberately contaminated before it was turned in to the museum. A hoaxer had molded plant and coal fragments with glue and worked them into a paste. This paste was penetrated into the crevices of the meteorite and hardened into what appeared to be a normal meteorite crust. No one had discovered the hoax for ninety-eight years; the identity or motivation of the hoaxer is now unclear.

Sources:

Anders, Edward, Eugene R. DuFresne, and Ryoichi Hayatsu. "Contaminated Meteorite." *Science* (November 27, 1964): 1157–61.

Curtis, Heber D. "The Comet-Seeker Hoax." *Popular Astronomy* 46 (1938): 71–75.

Ley, Willy. "Hoaxes" [The Fisher Hoax]. *Fantastic Adventures* (Chicago) (January 1940): 74–75.

McIver, Tom. "Ancient Tales and Space-Age Myths of Creationist Evangelism." *Skeptical Inquirer* 10 (Spring 1986): 258–76.

Mahan, Lloyd. *Russia's Space Hoax*. New York: Science and Mechanics News Book, 1966.

Show Business and Entertainment Hoaxes

This section will cover hoaxes involving music, cinema, theater, and dance. Most of the hoaxes happen to be in the field of music, although the musical hoaxes range from rock and roll to classical. While there is overlap between cinema and photography (See Photographic Hoaxes, p. 181), hoaxes involving commercially released motion pictures are covered under "Show Business," while other film hoaxes are found under "Photographic Hoaxes."

Backward Masking

Satan is a significant factor in the lives of many Fundamentalist Christians. He is purportedly always present, tempting people at every opportunity. With the assistance of his many demon helpers, he tries to get people to sin, reject Christianity, or follow him. Therefore, it was not surprising that Fundamentalist ministers—notably Gary Greenwald in the beginning—suggested that Satan had prodded rock groups record satanic messages backwards over the sound tracks of a number of rock albums. The messages could be heard clearly when the record or tape was played *backwards*, and sent subliminal messages to the brain when played forward.

Two questions need to be addressed. The first is whether humans can understand—consciously or subconsciously—spoken messages played backwards to them. The second is whether rock records contain any such messages. Obviously, if humans can't understand or perceive such messages, it matters little whether the messages exist. This distinction has been lost in Fundamentalist media about "backward masking." The term is actually a misnomer as applied to backwards subliminal messages, as it was "backmasking" originally and meant that louder music or lyrics were covering indistinct words in the background.

Another factor concerns whether ambiguous stimuli or sounds can be interpreted as meaningful words, even when they are not so intended. In other words, can messages of a satanic nature be manufactured *by the listener* from ambiguous, innocent, backwards sounds?

A significant technical development relevant to this issue involves Hal Becker's 1978 invention of a device that inserted audio subliminal messages (but not backwards) into music tapes. His messages, like "I am honest; I will not steal," were used by department stores at a very low volume in their background music. It was reported that shoplifting decreased, but it is unclear how controlled these "studies" were.

Several studies were well-controlled. In 1984, Throne and Himelstein showed how perception that a satanic message is present, when only ambiguous stimuli are present, comes from what people feel they *should* be perceiving. In other words, Fundamentalists told of a satanic message on a record are more likely to find a satanic message than others who do not expect to find such a message.

In 1985, researchers Don Vokey and John Read also did a well-conducted study in which they found that almost no one could consciously or unconsciously perceive or understand a backwards message, even one consisting of words that they already knew by heart. In other words, even if a backwards satanic message were on a record, no one playing that record's message backwards could understand it.

As with many rumors, a germ of truth is often part of a particular idea. With backward masking, there were a few records on which the rock group intentionally recorded something backwards, as a sort of perverse joke. For example, the group ELO (Electric Light Orchestra) has a backwards message on one of their albums that says "The music is reversible, but time is not. Turn back, turn back, turn back." A Pink Floyd album track has this deliberate backwards message "Congratulations! You've discovered the secret message. Please send your answer to Old Pink care of the funny farm. . . ." Neither message is satanic.

Charges have been made, however, that a number of specific recordings *do* have satanic messages. Among the ones listed by Fundamentalists are the Beatles, Black Oak Arkansas, ELO, Queen, Jefferson Starship, Led Zeppelin, Styx, Eagles, Rolling Stones, Venom, and Mötley Crüe. The backwards words supposedly include "It's better to reign in hell than to serve in heaven," "I love you said the Devil," and "Satan, move in our voices." When the backward words that supposedly say this are played forward, they *could* be interpreted to say what is claimed, but they could also be meaningless noises sounding something like what is claimed.

Much of the idea of subliminal messages of a "nasty" sort being included in ads or records comes from writer Wilson Bryan Key. His work, is totally discredited by his actions as reported by author Thomas Creed. Key sees sexual images everywhere, even when assured that a photograph was taken of an object just as it was and has not been doctored.

A side note to this whole matter is provided by the subject of "Christian rock." Many Fundamentalists claim that subliminal messages are present in Christian rock songs as well. Others say that since all rock music is inspired by the Devil, any subliminal messages—even the pro-Christian ones supposedly found in some of these songs—are demonically produced. Jimmy Swaggart has condemned "So-called Christian rock" as a "diabolical force undermining Christianity from within."

In short, the whole idea that satanic messages are hidden backwards under many rock recordings is simply a hoax perpetuated by Fundamentalists fearful of the bad effects of rock music upon young people. No real evidence exists that a conspiracy, human or demonic, to add such messages to songs is taking place.

Sources:

Aranza, Jacob. *Backward Masking Unmasked: Backward Satanic Messages of Rock and Roll Exposed.* Shreveport, LA: Huntington House, 1983.

Aranza, Jacob. *More Rock, Country and Backward Masking Unmasked.* Shreveport, LA: Huntington House, 1985.

Creed, Thomas L. "Subliminal Deception: Pseudoscience on the College Lecture Circuit." *Skeptical Inquirer* 11, no. 4 (1987): 358–66.

McIver, Tom. "Backward Masking, and Other Backward Thoughts About Music." *Skeptical Inquirer* 13 no. 1 (1988): 50–63.

Thorne, Stephen and Philip Himelstein. "The Role of Suggestion in the Perception of Satanic Messages in Rock-and-Roll Recordings." *Journal of Psychology* 116 (1984): 245–48.

Vokey, John and J. Don Read. "Subliminal Messages: Between the Devil and the Media." *American Psychologist* 40 no. 11 (1985): 1231–39.

Elvis Presley is Alive

The question of whether or not Elvis Presley, who reportedly died in 1977, is still alive raises important issues about evidence and proof of Presley's death. Elvis Aaron Presley (1935–1977) was probably the most popular American singer of the first seventy-five years of the twentieth century. When he died at the early age of forty-two, many fans suffered shock and disbelief, which set the stage for the idea that he might not really be dead.

Although Elvis's survival may be mere wishful thinking, it is at least *possible* that he faked his death and is still alive. This is coupled with many claimed sightings of Elvis, supposed phone calls from Elvis since 1977, and purported photographs. Nevertheless, the burden of proof is with those who say that he is still alive. As this prospect is fairly unlikely, given the evidence for his death and his absence of a public appearance since 1977, it will take strong evidence against his death having occurred before the idea should be given credence.

The circumstances of Elvis's death were rather strange. On August 16, 1977, he was found unconscious on the floor of the bathroom of his house—Graceland—in Memphis, Tennessee. Some reports say he was nude, others say he was in pajamas, the color of which varies with the source. All of the photographs of the death scene have disappeared from the coroner's files. Some reports said he was dead when found, others that he was near death. Supposedly, he was addicted to many prescription medications (not illegal drugs) and had overdosed on them. It is reported that Elvis took medication for high blood pressure, lupus, and glaucoma, as well as amphetamines and tranquilizers. He was at least sixty pounds overweight in August of 1977.

When the body was removed by the ambulance attendants, they did not recognize him. The law in Tennessee requires an autopsy in all cases of death at which no physician or witness was present. In this case, the family (evidently Vernon Presley, Elvis's father) gave permission for the autopsy. The results of an autopsy can be kept secret for fifty years. Some sources claim (without much justification, it would seem) that an autopsy was never performed. The cause of death was listed as heart problems (coronary artery disease). The stomach contents were taken for analysis, but no analysis seems to have been done. The coroner's office marked the case closed on the very day of his death, before any results of the autopsy were known. The death certificate was issued in October, several months later, supposedly to replace a lost original. The weight listed on the death certificate was 170 pounds (blank on some versions of the death certificate), although 250 pounds would have been more accurate. The official homicide report says that the body was found unconscious, while the medical examiner's report says that rigor mortis had already set in (e.g., he was dead for several hours) before the body was found.

The following are additional *claims* made about the death scene and the investigation of the death by various authors and investigators. The allegations are reported as additional considerations affecting the probability that Elvis really died as reported.

Paul Weist, a handwriting "expert" who appeared on the *Elvis Files* TV program, stated that it was his opinion after examining specimens of Elvis' handwriting, that the Medical Examiner's Report was filled out by Elvis Presley himself. The medical examiner who was supposedly in charge at the time was Dr. Jerry Francisco, who said that he had performed an autopsy. Dr. Francisco stated that he was present at the autopsy, and that such an autopsy *was* performed on Elvis Presley.

Elvis reportedly had read and been impressed by Hugh Schoenfield's book *The Passover Plot*, which postulates that Jesus faked his own death by taking some sort of drug that made him appear temporarily dead. Supposedly, Elvis was an expert on prescription medications. Elvis went to his dentist to have his teeth cleaned the night before his death, which indicated that he planned to go on an extended tour as scheduled the next week. However, he did not get his graying hair and sideburns dyed, as he usually did before a tour. More seriously, Elvis, who had gained so much weight that his concert costumes did not fit him any longer, did not get measured for any new costumes for the upcoming tour. No prescription medicines were found in the house (they were usually kept in a trailer outside the house). However, Elvis's girlfriend supposedly cleaned up *before* calling the paramedics.

At the funeral, people commented that the body in the open casket did not look exactly like Elvis. One relative noticed that one of Elvis' sideburns was becoming detached. The corpse also appeared to be "sweating." While it was quite hot and muggy that day in Memphis, corpses do not sweat. Comments have also been made about the weight of the coffin containing the body. It appeared to be several hundred pounds heavier than expected (900 pounds versus 500 pounds, though whether it was actually weighed is not clear). Also, unsubstantiated reports said that Vernon Presley, when told at the funeral that the body in the coffin did not look like Elvis, nodded and said that Elvis was "Upstairs. We had to show the fans something." Whether that meant that Elvis's *dead* body or the *living* Elvis was upstairs is not clear.

On "The Elvis Tape," purportedly a recording made of a telephone call received from Elvis in 1981, "Elvis" says that he *has* to perform in public. That was in 1981, and as of 1991, he still has not performed in public. An inventory of the estate left by Presley fails to list many of his personal items, such as jewelry, diaries, personal photographs of his family, and items of furniture.

Elvis's life insurance money was never collected. He was reportedly insured by Lloyds of London, but the amount is not clear. Of course, if Elvis were still alive, then collecting the insurance policy would be fraud.

The "sightings" and ambiguous photographs have not been precisely dated. Telephone calls were also made to friends or acquaintances, purportedly from Elvis. Voice analysis of some of these calls has reportedly shown that the calls were made by someone who had a nearly identical voice pattern to Elvis. The amount of confidence that should be placed on these results is open to dispute. Another story claims that Elvis was appointed an agent of the Drug Enforcement Agency (DEA). He *was* issued a DEA badge, but he also collected law enforcement badges. Whether his life was really in danger from organized crime because of his DEA activities cannot be determined at this time.

To sum up the evidence on both sides is difficult. A circumstantial case that Elvis has faked his death can be made. However, the probability of this being true seems slim. Against *this* evidence are the autopsy report, the fact that Elvis has not performed in public, the reports of relatives who saw the body, and the difficulty of pulling off a hoax involving a death. All of the police and coroner's office employees would have had to have been paid off or induced to keep silent. The disappearance of key documents, even from police files, is quite common in the case of the deaths of famous people (i.e., Robert Kennedy, Marilyn Monroe, etc). Even police can be souvenir hunters. Missing items do not necessarily mean a conspiracy or cover-up in the death.

A number of people have made a lot of money claiming that Elvis is still alive. Perhaps *they* are the real hoaxers. At this point one cannot tell for sure, but Elvis could certainly answer any doubts if he made a public appearance or conducted a press conference.

Sources:

Brewer-Giorgio, Gail. *The Elvis File: Was His Death Faked?* New York: Shapolsky Publishers, 1990.

———. *Is Elvis Alive?* New York: Tudor Publishing Co., 1988.

Cortez, Diego. *Private Elvis.* Stuttgart, Germany: Fey, 1978.

Griffin, David, producer. *The Elvis Files.* WPIX Television Network program aired August 14, 1991.

Marcus, Greil. *Dead Elvis.* New York: Doubleday, 1991.

Milli Vanilli

In November of 1990, the popular music world was startled with the announcement that the album "Girl You Know It's True"—the singing group Milli Vanilli's first album that sold over seven million copies—did not contain the group's singing. The band had won a 1989 Grammy Award as best new artist. Frank Farian, the German producer of the album, decided to make the hoax public when the group told him that they actually wanted to sing on their next album. Farian said that he didn't like the idea of Milli Vanilli actually singing as " . . . that's not really what I want to use on my records." Farian had recorded the hit song "Girl You Know It's True," which gave its name to the album, using different people, before he ever met the lead singers from Milli Vanilli, Rob Pilatus and Fab Morvan. It was Farian's idea to use the two men as the performers who appeared to have recorded the song. Pilatus and Morvan lip-synched the song in their concert appearances.

The National Academy of Recording Arts and Sciences, which awards the Grammy, stripped the group of its award before the group was able to return it as they intended. A telephone poll of the academy's thirty-four trustees was conducted. The trustees were furious and agreed the award should be revoked. The actual people who recorded the hit song were Brad Howell, Johnny Davis, and Charles Shaw. The academy finally decided that the revoked Grammy would not be awarded to anyone that year.

Sources:

Holden, Stephen. "Winner of Grammy Lost by Milli Vanilli: No One." *New York Times* (December 5, 1990): C23.

"Milli Vanilli Didn't Sing Its Pop Hits." *New York Times* (November 16, 1990): C20.

"Milli Vanilli Explains Its Lip-Synching." *New York Times* (November 21, 1990): C8.

Pareles, Jon. "Wages of Silence: Milli Vanilli Loses a Grammy Award." *New York Times* (November 20, 1990): C15, C22.

P.T. Barnum Hoaxes

Phineas Taylor Barnum (1810–1891) was the founder of the circus in America. He was also a showman and the perpetrator of many hoaxes, most in good fun, but some simply for money or publicity.

One of Barnum's earliest hoaxes was his exhibition of Joice Heth. Barnum had an agreement for the rights to exhibit her for a period of time in the 1830s. She was touted as being more than 160 years old and George Washington's nurse in his infancy. When Joice Heth died in 1836, an autopsy was performed. The story appeared in a 1836 newspaper that she was not 161 years old at the time of her death. However, the story in the *New York Herald* (February 27, 1836) claimed that the body autopsied was not really that of Joice Heth. She was still being exhibited in Connecticut. The hoax was really on the *Herald*, which had been supplied with erroneous information by Barnum's assistant, Levi Lyman. When confronted with the error of his ways, Lyman agreed to supply the *Herald* with the real story of Joice Heth. This ran in the *Herald* beginning on September 8, 1836, in six articles. The Joice Heth story was *again* a complete hoax. He said that Barnum had discovered an old black woman on a plantation in Kentucky. Barnum had her teeth extracted, taught her about George Washington, and gradually raised her age as he exhibited her. Heth's age crept up from 110 to 121, to 141, to 161 years old. Barnum revealed in his autobiography that Lyman made the story up.

Actually Barnum had bought the rights to exhibit Heth for ten months for $1,000. He opened an exhibit, employing Lyman as the "barker," in New York City. Soon Barnum was taking in $1,500 per week. It was his first success at show business. When the crowds in New York started to dwindle, Barnum took Heth on a tour of New England cities. After Heth died unexpectedly, Barnum arranged the autopsy. When that showed that Joice Heth could really not have been more than eighty years old, Lyman planted his "wrong body" story in the *Herald*, claiming that the person autopsied was an old black woman named "Aunt Nelly." Barnum supposedly made more than $10,000 from exhibiting Joice Heth.

P. T. Barnum.

Another hoax with which Barnum was closely associated was the Cardiff Giant (*See* Cardiff Giant, p. 13) Barnum's role here was to offer to buy the Giant from the exhibitors for a huge sum of money. When Barnum's offer was refused, he had his own version of the Cardiff Giant carved from a block of marble and exhibited it as if it were the original. Evidently, both specimens of the Giant brought in large sums of money for a while.

Another area of hoaxing in which Barnum played a prominent role was in the exhibition of fake animal composites (called Jenny Hanivers), such as mermaids made from a fish tail sewn to a monkey upper body and head (*See* Plant and Animal Hoaxes, p. 259). Both of Barnum's American Museums had a number of such specimens on exhibit. The remains of one is still on exhibit in the Barnum Museum in Bridgeport, Connecticut.

Barnum was not above using a little hoax to promote his otherwise legitimate acts. General Tom Thumb was the name Barnum gave to Charles Sherwood Stratton, a genuine American midget. Stratton was born in Connecticut and was not a general of any sort. At times Barnum depicted Tom as being from England, including when he was presented to Queen Victoria. One of Barnum's big publicity successes came when Tom married another midget, Lavinia Warren.

Some time later, Barnum had Tom and Lavinia's picture taken holding the seven-pound baby they had recently had. The baby was someone else's, as Tom and Lavinia were childless. The child soon disappeared from the scene.

Barnum was much impressed by the ingenuity of R.A. Locke's Moon Hoax (*See* Great Moon Hoax, p. 252) and wrote about it in his *Humbugs of the World*. He also appreciated Edgar Allan Poe's Balloon Hoax (*See* Edgar Allan Poe's Balloon Hoax, p. 47).

Sources:

Austin, James C. "Seeing the Elephant Again: P.T. Barnum and the American Art of Hoax." *Thalia* 4 (1) (1981): 14–18.

Barnum, P[hineas] T[aylor]. *The Life of Barnum the World-Renowned Showman.* Philadelphia: S.I. Bell & Co., [c. 1892].

———. *Struggles and Triumphs: Or, The Life of P.T. Barnum.* 2 vols. New York: A. Knopf, 1927.

Betts, John Rickards. "P.T. Barnum and the Popularization of Natural History." *Journal of the History of Ideas* 20 (1959): 353–68.

Harris, Neil. *Humbug: The Art of P.T. Barnum.* Boston: Little, Brown & Co., 1973.

Saxon, A.H. *P.T. Barnum: The Legend and the Man.* New York: Columbia University Press, 1989.

Rock Hudson's Marriage

Rock Hudson's marriage was done almost entirely as a public relations, image-boosting event. Rock Hudson was supposed to be the handsome heterosexual ideal of the 1950s; he was actually exclusively homosexual. When a lifestyle *appears* one way, but is actually another *by design*, it is a hoax. The perpetrator or instigator of this particular hoax was Hudson's manager, Henry Willson.

Hudson was born Roy Harold Scherer, Jr., but was later adopted by the Fitzgeralds, whose last name he took. He was raised by them in the Chicago suburbs. When Fitzgerald came into Henry Willson's office in Hollywood to see if Willson would become his manager, a life-long relationship was born. Willson was publicly recognized as a homosexual. He also travelled to Europe and elsewhere with Hudson, whose new name he devised. Yet it was not until just before the release of the film *Giant* (1955), which was actually Hudson's thirty-second film role, that public rumors of Hudson's own homosexuality threatened his reputation. *Confidential* magazine had been digging for a story on Hudson. Willson was frantic. He knew he had to protect his number one client, who was then being pushed as "America's number one heartthrob."

Supposedly, Willson made a deal with *Confidential*—although there is no hard evidence for this—to keep the story of Hudson's homosexuality out of the magazine in return for inside information on one or two of Willson's other clients. The story about Hudson never came out in *Confidential*, but a story did appear about Rory Calhoun, followed by another one about Tab Hunter, both Willson clients. This is suspicious, but by no means conclusive evidence of a deal.

Willson knew that the only way to really fend off rumors of Hudson's homosexuality would be to have him get married. Willson selected Phyllis Gates, a secretary in his own office. On November 11, 1955, she married Rock Hudson. The wedding, in Santa Barbara, California, was arranged at the last minute. Willson's plan to maximize press coverage included making the wedding *appear* secret. The press turned out in droves and the wedding was widely reported. It was a simple Protestant ceremony, conducted by a Lutheran minister.

Rock Hudson's best friend from childhood, Jim Matteoni, thought the marriage was sincere, although he knew that Hudson was afraid of marriage. Thirty years later, Hudson told his then lover, Marc Christian, that he really loved Phyllis and their relationship was both emotional and physical. Marriage, Hudson said later, had destroyed their relationship. Fan magazines, however, were filled with quotes about how happy they were.

Within a year of the wedding, rumors of the imminent breakup of the marriage began. In 1957, it was over. Phyllis received a reported cash settlement of $130,000 and never remarried. Hudson rarely talked about his marriage after it was over. It was not until his much publicized AIDS diagnosis was known (July of 1985) that the general public finally knew about Hudson's lifestyle.

Sources:

Hudson, Rock and Sara Davidson. *Rock Hudson: His Story*. New York: William Morrow & Co., 1986.

Oppenheimer, Jerry and Jack Vitek. *Idol/Rock Hudson: The True Story of an American Film Hero*. New York: Villard Books, 1986.

Rosemary Brown

Rosemary Brown is a British woman who claims that she can play newly composed music by long-dead, famous composers, by hearing the music in her head.

She cannot read music, so what she plays on the piano is transcribed onto paper by someone else. She claims her compositions are really by Liszt, Chopin, and others. It was once believed Rosemary Brown was sincere in her belief as to the origin of the music, but her mystery has been solved. Her performance is a hoax.

Brown's first book, *Unfinished Symphonies*, contained an illustration in its inside covers of the score of what she called *Valse Brilliante*, said to be dictated to her by Franz Liszt. Fortunately, this music was photocopied, enlarged, and studied by a professor of music, who is an expert of the work of Liszt and Chopin. Prof. Geoffrey Gibbs identified the source of Rosemary Brown's music in *Valse Brilliante* as *known* music of Chopin, written while Chopin was alive. Gibbs identified portions of *Valse Brilliante* as being from Chopin's *Scherzo in B Minor*. In fact, Gibbs thinks that the entire piece sounds much more like Chopin than Liszt. He feels that it is too "tame" even for a young Liszt.

Liszt's last piano works were rarely performed. It is therefore fairly unlikely that Rosemary Brown would have heard them played or heard them on records. This would mean that she was not likely to know how his style had evolved before his death. One would assume that he would not revert to an early style after his death, assuming that he *was* dictating post mortem compositions to Rosemary Brown.

"Playing by ear" is an often misunderstood phenomenon. The fact that a person who does not know how to read music can "hear" music in his or her head and then play it on an instrument, does not mean that the music is original with the player, or that it is being dictated from the afterlife. It is quite possible to sit down at a piano and play in the style of a particular composer. This could be new music, not written by that composer, or it could be a composition consisting of bits and pieces of the music of that composer, analyzed and strung together as one would imagine the famous composer would have done it. Gibbs feels that Brown's music in this case sounds "only like clever imitation and improvisation." It is not well conceived composition, but has features that sound somewhat like the music of Franz Liszt.

Brown's music is superficially attractive. The figuration is appropriate for a Romantic keyboard work and the chord changes and key modulations are typical of the nineteenth century. The music opens with a chromatic figuration in E Minor. The harmony at first glance might be suitable for early Liszt, but there is a part writing problem. For all of his experimentation, Liszt holds on to some of the old traditions for doubling tones and resolution of dissonance. In measure four, the music awkwardly doubles the leading tone (D#) between soprano and bass voices. Although Liszt uses thick sonorities to build resonance and obscures his musical lines with elaborate figuration, he seldom sacrifices good part writing between outer voices.

Later in the imitated work is a chain of seventh chords. Traditional handling requires that the seventh tone of each chord be resolved carefully. But Rosemary Brown jumps from one chord to another without regard to resolution of dissonance. This is typical of Jazz and popular Block harmony, and indicates that the commercial music of her day has also influenced her improvisation. To lengthen the music, directions are given to repeat the right hand up an octave. This is a casual way to fill out the music. Liszt would seldom resort to such an obvious method. His repetitions are variations on the theme with new ornamentation and figuration.

According to Gibbs, Liszt would not have missed the chance to enthrall his audience with a major run, a "sweeping figuration over the full keyboard in fast notes (32nds or 64ths). . . . It appears that Rosemary Brown is not capable of Liszt's level of virtuosity. . . . Overall, it is more like the keyboard writing of Chopin."

So, although Rosemary Brown is not necessarily a charlatan, she is also not likely a vehicle for the new compositions of now-dead composers. She has a good ear for style and a retentive memory for music she has heard. She has taken Chopin, dressed it up in the superficiality of Liszt's style, and claimed it as a new and original Liszt composition. Unfortunately, this piece is the only one given in sheet music in either of her two books. If other pieces were given, then an additional analysis could have also been done on those pieces, probably with similar results.

Sources:

Brown, Rosemary. *Immortals By My Side*. Chicago: Henry Regnery Co., 1974.

———. *Unfinished Symphonies: Voices from the Beyond*. New York: William Morrow, 1971.

Gibbs, Geoffrey. "Rosemary Brown's *Valse Brilliante*" [Unpublished manuscript, February 6, 1992. Available from Gordon Stein upon request.]

May, Antoinette. *Haunted Ladies: Exploring the Supernatural With Six Great Psychics*. San Francisco: Chronicle Books, 1975: 43–69.

Other Show Business and Entertainment Hoaxes

Fritz Kreisler's Hoaxes. The violinist and composer Fritz Kreisler (1875–1962) admitted that some of the pieces he played in his concerts as violin solos by Vivaldi, Couperin, Francoeur, Porpora, and Padre Martini, were really compositions of his own. Kreisler believed he was hampered by the lack of good solo violin music and therefore created his own. When he was questioned about the pieces, he said he found the music in libraries and monasteries in Paris, Venice, Rome, and Florence, and then copied them. Most critics called the pieces "little masterpieces."

Beatles Hoaxes. The group the Beatles has been both responsible for hoaxes and the subject of some. Perhaps the most common hoax facing famous popular musicians is the impostor. Groups of other musicians and individual musicians like to share in the fame of a popular group. Many cases involve one group impersonating another. In the case of the Beatles, perhaps the distinctive appearances and style of the group would appear to make this impersonation difficult. However, in the early days of "Beatlemania," namely in 1964, four young men from Liverpool, *Illinois*, grew their hair to Beatle length in preparation for the upcoming first series of American concerts by the Beatles. They learned to lip-synch to Beatles songs, and practiced British accents from movies. They got a friend to portray the Beatles manager, Brian Epstein. This friend also played the Beatles records backstage. The group started its tour in rural Illinois, but was soon playing Iowa, Montana, and other scenic spots. Then they moved on to Boise, Idaho, and Moose Jaw, Saskatchewan. On May 24, 1964, they were to play a concert at Rapid City, South Dakota, when the real Beatles made their third appearance on the Ed Sullivan show that very night. Federal marshalls were waiting for the fake Beatles at the stage door of the auditorium. The fake Beatles had to return all of their earnings in order to avoid jail time.

Another Beatles hoax involved the cover of the "Abbey Road" album as "evidence" that Paul McCartney was dead. The rumors of Paul's death were quite widespread, and may have been started by a Detroit disk jockey named Russ Gibbs, on October 19, 1969. The evidence was everywhere, he said. The cover of the "Abbey Road" album, where Paul is barefooted, is only one piece of that evidence. As Paul McCartney is still alive, the "Paul is dead" excitement can now be seen as a hoax.

Steve Allen's Hoaxes. Comedian, writer, and composer Steve Allen has used his great song-writing ability to cover several music hoaxes. Allen made an album containing boogie-woogie piano playing by "Buck Hammer." The album, issued in the 1950s, received three and a half stars from *Downbeat* magazine. Allen says that the "experts seemed to like my playing [as Hammer] much better when they thought I was black and dead rather than white and alive." Allen produced a second hoax album entitled "The Wild Piano of Mary Ann Jackson," illustrated by a cover photo of the Allen's housekeeper Mary Sears.

The Bob Dylan Hoax. Bob Dylan, the composer and folk singer, was the victim of a hoax that involved Dylan's song "Blowing in the Wind," a bestselling song of 1963. Henry Levin, an economics instructor at Rutgers University at the time, stated that Dylan had bought the song from a boy in New Jersey named Lorre Wyatt, who wrote it when he was fifteen. The payment was supposedly a $1,000 contribution to the charity CARE. Wyatt wrote to the magazine *Broadside* to disavow the Levin statement. Wyatt said that he had written a song called "Freedom is Blowing in the Wind," which had a similar title, but different music and different lyrics. The confusion originated with those who mixed up the two titles. In the February 1974 issue of *New Times*, Wyatt explained the whole situation.

Jo Stafford and Paul Weston's Hoax. Jo Stafford and Paul Weston, then husband and wife, made a hoax album in the 1950s under the names of Jonathan and Darlene Edwards. The album was a parody of everything they thought was wrong with contemporary popular music. Weston hit all the wrong chords and Stafford sang out of tune. Musicians saw the humor in it, even if the general public did not.

False Performers. Many old time rock and popular singers, especially those who haven't had a hit song in many years, give performances at smaller lounges and clubs around the country. However, many of these "stars" are fakes. A number of impersonators are trading in on the reputations of established performers. One of these, who had been impersonating the singer Bobby Vee, was unmasked when he filed for bankruptcy under both his real name and under "Bobby Vee." The real Bobby Vee was neither amused nor involved. Other singers and groups who have been impersonated include the Beatles, the Standells, and the Shirelles.

Claquers. Claquers, from the verb *claquer* which means "to clap" in French, refers to mercenary applauders who are hired by opera stars and others to applaud where appropriate. The practice evidently started in Italy in the early nineteenth century. It spread to France and England. The price (in Paris, c. 1850) for the services of claquers was as follows: "applause sufficient for a single curtain call, 150 francs," "overwhelming applause, 225 francs," "hissing a rival singer, 250 francs." Claquers were officially banned in 1935 at the Metropolitan Opera House in New York, although they were found there as late as 1960.

The TV Quiz Show Scandal. From 1955 to 1958, a number of popular quiz shows were on television—including "Dotto," "The $64,000 Question," "The $64,000 Challenge," and "Twenty-One"—that later turned out to be rigged. The rigging took several forms, including giving the contestants the answers in advance, telling them when they had to lose by answering incorrectly,

instructing them how to act in the isolation booths (including when to mop their brows), and even scripting their lines for them. Some contestants were innocent victims and did not cheat themselves. Among these was Joyce Brothers. Others went along unwillingly, then went to the authorities (e.g., Herb Stempel). The authorities refused to believe the shows were rigged until a stand-by contestant on "Dotto" produced a notebook that he saw a woman contestant referring to before she went on the air. To the stand-by contestant's amazement, all of the answers she gave to the questions asked were those he saw written down in her notebook. The stand-by contestant took the notebooks to the authorities in the District Attorney's office. They contacted CBS and the show was cancelled immediately. When another contestant produced registered letters he had sent to himself *before* the show, containing answers to the questions he was to be asked, a formal investigation was launched.

Although fixing a TV show was *not* illegal in New York State at the time, over 100 former contestants lied in front of the Grand Jury about whether they had been coached. Several were convicted of perjury and all received suspended sentences, including one producer. No one went to jail, although a new federal law against TV fraud was passed as a result of a subsequent Congressional investigation. Perhaps the one contestant whose whole life was ruined by the scandals was Charles Van Doren, the popular Columbia University English instructor, who won a good deal of money on the rigged shows. He went on to host the "Today" program on TV and then was exposed and fired as a participant in the rigging.

Among other frauds involved on these shows, the following should be noted. The IBM sorting machine—used on the game show "The $64,000 Question"—that appeared to be giving random packs of questions, was filled in such a way that the same questions were sorted into each of its bins. The so-called "soundproof" isolation booths were not soundproof, although the music piped into each during the contestant's thinking time did mask answers from the audience. The idea of rigging the shows was basically intended to heighten the dramatic impact of each show and to increase audience interest. It *did* do that. Recently, author Joseph Stone has written about the legal aspect of the investigation into the scandals, which he headed.

John Wilkes Booth's Mummy. The idea of exhibiting the mummy of a notorious person is something that is a bit foreign to us today, but in the days of P.T. Barnum (*See also* Outlaw Imposters, p. 112), it was almost sure to be an attraction. The mummy of Lincoln assassin John Wilkes Booth was displayed at carnivals and side shows after he supposedly committed suicide in Enid, Okla-

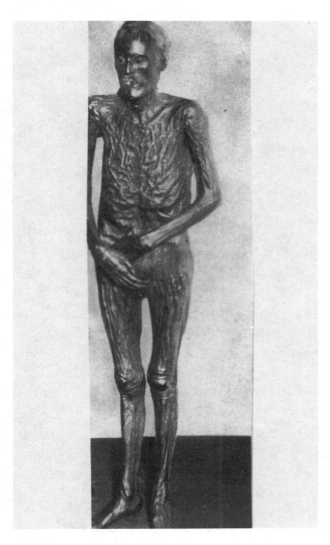

Supposed mummy of John Wilkes Booth.

homa, in 1903. This story contradicts the "official" version, which is probably correct, that Booth was killed in a barn in Virginia about thirty days after the assassination of Lincoln in 1865. Some people claimed that Booth had not been killed, but continued to live for a long time under various pseudonyms. One of these was David E. George, who "confessed" shortly before his death in Enid (as had forty others before or after him) that he was really John Wilkes Booth. The embalmed body was obtained by a lawyer named Finis Bates, as unclaimed at a mortuary. The preserved body was actually that of John St. Helen (apparently another name used by David E. George). It resembled Booth, both in identifying scars and by the presence of a signet ring in the stomach that appeared to have the initial "B" or "S" on it—visible only by X-ray. Other healed bone fractures appeared in places where Booth also had them. Although this is superficially interesting, the

evidence is strong that Booth was actually killed in Virginia in 1865. It was the secret way in which the U.S. government hid his body (attempting, no doubt, to prevent him being treated as a hero), that was largely responsible for the story that Booth was not really killed. Francis Wilson reviews evidence for Booth's death in his book, *John Wilkes Booth: Fact & Fiction of Lincoln's Assassination.*

Lip Synching. The recent scandal over Milli Vanilli (*See* Milli Vanilli, p. 284) and their lip synching only uncovered the tip of the iceberg. According to Handelman, writing in *Rolling Stone,* as of 1990 many groups use lip synching when giving concerts. This means that the voice of the performer is pre-recorded in a studio, and the performer simply moves his or her lips while on stage, but does not sing. As this intentionally deceives the audience—perhaps in the interest of obtaining a better sound for the vocalist—it is included among the hoaxes. How much of an effect the exposure of Milli Vanilli will have upon lip synching at future concerts will be difficult to tell, although in their case the artists on stage were not actually the ones singing. The whole subject is one that most performers will not discuss.

Sources:

Bird, Donald Allport, Stephen C. Holder, and Diane Sears. "Walrus Is Greek for Corpse: Rumor and the Death of Paul McCartney." *Journal of Popular Culture* 10 (1) (1976): 110–21.

Lees, Gene. "The Life and Times of Blind Orange Adams." *High Fidelity Magazine* 19 (10) (October 1969): 126.

"Long Parade of False Performers Marching Across Nation's Stages." *Variety* (November 25, 1987): 119.

Meisler, Andy. "The Beatles are Coming, The Beatles are Coming." *Games* (March/April 1982): 21.

Shelton, Robert. *No Direction Home: The Life and Music of Bob Dylan.* New York: Beachtree/William Morrow, 1986: 160–62.

Slominsky, Nicolas. "Claque," in *Lectionary of Music.* New York: McGraw-Hill, 1989: 86–87.

Stone, Joseph and Tim Yohn. *Prime Time and Misdemeanors: Investigating the 1950s T.V. Quiz Scandal–A D.A.'s Account.* New Brunswick, NJ: Rutgers University Press, 1992. See also the PBS-TV show of January 6, 1992, entitled "The TV Quiz Show Scandal."

Wilson, Francis. *John Wilkes Booth: Fact and Fiction of Lincoln's Assassination.* Boston: Houghton Mifflin, 1929.

The Sociology and Psychology of Hoaxes

Any comprehensive scientific analysis of hoaxes must be concerned with their description, prediction, explanation, and control. So far, little scientific analysis has been done on hoaxes, with only a smattering of literature on each of these topics, most of which is concerned with description of hoaxes (primarily in the form of case studies) and least of which is concerned with their prediction. Psychologist Ray Hyman, in his 1989 review of the state of "The Psychology of Deception," found an "absence of a systematic framework for, or theory of, deception." The same is true for sociology. Thus, this overview of social science approaches to hoaxes is more eclectic than systematic, but will try to give a fair representation of the research and analysis now available.

Because the hoax involves the duping of a hoaxee by a hoaxer, it fundamentally describes a social relationship—occurring between two or more actors—that is irreducible to a single individual. That is, one person on a desert island can not produce a hoax without some audience for it. Thus, the hoax is by definition a sociological rather than a psychological unit of analysis, and any comprehensive understanding of it must involve a sociological or social psychological theory.

For social science any understanding of hoaxes begins with conceptual clarification of the term itself. Two roughly distinct approaches to conceptual clarification are available: 1) a primarily, or at least initially, inductive examination of the term's use by existing groups (an approach some sociologists call *grounded theory*) which seeks to discover a common meaning; or 2) a mainly deductive approach which generates an abstract unit for analysis that is a *constructed type*, an idealized concept from which empirical cases are found to deviate by great or small degrees. The vast majority of sociological considerations of hoaxes have been of the inductive variety, usually case studies of individual episodes. Where theory rather than simply description has been involved at all, the hoax has usually been considered in the context of other more general or related theories, such as those of collective behavior or social deviance (rather than in terms of any specialized theory of hoaxes per se). A true theory of hoaxes may have to await further developments from the deductive approach briefly considered here, following a lengthier look at the far more extensive inductive efforts.

Primarily Inductive Approaches

Numerous books simply compiling hoax stories and the definitions of what constitutes a hoax have been found and vary greatly. In his classic collection, *Hoaxes*, Curtis D. MacDougall broadly defined a hoax as "a deliberately concocted untruth made to masquerade as truth." In *The World's Greatest Hoaxes*, Richard Saunders narrowed the definition substantially to "premeditated lies that pose as the truth . . . usually perpetrated by dedicated jokers in the spirit of mockery or just plain mischief." He then further reduced the meaning by adding that "At its best the hoax goes beyond its cousin the practical joke in that it is methodically planned and carried out in support of an attitude or conviction which is strongly felt by the hoaxer." Narrowing the concept still further, in *The Pleasures of Deception*, Norman Moss views the hoax as a "white and light hearted" lie that is "manufactured rather than told" and is fabricated by "an artist, in the sense in which Freud used the term when he said that an artist is a dreamer who is in control of his dreams." Similar ranges of meaning can be found in dictionaries, most of which give such broad definitions that they typically fail to differentiate a hoax from other forms of deception, or intentional misrepresentation.

Scientists remain divided on whether or not animals other than humans are capable of deception. Though most analysts have maintained that non-human animals do not have the cognitive capacities needed for the intentionality and symbolic abilities required for true deception, this view has been challenged by recent ethnological researchers and some sociobiologists. Much of this debate is reviewed in the essays to be found in Robert W. Mitchell and Nicholas S. Thompson's survey *Deception: Perspectives on Human and Nonhuman Deceit*. This topic has now produced a large literature. A recent exchange was initiated by comparative psychologists Andrew Whiten and Richard W. Byrne, who present strong evidence for tactical deception among primates. Aside from the recent experimental work, however, anecdotal evidence and lore suggest that many species (ranging from household pets to birds and elephants) may sometimes engage in both strategic and playful deceptions, the latter of which is called proto-hoaxes (much as the use of tools by some animals is currently termed proto-culture).

Among sociologists, Erving Goffman, in his *Frames of Meaning*, developed what is probably the most extensive overview of social *fabrications*, which he defined as "the intentional effort of one or more individuals to manage activity so that a party of one or more others will be induced to have a false belief about what it is that is going on." Goffman's general approach is one he termed *dramaturgical* since it views social activities through a theatrical analogy in which actors seek to control the impression formations of others, frequently masking their motives and misrepresenting themselves. Borrowing many of his concepts from the language of the theater, Goffman views human interactions in terms of such things as roles and scripts. His approach particularly lends itself to the study of hoaxes (which Goffman did not examine in detail) because one can similarly speak of the *backstage* (where those in on the fabrication plan and execute it) and *frontstage* (where those taken in by the hoax respond to it).

Before developing his own taxonomy of misrepresentations, Goffman noted numerous alternative ways to categorize fabrications. These might be in terms of 1) how long they last, 2) the number of persons contained by them, or 3) the materials that are manipulated (including such things as motives, statements, artifacts, personal identities, and conversations). Goffman chose to conduct his own analysis "based upon the end served by the fabrication." His two main categories are *other-induced* fabrications (deceptions) and *self-imposed* fabrications (illusions). The former category would include hoaxes, while the latter (which involves such things as dreams, dissociated states, and psychotic, hysterical, and hypnotic symptoms) does not. Within other-induced fabrications, Goffman subgroups these into *benign* versus *exploitative* fabrications.

Benign fabrications are those the fabricator claims are engineered in the interest of the benefit of—or at

least not against the interest of—the person(s) taken in. These include: 1) playful deceits (kidding, leg-pulling, practical jokes, surprise parties, larks or rags, and corrective hoaxing); 2) experimental hoaxing (such as conducted by psychologists who mislead their test subjects); 3) training hoaxes (where neophyte job trainees are not told that they are actually in a training simulation condition rather than a real one); 4) vital tests (as when a group member's loyalty is tested by setting up a potentially entrapping situation); 5) paternal constructions (where information is withheld or falsely given to spare pain or make the duped person more tractable, as when bad news is withheld from someone soon to die); and 6) purely strategic fabrications (as in games where particular kinds of misdirections are expected and have no moral character, like bluffing in poker).

Exploitative fabrications involve constructions clearly harmful to the private interests of those duped. Here Goffman considers: 1) nature's own fabrications produced in organisms for their protection or predation via the natural selection process (such things as camouflage, mimicry, and intimidation by animals); 2) exploitations within the law (as when police trick a perpetrator into confession) versus those outside it (frauds, swindles, etc.); 3) the tangle in relationships that discrediting can produce among the persons involved; and 4) indirect fabrications (where a definition of a second party is engineered to fool a third party, as with "plants" or "frame-ups"). Though these considerations are typically (and for Goffman apparently exclusively) found in exploitative arrangements, their relevance for some cases of benign fabrication, as in hoaxing, may arguably also be present.

Though fundamental to any developed sociological understanding of the phenomena, no reliable database shows the empirical extent and distribution of hoaxes. It seems reasonable to suppose, however, that hoax frequency should be related to some characteristics of social structure. Thus, a society's existing variations in norms and severity of sanctions should play a part in encouraging or discouraging hoaxes. Since hoaxes typically involve playfulness, one would expect to find them far more frequently in domains viewed as *profane* rather than *sacred* (sociologist Emile Durkheim's developed these terms), since joking is usually not permissible or openly appreciated in the latter realm. Also, since "fooling" people may be acceptable, while "making fools" of people typically is not—especially by the victim of the prank—one might expect a greater group tolerance for hoaxing when the hoaxer is of higher status than the hoaxee. This is because hoaxing here constitutes mockery, so it risks retribution from the more powerful. Yet many of the most memorable hoaxes have been those where a low status person managed to successfully deflate and embarrass a high status figure, as when previously presumed experts are taken in by a phony. A particularly fascinating aspect in these cases is the fact that embarrassment often precludes the higher status hoaxee from bringing retribution to the hoaxer; it often seems better to be viewed as the victim than as one who is humorless.

Other sociologists have produced writings on topics like trust and deception, some of which have relevance for future analysis of hoaxes. For example, following Orrin Klapp's analysis of social leadership types (in his *Heroes, Villains, and Fools: The Changing American Character*), one might classify hoaxes in terms of whether their social audiences view them as *heroic* (welcome and risk-taking, with socially beneficial results, as when evil is unmasked or social consciousness is raised), *villainous* (when harm is done to the social fabric, as in Goffman's exploitative fabrications), or *comical* (as when the hoax is viewed as purely playful entertainment, with no special moral message). Similar extrapolation might be fruitful from other sociological analyses not directly concerned with hoaxes. For example, Georg Simmel's early essay on "The Adventure" (further developed by authors Stanford M. Lyman and Marvin B. Scott) can be considered a general social type which would subsume cases of hoaxing as instances of extraordinary personal voyaging. Relevant here, too, is the now substantial social psychological literature on embarrassment (a result of hoaxing), particularly Erving Goffman's essay on "Embarrassment and Social Organization."

In terms of classification, hoaxes might be ordered along other dimensions than those alternatively noted by Goffman. The most obvious might be in terms of the medium through which misrepresentation takes place (face to face communication, print, radio, television, film, etc.). The literature on various media includes both case studies and compendia of hoaxes, for example, Fred Fedler's *Media Hoaxes* which looks at hoaxes both initiated by and put over upon journalists. Hoaxes might also be classified in terms of their elaborateness (from simple to complex, involving few or many elements), the scope and character of their consequences, or even in terms of their ethical or aesthetic dimensions (some hoaxes seem crude while others have an elegance about them).

A promising analytic approach is to classify hoaxes by the kind of deception involved. Author Barton S. Whaley's analysis of the structure of deception is an excellent starting point. Whaley first distinguishes two categories of deception (which he defines as one's intentional distortion of another's perceived reality): 1) *dissimulation* (hiding the real) and 2) *simulation* (showing the false). Under dissimulation he includes: a) *masking* (hiding the real by making it invisible), b)

repackaging (hiding the real by disguising), and c) *dazzling* (hiding the real by confusion). Under simulation he includes: a) *mimicking* (showing the false through imitation), b) *inventing* (showing the false by displaying a different reality), and c) *decoying* (showing the false by diverting attention). Since Whaley argues that "everything that exists can to some extent be both simulated and dissimulated," whatever the actual empirical frequencies, at least in principle hoaxing should be possible for any substantive area.

Since hoaxing involves persuasion, the now vast social psychological literature on attitude change is highly relevant. In discussing persuasion, psychologists conventionally examine it as a function of the characteristics of (1) the *source* (for us here, the hoaxer), (2) the *message* (here the fabrication), and (3) the *target* (here the hoaxee). There are literally scores of variables that have been experimentally examined and found to be linked to successful or unsuccessful persuasion (an excellent survey of this research can be found in *Age of Propaganda: The Everyday Use and Abuse of Persuasion* by psychologists Anthony Pratkanis and Elliot Aronson). Only a few correlates will be considered here. *Characteristics of the Hoaxer*. The existence of the hoaxer may be *visible* or *invisible*. In many instances, the message (hoax material) is planted or seemingly discovered by an independent, disinterested, or even anonymous source. In cases where the hoaxer is not visible to those involved, the principal determinant in acceptance of the hoax will be a function of the message material itself (e.g., the apparent integrity of a false document). A further fundamental problem with categorizing sources is that any generalizations or even speculations about hoaxers must be based on a) hoaxes that have been exposed (there are surely hoaxers whose fabrications remain undiscovered) and b) those cases of known hoaxes where the hoaxer has been identified (there are many hoaxes whose perpetrators remain a mystery). Where the hoaxer has been identified, the existing literature is suggestive about a) the social status and b) the likely motives of the fabricator.

There is a difference between hoaxers who *sometimes*—once or perhaps occasionally—engage in social fabrications and those who *frequently* produce them. It is important to note that some persons (e.g., the notorious Alan Abel and his Merry Pranksters or such widely publicized practical jokers as R.V. Jones and Hugh Troy) have gained reputations as regular and persistent public hoaxers. Such *serial* hoaxers have actually established a socially defined role (perhaps even a career) as public hoaxers (somewhat comparable in modern society to the earlier role of the feudal court jester), and some of their efforts have been viewed more as aesthetic happenings than mere pranks. The aesthetic and even moral dimensions of hoaxes in both art and social life have been analyzed by Jacob Brackman in his *The Put-On: Modern Fooling and Modern Mistrust.*

Hoaxers are more likely to be effective persuaders if they are viewed as credible. This includes the dimensions of perceived expertise (which pertains to the likelihood of the message's *validity*) and/or sincerity (which pertains to the likelihood of the honesty of the would-be persuader). As Pratkanis and Aronson have pointed out, in today's world of public relations, credibility can be manufactured rather than earned. Some analysts, notably Ian I. Mitroff and Warren Bennis in their *The Unreality Industry: The Deliberate Manufacturing of Falsehood and What It Is Doing to Our Lives,* suggest that contemporary society is dominated by media given pseudo-events (a concept introduced by historian Daniel Boorstin in *The Image: A Guide to Pseudo-Events in American Life*) and manufactured information, much of which is false (and often viewed as playful by the perpetrators if not the public) and therefore may be considered hoaxes.

Many factors contribute to credibility, including the speaker's likability, physical attractiveness, and perceived similarity to the recipient of the message. Typically, a hoaxer will be more successful if perceived to be either disinterested in the message's outcome or if relating the message seems to go against the hoaxer's own interest. Existing case studies suggest that elaborate hoaxes, at least in the United States, are less frequently perpetrated by children, women, and nonwhites. This is probably because this society is dominated by adult white males, but it may also be due to, at least in part, selective reporting in the literature.

Though there has been much speculation about the motives that compel hoaxers (particularly by some psychohistorians and psychoanalysts, e.g., see Lionel Finkelstein's analysis of impostors), most contemporary social psychologists recognize the difficulties and pitfalls in speculative efforts and usually eschew the imputation of motives. It seems likely that hoaxers are prompted by the vast array of psychological rewards available to humanity. But it also should be noted that some hoaxes have been perpetrated towards goals such as exposing gullibility (*instrumental* hoaxing) while others seem to have been done for their own sake or for pure amusement (*consummatory* hoaxing). Some hoaxing—especially where danger to the hoaxer is involved—may be indirectly driven, too, by some actors' greater needs for risk taking or sensation seeking (such *eudaemonism* or desire for what has been called "positive stress" has interested several psychologists, most notably Marvin Zuckerman). Since hoaxing involves social manipulations, there may be other personality traits correlated with being a hoaxer, for example, higher scores on R. Christie's Machiavellianism Scale, which measures cynicism and misanthropy.

Characteristics of the Message (the Fabrication)

A wide variety of possible classifications that can and have been applied to false information. In general, one can misrepresent through words, objects, and actions. A mere verbal lie seldom constitutes a hoax, which usually includes fabrication of some event (in a sense, *a lie writ large*)—the social consequences of a lie. There is vast psychological literature on lying and its detection (particularly by psychologist Paul Ekman), including extensive semantic and linguistic analysis (e.g., Eve E. Sweetser's analysis of the folk models of lies), much of which is relevant to hoaxing. However, most celebrated instances of hoaxing involve the fabrication of objects and actions. Most writers on hoaxes classify these in terms of their location in social institutions. Thus, one commonly finds writers dealing with hoaxes in art, science, religion, and politics. Such groupings are handy for readers but of less value to the social scientist seeking to find common processes that cut across such areas of social life.

Though nearly all information can be fabricated, the literature on hoaxes seems particularly concerned with such substantive instances as *impostures of identity* (including false representations of one's name, credentials, social rank, age, biological sex, and ethnic origins), *fakes and forgeries* (of documents, artifacts, artistic products, and scientific data), and *false discoveries and revelations* (ranging from facts of terrestrial history and geography to astronomical marvels).

Certain hoaxes might be termed *hoaxes of the second order* (a hoax alleging a "hoax"). There have been instances where a fabricator falsely asserts that a real event is a hoax—perpetrated either by himself or others. This seems most likely to occur when such a "confession" can gain fame or fortune for the fabricator of the "fabrication." Instances have been reported where persons have falsely "taken credit" for an admired real hoax actually produced by others. An unusual special instance of a second order hoax is the "sucker effect," commonly executed by stage magicians when the audience is duped into thinking the magician has revealed how his trick was done, only to learn after the magician repeats the effect by other means that it was a false revelation.

Characteristics of the Target (the Hoaxee)

As with the hoaxer, one can consider the hoaxee's status characteristics and motives or perceptual/cognitive inclinations towards acceptance of the fabrication. Most who write about hoaxing have concentrated on the latter.

Some people are probably more susceptible to hoaxing than are others. An extensive psychological literature deals with subject credulity or gullibility. This indicates that a small proportion of the general public has a propensity to accept almost any statement. Clearly, too, credulity is linked to both intelligence and education, although these relationships are far from uniform. Acceptance of statements, a form of conformity, has also been linked to some personality measures, particularly Thedoro W. Adorno's F (Fascism) Scale (a measure of Authoritarianism) and Milton Rokeach's (more politically balanced) Dogmatism Scale. However, empirical investigations of the correlates of general credulity fail to show its connection with some beliefs (where it was expected), such as belief in the paranormal or supernatural. It also seems less related than might have been expected to some measures of rationality.

In his classic study of hoaxes, Curtis D. MacDougall maintains that a hoax's success is the result of two sets of psychological forces acting within the hoaxee (rather like push and pull factors). The first consists of reasons why the hoaxee *fails to disbelieve* or set up barriers to belief (the internal factors that push towards acceptance). MacDougall lists the barriers as indifference, ignorance and superstition, suggestibility, and the authority or prestige of the source. The second set consists of incentives *to believe* the fabrication (external factors that pull towards acceptance). Incentives include financial gain, vanity, promotion of a cause, chauvinism, prejudices or "pet" theories, a thirst for vicarious thrills, and a supportive cultural climate. A vast literature can now be found on the psychological mechanisms of distortion by information recipients. Much of this is summarized in Charles K. West's *The Social and Psychological Distortion of Information*. Hoaxers have at one time or another made use of most of these perceptual and cognitive vulnerabilities.

In a rare social psychological survey analysis of hoaxing, sociologist Robert A. Stebbins polled a group of undergraduate students to learn about both any put-ons they had conducted and their motivations for doing so. Stebbins found three types. The *sporting* put-on, done simply for amusement or diversion, was—for his sample—by far the most frequent kind. Next came the *profitable* put-on, which produced some sort of psychological gain for the hoaxer (typically non-monetary and personal). The least frequent was the *discriminative* put-on, which was done to test—and expose—the hoaxee's judgement.

The social status of the hoaxer may be above, below, or equal to that of the hoaxee. Looking at these combinations in terms of Stebbins's three types, it seems reasonable to hypothesize: 1) *sporting* hoaxes should most likely target hoaxees of lower or equal status; 2) *profitable* hoaxes should most likely target hoaxees of equal or higher status; and 3) *discriminative*

hoaxes should most likely target hoaxes of higher status. Though these hypotheses need proper empirical testing, they do seem in line with most of the hoaxes surveyed.

Primarily Deductive Approaches

As indicated at the beginning of this essay, there has been little deductive effort in social science specifically to describe or explain hoaxes. Many theoretical efforts, however, indirectly relate to hoaxing. Most of this effort is found in the vast literature dealing with social deviance and with collective behavior, some of which includes case studies of hoaxes (for example, Erich Goode' *Collective Behavior*). Of particular related interest is a now extensive literature on trust, since a hoax often involves some betrayal of trust. A good analysis of the bases and correlates of trust can be found in J. David Lewis and Andrew Weigert's "Trust as a Social Reality."

Examination of the various inductive approaches to hoaxing discloses serious problems in conceptual definition. In particular, it shows confusion in demarcating different forms of deception from one another. Clearly, people in their everyday speech lump together a wide variety of synonyms for "hoax," such as "fraud," "humbug," "bamboozle," and "practical joke." One approach successfully used in other sociological areas, might be to consider the hoax as a constructed or idealized type. For example, it could be viewed as "a benign or only mildly exploitative fabrication by X (the hoaxer) to fool Y (the hoaxee), whose disclosure produces a reaction, typically more towards Y than X, from an audience Z (that may include Y)." Empirical instances will deviate from this constructed type, but such specification highlights some key features of most hoaxes, in contrast with, say, frauds. In these terms, the typical hoax demands its own exposure if it is to fulfill the hoaxer's goals. The goal of the hoaxer is usually to produce a reaction from some audience that learns of the fabrication. In any case, an acceptable taxonomy for deceptions, to include exclusive and exhaustive categories, should greatly facilitate the development of a comprehensive theory of hoaxes.

In broader perspective, hoaxing can be approached in terms of most of the existing "paradigms" in sociology, including the dominant perspectives of a) *functionalism,* b) *conflict theory,* and c) *symbolic interactionism.* The functionalist perspective would examine the positive and negative consequences, both manifest (anticipated) and latent (unanticipated) for the group or social system involved. Though hoaxes are frequently thought of as socially destructive, functional analysis—as has been demonstrated by applying this approach to other forms of deviance and conflict in society—suggests that hoaxes may make positive contributions to society by such consequences as exposing incompetence and providing some release from social stress by the introduction of humor and laughter.

Applying conflict theory to the study of hoaxes would investigate their relationships to power struggles in society. In many instances, those of lower social status have produced hoaxes to demonstrate the incompetence of the powerful and have thereby weakened them. An example of conflict analysis applied to fabrications is John F. Welsh's "The Social Psychology of Fraud: Dramatury, Carnegie and Puppet Theater," which examines the deeper social meanings of the fabrications taught in Dale Carnegie's courses on ingratiation and relates these to such Marxist issues as alienation, dehumanizing reification, and commodity fetishism.

The dominant sociological perspective that has been used to examine hoaxes—as evidenced by most of the inductive approaches surveyed above—is that of symbolic interactionism. This view emphasizes that humans engage in the manipulation of social symbols. Particularly relevant to hoaxing is the widely quoted dictum of W.I. Thomas: "If men define situations as real, they are real in their consequences." A hoax fabricates a reality upon which people will act and depend. Its disclosure then produces a new reality, the transition to which produces new actions. Symbolic interactionists have strongly contributed to the study of social deviance, and much of that theoretical work directly applies to the examination of hoaxes. *Labelling theory* views deviance in terms of how it is interpreted and viewed by group members. Deviance is placed "in the eye and actions of the beholder." Labelling theory is highly relevant in order to understand how groups determine when a fabrication is viewed and sanctioned as "playful," or "benign," and when an event is designated as "intentional" or a "fabrication."

Once theoretical explanation is available, it becomes possible to apply knowledge in attempts to control phenomena. Because certain forms of hoaxing need to be curtailed (for example, false announcements by terrorists that a bomb has been placed somewhere), there is a growing body of literature concerned with its disclosure and social control. Perhaps the most sophisticated of such efforts are to be found in the political arena, especially the literature on counteracting terrorism or investigating espionage. An excellent review in the latter field is H.H.A. Cooper and Lawrence J. Redlinger's *Catching Spies: Principles and Practices of Counterespionage.* On the everyday level of consumer detection of political hoaxing through the media, Martin A. Lee and Norman Solomon's *Unreliable Sources: A Guide to Detecting Bias in News Media* is particularly valuable.

This discussion of hoaxing has centered upon its substantive analysis. Mention should also be made of the study of hoaxing's possible methodological contributions. This is well exemplified in the analyses of physicist R.V. Jones (himself a renown hoaxer for his brilliant fabrications for British Intelligence in World War II) showing the benefits scientists can gain from studying the structure of practical jokes.

Marcello Truzzi

Sources:

Boorstin, Daniel. *The Image: A Guide to Pseudo-Events in America.* New York: Harper and Row, 1962.

Brackman, Jacob. *The Put-On: Modern Fooling and Modern Mistrust.* Chicago: Henry Regnery, 1971.

Cooper, H.H.A. and Lawrence J. Redlinger. *Catching Spies: Principles and Practices of Counterespionage.* Boulder, CO: Paladin Press, 1988.

Ekman, Paul. *Telling Lies: Clues to Deceit in the Marketplace, Politics and Marriage.* New York: W.W. Norton and Co., 1985.

Fedler, Fred. *Media Hoaxes.* Ames, IA: Iowa State University Press, 1989.

Finkelstein, Lionel. "The Impostor: Aspects of His Development." *The Psychoanalytic Quarterly* 43 no. 1 (1974): 85–114.

Goffman, Erving. "Embarrassment and Social Organization." In *Interaction Ritual.* Garden City, NY: Doubleday Anchor Books, 1967: 97–112.

———. *Frame Analysis: An Essay on the Organization of Experience.* New York: Harper Colophon Books, 1974.

Goode, Erich. *Collective Behavior.* New York: Harcourt Brace Jovanovich, 1992.

Hyman, Ray. "The Psychology of Deception." *Annual Review of Psychology* 40 (1989): 133–54.

Jones, R.V. "The Theory of Practical Joking—An Elaboration." *The Institute of Mathematics and Its Applications* (January-February 1972): 10–17.

———. "The Theory of Practical Joking—Its Relevance to Physics." *Bulletin of the Institute of Physics* (June 1957): 193–201.

———. *The Wizard War: British Scientific Intelligence, 1939–1945.* New York: Coward, McCann & Geoghegan, 1978.

Klapp, Orrin E. *Heroes, Villains, and Fools: The Changing American Character.* Englewood Cliffs, N.J.: Prentice-Hall Spectrum Books, 1962.

———. *Symbolic Leaders: Public Drama and Public Men.* Chicago: Aldine Publishing Co., 1964.

Koenig, Frederick. *Rumor in the Marketplace: The Social Psychology of Commercial Hearsay.* Dover, MA: Auburn House, 1985.

Lee, Martin A. and Norman Solomon. *Unrealiable Sources: A Guide to Detecting Bias in News Media.* New York: Lyle Stuart Book/Carol Publishing Group, 1990.

Lewis, J. David and Andrew Weigert. "Trust as a Social Reality." *Social Forces* 63 no. 4 (1985): 967–85.

Lyman, Stanford M. and Marvin B. Scott. "Adventures." In *The Drama of Social Reality.* New York: Oxford University Press, 1975: 147–58.

MacDougall, Curtis D. *Hoaxes.* New York: Dover Publications, 1958.

Mitchell, Robert W. and Nicholas S. Thompson, editors. *Deception: Perspectives on Human and Nonhuman Deceit.* Albany, NY: State University of New York Press, 1986.

Mitroff, Ian I. and Warren Bennis. *The Unreality Industry: The Deliberate Manufacturing of Falsehood and What It Is Doing to Our Lives.* New York: Birch Lane Press Book/Carol Publishing Group, 1989.

Moss, Norman. *The Pleasures of Deception.* London: Chatto & Windus, 1977.

Pratkanis, Anthony and Elliot Aronson. *Age of Propaganda: The Everyday Use and Abuse of Persuasion.* New York: W.H. Freeman, 1992.

Saunders, Richard. *The World's Greatest Hoaxes.* New York: Playboy Press Paperbacks, 1980.

Simmel, Georg. "The Adventure." In *Essays on Sociology and Aesthetics.* Edited by Kurt H. Wolf. New York: Harper and Row, 1985: 243–58.

Stebbins, Robert A. "Putting People On: Deception of Our Fellow Man in Everyday Life." *Sociology and Social Research* 59 no. 1 (1975): 189–200.

Sweetser, Eve E. "The Definition of *Lie*: An Examination of the Folk Models Underlying a Semantic Prototype." In *Cultural Models in Language and Thought.* Edited by Dorothy Holland and Naomi Quinn. New York: Cambridge University Press, 1987: 43–66.

Welsh, John F. "The Social Psychology of Fraud: Dramaturgy, Carnegie and Puppet Theater." *Mid-American Review of Sociology* 11 no. 1 (1986): 45–66.

West, Charles K. *The Social and Psychological Distortion of Information.* Chicago: Nelson-Hall, 1981.

Whaley, Bart. "Toward a General Theory of Deception." *Epoptica: A Review of Current Magic Literature and Apparatus* no. 5 (January 1984): 270–77. [An extended revision of a prior version in the 1983 *Journal of Strategic Studies.*]

Whiten, Andrew and Richard W. Byrne. "Tactical Deception in Primates." *Behavioral and Brain Sciences* 11 (1988): 233–73.

Zuckerman, Marvin. "The Sensation Seeking Motive." In *Progress in Experimental Personality Research.* Vol. 7. Edited by B.A. Maher. New York: Academic Press, 1974: 79–148.

Sports and Games Hoaxes

Abner Doubleday and Baseball

Most people believe that Abner Doubleday invented the game of baseball. He was given this honor by the Baseball Hall of Fame in Cooperstown, New York. Yet, few people know much about Doubleday or and about his real connection with baseball. Actually, the story that he invented baseball was a deliberate falsehood—a hoax.

Abner Doubleday (1819–1893) was born in upstate New York. He went to West Point and was commissioned into the United States Army. Doubleday served in battles in the Mexican War and was promoted to captain in 1855 and to major in 1861. He fired the first shot from Fort Sumter against the Confederates in the attack that began the Civil War. He was a brigadier general in the volunteers at the beginning of the Civil War, but was promoted to major general in 1862. He played a role in the Battle of Bull Run, at Antietam, Fredricksburg, and at Gettysburg. After General Reynolds was killed on the battlefield, Doubleday assumed the command of the Union forces at the battle of Gettysburg. After the battle, he was replaced as commanding officer by his classmate, Newton, from West Point. For this, he never forgave General Meade. He spent the rest of the Civil War in Washington. After the war, he was promoted to Lieutenant Colonel in the regular army and finally to colonel in 1867. Doubleday retired from the service in 1873 and moved to New Jersey. He was buried in Arlington National Cemetery.

In 1906, a Special Baseball Commission was set up to determine if baseball was truly an American invention. It was charged with discovering the early history of the game. The high commission of baseball experts made a report in 1907. In their report, the commission said that while Doubleday was at school in Cooperstown in 1839, he created the game of baseball out of the popular bat-and-ball games of "one old cat"

Abner Doubleday.

and its variants. He invented the diamond-shaped field, the assignment of definite playing positions, and the name "baseball" for the game, the commission said.

The main proponent of the American origin of the game was Albert Spaulding. He had partly relied on the statements of an old man named Abner Graves of Denver, given in writing to James E. Sullivan. Graves stated that he was certain that Doubleday had invented the game because when Doubleday was a pupil at Green's Select School in Cooperstown in 1839, the pupils played a game called Town Ball. Doubleday improved this game by assigning definite teams or sides, calling the game "Base Ball," having eleven players on each side, placing four bases around a diamond where players could rest, and putting the pitcher in a six-foot ring in the center of the diamond. This information (although demonstrably false, since Doubleday was at West Point in 1839), was just the information that Spaulding needed to bolster his idea that the game had an American origin.

The major advocate for the foreign origin of the game of baseball was Henry Chadwick. He was born in England and was the first real baseball reporter. He also originated the box score and would become known later as "the Father of Baseball." Chadwick said that he could clearly remember playing a British game known as rounders when he was a child. This, as modified by passing through an American version called "town ball," led to baseball. Rounders had been brought to America at least 100 years before 1839. The term "baseball" was actually in use at least by 1744, as it is mentioned in a children's book of that year. It was thought by Chadwick that rounders probably derived from cricket. It was not until 1845 that Alexander J. Cartwright drew up a set of rules that formalized what is now called baseball. He drew the ninety-foot baselines, moved the batter to home plate, and outlawed throwing the batter out by hitting him with the ball.

It is clear today that printed rules for rounders existed, dating from 1829 in England and, under the name "baseball," from 1834 in the United States. It looks like the game as now known was first played in New York City in 1842.

The question remains as to how Abner Doubleday was the one credited with the invention of baseball. A possible solution is that A.G. Mills, former National League president, who served as the most active member of the Special Baseball Commission, had been a classmate of Abner Doubleday's at West Point. Perhaps he simply wanted to honor his old friend, especially in light of the weak but plausible evidence of Mr. Graves that Doubleday really did play a role in the game's invention. Graves was mistaken, but Doubleday still has the honor of inventing baseball in the public's mind, and Cooperstown is still honored as the place where the game was invented.

Sources:

Bartlett, Arthur. *Baseball and Mr. Spalding: The History and Romance of Baseball.* New York: Farrar, Straus & Young, 1951: 6–9.

Danzig, Allison and Joe Reichler. *Baseball: Its Great Players, Teams and Managers.* Englewood Cliffs, NJ: Prentice-Hall, 1959: 19–31.

Henderson, Robert W. "Baseball and Rounders." *Bulletin of the New York Public Library* 43 (4) (April 1939): 303–14.

———. "How Baseball Began." *Bulletin of the New York Public Library* 41 (4) (April 1937): 287–91.

Peterson, Harold. *The Man Who Invented Baseball.* New York: Charles Scribner's Sons, 1973.

The Great Chess Automaton

In the 1700s, the complexity of mechanical devices, such as those employing fine clockwork-type mechanisms increased. European craftsmen made most of these devices, which included mechanically operated figures and clocks. Among the devices that were introduced at this time (1769) was the Great Chess Automaton, a complex machine that was able to play chess against a human opponent.

This automaton was (or appeared to be) several orders of magnitude more complex than any other mechanical device of its time. Today computer programs can play a strong game of chess, but to design such a device using only mechanical, not electronic, parts would be nearly impossible then *or now*. People suspected that a human being was concealed within the automaton's mechanism. The Great Chess Automaton was said to have been dismantled by its inventor, Kempelen, in 1773, after having impressed the court of Empress Maria Theresa in Vienna for three years.

The Chess Player was built in the shape of a life-size man, who was sitting at a table-like chest. The chest was about four and a half feet wide, two feet deep, and three and a half feet high. The chest moved on brass casters, which raised the bottom of the chest several inches off the floor. The "man" was made of wood and clothed in Turkish garb of the time. In fact, he was usually referred to as "the Turk." The lower portion of the torso (not visible from the front) consisted only of an oblong box supported on a ledge projecting from the chest. On the chest, beside the chess board and pieces, rested two three-candle candelabras.

Before the automaton was used, all of the doors of the cabinet were opened on opposite sides (one pair at a time) and a candle's light shined through. The first third of the cabinet was filled with clockwork gears, while the rest was more or less empty.

Before proceeding with a game of chess, the human operator of the device took out his keys and unlocked each of the doors, showing the inner works and the candlelight through the cabinet. He then took out a chessboard and pieces, which were placed on an adjoining table for the use of the opponent. The opponent played on a separate table with a separate board and pieces. Then a large key was used to wind up the automaton's mechanism. The automaton was then wheeled to the location desired.

The automaton always played white, so it always went first. The operator started the game by reaching inside the small door in the torso of the automaton and flipping a switch. The Turk then raised its left hand (the right was rarely used) and grasped the piece to be moved, moved it, and set it down. The operator waited for the opponent to move on his own board, after which he duplicated the move on the automaton's board. The sound of machinery could be heard each time the automaton moved. Occasionally the device was re-wound with the key. Games lasted only thirty minutes, after which the automaton was wheeled offstage.

When the opponent's queen was in danger of being taken, the Turk nodded his head twice. When it was a check, he nodded three times. If an illegal move was made by the opponent, the Turk would pound the table once with his right hand and shake his head vigorously. Repeated illegal moves would result in the Turk sweeping the pieces from the board with his left hand, ending the game. However, the Turk was a good player and usually won. There was an occasional en-core when the automaton answered questions from the audience by pointing to a sort of ouija board of letters and spelling out its response with its finger.

The working of this device was far too complex to be the product of mechanical gears. Soon pamphlets were published suggesting that there was more to the Turk than met the eye. Some suggested that magnetism was involved in the operation. This was countered by the operator allowing a large magnet to be placed upon the chest while the automaton was operating. It was suggested that a child was concealed in the chest and that the child saw the moves made on the board by means of a mirror on the ceiling.

When the automaton was taken out of storage, renovated, and taken on exhibition for many years around Europe by Johann Nepomuk Maelzel, it was the subject of even more intense speculation as to its mode of operation. It was noted that the Turk answered questions from the audience in the language of the country. A breakthrough in the understanding of the mechanism came when Baron Racknitz noted in 1789 that the Turk never played two games consecutively, but was always wheeled out of the room between games. Robert Willis (1821) noted that the amount of winding was unrelated to the number of moves played, and therefore, was a ruse. He noted that because the doors were opened one at a time, no one noticed that there was sufficient room for a small adult to hide in the cabinet. The adult had enough room to sit inside and operate the Turk's arm with a pantograph that dupli-

cated his own arm's movements as he moved pieces on his interior chessboard. This concealed agent could follow the opponent's moves by means of magnetic dials that were placed under each square of the chess-board on the cabinet. Each chess piece had a core of iron. When it was lifted from the board, a small dial under that square rotated. The same happened when that piece was replaced on another square. The cande-labra were required to mask the odor of burning wax from the candle inside the cabinet that provided the needed light to the agent.

When the automaton toured the United States in the 1820s and 1830s, among those who observed it and tried to explain it was Edgar Allan Poe. His anonymous 1836 article about the Turk liberally quoted (without attribution) from previous works. Poe came up with one new and correct piece of information, namely that the man inside the cabinet was, while the automaton was in the United States, William Schlumberger, a man six-feet tall. He deduced this from the fact that Schlumberger was always suddenly missing when the automaton was wheeled on stage.

The end of the automation came when Schlumberger contracted yellow fever in Havana and died. By then Poe's article had appeared and the former agent, Mouret, had confessed to his role in a French magazine article. Maelzel died soon after aboard a ship from Havana to Europe. The Turk was bought at an auction of Maelzel's effects by John F. Ohl of Philadelphia. He restored the automaton, but it was little used, eventually coming to rest in the Chinese Museum in Philadelphia. In 1854, a fire broke out across the street from the museum, soon spreading to the museum itself. The Turk was de-stroyed in the fire, thus ending the career of one of the cleverest hoaxes of the last century.

Sources:

Carroll, Charles Michael. *The Great Chess Automaton.* New York: Dover Publications, 1975.

[Poe, Edgar Allan]. "Maelzel's Chess Player." *Southern Literary Messenger* 2 (1836): 318–26.

von Racknitz, Joseph Friedrich Freiherr. *Über den Schachspieler des Herrn von Kempelen und dessen Nachbildung.* Leipzig & Dresden: J.G.I. Breitkopf, 1789.

[Willis, Robert]. *An Attempt to Analyse the Automaton Chess Player of Mr. von Kempelen.* London: Booth, 1821.

Rosie Ruiz and the Boston Marathon

The Boston Marathon is a twenty-six-mile, 385-yard foot race, held once a year in April. The 1980 race women's division winner—with the third best time ever of two hours, thirty-one minutes, fifty-six seconds—was Rosie Ruiz. Miss Ruiz, then a twenty-six-year-old administrative assistant from New York City, was immediately crowned with the winner's wreath. However, there were immediate doubts about her victory. No one seems to have seen her among the leaders of the race during the critical period before the final mile. There had been 449 women in the race.

Monitors of the race had stationed photographers at six checkpoints along the route. They were to photograph the leading runners at each point, and *not* specifically the leading *women*. Since 146 men finished ahead of her, the photographs of the leaders at each checkpoint showed only men. The second woman to cross the finish line was Jacqueline Gareau of Montreal, who was the 203rd person to finish the race. She claimed that the first time she saw Rosie Ruiz was when she saw Rosie sitting with the winner's wreath on her head.

It was noted that Ruiz did not look exhausted, as most finishers of the marathon do. She had finished the New York Marathon six months previously in 663rd place overall, and twenty-fourth among the women.

An investigation soon revealed that although Miss Ruiz said that she would be willing to take a lie detector test, none was given. That was probably because several witnesses came forth who said that they saw Jacqueline Gareau leading the women all along, with Patti Lyons as the second place woman. Several sportscasters who were commenting on the race for radio and TV also said they did not see Miss Ruiz near the front of the pack, or at all. A woman came forward to say that Miss Ruiz could not have run the entire *New York* marathon because she had seen her on the subway during the race. The witness, Susan Morrow, said that she had ridden with Miss Ruiz from the ten-mile point of the race to Columbus Circle (near the finish), and had then walked with Miss Ruiz to the finish line. Rosie Ruiz had been in her contestant's running uniform at the time. They had spoken and exchanged names and phone numbers. Miss Ruiz's time in the New York Marathon qualified her to participate in the Boston Marathon. Two runners assigned by WGBH-TV in Boston to watch for the lead man and woman at the halfway point, both said that they never saw Rosie Ruiz. On the other side, several witnesses said they saw Miss Ruiz at the twenty-five-mile point in the woman's lead and at other points in the race.

Officials of the Boston Marathon, who had compiled five lists of runners in the lead during the first twenty-four miles, pointed out that Rosie Ruiz's name did not appear on any of the lists. Miss Ruiz denied ever meeting or talking with Susan Morrow during the New York race. Suspicion against Miss Ruiz's honesty

seemed to be growing. Two Harvard students finally came forward to say that they had seen Miss Ruiz jump back into the race less than a mile from the finish.

Rosie Ruiz was stripped of her New York Marathon time; Boston Marathon officials declared Jacqueline Gareau the winner of that race. A seven-day intensive investigation and the review of more than 10,000 photographs of the race had failed to show her at any point before the final mile.

Sources:

Amdur, Neil. (A series of articles in the *New York Times*, as follows): April 22, 1980: A1, B15; April 23, 1980: B13; April 25, 1980: 24; April 26, 1980: 24; April 27, 1980: E6.

"Miss Ruiz Loses Her Title." *New York Times* (April 30, 1980): B8.

Moran, Malcolm. "Doubts Rise on Woman's Feat; 'I Ran Race,' She Says." *New York Times* (April 22, 1980): B15, B17.

Other Sports and Games Hoaxes

The Case of Sidd Finch. Although this was an April Fool's Day hoax (*See* April Fool's Day Hoaxes, p. 9), it involved sports to such an extent that it was placed here. George Plimpton told the story of Hayden (Sidd) Finch in the April 1, 1985, issue of *Sports Illustrated*. It seems that Finch was a baseball pitcher able to throw a fast ball at 168 miles an hour. The 6' 4" twenty-eight-year-old pitcher was still in the New York Mets St. Petersburg, Florida, spring training camp. Finch was from England, but had perfected his fast ball during several years of practice in Tibet. His father was an archeologist, who was killed in a plane crash in Nepal, where he had gone to work.

Finch had attended Harvard for a semester, then dropped out. He was first seen by Mets scout Bob Schaefer in Maine, where he was at the Mets' AAA Farm Club. Schaefer was amazed at the speed and accuracy of Finch's fast ball. Finch was invited to appear at the St. Petersburg spring training camp, but would only go if secrecy and several other conditions were observed. The Mets agreed.

Plimpton's article was heavily illustrated with photos of Finch and Mets players and trainers taken in St. Petersburg. The article aroused reader interest, especially among sports writers. It later turned out that Plimpton and the editor of *Sports Illustrated*, Mark Mulvoy, had decided to do an April Fool's article for the first time. Plimpton came up with the subject, and an arrangement was made with the real Mets at St. Petersburg to allow the photographs to be taken. Sidd

Finch was portrayed by a friend of the photographer. His real name was not recorded, but it is thought that he was a school teacher from Chicago. The hoax was finally revealed by the magazine when it was deluged with calls about Finch from the readers. Plimpton's article was so well written that there was scarcely a clue that it was a hoax.

The April 8 issue of *Sports Illustrated* reported that Finch lost his pinpoint accuracy. As a result, after a press conference, he simply gave a wave to the crowd and walked away from professional baseball. Almost no one had noticed that the first letter of each word in the first paragraph of the original article spelled "H-A-P-P-Y-A-P-R-I-L-F-O-O-L-S-D-A-Y."

The Plainfield Teachers. In 1941, Morris Newburger, a Wall Street stockbroker, created a fictitious football team at Plainfield Teachers' College in Newark, New Jersey. The school was also fictitious. Newburger called the New York *Herald-Tribune*, the Associated Press, the United Press International, and the *New York Times*, and told them that Plainfield's team had defeated the Benson Institute team by a score of twenty to zero. In those days, many small college scores were simply phoned in by informants. A week later, they reported that Plainfield had beaten Scott by twelve to zero. The mythical team's quarterback was John Chung. The team's scores were reported for their first seven games. Then people got suspicious. Newburger, when questioned, begged the papers to "let Plainfield finish the season." The newspapers refused. Newburger then issued a final press release, in which he stated that the team's coach had cancelled the rest of the season's games after six of their fifteen players had flunked their midterm exams.

The Australian Soccer Tourney. In March of 1982, thousands of Canadians were thrilled to read about an Ontario teenager who led the Canadian junior soccer team to victory in a World Cup championship in Sydney, Australia. Unfortunately, the tournament and the victory were created by a teenager who was pulling an elaborate hoax.

Victor Notaro was the teenager. He began his hoax by sending information from Kalamazoo, Michigan—where he attended college—to his hometown newspaper in Canada. The material sent included information about the upcoming tournament in February, and Notaro's role on the Canadian team that would be playing in Australia. Canada beat West Germany, Brazil, and the Soviet Union, all with Notaro's help. Notaro gave detailed telephone reports to the local newspaper, the *Welland (Ontario) Tribune*, after each victory. The *Tribune* passed the information on to the Canadian Press Agency after writing their article. Other newspapers all over Canada picked the news up from the agency. Soon, some of the other papers checked into the story and found that the tournament did not exist. Notaro, when confronted by reporters, admitted that he made the story up. He claimed that he didn't realize that the story would spread beyond his hometown paper, where he was just looking to be awarded a local sports trophy.

Sources:

Cooke, Bob. "Plainfield's Phantom Football Team." *Reader's Digest* (December 1974): 233.

Malcolm, Andrew H. "Canadian Papers Hoaxed on 'Soccer Tourney'." *New York Times* (March 18, 1982): A6.

Plimpton, George. "The Curious Case of Sidd Finch." *Sports Illustrated* (April 1, 1985): 58–76.

Bibliography

Anthropology Hoaxes

ABC News. "The Tribe That Never Was." Transcript of "20/20" television program for August 14, 1986.

Castaneda, Carlos. *Journey to Ixtlan: The Lessons of Don Juan*. New York: Simon & Schuster, 1972.

Castaneda, Carlos. *A Separate Reality: Further Conversations with Don Juan*. New York: Simon & Schuster, 1971.

Castaneda, Carlos. *The Teachings of Don Juan: A Yaqui Way of Knowledge*. Berkeley, CA: University of California Press, 1968.

Chang, Chen Chi. "Tibetan Phantasies." *Tomorrow* 6 (1958): 13–16.

de Mille, Richard. *Castaneda's Journey: The Power and the Allegory*. Santa Barbara, CA: Capra Press, 1976.

de Mille, Richard, ed. *The Don Juan Papers: Further Castaneda Controversies*. Santa Barbara, CA: Ross-Erikson Publishers, 1980.

Drury, Nevill. *Don Juan, Mescalito and Modern Magic*. London: Routledge & Kegan Paul, 1978.

Ellis, John M. *One Fairy Story Too Many: The Brothers Grimm and Their Tales*. Chicago: University of Chicago Press, 1983.

Foley, Frederic J. *The Great Formosan Impostor*. St. Louis, MO: Jesuit Historical Institute, 1968.

Freeman, Derek. "Fa'apua'a Fa'amu and Margaret Mead." *American Anthropologist* 91 (1989): 1017–22.

"George Psalmanazar." *Temple Bar* (July 1865): 385–395.

"High Hoax: Those Not-So-Old Ecuadorians." *Time* (March 27, 1978): 87–88.

McIlroy, William. "Jottings." *The Freethinker* (March 1981): 39.

MacLeish, Kenneth. "The Tasadays: Stone Age Cavemen of Mindanao." *National Geographic* 142 (August 1972): 219–49.

Marshall, Eliot. "Anthropologists Debate Tasaday Hoax Evidence." *Science* 1 (December 1989): 1113–14.

Maycock, A.L. "The Amazing Story of George Psalmanazar." *Blackwood's Magazine* 235 (1934): 797–808.

Molony, Carol. "The Truth About the Tasaday." *Sciences* 28 (September/October 1988): 12–20; letters in response, 29 (March/April 1989): 8, 10.

Nance, John. *The Gentle Tasaday*. New York: Harcourt Brace Jovanovich, 1975.

Noel, Daniel. *Seeing Castaneda: Reactions to the "Don Juan" Writings of Carlos Castaneda*. New York: Capricorn/G.P. Putnam's Sons, 1976.

Psalmanazar, George. *An Historical and Geographical Description of Formosa. . . .*, 1704. Reprint. Edited by Norman M. Penzer. London: Robert Holden & Co., 1926.

Psalmanazar, George. *Memoirs of ****. Commonly Known by the Name of George Psalmanazar*. London: Printed for R. Davis, 1765.

Rampa, T. Lobsang [Cyril Henry Hoskins]. *The Rampa Story*. London: Souvenir Press, 1960.

Rampa, T. Lobsang [Cyril Henry Hoskins]. *The Third Eye*. Garden City, NY: Doubleday, 1956.

"The Tibetan Lama Hoax." *Tomorrow* 6 (1958): 9--13.

April Fool's Day

Calonius, L. Erik. "Stiff Upper Lips Get a Bit More Relaxed on the First of April." *Wall Street Journal* (March 30, 1984): 1, 17.

Cohen, Hennig, and Tristam Potter Coffin, eds. *The Folklore of American Holidays.* Detroit: Gale Research Inc., 1987.

Hatch, Jane M. *The American Book of Days.* New York: H. W. Wilson Co., 1978, 3rd ed.

Phillips, Richard. "April Fool's Prank Catches Bank Off Balance." *Chicago Tribune* (April 3, 1977): I3.

Archaeology Hoaxes

Anderson, Ian. "Himalayan Scandal Rocks Indian Science." *New Scientist* (February 9, 1991): 17.

Anderson, Ian. "Researcher Faces Charges Over Himalayan Fossils Scandal." *New Scientist* (February 23, 1991): 17.

Bainbridge, William Sims. "Chariots of the Gullible." *The Skeptical Inquirer* 3, no. 2 (Winter 1978): 33–48.

Beringer, Johann B. A. *The Lying Stones of Dr. Johann Bartolomew Adam Beringer Being His Lithographiae Wirceburgensis.* Translated and annotated by Melvin E. Jahn & Daniel J. Woolf. Berkeley, CA: University of California Press, 1963.

Blinderman, Charles. *The Piltdown Quest.* Buffalo, NY: Prometheus Books, 1986.

Booher, Harold R. "Science Fraud at Piltdown: The Amateur and the Priest." *The Antioch Review* 44 (Fall 1986): 389–407.

Brackman, Arnold C. *The Search for the Gold of Tutankamen.* New York: Mason/Charter, 1976.

Carter, Howard. *The Tomb of Tut-ankh-Amen.* 3 vols. New York: Cooper Square Publishers, 1963.

Cazeau, Charles J., and Stuart D. Scott, Jr. *Exploring the Unknown: Great Mysteries Reexamined.* New York: Plenum Press, 1979.

Costello, Peter. "The Piltdown Hoax Reconsidered." *Antiquity* 59 (1985): 167–73. See also letters in response to this article in vol. 60 (1986), p.59–60, and Costello's response, p. 145–47.

Dexter, Ralph W. "Historical Aspects of the Calaveras Skull Controversy." *American Antiquity* 51, no. 2 (1986): 365–69.

Domenech, Em[manuel]. *Manuscrit Pictographique Américain.* Paris: Gide Librarie-Editeur, 1860.

Dunn, James Taylor. "The Cardiff Giant Hoax." *New York History* 29, no. 3 (1948): 367–77.

Feder, Kenneth L. *Frauds, Myths, and Mysteries: Science and Pseudoscience in Archeology.* Mountain View, CA: Mayfield Publishing Co., 1990.

Franco, Barbara. "The Cardiff Giant: A Hundred Year Old Hoax." *New York History* 50, no. 4 (1969): 421–40.

Griffin, James B., and others. "A Mammoth Fraud in Science." *American Antiquity* 53, no. 3 (July 1988): 578–82.

Grigson, Caroline. "Missing Links in the Piltdown Fraud." *New Scientist* (January 13, 1990): 55–58.

"Himalayan Hoax." *Nature* (April 20, 1989): 604.

Hoving, Thomas. *Tutankhamun: The Untold Story.* New York: Simon & Schuster, 1979.

Kimball, Stanley B. "Kinderhook Plates Brought to Joseph Smith Appear to be a Nineteenth-Century Hoax." *The Ensign* (August 1981): 66–74.

Matthews, L. Harrison. "Piltdown Man: The Missing Links" (multiple part article). *New Scientist* (April 30, 1981): 280–82; May 7, 1981, p. 376; May 14, 1981, p. 430; May 21, 1981, pp. 515–16; May 28, 1981, pp. 578–79; June 4, 1981, pp. 647–48; June 11, 1981, pp. 710–11; June 18, 1981, p. 785; June 25, 1981, pp. 861–62; July 2, 1981, pp. 26–28.

Meissner, J. P. *Erklärung des "Buches der Wilden."* Leipzig: Friedrich Ludwig Herbig, 1862.

Munro, Robert. *Archeology and False Antiquities.* London: Methuen & Co., 1905.

Nickell, Joe. "The Nazca Drawings Revisited: Creation of a Full-Sized Duplicate." *The Skeptical Inquirer* 8 (Spring 1983): 36–47.

Oakley, Kenneth P. "The Piltdown Problem Reconsidered." *Antiquity* 50 (1976): 9–13.

Petzholdt, J. *"Das Buch der Wilden" im Lichte Französischer Civilization.* Dresden [Germany]: G. Schönfeld's Buchhandlung, 1861.

Rieth, Adolf. *Archeological Fakes.* New York: Praeger Publishers, 1970.

Sears, Stephen W. "The Giant in the Earth." *American Heritage* 26, no. 5 (August 1975): 94–99.

Shipman, Pat. "On the Trail of the Piltdown Fraudsters." *New Scientist* (October 6, 1990): 52–54. Also letters in response on October 20, 1990, p. 59.

Spencer, Frank. *Piltdown: A Scientific Forgery.* London: Oxford University Press, 1990. See also the companion volume of documentation, *The Piltdown Papers.*

Story, Ronald. *Guardians of the Universe?* New York: St. Martin's Press, 1980.

Story, Ronald. *The Space Gods Revealed: A Close Look at the Theories of Erich von Däniken.* New York: Harper & Row, 1976.

Talent, John. "The Case of the Peripatetic Fossils." *Nature* (April 20, 1989): 613–15.

Thomson, Keith Stewart. "Piltdown Man: The Great English Mystery Story." *American Scientist* 79 (May/June 1991): 194–201.

Vandenberg, Philipp. *The Curse of the Pharaohs.* Philadelphia: J.B. Lippincott Co., 1975.

Vayson de Pradenne, Andre. *Les Fraudes en Archéologie Préhistorique, avec quelques examples de comparison en archéologie générale et sciences naturelles.* Paris: E. Nourry, 1932.

Weiner, J[oseph] S. *The Piltdown Forgery.* Oxford: Oxford University Press, 1955.

West, J. A. "Pyramidology." In *Man, Myth & Magic* 17 (1970).

Williams, Stephen. *Fantastic Archeology: The Wild Side of North American Prehistory.* Philadelphia: University of Pennsylvania Press, 1991.

Wilson, Clifford. *Crash Go the Chariots: An Alternative to Chariots of the Gods.* New York: Lancer Books, 1972.

Art Hoaxes

Arnau, Frank [H. Schmitt]. *The Art of the Faker.* Boston: Little Brown, 1961.

Bredius, Abraham. "A New Vermeer." *Burlington Magazine* 71 (November 1937): 210–11.

Bredius, Abraham. "An Unpublished Vermeer." *Burlington Magazine* 61 (October 1932): 145.

Bulley, M. H. *Art and Counterfeit.* London: Methuen, 1925.

Coremans, P. B. *Van Meegeren's Faked Vermeers and de Hooghs.* Translated by A. Hardy and C. Hutt. London: Cassel, 1949.

Drachsler, Leo M., ed. *Forgery in Art and the Law: A Symposium.* New York: Federal Legal Publishers, 1956.

Dutton, Dennis, ed. *The Forger's Art: Forgery and the Philosophy of Art.* Berkeley, CA: University of California Press, 1983.

Friedlander, Max J. *Genuine and Counterfeit.* New York: A. & C. Bonni, 1930.

Gerald, W. R. *The Eye of the Beholder: Fakes, Replicas, and Alterations in American Art.* New Haven, CT: Yale University Press, 1977.

Godley, John. *Van Meegeren, Master Forger.* New York: Charles Scribner's Sons, 1967.

Goodman, Nelson. *Languages of Art.* Indianapolis: Hackett, 1976.

Goodrich, David L. *Art Fakes in America.* New York: Viking Press, 1973.

Goodrich, Lloyd. *The Problem of Authenticity in American Art.* New York: Whitney Museum, 1942.

Hollander, Barnett. *The International Law of Art.* London: Bowes and Bowes, 1959.

Irving, Clifford. *Fake! The Story of Elmyr de Hory, the Greatest Art Forger of Our Time.* New York: McGraw-Hill, 1969.

Business Hoaxes

"Admits $5,000,000 Fraud." *New York Times* section 2 (May 25, 1930): 1. See also other reports of the case in the *New York Times,* as follows: December 11, 1930: 12; December 12, 1930: 18; December 24, 1930: 13; and March 27, 1931: 11.

Beckford, William. *Biographical Memoirs of Extraordinary Painters.* Rutherford, NJ: Fairleigh Dickinson University Press, 1969 (reprint).

Bloom, Murray Teigh. *The Man Who Stole Portugal.* New York: Charles Scribner's Sons, 1966.

Bredius, Abraham. "A New Vermeer." *Burlington Magazine* 71 (November 1937): 210–211.

Bredius, Abraham. "An Unpublished Vermeer." *Burlington Magazine* 61 (October 1932): 145.

Chapman, Guy. *Beckford.* London: Rupert Hart-Davis, 1952.

Checkland, Sarah Jane. "Works of a Great Faker Come to Auction." *London Times* (March 30, 1990): 4.

Coremans, P. B. *Van Meegeren's Faked Vermeers and de Hooghs.* London: Cassel, 1949.

DeVoe, Thomas F. *The Market Book, Containing a Historical Account of the Public Markets. . . .* 1862. Reprint. New York: Augustus M. Kelley, 1970.

Gemmett, Robert J. "Introduction" to Beckford's *Biographical Memoirs.* Rutherford, NJ: Fairleigh Dickinson University Press, 1969.

Godley, John [John Raymond Godley Kilbracken]. *Van Meegeren, Master Forger.* New York: Charles Scribner's Sons, 1967.

Harpending, Asbury. *The Great Diamond Hoax and Other Stirring Incidents in the Life of Asbury Harpending.* Norman, OK: University of Oklahoma Press, 1958.

Irving, Clifford. *Fake! The Story of Elmyr de Hory, The Greatest Art Forger of Our Time.* New York; McGraw-Hill, 1969.

Jones, Mark, ed. *Fake? The Art of Detection.* Berkeley, CA: University of California Press, 1990.

Klein, Alexander. *Grand Deception.* Philadelphia: J. B. Lippincott, 1955.

Koestler, Arthur. *The Act of Creation.* New York: Macmillan, 1964.

Koobatian, James, ed. *Faking It: An International Bibliography of Art and Literary Forgeries, 1949–1986.* Washington, DC: Special Libraries Association, 1987.

Kurz, Otto. *Fakes: A Handbook for Collectors and Students.* New York: Dover, 1967.

MacDougall, Curtis D. *Hoaxes.* New York: Macmillan, 1940.

Madigan, Charles. "A Story of Satan that is Rated P&G." *Chicago Tribune* (July 18, 1982): 1, 12.

Mehling, Harold. *The Scandalous Scamps.* New York: Henry Holt, 1959.

Monkman, Carol Smith. "The Case of the Paper Empire." *Forbes* 138 (October 27, 1986): 354–55.

Moore, Timothy E. "Subliminal Perception: Facts and Fallacies." *Skeptical Inquirer* 16, no. 3 (Spring 1992): 273–81.

"P&G Rumor Blitz Looks Like a Bomb." *Advertising Age* (August 9, 1982): 1, 68–69.

Phillips, Perrott, ed. "Crooked Washerwoman Cleaned Up a Fortune." In *Out of This World: The Illustrated Library of the Bizarre and Extraordinary.* New York: Columbia House, 1978, vol. 5.

Pratkanis, Anthony R. "The Cargo-Cult Science of Subliminal Persuasion." *Skeptical Inquirer* 16, no. 3 (Spring 1992): 260–72.

Puzo, Daniel P. "The Great Neiman Marcus Cookie Recipe Hoax." *Providence Journal* (February 12, 1992): F7. From the *Los Angeles Times.*

Redding, Cyrus. *Memoirs of William Beckford of Fonthill: Author of Vathek.* 2 vols. London: Charles Skeet, 1859.

Reisener, Robert George, ed. *Fakes and Forgeries in the Fine Arts [1848–1948]: A Bibliography.* New York: Special Libraries Association, 1950.

Sachs, Samuel. *Fakes and Forgeries.* Minneapolis: Minneapolis Institute of Arts, 1973.

Savage, George. *Forgeries, Fakes, and Reproductions.* London: Barrie and Rockliff, 1963.

"A Storm Over Tropical Fantasy." *Newsweek* (April 22, 1991): 34.

Tietze, Hans. *Genuine and False.* London: Max Parrish & Co., 1948.

Van Bemmelen, J. M., and others, eds. *Aspects of Art Forgery.* The Hague: Martinus Nijhoff, 1962.

Wall, Joseph Frazier. *Andrew Carnegie.* New York: Oxford University Press, 1970.

Werness, Hope B. "Han van Meegeren Fecit." In *The Forger's Art: Forgery and the Philosophy of Art.* Edited by Denis Dutton. Berkeley, CA: University of California Press, 1983.

"William Beckford, Esq., of Fonthill." *European Magazine & London Review* (September 1797): 147–150.

Disappearance Hoaxes

Berlitz, Charles. *The Bermuda Triangle.* New York: Doubleday, 1974.

Bierce, Ambrose. "Mysterious Disappearances." In *Can Such Things Be?* New York: Albert & Charles Boni, 1924.

Edwards, Frank. *Strangest of All.* New York: Signet Books, 1962: 102–03.

Gaddis, Vincent. *Invisible Horizons: True Mysteries of the Sea.* Philadelphia: Chilton, 1965.

Kusche, Lawrence David. *The Bermuda Triangle Mystery—Solved.* New York: Harper & Row, 1975.

Nash, Jay Robert. *Among the Missing.* New York: Simon and Schuster, 1978: 327–30.

Neale, Walter. *Life of Ambrose Bierce.* New York: AMS Press, 1969.

Nickell, Joe. *Ambrose Bierce Is Missing and Other Historical Mysteries.* Lexington, KY: University Press of Kentucky, 1991.

Nickell, Joe. "The Oliver Lerch Disappearance: A Postmortem." *Fate* (March 1980): 61–65.

Parrott, Wanda Sue. "Public Mystery Number One—Or Just a Hoax? An Interview With Lawrence David Kusche." In *The Riddle of the Bermuda Triangle.* Edited by Martin Ebon. New York: Signet Books, 1975.

Rosenberger, Joseph. "What Happened to Oliver Lerch?" *Fate* (September 1950): 28–31.

Schadewald, Robert. "David Lang Vanishes . . . Forever." *Fate* (December 1977): 54–60.

Winer, Richard. *The Devil's Triangle.* New York: Bantam Books, 1974.

Education Hoaxes

Bear, John. *How to Get the Degree You Want.* Berkeley, CA: Ten Speed Press, 1982.

Leibowitz, Brian M. *The Journal of the Institute for Hacks, Tomfoolery & Pranks at M.I.T.* Cambridge, MA: M.I.T. Museum, 1990.

Poundstone, William. "Judging How Easy," In *The Ultimate.* New York: Doubleday, 1990.

"A Question of Degree." *Time* (February 5, 1979): 125.

Exploration and Travel Hoaxes

Abramson, Howard S. *Hero in Disgrace: The Life of Arctic Explorer Frederick A. Cook.* New York: Paragon House, 1991.

Adams, Perry G. *Travelers and Travel Liars, 1660–1800.* New York: Dover Publications, 1980. Originally published by the University of California Press in 1962.

Babcock, William H. *Legendary Islands of the Atlantic.* New York: American Geographic Society, 1922.

Bernard, Raymond [Walter Siegmeister]. *The Hollow Earth: The Greatest Geographical Discovery in History.* New York: Fieldcrest Publishing, 1964.

Blegen, Theodore C. *The Kensington Rune Stone: New Light on an Old Riddle.* St. Paul, MN: Minnesota Historical Society, 1968.

Bourne, Edward Gaylord. "The Travels of Jonathan Carver." *American Historical Review,* 11 (1906):287–302.

Corrigan, Douglas. *That's My Story.* New York: E. P. Dutton, 1938.

"Chappell, George Shepard (Walter E. Traprock)." *Book Review Digest* (1921): 79.

de Camp, L. Sprague. *Lost Continents: The Atlantis Theme in History, Science and Literature.* New York: Dover Publications, 1970.

Dean, Paul. "Return of 'Wrong Way,'" *Los Angeles Times* Sect. V (August 16, 1988): 1, 3.

Delanglez, Jean. "Hennepin's *Description of Louisiana*: A Critical Essay." *Mid-America* 23, no. 1 (1941): 3–44; 23, no. 2 (1941): 99–137.

Donnelly, Ignatius. *Atlantis: The Antediluvian World.* New York: Harper Brothers, 1882.

Eames, Hugh. *Winner Lose All: Dr. Cook and the Theft of the North Pole.* Boston: Little Brown, 1973.

Falk, Doris V. "Thomas Low Nichols, Poe, and the 'Balloon Hoax'." *Poe Newsletter* 5 (1972): 48–49.

Freeman, Andrew A. *The Case for Doctor Cook.* New York: Coward-McCann, 1961.

Gudde, Erwin G. "The Vizetelly Hoax." *Pacific Historical Review* 28, no. 3 (1959): 233–36.

Harrisse, Henry. *Apocrypha Americana: Examen Critique de Deux Décisions de Tribunaux Américains en Favor d'une Falsification Enhontée de la Lettre Imprimée de Christophe Columb en Espagnol Annonçant la Decouverte de Nouveau Monde, et Vendue Comme Authentique un Prix Enorme.* Leipzig [Germany]: Harrassowitz, 1902.

Harrisse, Henry. *John Cabot the Discoverer of North America and Sebastian Cabot His Son.* London: B. F. Stephens, 1896.

Herbert, Wally. *The Noose of Laurels: Robert E. Peary and the Race to the North Pole.* New York: Atheneum, 1989.

"Ives v. Ellis." 370 *New York State Reports & Session Laws 399*, (April Term, 1900).

Kafton-Minkel, Walter. *Subterranean Worlds: 100,000 Years of Dragons, Dwarfs, the Dead, Lost Races and UFOs from Inside the Earth.* Port Townsend, WA: Loompanics Unlimited, 1989.

Keating, Laurence J. *The Great Mary Celeste Hoax: A Famous Sea Mystery Exposed.* London: Heath Cranton, 1929.

Ley, Willy. "For Your Information: The Hollow Earth." *Galaxy Science Fiction* 2, no. 5 (March 1956): 71–81.

Mamak, Zbigniew. "Is the Earth Hollow?" *Fate.* Part I, 33, no. 7 (July 1980): 47–52; Part II, 33, no. 8 (August 1980):80–86.

McCrone, Walter. "The Vinland Map." *Analytical Chemistry* 60 (1988): 1009–18.

Mavor, James W. *Voyage to Atlantis.* New York: G. P. Putnam's Sons, 1969.

Michell, John. *Eccentric Lives and Peculiar Notions.* San Diego, CA: Harcourt Brace Jovanovich, 1984.

Norris, Walter B. "Poe's Balloon Hoax." *The Nation* (October 27, 1910): 389–90.

Pellegrino, Charles. *Uncovering Atlantis.* New York: Random House, 1990.

[Poe, Edgar Allan]. "The Atlantic Crossed in Three Days!" *New York Extra Sun* (April 13, 1844): 1.

Rae, Julia E. S., ed. *The Letter in Spanish of Christopher Columbus, Written on His Return from His First Voyage, and Addressed to Luis de Sant Angel, 15 Feb.–14 March, 1493. Announcing the Discovery of the New World.* London: Ellis & Elvey, 1889.

Ramage, Edwin, S., ed. *Atlantis: Fact or Fiction?* Bloomington, IN: Indiana University Press, 1978.

Rawlins, Dennis. *Peary at the North Pole: Fact or Fiction?* Washington, DC: Robert B. Luce, 1973.

Roberts, David. *Great Exploration Hoaxes.* San Francisco: Sierra Club Books, 1982.

St. Elmo, Walter M. *The Alleged Remains of Christopher Columbus in Santo Domingo. Removing the Mask from This Most Amazing Hoax.* San Juan, Puerto Rico: Author, 1929.

Scudder, Harold H. "Poe's Balloon Hoax." *American Literature* 21 (May 1949): 179–90.

Shaver, Richard S. "I Remember Lemuria!" *Amazing Stories* 19, no. 1 (March 1945): 12–70.

Skelton, R. A., T. E. Marston, and G. D. Painter. *The Vinland Map and the Tarter Relation.* New Haven, CT: Yale University Press, 1965.

Spence, Lewis. *The Problem of Atlantis.* London: H. Rider & Son, 1924.

Tomalin, Nicholas, and Ron Hall. *The Strange Last Voyage of Donald Crowhurst.* New York: Stein & Day, 1970.

Traprock, Walter E. [pseud.]. *The Cruise of the Kawa.* New York: G. P. Putnam's Sons, 1921.

Wahlgren, Erik. "The Case of the Kensington Rune Stone." *American Heritage.* 10, no. 3 (April 1959): 34–35, 101–05.

Wallace, Birgitta. "Viking Hoaxes." In *Vikings in the West.* Edited by Eleanor Guralnick. New York: Archeological Institute of America, 1982.

Walton, Bruce A. *A Guide to the Inner Earth.* Jane Lew, WV: New Age Books, 1983.

Watson, Douglas. "Spurious Californiana." *California Historical Society Quarterly* 11 (1932): 65–68.

Weems, John Edward. *Peary: The Explorer and the Man.* Boston: Houghton Mifflin, 1967.

Wilkinson, Ronald Sterne. "'Poe's Balloon-Hoax' Once More." *American Literature* 32 (November 1960): 313–17.

History Hoaxes

Ainszstein, Reuben. "How Hitler Died: The Soviet Version." *International Affairs* 43 (April 1967): 307–18.

Allen, Don Cameron. *Doubt's Boundless Sea: Skepticism and Faith in the Renaissance.* Baltimore, MD: Johns Hopkins Press, 1964. 224–43.

Almack, Edward. *Bibliography of the King's Book or Eikon Basilike.* London: Blades, East & Blades, 1896.

Almack, Edward, ed. *Eikon Basilike, Or The King's Book.* London: Alexander Moring, 1904. See especially the preface (ix–xxiii) and appendices I–IV (286–99).

Anson, Jay. *The Amityville Horror: A True Story.* Englewood Cliffs, NJ: Prentice Hall, 1977.

Bahr, Robert. *Least of All the Saints: The Story of Aimée Semple McPherson.* Englewood Cliffs, NJ: Prentice-Hall, 1979.

Barnhart, John Hendley. "Some Fictitious Botanists." *Journal of the New York Botanical Garden* 20 (September 1919): 171–81.

Begg, Paul. *Jack the Ripper: The Uncensored Facts.* New York: Robson/Parkwest Publications, 1989.

Bernstein, Herman. *The Truth About "The Protocols of Zion"; A Complete Exposure.* New York: Ktav Publishing House, 1971.

Berti, Silvia. "The First Edition of the *Traité des Trois Imposteurs* and its Debt to Spinoza's *Ethics*" in Michael Hunter and David Woston, eds. *Atheism from the Reformation to the Enlightenment.* Oxford, UK: Clavender Press, 1992.

Berti, Silvia. "Jan Vroesen, Autore del 'Traité des Trois Imposteurs'." *Rivista Storica Italiana* 8, no. 2 (1991): 528–43.

Bezymensky, Lev. *The Death of Adolf Hitler: Unknown Documents from Soviet Archives.* New York: Harcourt, Brace & World, 1968.

Binyon, Michael. "Hitler's Secret Diaries: Germans Greet Find With Great Skepticism." *Times of London* (April 25, 1983): 1–2.

Bracker, Milton. "The Hope Diamond Is Off in the Mail." *New York Times* (November 9, 1958): 56.

Bracker, Milton. "Winston Gives Hope Diamond to Smithsonian for Gem Hall." *New York Times* (November 8, 1958): 1, 28.

Bradley, Henry. "Charles Bertram." *Dictionary of National Biography.* London: Oxford University Press, 1922.

Bridgeman, William S. "Famous Hoaxes." *Munsey's Magazine* 29 (August 1903): 730–34.

Brooke, Christopher. *Medieval Church and Society: Collected Essays.* London: Sidgwick & Jackson, 1971.

Cazeau, Charles J. "Prophecy: The Search for Certainty." *Skeptical Inquirer* 7, no. 1 (Fall 1982): 20–29.

Clarity, James F. "Swiss Give Edith Irving 2 Years." *New York Times* (March 6, 1973): 47.

Cohen, Daniel. *Encyclopedia of the Strange.* New York: Dodd, Mead & Co., 1985: 254–58.

Cohn, Norman R. C. *Warrant for Genocide: The Myth of the Jewish World Conspiracy and the Protocols of the Elders of Zion.* New York: Harper & Row, 1967.

Coleman, Christopher B., ed. *The Treatise of Lorenzo Valla on the Donation of Constantine. Text and Translation into English.* New Haven, CT: Yale University Press, 1922.

Corry, John, and Richard Eder. "Irving: Gulling Experts for Fun and Fame." *New York Times* (March 12, 1972): 68.

Daniloff, Ruth. "A Cipher's the Key to the Treasure in Them Thar Hills." *Smithsonian Magazine* (April 1981): 126–128, 130, 132, 134, 136, 138, 140, 142, 144.

Davenport, E. H. *The False Decretals.* Oxford, England: B. H. Blackwell, 1916.

Doble, C. E. "Notes and Queries on the 'Eikon Basilike'." *The Academy* (May 12, 1883): 330–332; May 26, 1883: 367–368; June 9, 1883: 402–3; June 30, 1883: 457–59.

Fay, Stephen, Lewis Chester, and Magnus Linklater. *Hoax: The Inside Story of the Howard Hughes-Clifford Irving Affair.* New York: Viking Press, 1972.

Fedler, Fred. *Media Hoaxes.* Ames, IA: Iowa State University Press, 1989.

Ford, Worthington Chauncey. "Dr. S. Millington Miller and the Mecklenburg Declaration." *American Historical Review* 11 (April 1906): 548–58.

Gilreath, James. *The Judgment of Experts: Essays and Documents About the Investigation of the Forging of the Oath of a Freeman.* Worcester, MA: American Antiquarian Society, 1991.

Girard, Georges. *Le Parfait Secrétaire des Grandes Hommes, ou Lettres de Sapho, Platon, Vercingetorix, Cleopatre, Marie-Madeleine, Charlemagne, Jeanne d'Arc et Autres Personnages Illustres, Mises en Jour par Vrain-Lucas.* Paris: La Cité des Livres, 1924.

Goffert, Walter. *The Le Mans Forgeries.* Cambridge, MA: Harvard University Press, 1966.

Goodwin, Gordon. "John Gauden." *Dictionary of National Biography.* Oxford: Oxford University Press, 1922.

Gordon, Michael R. "Plant Said to Make Poison Gas in Libya is Reported on Fire." *New York Times* (March 15, 1990): 1; (March 16, 1990): 3; (June 19, 1990): 8.

Graham, George W. *The Mecklenburg Declaration of Independence. May 20, 1775 and Lives of Its Signers.* New York: Neale Publishing Co., 1905.

Graham, William A. *The Address of Hon. Wm. A. Graham on the Mecklenburg Declaration of Independence of the 20th of May 1775.* New York: E. J. Hale & Son, 1875.

Graves, Philip. *The Truth About "The Protocols": A Literary Forgery.* London: Times Publishing Co., 1921.

Griffith-Jones, G. C. *Monkanna Unveiled: An Essay on Charles R. Mackay's "Life of Charles Bradlaugh, M. P." with an Addendum on Secularism and Politics.* London: D. J. Gunn [false imprint c. 1889].

Gwyer, John. *Portraits of Mean Men: A Short History of the Protocols of the Elders of Zion.* London: Cobden-Sanderson, 1938.

Hamblin, Dora Jane. "Anyone for Fake 'Duce' Diaries?" *Life* (May 3, 1968): 73–74, 77–78.

Hamilton, Charles. *The Hitler Diaries: Fakes That Fooled the World.* Lexington, KY: University Press of Kentucky, 1991.

Hammer, Carl. "Signature Simulation and Certain Cryptographic Codes." *Communications of the ACM* 14, no. 1 (January 1971): 3–14.

Harris, Melvin. *Jack the Ripper: The Bloody Truth.* London: Columbus Books, 1987.

Harris, Melvin. *Sorry—You've Been Duped.* London: Weidenfeld and Nicholson, 1986.

Harris, Robert. *Selling Hitler.* New York: Pantheon Books, 1986.

Hewett, David. "Is the White Salamander Letter a Fake? Many Don't Think So." *Maine Antiques Digest* (April 1986): 10–13.

Horn, W. F. *The Horn Papers: Early Westward Movement on the Monongahela and Upper Ohio, 1765–1795.* 3 vols. Scottsdale, PA: Published by a Committee of the Greene County Historical Society, by the Herald Press, 1945.

Hoyt, William Henry. *The Mecklenburg Declaration of Independence.* New York: DaCapo Press, 1972. Reprint.

Huyghebaert, Nicolas. "La Donation de Constantine ramenée à ses veritables dimensions." *Revue d'Histoire Ecclésiastique* 71 (1971): 45–69.

Innis, Pauline B., and Walter Deane Innis. *Gold in the Blue Ridge: The True Story of the Beale Treasure.* Washington, DC: Robert B. Luce, 1973. Contains a complete reprint of James Ward's *The Beale Papers* pamphlet.

Irving, Clifford. *What Really Happened: His Untold Story of the Hughes Affair.* New York: Grove Press, 1972.

Jacob, Margaret C. *The Radical Enlightenment: Pantheists, Freemasons and Republicans.* London: George Allen & Unwin, 1981.

Kelly, Alexander. *Jack the Ripper: A Bibliography and Review of the Literature.* London: Association of Assistant Librarians, 1973.

Kingsley, William L. "The Blue Laws." *The New Englander and Yale Review* (April 1871): 243–304. .

Knight, Stephen. *Jack the Ripper: The Final Solution.* New York: David McKay Co., 1976.

Leoni, Edgar. *Nostradamus and His Prophecies.* New York: Exposition Press, 1961.

LeVert, Liberte [Everett Bleiler]. *The Prophecies and Enigmas of Nostradamus.* Glen Rock, NJ: Firebell Books, 1979.

Lindsay, Robert. *A Gathering of Saints: A True Story of Money, Murder and Deceit.* New York: Simon & Schuster, 1988.

Lowe, Ed. "The Relentless Horror of the Amityville Tourists." *Chicago Tribune Magazine* (May 2, 1980): 13, 42–43, 47.

McKale, Donald M. *Hitler: The Survival Myth.* New York: Stein and Day, 1981.

Mackay, Charles R. *Balak Secundus: Being a Preliminary Exposure of William Stewart Ross, Trading as W. Stewart & Co. . . . .* London: D. J. Gunn [false imprint c. 1889].

Mackay, Charles R. *Life of Charles Bradlaugh, M. P.* London: D. J. Gunn [false imprint], 1888.

Mann, Georg. "Literary Hoaxes Live On!" *Science Digest* (August 1948): 57–61.

Mayor, J. E. B., ed. *Ricardi de Cirencestri Speculum Historiale, Vol. 2.* London: Longmans Green, 1869.

Mencken, H. L. *The Bathtub Hoax and Other Blasts and Bravos.* New York: Alfred A. Knopf, 1958: 4–10.

Mencken, H. L. "A Neglected Anniversary." New York *Evening Mail* (December 28, 1917): 9.

Middleton, Arthur Price, and Douglass Adair. "The Mystery of the Horn Papers." *William & Mary Quarterly,* 4, no. 4 (1947): 409–45.

Morris, Robert L. "The Amityville Horror." *The Skeptical Inquirer* (Spring/Summer 1978): 95–102.

[Morrow, Lance, and Frank McCulloch]. "The Fabulous Hoax of Clifford Irving." *Time* (February 21, 1972): 12–18, 21.

Naifeh, Steven. *The Mormon Murders: A True Story of Greed, Forgery, Deceit and Death.* New York: Weidenfeld & Nicholson, 1988.

Nasier, Alcofribas [pseud.], ed. *De Tribus Impostoribus, A. D. 1230. The Three Impostors Translated (with Notes and Comments) from a French Manuscript of the Work Written in the Year 1716, with a Dissertation on the Origin of the Treatise and a Bibliography of the Various Editions by Alcofribas Nasier, the Later.* Privately printed, 1904.

Nickell, Joe. "Discovered: The Secret of Beale's Treasure." *The Virginia Magazine of History and Biography* 90, no. 3 (July 1982): 310–324.

[Nilus, Sergey, ed.] *The Protocols and World Revolution, Including a Translation and Analysis of the "Protocols of the Meetings of the Zionist Men of Wisdom."* Boston: Small, Maynard & Co, 1920.

Peters, Samuel. *General History of Connecticut. . . .* Freeport, NY: Books For Libraries Press, 1969.

Philomeste Junior [Gustave Brunet]. *Le Traité des Trois Imposteurs (De Tribus Impostoribus, MDIIC).* Paris: La Libraire de l'Academie des Bibliophiles, 1867.

Presser, J. *Das Buch "De Tribus Impostoribus" (Von Den Drei Betrugern).* Amsterdam: H. J. Paris, 1926.

Randall, H. J. "Splendide Mendax." *Antiquity* 7 (1933): 49–60.

Randi, James. *The Mask of Nostradamus.* New York: Charles Scribner's Sons, 1990.

Ross, William S. *Bradlaugh Papers.* Item 1631, Bishopsgate Institute, London, or microfilm of same.

Rumbelow, Donald. *The Complete Jack the Ripper.* Boston: New York Graphic Society, 1975.

Schindler, Margaret Castle. "Fictitious Biography." *American Historical Review* 42 (1937): 680–90.

Schumaker, John N. "The Authority of the Writings Attributed to Father José Burgos." *Philippine Studies* 18, no. 1 (1970): 3–51.

Sillitoe, Linda and Allen Roberts. *Salamander: The Story of the Mormon Forgery Murders.* Salt Lake City: Signature Books, 1988.

Smith, Beverly. "The Curious Case of the President's Bathtub." *Saturday Evening Post* (August 23, 1952): 25, 91–94.

Stefansson, Vilhjalmur. *Adventures in Error.* New York: Robert McBride & Co., 1936: 279–99.

Stukeley, William. *An Account of Richard of Cirencester . . . With His Ancient Map of Roman Brittain . . . The Itinerary Thereof, . . .* London: Richard Hett, 1757.

Tanner, Jerald. "LDS Documents & Murder." *Salt Lake City Messenger* no. 59 (January 1986): 1–25.

Thomas, Lately. *Storming Heaven: The Lives and Turmoils of Minnie Kennedy and Aimée Semple McPherson.* New York: William Morrow & Co., 1970.

Thomas, Lately. *The Vanishing Evangelist: The Aimée Semple McPherson Kidnaping Affair.* New York: Viking Press, 1959.

Tout, T. F. "Medieval Forgers and Forgeries." *Bulletin of the John Rylands Library* 5 (1919): 208–34.

Trevor-Roper, H. R. *The Last Days of Hitler,* 3rd ed. New York: Macmillan Co., 1965.

Tribe, David. *President Charles Bradlaugh, M. P.* London: Elek Books, 1971.

Trumbull, J. Hammond. *The True Blue Laws of Connecticut and New Haven and the False Blue Laws Invented by the Rev. Samuel Peters to Which are Added Specimens of the Laws and Judicial Proceedings of Other Colonies and Some Blue-Laws of England in the Reign of James I.* Hartford, CT: American Publishing Co., 1876.

Vale, Gilbert, ed. *The Three Impostors. Translated (with notes and Illustrations) from the French Edition of the Works, Published at Amsterdam, 1776.* New York: G. Vale, 1846.

Wade, Ira O. *The Clandestine Organization and Diffusion of Philosophic Ideas in France from 1700 to 1750.* Princeton, NJ: Princeton University Press, 1938.

West, D. J. "The Identity of Jack the Ripper." *Journal of the Society for Psychical Research* 35 (1949): 76–80.

Whibley, Charles. "Of Literary Forgers." *Cornhill Magazine* 12 (1902): 625–36.

Williams, Schafer. "The Oldest Text of the 'Constitutum Constantini'." *Traditio* 20 (1964): 448–61.

Williams, Schafer. "The Pseudo-Isidorian Problem Today." *Speculum* 29 (1954): 702–7.

Wolf, A[braham], ed. *The Oldest Biography of Spinoza.* New York: The Dial Press, 1928.

Wolf, Lucien. *The Myth of the Jewish Menace in World Affairs, or The Truth About the Forged Protocols of the Elders of Zion.* New York: Macmillan, 1921.

Woodward, B. B. "A Literary Forgery: Richard of Cirencester's Tractate on Britain." *Gentleman's Magazine & Historical Review* 1 (1866): 301–8, 617–24; 2: 458–66; 4 (1867): 443–51.

Wordsworth, Christopher. *King Charles the First. Author of Icon Basilike.* London: John Murray, 1828.

Wordsworth, Christopher. *Who Wrote Eikon Basilike? Two Letters to the Archbishop of Canterbury.* London: J. Murray, 1824.

Zindler, Frank. "The Amityville Humbug." *American Atheist* (January 1986) 28: Part I: 20–24; Part II (February 1986): 23–26; Part III (March 1986): 29–33.

Hoaxes That Were Not Hoaxes

Allegro, John Marco. *The Shapira Affair.* Garden City, NY: Doubleday & Co., 1965.

Arens, W[illiam]. *The Man-Eating Myth: Anthropology and Anthropophagy.* New York: Oxford University Press, 1979.

Blinkhorn, Steve. "Was Burt Stitched Up?" *Nature* 340 (August 10, 1989): 439–40.

Brown, Paula, and Donald Tuzin. *The Ethnography of Cannibalism.* Washington, DC: Society for Psychological Anthropology, 1983.

Burt, Cyril. "The Genetic Determination of Differences in Intelligence: A Study of Monozygotic Twins Reared Together and Apart." *British Journal of Psychology* 57 (1966): 137–53.

Cantril, Hadley. *The Invasion from Mars: A Study in the Psychology of Panic, With the Complete Script of the Famous Orson Welles Broadcast.* Princeton, NJ: Princeton University Press, 1949.

Charig, Alan, and others. "Archeopteryx Is Not a Forgery." *Science* 232 (May 2, 1988): 622–25.

Davis, E. Wade. "The Ethnobiology of the Haitian Zombie." *Caribbean Review* 12, no. 3 (Summer 1983): 18–21, 47.

Davis, E. Wade. *The Serpent and the Rainbow.* New York: Simon & Schuster, 1985.

Dennett, Michael R. "Firewalking: Reality or Illusion?" *The Skeptical Inquirer* 10, no. 1 (Fall 1985): 36–40.

Diederich, Bernard. "On the Nature of Zombie Existence." *Caribbean Review* 12, no. 3 (Summer 1983): 14–17, 43–46.

Koper, Peter. "In Search of Zombies: A Tale of Voodoo Potions and the Curse of Living Death." *Chicago Tribune* (August 21, 1983) Sect. 15: 1, 4.

Fletcher, Ronald. *Science, Ideology & the Media: The Cyril Burt Scandal.* New Brunswick, NJ: Transaction Publishers, 1991.

Forsyth, Donald W. "Three Cheers for Hans Staden: The Case for Brazilian Cannibalism." *Ethnohistory* 32, no. 1 (1985): 17–36.

Gillie, Oliver. "Burt: The Scandal and the Cover-Up" In *A Balance Sheet on Burt,* edited by H. Beloff. Supplement to *Bulletin of the British Psychological Society,* vol. 33 (1980): 9–16.

Gould, Stephen Jay. "The Archeopteryx Flap." *Natural History* 95, no. 9 (September 1986): 16–25.

Griffiths, Mervyn. *The Biology of the Monotremes.* New York: Academic Press, 1978.

Harry, Myriam [pseud]. *La Petite Fille de Jerusalem.* Paris: Librairie Artheme Fayard, 1925.

Hearnshaw, L. S. *Cyril Burt: Psychologist.* Ithaca, NY: Cornell University Press, 1979.

Hoyle, Fred and C. Wickramasinghe. *Archeopteryx, the Primordial Bird: A Case of Fossil Forgery.* Swansea, England: C. Davies, 1986.

Joynson, Robert B. *The Burt Affair.* London: Routledge, 1989.

Kamin, Leon J. *The Science and Politics of IQ.* New York: John Wiley, 1974.

Klarsfeld, Serge, ed. *The Holocaust and the Neo-Nazi Mythomania.* New York: Beatte Klarsfeld Foundation, 1978.

Koch, Howard. *The Panic Broadcast: Portrait of an Event.* Boston: Little, Brown & Co., 1970.

Kolata, Gina. "Are the Horrors of Cannibalism Fact—or Fiction?" *Smithsonian* (March 1987) 17: 150–70.

Leikind, Bernard J., and William J. McCarthy. "Firewalking." *Experientia* 44 (1988): 310–15.

Leikind, Bernard J., and William J. McCarthy. "An Investigation of Firewalking." *The Skeptical Inquirer* 10, no. 1 (Fall 1985): 23–34.

Lesy, Michael. "Dark Carnival: The Death and Transfiguration of Floyd Collins." *American Heritage* 27, no. 6 (October 1976): 34–45.

Lewis, L. E. "The Fire-walking Hindus of Singapore." *National Geographic* 59 (1931): 513–22.

Lynn, Kenneth S. "The Masterpiece That Became a Hoax." *New York Times Book Review* (April 26, 1981): 9, 36.

McAskie, M. "Carelessness or Fraud in Sir Cyril Burt's Kinship Data: A Critique of Jensen's Analysis." *American Psychologist* 33 (1978): 496–98.

Marcuse, Michael J. "The Scourge of Impostors, the Terror of Quacks: John Douglas and the Expose of William Lauder." *Huntington Library Quarterly* 42, no. 3 (1979): 231–61.

"'Mars Raiders' Cause Quito Panic; Mob Burns Radio Plant; Kills 15." *New York Times* (February 14, 1949): 1, 7.

"Martian Invasion Terrorizes Chile." *New York Times* (November 14, 1944): 1.

Pomerantz, Bruce and Gabriel Stux, eds. *Scientific Bases of Acupuncture.* Berlin and New York: Springer Verlag, 1989.

"Radio Listeners in Panic, Taking War Drama as Fact." *New York Times* (October 31, 1938): 1, 4.

Sanday, Peggy Reeves. *Divine Hunger: Cannibalism as a Cultural System,* Cambridge, England: Cambridge University Press, 1986.

Secord, Arthur W. *Robert Drury's Journal and Other Studies.* Urbana, IL: University of Illinois Press, 1961: 1–71.

Steadman, Lyle B., and Charles F. Merbs. "Kuru and Cannibalism?" *American Anthropologist* 84 (1982): 611–27.

Wellnhofer, Peter. "Archeopteryx." *Scientific American* 262 (May 1990): 70–77.

Woodward, C. Vann, and Elisabeth Muhlenfeld. *The Private Mary Chestnut: The Unpublished Civil War Diaries.* New York: Oxford University Press, 1984: especially introduction, ix–xxix.

Impostors

"At Duke U., Bogus Baron Fit Right In." *New York Times* (February 20, 1990): A18.

Atlay, J[ames] B. *The Tichburne Case.* London: W. Hodge, 1916.

Bahn, Paul, and Tim Rayment. "Remains of Tsar and Family Found in Forest Grave." *London Sunday Times* (May 10, 1992): 1, 22.

Barringer, Felicity. "The Czar? Sverdlovsk Keeps Its Secrets." *New York Times* (September 23, 1991): A-12.

Barron, James. "Princeton Man is Held as Fugitive, Unmasked and Undone." *New York Times* (February 28, 1991): B1–B2.

Barton, Margaret. *Sober Truth: A Collection of Nineteenth Century Episodes, Fantastic, Grotesque and Mysterious.* London: Duckworth, 1930.

Botkin, Gleb. *The Woman Who Rose Again: The Story of the Grand Duchess Anastasia.* New York: Fleming Revell, 1937.

Byrne, Gregory. "Did Billy Really Die a Kid?" *Science* 243 (February 3, 1989): 610.

Caraboo: A Narrative of a Singular Imposition Practiced Upon the Benevolence of a Lady Residing in the Vicinity of Bristol. Bristol [U.K.]: J.M. Gutch, 1817.

"Computer Upholds Billy the Kid Legend." *Lexington Herald-Leader* (March 4, 1990).

Cowan, Robert Ernest. "Norton I Emperor of the United States and Protector of Mexico." *California Historical Society Quarterly* 2 (1923): 237–245.

Creason, Joe. *Joe Creason's Kentucky.* Louisville: The Courier-Journal and the Louisville Times, 1972: 230.

Crichton, Robert. *The Great Impostor.* New York: Random House, 1959.

Croffut, W. A. "Lord Gordon-Gordon: A Bogus Peer and His Distinguished Dupes." *Putnam's Magazine* 7 (January 1910): 416–428.

Davis, Natalie Zemon. "AHR Forum: The Return of Martin Guerre 'On The Lane.'" *American Historical Review* 93, no. 3 (1988): 572–603.

Davis, Natalie Zemon. *The Return of Martin Guerre.* Cambridge, MA: Harvard University Press, 1983.

de Coras, Jean. *Arrest Memorable, du Parlement de Tolose* [Toulouse], *Contenant une Histoire Prodigieuse, de nostre temps. . . .* Lyon, [France]: Antoine Vincent, 1561.

Deutsch, Helene. "The Impostor: Contribution to Ego Psychology of a Type of Psychopath." *Psychoanalytic Quarterly* 24 (1955): 483–505.

Dickson, Lovat. *Wilderness Man: The Strange Story of Grey Owl.* Toronto: Macmillan of Canada, 1973.

"Dr. Reid L. Brown." *Life* (June 12, 1968): 32–32A.

Domela, Harry. *A Sham Prince: The Life and Adventures of Harry Domela as Written by Himself in Prison at Cologne, January to June, 1927.* London: Hutchinson, 1928.

Dorson, Richard M. *American Folklore.* Chicago: University of Chicago Press, 1959: 243.

Dressler, Albert. *Emperor Norton.* San Francisco: Albert Dressler, 1927.

Drury, William. *Norton I: Emperor of the United States.* New York: Dodd, Mead & Co., 1986.

"Ferdinand Waldo Demara, 60, An Impostor in Varied Fields" (obituary). *New York Times* (June 9, 1982): Section 2, 16.

Finger, Charles Joseph. *Romantic Rascals.* Freeport, NY: Books For Libraries, 1969.

Finlay, Robert. "AHR Forum: The Return of Martin Guerre—The Refashioning of Martin Guerre." *American Historical Review,* 93, no. 3 (1988): 553–71.

Garvey, Jack. "Ferdinand Demara, Jr.: His Undoing Was Usually That He Did So Well." *American History* (October 1985): 20–21.

Greenacre, Phyllis. "The Imposter." *Psychoanalytic Quarterly* 27 (1958): 359–82.

Greenacre, Phyllis. "The Relation of the Imposter to the Artist." *Psychoanalytic Study of the Child* 13 (1958): 521–40.

Hynd, Alan. "The Fabulous Fraud from Brooklyn." *True* (March 1953): 55–56, 68–71.

Kurth, Peter. *Anastasia: The Riddle of Anna Anderson.* Boston: Little, Brown & Co., 1983.

Lane, Allen Stanley. *Emperor Norton, the Mad Monarch of America.* Caldwell, ID: The Caxton Printers, 1939.

Larsen, Egon. *The Deceivers: Lives of Great Imposters.* New York: Roy Publishers, 1966.

Long Lance, Chief Buffalo Child [pseud]. *Long Lance.* New York: Cosmopolitan Book Corporation, 1928.

Lovell, James Blair. *Anastasia: The Lost Princess.* Washington, DC: Regnery Gateway, 1991.

McCarthy, Joe. "The Master Impostor: An Incredible Tale." *Life* (January 28, 1952): 79–86, 89.

MacDougall, Curtis. *Hoaxes.* New York: Dover Books, 1958.

[Mann, Herman]. *The Female Review: Life of Deborah Sampson, the Female Soldier in the War of the Revolution.* Boston: J. K. Wiggin and Wm. Parsons Lunt, 1866.

Maugham, Lord [F. H.]. *The Tichborne Case.* London: Hodder & Staughton, 1936.

"Musician's Death at 74 Reveals He Was a Woman." *New York Times* (February 2, 1989): A18.

Nogly, Hans. *Anastasia.* London: Methuen, 1959.

Oulahan, Richard, Jr. "Barrel of Fun for Cynics." *Life* (December 7, 1962): 25.

"'Our Gang' Imposter Dupes Staff of '20/20'." *New York Times* (October 8, 1990): A15.

Racster, Olga, and Jessica Grove. *Dr. James Barry: Her Secret Story.* London: G. Howe, 1932.

Settle, William A., Jr. *Jesse James Was His Name.* Lincoln, NE: University of Nebraska Press, 1977.

Smith, Donald B. *Long Lance: The True Story of an Impostor.* Toronto: Macmillan of Canada, 1982.

Smith, Ralph Lee. "Strange Tales of Medical Impostors." *Today's Health* 46 (October 1968): 45–47, 69–70.

Summers, Anthony, and Tom Mangold. *The File on the Tsar.* New York: Harcourt Brace Jovanovich, 1978.

Wasserman, Jacob. *Caspar Hauser: The Enigma of a Century.* New York: Horace Liveright, 1928.

Williams, Greer. "The Doctor Was a Fake." *Saturday Evening Post* (November 13, 1954): 17–19, 53, 55, 57–58, 60.

Wilton, Robert. *The Last Days of the Romanovs.* New York: G. Doran, 1920.

Witchel, Alex. "The Life of Fakery and Delusion in John Guare's 'Six Degrees.'" *New York Times* (June 21, 1990): C17, C20.

Woodruff, Douglas. *The Tichborne Claimant.* New York: Farrar, Straus & Cudahy, 1957.

Wyden, Peter. "Thirty Years a Fake Doctor." *Coronet* (August 1953).

''Young Man Claiming to Be Son of Sidney Poitier Hits Rich New Yorkers for Loans.'' *Jet* 65 no. 9 (November 7, 1983): 59.

Invention Hoaxes

Angrist, Stanley W. ''Perpetual Motion Machines.'' *Scientific American* 218 (January 1968): 114–22.

Beller, William. ''Consultant's Report Overrides Dean Space Drive.'' *Missiles and Rockets* 9 (June 12, 1961): 24–25, 42.

Bloomfield-Moore, C. S. *Keeley and His Discoveries.* Secaucus, NJ: University Books, [1972]. Reprint.

Dircks, Henry C. E. *Perpetuum Mobile.* London: E. F. Spon, 1861 (Vol. 1), 1870 (Vol. 2).

Gardner, Martin. ''Perpetual Motion: Illusion and Reality.'' *Foote Prints* 47, no. 2 (1984): 21–35.

Gibbs-Smith, C[harles] H. *Flight Through the Ages.* New York: Thomas Y. Crowell, 1974.

Haining, Peter. *The Compleat Birdman: An Illustrated History of Man-Powered Flight.* New York: St. Martin's Press, 1977.

Hart, Clive. *The Dream of Flight: Aeronautics from Classical Times to the Renaissance.* London: Faber & Faber, 1972.

Hunt, Inez, and Wanetta W. Draper. *Lightning in His Hand: The Life Story of Nikola Tesla.* Denver: Sage Books, 1964.

Jones, David ''Daedalus''. ''I, Fraudulous.'' *New Scientist* 100 (December 1983): 915–17.

LaFond, Charles D. ''The Controversial Dean System Space Drive.'' *Missiles and Rockets* 8 (May 1, 1961): 24, 34, 46.

Ord-Hume, Arthur W. J. G. *Perpetual Motion: The History of an Obsession.* New York: St. Martin's Press, 1977.

[Stewart, Oliver], Frank Howard, and Bill Gunston. *The Conquest of the Air.* New York: Random House, 1974.

Valentine, Tom. ''The Man Below Is Turning Tap Water Into Gasoline.'' *The National Exchange* 1, no. 3 (June 1977): 6–7.

White, Lynn, Jr. ''Eilmer of Malmesbury, an Eleventh Century Aviator.'' *Technology and Culture* 2 (1961): 97–111.

Journalism

[Arrowsmith, John]. ''Railways and Revolvers in Georgia.'' London *Times* (October 15, 1856): 6.

Arrowsmith, John. ''Railways and Revolvers in Georgia.'' London *Times* (October 24, 1856): 7.

''Awful Calamity.'' New York *Herald* (November 9, 1874): 1.

Bird, S. Elizabeth. *For Enquiring Minds: A Cultural Study of Supermarket Tabloids.* Knoxville, TN: University of Tennessee Press, 1992.

''Burned Alive!'' *Chicago Times* (February 13, 1875): 1.

Castelli, Jim. ''The Curse of the Phantom Petition.'' *TV Guide* (July 24, 1976): 4–6.

''Coast Guard Acts to Close Cabaret 15 Miles Out at Sea.'' *New York Times* (August 17, 1924): 1.

''The Conclusions.'' *Washington Post* (April 19, 1981): A12–A15.

''The Confession.'' *Washington Post* (April 19, 1981): A12–A15.

Connery, Thomas B. ''A Famous Newspaper Hoax.'' *Harper's Weekly* (June 3, 1893): 534–35.

Dart, John. ''Rumor of Atheist Radio Move Proves Persistent.'' *Los Angeles Times* (December 1, 1964) II: 6.

''The Doubts.'' *Washington Post* (April 19, 1981): A12–A15.

Federal Communications Commission. *Fact Sheet RM-2493.* Washington, DC: Federal Communications Commission, 1990.

Fedler, Fred. *Media Hoaxes.* Ames, IA: Iowa State University Press, 1989.

Griffith, Thomas. ''The Pulitzer Hoax—Who Can Be Believed?'' *Time* 117 (May 4, 1981): 50–51.

[H. C. W.]. ''Railways and Revolvers in Georgia.'' London *Times* (October 18, 1856): 8.

Hirsley, Michael. ''Rumor That Wouldn't Die.'' *Chicago Tribune* (December, 1988).

Jarrell, Sanford. ''New Yorkers Drink Sumptuously on 17,000-Ton Floating Cafe at Anchor 15 Miles Off Long Island.'' *New York Herald Tribune* (August 16, 1924): 1.

Lancaster, Paul. "Faking It." *American Heritage* 33, no. 6 (October/November 1982): 50–57.

Muldavin, Mark, and Alexander Klein, eds. "The Fake That Made Violent History." *The Double Dealers.* Philadelphia: J. B. Lippincott, 1958.

Munson, Naomi. "The Case of Janet Cooke." *Commentary* 72, no. 2 (August 1981): 46–50.

Noah, Timothy. "Jimmy's Big Brothers." *New Republic* 184 (May 16, 1981): 14–16.

"The Ombudsman." *Washington Post* (April 19, 1981): A12–A15.

The Phantom Phenomenon Christiansanity Strikes Again! Austin, TX: American Atheist Center, [ca. 1982]: 29.

"The Players." *Washington Post* (April 19, 1981): A12–A15.

"The Pressures." *Washington Post* (April 19, 1981): A12–A15.

"The Prize." *Washington Post* (April 19, 1981): A12–A15.

"A Prodigious Hoax." *New York Times* (November 1, 1856): 4.

"The Publication." *Washington Post* (April 19, 1981): A12–A15.

"Pulitzer Board Withdraws Post Reporter's Prize." *Washington Post* (April 16, 1981): A25.

"The Reporter." *Washington Post* (April 19, 1981): A12–A15.

Smith, Jack. "The Great Gambling Ship Hoax and How it Was Blown Out of the Water." *Los Angeles Times* (July 11, 1984): Section 5: 1.

"The Story." *Washington Post* (April 19, 1981): A12–A15.

[Untitled letter]. London *Times* (October 18, 1856): 8.

"'The Winsted Liar.' A News-Fictionist Whose Fame Is in Whoppers." *Literary Digest* (September 11, 1920): 62.

Language Hoaxes

Adler, Jerry, and Niko Price. "The Melting of a Mighty Myth. Guess What: Eskimos Don't Have 23 Words for Snow." *Newsweek* (July 22, 1991): 23.

Goddard, Ives. "Time to Retire an Indian Place Name Hoax." *New York Times* (September 29, 1990): 22.

Martin, Laura. "Eskimo Words for Snow: A Case Study in the Genesis and Decay of an Anthropological Example." *American Anthropologist* 88 (1986): 418–23.

Pullum, Geoffrey K. "The Great Eskimo Vocabulary Hoax." *Natural Language and Linguistic Theory* 7 (1989): 275–81.

Roberts, Majory. "A Linguistic 'Nay' to Channeling." *Psychology Today* (October 1989): 64–66.

Shetter, William Z. "That Thusendigste Jär." *Language* 34 (1958): 131–34.

Worf, Benjamin Lee. "Science and Linguistics." *Technology Review (MIT)* 42 (1940): 229–31, 247–48. Reprinted in S. I. Hayakawa's *Language in Action.*

Legal Hoaxes

"As Barnum Said." *New Outlook* (October 29, 1924): 317–18.

Head, Franklin H. "Captain Kidd and the Astor Fortune." *The Forum* (July 1931): 56–64.

Rhoden, Harold. *High Stakes: The Gamble for Howard Hughes' Will.* New York: Crown Publishers, 1980.

Turner, Wallace. "Ex-Aide to Hughes Is Seeking Probate of Purported Will." *New York Times* (May 1, 1976): 1, 20.

Turner, Wallace. "Probate Judge in Texas Rules That No Will Was Left by Howard Hughes." *New York Times* (February 19, 1981): A21.

Turner, Wallace. "Purported Will of Hughes Found at Mormon Office." *New York Times* (April 30, 1976): 1, 17.

Turner, Wallace. "Students of Hughes's Life Doubt Will's Authenticity." *New York Times* (May 3, 1976): 1, 40.

Literary Hoaxes

Aldridge, Alfred Owen. "A Religious Hoax by Benjamin Franklin." *American Literature* 36 no. 2 (May 1964): 204–09.

Bales, Jack. "Herbert R. Mayes and Horatio Alger, Jr.; Or the Story of a Unique Literary Hoax." *Journal of Popular Culture* 8, no. 2 (1974): 317–19.

Barker, Nicolas, and John Collins. *A Sequel to An Enquiry into the Nature of Certain Nineteenth Century Pamphlets by John Carter and Graham Pollard: The Forgeries of H. Buxton Forman & T. J. Wise Re-Examined.* London: Scholar Press, 1983.

Bickerstaff, Isaac [Jonathan Swift]. *Predictions for the Year 1708.* London: John Morphew, 1708.

Bruns, Bill. "Naked Truth About the Great Novel Hoax." *Life* (August 22, 1969): 69–70.

Carter, John, and Graham Pollard. *An Enquiry into the Nature of Certain Nineteenth Century Pamphlets.* London: Constable & Co., 1934.

Carter, John, and Graham Pollard. *The Firms of Charles Ottley, Landon & Company: A Footnote to an Enquiry.* London: Rupert Hart-Davis, 1948.

Chatterton, Thomas. *The Complete Poetical Works of Thomas Chatterton.* 2 vols. London: George Routledge & Sons, 1906.

Collins, John. *The Two Forgers.* Newark, DE: Oak Knoll Publications, 1992.

Curtis, Lewis B. "Forged Letters of Laurence Stern." *Papers of the Modern Language Ass'n.* 50 (1935): 1076–106.

Durnell, Jane B. "An Irrepressible Deceiver." *PNLA Quarterly* 36 (Fall, 1971): 17–23.

Farrer, J. A. *Literary Forgeries.* London: Longman, Green & Co., 1907.

Fatout, Paul. *Mark Twain in Virginia City.* Bloomington, IN: Indiana University Press, 1964.

Fedler, Fred. *Media Hoaxes.* Ames, IA: Iowa State University Press, 1989.

Ferguson, DeLancy. "Mark Twain's Comstock Duel: The Birth of a Legend." *American Literature* 14 (1942): 66–70.

Foxon, D[avid] F. "Another Skeleton in Thomas J. Wise's Cupboard." *Times Literary Supplement* (October 19, 1956): 624.

Ganzel, Dewey. *Fortune and Men's Eyes: The Career of John Payne Collier.* New York: Oxford University Press, 1982.

Grebanier, Bernard. *The Great Shakespeare Forgery.* New York: W. W. Norton & Co., 1965.

Haines, Helen E. "The Old Librarian's Almanack." *The Nation* 90 (February 24, 1910): 185.

Hall, Carroll D. *Bierce and the Poe Hoax.* San Francisco: Book Club of California, 1934.

Hall, Max. "An Amateur Detective on the Trail of B. Franklin, Hoaxer." *Massachusetts Historical Society Proceedings* 84 (1972): 26–43.

Hall, Max. *Benjamin Franklin & Polly Baker: The History of a Literary Deception.* Chapel Hill, NC: University of North Carolina Press, 1960.

Hamilton, Charles. *In Search of Shakespeare: A Reconnaissance into the Poet's Life and Handwriting.* San Diego: Harcourt Brace Jovanovich, 1985.

Haywood, Ian. *The Making of History: A Study of the Literary Forgeries of James MacPherson and Thomas Chatterton in Relation to Eighteenth-Century Ideas of History and Fiction.* Rutherford, NJ: Fairleigh Dickinson University Press, 1986.

Ingleby, Clement M. *A Complete View of the Shakspere [sic] Controversy Concerning the Authenticity and Genuineness of the MS. Matter Affecting the Works and Biography of Shakspere, Published by Mr. J. Payne Collier as the Fruits of His Researches.* London: Nattali & Bond, 1861.

Ireland, William Henry. *Confessions of William Henry Ireland Containing the Particulars of His Fabrication of the Shakespeare Manuscripts; Together With Anecdotes and Opinions of Many Distinguished Persons in the Literary, Political and Theatrical World.* New York: Burt Franklin, 1969. Reprint of 1879 edition.

Kaplan, Louise J. *The Family Romance of the Impostor-Poet Thomas Chatterton.* New York: Atheneum, 1988.

Klinefelter, Walter. *The Fortsas Bibliohoax.* New York: Press of the Wooly Whale, 1942: 72.

Lehman, David. "The Ern Malley Hoax: Australia's 'National Poet'." *Shenandoah* 34, no. 4 (1983): 47–73.

Lethwidge, Arnold. "The Library of M. Le Comte de Fortsas." *Literary Collector* 7 (November 1903): 6–11.

Lillard, Richard G. "Dan De Quille, Comstock Reporter and Humorist." *Pacific Historical Review* 13, no. 3 (1944): 251–59.

Loomis, C. Grant. "The Tall Tales of Dan De Quille." *Western Folklore* [*California Folklore Quarterly*] 5, no. 1 (1946): 26–27.

McGrady, Mike. *Stranger Than Naked; Or, How to Write Dirty Books for Profit; A Manual.* New York: P. H. Wyden, 1970.

Malone, Edmund. *Inquiry Into the Authenticity of Certain Miscellaneous Papers*. New York: A. M. Kelley, 1970. Reprint of 1796 edition.

Mayhew, George P. "Swift's Bickerstaff Hoax as an April Fool Joke." *Modern Philology* 61 (May 1964): 270–80.

Meyerstein, E. H. W. *A Life of Thomas Chatterton*. New York: Russell & Russell, 1972. Reprint of 1930 edition.

Newell, John Cranstoun. *Thomas Chatterton*. Port Washington, NY: Kennikat Press, [ca. 1970]. Reprint of 1948 edition.

Partington, Wilfred. *Forging Ahead: The True Story of the Upward Progress of Thomas James Wise, Prince of Book Collectors, Bibliographer Extraordinary and Otherwise*. New York: G. P. Putnam's Sons, 1939.

Partridge, John. *Merlinus Liberatus for 1709*. London: John Partridge, 1709.

Paull, H. M. *Literary Ethics: A Study in the Growth of Literary Conscience*. Port Washington, NY: Kennikat Press, 1968. Reprint of 1928 edition.

[Pearson, Edmund Lester] "Philobiblos." *The Old Librarian's Almanack*. Woodstock, VT: Elm Tree Press, 1909.

Pullar, Philippa. *Frank Harris*. London: Hamish Hamilton, 1975.

Reid, Calvin. "Widow of 'Little Tree' Author Admits He Changed Identity." *Publishers Weekly* (October 25, 1991): 16–17.

Rosenwald, Lessing J. *The Fortsas Catalogue: A Facsimilie With an Introduction by Lessing J. Rosenwald*. North Hills, PA: Bird & Bull Press, 1970.

Russell, Charles Edward. *Thomas Chatterton: The Marvelous Boy*. New York: Moffat, Yard & Co., 1908.

Schwartz, Joel S. "Alfred Russel Wallace and 'Leonainie': A Hoax That Would Not Die." *Victorian Periodicals Review* 17 (1984): 1–2, 3–15.

Silverman, Kenneth. *Edgar A. Poe: Mournful and Never-Ending Remembrance*. New York: Harper-Collins, 1991.

Smith, William Jay. *The Spectra Hoax*. Middletown, CT: Wesleyan University Press, 1961.

Sullivan, Howard. "The Old Librarian and His Almanack." *Library Journal* 89 (March 15, 1964): 1188–92.

Tannenbaum, Samuel A. *Shakespeare Forgeries in the Revels Accounts*. Port Washington, NY: Kennikat Press, 1966. Reprint of 1928 edition.

Taylor, Donald S. *Thomas Chatterton's Art: Experiments in Imagined History*. Princeton, NJ: Princeton University Press, 1978.

Thomas, Dwight, and David K. Jackson, eds. *The Poe Log: A Documentary Life of Edgar Allan Poe*. Boston: G. K. Hall, 1987.

"Timeless Tentmaker" [Omar Khayyam]. *MD* (May 1978): 111–16.

Todd, William B., ed. *Thomas J. Wise Centenary Studies*. Austin, TX: University of Texas Press, 1959.

Van Der Bellen, Liana. "The Fortsas Catalogue." *Osler Library Newsletter* no. 9 (February 1972).

Weissbuch, Ted N. "Edgar Allan Poe: Hoaxer in the American Tradition." *New York Historical Society Quarterly* 45 (1961): 290–309.

Wertheim, Stanley. "The Adventure of the Arthur Conan Doyle Bookplate." *Manuscripts* 34, no. 4 (Fall 1982): 279–89.

Whitehead, John. *This Solemn Mockery: The Art of Literary Forgery*. London: Arlington Books, 1973.

Wiegand, Wayne A. *The History of a Hoax: Edmund Lester Pearson, John Cotton Dana, and The Old Librarian's Almanack*. Pittsburgh, PA: Beta Phi Mu, 1979.

Wormser, Richard. "Fabulous Fiction." *Papers of the Bibliographical Society of America*. 47 (1953): 231–47.

Medical Hoaxes

Adler, Jerry, and Peter Annin. "A Hard Lesson or a Hoax?" *Newsweek* (March 2, 1992): 77.

"Alarming in Texas." *New York Times* (October 27, 1991): E7.

Armstrong, David, and Elizabeth Metzger Armstrong. *The Great American Medicine Show*. New York: Prentice Hall, 1991.

Bainbridge, William Sims. "Biorhythms: Evaluating a Pseudoscience." *Skeptical Inquirer* (Spring/Summer 1978): 41–56.

Beall, Otho T., Jr. "*Aristotle's Masterpiece* in America: A Landmark in the Folklore of Medicine." *William & Mary Quarterly* (3rd Series) 20 (1963): 207–22.

Bettany, George Thomas. "James Graham." In *Dictionary of National Biography,* Oxford, UK: Oxford University Press, 1921–1922, Vol. 8.

"The Big Banana Hoax." *Science Digest* 63 (February 1968): 62–63.

Blackman, Janet. "Popular Theories of Generation: The Evolution of Aristotle's Works, the Study of an Anachronism." In John Woodward and David Richards, eds. *Health Care and Popular Medicine in Nineteenth-Century England.* New York: Holmes & Meier, 1977.

Branyan, Helen B. "Medical Charlatanism: The Goat Gland Wizard of Milford, Kansas." *Journal of Popular Culture,* 25, no. 1 (Summer 1991): 31–37.

Carson, Gerald. *The Roguish World of Doctor Brinkley.* New York: Rhinehart, 1960.

Christopher, Milbourne. *Mediums, Mystics & the Occult.* New York: Thomas Y. Crowell, 1975.

Clugston, William George. *Rascals in Democracy.* New York: R. R. Smith, 1940.

Cramp, Arthur J., ed. *Nostrums and Quackery.* Vol. 1 (1911); Vol. 2 (1921); Vol. 3 (1936). Chicago: American Medical Association.

Fuller, John G. *Arigo: Surgeon of the Rusty Knife.* New York: Thomas Y. Crowell Co., 1974.

Gittelson, Bernard. *Bio-Rhythm: A Personal Science.* New York: Warner Books, 1977.

Hines, Terence M. "Biorhythm Theory: A Critical Review." *The Skeptical Inquirer* 3, no. 4 (Summer 1979): 26–36.

Holbrook, Stewart. *The Golden Age of Quackery.* New York: Macmillan, 1959.

Ireland, Patricia, Joseph D. Sapira, and Bryce Templeton. "Munchausen's Syndrome: Review and Report of a Case." *American Journal of Medicine* 43 (1967): 579–92.

Jameson, Eric. *The Natural History of Quackery.* Springfield, IL: Charles C. Thomas, 1981.

Jay, Ricky. *Learned Pigs & Fireproof Women.* New York: Villard Books, 1986.

Kane, Steven M. "Holiness Ritual Fire Handling: Ethnographic and Psychophysiological Considerations." *Ethos* 10, no. 4 (Winter 1982): 369–84.

Kantowitz, Barbara. "Anatomy of a Drug Scare: A Phony LSD Warning?" *Newsweek* 108, no. 21 (November 24, 1986): 85.

Kantowitz, Barbara, and Karen Springen. "Parental Indiscretion." *Newsweek* (April 22, 1991): 64.

Lawn, Brian. *The Salernitan Questions: An Introduction to the History of Medieval and Renaissance Problem Literature.* Oxford: The Clarendon Press, 1963.

Leikind, Bernard J., and William J. McCarthy. "An Investigation of Firewalking." *Skeptical Inquirer* 10, no. 1 (Fall 1985): 23–34.

Leventhal, Todd. "Traffic in Baby Parts Has No Factual Basis." *New York Times* (February 26, 1992): A20.

Luce, Gay Gaer. *Body Time: Physiological Rhythms and Social Stress.* New York: Pantheon Books, 1971.

McNamara, Brooks. *Step Right Up.* New York: Doubleday, 1976.

Manningham, Richard. *An Exact Diary of What Was Observ'd During a Close Attendance Upon Mary Toft. . . .* London: J. Roberts, 1726.

Mannix, Dan. *Step Right Up!* New York: Harper & Brothers, 1950.

Maple, Eric. *Magic, Medicine and Quackery.* New York: A. S. Barnes & Co, 1968.

Mehling, Harold. *The Scandalous Scamps.* New York: Henry Holt & Co., 1959.

Palmer, John D. *An Introduction to Biological Rhythms.* New York: Academic Press, 1976.

Pankrantz, Loren. "Fire Walking and the Persistence of Charlatans." *Perspectives in Biology and Medicine* 31, no. 2 (Winter 1988): 291–98.

Pankratz, Loren. "A Review of the Munchausen Syndrome." *Clinical Psychology Review* 1 (1981): 65–78.

Power, D'Arcy. "Aristotle's Masterpiece." In *The Foundations of Medical History.* Baltimore: Williams & Wilkins, 1931.

Randi, James. *Flim-Flam!: The Truth About Unicorns, Parapsychology and Other Delusions.* New York: Lippincott & Crowell, 1980.

St. Andre, Nathanael. *A Short Narrative of an Extraordinary Delivery of Rabbits Perform'd by Mr. John Howard, Surgeon at Guilford.* London: J. Clarke, 1726.

Sakula, Alex. "Munchausen: Fact and Fiction." *Journal of the Royal College of Physicians* 12, no. 3 (1978): 286–92.

Schadewald, Robert. "Biorhythms: A Critical Look at Critical Days." *Fate* (February 1979): 75–80.

Seligman, S. A. "Mary Toft—The Rabbit Breeder." *Medical History* 5 (1961): 349–60.

Spiro, Herzl R. "Chronic Factitious Illness: Munchausen's Syndrome." *Archives of General Psychiatry* 18 (1968): 569–79.

Taberner, P. V. *Aphrodisiacs: The Science and the Myth.* Philadelphia: University of Pennsylvania Press, 1985.

"Texas Health Officials Unable to Verify School HIV Report." *New York Times* (February 27, 1992): A20.

Tissot, [S. A. D.]. *Onanism: Or, a Treatise Upon the Disorders Produced by Masturbation: Or, the Dangerous Effects of Secret and Excessive Venery.* London: Printed for A. Hume, 1766.

Valentine, Tim. *Psychic Surgery.* Chicago: Henry Regnery Co., 1973.

Wall, L. Lewis. "The Strange Case of Mary Toft (Who Was Delivered of Sixteen Rabbits and a Tabby Cat in 1726)." *Medical Heritage* 1 (1985): 199–212.

Young, James Harvey. *The Medical Messiahs: A Social History of Health Quackery in Twentieth Century America.* Princeton, NJ: Princeton University Press, 1967.

Military Hoaxes

Augustus, C. *Paul Jones, Founder of the American Navy, A History,* 2 vols. New York: Charles Scribner's Sons, 1900.

Begg, Paul. "Immaterial Evidence." in *The Unexplained.* Peter Brooksmith, ed. London: Marshall Cavendish, 1985: 1206–10.

Breeden, James O. "'The Case of the Miraculous Bullet' Revisited." *Military Affairs* 45, no. 1 (February 1981): 23–26.

Brown, Raymond Lemmont. *The Phantom Soldiers.* New York: Drake Publishers, 1975.

Capers, LeGrand G. "Attention Gynecologists!—Notes from the Diary of a Field and Hospital Surgeon, C. S. A." *American Medical Weekly* 1 (1874): 233–34.

Cooper, A. Duff. *Operation Heartbreak.* New York: Viking Press, 1950.

De Koven, Anna F. *The Life and Letters of John Paul Jones,* 2 vols. New York: Charles Scribner's Sons, 1913.

De Koven, Mrs. [Anna] Reginald. "A Fictitious Paul Jones Masquerading as the Real." *New York Times* (June 10, 1906) Section 3: 1–2.

Dewar, Michael. *The Art of Deception in Warfare.* Newton Abbot, England: David & Charles, 1989.

Frazer, R. M., Jr. *The Trojan War: The Chronicles of Dictys of Crete and Dares the Phrygian.* Bloomington, IN: Indiana University Press, 1966: 112–13.

Gaillard, E. S. "Miscellaneous." *American Medical Weekly* 1 (1874): 263–64.

Goerman, Robert A. "Alias Carlos Allende." *Fate* (October 1980): 69–75.

Gould, George M., and Walter L. Pyle. *Anomalies and Curiosities of Medicine.* Philadephia: W. B. Saunders, 1900.

Hamilton, Milton W. "Augustus C. Buell, Fraudulent Historian." *Pennsylvania Magazine of History and Biography* 80 (1956): 478–92.

Harris, Melvin. *Sorry—You've Been Duped.* London: Weidenfeld and Nicholson, 1986.

Highet, Gilbert. "The Art of the Hoax." *Horizon* 3, no. 3 (January 1961): 66–72.

Hone, Joseph. "The Serious Art of Hoaxing." *Living Age* (December 1940): 365–68.

[Lorenzen, Bill, and Coral Lorenzen]. "Allende Letters a Hoax." *A. P. R. O. Bulletin* (July/August 1969): 1, 3.

Machen, Arthur. *The Angels of Mons: The Bowman and Other Legends.* New York: G. P. Putnam's Sons, 1915.

Montagu, Ewen. *Beyond Top Secret U.* London: P. Davies, 1977.

Montagu, Ewen. *The Man Who Never Was.* London: Evans Brothers, 1953.

Moore, William L., and Charles Berlitz. *The Philadelphia Experiment.* New York: Grosset & Dunlap, 1979.

Morison, Samuel Eliot. *John Paul Jones: a Sailor's Biography.* Boston: Little, Brown & Co., 1959.

Napolitani, F. Donald. "The Case of the Miraculous Bullet." *American Heritage* 23, no. 1 (December 1971): 99.

Painton, Priscilla, and Scot Thurston. "Con Man Had Run of Entire Army Base." *Atlanta Constitution* (April 20, 1985) "Weekend" section: 1, 13.

Paullin, Charles Oscar. "When Was Our Navy Founded? A Criticism of Augustus C. Buell's 'Paul Jones, Founder of the American Navy.'" *Proceedings of the U.S. Naval Institute* 36, no. 1 (March 1910): 255–67.

Sklar, Dusty. *The Nazis and the Occult.* New York: Dorset Press, 1977.

Steiger, Brad, and Joan Whritenour. *New UFO Breakthrough: The Allende Affair.* New York: Award Books, 1968.

Stephen, Adrian. *The "Dreadnought" Hoax.* London: Leonard and Virginia Woolf at the Hogarth Press, 1936.

Wulff, Wilhelm. *Zodiac and Swastika: How Astrology Guided Hitler's Germany.* New York: Coward, McCann & Geoghegan, 1973.

Photographic Hoaxes

Barlow, Fred, and W. Rampling-Rose. "Report of an Investigation into Spirit Photography." *Proceedings of the Society for Psychical Research* 41 (1933): 121–38.

Browne, Malcolm W. "Computer as an Accessory to Photo Fakery." *New York Times* (July 24, 1991): A6.

Clark, Jerome. "The Cottingley Fairies: The Last Word." *Fate* (November 1978) 68–71.

Cooper, Joe. *The Case of the Cottingley Fairies.* London: Robert Hale, 1990.

"Dome Topples Off Statehouse." Madison (WI) *Capital Times* (April 1, 1933): 1.

Doyle, Arthur Conan. *The Coming of the Fairies.* New York: George H. Doran, 1922.

Edmunds, Simeon. *Spirit Photography.* London: Society for Psychical Research, 1965.

Eisenbud, Jule. *The World of Ted Serios.* New York: William Morrow, 1967.

Fielding, Raymond. *The Technique of Special Effects Cinematography,* 4th ed. London: Focus Press, 1985.

Gardner, Edward L. *Fairies: The Cottingley Fairies and Their Sequel,* 3rd ed. London: Theosophical Publishing House, 1957.

Gettings, Fred. *Ghosts in Photographs: The Extraordinary Story of Spirit Photography.* New York: Harmony Books, 1978.

Goldsmith, Arthur. "Photos Always Lied." *Popular Photography* (November 1991): 68–75.

Krippner, Stanley, and Daniel Rubin, eds. *The Energies of Consciousness.* New York: Gordon & Breach, 1975.

Krippner, Stanley, and Daniel Rubin, eds. *The Kirlian Aura: Photographing the Galaxies of Life.* Garden City, NY: Anchor Books, 1974.

Park, Edwards. "The Greatest Aerial Warfare Photos Go Down in Flames." *Smithsonian Magazine* 15, no. 10 (January 1985): 102–8.

Pehek, John O., Harry J. Kyler, and David L. Faust. "Image Modulation in Corona Discharge Photography." *Science* 194 (October 15, 1976): 263–70.

Permutt, Cyril. *Photographing the Spirit World: Images from Beyond the Spectrum.* Wellingborough, England: Aquarian Press, 1988.

Randi, James. *Flim-Flam: The Truth About Unicorns, Parapsychology, and Other Delusions.* New York: Lippincott & Crowell, 1980.

Reynolds, Charles, and David B. Eisendrath. "An Amazing Weekend with the Amazing Ted Serios." *Popular Photography* (October 1967): 81–87, 131–41, 158.

Ronnie, Art. "Houdini's High-Flying Hoax." *American Heritage* 23, no. 3 (1972): 106–9.

Rosenbaum, Naomi. *A World History of Photography.* New York: Abbeville Press, 1984.

Shaeffer, Robert. "The Cottingley Fairies: A Hoax?" *Fate* (June 1978): 76–83.

Sidgwick, Mrs. Henry [Eleanor]. "On Spirit Photographs, a Reply to Mr. A. R. Wallace." *Proceedings of the Society for Psychical Research* 8 (1891): 268–89.

Smith, Thomas G. *Industrial Light & Magic: The Art of Special Effects.* New York: Ballantine Books, 1986.

Szumanki, Richard. "A New Hard Look at Kirlian Photography: Has It Lost Its Halo?" *Fate* Part I (Jan 1976) 30–38; Part II (February 1976): 78–85.

Watkins, Arleen J., and William S. Bickell. "A Study of the Kirlian Effect." *The Skeptical Inquirer* 10 (Spring 1986): 244–57.

Welch, Paul. "A Man Who Thinks Pictures." *Life* 63 (September 22, 1967): 112–14.

Political Hoaxes

Anderson, Frank Maloy. *The Mystery of "A Public Man."* Minneapolis: University of Minnesota Press, 1948.

Barnum, P. T. "The Miscegenation Hoax." In *Humbugs of the World.* Detroit: Singing Tree Press, 1970 (reprint).

Brunvand, Jan Harold. *The Mexican Pet: More "New" Urban Legends and Some Old Favorites.* New York: W. W. Norton & Co., 1986.

"Cairo Fakes Pictures and Foils Libyan Death Plot." *New York Times* (November 18, 1984): 1, 13.

"The Diary of a Public Man: Unpublished Passages of the Secret History of the American Civil War." *North American Review* 129 (August, September, October, November 1879): 125–40, 259–73, 375–88, 484–96.

Farber, M. A. "The Hoax of the Sentry Catches Police Off Guard." *New York Times* (May 18, 1982): B1, B9.

Goodman Croly, David. *Miscegenation: The Theory of the Blending of the Races, Applied to the American White Man and Negro.* New York: H. Dexter, Hamilton & Co., 1864.

Greene, Bob. "A Communist Master Plan? The Plot Thins." *Chicago Tribune* (March 23, 1981) section 2: 1.

Jonas, Frank H. *The Story of a Political Hoax.* Salt Lake City: Institute of Government, University of Utah, 1966.

Kominsky, Morris. *The Hoaxers: Plain Liars, Fancy Liars, and Damned Liars.* Boston: Branden Press, 1970.

[Lee, Sidney]. "Charles Stewart Parnell." In *Dictionary of National Biography.* Edited by Lee and Sidney. Oxford: Oxford University Press, 1921.

[Lewin, Leonard C.?]. *Report from Iron Mountain on the Possibility and Desirability of Peace.* New York: Dial Press, 1967. Reviewed in the *New York Times* (November 20, 1967): 45; (November 27, 1967) Section VII: 70–71.

"Libya Says Its Squads Killed Ex-Prime Minister." *New York Times* (November 17, 1984): 5.

Lokken, Roy N. "Has the Mystery of 'A Public Man' Been Solved?" *Mississippi Valley Historical Review* 40 (December 1953): 419–40.

Luthin, Reinhard H. "Fakes and Frauds in Lincoln Literature." *Saturday Review* (February 14, 1959): 15–16, 54.

Page, Evelyn. "The Diary and the Public Man." *New England Quarterly* 22 (June 1949): 147–72.

Stephan, John J. "The Tanaka Memorial (1927): Authentic or Spurious?" *Modern Asian Studies* 7, no. 4 (1973): 733–45.

Tuck, Dick. *An Evening with Dick Tuck: The Confessions of a Political Prankster.* [audiotape] North Hollywood, CA: Center for Cassette Studies, 1973.

Wolfe, Bertram D. "Adventures in Forged Sovietica." *New Leader* (July 25, 1955): 13–14; (August 1, 1955): 11–14; (August 8, 1955): 21–22.

Psychology Hoaxes

Abbott, David P. *Behind the Scenes With the Mediums.* Chicago: Open Court Publishing Co., 1907.

Bernstein, Morey. *The Search for Bridey Murphy.* New York: Avon Publishers, 1965. Revised edition.

Borgatta, Edgar F. "Sidesteps Toward a Nonspecial Theory." *Psychological Review* 61, no. 5 (1954): 343–52.

Brean, Herbert. "Bridey Murphy Puts Nation in a Hypnotizzy." *Life* (March 19, 1956): 28–35.

Broad, William J. "Magician's Effort to Debunk Scientists Raises Ethical Issues." *New York Times* (February 15, 1983): 19, 21.

Christopher, Milbourne. *ESP, Seers and Psychics.* New York: Thomas Y. Crowell, 1970.

Christopher, Milbourne. *Houdini: The Untold Story.* New York: Thomas Y. Crowell, 1969.

Christopher, Milbourne. *Mediums, Mystics & the Occult.* New York: Thomas Y. Crowell, 1975.

Churchill, Edward. "Houdini Message a Big Hoax." *New York Graphic* (January 10, 1929): 1.

Clark, Jerome. "Scandal in the Spirit World." *Fate* 36, no. 11 (November 1983): 63–67.

Clark, Jerome, and Loren Coleman. "The Mad Gasser of Mattoon." *Fate* (February 1972): 38–47.

Cohen, Daniel. *The Mysteries of Reincarnation.* New York: Dodd, Mead & Co., 1975.

Collins, Harry. "Magicians in the Laboratory: A New Role to Play." *New Scientist* (June 30, 1983): 929–31.

Dingwall, Eric J. "The Woman Who Never Was." *Tomorrow* 4, no. 4 (Summer 1956): 6–15.

Evans, Henry Ridgley. *The Spirit World Unmasked*. Chicago: Laird & Lee, (c. 1908).

Frazier, Kendrick, and James Randi. "Prediction After the Fact: Lessons of the Tamara Rand Hoax." *Skeptical Inquirer* 6 (Fall 1981): 4–7.

Gardner, Martin. *Science: Good, Bad and Bogus*. Buffalo, NY: Prometheus Books, 1981.

Gauld, Alan, and A. D. Cornell. *Poltergeists*. London: Routledge & Kegan Paul, 1979.

Gresham, William Lindsay. *Houdini: The Man Who Walked Through Walls*. New York: Holt, Rinehart and Winston, 1959.

Grove, Bob. "Atlanta's 'Infamous House of Blood' Case Closed." *Skeptical Inquirer* 13, no. 3 (Spring 1989): 248–49.

Jacobs, Norman. "The Phantom Slasher of Taipei: Mass Hysteria in a Non-Western Society." *Social Problems* 12 (1965): 318–28.

Johnson, Donald M. "The 'Phantom Anesthetist' of Mattoon: A Field Study of Mass Hysteria." *Journal of Abnormal and Social Psychology* 40 (1945): 175–86.

Keene, M. Lamar. *The Psychic Mafia*. New York: St. Martin's Press, 1976.

Kellock, Harold. *Houdini, His Life Story*. New York: Harcourt, Brace & Co., 1928.

Kerckhoff, Alan C., and Kurt W. Back. *The June Bug: A Study of Hysterical Contagion*. New York: Appleton-Century-Crofts, 1968.

Kline, Milton V. *A Scientific Report on "The Search for Bridey Murphy."* New York: Julian Press, 1956.

Marwick, Betty. "The Establishment of Data Manipulation in the Soal-Shackleton Experiments." In *A Skeptic's Handbook of Parapsychology*. Edited by Paul Kurtz. Buffalo, NY: Prometheus Books, 1985.

Marwick, Betty. "The Soal-Goldney Experiments With Basil Shackleton: New Evidence of Data Manipulation." *Proceedings of the Society for Psychical Research* 56, no. 211 (1978): 250–81.

Medalia, Nahum Z., and Otto N. Larsen. "Diffusion and Belief in a Collective Delusion: The Seattle Windshield Pitting Epidemic." *American Sociological Review* 23 (1958): 180–86.

Oppenheim, Janet. *The Other World: Spiritualism and Psychical Research in England, 1850–1914*. Cambridge, England: Cambridge University Press, 1985.

Patterson, Francine "Penny." "Conversations With a Gorilla." *National Geographic Magazine* (October 1978): 438–65.

Pfungst, Oskar. *Clever Hans (the Horse of Mr. Van Osten): A Contribution to Experimental and Human Psychology*. New York: Holt, Rinehart and Winston, 1911.

Randi, James. "The Columbus Poltergeist Case." *Skeptical Inquirer* 9, no. 3 (Spring 1985): 221–35.

Randi, James. "The Project Alpha Experiment." *The Skeptical Inquirer* Part I: 7, no. 4 (Summer 1983): 24–35; Part II: 8, no. 1 (Fall 1983): 36–45.

Randi, James. "The Psychology of Conjuring." *Technology Review* (January 1978): 56–63.

Revelations of a Spirit Medium. London: Kegan Paul Trench, Trubner, 1922 [facsimile ed.].

Rhine, J. B. "A New Case of Experimenter Unreliability." *Journal of Parapsychology* 38 (1974): 215–225.

Rhine, J. B. "Second Report on a Case of Experimenter Fraud." *Journal of Parapsychology* 39 (1975): 306–25.

Rogo, D. Scott. "J. B. Rhine and the Levy Scandal." In *A Skeptic's Handbook of Parapsychology*. Edited by Paul Kurtz. Buffalo, NY: Prometheus Books, 1985.

Rogo, D. Scott. *On the Track of the Poltergeist*. Englewood Cliffs, NJ: Prentice-Hall, 1986.

Schuler, Edgar A., and Vernon J. Parenton. "A Recent Epidemic of Hysteria in a Louisiana High School." *Journal of Social Psychology* 17 (1943): 221–35.

Scott, Christopher, and Philip Haskell. "Fresh Light on the Shackleton Experiments." *Proceedings of the Society for Psychical Research* 56, no. 209 (1974): 43–72. See also papers by K. M. Goldney (73–84), C. W. K. Mundle (85–87), Robert H. Thouless (88–92), John Beloff (93–96), J. G. Pratt (97–111), M. R. Barrington (112–16), Ian Stevenson (117–129), and J. R. Smythies (130–31) in the same issue.

Seboek, Thomas A., and Donna Jean Umiker-Seboek, eds. *Speaking of Apes*. New York: Plenum Press, 1980.

Seboek, Thomas A., and Robert Rosenthal, eds. *The Clever Hans Phenomenon: Communication With Horses, Whales, Apes and People*. New York: The New York Academy of Sciences, 1981.

Sirois, François. *Epidemic Hysteria*. Published as Supplementum 252 to *Acta Psychiatrica Scandinavica*. Copenhagen: Munksgaard, 1974.

"Skeptical Eye: Psychic Abscam." *Discover* (March 1983): 10, 13.

Stein, Gordon. "Does the Near Death Experience Give Proof of an Afterlife?" *American Rationalist* (March/April 1983): 84–88.

Terrace, Herbert. *Nim*. New York: A. A. Knopf, 1979.

Terrace, Herbert, and others. "Can an Ape Create a Sentence?" *Science* 206 (November 23, 1979): 891–902.

Truzzi, Marcello. "Reflections on 'Project Alpha': Scientific Experiment or Conjuror's Illusion?" *Zetetic Scholar* 12/13 (1987): 73–98.

"TV Host, Psychic Admit Reagan Hoax." *Chicago Tribune* (April 6, 1981): 1, 4.

Umiker-Seboek, Jean, and Thomas A. Seboek. "Clever Hans and Smart Simians." *Anthropus* 76 (1981): 89–165.

Public Relations Hoaxes

Aaron, Andy, and Joe Queenan. "Let Them Eat Bunnies." *Spy* (April 1992): 56–62.

Abel, Alan. *The Great American Hoax*. New York: Trident Press, 1966.

Abel, Alan. *How to Thrive on Rejection: A Manual for Survival*. New York: Dembner Books, 1984.

Abel, Alan. "Omar the Beggar." *The Panhandler's Handbook*. New York: Zebra Books, 1977.

Ball, Edward. "$35 M[illion] and She's Single." *New York Post* (January 8, 1990): 1.

Blau, Eleanor. "Rare Thrill for Tass: Joshing Over Its U.F.O. Report." *New York Times* (October 12, 1989): A18.

The Confessions of a Hoaxer. New York: Macmillan, 1970.

Fein, Esther B. "Hot News from Tass: Tourists from Space." *New York Times* (October 10, 1989): A1, 10.

Fein, Esther B. "U.F.O. Landing Is Fact, Not Fantasy, Russians Insist." *New York Times* (October, 1989): A6.

"Final Tributes Paid to H. L. Reichenbach." *New York Times* (July 10, 1931): 26.

Fuhrman, Candice Jacobson. *Publicity Stunt!* San Francisco: Chronicle Books, 1989.

Gehman, Richard. "The Little World of Jim Moran." *Playboy* (September 1981): 68–69, 123–29.

"H. L. Reichenbach, Press Agent, Dead." *New York Times* (July 4, 1931): 13.

"Home Office and Mr. Power: Kitchener Allegations Refuted." *Times of London* (September 10, 1926): 9.

Hynd, Alan. *Professors of Perfidy*. New York: A. S. Barnes & Co., 1963: 40–88.

"Lord Kitchener: An Empty Coffin Opened." *Times of London* (August 17, 1926): 12.

"The Lord Kitchener Body Myth." *Times of London* (November 16, 1926): 5.

"Lord Kitchener: Coffin Removed by Scotland Yard." *Times of London* (August 16, 1926): 12.

Maurice, Frederick Burton. "Horatio Herbert Kitchener." *Dictionary of National Biography, 1912–1921*. Oxford: Oxford University Press, 1927: 306–14.

Paar, Jack. *I Kid You Not*. Boston: Little, Brown & Co., 1960.

Pranks. San Francisco: Research, 1987: 103–09.

Reichenbach, Harry, and David Freedman. *Phantom Fame: The Anatomy of Ballyhoo*. New York: Simon & Schuster, 1931.

Smith, H. Allen. *The Compleat Practical Joker*. New York: Doubleday & Co., 1953.

Smith, H. Allen. *Lost In the Horse Latitudes*. Garden City, NY: Doubleday, Doran & Co., 1944.

Smith, H. Allen. *Low Man on a Totem Pole*. Garden City, NY: Doubleday, Doran & Co., 1941.

Troy, Con. *Laugh With Hugh Troy, World's Greatest Practical Joker*. Wyomissing, PA: Trojan Books, 1983.

Religion Hoaxes

Alvarez, José Luis [James Randi]. *The Teachings of Carlos*. [N. P.]: The Author, 1988.

Alzog, John B. *History of the Church*. Vol. 2. New York: Benziger Brothers, 1912.

Anderson, Richard Lloyd. "The Fraudulent Archko Volume." *Brigham Young University Studies* 15 no. 1 (Autumn 1974): 43–64.

"Awful Disclosures of Maria Monk." *Dublin Review* 1 no. 1 (May 1836): 151–74.

Awful Exposure of the Atrocious Plot Formed by Certain Individuals Against the Clergy and Nuns of Lower Canada, Through the Intervention of Maria Monk. New York: Printed for Jones & Co. of Montreal, 1836.

Bailey, Lloyd R. *Noah: The Person and the Story in History and Tradition.* Columbia, SC: University of South Carolina Press, 1989.

Bataille, Dr. (Léo Taxil). *Le Diable au XIXe Siècle.* Paris: Delhomme et Briguet, (c. 1893).

Bentley, James. *Restless Bones: The Story of Relics.* London: Constable, 1985.

Billington, Ray Allen. *The Protestant Crusade, 1800–1860: A Study of the Origins of American Nativism.* New York: Macmillan Co., 1958.

Bright, John. "Has Archeology Found Evidence of the Flood?" *The Biblical Archeologist* 5 (1942): 55–61.

Browne, Malcolm W. "How Carbon 14 Was Used to Fix Date of Shroud." *New York Times* (October 14, 1988): 10.

Buhler, Rich. "Scientists Discover Hell in Siberia." *Christianity Today* 34, no. 10 (July 16, 1990): 28–29.

Bullett, Gerald. "Introduction" to the Thinker's Library edition of *The Fair Haven.* C. A. Watts & Co., 1938: vii–ix.

[Butler, Samuel]. *The Fair Haven.* London: Trubner, 1873.

[Butler, Samuel]. *The Note-Books of Samuel Butler.* New York: E. P. Dutton, 1907.

Calvin, John. *A Treatise on Relics.* Edinburgh: Johnstone, Hunter & Co., [c. 1854].

Carlson, Shawn, and Gerald Larue, eds. *Satanism in America.* El Cerrito, CA: Gaia Press, 1989.

Damon, Paul, and others. "Radiocarbon Dating of the Shroud of Turin." *Nature* 337, no. 16 (February 16, 1989): 611–15.

Douglas, J. Archibald. "The Chief Lama of Himis on the Alleged 'Unknown Life of Christ'." *Nineteenth Century* 39 (1896): 667–78.

Duhr, Bernhard. *Jesuiten-Fabeln.* Freiburg [Germany]: Herderische Verlagshandlung, 1892.

Dundes, Alan, ed. *The Blood Libel Legend: A Casebook in Anti-Semitic Folklore.* Madison, WI: University of Wisconsin Press, 1991.

Fasold, David. *The Ark of Noah.* New York: Wynwood Press, 1988.

Frame, Randy. "A Hoax Observed." *Christianity Today* 33 (June 16, 1989): 64–65.

Garlaschelli, Luigi, Franco Ramaccini, and Sergio Della Sala. "Working Bloody Miracles." *Nature* 353 (October 10, 1991): 507.

Garrett, Edmund. *Isis Very Much Unveiled, Being the Story of the Great Mahatma Hoax.* London: Westminster Gazette, [c. 1894].

Goodspeed, Edgar J. "Pilate's Court and the Archko Volume." In *Strange New Gospels.* Chicago: University of Chicago Press, 1931.

Goodspeed, Edgar J. *Strange New Gospels.* Chicago: University of Chicago Press, 1931.

Griffin, William. *Clive Staples Lewis: A Dramatic Life.* San Francisco: Harper & Row, 1986.

Harney, Martin P. *The Jesuits in History: The Society of Jesus Through Four Centuries.* New York: The America Press, 1941: 464–465.

Harrison, William H. *Mother Shipton Investigated.* London: W. H. Harrison, 1881. Reprinted by Norwood Editions, 1976.

Hering, Daniel W. *Foibles and Fallacies of Science.* New York: D. Van Nostrand & Co., 1924: 213–18.

Hicks, Robert D. *In Pursuit of Satan: The Police and the Occult.* Buffalo, NY: Prometheus Books, 1991.

Holt, Lee E. *Samuel Butler.* New York: Twayne, 1964.

Jastrow, Joseph. *Error and Eccentricity in Human Belief.* New York: Dover Publications, 1962.

Kagan, Daniel, and Ian Summers. *Mute Evidence.* New York: Bantam Books, 1984.

Koromvokis, Lygeri. "Faith Healers in the Laboratory." *Science Digest* (May 1982): 88–92, 95.

Kurtz, Paul. "Does Faith-Healing Work?" *Free Inquiry* 6, no. 2 (Spring 1986): 30–36.

Lea, Henry Charles. *Léo Taxil, Diana Vaughan et l'Eglise Romaine.* Paris: Société Nouvelle de Librarie et d'Edition, 1901.

[Léo Taxil]. *Memoires d'une Ex-Palladiste.* A Monthly Publication. Paris: A. Pierret, 1895–1897.

Lindskoog, Kathryn. *The C. S. Lewis Hoax*. Portland, OR: Multnomah, 1988.

McCrone, Walter. "The Shroud of Turin: Blood or Artist's Pigment?" *Accounts of Chemical Research* 23 (March 1990): 77–83.

Mahan, William D. *The Archko Volume*. New Canaan, CT: Keats Publishing, 1975.

Mann, Horace K. *The Lives of the Popes in the Early Middle Ages*. Vols. 2, 3. St. Louis: B. Herder, 1906: 328 (v. 2); 263 (v. 3).

Meade, Marion. *Madame Blavatsky: The Woman Behind the Myth*. New York: G. P. Putnam's Sons, 1980.

Monk, Maria. *Awful Disclosures of Maria Monk*. New York: Howe & Bates, 1836.

Moore, Robert A. "The Impossible Voyage of Noah's Ark." *Creation/ Evolution* no. 11 (Winter 1983): 1–43.

Mueller, F. Max. "The Alleged Sojourn of Christ in India." *Nineteenth Century* 36 (1894): 515.

Nickell, Joe. *Inquest on the Shroud of Turin*. 2nd ed. Buffalo, NY: Prometheus Books, 1988.

Nolen, William. *Healing: A Doctor in Search of a Miracle*. New York: Random House, 1974.

Notovitch, Nicolas. *The Unknown Life of Jesus Christ*. Santa Monica, CA: Leaves of Healing Publications, 1980.

Olsen, Chris. *Pope Joan: A Riddle of the Dark Ages*. St. Louis: Rationalist Publications, [c. 1960].

Passantino, Gretchen, Bob Passantino, and Jon Trott. "Satan's Sideshow." *Cornerstone* 18, no. 90 (1990): 23–28.

Raby, Peter. *Samuel Butler: A Biography*. Iowa City, IA: University of Iowa Press, 1991.

Randi, James. "'Be Healed in the Name of God!': An Exposé of the Reverend W. V. Grant." *Free Inquiry* (Spring 1986): 8–19.

Randi, James. *The Faith Healers*. Buffalo, NY: Prometheus Books, 1989.

Randi, James. "Peter Popoff Reaches Heaven Via 39.17 Megahertz." *Free Inquiry* 6, no. 3 (Summer 1986): 6–9.

Reiber, Johannes B. *Monita Secreta. Die geheimen Instruktionen der Jesuiten verglicten mit den amtlichen Quellen des Ordens*. Augsburg [Germany]: Litterar Institut von Dr. R. Huttler, 1892.

Reinach, Solomon. *Orpheus: A History of Religions*. New York: Horace Liveright, 1930.

Rhoidis, Emmanuel. *Pope Joan (The Female Pope): An Historical Study*. London: George Redway, 1886.

Rhys, Jocelyn. *The Reliquary: A Collection of Relics*. New York: Freethought Press Association, 1931.

Richardson, James T., Joel Best, and David G. Bromley, eds. *The Satanism Scare*. New York: Aldine De Gruyter, 1991.

The Secret Instructions of the Jesuits. New York: Truth Seeker Co., [c. 1910].

Secret Instructions of the Jesuits. Printed Verbatim from the London Copy of 1725. To Which Is Prefaced an Historical Essay; With an Appendix of Notes, by the Editor of The Protestant. Princeton, NJ: J. & T. Simpson, 1831.

Shipton, Ursula. *The Strange and Wonderful History of Mother Shipton*. London: Printed for E. Pearson by J. Davy, 1870.

Sloan, Pat. "Demythologizing Darwin." *The Humanist* (London), (April 1965): 106–10.

Sloan, Pat. "The Myth of Darwin's Conversion." *The Humanist* (London), (March 1960): 70–72.

Stein, Gordon. "Deathbeds of Unbelievers." In *Encyclopedia of Unbelief*. Buffalo, NY: Prometheus Books, 1985.

Stone, William Leete. *A Refutation of the Fabulous History of the Arch-Impostor Maria Monk, Being the Result of a Minute and Searching Inquiry by William L. Stone, Esq. of New York, To Which Are Added Other Interesting Testimonies*. N.P., 1836: 46.

Stratford, Lauren [Laurel Rose Willson]. *Satan's Underground*. Eugene, OR: Harvest House Publishers, 1988.

Suro, Robert. "Church Says Shroud of Turin Isn't Authentic." *New York Times* (October 14, 1988): 1–6.

Symonds, John. *The Lady with the Magic Eyes: Madame Blavatsky— Medium and Magician*. New York: Thomas Yoseloff, 1959.

Taxil, Léo. *Confessioni di un Ex-Libero-Pensatore*. Florence, Italy: Tipografia Editrice di A. Ciardi, 1887.

Teeple, Howard M. *The Noah's Ark Nonsense*. Evanston, IL: Religion and Ethics Institute, 1978.

Thompson, Ralph. "The Maria Monk Affair." *The Colophon* Part 17, no. 6 (1934).

Thurston, Herbert. *No Popery: Chapters on Anti-Papal Prejudice.* London: Longmans Green & Co., 1930.

Vaughan, Diana [Léo Taxil]. *La Restauration du Paganisme.* "Written by Albert Pike, translation by Diana Vaughan." Paris: A. Pierret, (c. 1896).

Waite, Arthur Edward. *Devil-Worship in France.* London: George Redway, 1896.

Wakefield, Sherman D. "Washington's Prayer." *Progressive World* 7, no. 6 (June 1953): 331–32.

[Ware, Robert]. *Pope Joan: Or, An Account Collected Out of the Romish Authors, Proved to Be of the Clergy and Members of That Church, Before Luther Left Her Doctrine; and Also of Romish Authors Since Luther Departed from Rome; Testifying That There Was a She-Pope, Who Sate [sic] in That See, and Ruled the Same.* London: William Miller, 1689.

Wilson, A(ndrew) N(orman). *C. S. Lewis: A Biography.* New York: W. W. Norton, 1990.

Wilson, A(ndrew) N(orman). "C. S. Lewis, Sins and All." *New York Times Book Review* (December 24, 1989): 1, 26–27.

Wilson, Ian. *The Mysterious Shroud.* Garden City, NY: Doubleday, 1986.

Wood, Clement. *The Woman Who Was Pope: A Biography of Pope Joan, 853–855 a.d.* New York: William Faro, 1931.

Science Hoaxes

Allen, Woody, director. *Zelig.* Orion Pictures, 1983.

Anders, Edward, Eugene R. DuFresne, and Ryoichi Hayatsu. "Contaminated Meteorite." *Science* (November 27, 1964): 1157–61.

Aronson, Lester R. The Case of *The Case of the Midwife Toad.*" *Behavior Genetics* 5, no. 2 (1975): 115–1025.

Bartholomew, Paul, and Bob Bartholomew, William Brann, and Bruce Hallenbeck. *Monsters of the Northwoods: An In-Depth Investigation of Bigfoot in New York and Vermont.* The Authors, 1992.

Bateson, William. "Dr. Kammerer's Alytes." *Nature* 111 (1923): 738–39.

Benwell, Gwen, and Arthur Waugh. *Sea Enchantress: The Tale of the Mermaid and Her Kin.* London: Hutchinson, 1961.

Binns, Ronald. *The Loch Ness Mystery Solved.* Buffalo, NY: Prometheus Books, 1984.

Bord, Janet, and Colin Bord. *The Bigfoot Casebook.* Harrisburg, PA: Stackpole Books, 1982.

Bord, Janet, and Colin Bord. *The Evidence for Bigfoot and Other Man-Beasts.* Wellingborough, UK: Aquarian Press, 1984.

Broad, William J. "Harvard Delays in Reporting Fraud." *Science* 215 (1982): 478–82.

Broad, William J. "Report Absolves Harvard in Case of Fakery." *Science* 215 (1982): 874–76.

Broad, William J. "Saga of Boy Clone Ruled a Hoax." *Science* 211 (February 27, 1981): 902.

Broad, William, and Nicholas Wade. *Betrayers of the Truth: Fraud and Deceit in the Halls of Science.* New York: Touchstone/Simon & Schuster, 1982.

Bromhall, Derek. "The Great Cloning Hoax." *New Statesman* (June 2, 1978): 734–36.

Cameron, Grant R., T. Scott Crain, and Chris Rutkowski. "In the Land of Dreams." *International UFO Reporter* 15, no. 5 (September/October 1990): 4–8.

Campbell, Stewart. "The Surgeon's Monster Hoax." *British Journal of Photography* (April 20, 1984): 402–05, 410.

Chorost, Michael. *Circles of Note: A Reader's Guide to the Crop Circle Phenomenon.* San Antonio, TX: Dennis Stacey, c. 1991.

Clair, Colin. *Unnatural History: An Illustrated Bestiary.* New York: Abelard-Schuman, 1967.

Clark, Jerome. *The Emergence of a Phenomenon: The UFO Encyclopedia,* Volume 2. Detroit, MI: Apogee Books, 1992.

Clark, Jerome. *UFOs in the 1980s: The UFO Encyclopedia,* Volume 1. Detroit, MI: Apogee Books, 1990.

Clements, Warner. "Levitation: Some Phantasy and Some Physics." *Skeptical Inquirer* 13, no. 3 (Spring 1989): 289–95.

Cohen, Daniel. *The Great Airship Mystery: A UFO of the 1890s.* New York: Dodd, Mead, 1981.

Crowe, Michael J. *The Extraterrestrial Life Debate, 1750–1900.* Cambridge, England: Cambridge University Press, 1986.

Culliton, Barbara. "The Sloan-Kettering Affair: A Story Without a Hero." *Science* 184 (1974): 644–50.

Curtis, Heber D. "The Comet-Seeker Hoax." *Popular Astronomy* 46 (1938): 71–75.

Dance, Peter. *Animal Fakes & Frauds.* Maidstone, England: Sampson Low, 1975.

Delgado, Pat, and Colin Andrews. *Circular Evidence: A Detailed Investigation of the Flattened Swirled Crops Phenomenon.* Grand Rapids, MI: Phanes Press, 1989.

Dolby, R. G. A. "Science and Pseudo-science: The Case of Creationism." *Zygon* 22, no. 2 (1987): 195–212.

Ellis, Bill. "The US-EBE 'Secret Treaty': Folklorists Should Be Appalled." *Foaftale News* 17 (March 1990): 6–8.

Emboden, William A. *Bizarre Plants: Magical, Monstrous, Mythical.* New York: Macmillan, 1974.

Emery, C. Eugene, Jr. "News and Comment: Sasquatchsicle: The Monster, the Model and the Myth." *Skeptical Inquirer* 6, no. 2 (Winter 1981–82): 2–4.

Evans, David S. "The Great Moon Hoax I" and "II." *Sky and Telescope* 62 (September 1981): 196–98 and 62 (October 1981): 308–11. See also issue of November 1981, pages 428–429 for related article by Michael J. Crowe.

Eve, Raymond A. and Francis B. Harrold. *The Creationist Movement in Modern America.* Boston: Twayne Publishers, 1991.

"'Eyeless Vision' Unmasked." *Scientific American* 212 (March 1965): 57.

Flammonde, Paris. *The Age of Flying Saucers: Notes on a Projected History of Unidentified Flying Objects.* New York: Hawthorn Books, 1971.

Fox, H. Munro. "Note on Kammerer's Experiments with *Ciona* Concerning the Inheritance of an Acquired Character." *Journal of Genetics* 14 (1924): 89–91.

Fuller, Paul, and Jenny Randles. *Controversy of the Circles.* London: BUFORA, [c. 1989.

Gardner, Martin. "Dermo-optical Perception: A Peek Down the Nose." *Science* 151 (February 11, 1966): 654–57.

Green, John, and Sabina W. Sanderson. "Alas, Poor Jacko." *Pursuit* 8, no. 1 (January 1975): 18–19.

Gudge, E. W. "Jenny Hanivers, Dragons and Basilisks in the Old Natural History Books and in Modern Times." *Scientific Monthly* 38 (June 1934): 511–23; 211 (February 27, 1981): 902.

Hall, Trevor H. *The Enigma of D. D. Home: Medium or Fraud?* Buffalo, NY: Prometheus Books, 1984.

Heuvelmans, Bernard. "The Monsters of Loch Ness. By Roy Mackal" [book review]. *The Zetetic* (Fall/Winter 1977): 110–21.

Hixson, Joseph. *The Patchwork Mouse.* New York: Doubleday, 1976.

Jenkins, Patrick. "Jersey Devil Struggles for His Due in Face of Fiendish Development." *Newark Star-Ledger* (October 31, 1985): 61.

Keel, John. *Jadoo.* New York: Julian Messner, 1957.

Koestler, Arthur. *The Case of the Midwife Toad.* New York: Random House, 1971.

Langford, David. "Myths in the Making." *New Scientist* (May 26, 1988): 78.

Lemonick, Michael B. "Defeat for Strict Creationists." *Time* (June 30, 1986): 75.

Leroy, Olivier. *La Levitation.* Paris: Librarie Valois, 1928.

Ley, Willy. "Hoaxes" [The Fisher Hoax]. *Fantastic Adventures* (January 1940): 74–75.

[Locke, Richard Adams]. "Great Astronomical Discoveries." *The New York Sun* (August 25, 1835): 1–2.

Locke, Richard Adams. *The Moon Hoax: or a Discovery that the Moon Has a Vast Population of Human Beings.* New York: William Gowans, 1859. Reprint published by Gregg Press (Boston), 1975.

Loosley, William Robert [David Langford]. *An Account of a Meeting With Denizens of Another World.* Newton Abbot, England: David & Charles, 1979. American edition: New York: St. Martin's Press, 1980.

McCloy, James F., and Ray Miller, Jr. *The Jersey Devil.* Wallingford, PA: Middle Atlantic Press, 1976.

McIver, Tom. "Ancient Tales and Space-Age Myths of Creationist Evangelism." *Skeptical Inquirer* 10 (Spring 1986): 258–76.

Mahan, Lloyd. *Russia's Space Hoax.* New York: Science and Mechanics News Book, 1966.

Meaden, G. Terence. *The Goddess of the Stones.* London: Souvenir Press, 1991.

Meurger, Michel, and Claude Gagnon. *Lake Monster Traditions: A Cross-Cultural Analysis.* London: Fortean Tomes, 1988.

Moore, William L. "Crashed Saucers: Evidence in Search of Proof." In *MUFON 1985 UFO Symposium Pro-*

ceedings. Edited by Walter H. Andrus, Jr., and Richard H. Hall. Seguin, TX: Mutual UFO Network, 1985.

Napier, John. *Bigfoot: The Yeti and Sasquatch in Myth and Reality*. New York: E. P. Dutton, 1973.

Nebel, Long John. *The Way Out World*. Englewood Cliffs, NJ: Prentice-Hall, 1961.

Noyes, Ralph, ed. *The Crop Circle Enigma*. Bath, England: Gateway Books, 1990.

Oudemans, A. C. *The Great Sea Serpent*. Leiden, Netherlands: E.J. Brill, 1892.

Pastner, Stephen, and William Haviland. "Confronting the Creationists." *Northeastern Anthropological Association Occasional Proceedings* no. 1 (1982).

Perry, James M. "Run for Your Life! That Thing Could be the Loch Ness Monster." *Wall Street Journal* (August 1, 1983): 1, 8.

Price, George R. "The Day They Discovered Men on the Moon." *Popular Science* 173 (July 1958): 61–64.

Przibram, Hans. "The Nuptial Pad of Kammerer's Water-Bred Alytes." *Nature* 119 (1926): 635–36.

"Publisher Lippincott Is Sued for $7 Million Over Cloning Book." *Wall Street Journal* (July 11, 1978): 37.

Rickard, R. J. M. "Walking, Sitting and Lying on Air." *Fortean Times* no. 21 (1977): 16–24.

Robinson, Leonard Wallace. "We Have More than Five Senses." *New York Times Magazine* (March 15, 1964): 30–34, 106–08.

Romains, Jules. *Eyeless Vision*. New York: G. P. Putnam, 1924.

Rosenfeld, A. "Seeing Color With the Fingers." *Life* (June 12, 1964): 102–13.

Sanderson, Ivan T. *Abominable Snowmen: Legend Come to Life*. Philadelphia: Chilton Company, 1961.

Sanderson, Ivan T. "The Missing Link." *Argosy* (May 1969): 23–31.

Schadewald, Robert. "Creationist Pseudoscience." *Skeptical Inquirer* 8, no. 1 (Fall 1983): 22–35.

[Seaman, Barbara]. "Penthouse Interview: David Rorvik." *Penthouse* (June 1978): 93–98, 176–79.

Skinner, Bob, and others. "The Crop Circle Phenomenon." *Fortean Times* 90, no. 53 (Winter 1989): 32–57.

Skinner, Charles. *American Myths and Legends*. Philadelphia: J. B. Lippincott, 1903.

Stein, Gordon. "The Amazing Medium Mirabelli." *Fate* (March 1991): 86–95.

Strahler, Arthur N. "Toward a Broader Perspective in the Evolutionist-Creationist Debate." *Journal of Geological Education* 31 (1983): 87–94.

"Suit Over Cloning Book Settled Out of Court." *Publishers Weekly* (April 23, 1982): 12–13.

Sullivan, Jeremiah J., and James F. McCloy. "The Jersey Devil's Finest Hour." *New York Folklore Quarterly* 30 (September 1974): 231–38.

U.S. House of Representatives, 97th Congress. *Fraud in Biomedical Research*. Hearings before the Subcommittee on Investigations and Oversight of the Committee on Science and Technology, March 31–April 1, 1981. Washington, DC: United States Government Printing Office, 81: 14950.

Show Business and Entertainment Hoaxes

Aranza, Jacob. *Backward Masking Unmasked: Backward Satanic Messages of Rock and Roll Exposed*. Shreveport, LA: Huntington House, 1983.

Aranza, Jacob. *More Rock, Country and Backward Masking Unmasked*. Shreveport, LA: Huntington House, 1985.

Austin, James C. "Seeing the Elephant Again: P.T. Barnum and the American Art of Hoax." *Thalia* 4 (1) (1981): 14–18.

Barnum, P[hineas] T[aylor]. *The Life of Barnum the World-Renowned Showman*. Philadelphia: S.I. Bell & Co., [c. 1892].

Barnum, P[hineas] T[aylor]. *Struggles and Triumphs: Or, The Life of P.T. Barnum*. 2 vols. New York: A. Knopf, 1927.

Betts, John Rickards. "P.T. Barnum and the Popularization of Natural History." *Journal of the History of Ideas* 20 (1959): 353–68.

Brewer-Giorgio, Gail. *Is Elvis Alive?* New York: Tudor Publishing Co., 1988.

Brewer-Giorgio, Gail. *The Elvis File: Was His Death Faked?* New York: Shapolsky Publishers, 1990.

Brown, Rosemary. *Immortals by My Side*. Chicago: Henry Regnery Co., 1974.

Brown, Rosemary. *Unfinished Symphonies: Voices from the Beyond.* New York: William Morrow, 1971.

Cortez, Diego. *Private Elvis.* Stuttgart, Germany: Fey, 1978.

Creed, Thomas L. "Subliminal Deception: Pseudoscience on the College Lecture Circuit." *Skeptical Inquirer* 11, no. 4 (1987): 358–66.

Gibbs, Geoffrey. "Rosemary Brown's *Valse Brilliante*" [Unpublished manuscript, February 6, 1992. Available from Gordon Stein upon request.]

Griffin, David, producer. *The Elvis Files.* WPIX Television Network. Program aired August 14, 1991.

Harris, Neil. *Humbug: The Art of P. T. Barnum.* Boston: Little, Brown & Co., 1973.

Holden, Stephen. "Winner of Grammy Lost by Milli Vanilli: No One." *New York Times* (December 5, 1990): C23.

Hudson, Rock, and Sara Davidson. *Rock Hudson: His Story.* New York: William Morrow & Co., 1986.

Lees, Gene. "The Life and Times of Blind Orange Adams." *High Fidelity Magazine* 19, no. 10 (October 1969): 126.

"Long Parade of False Performers Marching Across Nation's Stages." *Variety* (November 25, 1987): 119.

McIver, Tom. "Backward Masking, and Other Backward Thoughts About Music." *Skeptical Inquirer* 13, no. 1 (1988): 50–63.

Marcus, Greil. *Dead Elvis.* New York: Doubleday, 1991.

May, Antoinette. *Haunted Ladies: Exploring the Supernatural With Six Great Psychics.* San Francisco: Chronicle Books, 1975: 43–69.

Bird, Donald Allport, Stephen C. Holder, and Diane Sears. "Walrus Is Greek for Corpse: Rumor and the Death of Paul McCartney." *Journal of Popular Culture* 10, no. 1 (1976): 110–21.

Meisler, Andy. "The Beatles Are Coming, The Beatles Are Coming." *Games* (March/April 1982): 21.

"Milli Vanilli Didn't Sing Its Pop Hits." *New York Times* (November 16, 1990): C20.

"Milli Vanilli Explains Its Lip-Synching." *New York Times* (November 21, 1990): C8.

Oppenheimer, Jerry, and Jack Vitek. *Idol/Rock Hudson: The True Story of an American Film Hero.* New York: Villard Books, 1986.

Pareles, Jon. "Wages of Silence: Milli Vanilli Loses a Grammy Award." *New York Times* (November 20, 1990): C15, C22.

Saxon, A. H. *P. T. Barnum: The Legend and the Man.* New York: Columbia University Press, 1989.

Shelton, Robert. *No Direction Home: The Life and Music of Bob Dylan.* New York: Beachtree/William Morrow, 1986: 160–62.

Slominsky, Nicolas. "Claque." In *Lectionary of Music.* New York: McGraw-Hill, 1989.

Stone, Joseph, and Tim Yohn. *Prime Time and Misdemeanors: Investigating the 1950s T.V. Quiz Scandal–A D.A.'s Account.* New Brunswick, NJ: Rutgers University Press, 1992. See also the PBS-TV show of January 6, 1992, entitled "The TV Quiz Show Scandal."

Thorne, Stephen, and Philip Himelstein. "The Role of Suggestion in the Perception of Satanic Messages in Rock-and-Roll Recordings." *Journal of Psychology* 116 (1984): 245–48.

Vokey, John, and J. Don Read. "Subliminal Messages: Between the Devil and the Media." *American Psychologist* 40, no. 11 (1985): 1231–39.

Wilson, Francis. *John Wilkes Booth: Fact and Fiction of Lincoln's Assassination.* Boston: Houghton Mifflin, 1929.

Sociology and Psychology of Hoaxes

Boorstin, Daniel. *The Image: A Guide to Pseudo-Events in America.* New York: Harper and Row, 1962.

Brackman, Jacob. *The Put-On: Modern Fooling and Modern Mistrust.* Chicago: Henry Regnery, 1971.

Cooper, H. H. A., and Lawrence J. Redlinger. *Catching Spies: Principles and Practices of Counterespionage.* Boulder, CO: Paladin Press, 1988.

Ekman, Paul. *Telling Lies: Clues to Deceit in the Marketplace, Politics and Marriage.* New York: W. W. Norton and Co., 1985.

Fedler, Fred. *Media Hoaxes.* Ames, IA: Iowa State University Press, 1989.

Finkelstein, Lionel. "The Impostor: Aspects of His Development." *The Psychoanalytic Quarterly* 43, no. 1 (1974): 85–114.

Goffman, Erving. "Embarrassment and Social Organization." In *Interaction Ritual.* Garden City, NY: Doubleday Anchor Books, 1967: 97–112.

Goffman, Erving. *Frame Analysis: An Essay on the Organization of Experience.* New York: Harper Colophon Books, 1974.

Goode, Erich. *Collective Behavior.* New York: Harcourt Brace Jovanovich, 1992.

Hyman, Ray. "The Psychology of Deception." *Annual Review of Psychology* 40 (1989): 133–54.

Jones, R. V. "The Theory of Practical Joking—An Elaboration." *The Institute of Mathematics and Its Applications* (January-February 1972): 10–17.

Jones, R. V. "The Theory of Practical Joking—Its Relevance to Physics." *Bulletin of the Institute of Physics* (June 1957): 193–201.

Jones, R. V. *The Wizard War: British Scientific Intelligence, 1939–1945.* New York: Coward, McCann & Geoghegan, 1978.

Klapp, Orrin E. *Heroes, Villains, and Fools: The Changing American Character.* Englewood Cliffs, N.J.: Prentice-Hall Spectrum Books, 1962.

Klapp, Orrin E. *Symbolic Leaders: Public Drama and Public Men.* Chicago: Aldine Publishing Co., 1964.

Koenig, Frederick. *Rumor in the Marketplace: The Social Psychology of Commercial Hearsay.* Dover, MA: Auburn House, 1985.

Lee, Martin A., and Norman Solomon. *Unrealiable Sources: A Guide to Detecting Bias in News Media.* New York: Lyle Stuart Book/Carol Publishing Group, 1990.

Lewis, J. David, and Andrew Weigert. "Trust as a Social Reality." *Social Forces* 63, no. 4 (1985): 967–85.

Lyman, Stanford M. and Marvin B. Scott. "Adventures." In *The Drama of Social Reality.* New York: Oxford University Press, 1975.

MacDougall, Curtis D. *Hoaxes.* New York: Dover Publications, 1958.

Mitchell, Robert W., and Nicholas S. Thompson, editors. *Deception: Perspectives on Human and Nonhuman Deceit.* Albany, NY: State University of New York Press, 1986.

Mitroff, Ian I., and Warren Bennis. *The Unreality Industry: The Deliberate Manufacturing of Falsehood and What It Is Doing to Our Lives.* New York: Birch Lane Press Book/Carol Publishing Group, 1989.

Moss, Norman. *The Pleasures of Deception.* London: Chatto & Windus, 1977.

Pratkanis, Anthony, and Elliot Aronson. *Age of Propaganda: The Everyday Use and Abuse of Persuasion.* New York: W.H. Freeman, 1992.

Saunders, Richard. *The World's Greatest Hoaxes.* New York: Playboy Press Paperbacks, 1980.

Simmel, Georg. "The Adventure." In *Essays on Sociology and Aesthetics.* Edited by Kurt H. Wolf. New York: Harper and Row, 1985: 243–58.

Stebbins, Robert A. "Putting People On: Deception of Our Fellow Man in Everyday Life." *Sociology and Social Research* 59, no. 1 (1975): 189–200.

Sweetser, Eve E. "The Definition of *Lie*: An Examination of the Folk Models Underlying a Semantic Prototype." In *Cultural Models in Language and Thought.* Edited by Dorothy Holland and Naomi Quinn. New York: Cambridge University Press, 1987.

Welsh, John F. "The Social Psychology of Fraud: Dramaturgy, Carnegie and Puppet Theater." *Mid-American Review of Sociology* 11, no. 1 (1986): 45–66.

West, Charles K. *The Social and Psychological Distortion of Information.* Chicago: Nelson-Hall, 1981.

Whaley, Bart. "Toward a General Theory of Deception." *Epoptica: A Review of Current Magic Literature and Apparatus* no. 5 (January 1984): 270–77. [An extended revision of a prior version in the 1983 *Journal of Strategic Studies.*]

Whiten, Andrew, and Richard W. Byrne. "Tactical Deception in Primates." *Behavioral and Brain Sciences* 11 (1988): 233–73.

Zuckerman, Marvin. "The Sensation Seeking Motive." In *Progress in Experimental Personality Research.* Vol. 7. Edited by B.A. Maher. New York: Academic Press, 1974.

Sports and Games Hoaxes

Amdur, Neil. (A series of articles in the *New York Times,* as follows): April 22, 1980: A1, B15; April 23, 1980: B13; April 25, 1980: 24; April 26, 1980: 24; April 27, 1980: E6.

Bartlett, Arthur. *Baseball and Mr. Spalding: The History and Romance of Baseball.* New York: Farrar, Straus & Young, 1951.

Carroll, Charles Michael. *The Great Chess Automaton.* New York: Dover Publications, 1975.

Cooke, Bob. "Plainfield's Phantom Football Team." *Reader's Digest* (December 1974): 233.

Danzig, Allison, and Joe Reichler. *Baseball: Its Great Players, Teams and Managers.* Englewood Cliffs, NJ: Prentice-Hall, 1959.

Henderson, Robert W. "Baseball and Rounders." *Bulletin of the New York Public Library* 43, no. 4 (April 1939): 303–14.

Henderson, Robert W. "How Baseball Began." *Bulletin of the New York Public Library* 41, no. 4 (April 1937): 287–91.

Malcolm, Andrew H. "Canadian Papers Hoaxed on 'Soccer Tourney'." *New York Times* (March 18, 1982): A6.

"Miss Ruiz Loses Her Title." *New York Times* (April 30, 1980): B8.

Moran, Malcolm. "Doubts Rise on Woman's Feat; 'I Ran Race,' She Says." *New York Times* (April 22, 1980): B15, B17.

Peterson, Harold. *The Man Who Invented Baseball.* New York: Charles Scribner's Sons, 1973.

Plimpton, George. "The Curious Case of Sidd Finch." *Sports Illustrated* (April 1, 1985): 58–76.

[Poe, Edgar Allan]. "Maelzel's Chess Player." *Southern Literary Messenger* 2 (1836): 318–26.

von Racknitz, Joseph Friedrich Freiherr. *Über den Schachspieler des Herrn von Kempelen und dessen Nachbildung.* Leipzig & Dresden: J. G. I. Breitkopf, 1789.

[Willis, Robert]. *An Attempt to Analyse the Automaton Chess Player of Mr. de Kempelen.* London: Booth, 1821.

Index